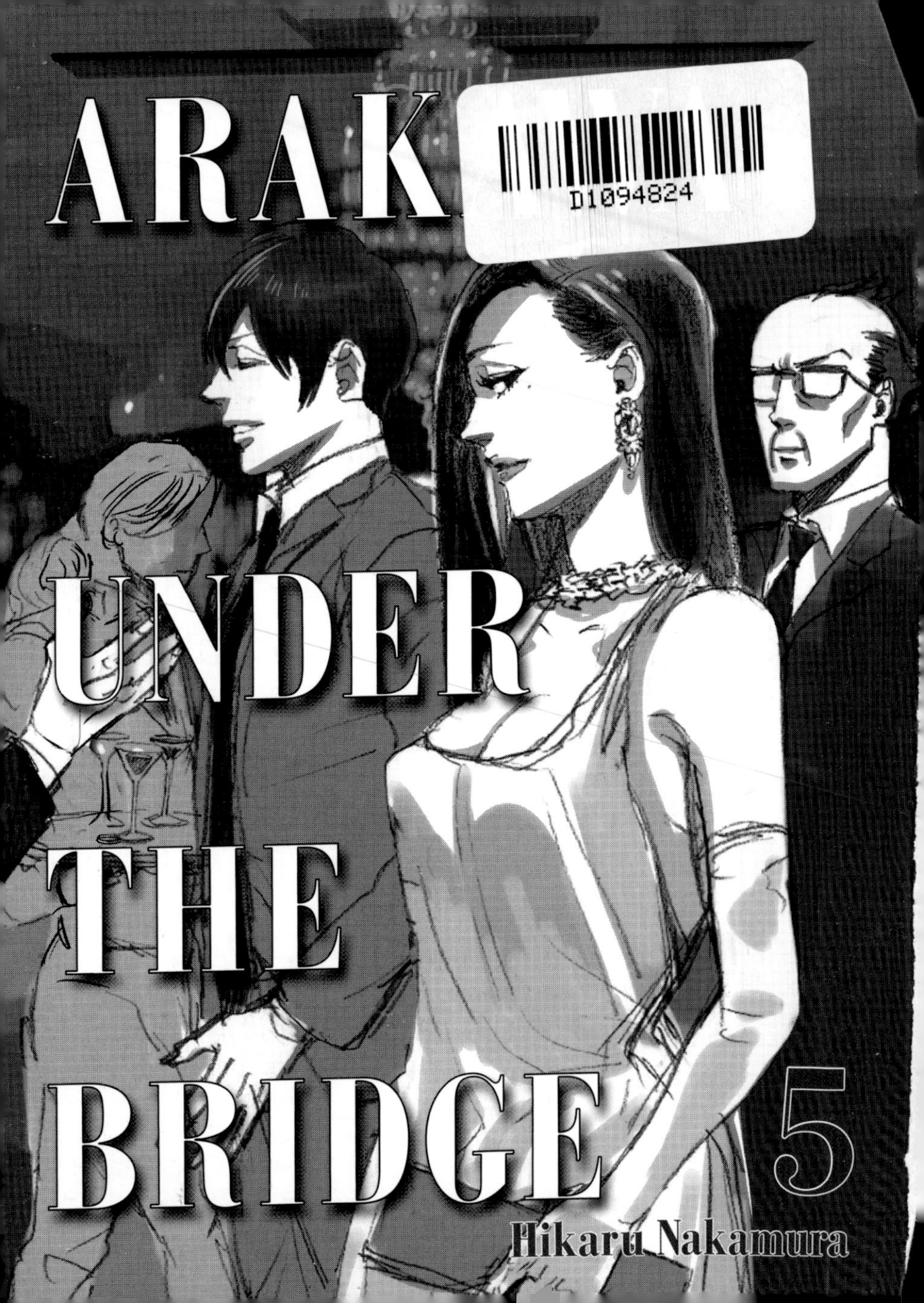
ARAK
D1094824
UNDER
THE
BRIDGE
5
Hikaru Nakamura

CONTENTS

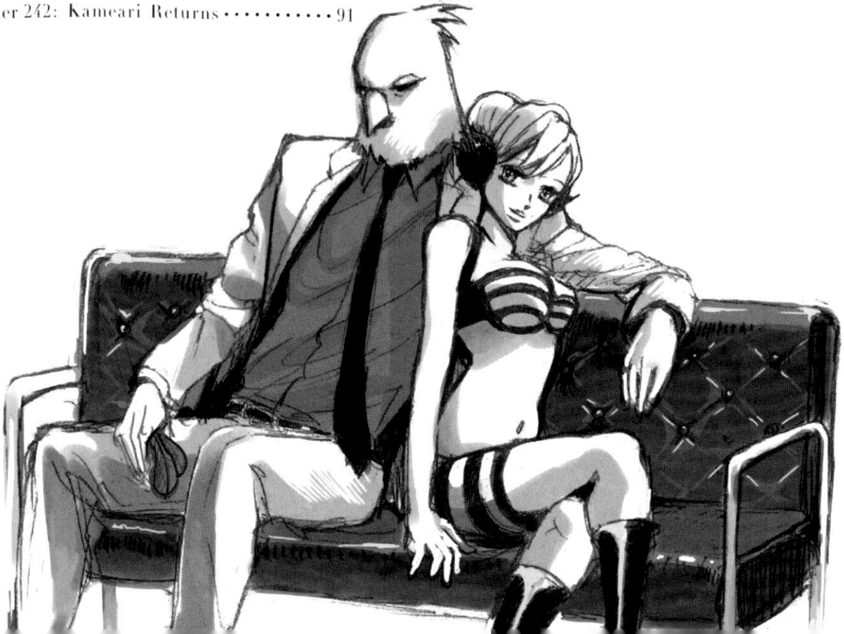

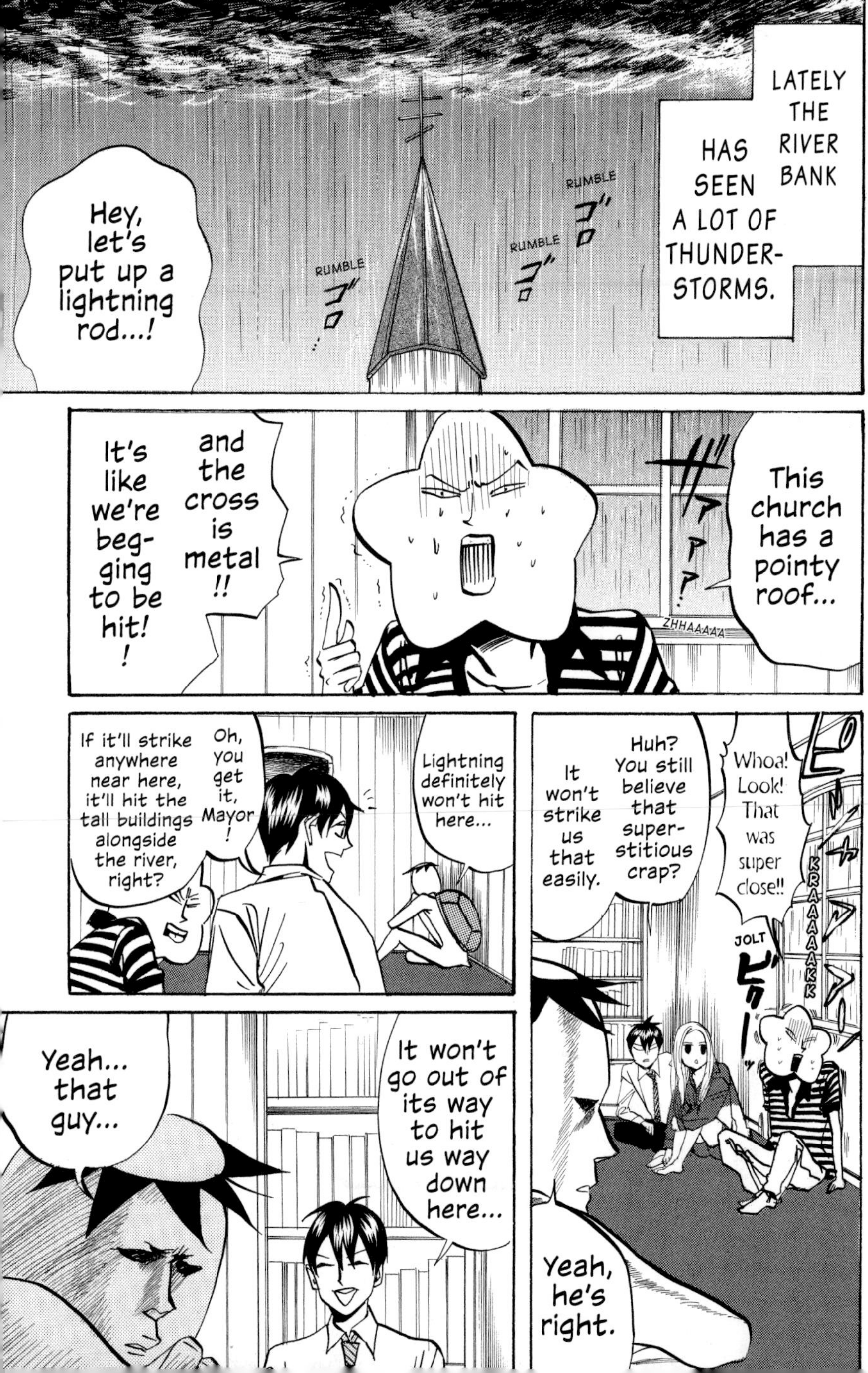
LATELY THE RIVER BANK HAS SEEN A LOT OF THUNDER-STORMS.
RUMBLE
RUMBLE
RUMBLE
Hey, let's put up a lightning rod...!
This church has a pointy roof...
ZHHAAAAA
and the cross is metal!!
It's like we're beg-ging to be hit!!
Whoa! Look! That was super close!!
KRAAAAAAKK
JOLT
Huh? You still believe that super-stitious crap?
It won't strike us that easily.
Yeah, he's right.
Lightning definitely won't hit here...
Oh, you get it, Mayor!
If it'll strike anywhere near here, it'll hit the tall buildings alongside the river, right?
It won't go out of its way to hit us way down here...
Yeah... that guy...

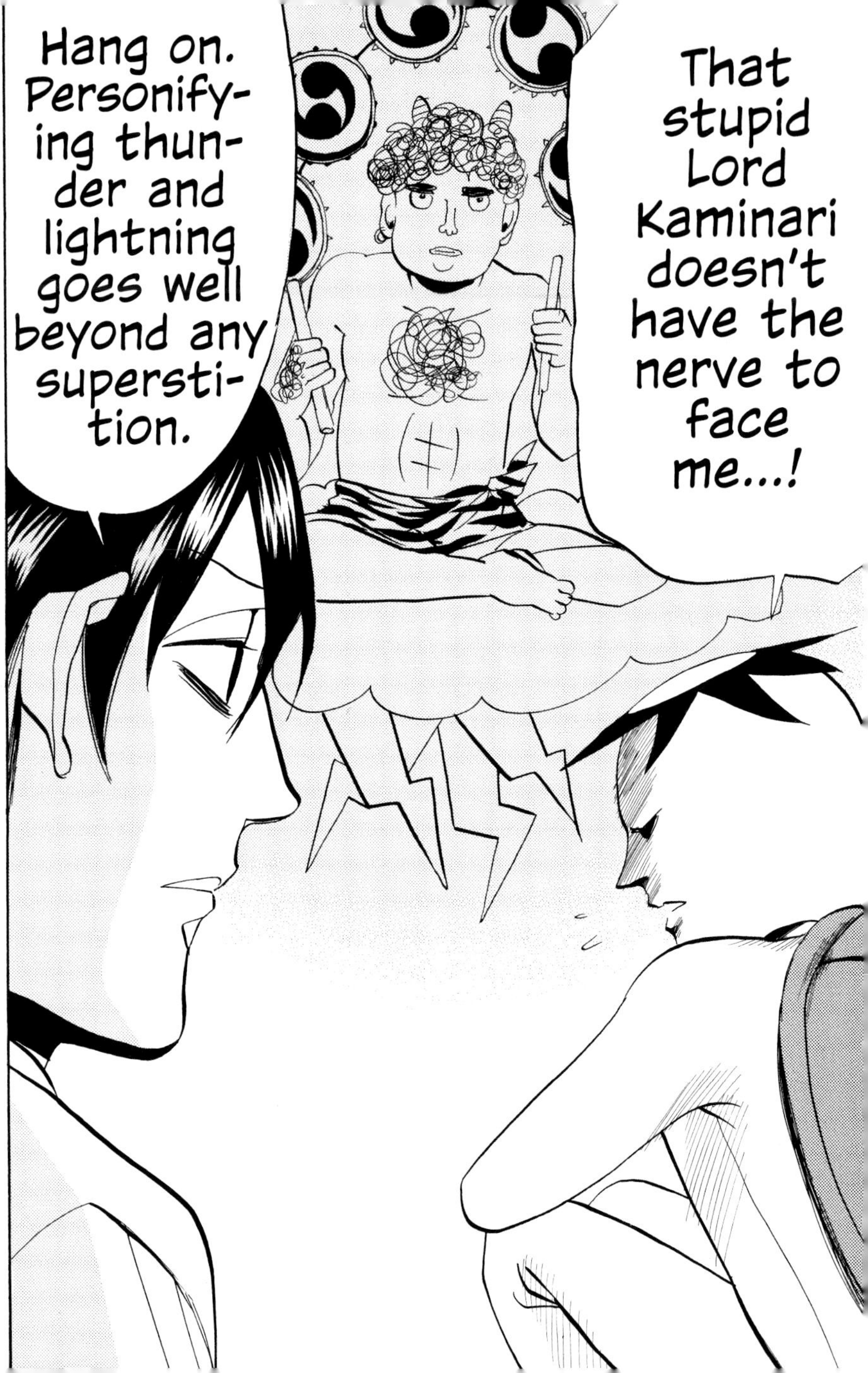
That stupid Lord Kaminari doesn't have the nerve to face me...!
Hang on. Personifying thunder and lightning goes well beyond any superstition.

Chapter 226: The Mayor's Memory

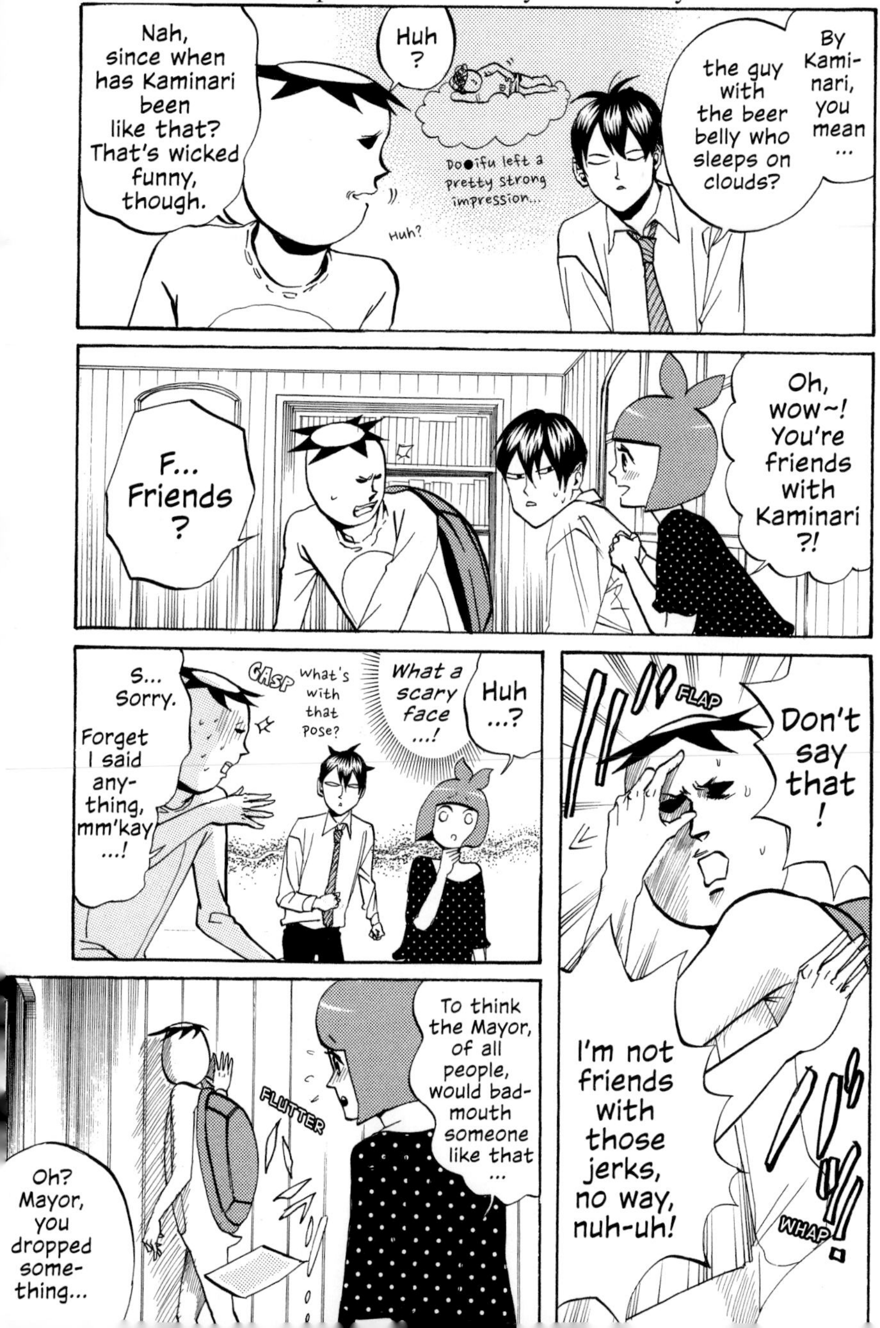
By Kaminari, you mean ...
the guy with the beer belly who sleeps on clouds?
Huh?
Do●ifu left a pretty strong impression...
Nah, since when has Kaminari been like that? That's wicked funny, though.
Huh?
Oh, wow~! You're friends with Kaminari?!
F... Friends?
FLAP
Don't say that!
I'm not friends with those jerks, no way, nuh-uh!
WHAP
Huh ...?
What a scary face ...!
What's with that pose?
GASP
S... Sorry. Forget I said any-thing, mm'kay ...!
To think the Mayor, of all people, would bad-mouth someone like that ...
FLUTTER
Oh? Mayor, you dropped some-thing...

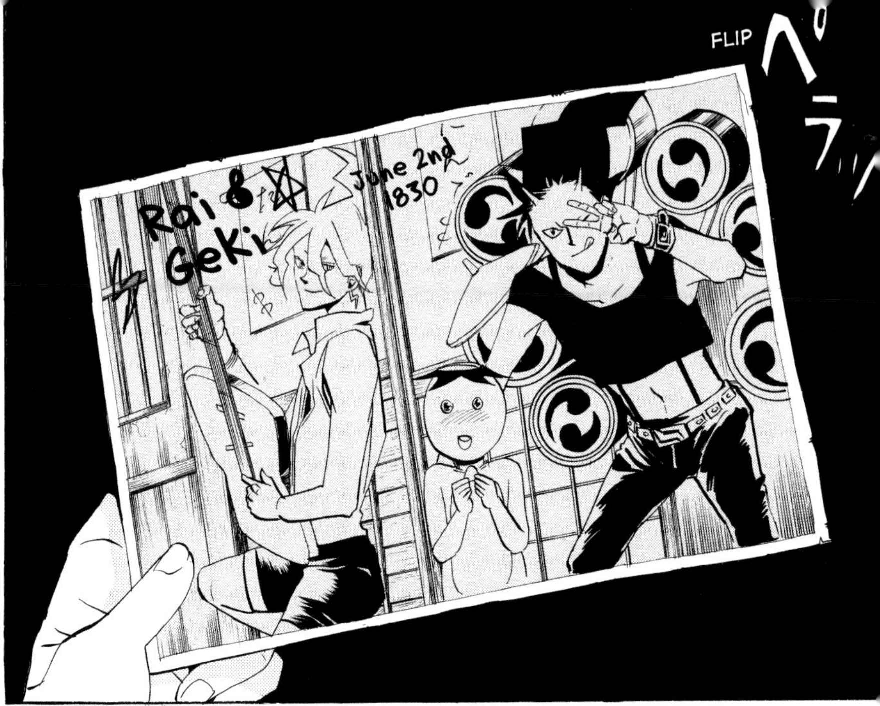
FLIP
Rai & Geki
June 2nd 1830

※ Meaning, "lighting strike"

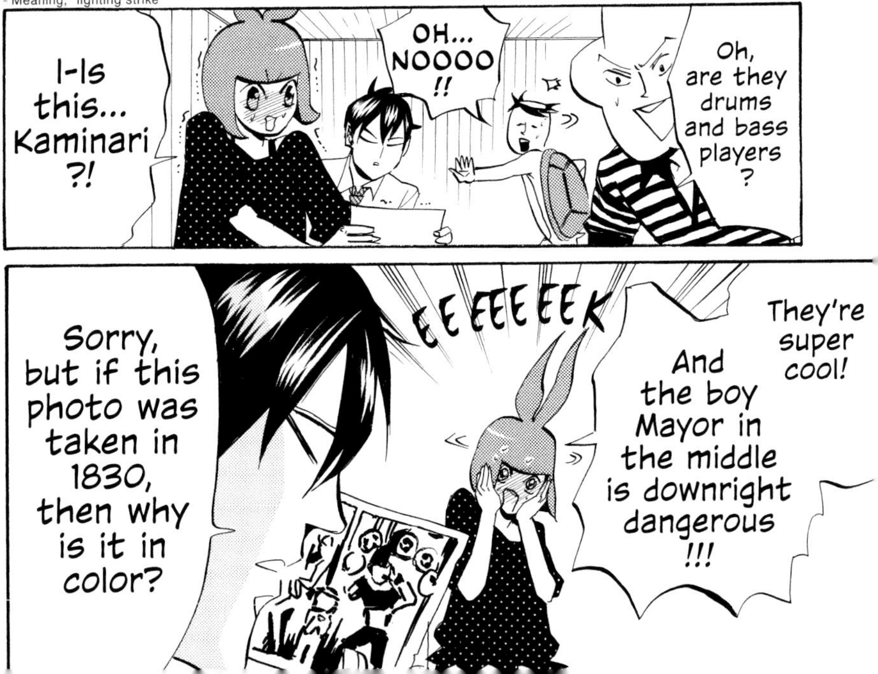
Oh, are they drums and bass players?
OH... NOOOO!!
I-Is this... Kaminari?!
They're super cool!
And the boy Mayor in the middle is downright dangerous!!!
EEEEEEEK
Sorry, but if this photo was taken in 1830, then why is it in color?

Chapter 227: Sad Break-Up

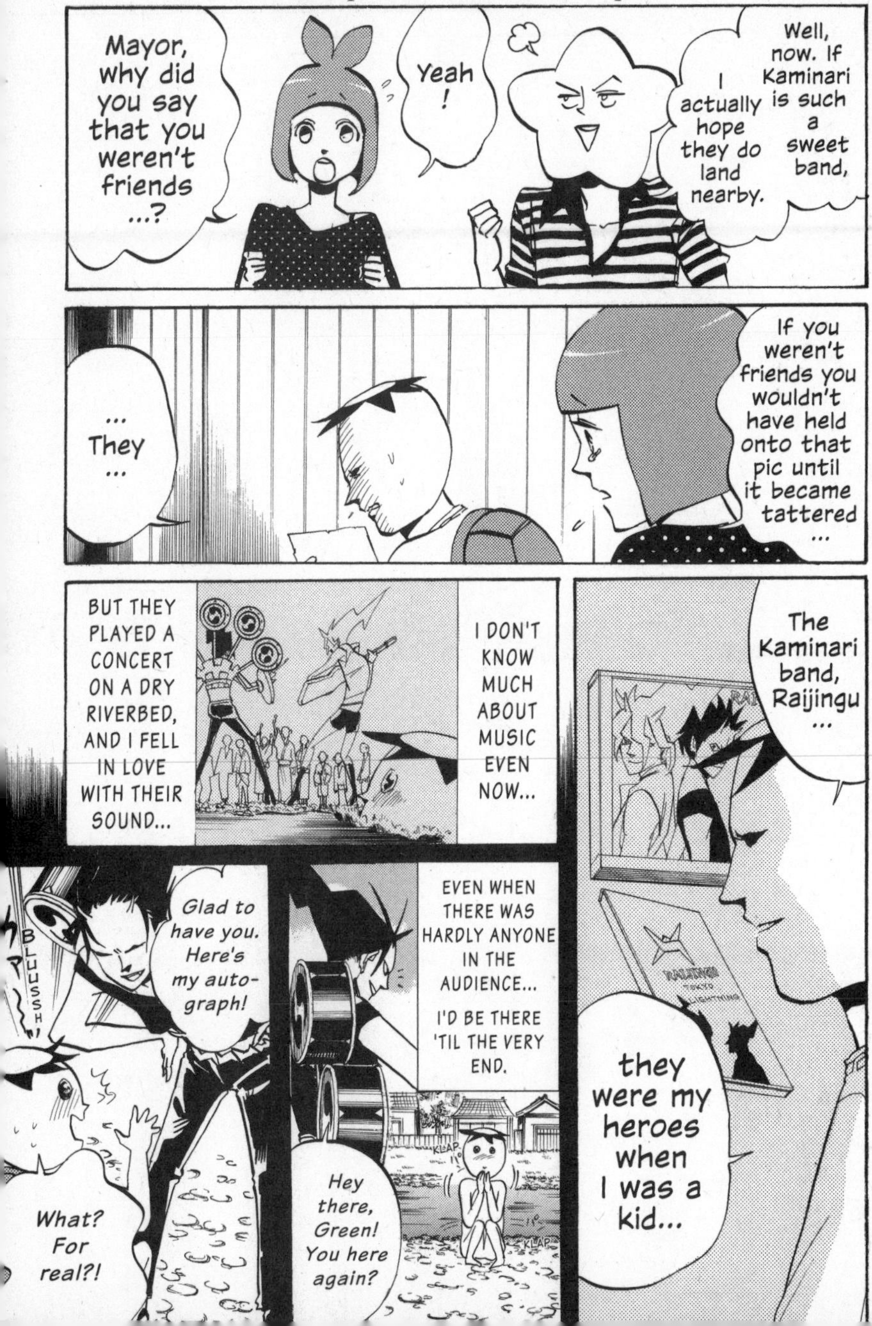
Well, now. If Kaminari is such a sweet band,
I actually hope they do land nearby.
Yeah!
Mayor, why did you say that you weren't friends ...?
If you weren't friends you wouldn't have held onto that pic until it became tattered ...
... They ...
The Kaminari band, Raijingu ...
they were my heroes when I was a kid...
I DON'T KNOW MUCH ABOUT MUSIC EVEN NOW...
BUT THEY PLAYED A CONCERT ON A DRY RIVERBED, AND I FELL IN LOVE WITH THEIR SOUND...
EVEN WHEN THERE WAS HARDLY ANYONE IN THE AUDIENCE...
I'D BE THERE 'TIL THE VERY END.
KLAP
KLAP
Hey there, Green! You here again?
Glad to have you. Here's my auto-graph!
BLUUSSH
What? For real?!

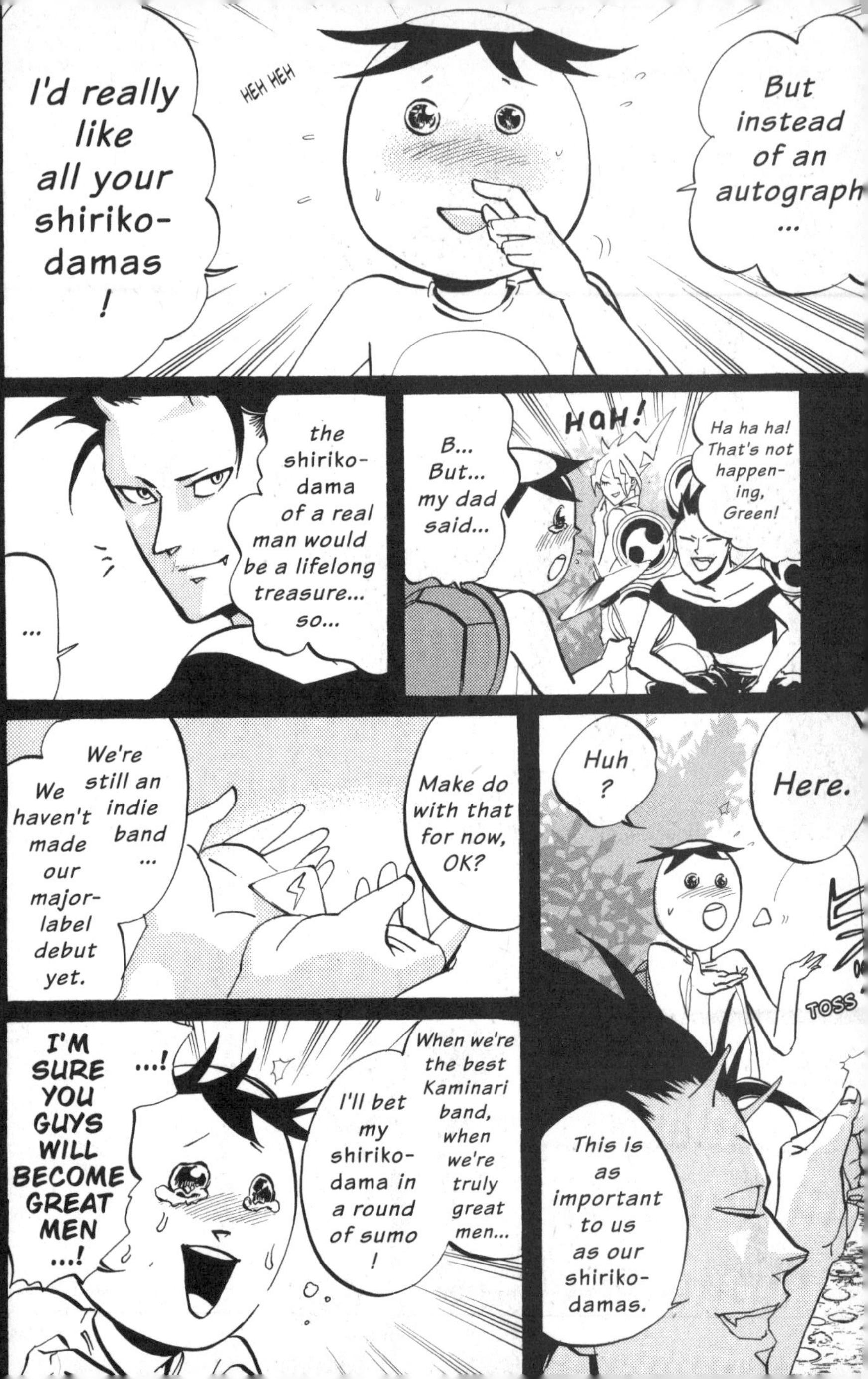
But instead of an autograph...
HEH HEH
I'd really like all your shiriko-damas!
Ha ha ha! That's not happen-ing, Green!
HAH!
B... But... my dad said...
the shiriko-dama of a real man would be a lifelong treasure... so...
...
Here.
Huh?
TOSS
Make do with that for now, OK?
We're still an indie band...
We haven't made our major-label debut yet.
This is as important to us as our shiriko-damas.
When we're the best Kaminari band, when we're truly great men...
I'll bet my shiriko-dama in a round of sumo!
...!
I'M SURE YOU GUYS WILL BECOME GREAT MEN...!

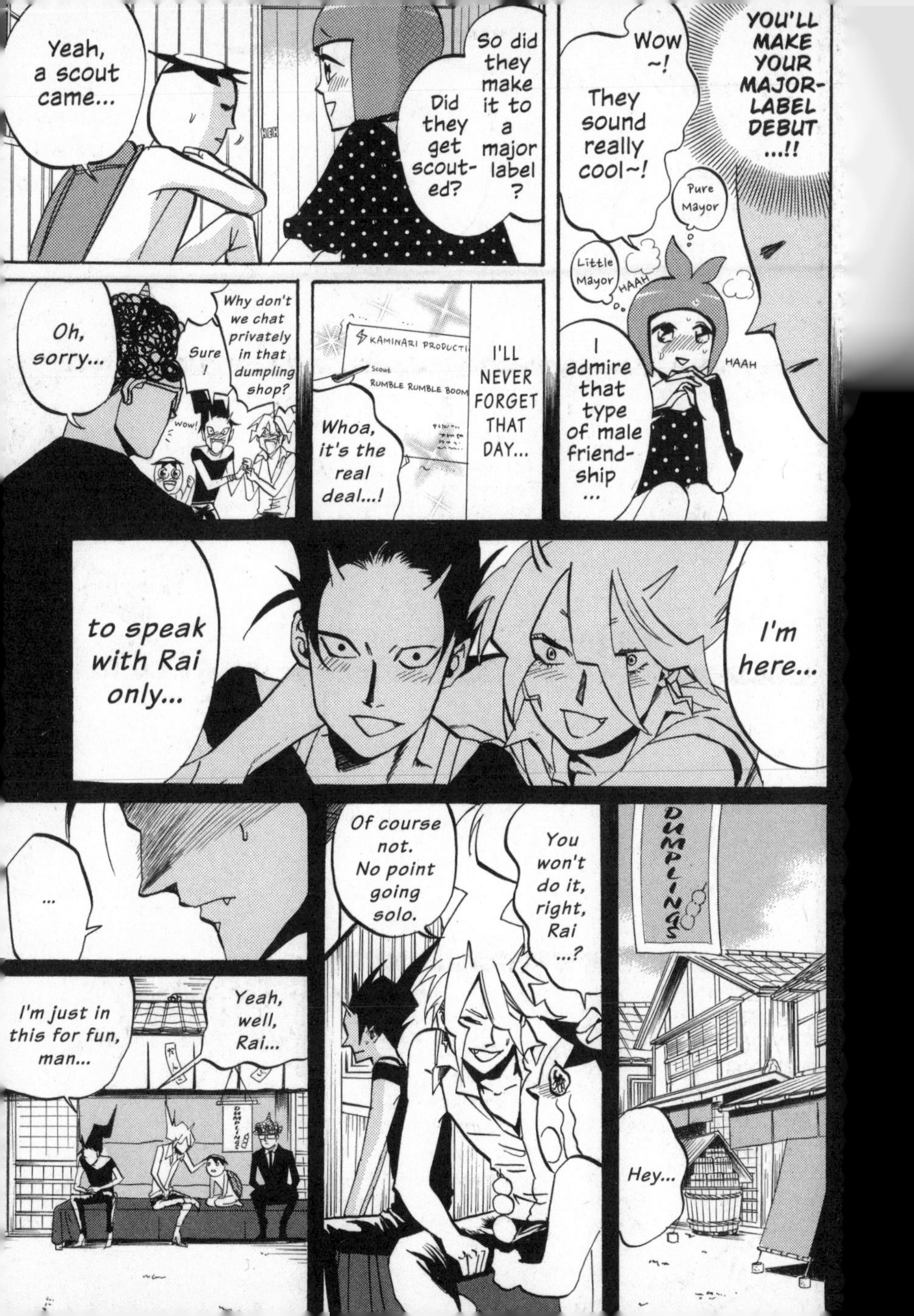
YOU'LL MAKE YOUR MAJOR-LABEL DEBUT ...!!
Wow ~! They sound really cool~!
Pure Mayor
Little Mayor
HAAH
HAAH
I admire that type of male friendship ...
So did they make it to a major label?
Did they get scout-ed?
Yeah, a scout came...
HEH
I'LL NEVER FORGET THAT DAY...
KAMINARI PRODUCTI
Scout
RUMBLE RUMBLE BOOM
Whoa, it's the real deal...!
Why don't we chat privately in that dumpling shop?
Sure!
Oh, sorry...
Wow!
I'm here...
to speak with Rai only...
DUMPLINGS
Hey...
You won't do it, right, Rai ...?
Of course not. No point going solo.
...
Yeah, well, Rai...
I'm just in this for fun, man...
DUMPLINGS

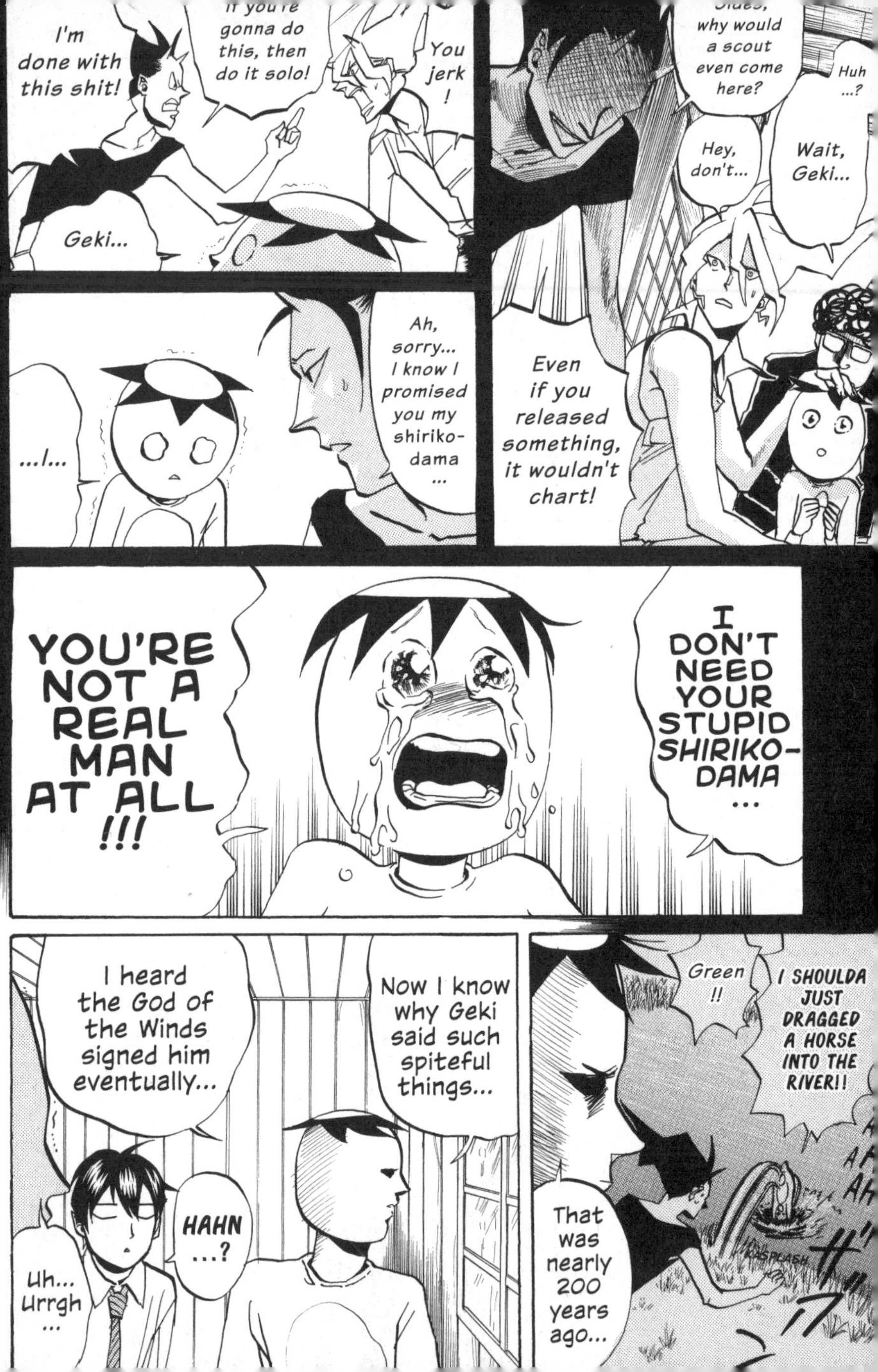
Sides, why would a scout even come here?
Huh ...?
Wait, Geki...
Hey, don't...
Even if you released something, it wouldn't chart!
You jerk !
if you're gonna do this, then do it solo!
I'm done with this shit!
Geki...
Ah, sorry... I know I promised you my shiriko-dama ...
...I...
I DON'T NEED YOUR STUPID SHIRIKO-DAMA ...
YOU'RE NOT A REAL MAN AT ALL !!!
Green !!
I SHOULDA JUST DRAGGED A HORSE INTO THE RIVER!!
KASPLASH
That was nearly 200 years ago...
Now I know why Geki said such spiteful things...
I heard the God of the Winds signed him eventually...
HAHN ...?
Uh... Urrgh ...

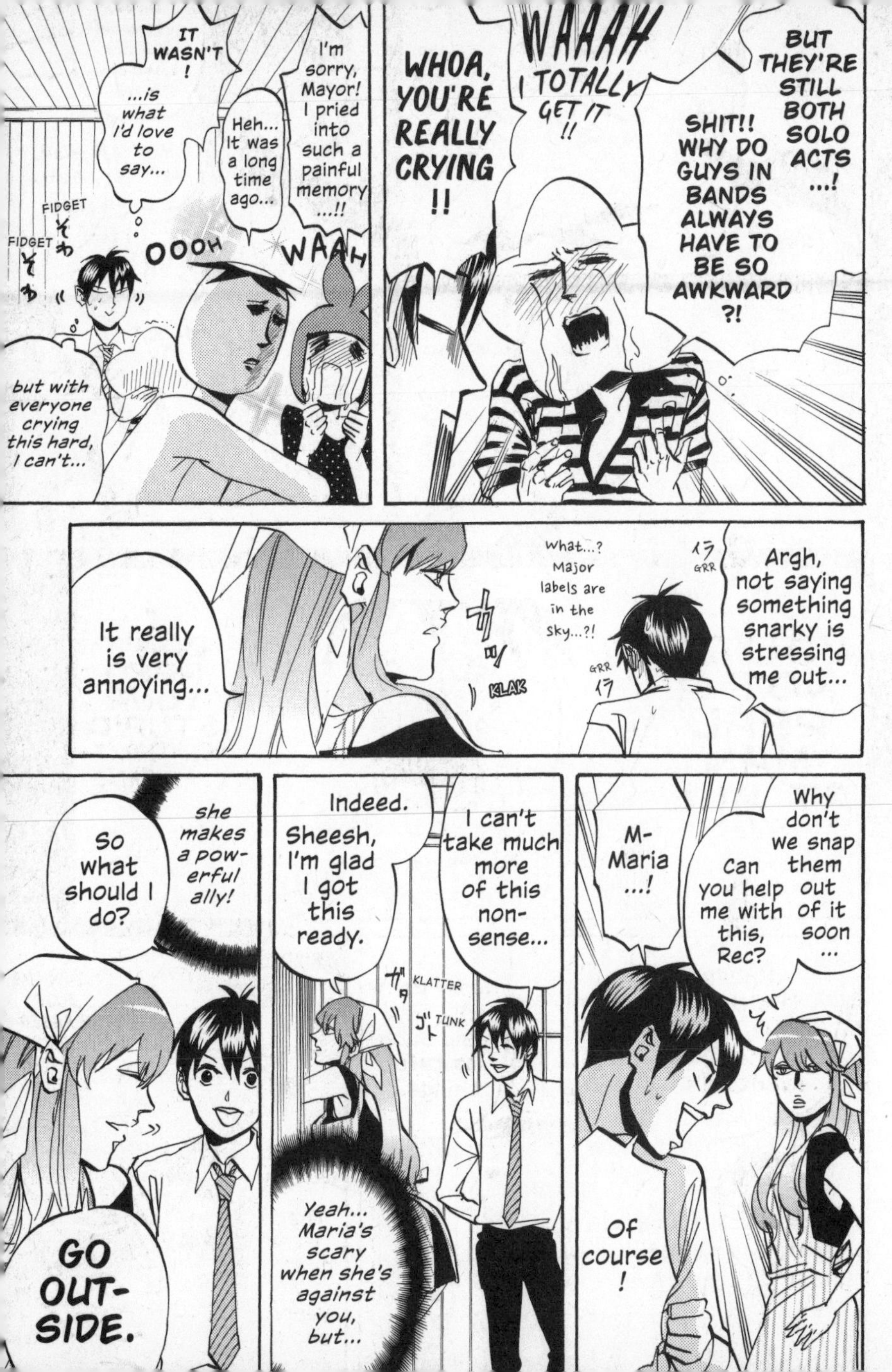
BUT THEY'RE STILL BOTH SOLO ACTS ...!
SHIT!! WHY DO GUYS IN BANDS ALWAYS HAVE TO BE SO AWKWARD ?!
WAAAH
I TOTALLY GET IT !!
WHOA, YOU'RE REALLY CRYING !!
I'm sorry, Mayor! I pried into such a painful memory ...!!
WAAAH
Heh... It was a long time ago...
OOOH
IT WASN'T !
...is what I'd love to say...
FIDGET
FIDGET
but with everyone crying this hard, I can't...
Argh, not saying something snarky is stressing me out...
GRR
What...? Major labels are in the sky...?!
GRR
KLAK
It really is very annoying...
Why don't we snap them out of it soon ...
M-Maria ...!
Can you help me with this, Rec?
Of course !
I can't take much more of this non-sense...
Indeed.
Sheesh, I'm glad I got this ready.
KLATTER
TUNK
Yeah... Maria's scary when she's against you, but...
she makes a pow-erful ally!
So what should I do?
GO OUT-SIDE.

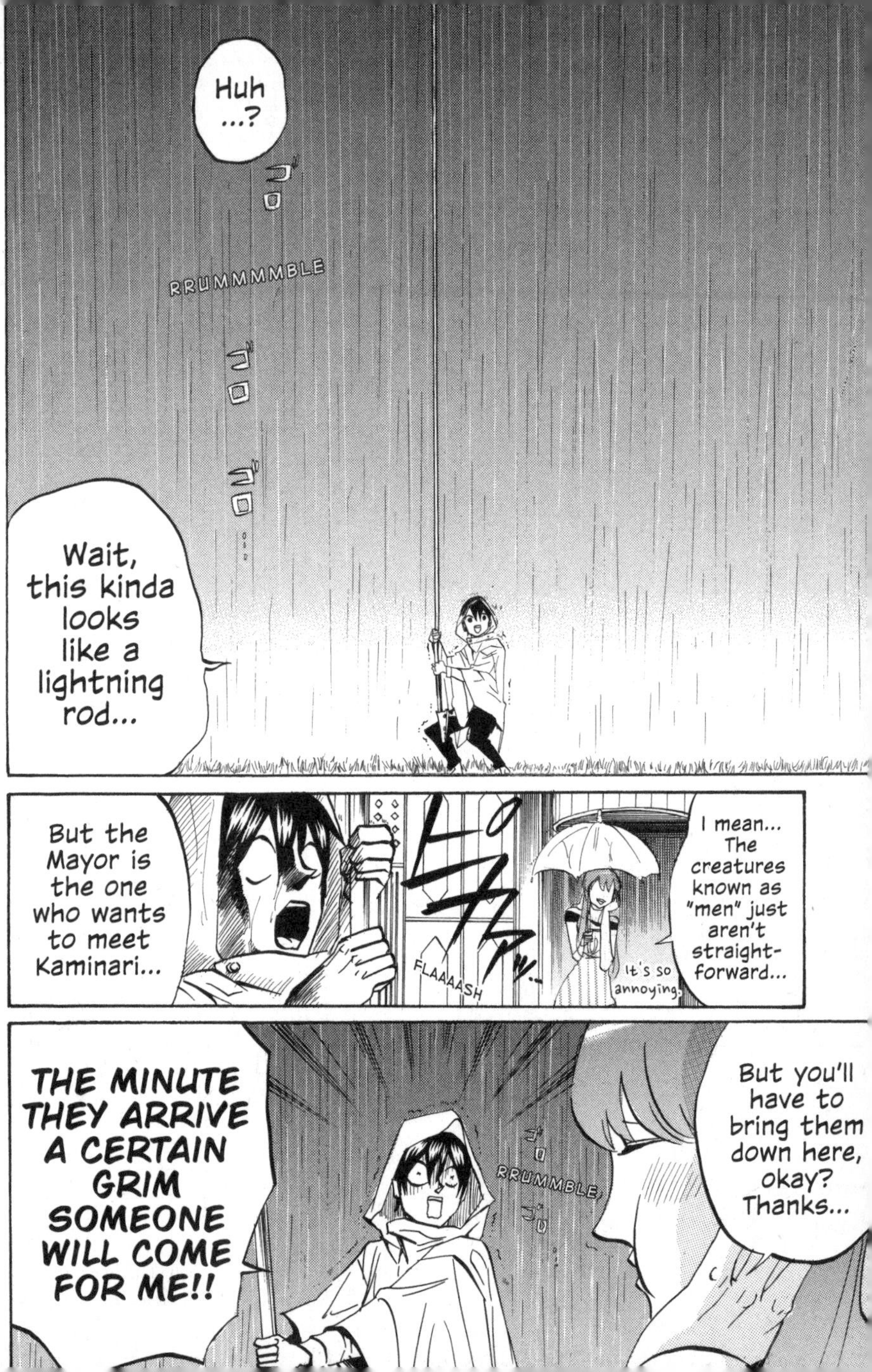
Huh ...?
ゴロ
RRUMMMMBLE
ゴロ
ゴロ...
Wait, this kinda looks like a lightning rod...
I mean... The creatures known as "men" just aren't straight-forward...
It's so annoying.
FLAAAASH
But the Mayor is the one who wants to meet Kaminari...
But you'll have to bring them down here, okay? Thanks...
RRUMMBLE
THE MINUTE THEY ARRIVE A CERTAIN GRIM SOMEONE WILL COME FOR ME!!

Chapter 228: Best Act

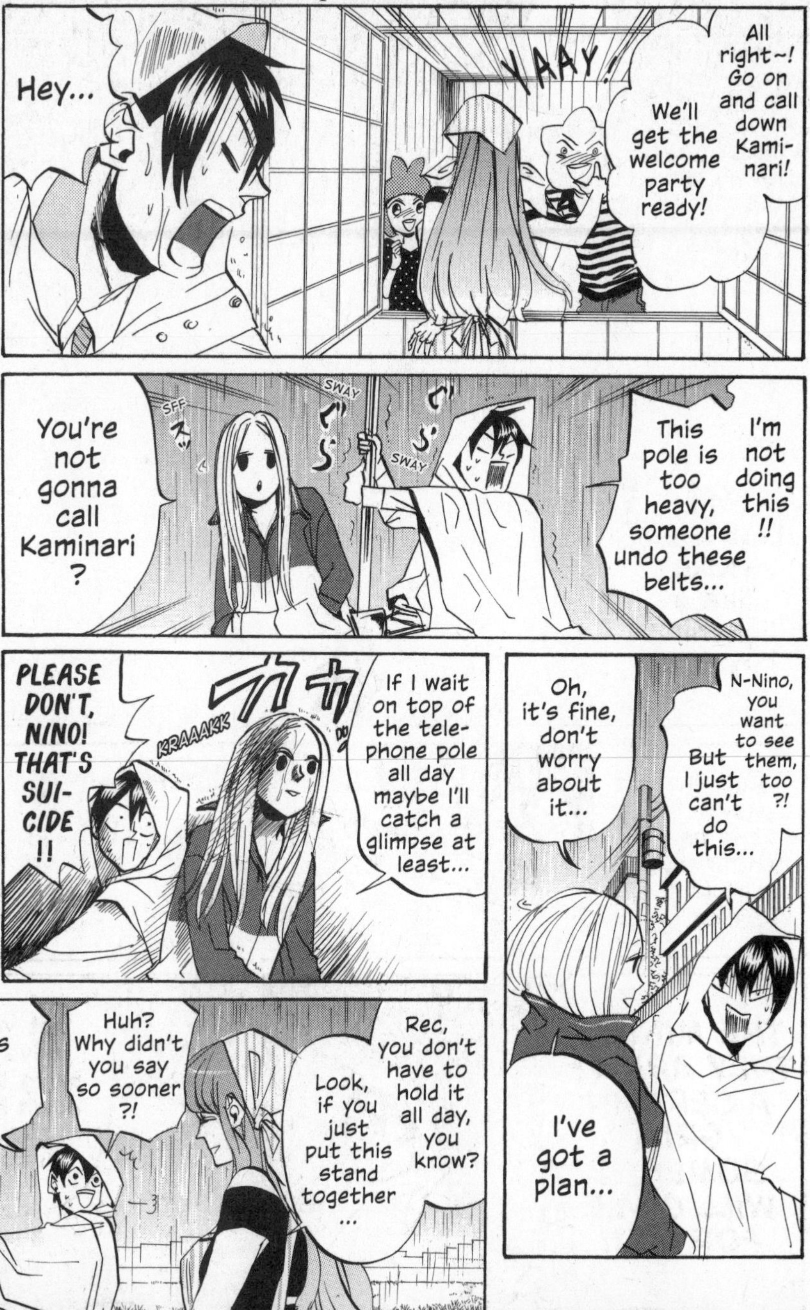

All right~! Go on and call down Kaminari!
We'll get the welcome party ready!
YAAY!
Hey...
I'm not doing this!!
This pole is too heavy, someone undo these belts...
SWAY
SWAY
SFF
You're not gonna call Kaminari?
N-Nino, you want to see them, too?!
But I just can't do this...
Oh, it's fine, don't worry about it...
I've got a plan...
If I wait on top of the telephone pole all day maybe I'll catch a glimpse at least...
KRAAAKK
PLEASE DON'T, NINO! THAT'S SUICIDE!!
Rec, you don't have to hold it all day, you know?
Look, if you just put this stand together...
Huh? Why didn't you say so sooner?!
Let's get it...

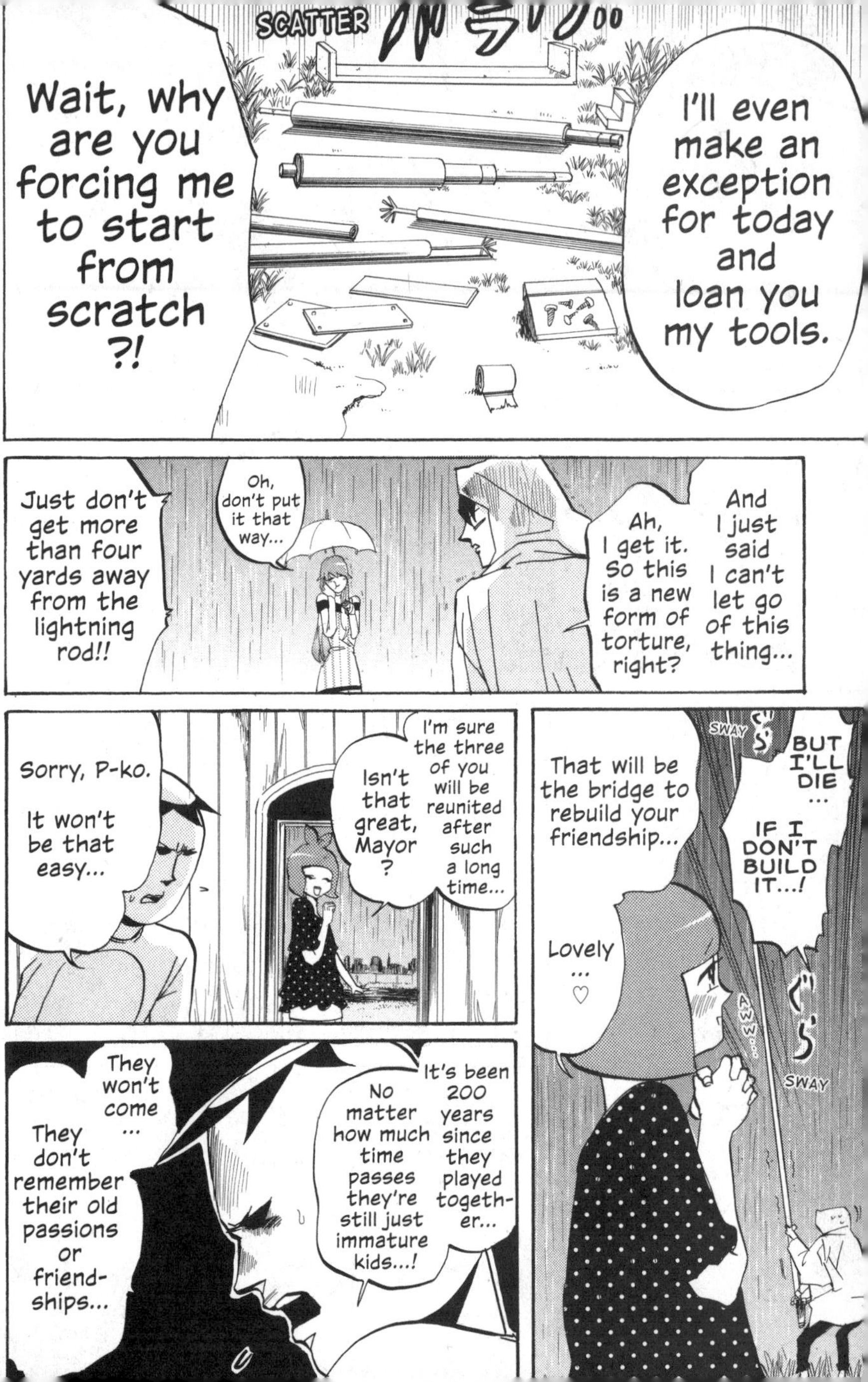
SCATTER
I'll even make an exception for today and loan you my tools.
Wait, why are you forcing me to start from scratch ?!
And I just said I can't let go of this thing...
Ah, I get it. So this is a new form of torture, right?
Oh, don't put it that way...
Just don't get more than four yards away from the lightning rod!!
SWAY
BUT I'LL DIE... IF I DON'T BUILD IT...!
That will be the bridge to rebuild your friendship...
Lovely... ♡
AWW...
SWAY
I'm sure the three of you will be reunited after such a long time...
Isn't that great, Mayor?
Sorry, P-ko. It won't be that easy...
It's been 200 years since they played togeth-er...
No matter how much time passes they're still just immature kids...!
They won't come...
They don't remember their old passions or friend-ships...

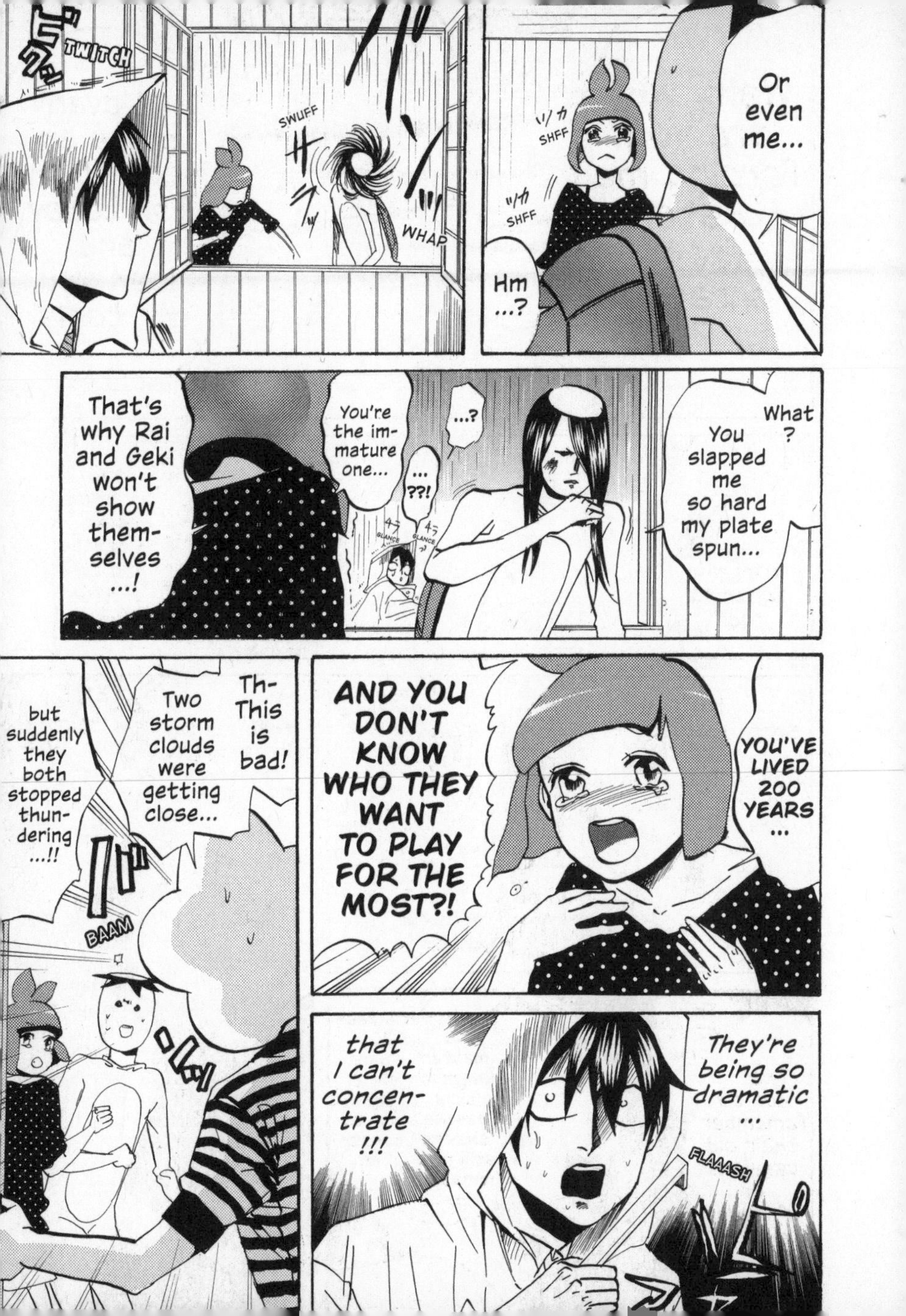
Or even me...
ツカ SHFF
ツカ SHFF
Hm ...?
SWUFF
WHAP
TWITCH
What? You slapped me so hard my plate spun...
...?
You're the im-mature one...
... ??!
GLANCE
GLANCE
That's why Rai and Geki won't show them-selves ...!
YOU'VE LIVED 200 YEARS ...
AND YOU DON'T KNOW WHO THEY WANT TO PLAY FOR THE MOST?!
They're being so dramatic ...
that I can't concen-trate !!!
FLAAASH
Th-This is bad!
Two storm clouds were getting close...
but suddenly they both stopped thun-dering ...!!
BAAM

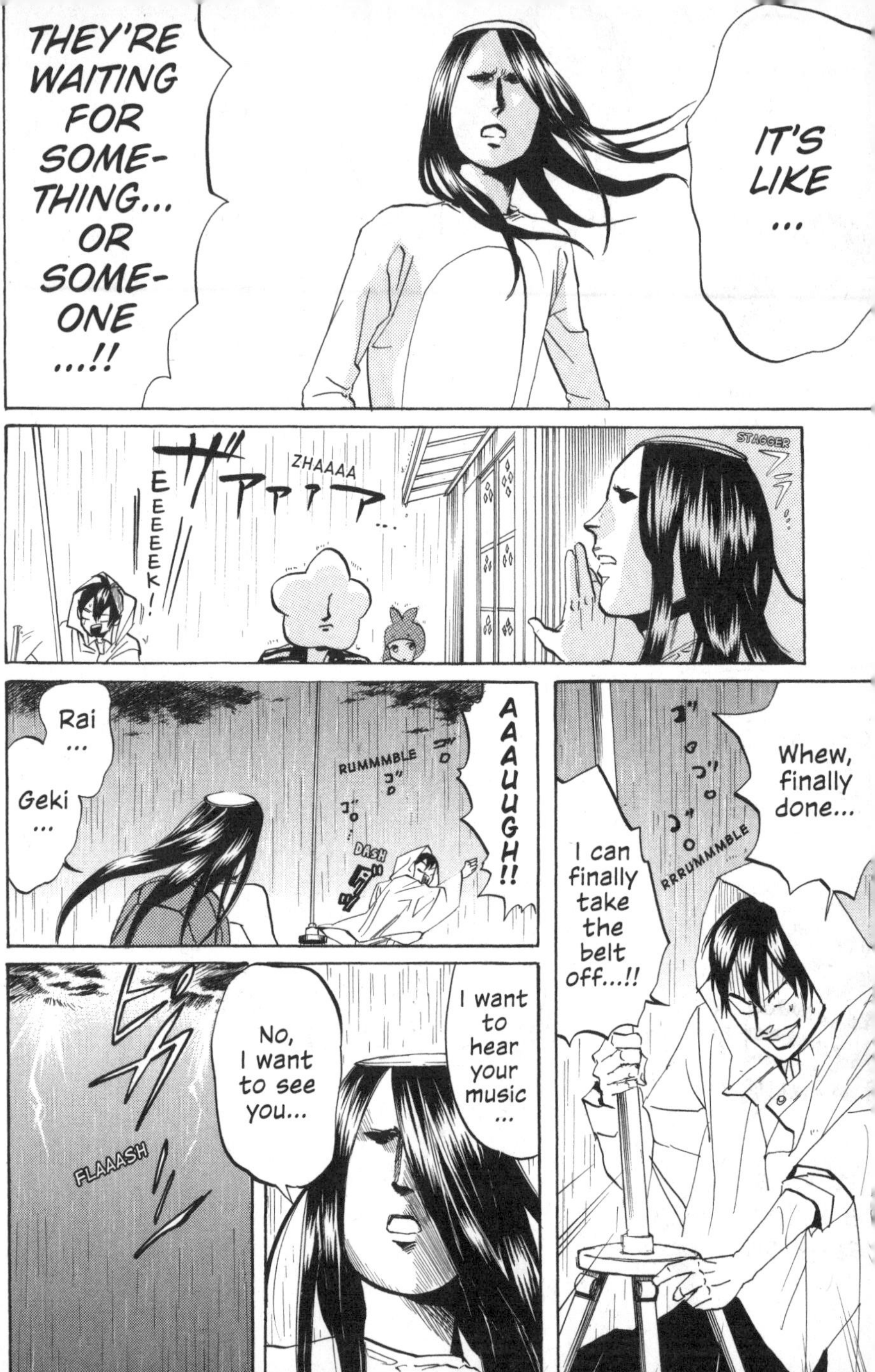
IT'S LIKE ...
THEY'RE WAITING FOR SOME-THING... OR SOME-ONE ...!!
STAGGER
ザァァァァ
ZHAAAA
EEEEEEK!
Whew, finally done...
I can finally take the belt off...!!
RRRUMMMBLE
AAAAUGH!!
RUMMMBLE
DASH
Rai ...
Geki ...
I want to hear your music ...
No, I want to see you...
FLAAASH

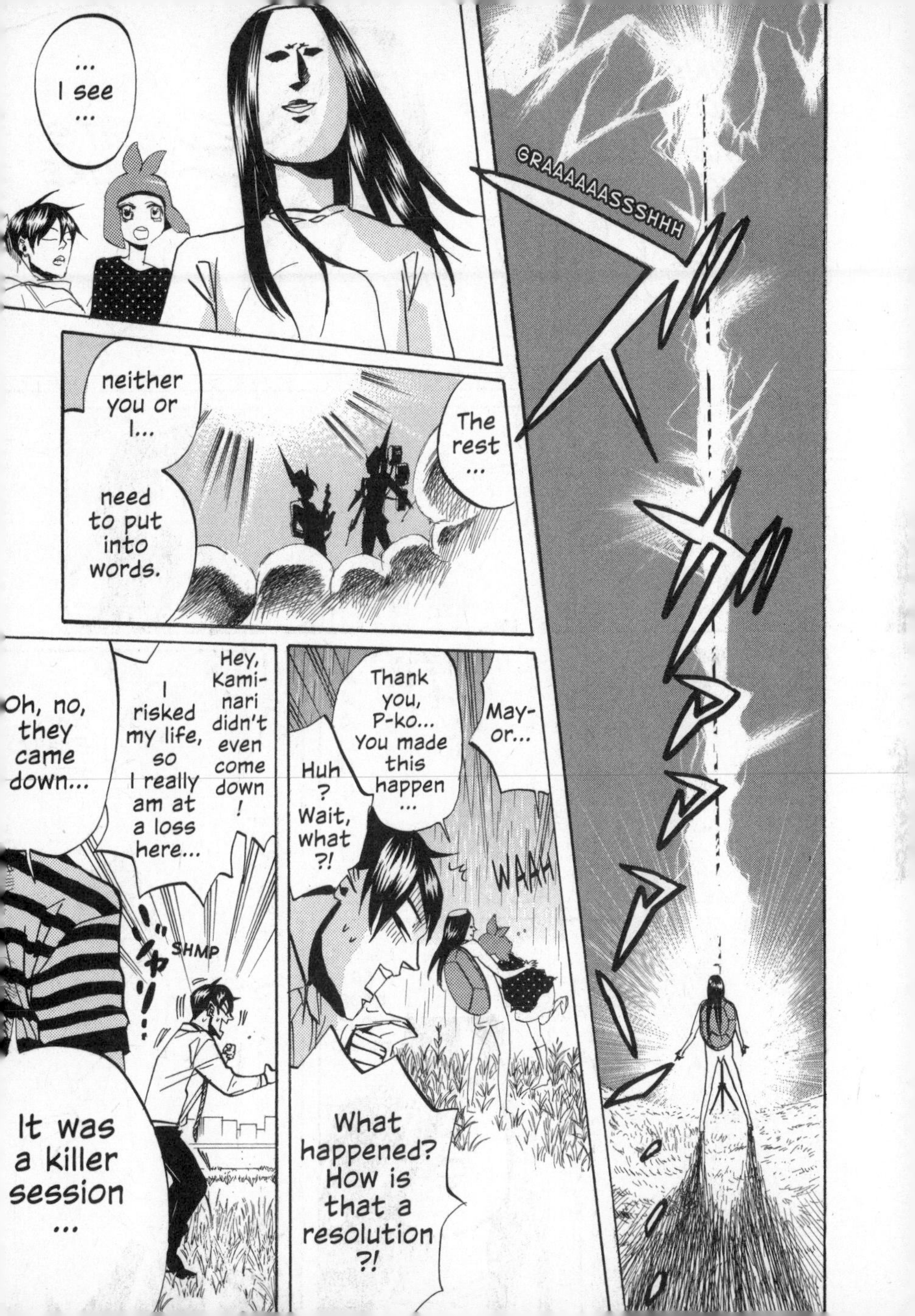
GRAAAAAASSSHHH
... I see ...
The rest ...
neither you or I...
need to put into words.
May-or...
Thank you, P-ko... You made this happen ...
Huh? Wait, what?!
WAAH
What happened? How is that a resolution?!
Hey, Kami-nari didn't even come down!
I risked my life, so I really am at a loss here...
Oh, no, they came down...
SHMP
It was a killer session ...

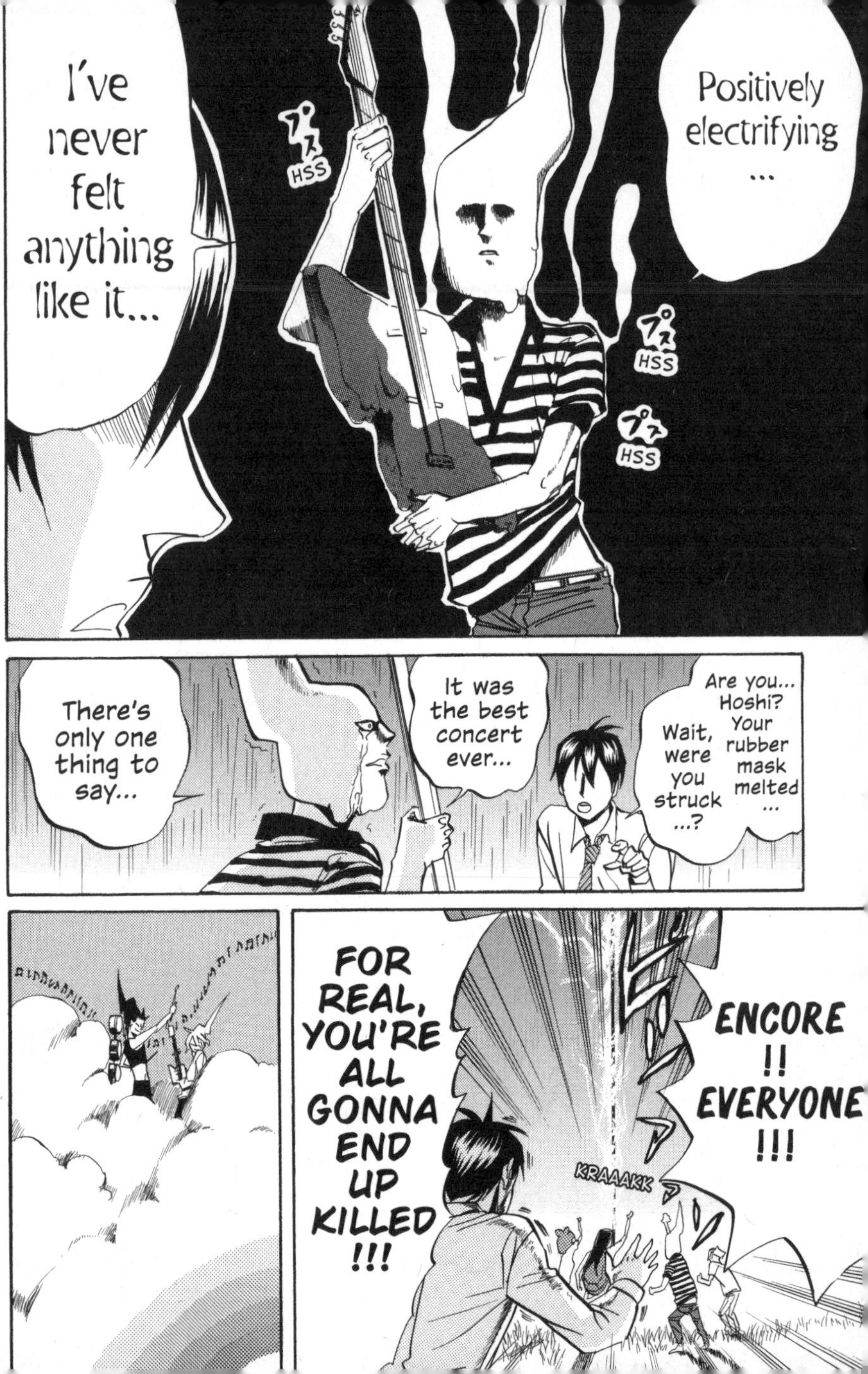
Positively electrifying ...
プス
HSS
プス
HSS
プス
HSS
I've never felt anything like it...
Are you... Hoshi? Your rubber mask melted ...
Wait, were you struck ...?
It was the best concert ever...
There's only one thing to say...
ENCORE !! EVERYONE !!!
KRAAAKK
FOR REAL, YOU'RE ALL GONNA END UP KILLED !!!

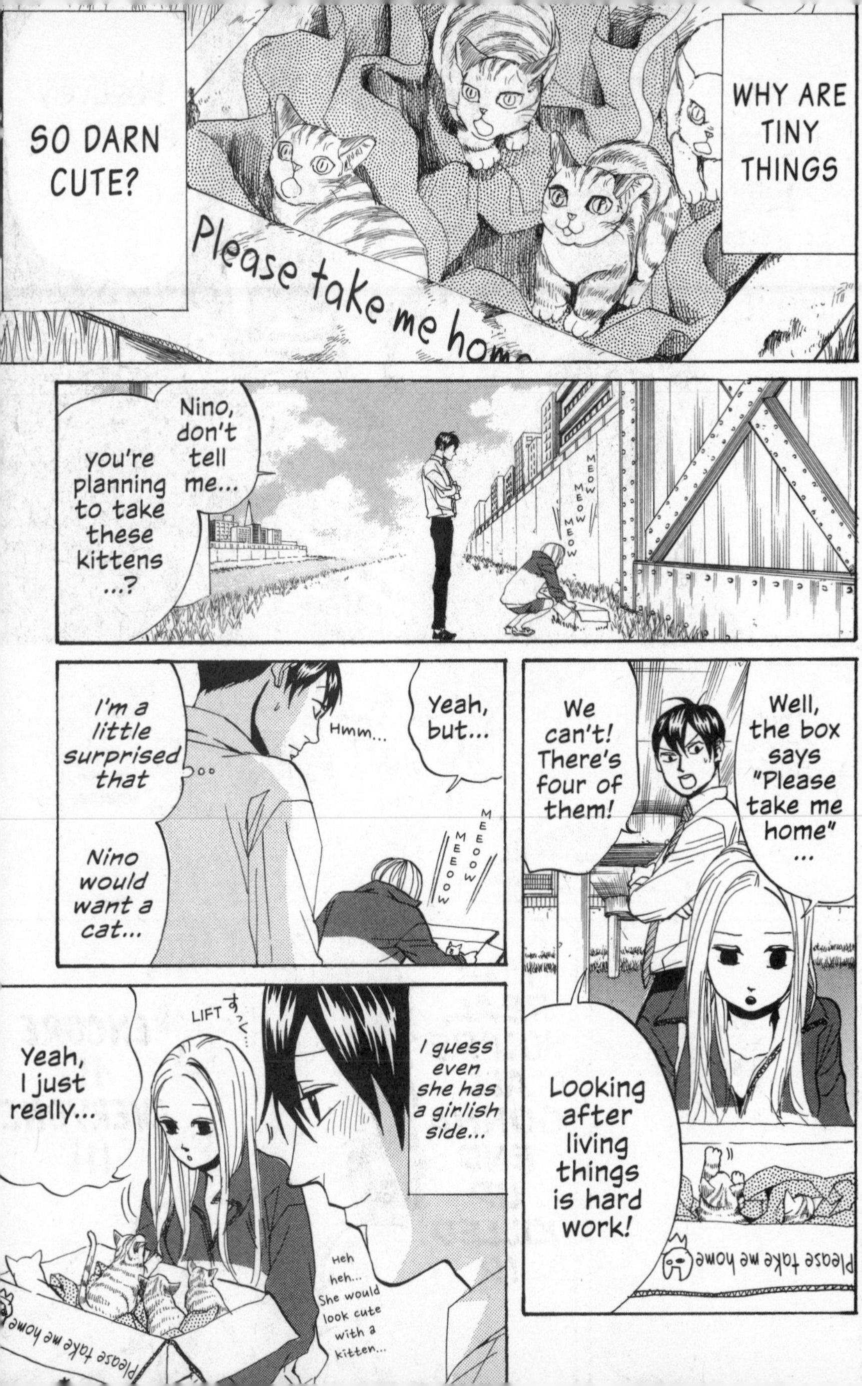
WHY ARE TINY THINGS
SO DARN CUTE?
Please take me hom
Nino, don't tell me...
you're planning to take these kittens ...?
MEOW
MEOW
MEOW
MEOW
Well, the box says "Please take me home" ...
We can't! There's four of them!
Looking after living things is hard work!
Please take me home
Yeah, but...
Hmm...
I'm a little surprised that
Nino would want a cat...
MEEOOW
MEEOOW
I guess even she has a girlish side...
LIFT すっ...
Yeah, I just really...
Heh heh... She would look cute with a kitten...
Please take me home

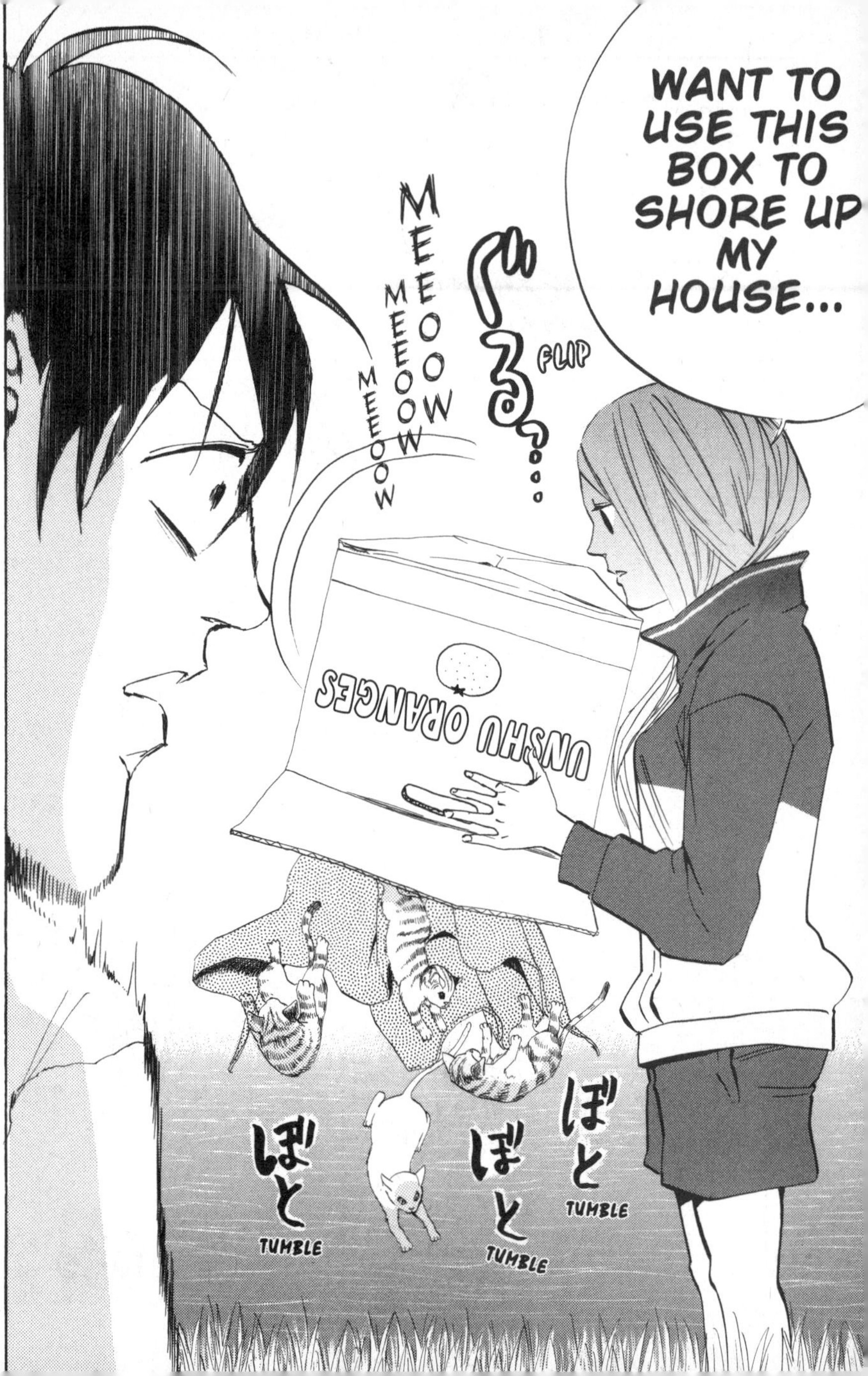
WANT TO USE THIS BOX TO SHORE UP MY HOUSE...
FLIP
MEEEOOW
MEEEOOW
MEEEOOW
UNSHU ORANGES
ぼと
TUMBLE
ぼと
TUMBLE
ぼと
TUMBLE

Chapter 229: Cat Magic

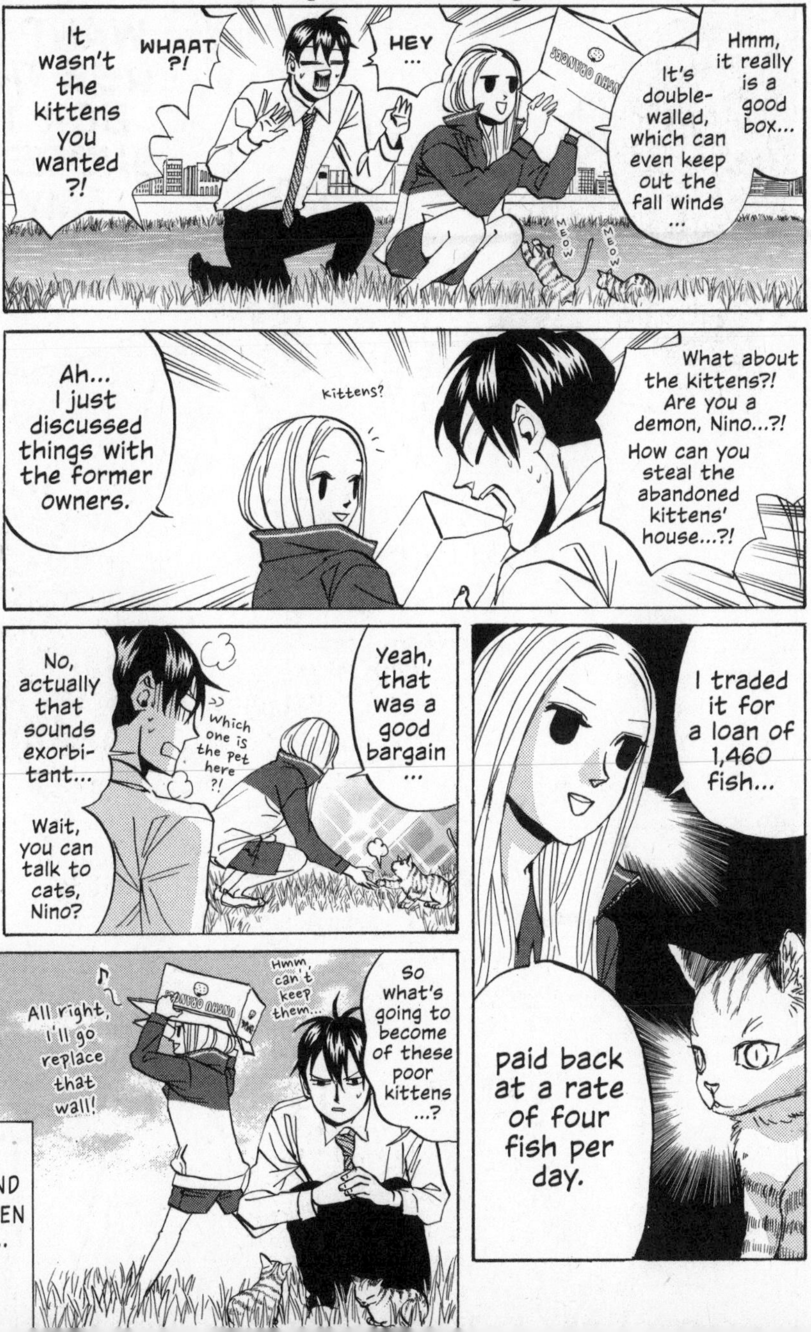
Hmm, it really is a good box...
It's double-walled, which can even keep out the fall winds ...
UNSHU ORANGES
HEY ...
WHAAT ?!
It wasn't the kittens you wanted ?!
MEOW
MEOW
What about the kittens?! Are you a demon, Nino...?!
How can you steal the abandoned kittens' house...?!
Kittens?
Ah... I just discussed things with the former owners.
I traded it for a loan of 1,460 fish...
paid back at a rate of four fish per day.
Yeah, that was a good bargain ...
Which one is the pet here ?!
No, actually that sounds exorbitant...
Wait, you can talk to cats, Nino?
So what's going to become of these poor kittens ...?
Hmm, can't keep them...
UNSHU ORANGES
All right, I'll go replace that wall!
AND THEN ...

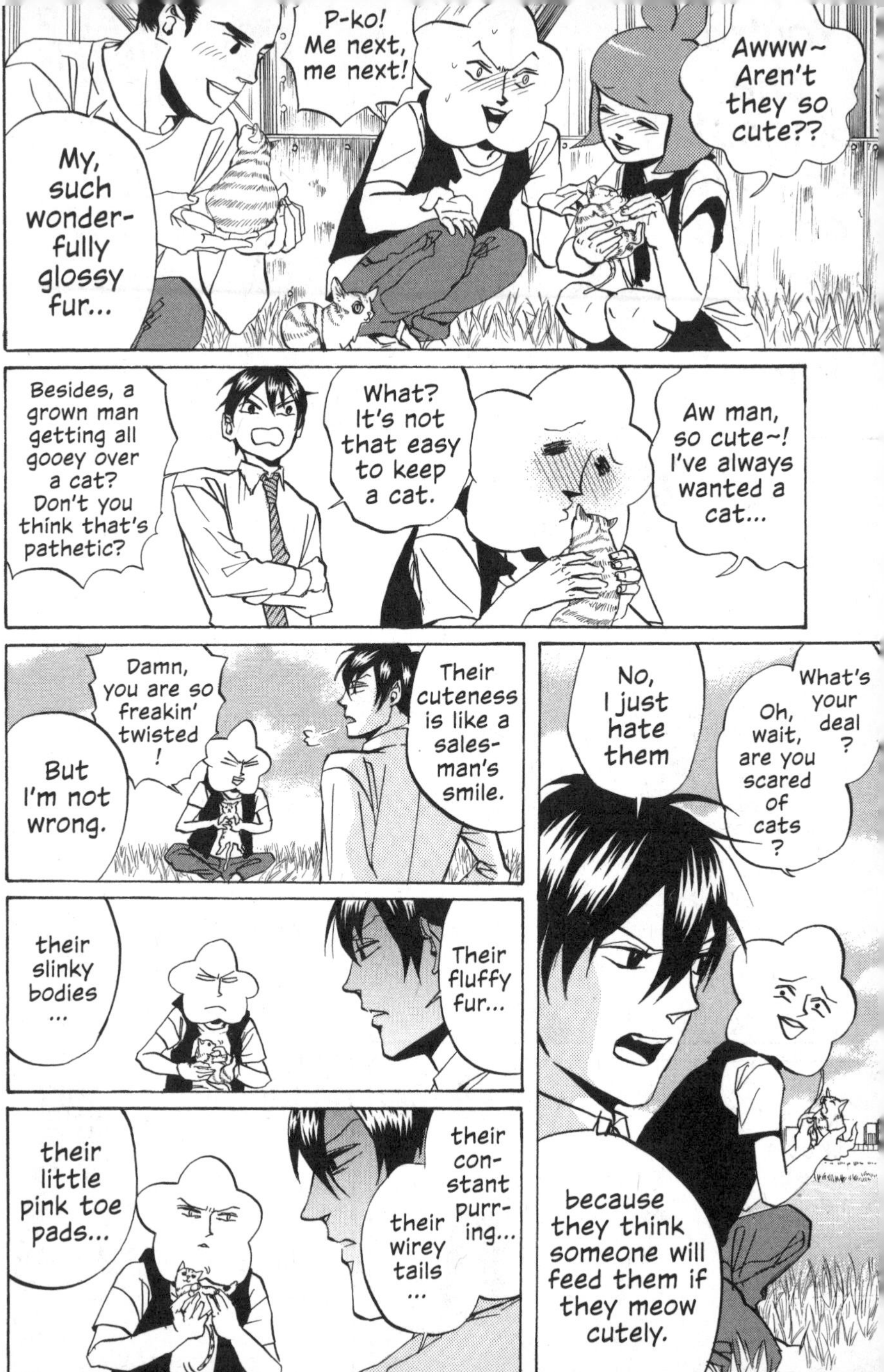
Awww~ Aren't they so cute??
P-ko! Me next, me next!
My, such wonderfully glossy fur...
Aw man, so cute~! I've always wanted a cat...
What? It's not that easy to keep a cat.
Besides, a grown man getting all gooey over a cat? Don't you think that's pathetic?
What's your deal ?
Oh, wait, are you scared of cats ?
No, I just hate them
because they think someone will feed them if they meow cutely.
Their cuteness is like a salesman's smile.
Damn, you are so freakin' twisted !
But I'm not wrong.
Their fluffy fur...
their slinky bodies ...
their constant purring...
their wirey tails ...
their little pink toe pads...

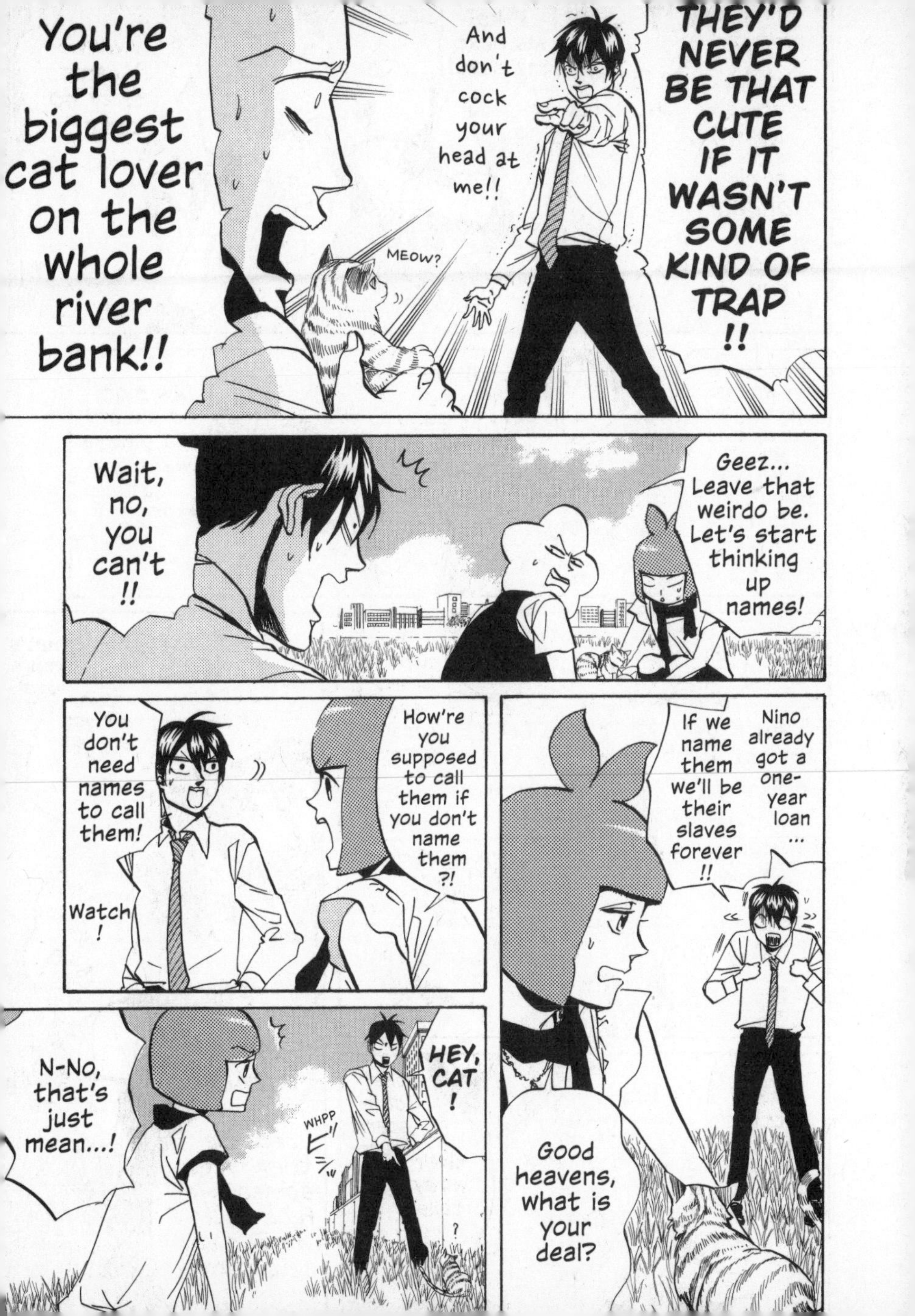
THEY'D NEVER BE THAT CUTE IF IT WASN'T SOME KIND OF TRAP!!
And don't cock your head at me!!
MEOW?
You're the biggest cat lover on the whole river bank!!
Geez... Leave that weirdo be. Let's start thinking up names!
Wait, no, you can't!!
Nino already got a one-year loan...
If we name them we'll be their slaves forever!!
Good heavens, what is your deal?
How're you supposed to call them if you don't name them?!
You don't need names to call them!
Watch!
HEY, CAT!
WHPP
N-No, that's just mean...!

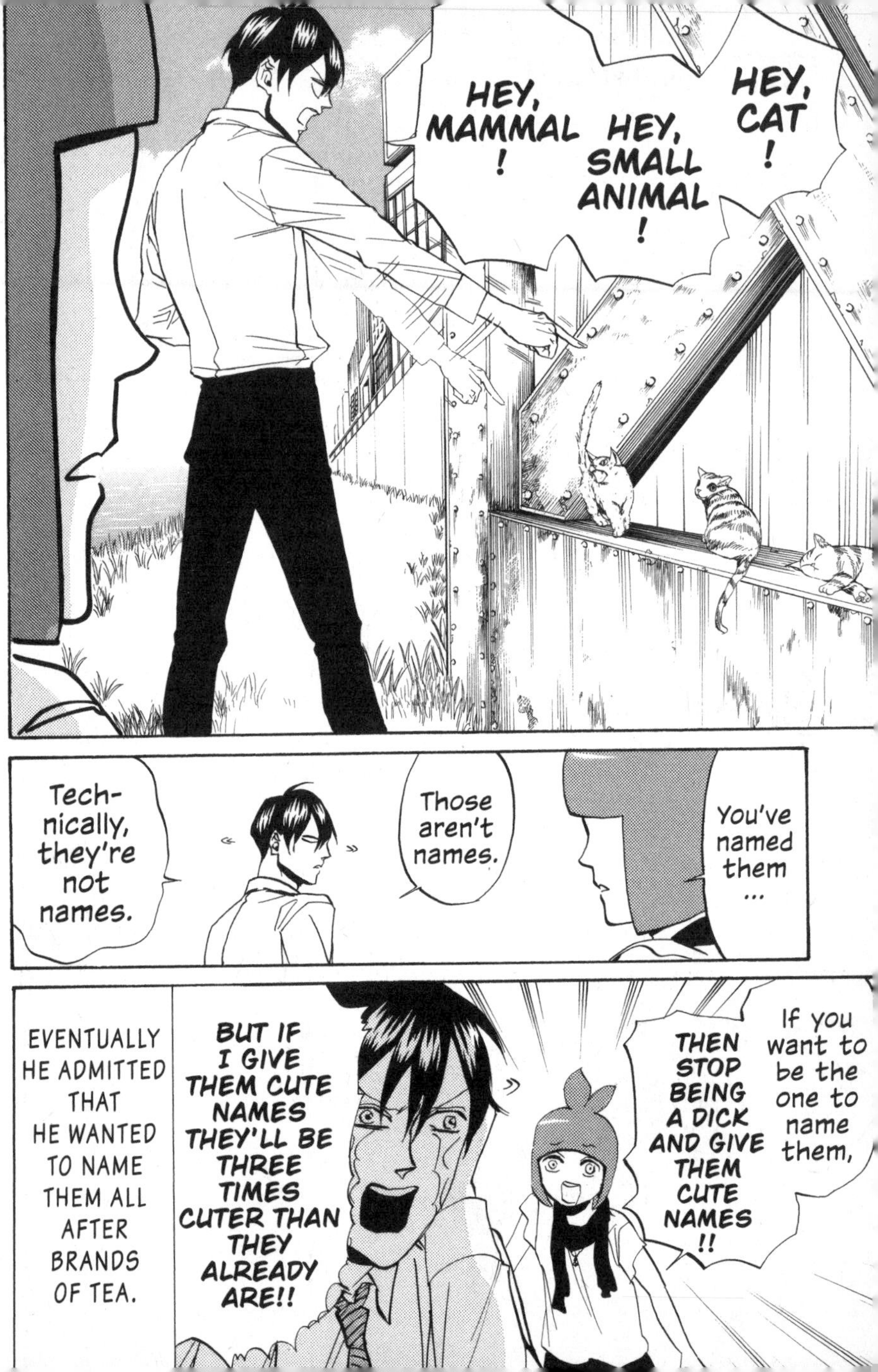
HEY, CAT!
HEY, SMALL ANIMAL!
HEY, MAMMAL!
You've named them ...
Those aren't names.
Tech-nically, they're not names.
If you want to be the one to name them,
THEN STOP BEING A DICK AND GIVE THEM CUTE NAMES!!
BUT IF I GIVE THEM CUTE NAMES THEY'LL BE THREE TIMES CUTER THAN THEY ALREADY ARE!!
EVENTUALLY HE ADMITTED THAT HE WANTED TO NAME THEM ALL AFTER BRANDS OF TEA.

Chapter 230: Arakawa-style Training

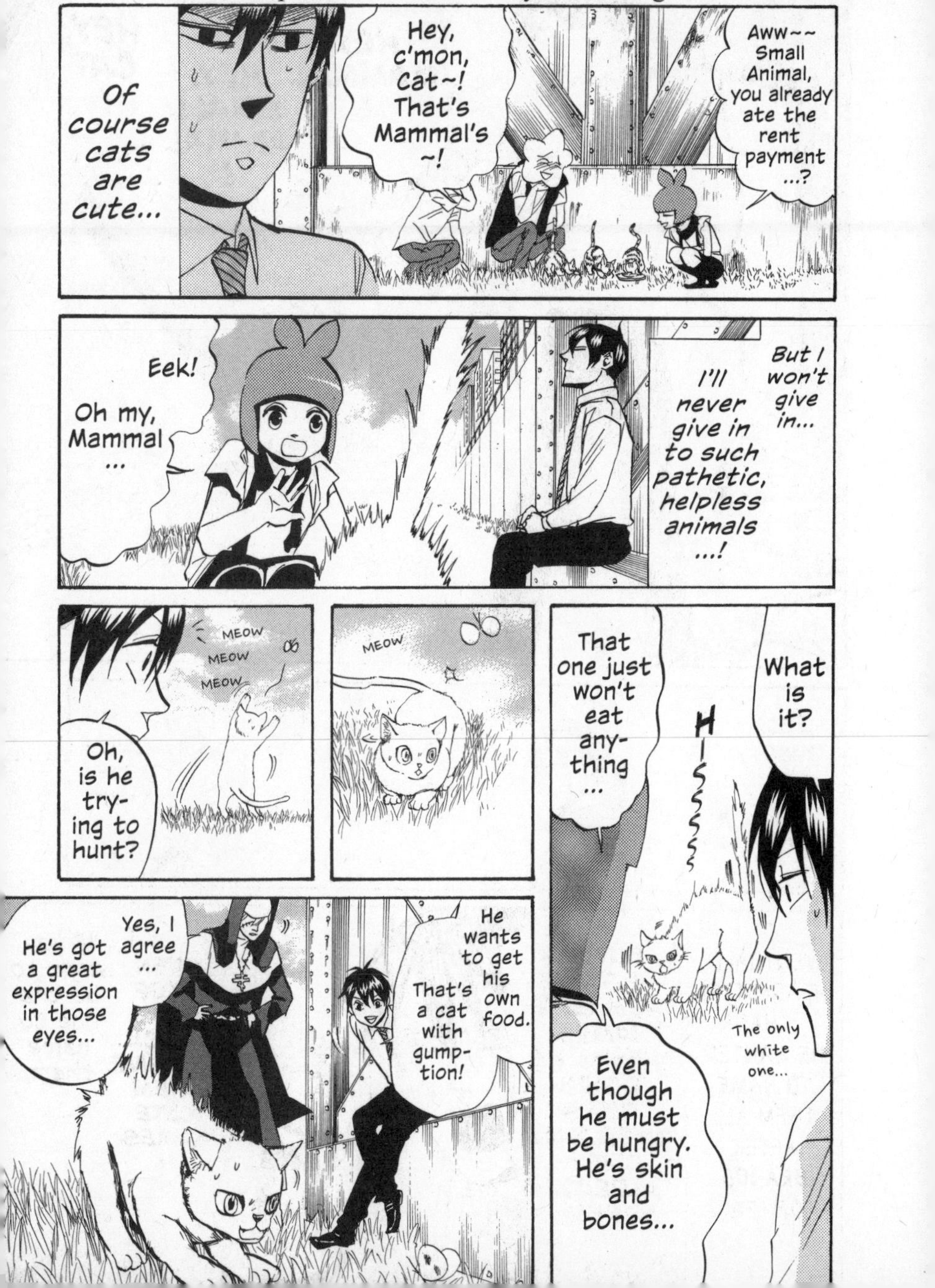
Aww~~ Small Animal, you already ate the rent payment ...?
Hey, c'mon, Cat~! That's Mammal's ~!
Of course cats are cute...
But I won't give in...
I'll never give in to such pathetic, helpless animals ...!
Eek!
Oh my, Mammal ...
What is it?
That one just won't eat anything ...
HISSSS
The only white one...
Even though he must be hungry. He's skin and bones...
MEOW
MEOW
MEOW
MEOW
Oh, is he trying to hunt?
He wants to get his own food.
That's a cat with gumption!
Yes, I agree ...
He's got a great expression in those eyes...

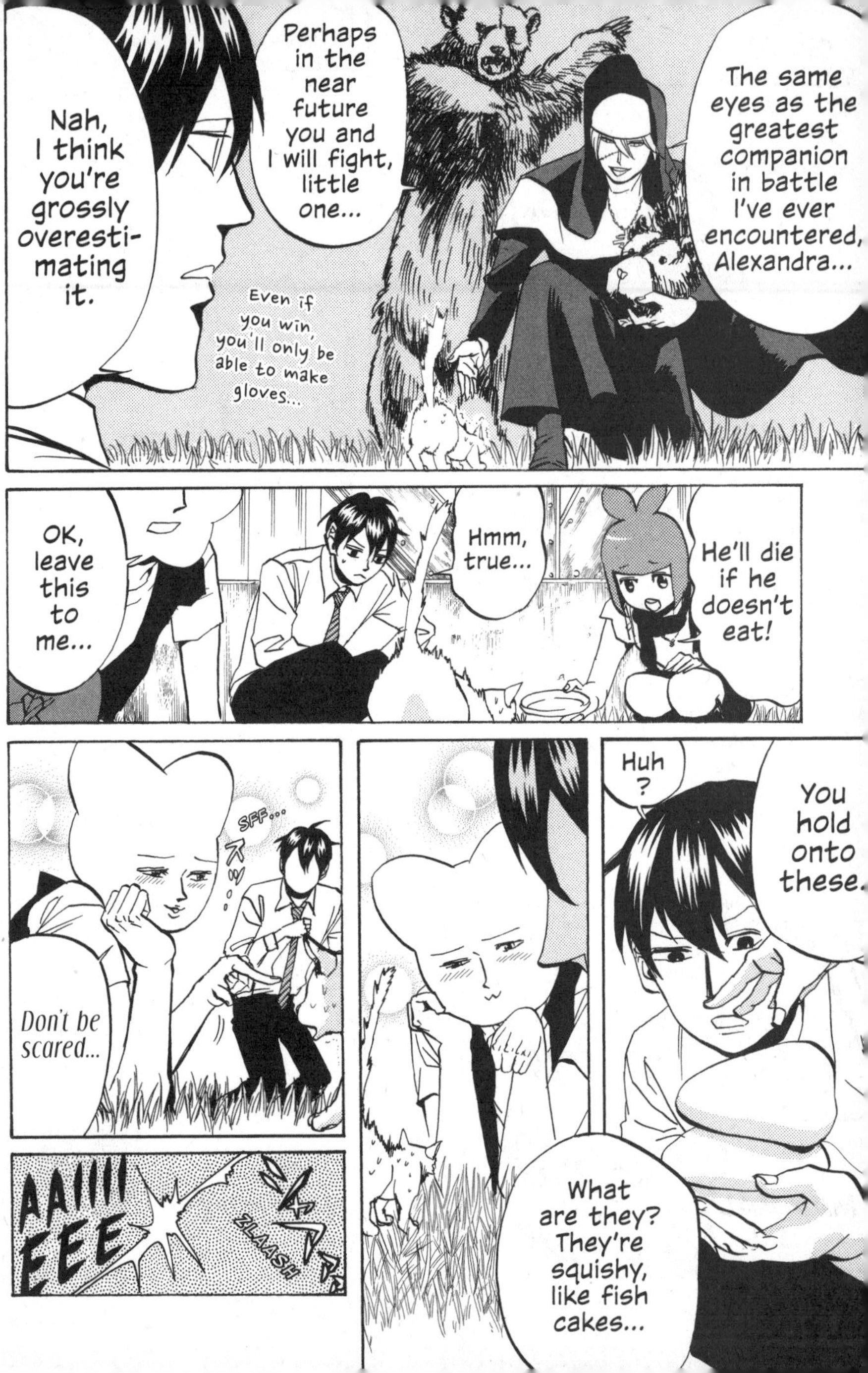
The same eyes as the greatest companion in battle I've ever encountered, Alexandra...
Perhaps in the near future you and I will fight, little one...
Nah, I think you're grossly overesti-mating it.
Even if you win, you'll only be able to make gloves...
He'll die if he doesn't eat!
Hmm, true...
OK, leave this to me...
You hold onto these.
Huh?
What are they? They're squishy, like fish cakes...
SFF...
Don't be scared...
AAIIII EEE
ZLAASH

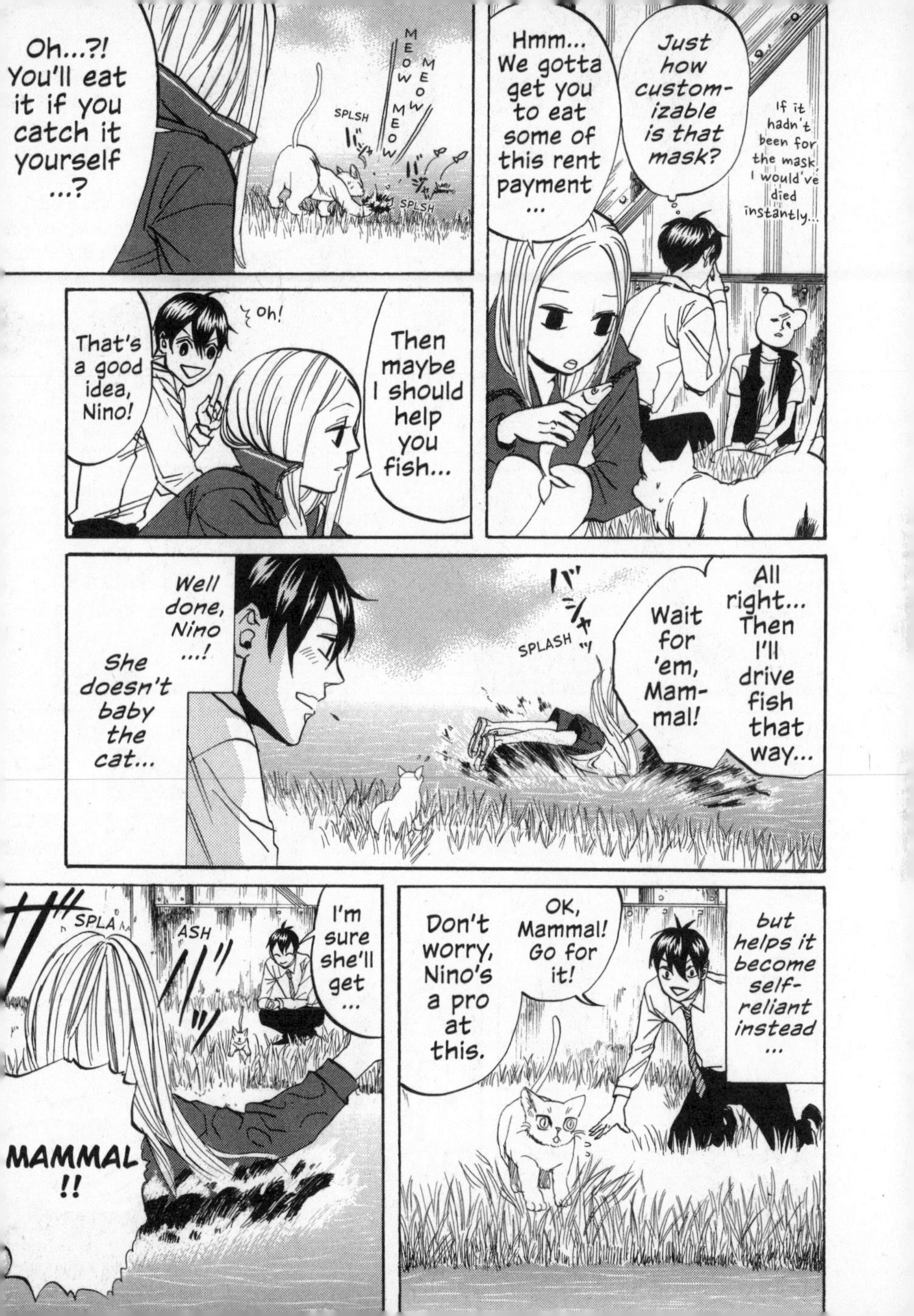
Just how customizable is that mask?
If it hadn't been for the mask I would've died instantly...
Hmm... We gotta get you to eat some of this rent payment ...
Oh...?! You'll eat it if you catch it yourself ...?
MEOW MEOW
MEOW MEOW
SPLSH
SPLSH
Oh!
Then maybe I should help you fish...
That's a good idea, Nino!
All right... Then I'll drive fish that way...
Wait for 'em, Mammal!
SPLASH
Well done, Nino ...!
She doesn't baby the cat...
but helps it become self-reliant instead ...
OK, Mammal! Go for it!
Don't worry, Nino's a pro at this.
I'm sure she'll get ...
SPLA
ASH
MAMMAL !!

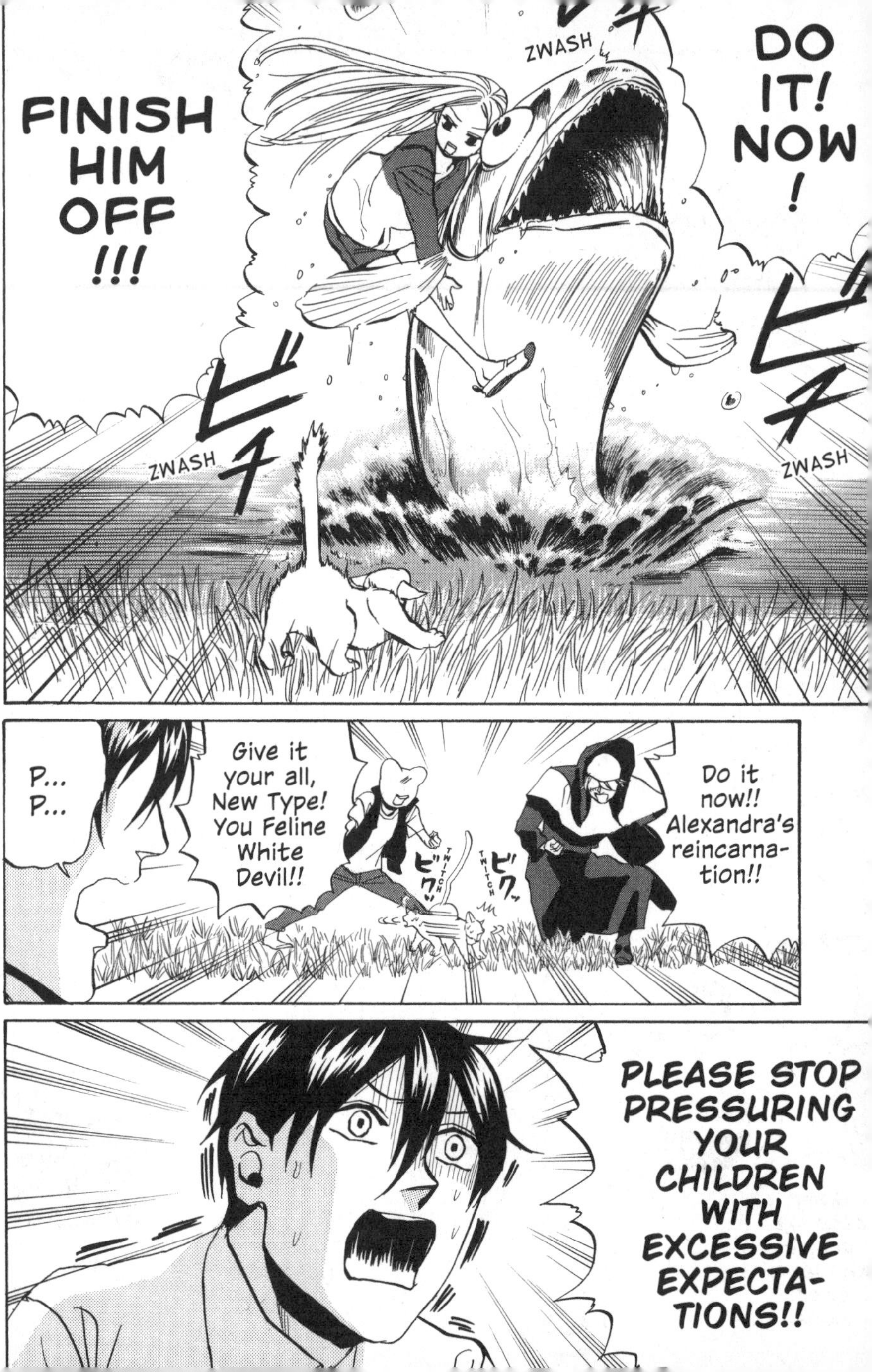

ZWASH
DO IT! NOW!
FINISH HIM OFF!!!
ZWASH
ZWASH
Do it now!! Alexandra's reincarnation!!
TWITCH
TWITCH
Give it your all, New Type! You Feline White Devil!!
P... P...
PLEASE STOP PRESSURING YOUR CHILDREN WITH EXCESSIVE EXPECTATIONS!!

Chapter 231: Open Your Heart

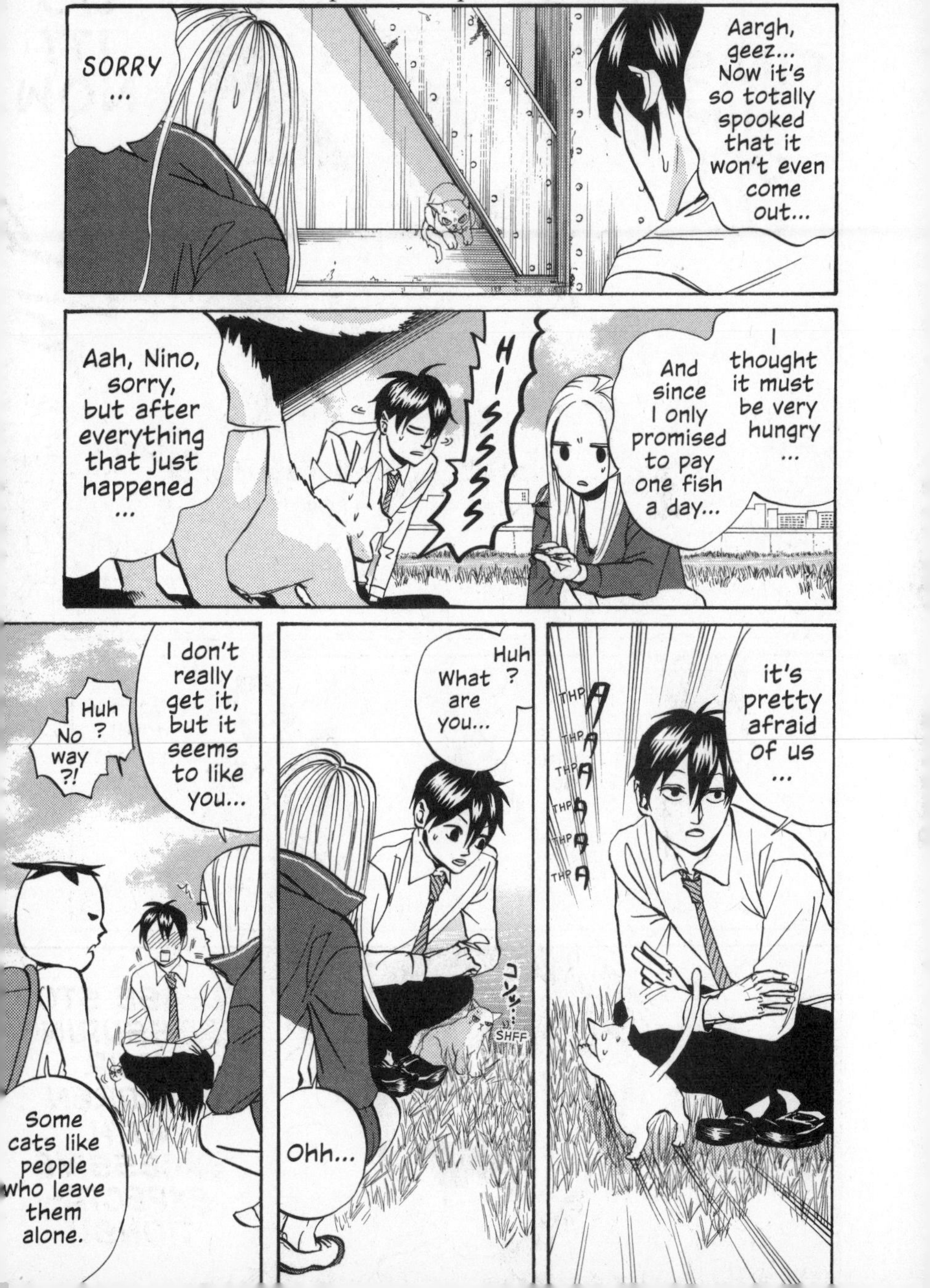
Aargh, geez... Now it's so totally spooked that it won't even come out...
SORRY ...
I thought it must be very hungry ...
And since I only promised to pay one fish a day...
HISSSSS
Aah, Nino, sorry, but after everything that just happened ...
THP
THP
THP
THP
THP
THP
it's pretty afraid of us ...
Huh ?
What are you...
SHFF
Ohh...
I don't really get it, but it seems to like you...
Huh ?
No way ?!
Some cats like people who leave them alone.

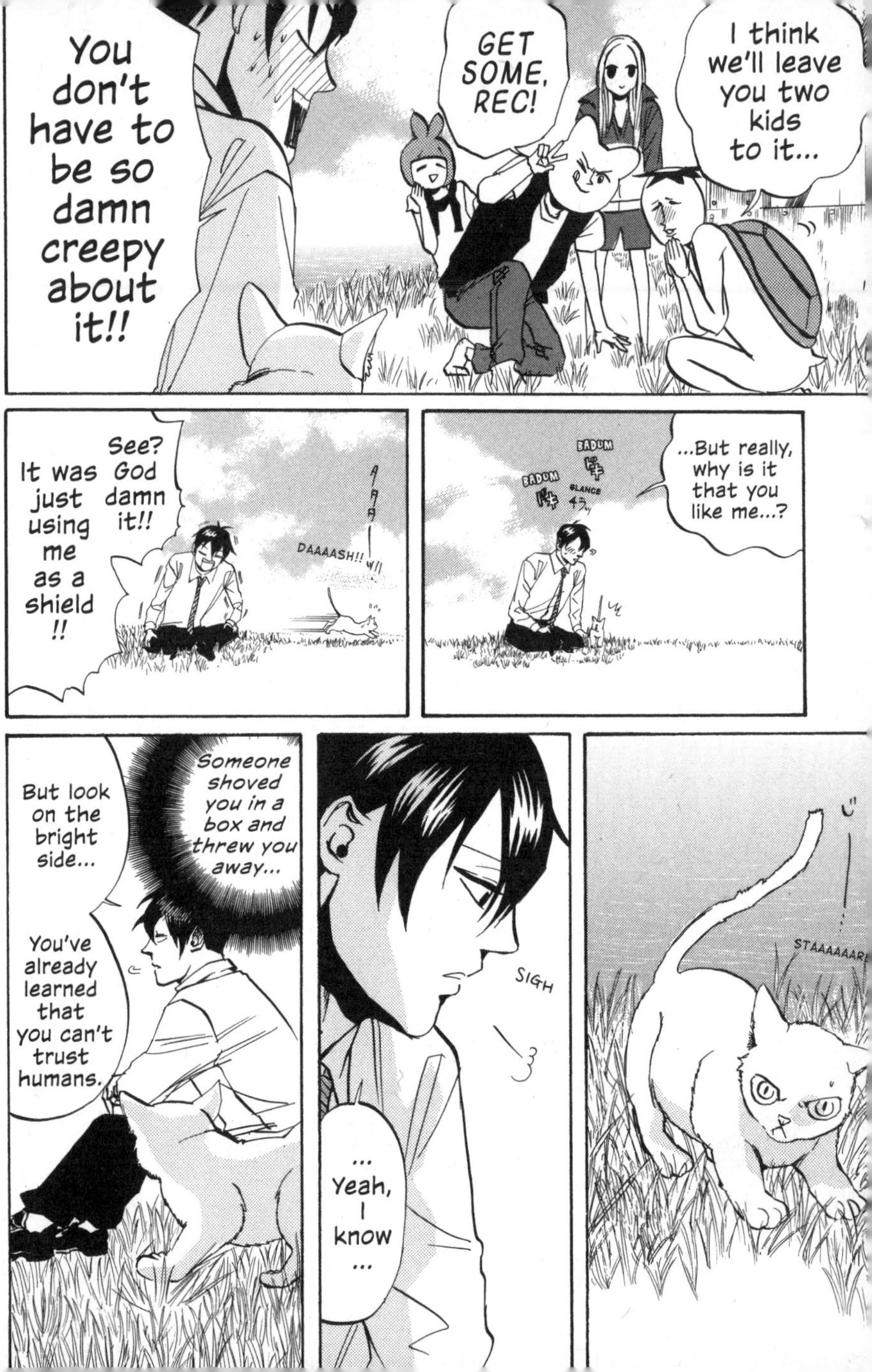
I think we'll leave you two kids to it...
GET SOME, REC!
You don't have to be so damn creepy about it!!
BADUM
BADUM
GLANCE
...But really, why is it that you like me...?
See? God damn it!!
It was just using me as a shield !!
DAAAASH!!
STAAAAAARE
SIGH
... Yeah, I know ...
Someone shoved you in a box and threw you away...
But look on the bright side...
You've already learned that you can't trust humans.

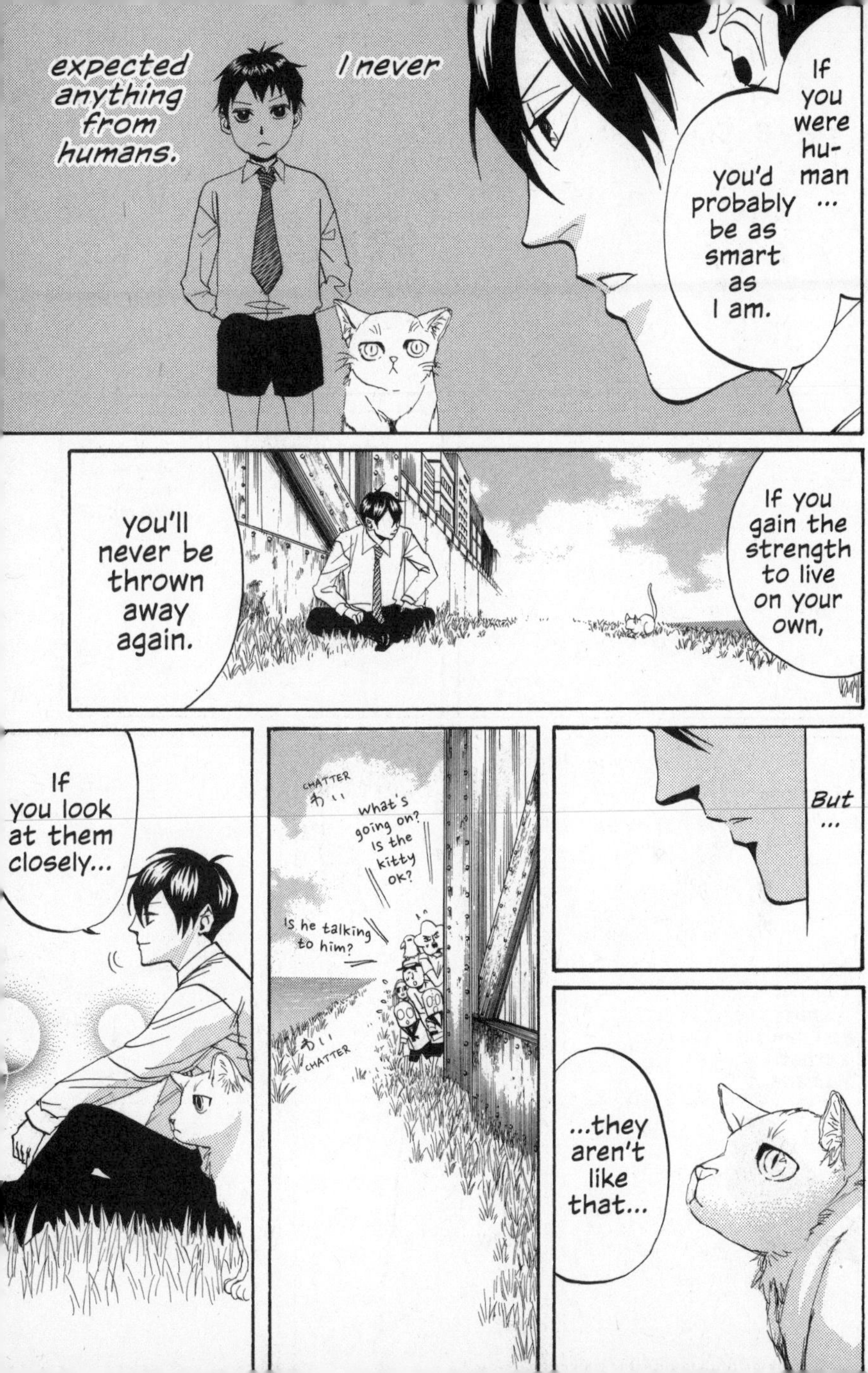
If you were human... you'd probably be as smart as I am.
I never
expected anything from humans.
If you gain the strength to live on your own,
you'll never be thrown away again.
But...
...they aren't like that...
CHATTER
わい
what's going on? Is the kitty OK?
Is he talking to him?
わい
CHATTER
If you look at them closely...

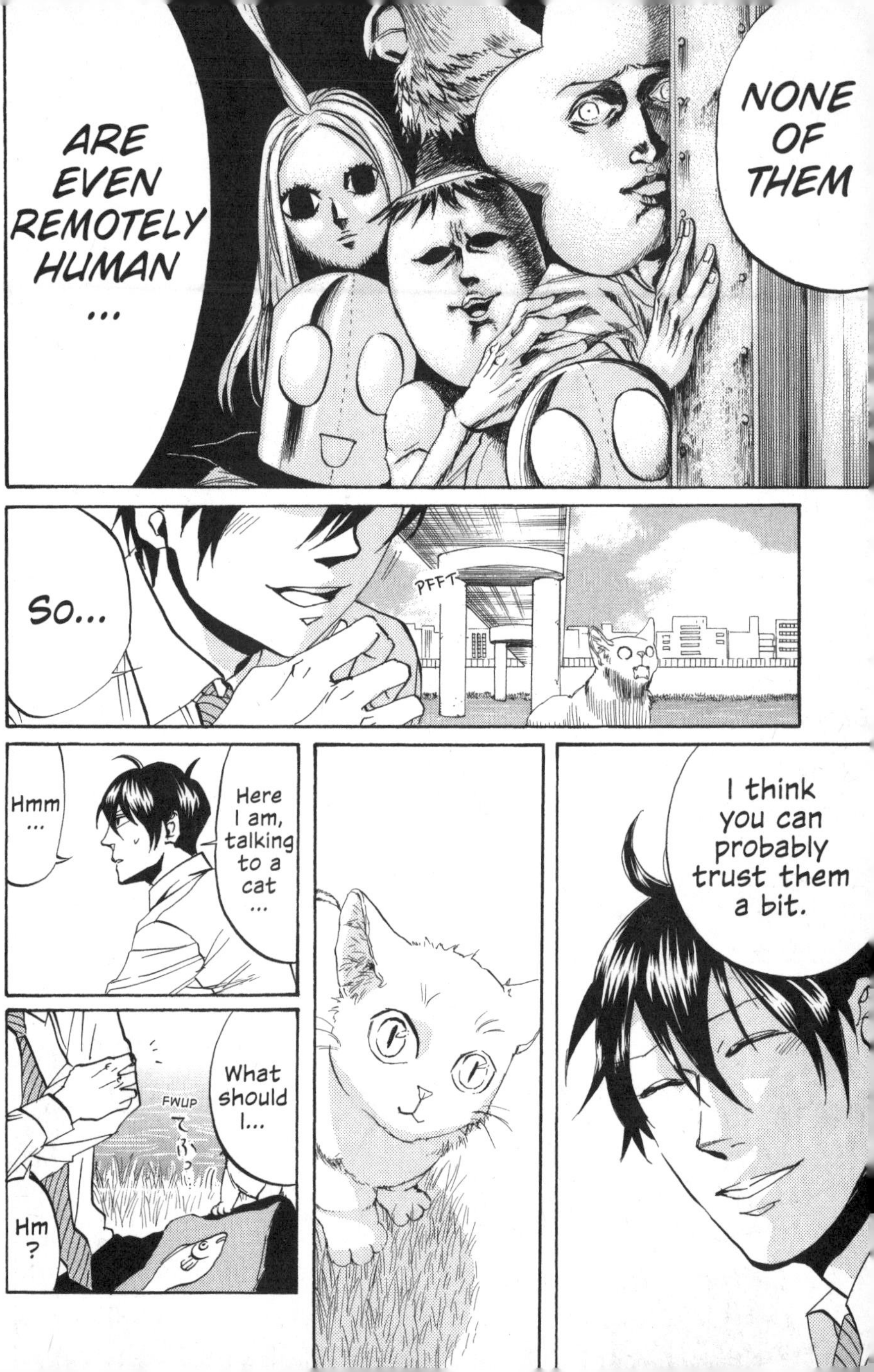
NONE OF THEM
ARE EVEN REMOTELY HUMAN ...
So...
PFFT
I think you can probably trust them a bit.
Here I am, talking to a cat ...
Hmm ...
What should I...
FWUP
Hm ?

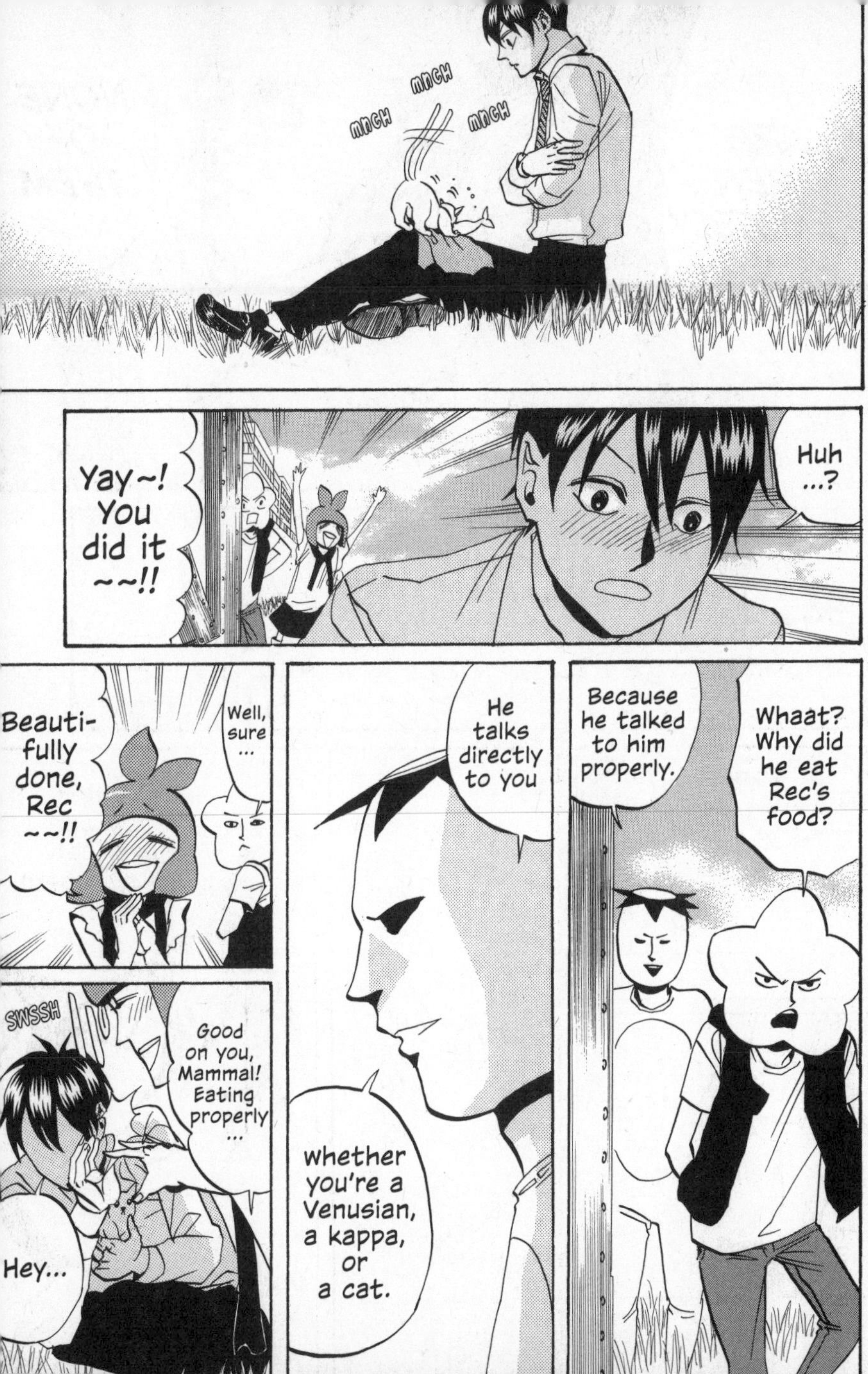
MNCH
MNCH
MNCH
Huh ...?
Yay~! You did it ~~!!
Whaat? Why did he eat Rec's food?
Because he talked to him properly.
He talks directly to you
whether you're a Venusian, a kappa, or a cat.
Well, sure ...
Beauti-fully done, Rec ~~!!
SWSSH
Good on you, Mammal! Eating properly ...
Hey...

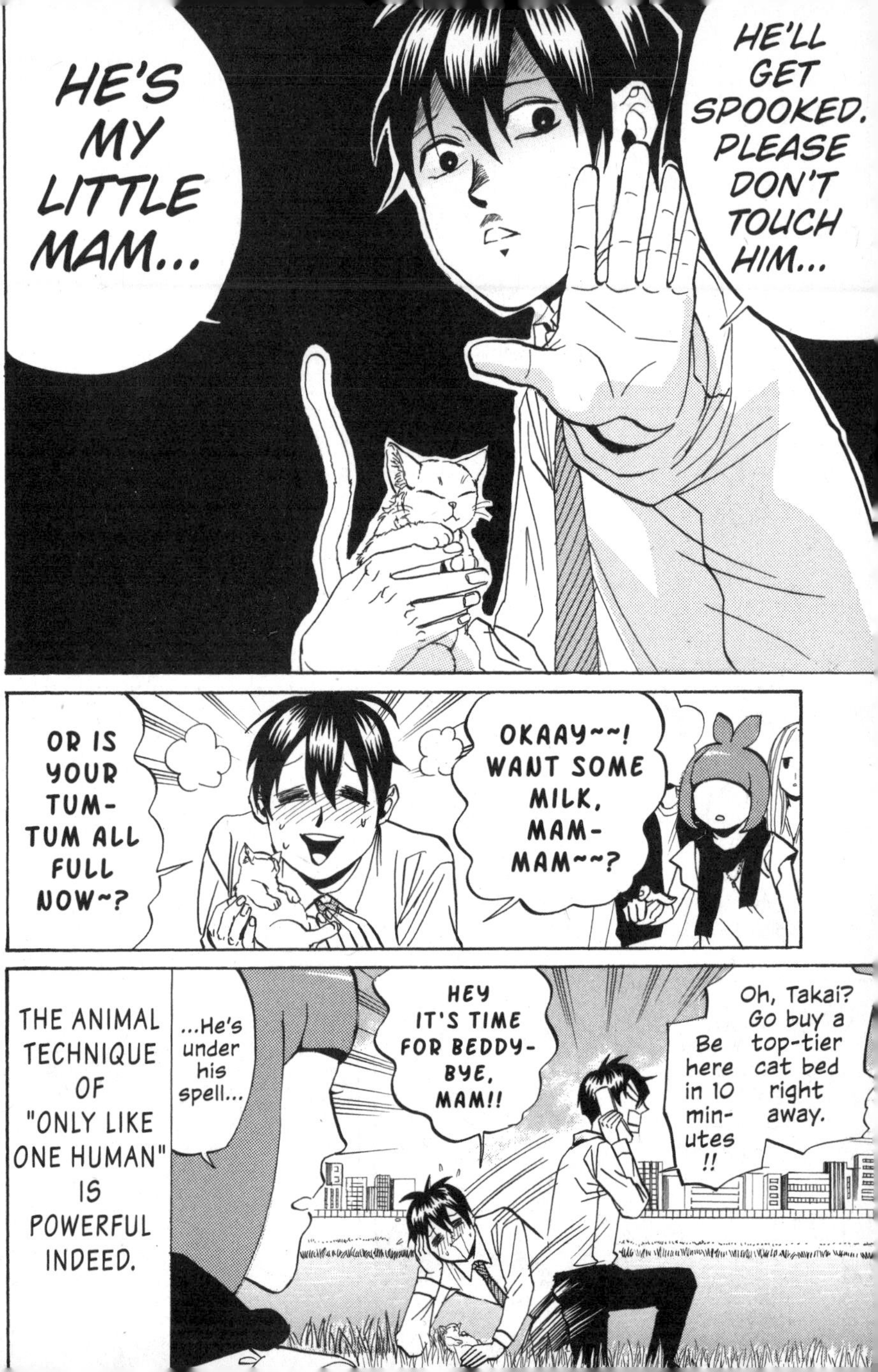
HE'LL GET SPOOKED. PLEASE DON'T TOUCH HIM...
HE'S MY LITTLE MAM...
OKAAY~~! WANT SOME MILK, MAM-MAM~~?
OR IS YOUR TUM-TUM ALL FULL NOW~?
Oh, Takai? Go buy a top-tier cat bed right away.
Be here in 10 min-utes !!
HEY IT'S TIME FOR BEDDY-BYE, MAM!!
...He's under his spell...
THE ANIMAL TECHNIQUE OF "ONLY LIKE ONE HUMAN" IS POWERFUL INDEED.

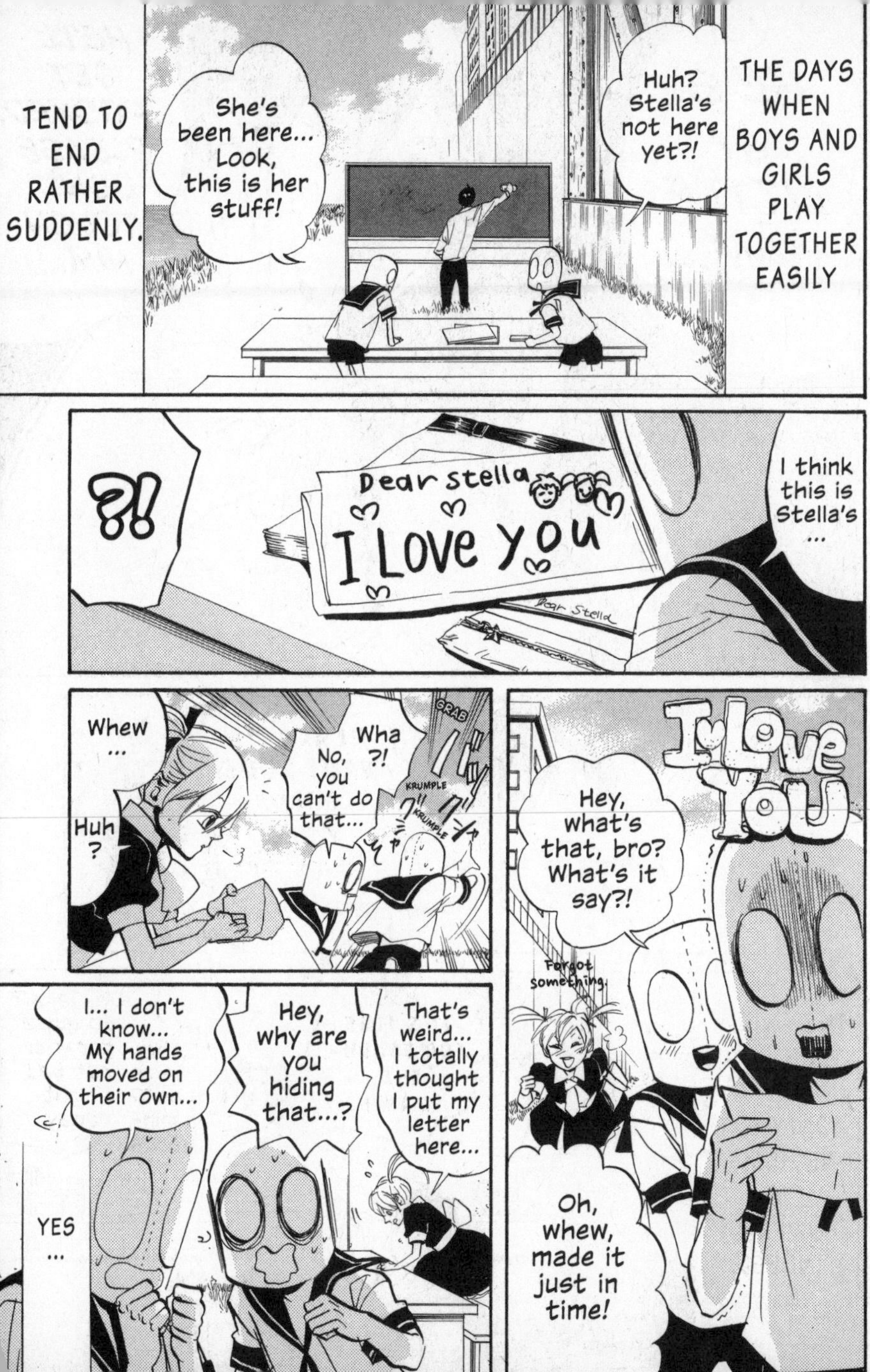
THE DAYS WHEN BOYS AND GIRLS PLAY TOGETHER EASILY
Huh? Stella's not here yet?!
She's been here... Look, this is her stuff!
TEND TO END RATHER SUDDENLY.
I think this is Stella's ...
Dear stella
I Love you
Dear Stella
?!
I Love YOU
Hey, what's that, bro? What's it say?!
Forgot something.
Oh, whew, made it just in time!
GRAB
Wha ?!
No, you can't do that...
KRUMPLE
KRUMPLE
Whew ...
Huh ?
That's weird... I totally thought I put my letter here...
Hey, why are you hiding that...?
I... I don't know... My hands moved on their own...
YES ...

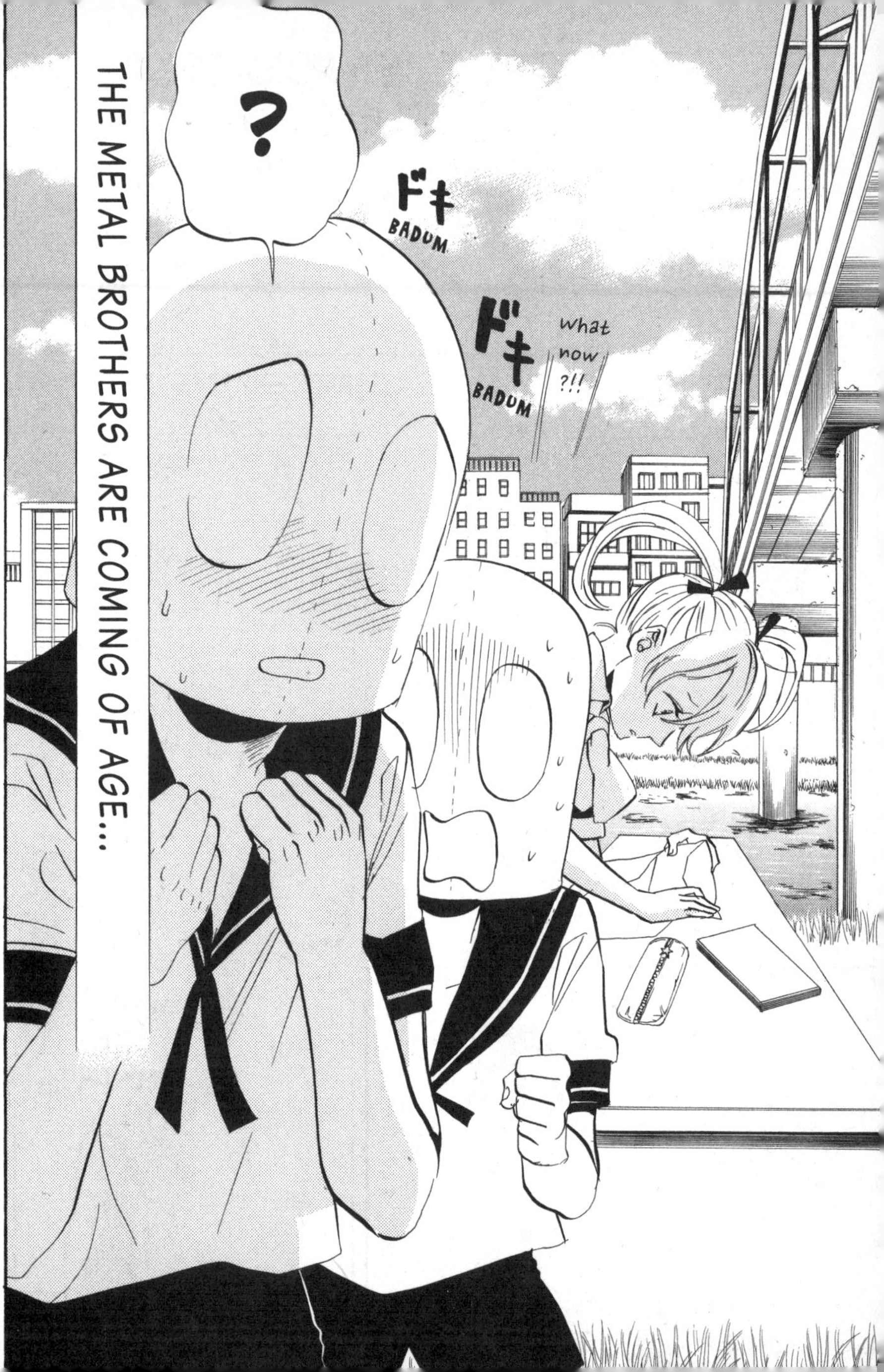

what now ?!!
ドキ BADUM
ドキ BADUM
?
THE METAL BROTHERS ARE COMING OF AGE...

Chapter 232: First Love

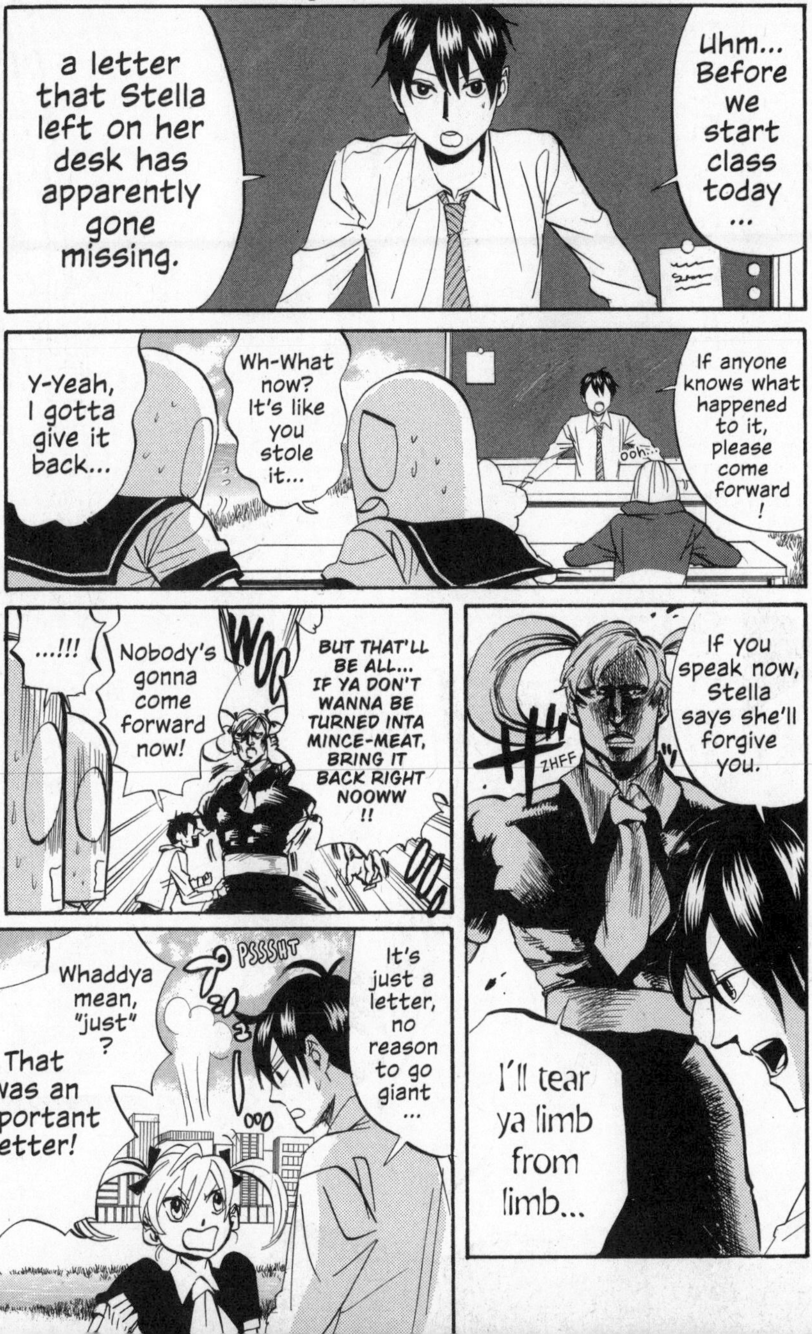
Uhm... Before we start class today ...
a letter that Stella left on her desk has apparently gone missing.
If anyone knows what happened to it, please come forward !
ooh...
Wh-What now? It's like you stole it...
Y-Yeah, I gotta give it back...
If you speak now, Stella says she'll forgive you.
ZHFF
I'll tear ya limb from limb...
BUT THAT'LL BE ALL... IF YA DON'T WANNA BE TURNED INTA MINCE-MEAT, BRING IT BACK RIGHT NOOWW !!
WOO
Nobody's gonna come forward now!
...!!!
It's just a letter, no reason to go giant ...
PSSSHT
Whaddya mean, "just" ?
That was an important letter!
OOO

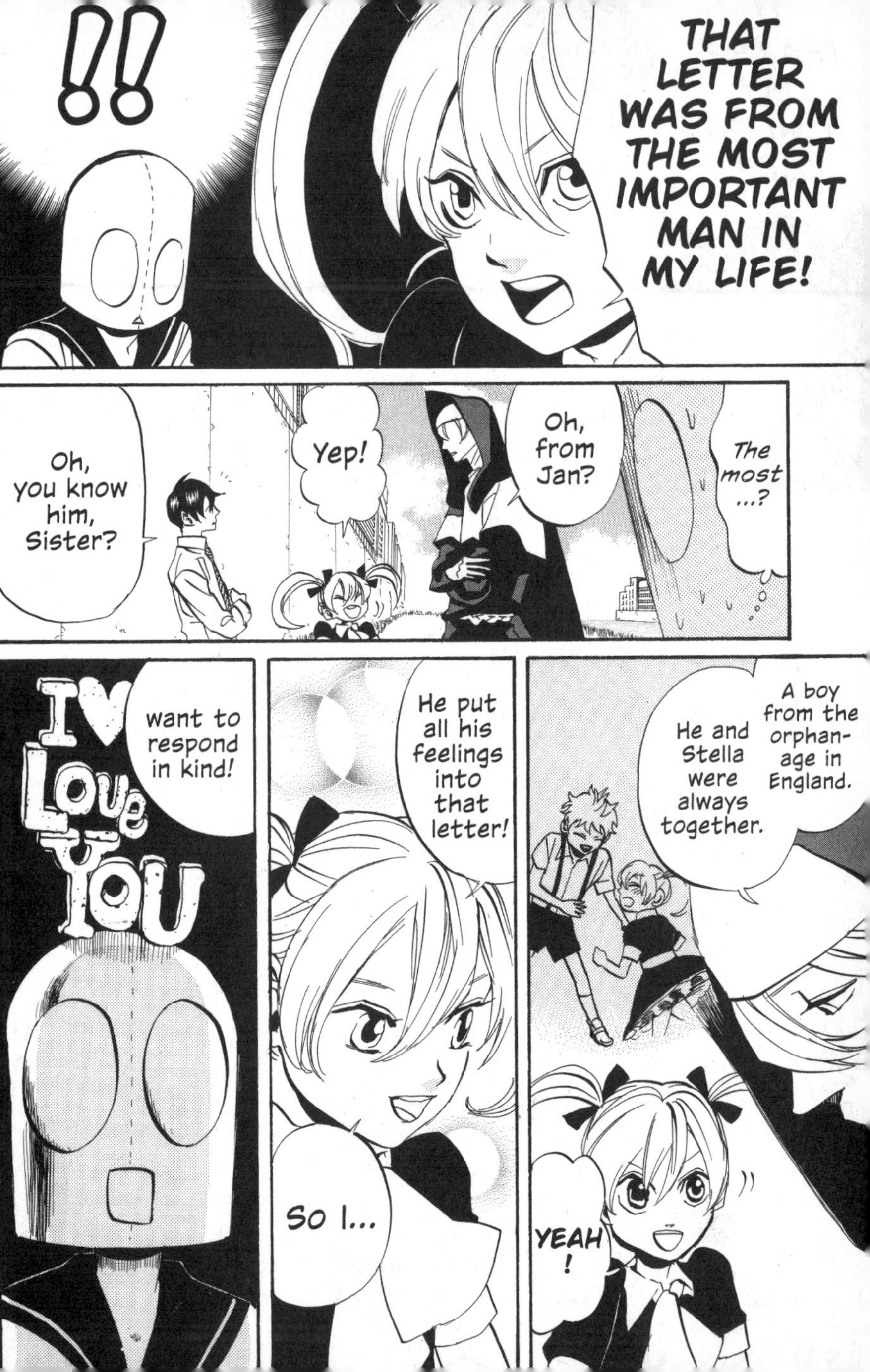
THAT LETTER WAS FROM THE MOST IMPORTANT MAN IN MY LIFE!
!!
The most ...?
Oh, from Jan?
Yep!
Oh, you know him, Sister?
A boy from the orphan-age in England.
He and Stella were always together.
YEAH!
He put all his feelings into that letter!
So I...
want to respond in kind!
I ♥ Love You

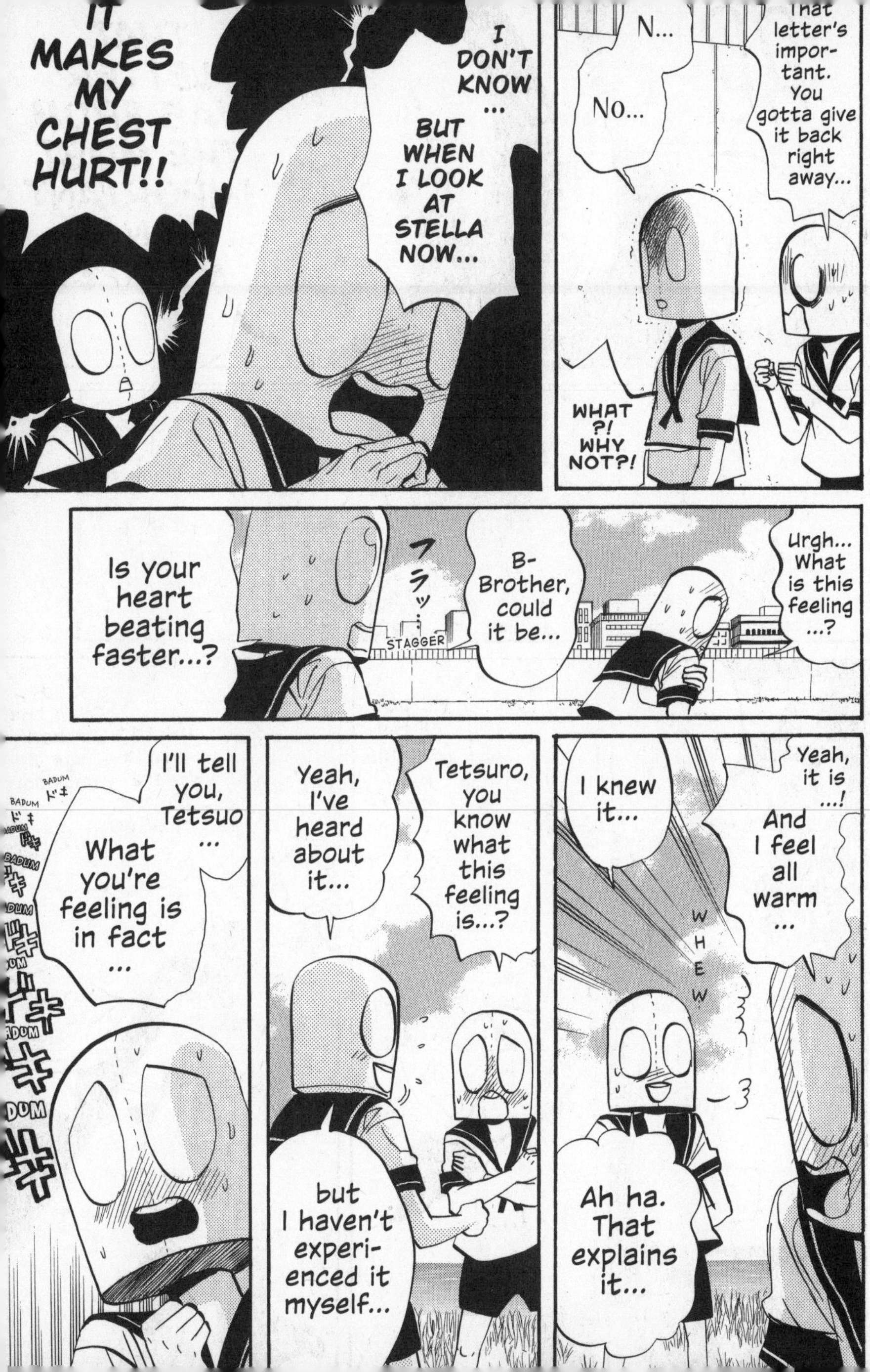
That letter's important. You gotta give it back right away...
N...
No...
WHAT?! WHY NOT?!
I DON'T KNOW... BUT WHEN I LOOK AT STELLA NOW...
IT MAKES MY CHEST HURT!!
Urgh... What is this feeling...?
B-Brother, could it be...
フラッ
STAGGER
Is your heart beating faster...?
Yeah, it is...! And I feel all warm...
I knew it...
WHEW
Ah ha. That explains it...
Tetsuro, you know what this feeling is...?
Yeah, I've heard about it...
but I haven't experienced it myself...
BADUM
ドキ
I'll tell you, Tetsuo...
What you're feeling is in fact...

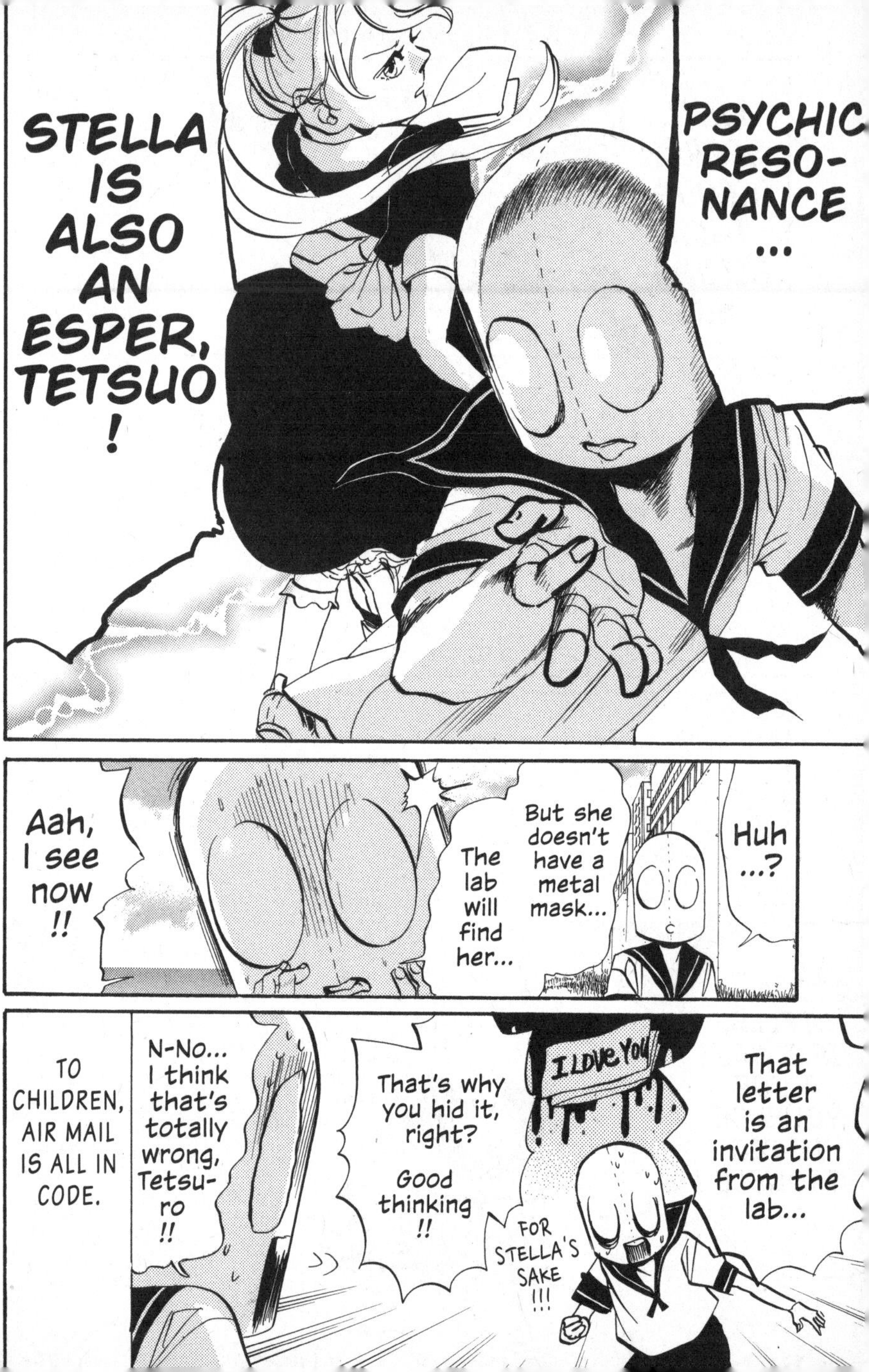
PSYCHIC RESONANCE...
STELLA IS ALSO AN ESPER, TETSUO!
Huh...?
But she doesn't have a metal mask...
The lab will find her...
Aah, I see now!!
That letter is an invitation from the lab...
I LOVE YOU
FOR STELLA'S SAKE!!!
That's why you hid it, right?
Good thinking!!
N-No... I think that's totally wrong, Tetsuro!!
TO CHILDREN, AIR MAIL IS ALL IN CODE.

Chapter 233: Inspection

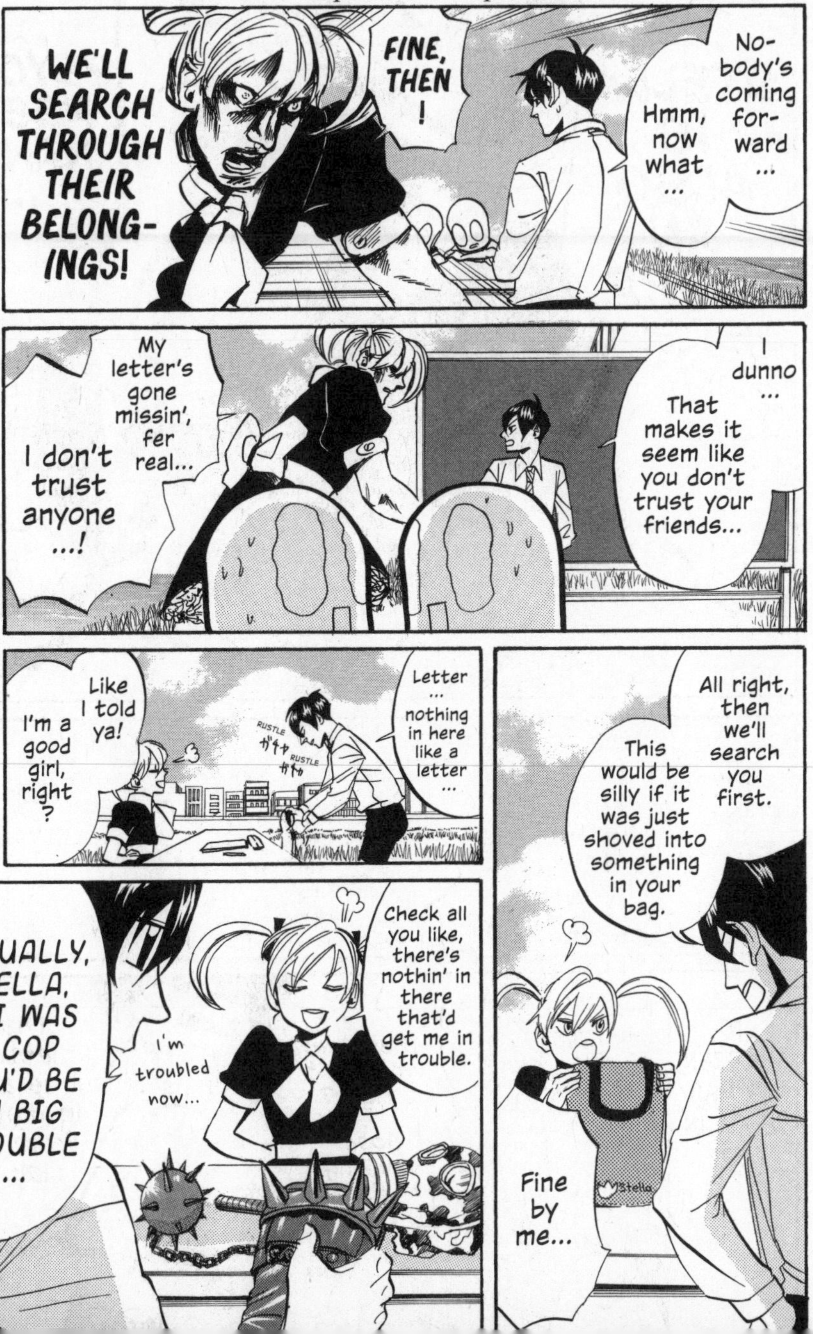

No-body's coming for-ward ...
Hmm, now what ...
FINE, THEN!
WE'LL SEARCH THROUGH THEIR BELONG-INGS!
I dunno ...
That makes it seem like you don't trust your friends...
My letter's gone missin', fer real...
I don't trust anyone ...!
All right, then we'll search you first.
This would be silly if it was just shoved into something in your bag.
Stella
Fine by me...
Letter ... nothing in here like a letter ...
RUSTLE
RUSTLE
Like I told ya!
I'm a good girl, right?
Check all you like, there's nothin' in there that'd get me in trouble.
I'm troubled now...
ACTUALLY, STELLA, IF I WAS A COP YOU'D BE IN BIG TROUBLE ...

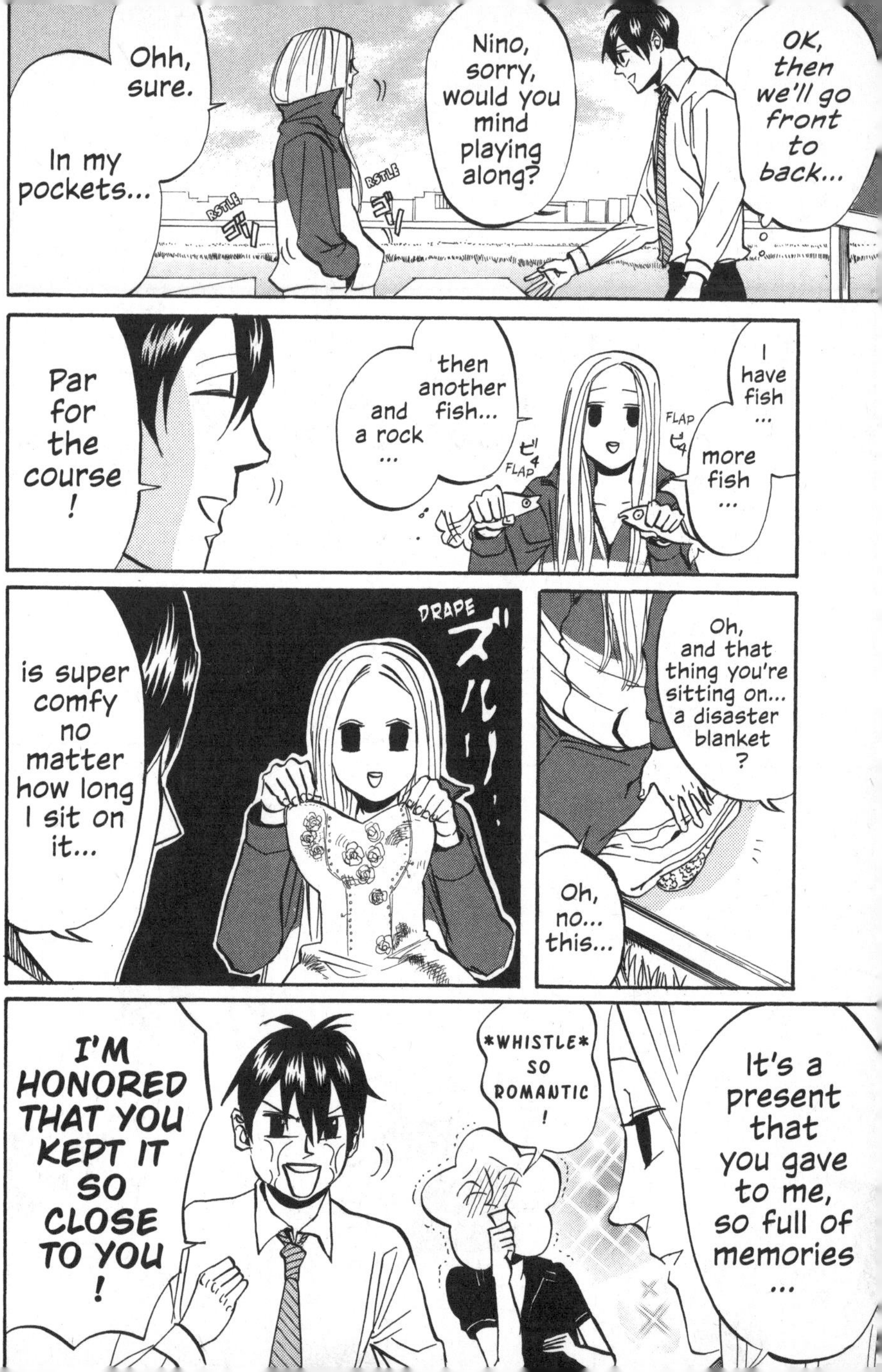
OK, then we'll go front to back...
Nino, sorry, would you mind playing along?
RSTLE
RSTLE
Ohh, sure.
In my pockets...
I have fish... more fish...
FLAP
FLAP
then another fish... and a rock...
Par for the course!
Oh, and that thing you're sitting on... a disaster blanket?
Oh, no... this...
DRAPE
is super comfy no matter how long I sit on it...
It's a present that you gave to me, so full of memories...
WHISTLE SO ROMANTIC!
I'M HONORED THAT YOU KEPT IT SO CLOSE TO YOU!

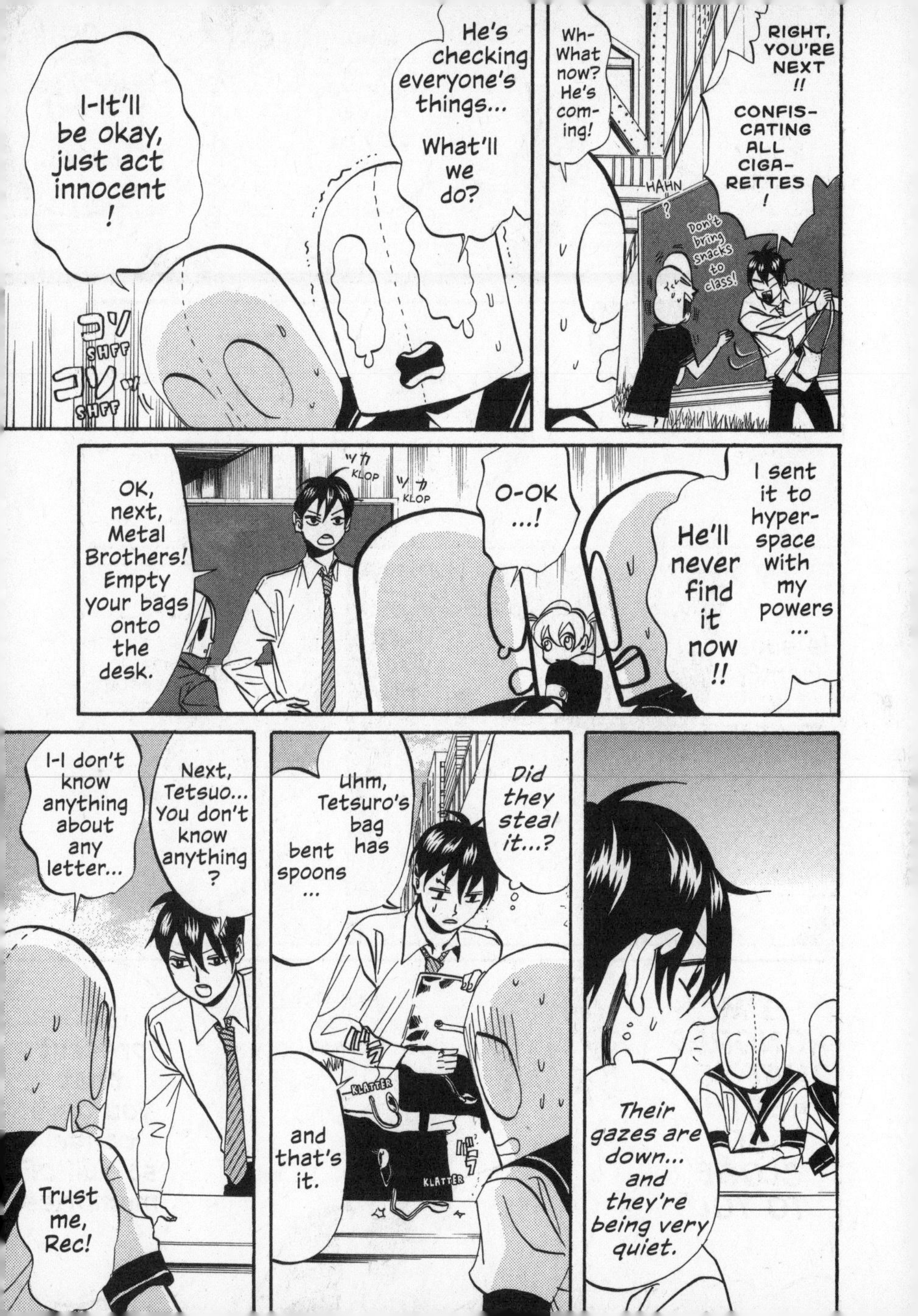
RIGHT, YOU'RE NEXT!!
CONFISCATING ALL CIGARETTES!
HAHN
Don't bring snacks to class!
Wh-What now? He's coming!
He's checking everyone's things...
What'll we do?
I-It'll be okay, just act innocent!
SHFF
SHFF
I sent it to hyperspace with my powers...
He'll never find it now!!
O-OK...!
KLOP
KLOP
OK, next, Metal Brothers! Empty your bags onto the desk.
Their gazes are down... and they're being very quiet.
Did they steal it...?
Uhm, Tetsuro's bag has bent spoons...
KLATTER
KLATTER
and that's it.
Next, Tetsuo... You don't know anything?
I-I don't know anything about any letter...
Trust me, Rec!

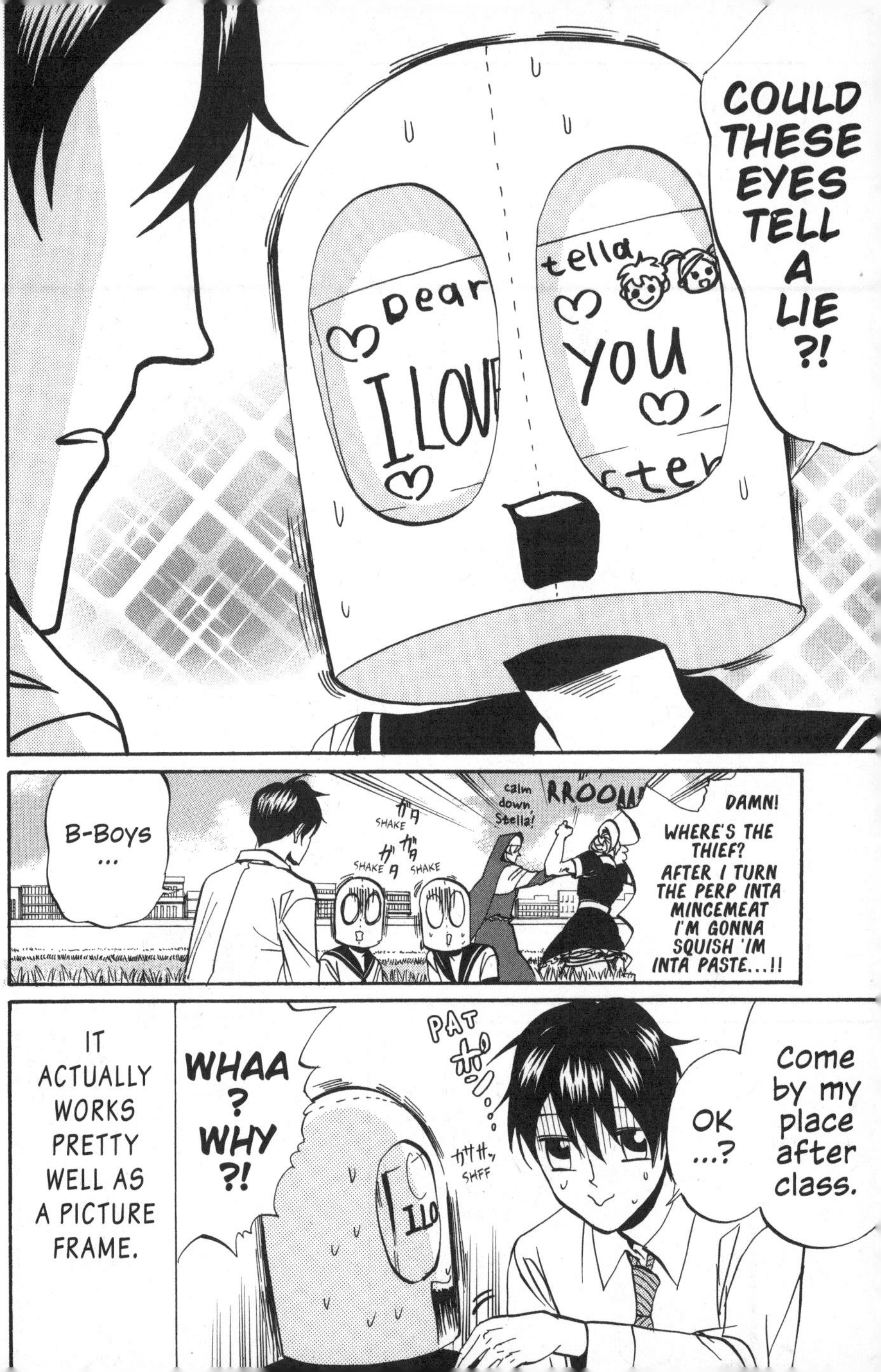
COULD THESE EYES TELL A LIE ?!
Dear
tella
YOU
DAMN! WHERE'S THE THIEF? AFTER I TURN THE PERP INTA MINCEMEAT I'M GONNA SQUISH 'IM INTA PASTE...!!
calm down, Stella!
SHAKE
SHAKE
SHAKE
B-Boys ...
Come by my place after class.
OK ...?
PAT
SHFF
WHAA ? WHY ?!
IT ACTUALLY WORKS PRETTY WELL AS A PICTURE FRAME.

Chapter 234: Confession

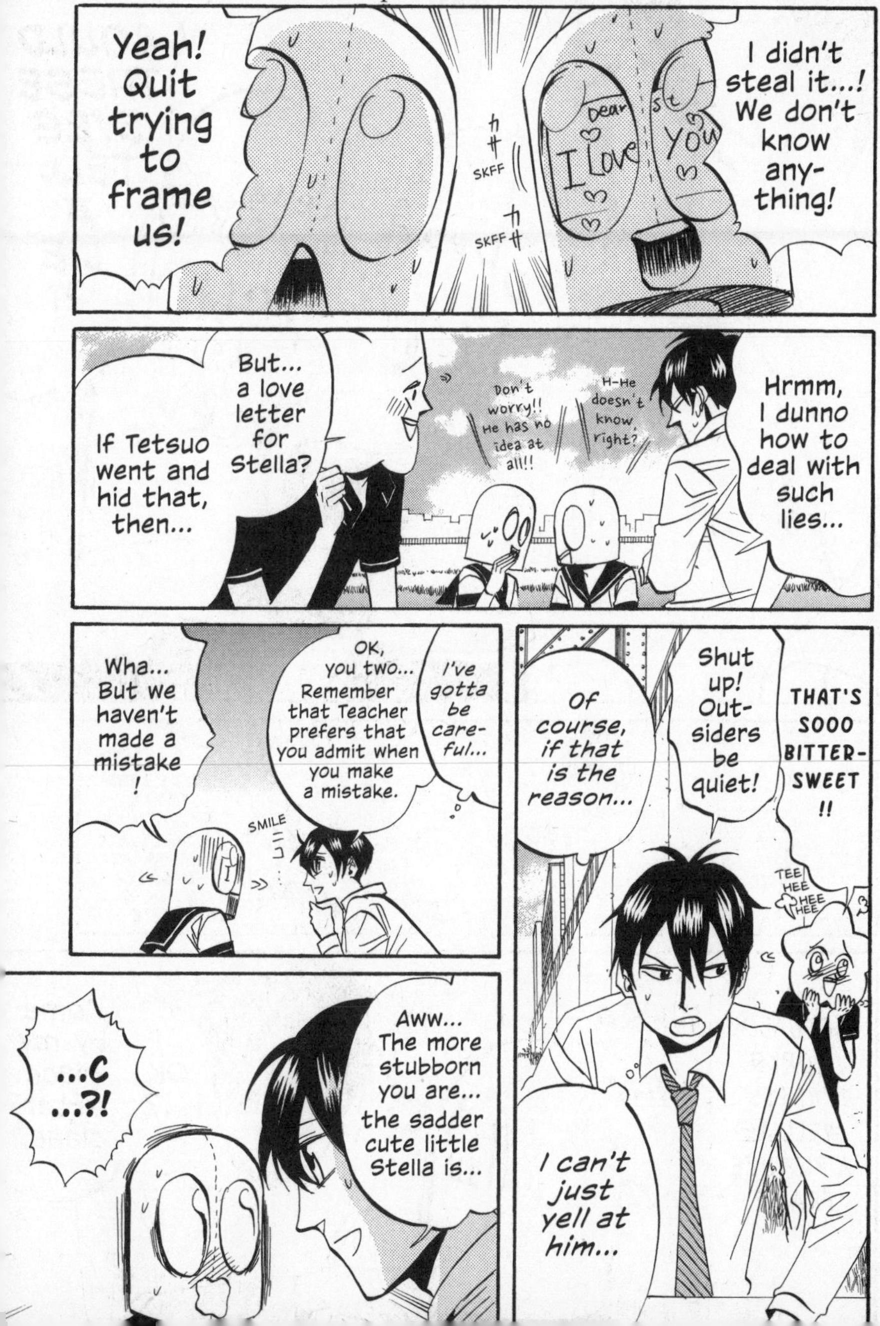
I didn't steal it...! We don't know anything!
Dear St
I Love You
SKFF
SKFF
Yeah! Quit trying to frame us!
Hrmm, I dunno how to deal with such lies...
H-He doesn't know, right?
Don't worry!! He has no idea at all!!
But... a love letter for Stella?
If Tetsuo went and hid that, then...
THAT'S SOOO BITTER-SWEET!!
TEE HEE HEE HEE
Shut up! Outsiders be quiet!
Of course, if that is the reason...
I can't just yell at him...
I've gotta be careful...
OK, you two... Remember that Teacher prefers that you admit when you make a mistake.
SMILE
Wha... But we haven't made a mistake!
Aww... The more stubborn you are... the sadder cute little Stella is...
...C ...?!

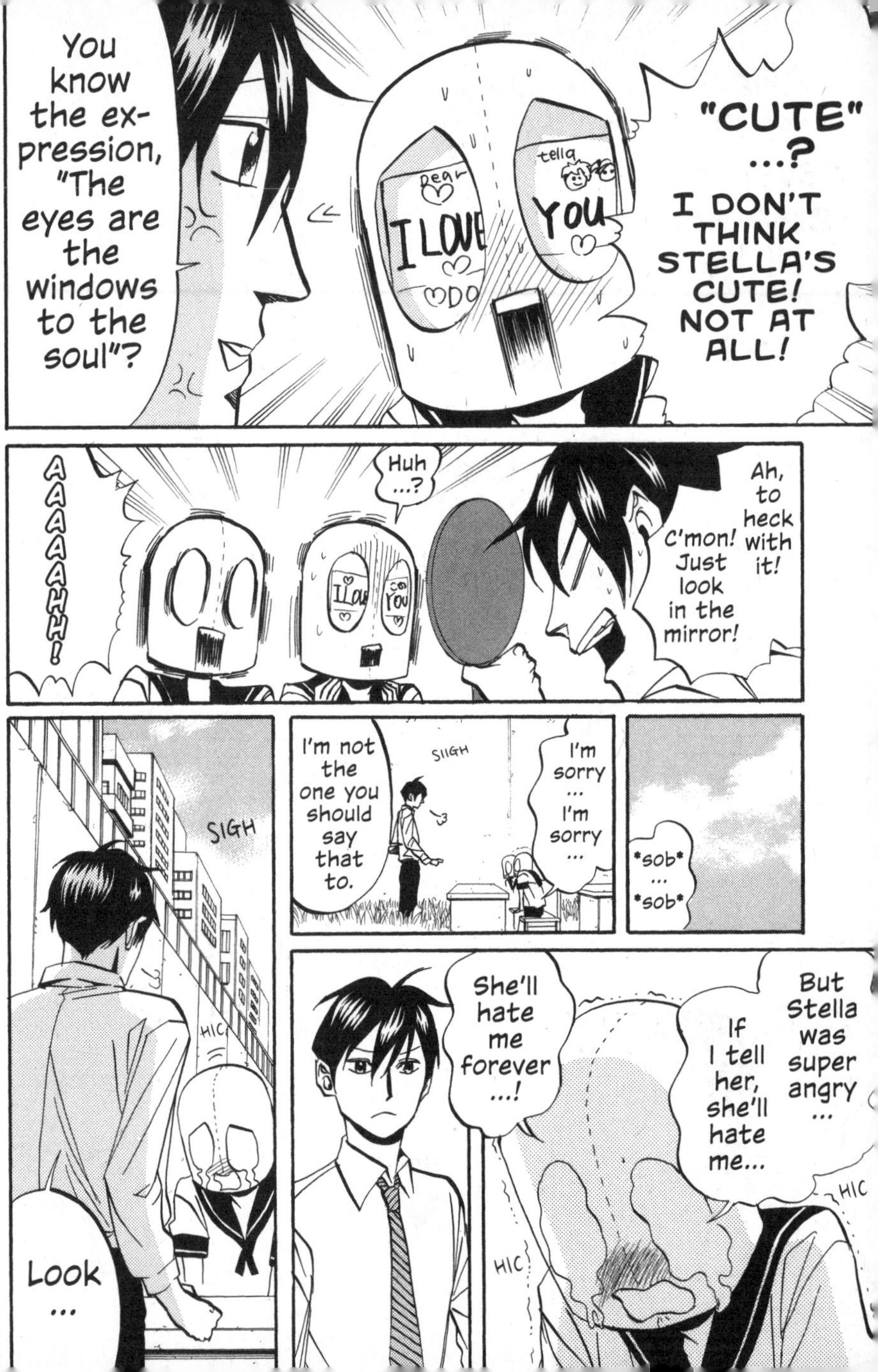
"CUTE" ...? I DON'T THINK STELLA'S CUTE! NOT AT ALL!
I LOVE YOU
You know the expression, "The eyes are the windows to the soul"?
Ah, to heck with it!
C'mon! Just look in the mirror!
Huh ...?
AAAAAAAHH!
sob ... *sob*
I'm sorry ... I'm sorry ...
SIIGH
I'm not the one you should say that to.
But Stella was super angry ...
If I tell her, she'll hate me...
She'll hate me forever ...!
HIC
HIC
SIGH
HIC
Look ...

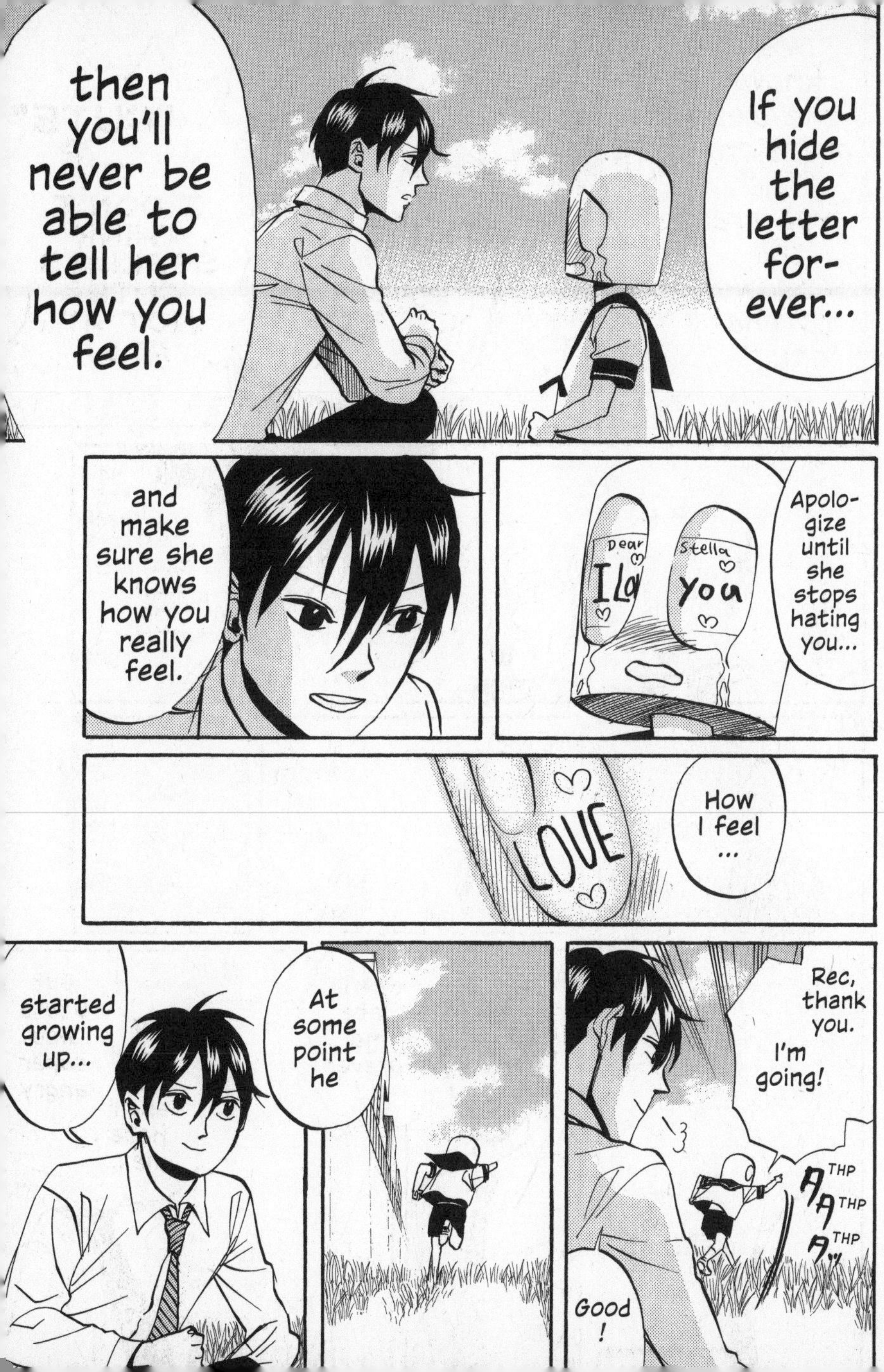
If you hide the letter for-ever...
then you'll never be able to tell her how you feel.
Apolo-gize until she stops hating you...
Dear
Stella
you
and make sure she knows how you really feel.
How I feel ...
LOVE
Rec, thank you.
I'm going!
THP
THP
THP
Good!
At some point he
started growing up...

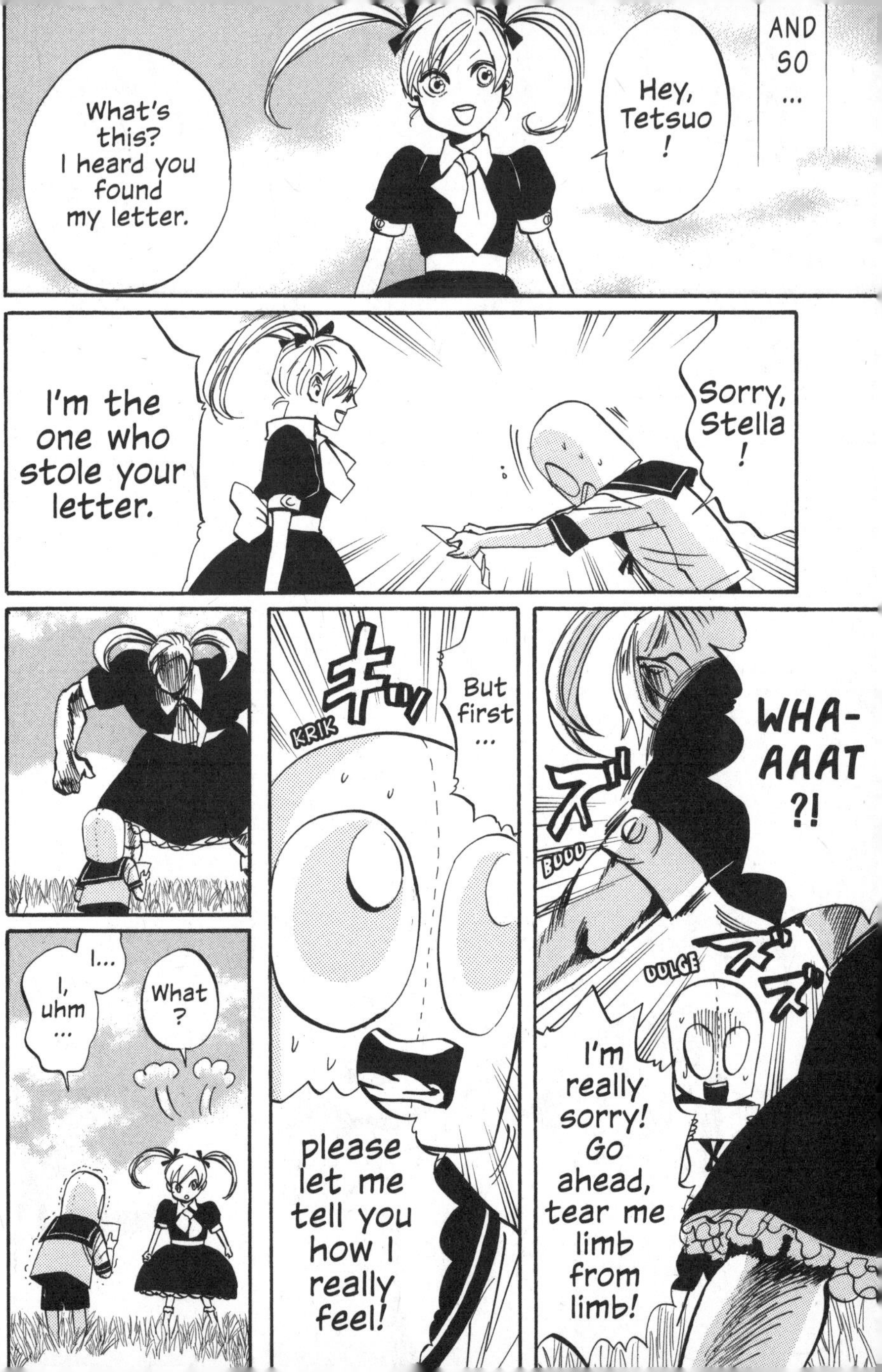
AND SO ...
Hey, Tetsuo!
What's this? I heard you found my letter.
Sorry, Stella!
I'm the one who stole your letter.
WHA-AAAT?!
BOOO
BULGE
I'm really sorry! Go ahead, tear me limb from limb!
KRIK
But first ...
please let me tell you how I really feel!
I, uhm ...
What?
I...

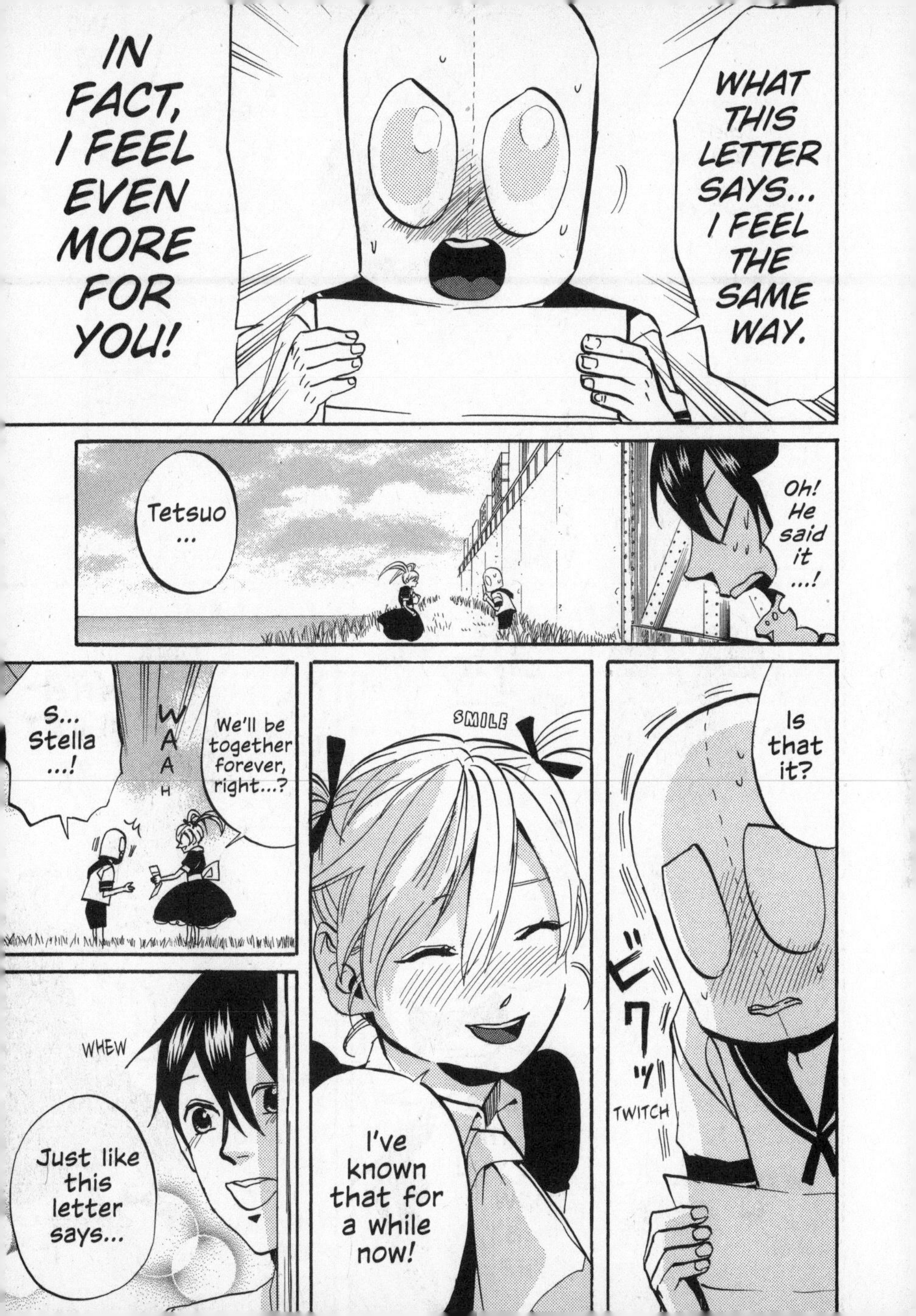
WHAT THIS LETTER SAYS... I FEEL THE SAME WAY.
IN FACT, I FEEL EVEN MORE FOR YOU!
Oh! He said it ...!
Tetsuo ...
Is that it?
ビクッ
TWITCH
SMILE
I've known that for a while now!
We'll be together forever, right...?
WAAH
S... Stella ...!
WHEW
Just like this letter says...

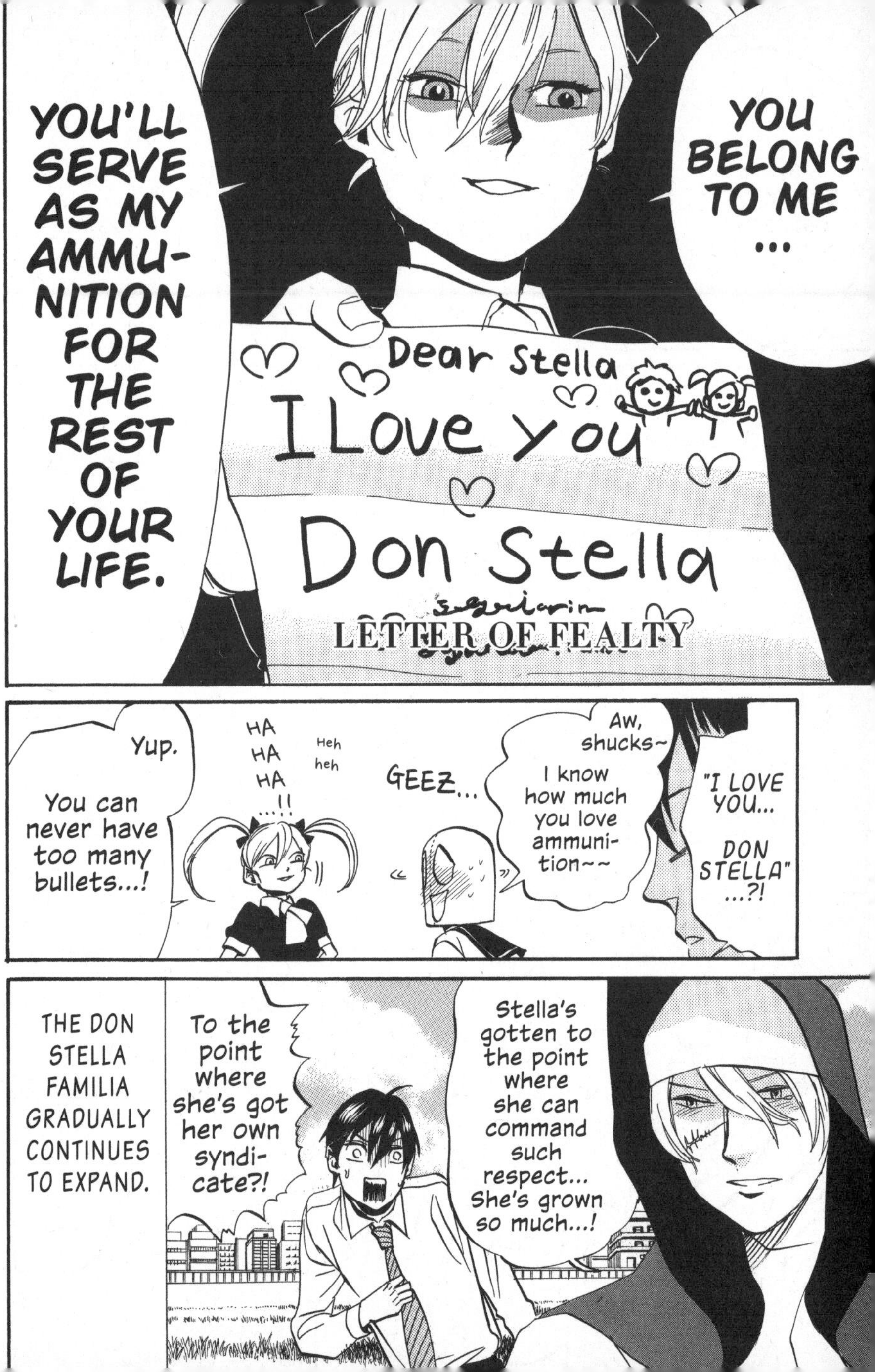
YOU BELONG TO ME ...
YOU'LL SERVE AS MY AMMUNITION FOR THE REST OF YOUR LIFE.
Dear Stella
I Love you
Don Stella
LETTER OF FEALTY
"I LOVE YOU... DON STELLA" ...?!
Aw, shucks~
I know how much you love ammunition~~
GEEZ...
Heh heh
HA HA HA ...!!
Yup.
You can never have too many bullets...!
Stella's gotten to the point where she can command such respect... She's grown so much...!
To the point where she's got her own syndicate?!
THE DON STELLA FAMILIA GRADUALLY CONTINUES TO EXPAND.

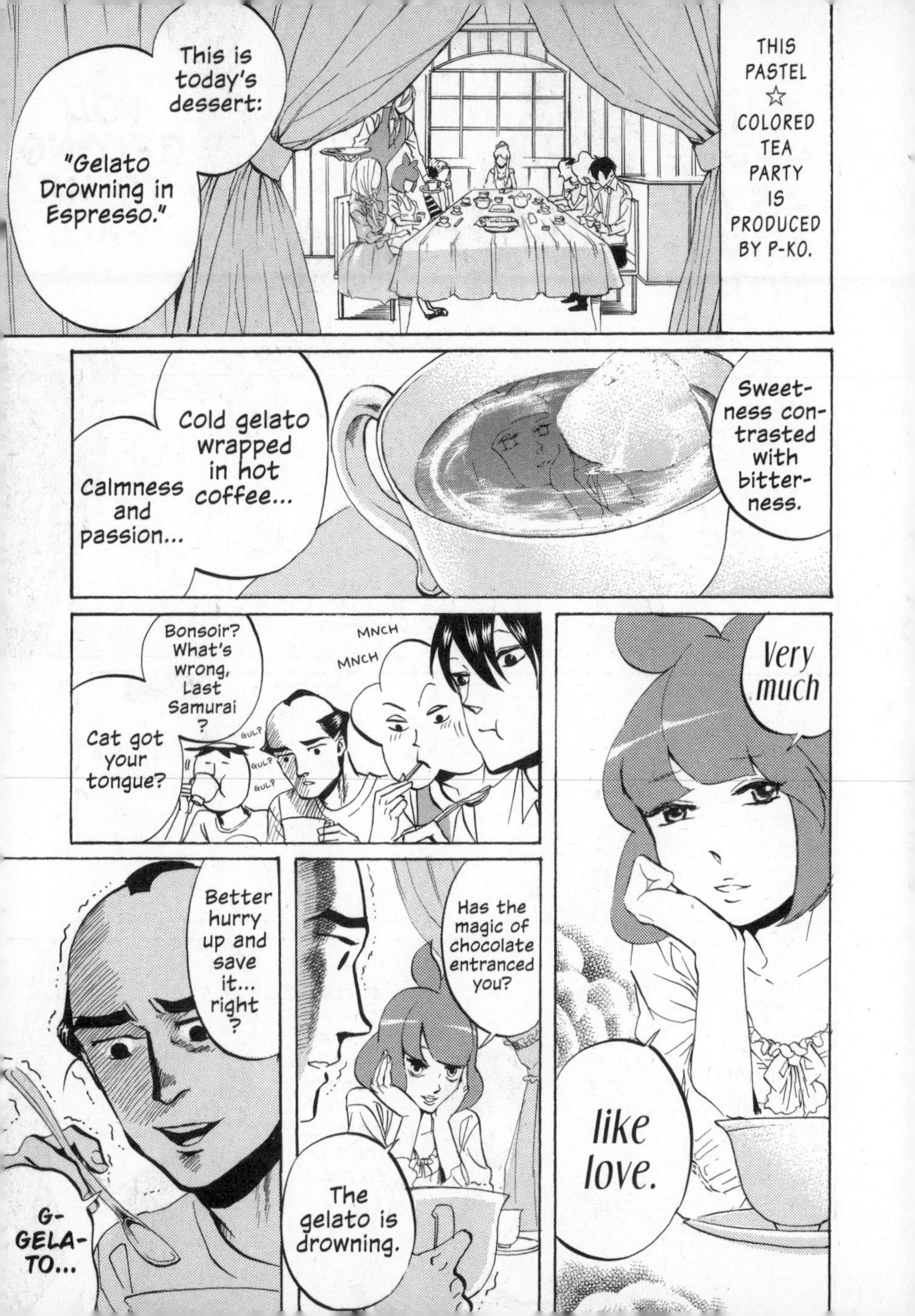
THIS PASTEL ☆ COLORED TEA PARTY IS PRODUCED BY P-KO.
This is today's dessert:
"Gelato Drowning in Espresso."
Sweetness contrasted with bitterness.
Cold gelato wrapped in hot coffee...
Calmness and passion...
Very much
like love.
MNCH
MNCH
Bonsoir? What's wrong, Last Samurai?
Cat got your tongue?
GULP
GULP
GULP
Has the magic of chocolate entranced you?
The gelato is drowning.
Better hurry up and save it... right?
G-GELATO...

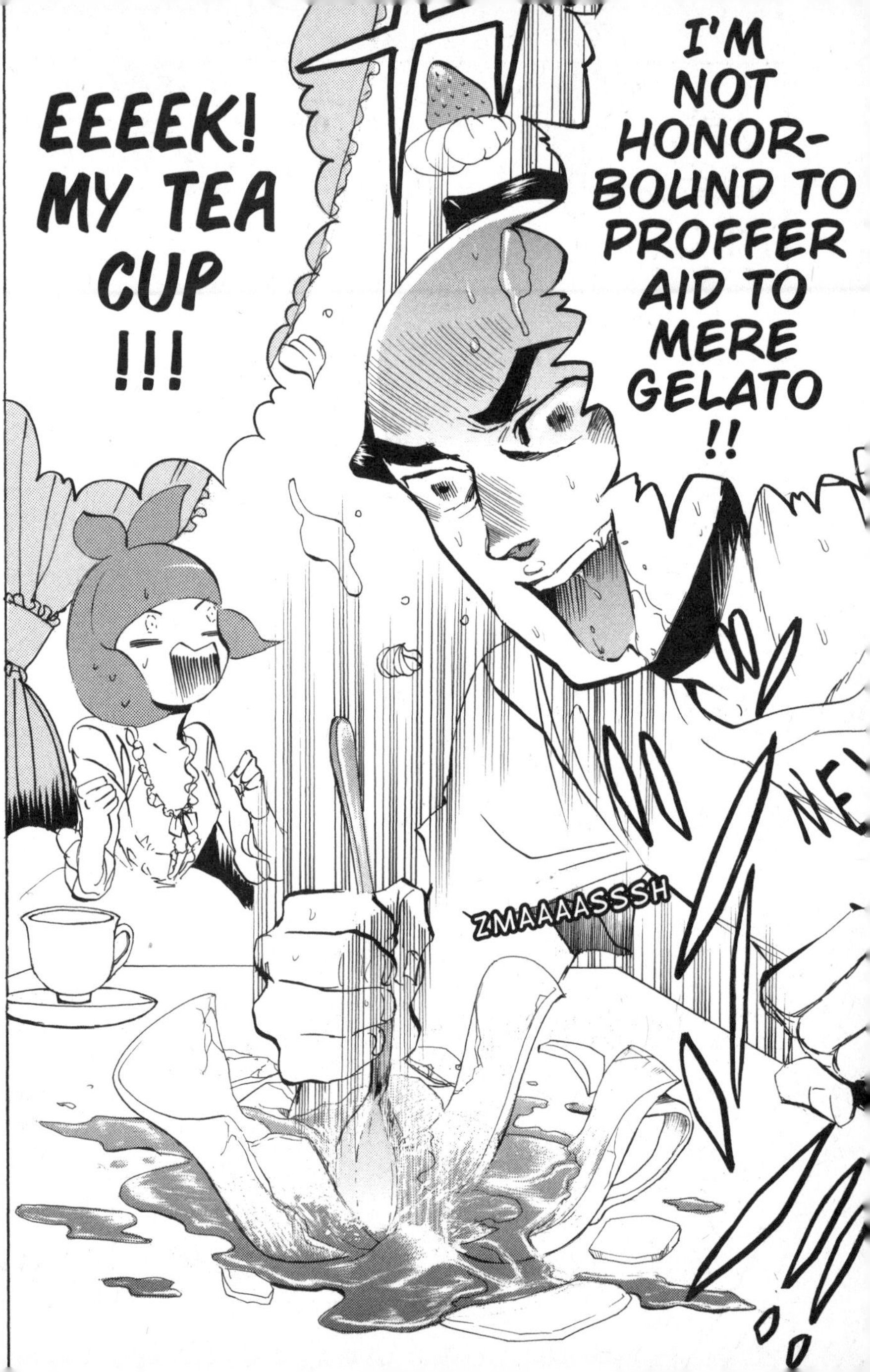
I'M NOT HONOR-BOUND TO PROFFER AID TO MERE GELATO!!
EEEEK! MY TEA CUP!!!
ZMAAAASSSH

Chapter 235: Know Your *Wa*

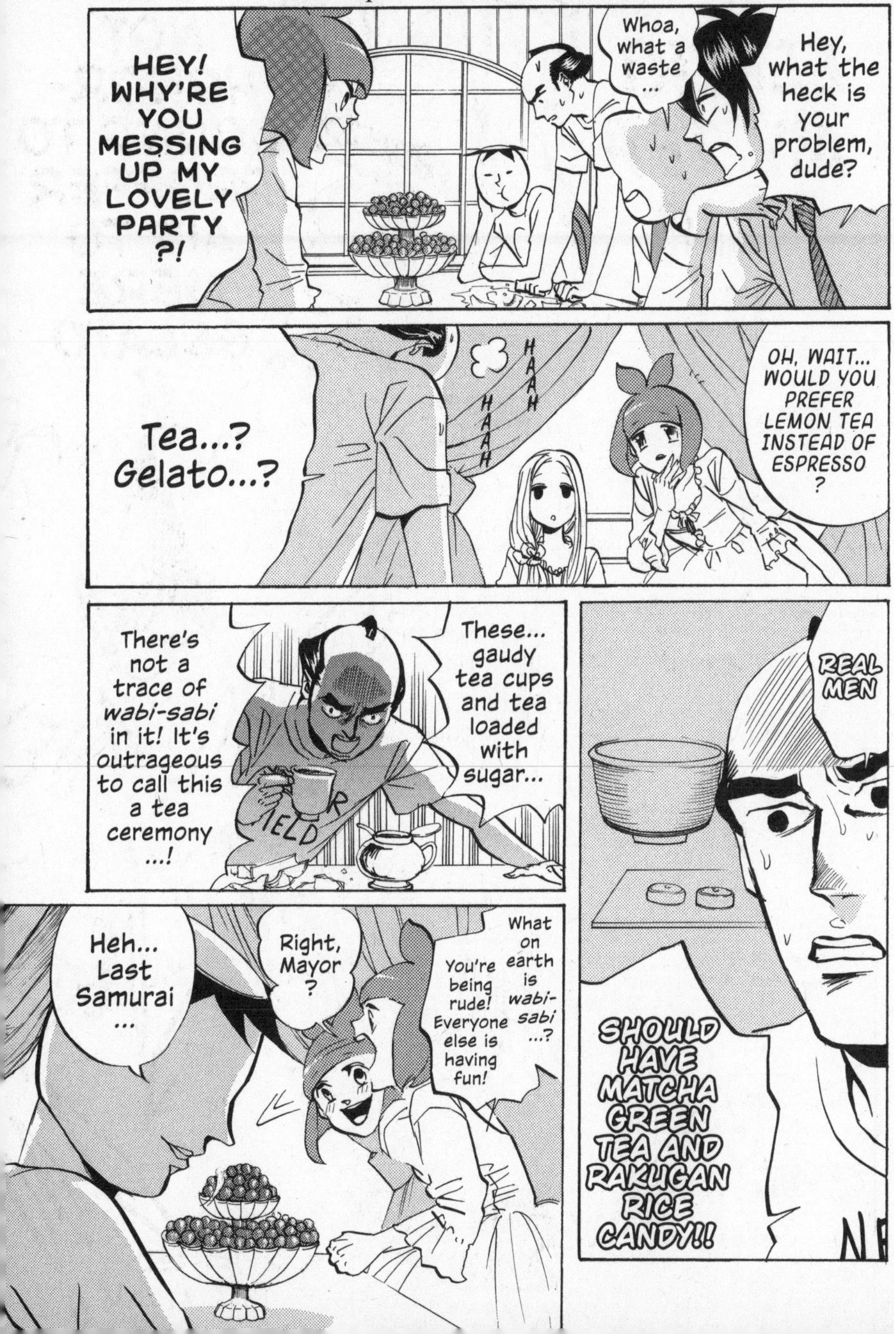
Hey, what the heck is your problem, dude?
Whoa, what a waste...
HEY! WHY'RE YOU MESSING UP MY LOVELY PARTY?!
OH, WAIT... WOULD YOU PREFER LEMON TEA INSTEAD OF ESPRESSO?
HAAH
HAAAH
Tea...? Gelato...?
REAL MEN
SHOULD HAVE MATCHA GREEN TEA AND RAKUGAN RICE CANDY!!
These... gaudy tea cups and tea loaded with sugar...
There's not a trace of wabi-sabi in it! It's outrageous to call this a tea ceremony...!
What on earth is wabi-sabi...?
You're being rude! Everyone else is having fun!
Right, Mayor?
Heh... Last Samurai...

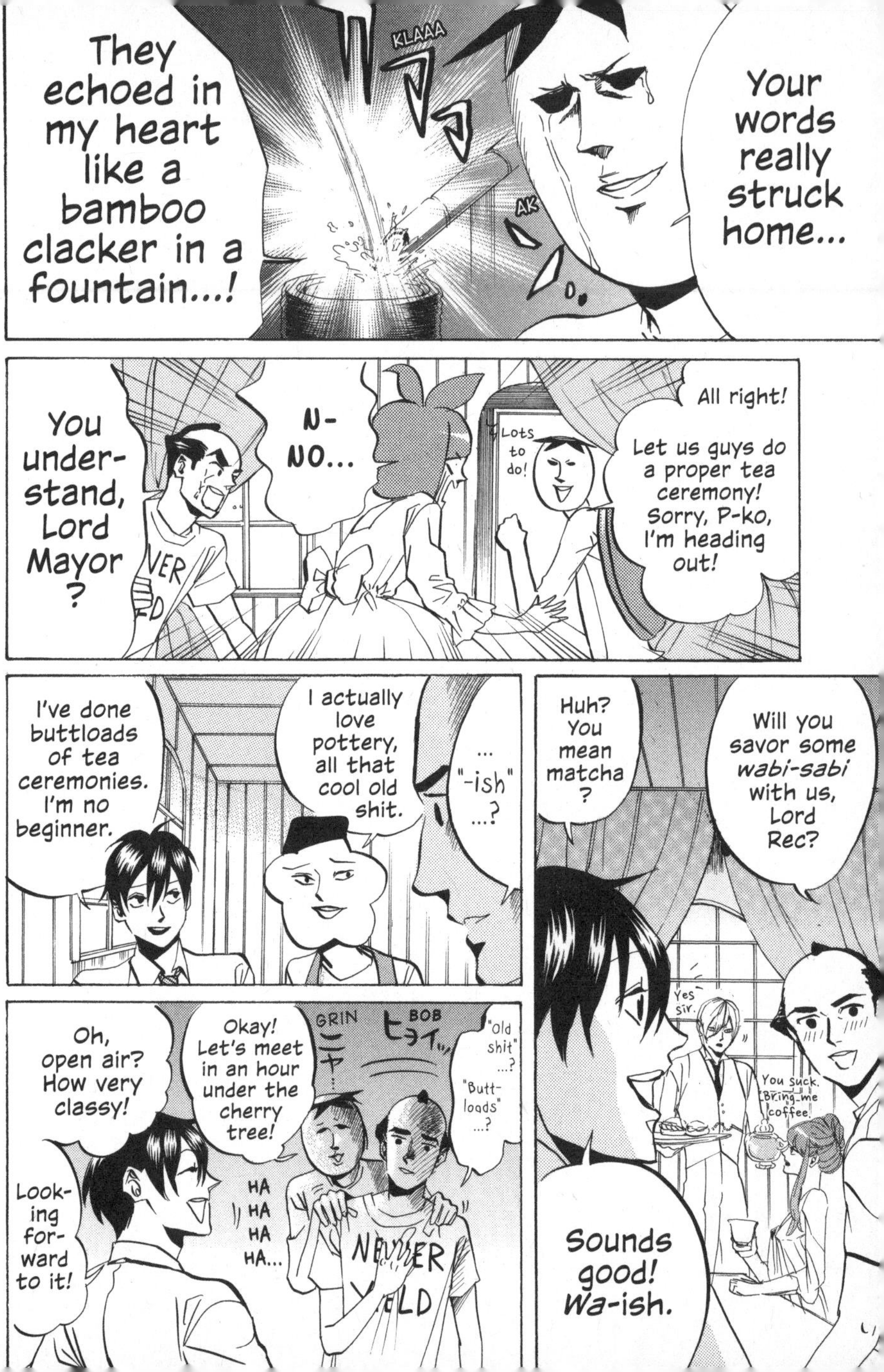
Your words really struck home...
KLAAA
AK
They echoed in my heart like a bamboo clacker in a fountain...!
All right!
Let us guys do a proper tea ceremony! Sorry, P-ko, I'm heading out!
Lots to do!
N-NO...
You understand, Lord Mayor?
Will you savor some *wabi-sabi* with us, Lord Rec?
Huh? You mean matcha?
Yes sir.
You suck. Bring me coffee.
Sounds good! Wa-ish.
... "-ish" ...?
I actually love pottery, all that cool old shit.
I've done buttloads of tea ceremonies. I'm no beginner.
"old shit" ...?
"Butt-loads" ...?
BOB
GRIN
Okay! Let's meet in an hour under the cherry tree!
Oh, open air? How very classy!
HA HA HA HA...
Looking forward to it!

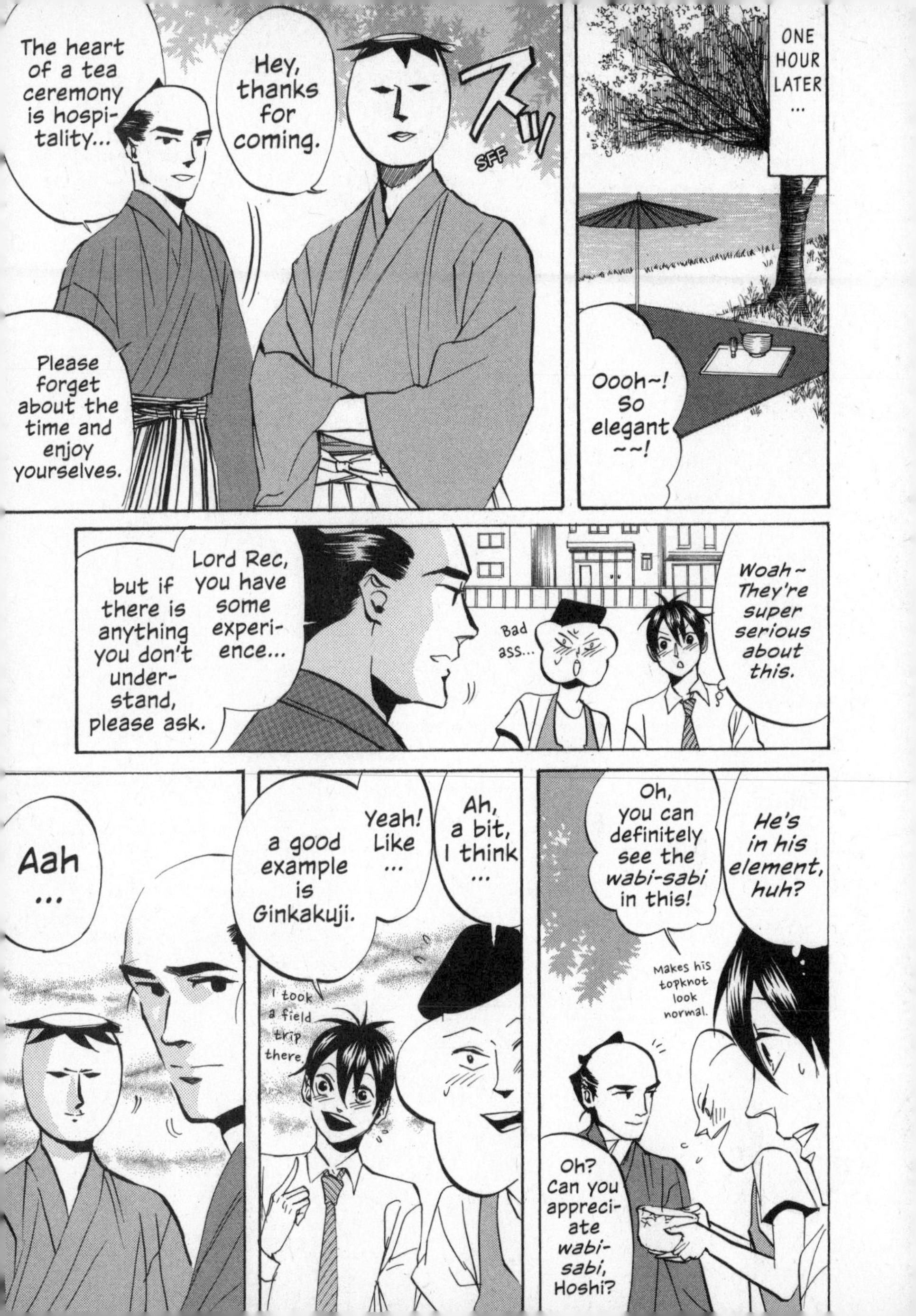
ONE HOUR LATER ...
Oooh~! So elegant ~~!
Hey, thanks for coming.
SFF
The heart of a tea ceremony is hospitality...
Please forget about the time and enjoy yourselves.
Woah~ They're super serious about this.
Bad ass...
Lord Rec, you have some experience...
but if there is anything you don't understand, please ask.
He's in his element, huh?
Oh, you can definitely see the wabi-sabi in this!
Makes his topknot look normal.
Oh? Can you appreciate wabi-sabi, Hoshi?
Ah, a bit, I think ...
Yeah! Like ...
a good example is Ginkakuji.
I took a field trip there.
Aah ...

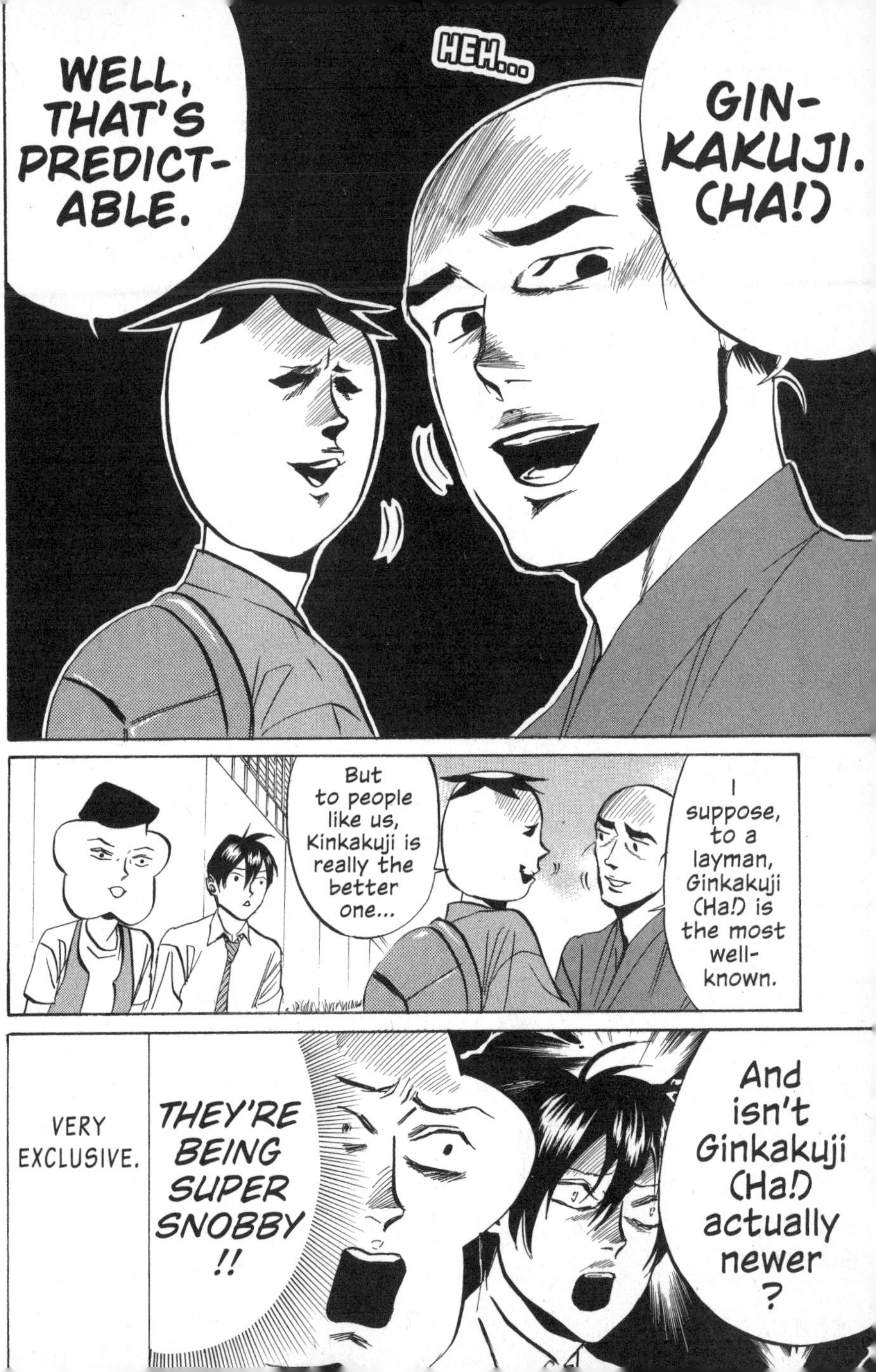
GIN-KAKUJI. (HA!)
HEH...
WELL, THAT'S PREDICT-ABLE.
I suppose, to a layman, Ginkakuji (Ha!) is the most well-known.
But to people like us, Kinkakuji is really the better one...
And isn't Ginkakuji (Ha!) actually newer?
THEY'RE BEING SUPER SNOBBY!!
VERY EXCLUSIVE.

Chapter 236: *Wabi-Sabi*

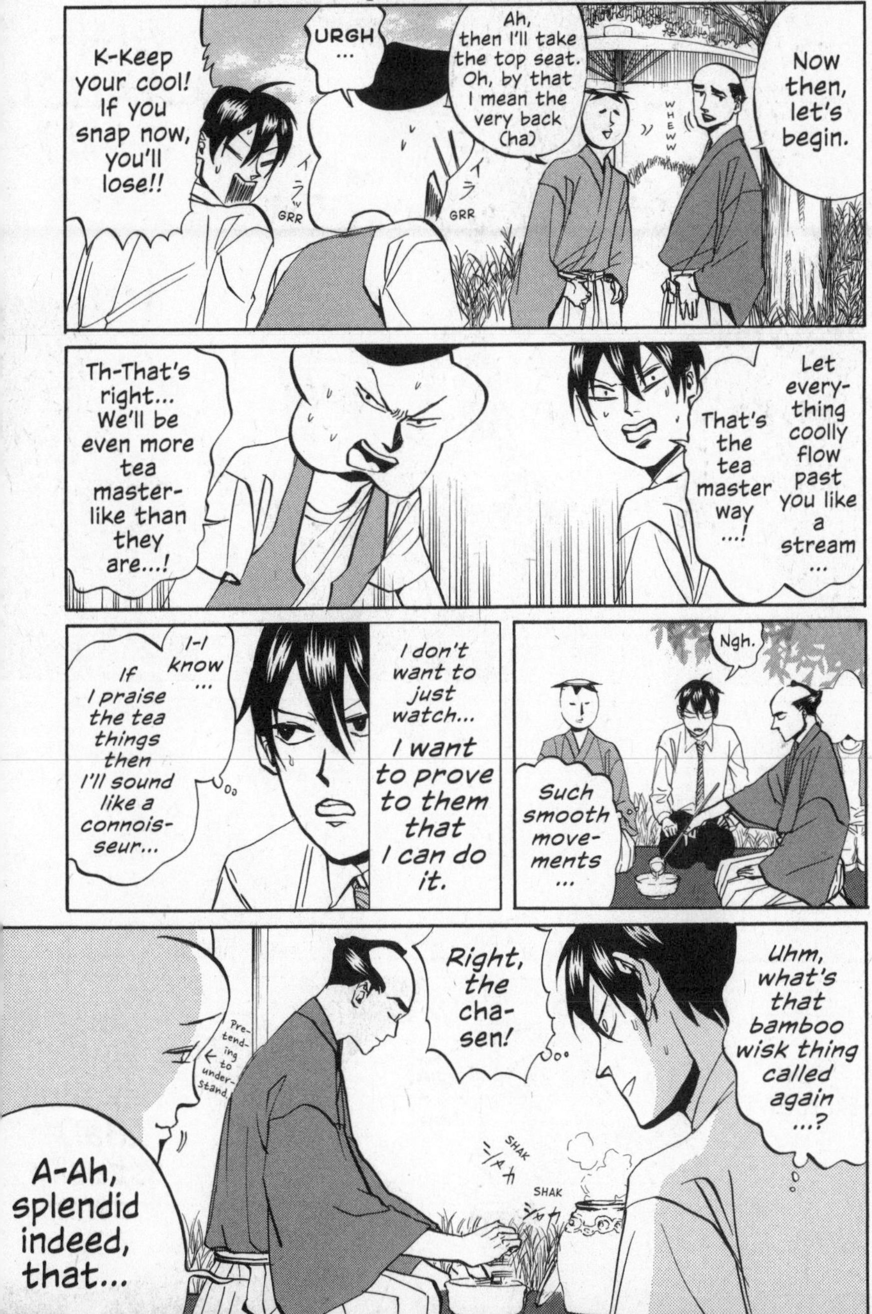
Now then, let's begin.
WHEWW
Ah, then I'll take the top seat. Oh, by that I mean the very back (ha)
URGH ...
GRR
GRR
K-Keep your cool! If you snap now, you'll lose!!
Let everything coolly flow past you like a stream ...
That's the tea master way ...!
Th-That's right... We'll be even more tea master-like than they are...!
Ngh.
Such smooth movements ...
I don't want to just watch...
I want to prove to them that I can do it.
I-I know ...
If I praise the tea things then I'll sound like a connoisseur...
Uhm, what's that bamboo wisk thing called again ...?
Right, the cha-sen!
SHAK
SHAK
Pretending to understand.
A-Ah, splendid indeed, that...

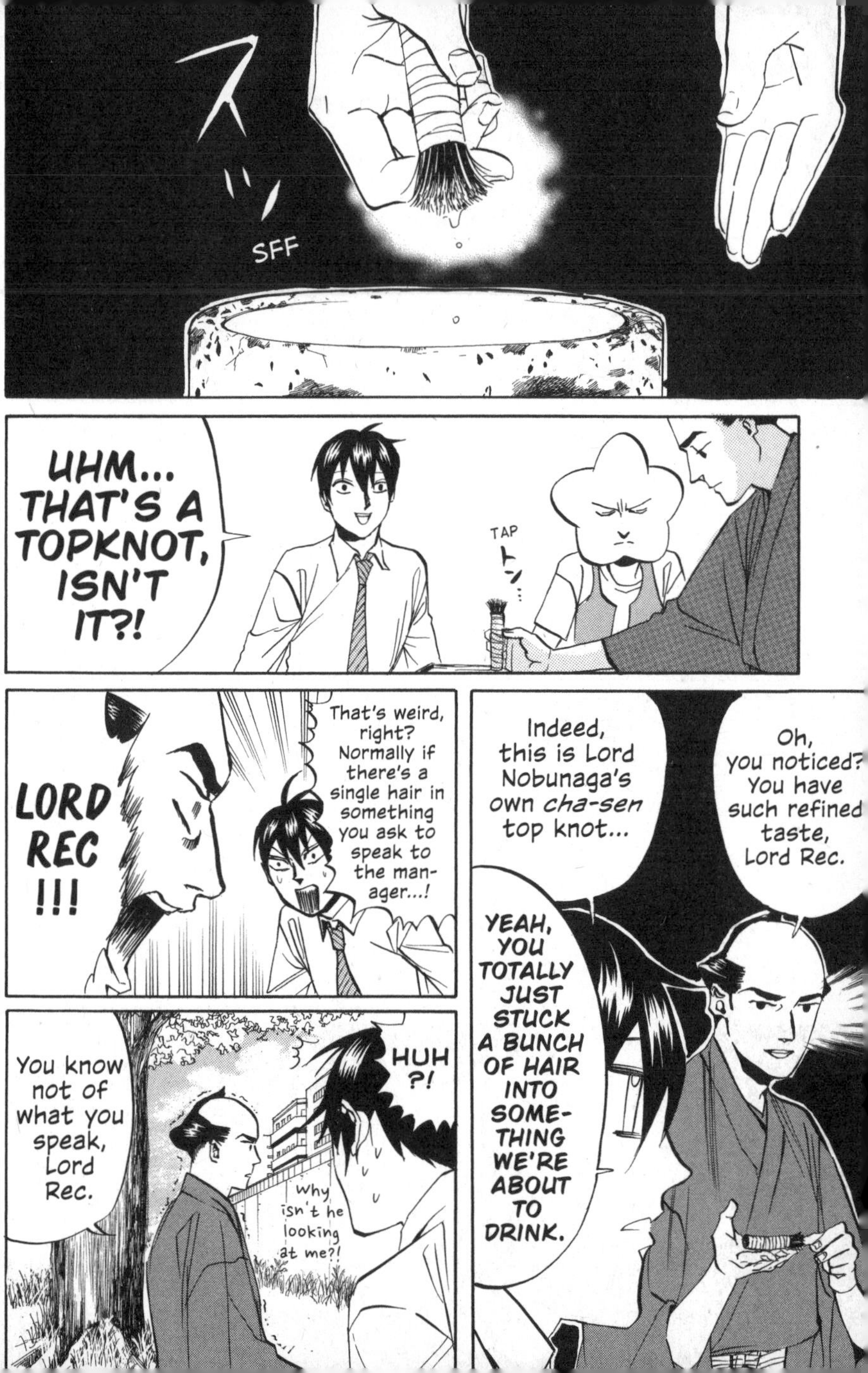
SFF
TAP
UHM... THAT'S A TOPKNOT, ISN'T IT?!
Oh, you noticed? You have such refined taste, Lord Rec.
Indeed, this is Lord Nobunaga's own *cha-sen* top knot...
YEAH, YOU TOTALLY JUST STUCK A BUNCH OF HAIR INTO SOME-THING WE'RE ABOUT TO DRINK.
That's weird, right? Normally if there's a single hair in something you ask to speak to the man-ager...!
LORD REC!!!
HUH?!
Why isn't he looking at me?!
You know not of what you speak, Lord Rec.

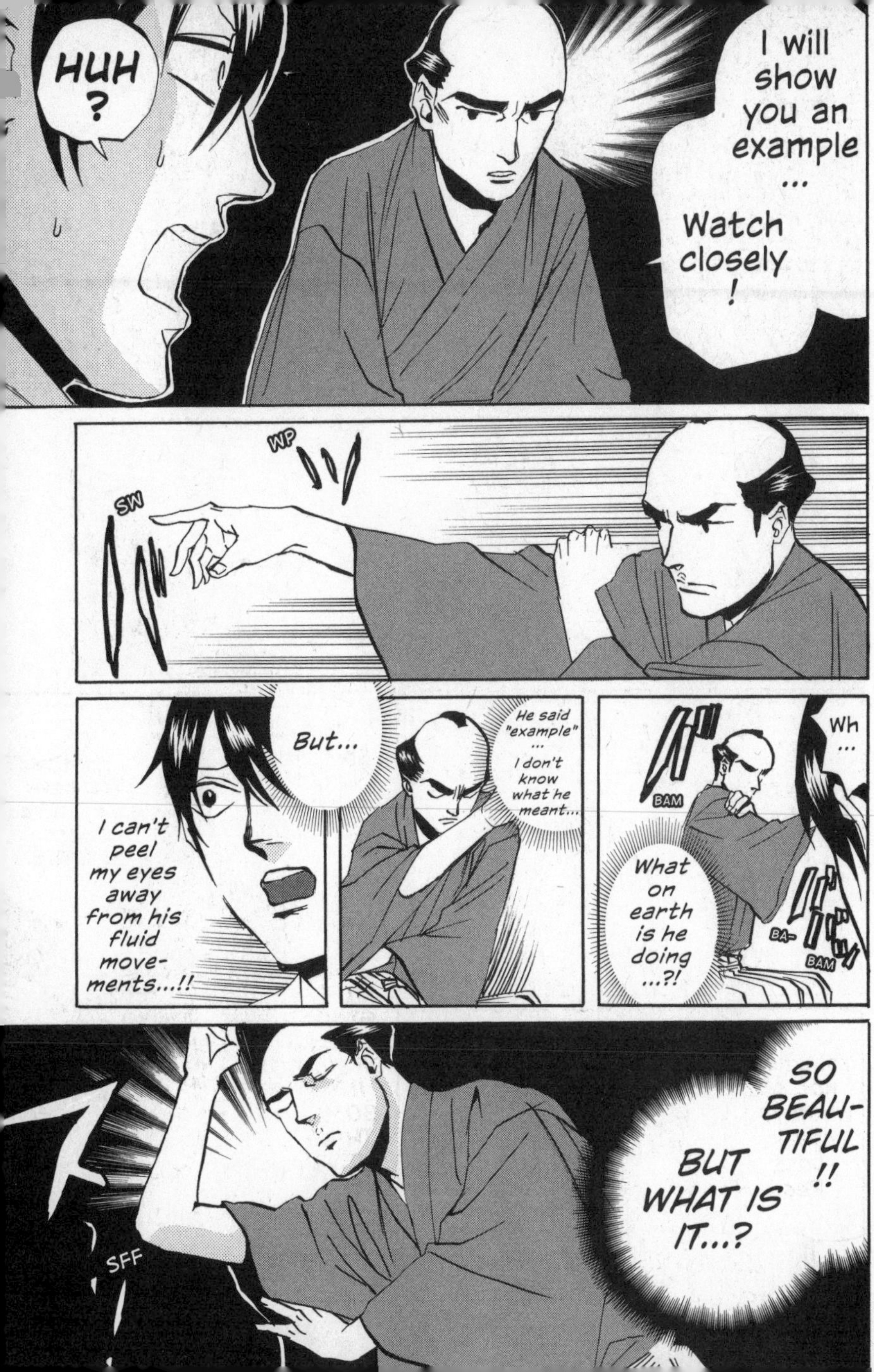
I will show you an example ... Watch closely!
HUH?
WP
SW
Wh ...
BAM
What on earth is he doing ...?!
BA-BAM
He said "example" ... I don't know what he meant...
But...
I can't peel my eyes away from his fluid movements...!!
SO BEAU-TIFUL!!
BUT WHAT IS IT...?
SFF

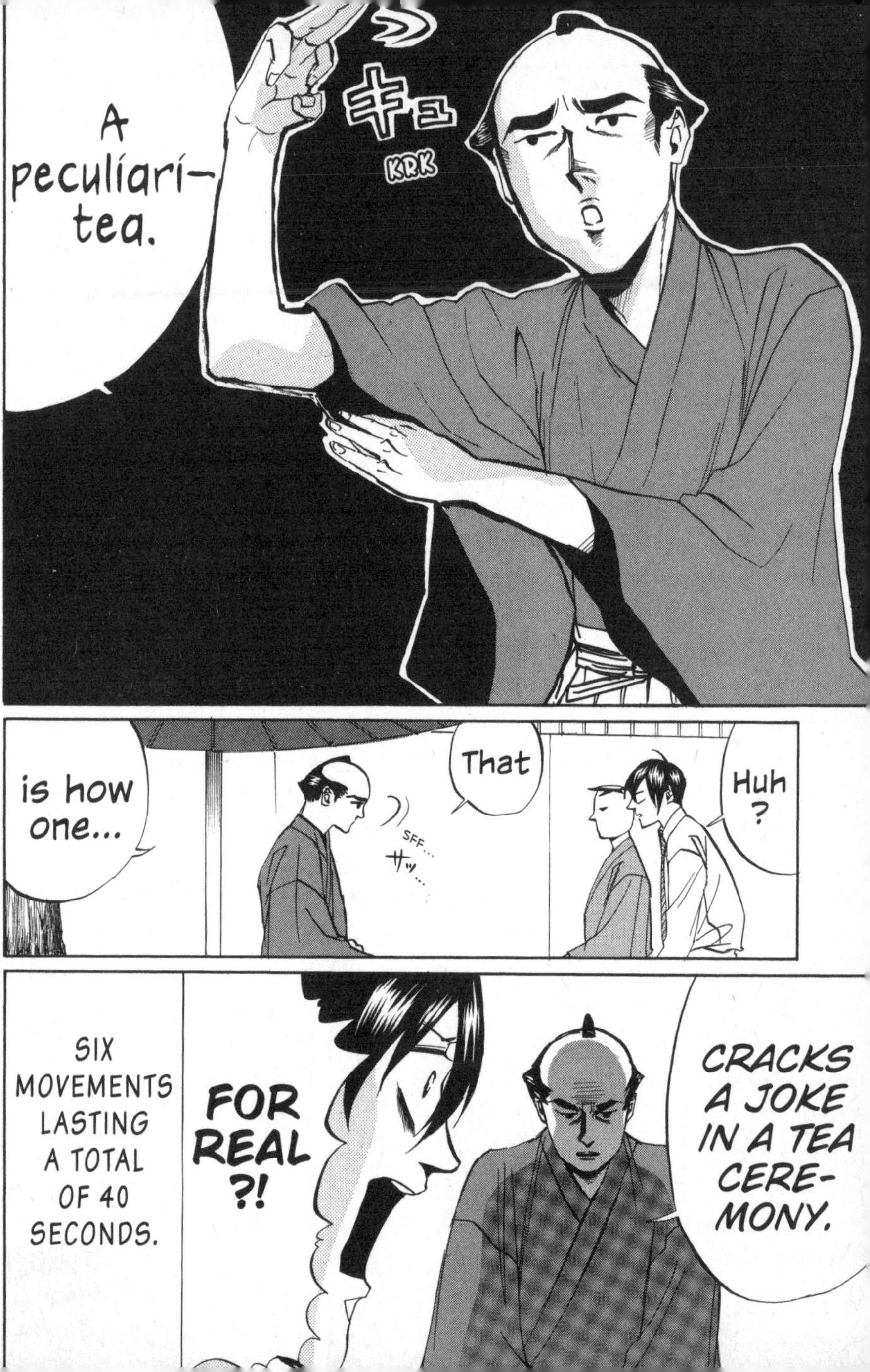
キュ
KRK
A peculiari-tea.
Huh?
That
SFF... サッ...
is how one...
CRACKS A JOKE IN A TEA CEREMONY.
FOR REAL?!
SIX MOVEMENTS LASTING A TOTAL OF 40 SECONDS.

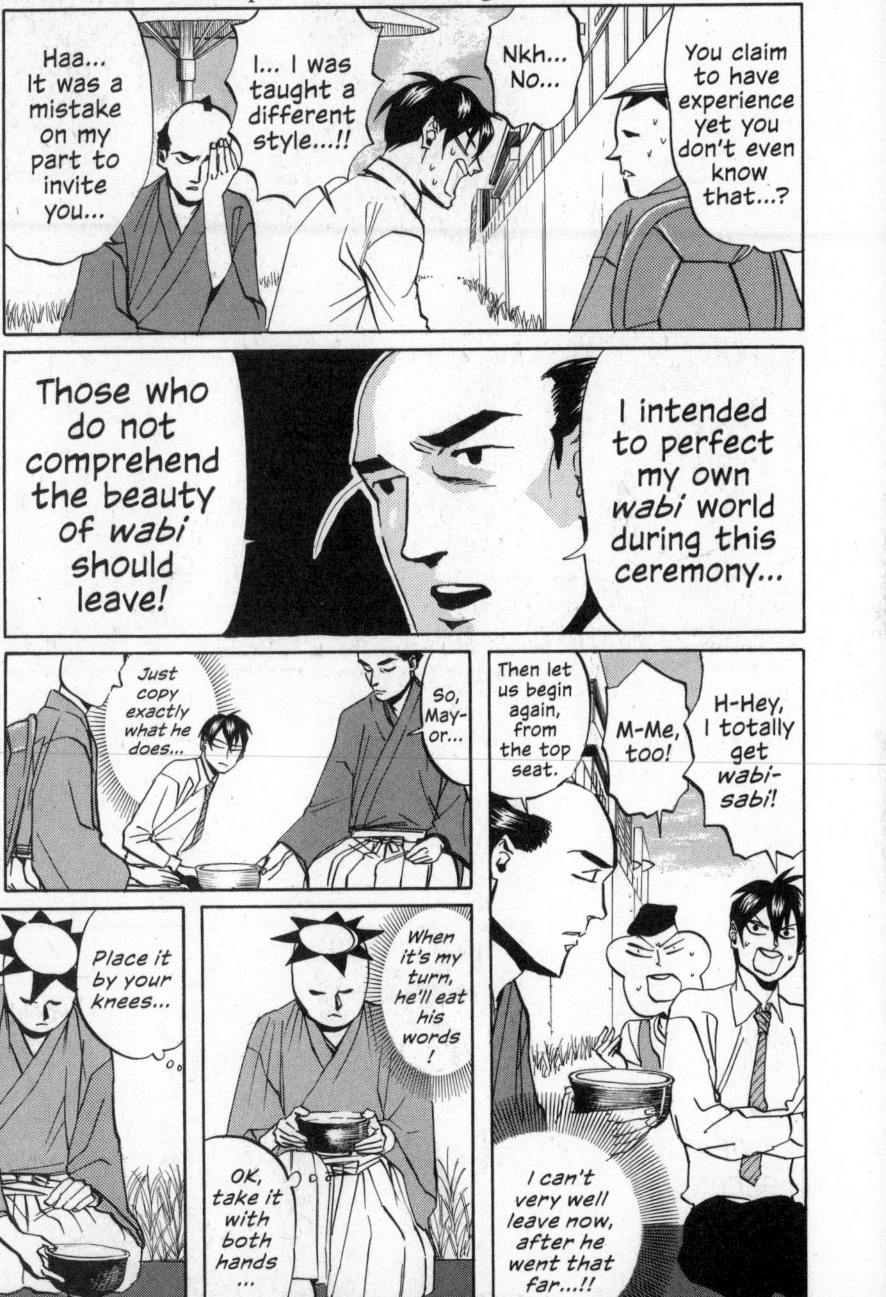

You claim to have experience yet you don't even know that...?
Nkh... No...
I... I was taught a different style...!!
Haa... It was a mistake on my part to invite you...
I intended to perfect my own wabi world during this ceremony...
Those who do not comprehend the beauty of wabi should leave!
H-Hey, I totally get wabi-sabi!
M-Me, too!
Then let us begin again, from the top seat.
I can't very well leave now, after he went that far...!!
So, Mayor...
Just copy exactly what he does...
When it's my turn, he'll eat his words!
OK, take it with both hands...
Place it by your knees...

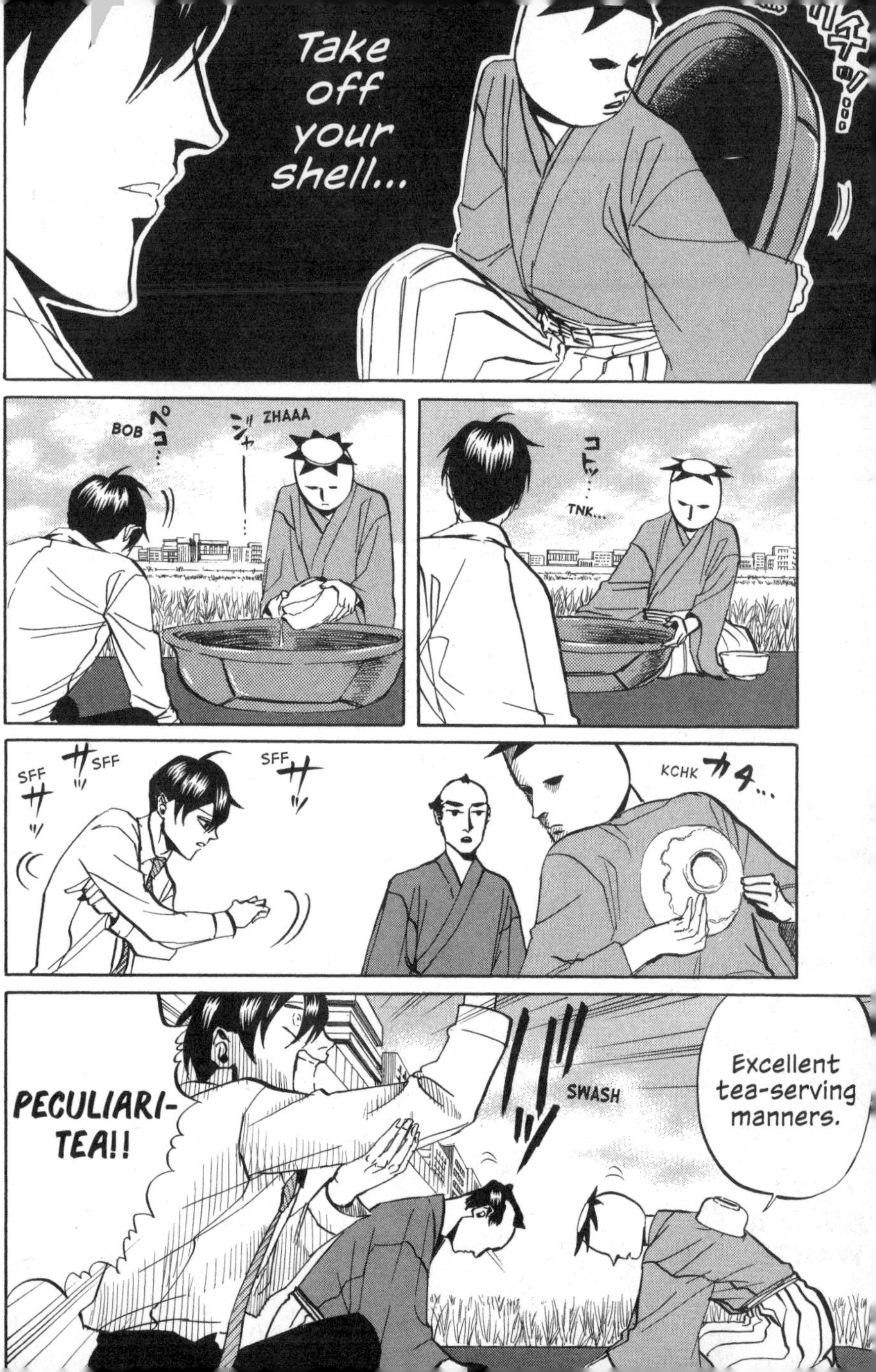
Take off your shell...
コトッ...
TNK...
ペコ...
BOB
ジャー
ZHAAA
カタ...
KCHK
サッ
SFF
サッ
SFF
サッ
SFF
Excellent tea-serving manners.
SWASH
PECULIARI-TEA!!

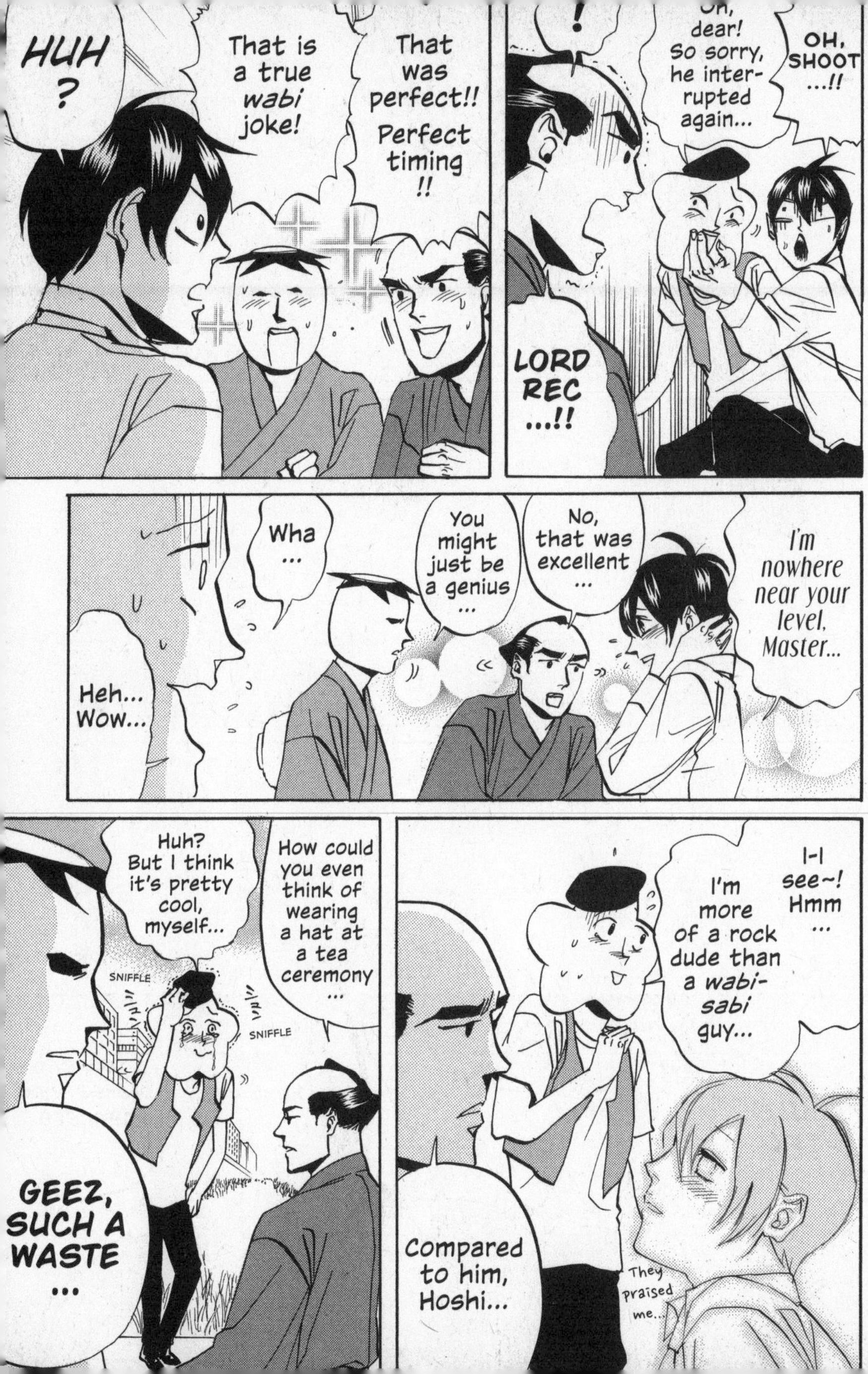
OH, SHOOT ...!!
Oh, dear! So sorry, he inter-rupted again...
!
LORD REC ...!!
That was perfect!! Perfect timing !!
That is a true *wabi* joke!
HUH ?
I'm nowhere near your level, Master...
No, that was excellent ...
You might just be a genius ...
Wha ...
Heh... Wow...
I-I see~! Hmm ...
I'm more of a rock dude than a *wabi-sabi* guy...
They praised me...
Compared to him, Hoshi...
How could you even think of wearing a hat at a tea ceremony ...
Huh? But I think it's pretty cool, myself...
SNIFFLE
SNIFFLE
GEEZ, SUCH A WASTE ...

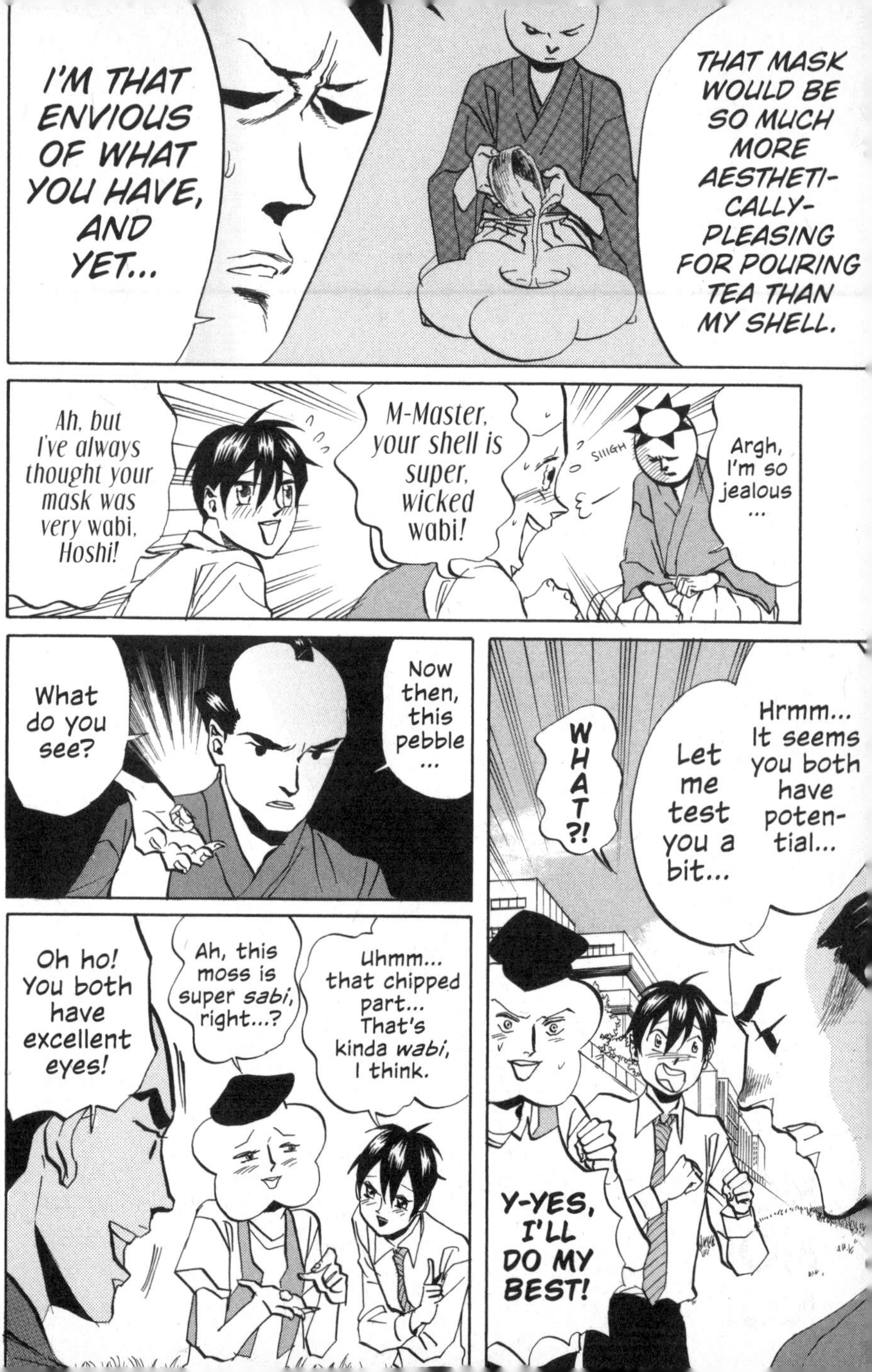
THAT MASK WOULD BE SO MUCH MORE AESTHETI-CALLY-PLEASING FOR POURING TEA THAN MY SHELL.
I'M THAT ENVIOUS OF WHAT YOU HAVE, AND YET...
Argh, I'm so jealous ...
SIIIGH
M-Master, your shell is super, wicked wabi!
Ah, but I've always thought your mask was very wabi, Hoshi!
Hrmm... It seems you both have poten-tial...
Let me test you a bit...
WHAT?!
Y-YES, I'LL DO MY BEST!
Now then, this pebble ...
What do you see?
Uhmm... that chipped part... That's kinda *wabi*, I think.
Ah, this moss is super *sabi*, right...?
Oh ho! You both have excellent eyes!

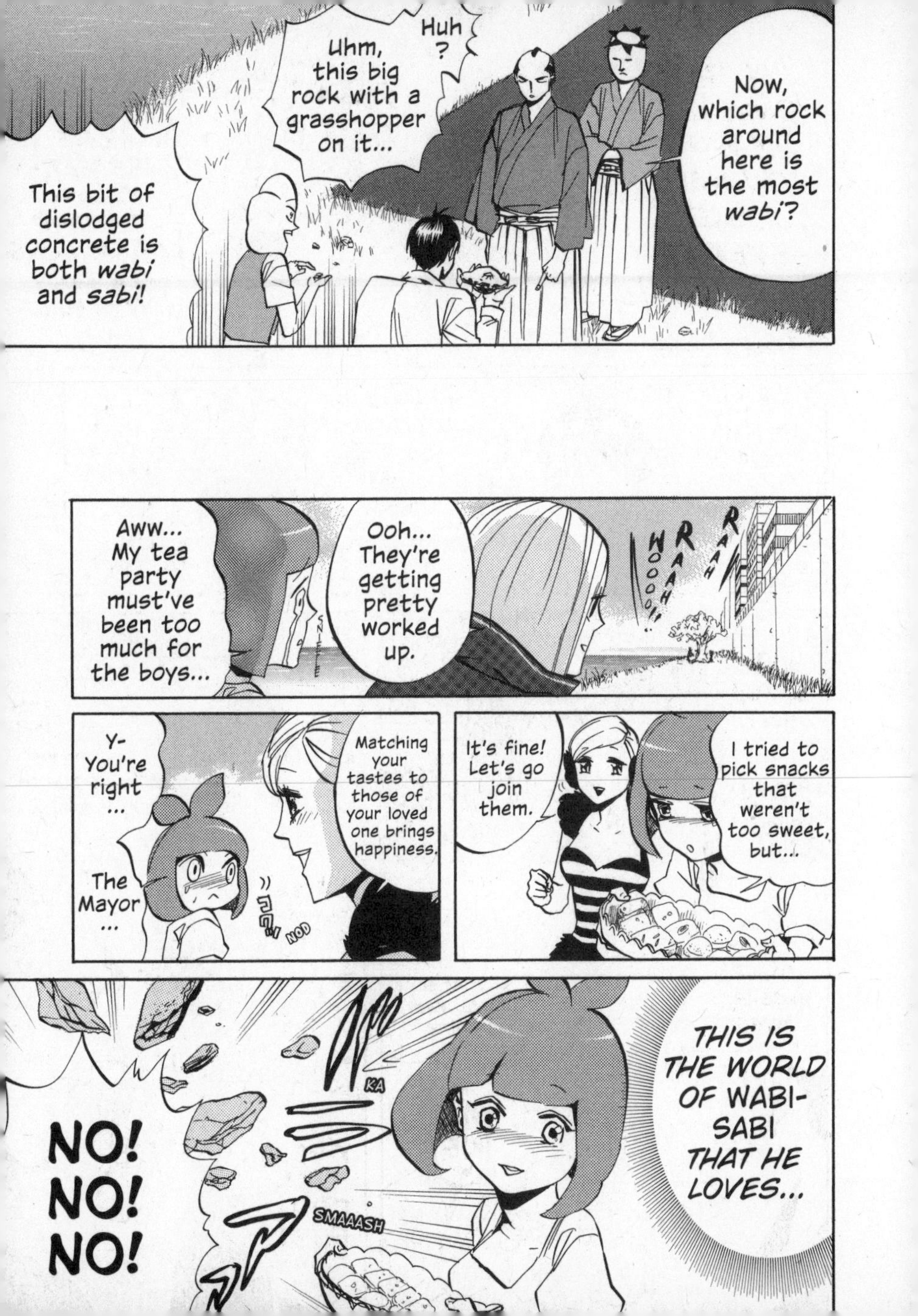
Now, which rock around here is the most *wabi*?
Huh?
Uhm, this big rock with a grasshopper on it...
This bit of dislodged concrete is both *wabi* and *sabi*!
RAAH
RAAH
WOOOO!!
Ooh... They're getting pretty worked up.
Aww... My tea party must've been too much for the boys...
I tried to pick snacks that weren't too sweet, but...
It's fine! Let's go join them.
Matching your tastes to those of your loved one brings happiness.
NOD
Y- You're right ...
The Mayor ...
THIS IS THE WORLD OF WABI-SABI THAT HE LOVES...
KA
SMAAASH
NO! NO! NO!

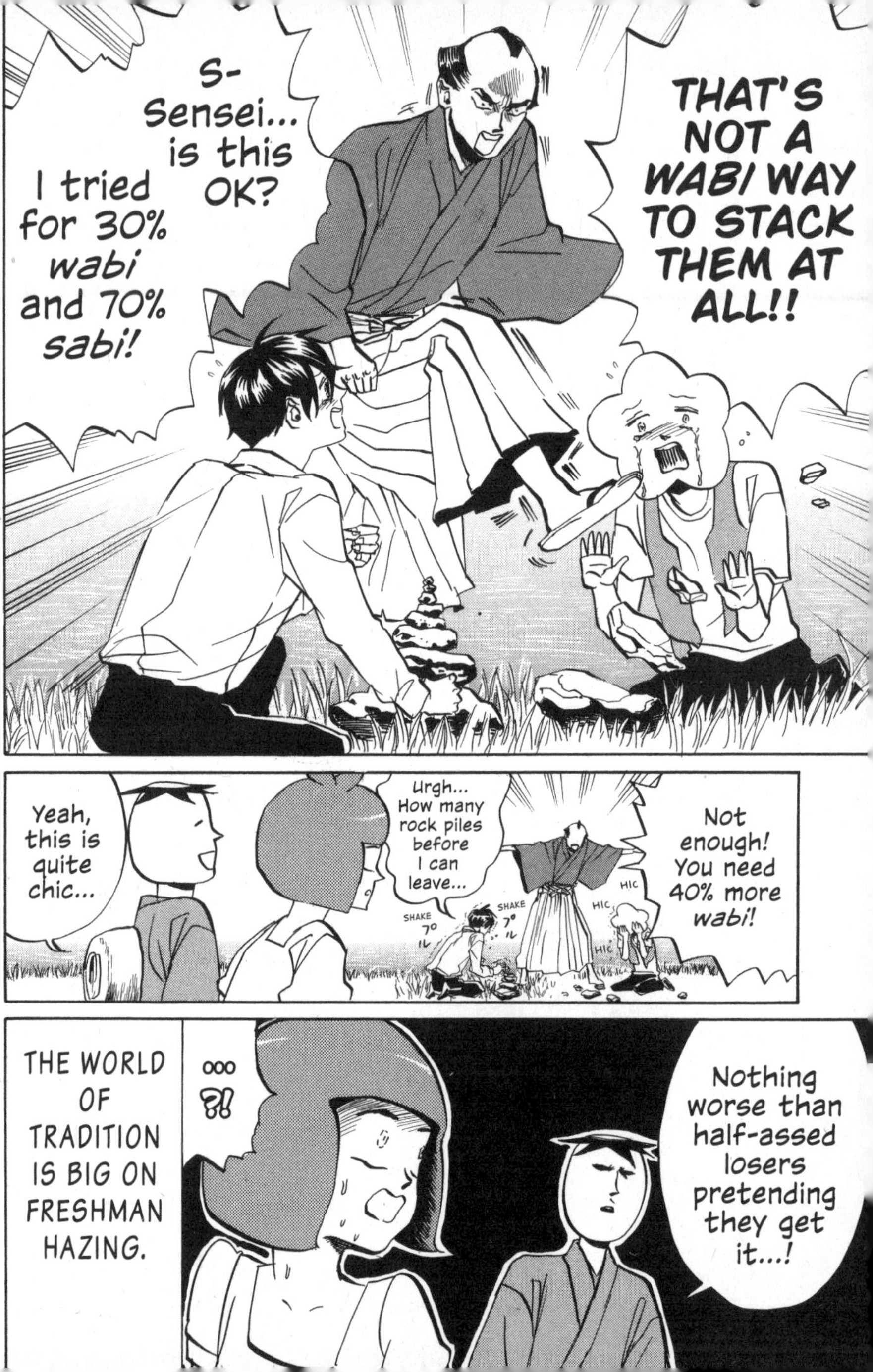
THAT'S NOT A WABI WAY TO STACK THEM AT ALL!!
S-Sensei... is this OK?
I tried for 30% wabi and 70% sabi!
Not enough! You need 40% more wabi!
HIC
HIC
HIC
SHAKE
SHAKE
Urgh... How many rock piles before I can leave...
Yeah, this is quite chic...
Nothing worse than half-assed losers pretending they get it...!
ooo ?!
THE WORLD OF TRADITION IS BIG ON FRESHMAN HAZING.

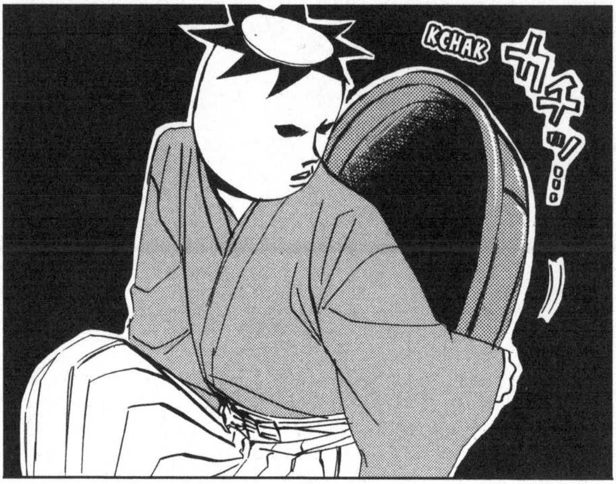
KCHAK
カチッ…

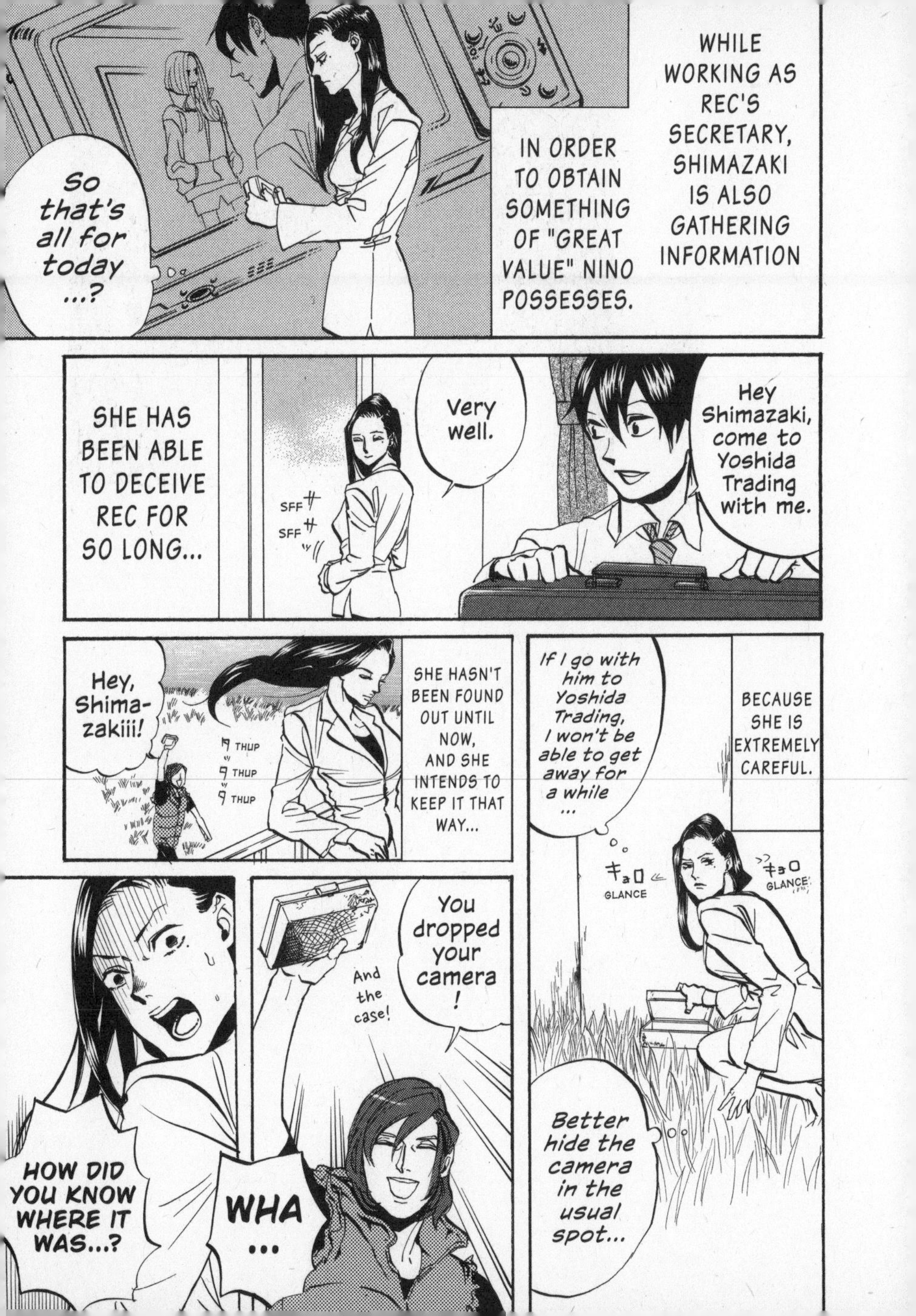
WHILE WORKING AS REC'S SECRETARY, SHIMAZAKI IS ALSO GATHERING INFORMATION
IN ORDER TO OBTAIN SOMETHING OF "GREAT VALUE" NINO POSSESSES.
So that's all for today ...?
Hey Shimazaki, come to Yoshida Trading with me.
Very well.
SFF
SFF
SHE HAS BEEN ABLE TO DECEIVE REC FOR SO LONG...
BECAUSE SHE IS EXTREMELY CAREFUL.
If I go with him to Yoshida Trading, I won't be able to get away for a while ...
キョロ GLANCE
キョロ GLANCE
Better hide the camera in the usual spot...
SHE HASN'T BEEN FOUND OUT UNTIL NOW, AND SHE INTENDS TO KEEP IT THAT WAY...
Hey, Shimazakiii!
THUP
THUP
THUP
You dropped your camera!
And the case!
WHA ...
HOW DID YOU KNOW WHERE IT WAS...?

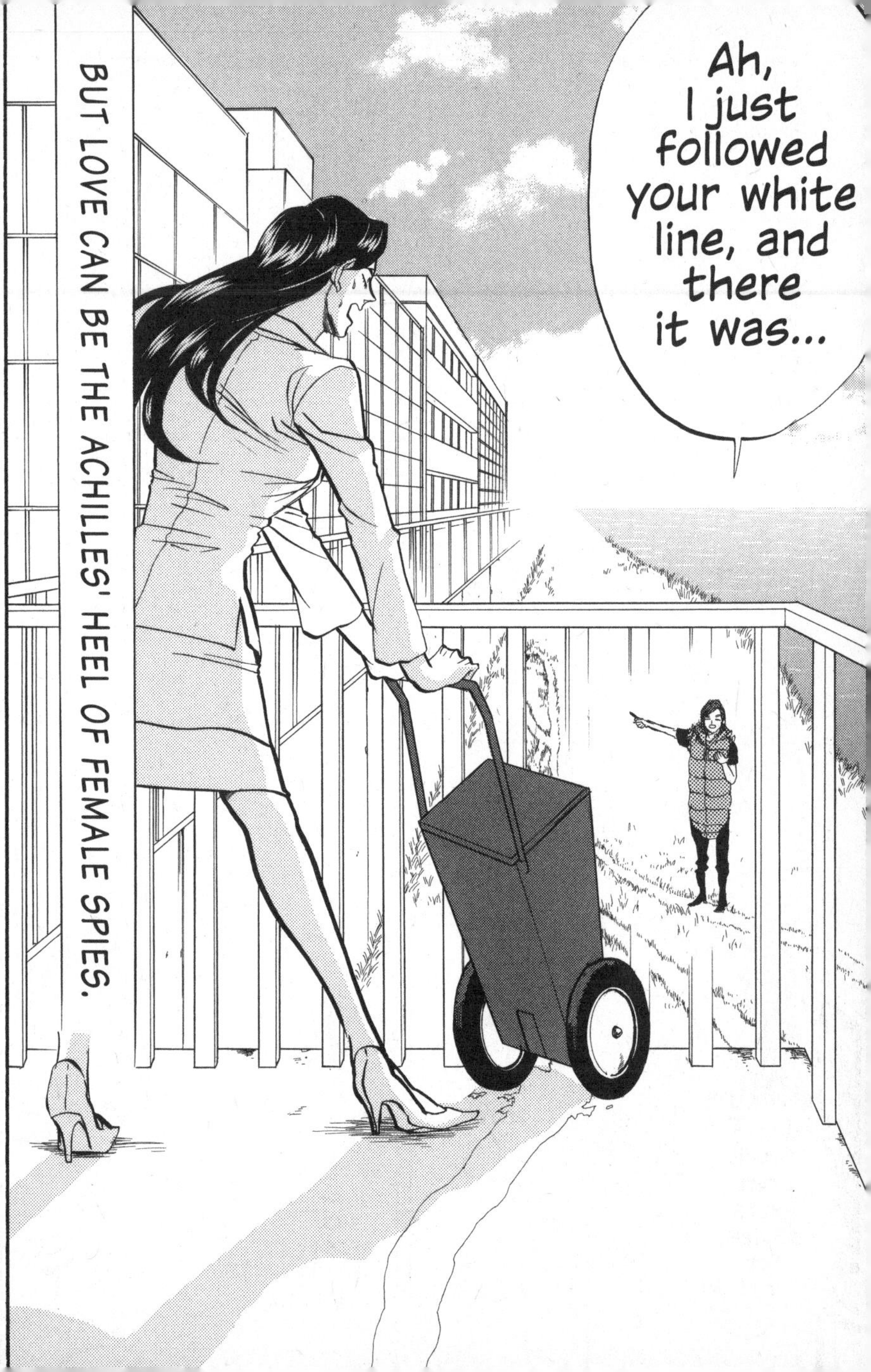
Ah, I just followed your white line, and there it was...
BUT LOVE CAN BE THE ACHILLES' HEEL OF FEMALE SPIES.

Chapter 238: Photos

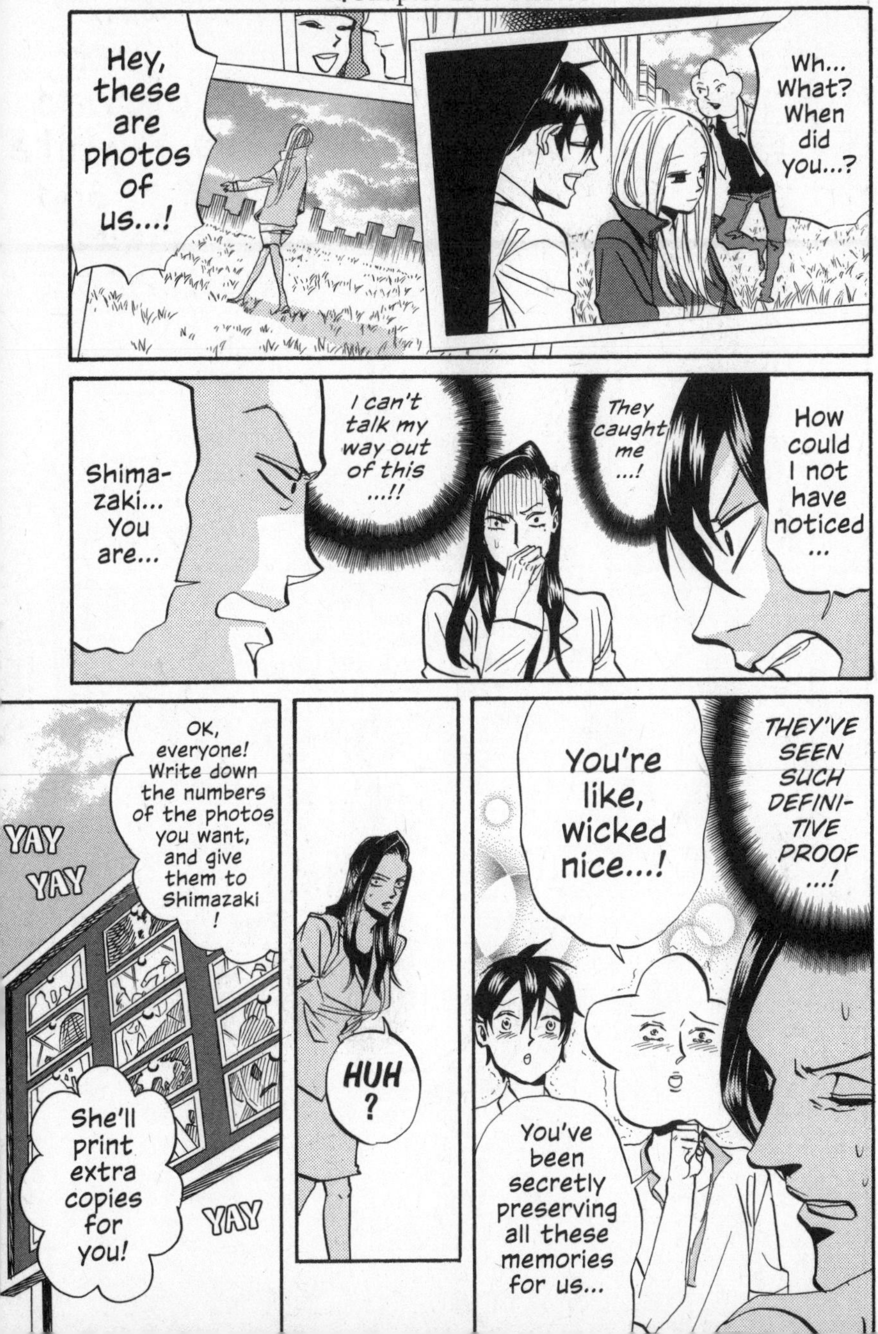

Wh... What? When did you...?
Hey, these are photos of us...!
How could I not have noticed ...
They caught me ...!
I can't talk my way out of this ...!!
Shimazaki... You are...
THEY'VE SEEN SUCH DEFINITIVE PROOF ...!
You're like, wicked nice...!
You've been secretly preserving all these memories for us...
HUH?
OK, everyone! Write down the numbers of the photos you want, and give them to Shimazaki!
YAY
YAY
She'll print extra copies for you!
YAY

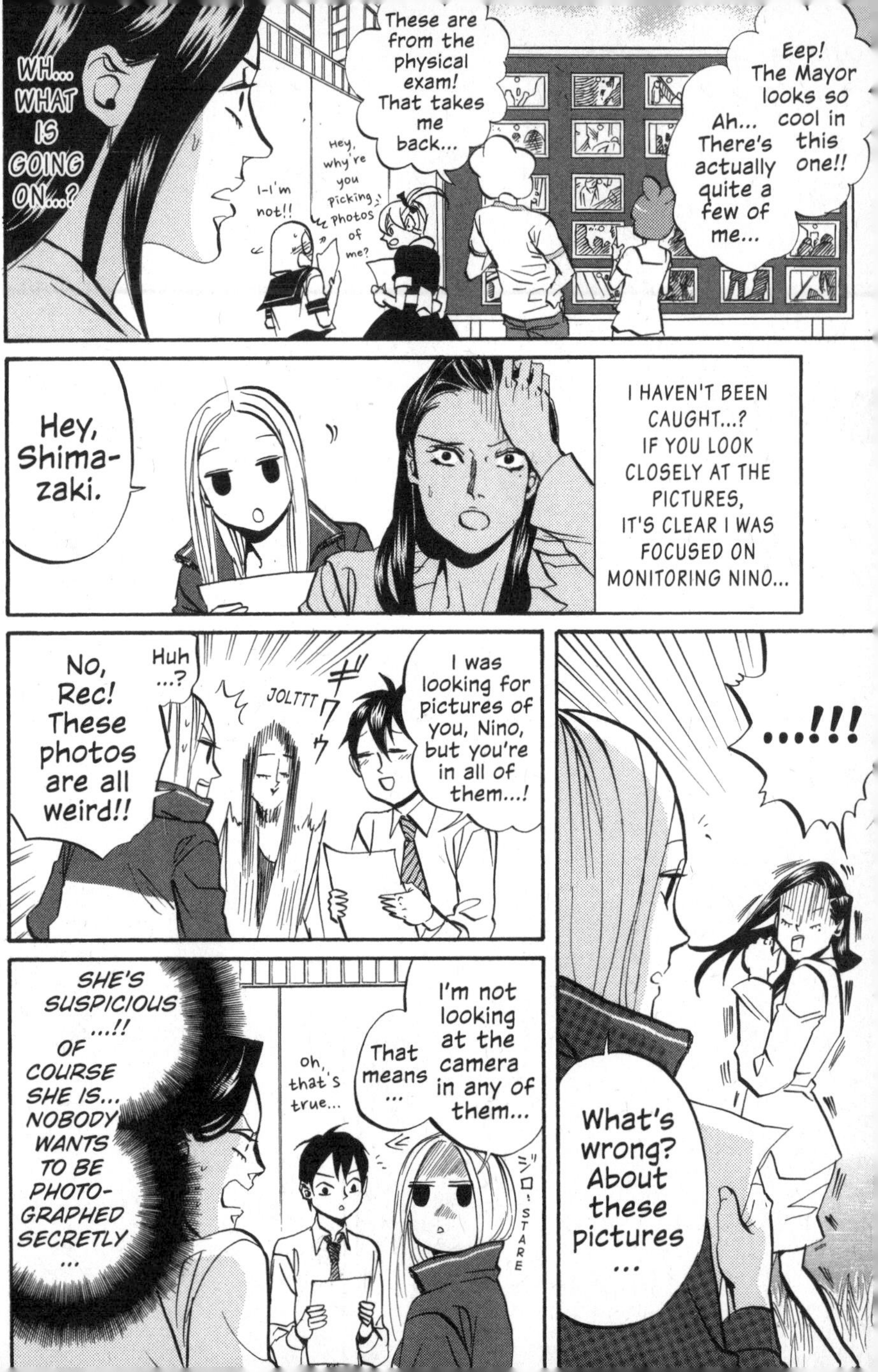

Eep! The Mayor looks so cool in this one!!
Ah... There's actually quite a few of me...
These are from the physical exam! That takes me back...
Hey, why're you picking photos of me?
I-I'm not!!
WH... WHAT IS GOING ON...?
I HAVEN'T BEEN CAUGHT...? IF YOU LOOK CLOSELY AT THE PICTURES, IT'S CLEAR I WAS FOCUSED ON MONITORING NINO...
Hey, Shimazaki.
...!!!
What's wrong? About these pictures...
I was looking for pictures of you, Nino, but you're in all of them...!
JOLTTT
Huh...?
No, Rec! These photos are all weird!!
I'm not looking at the camera in any of them...
That means...
STARE
Oh, that's true...
SHE'S SUSPICIOUS...!! OF COURSE SHE IS... NOBODY WANTS TO BE PHOTOGRAPHED SECRETLY...

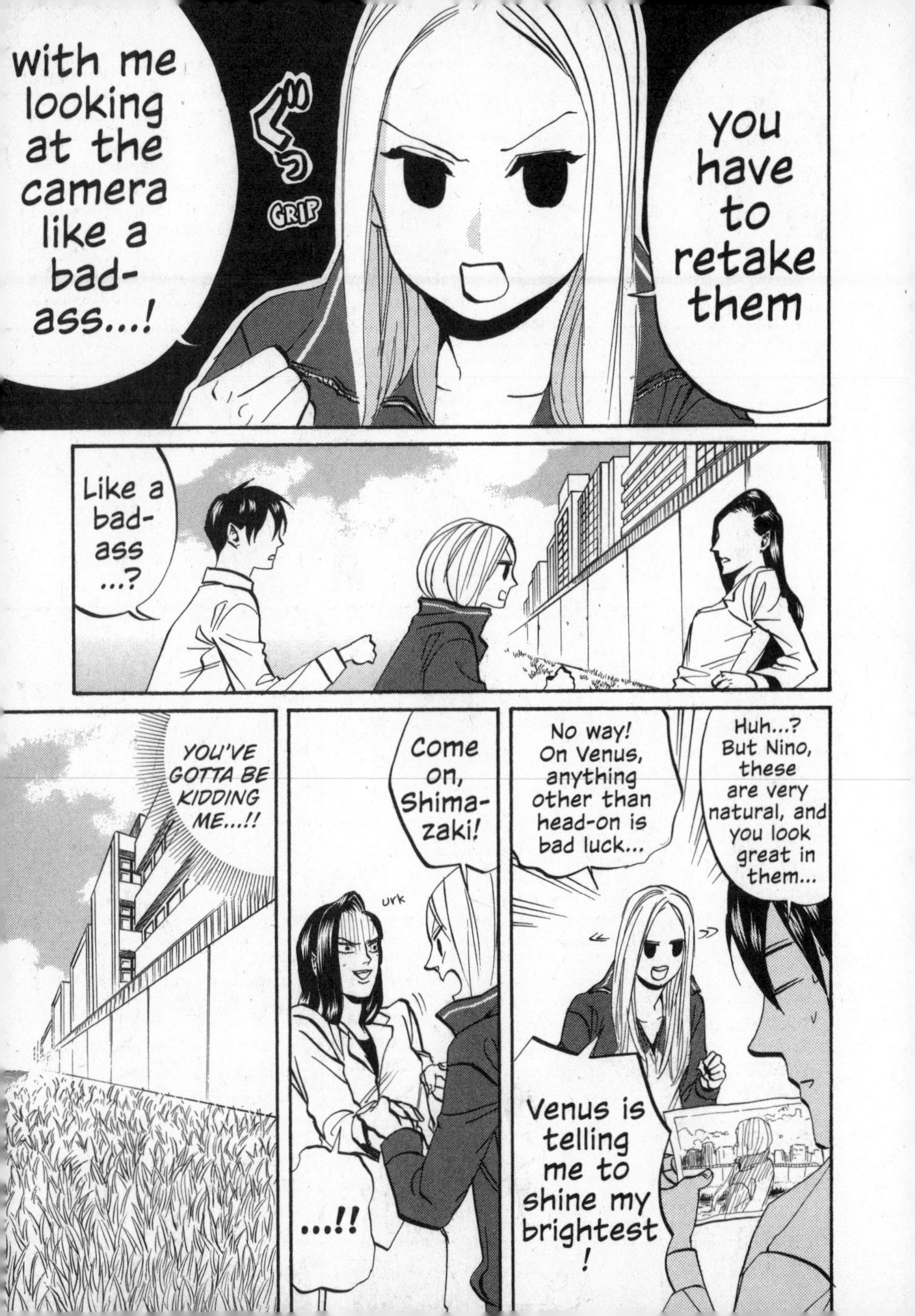

you have to retake them
ぐっ
GRIP
with me looking at the camera like a bad-ass...!
Like a bad-ass...?
Huh...? But Nino, these are very natural, and you look great in them...
No way! On Venus, anything other than head-on is bad luck...
Venus is telling me to shine my brightest!
Come on, Shimazaki!
urk
...!!
YOU'VE GOTTA BE KIDDING ME...!!

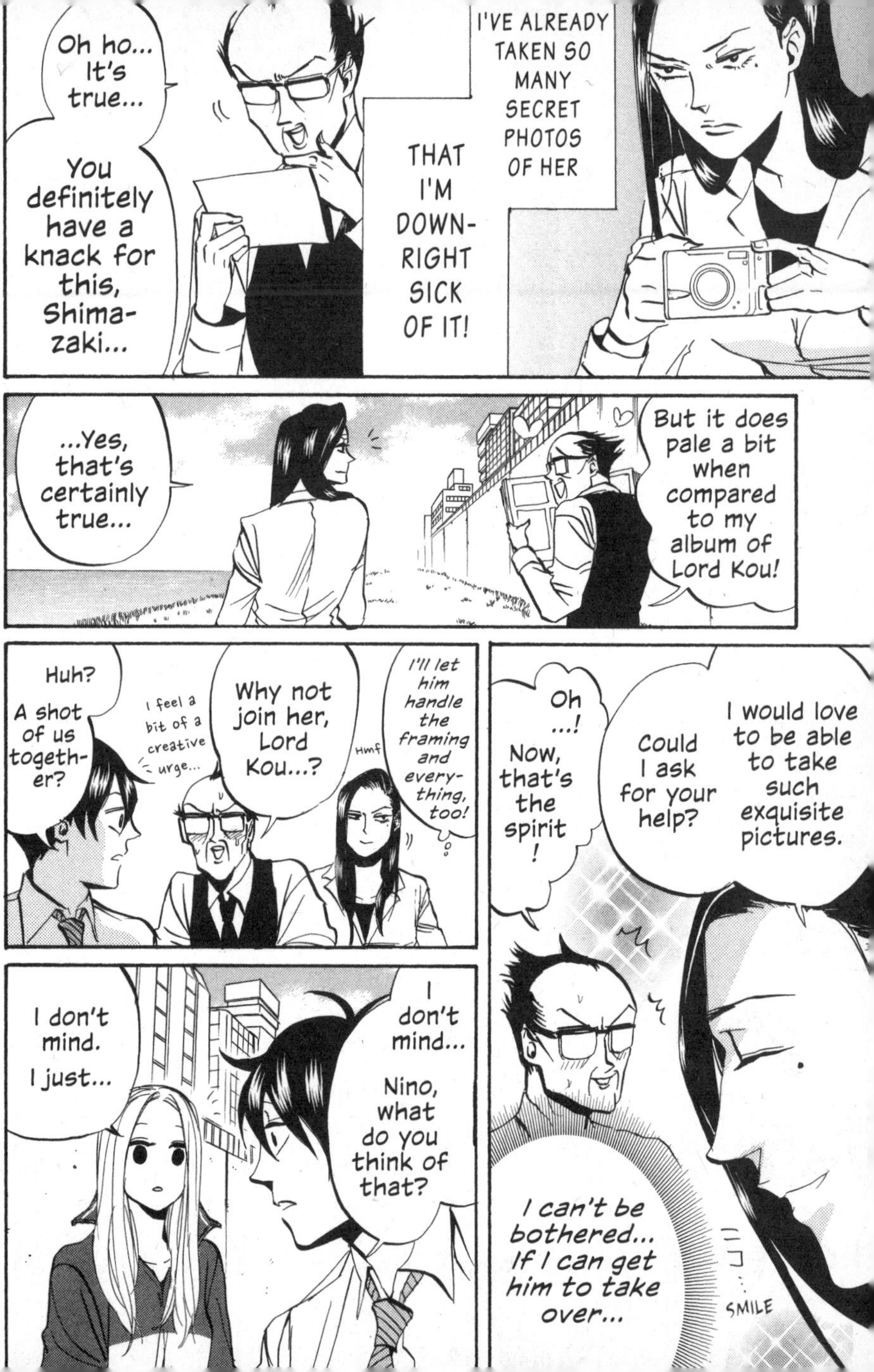
I'VE ALREADY TAKEN SO MANY SECRET PHOTOS OF HER
THAT I'M DOWN-RIGHT SICK OF IT!
Oh ho... It's true...
You definitely have a knack for this, Shima-zaki...
But it does pale a bit when compared to my album of Lord Kou!
...Yes, that's certainly true...
I would love to be able to take such exquisite pictures.
Could I ask for your help?
Oh ...! Now, that's the spirit!
I can't be bothered... If I can get him to take over...
SMILE
I'll let him handle the framing and everything, too!
Hmf
Why not join her, Lord Kou...?
I feel a bit of a creative urge...
Huh? A shot of us together?
I don't mind...
Nino, what do you think of that?
I don't mind. I just...

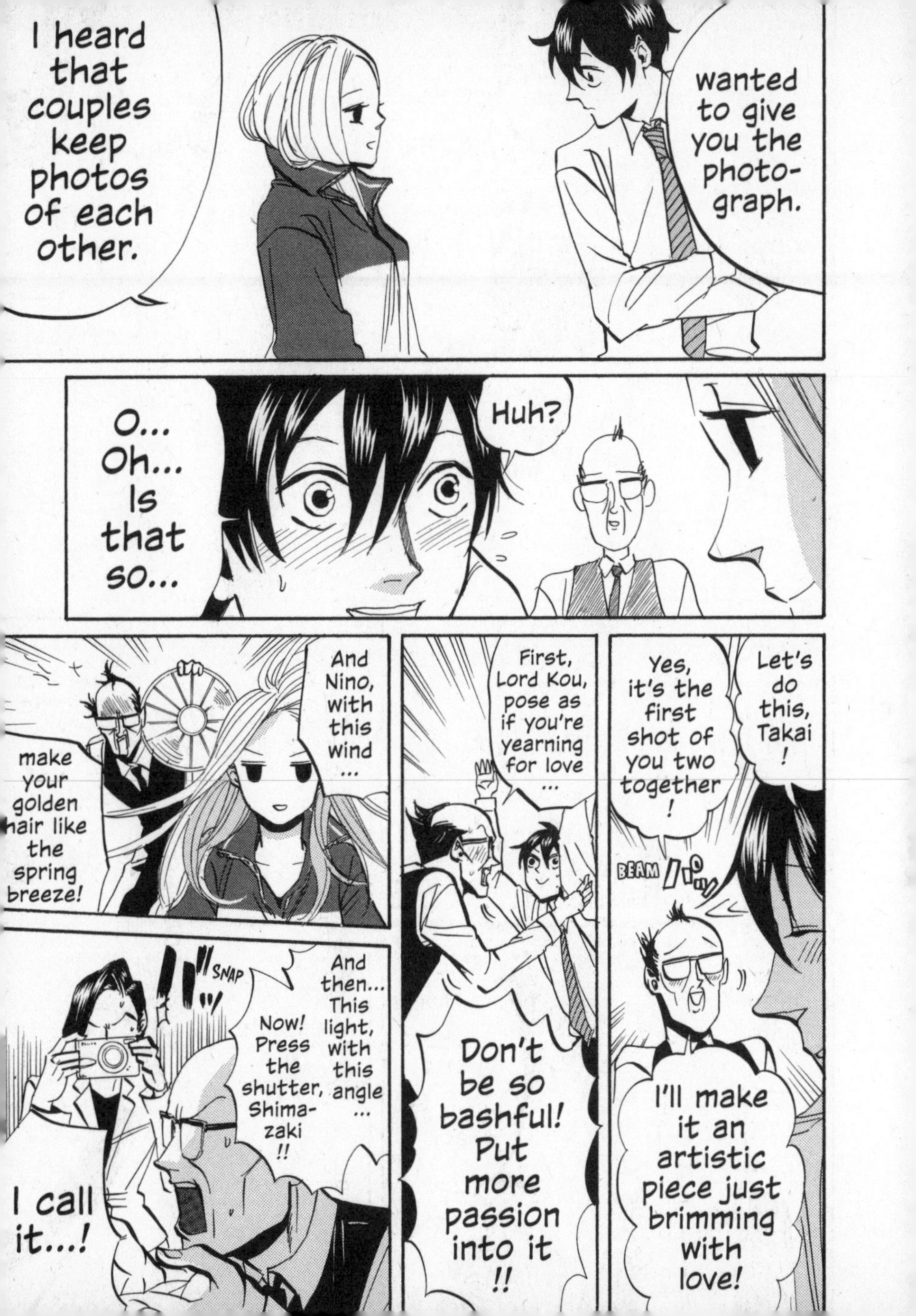
wanted to give you the photograph.
I heard that couples keep photos of each other.
Huh?
O... Oh... Is that so...
Let's do this, Takai!
Yes, it's the first shot of you two together!
BEAM
I'll make it an artistic piece just brimming with love!
First, Lord Kou, pose as if you're yearning for love...
Don't be so bashful! Put more passion into it!!
And Nino, with this wind...
make your golden hair like the spring breeze!
And then... This light, with this angle...
Now! Press the shutter, Shimazaki!!
SNAP
I call it...!

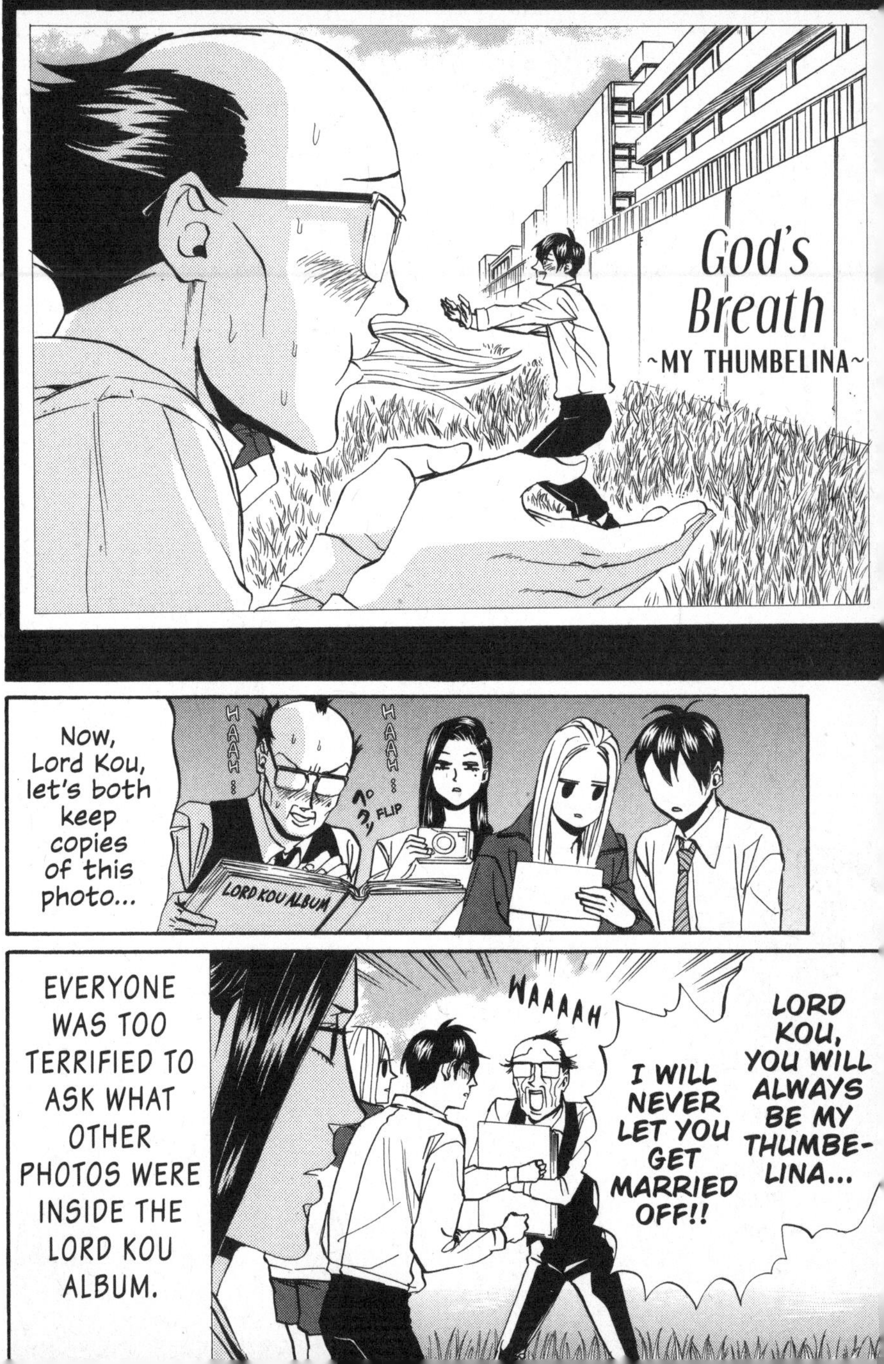
God's Breath
~MY THUMBELINA~
HAAAH...
FLIP
HAAAH...
Now, Lord Kou, let's both keep copies of this photo...
LORD KOU ALBUM
LORD KOU, YOU WILL ALWAYS BE MY THUMBE-LINA...
I WILL NEVER LET YOU GET MARRIED OFF!!
WAAAAH
EVERYONE WAS TOO TERRIFIED TO ASK WHAT OTHER PHOTOS WERE INSIDE THE LORD KOU ALBUM.

Chapter 239: Don't Look Away

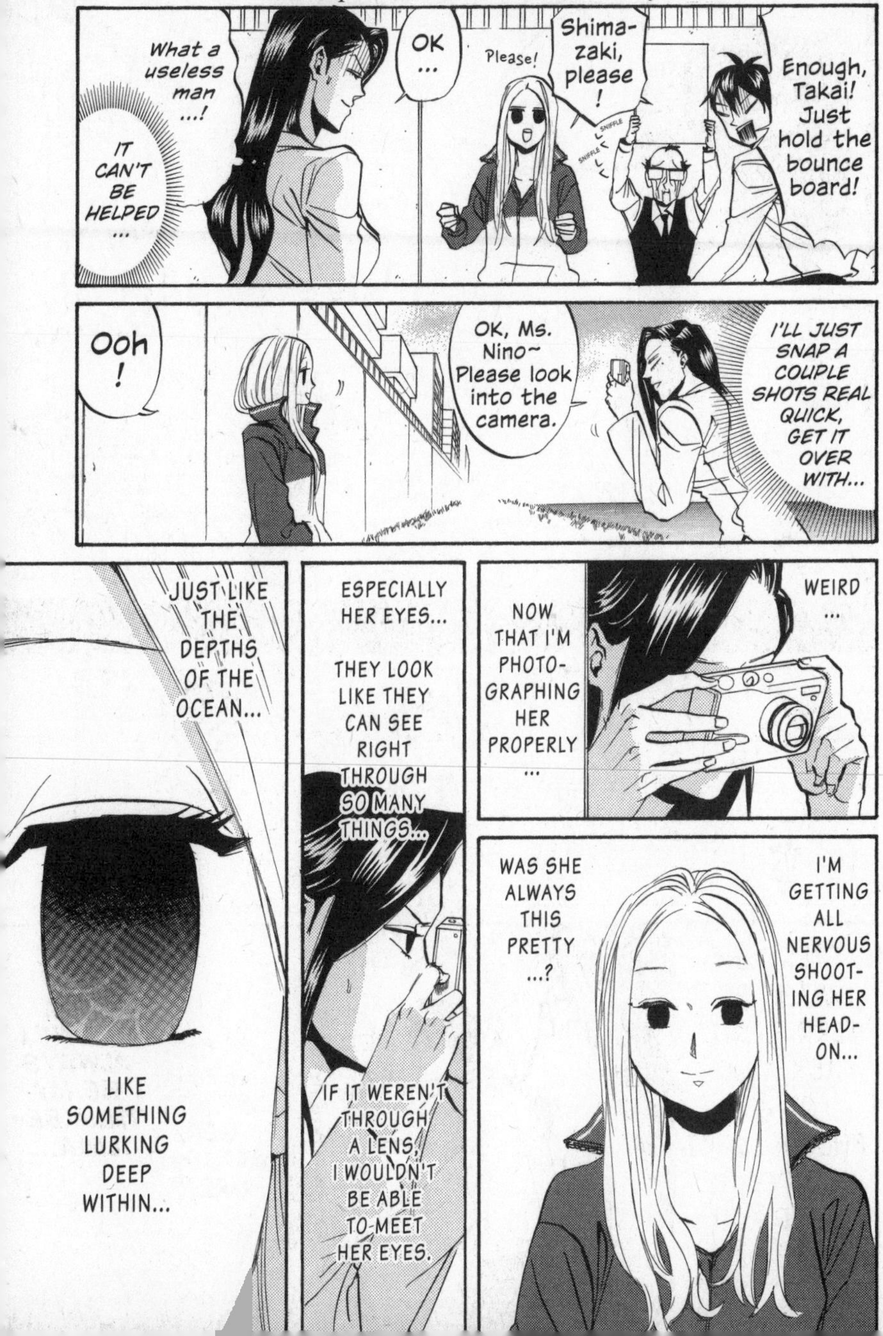
Enough, Takai! Just hold the bounce board!
Shimazaki, please!
SNIFFLE
SNIFFLE
Please!
OK ...
What a useless man ...!
IT CAN'T BE HELPED ...
I'LL JUST SNAP A COUPLE SHOTS REAL QUICK, GET IT OVER WITH...
OK, Ms. Nino~ Please look into the camera.
Ooh!
WEIRD ...
NOW THAT I'M PHOTOGRAPHING HER PROPERLY ...
I'M GETTING ALL NERVOUS SHOOTING HER HEAD-ON...
WAS SHE ALWAYS THIS PRETTY ...?
ESPECIALLY HER EYES...
THEY LOOK LIKE THEY CAN SEE RIGHT THROUGH SO MANY THINGS...
IF IT WEREN'T THROUGH A LENS, I WOULDN'T BE ABLE TO MEET HER EYES.
JUST LIKE THE DEPTHS OF THE OCEAN...
LIKE SOMETHING LURKING DEEP WITHIN...

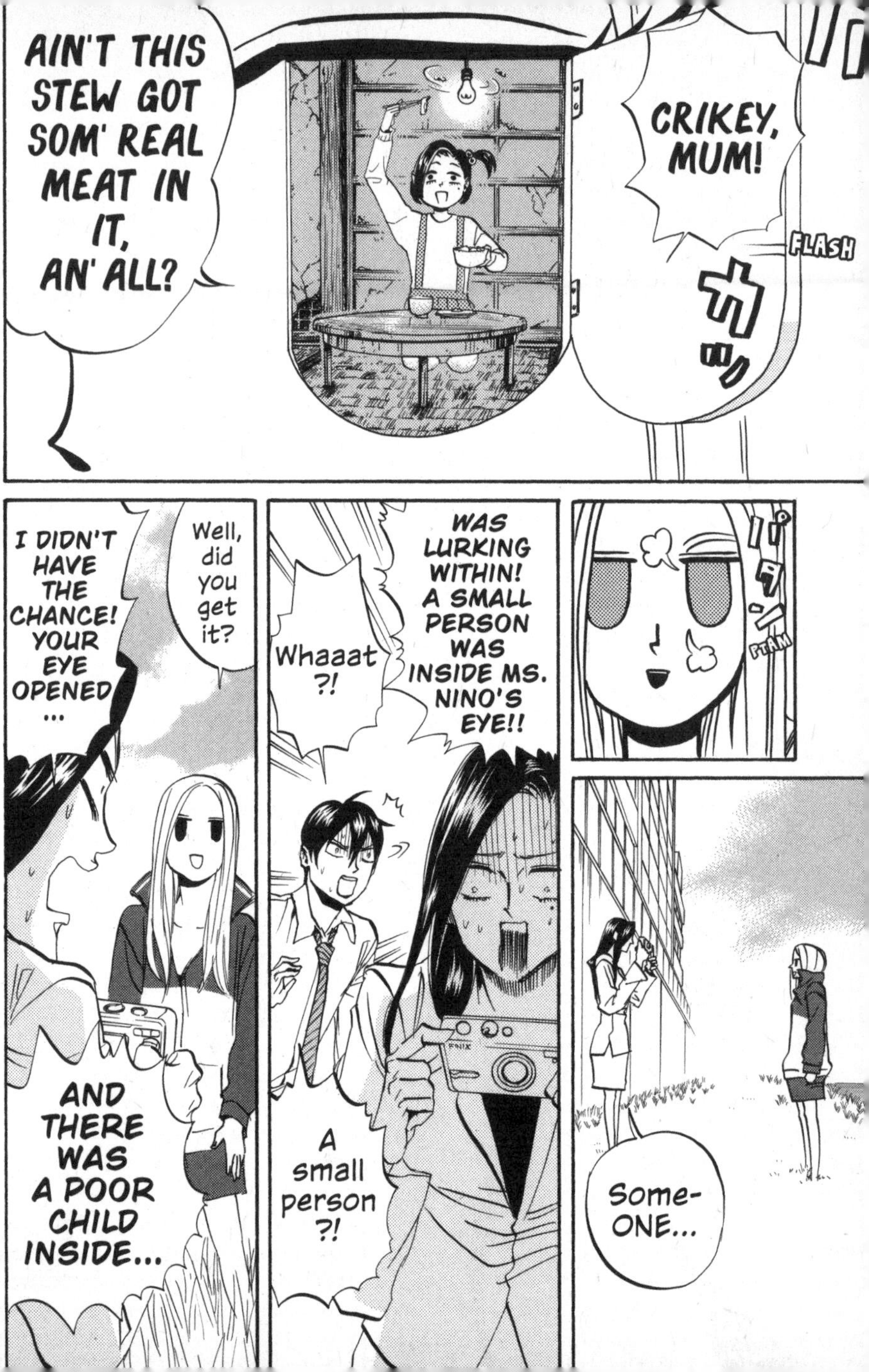
CRIKEY, MUM!
FLASH
AIN'T THIS STEW GOT SOM' REAL MEAT IN IT, AN' ALL?
PTAM
Some-ONE...
WAS LURKING WITHIN! A SMALL PERSON WAS INSIDE MS. NINO'S EYE!!
Whaaat?!
A small person?!
Well, did you get it?
I DIDN'T HAVE THE CHANCE! YOUR EYE OPENED...
AND THERE WAS A POOR CHILD INSIDE...

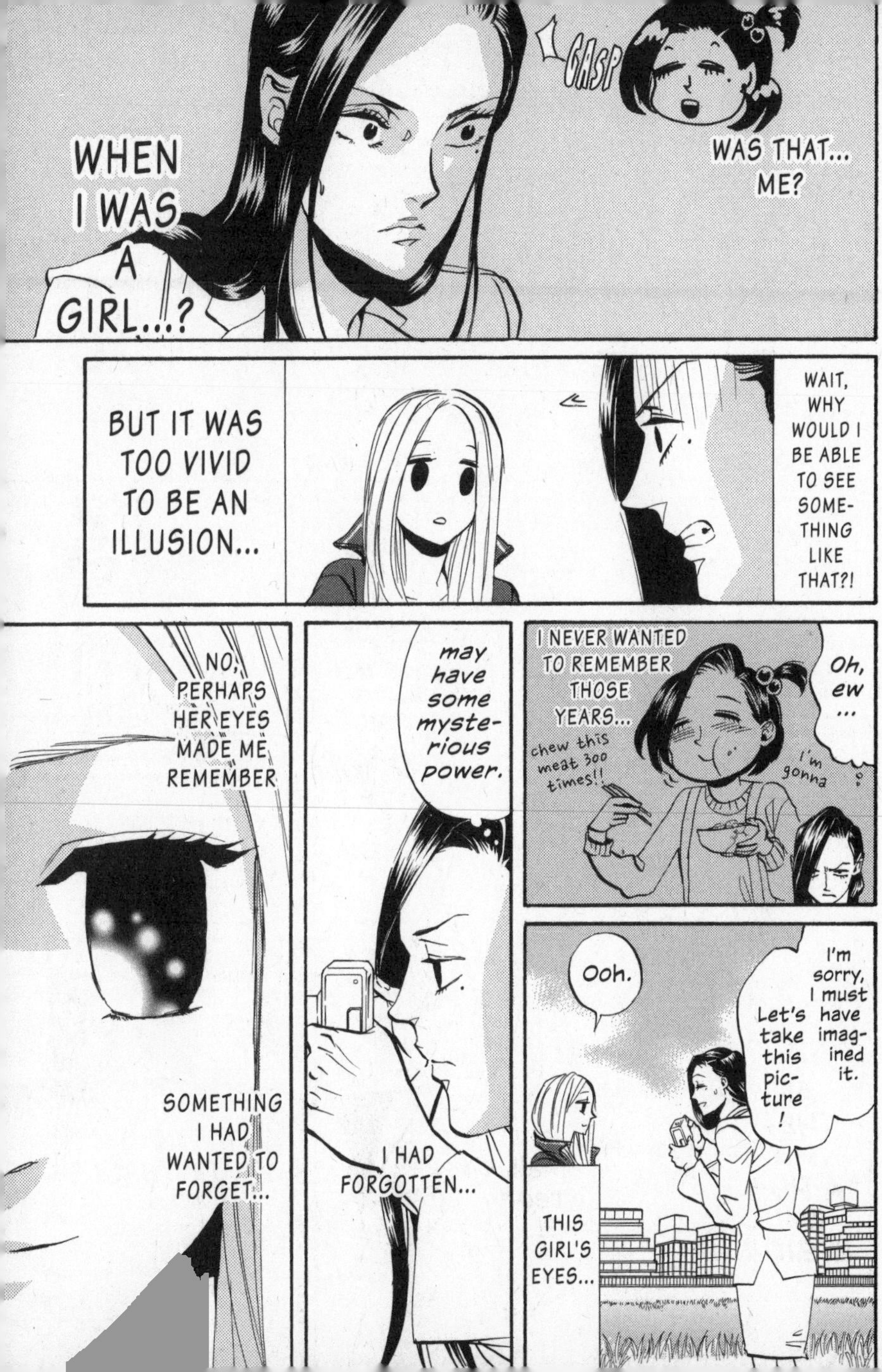
GASP
WAS THAT... ME?
WHEN I WAS A GIRL...?
WAIT, WHY WOULD I BE ABLE TO SEE SOME-THING LIKE THAT?!
BUT IT WAS TOO VIVID TO BE AN ILLUSION...
I NEVER WANTED TO REMEMBER THOSE YEARS...
Oh, ew...
I'm gonna
chew this meat 300 times!!
I'm sorry, I must have imag-ined it.
Let's take this pic-ture!
Ooh.
THIS GIRL'S EYES...
may have some myste-rious power.
I HAD FORGOTTEN...
NO, PERHAPS HER EYES MADE ME REMEMBER
SOMETHING I HAD WANTED TO FORGET...

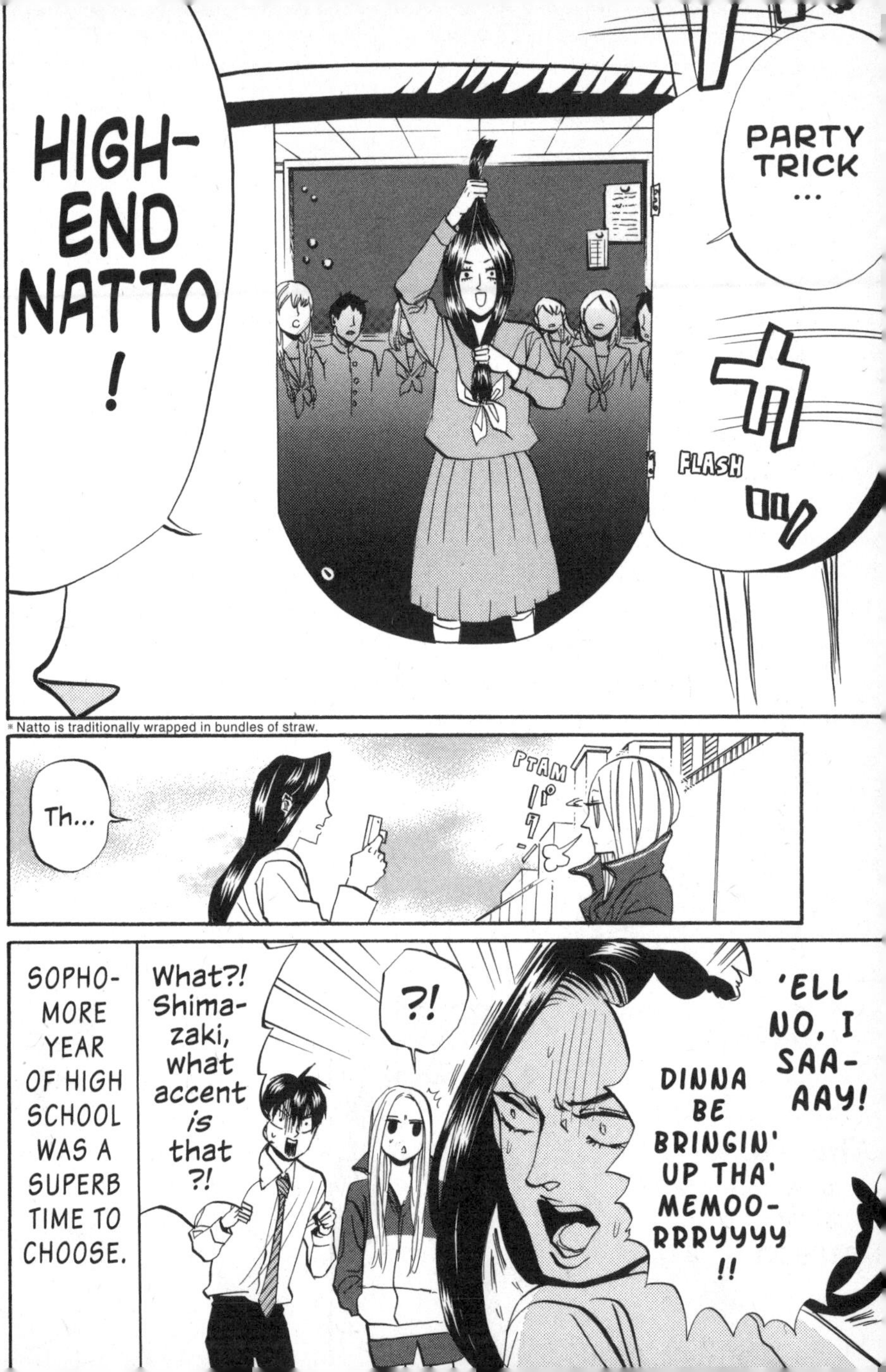
PARTY TRICK ...
FLASH
HIGH-END NATTO!
PTAM
Th...
'ELL NO, I SAAAAY!
DINNA BE BRINGIN' UP THA' MEMOO-RRRYYYY!!
?!
What?! Shimazaki, what accent *is* that?!
SOPHOMORE YEAR OF HIGH SCHOOL WAS A SUPERB TIME TO CHOOSE.

※ Natto is traditionally wrapped in bundles of straw.

Chapter 240: Beyond the Lens

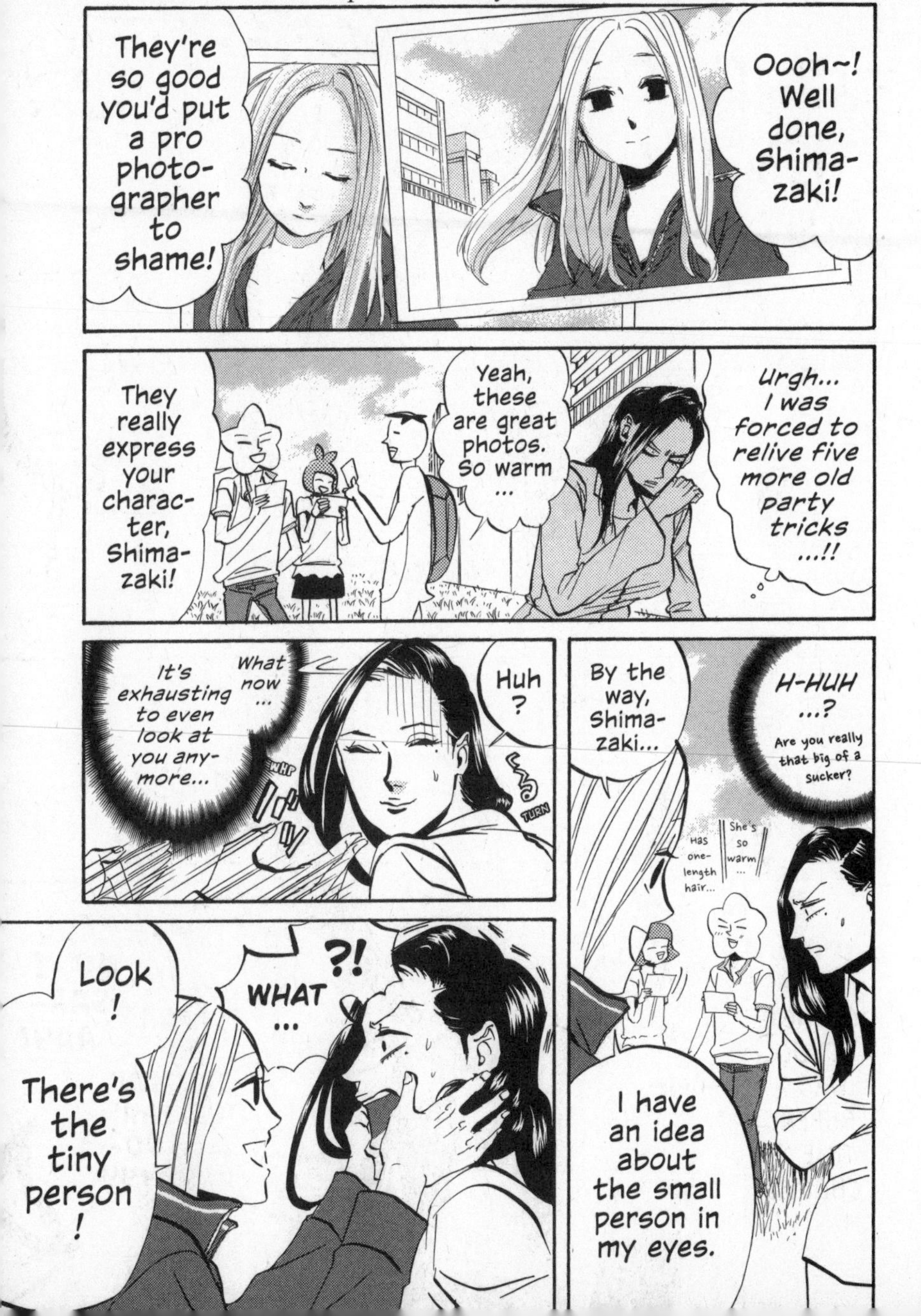

Oooh~! Well done, Shimazaki!
They're so good you'd put a pro photographer to shame!
Urgh... I was forced to relive five more old party tricks ...!!
Yeah, these are great photos. So warm ...
They really express your character, Shimazaki!
H-HUH ...?
Are you really that big of a sucker?
By the way, Shimazaki...
She's so warm ...
Has one-length hair...
I have an idea about the small person in my eyes.
Huh ?
What now ...
It's exhausting to even look at you anymore...
WHP
くる
TURN
?!
WHAT ...
Look !
There's the tiny person !

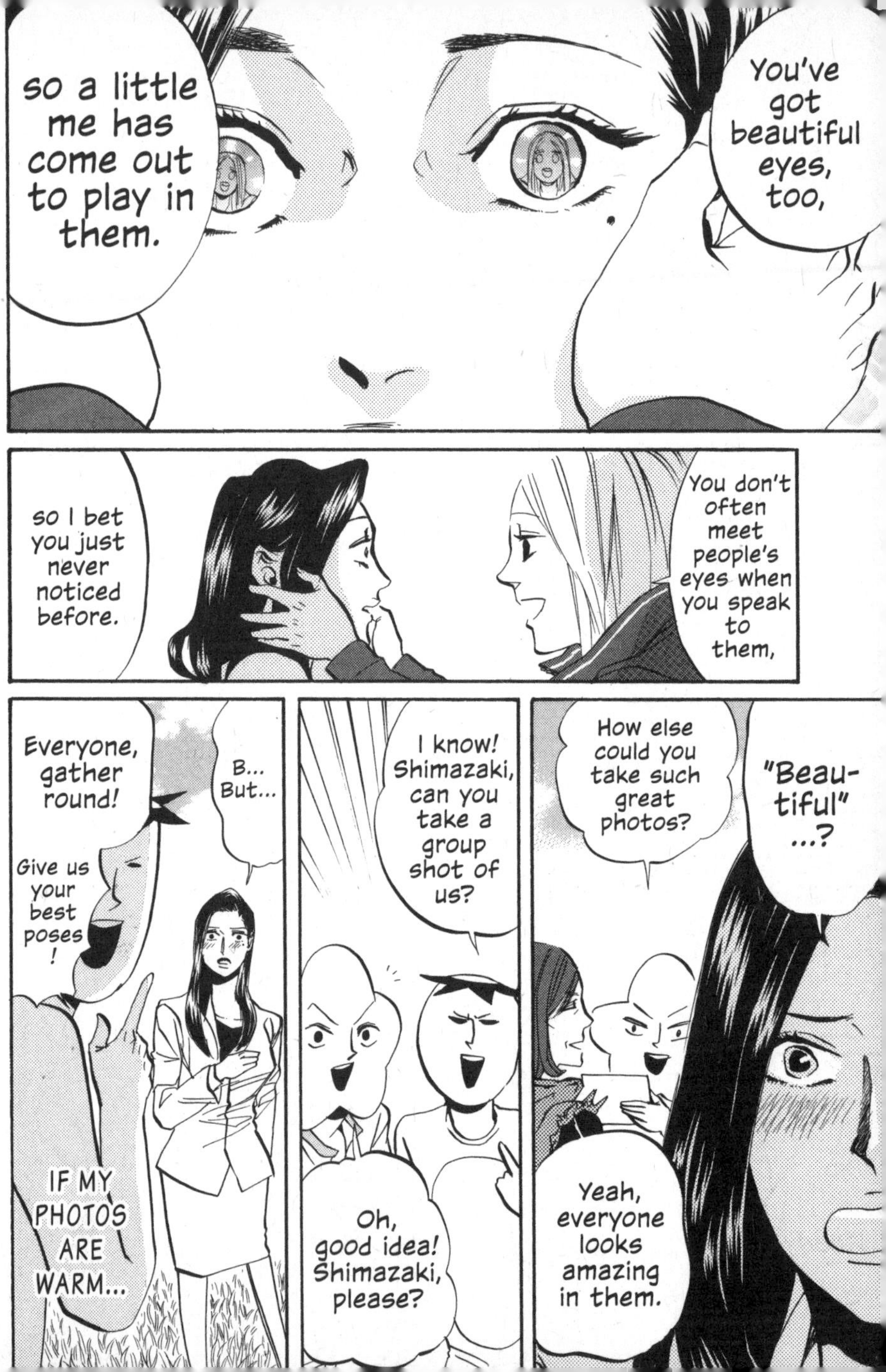
You've got beautiful eyes, too,
so a little me has come out to play in them.
You don't often meet people's eyes when you speak to them,
so I bet you just never noticed before.
"Beau-tiful" ...?
How else could you take such great photos?
Yeah, everyone looks amazing in them.
I know! Shimazaki, can you take a group shot of us?
Oh, good idea! Shimazaki, please?
B... But...
Everyone, gather round!
Give us your best poses!
IF MY PHOTOS ARE WARM...

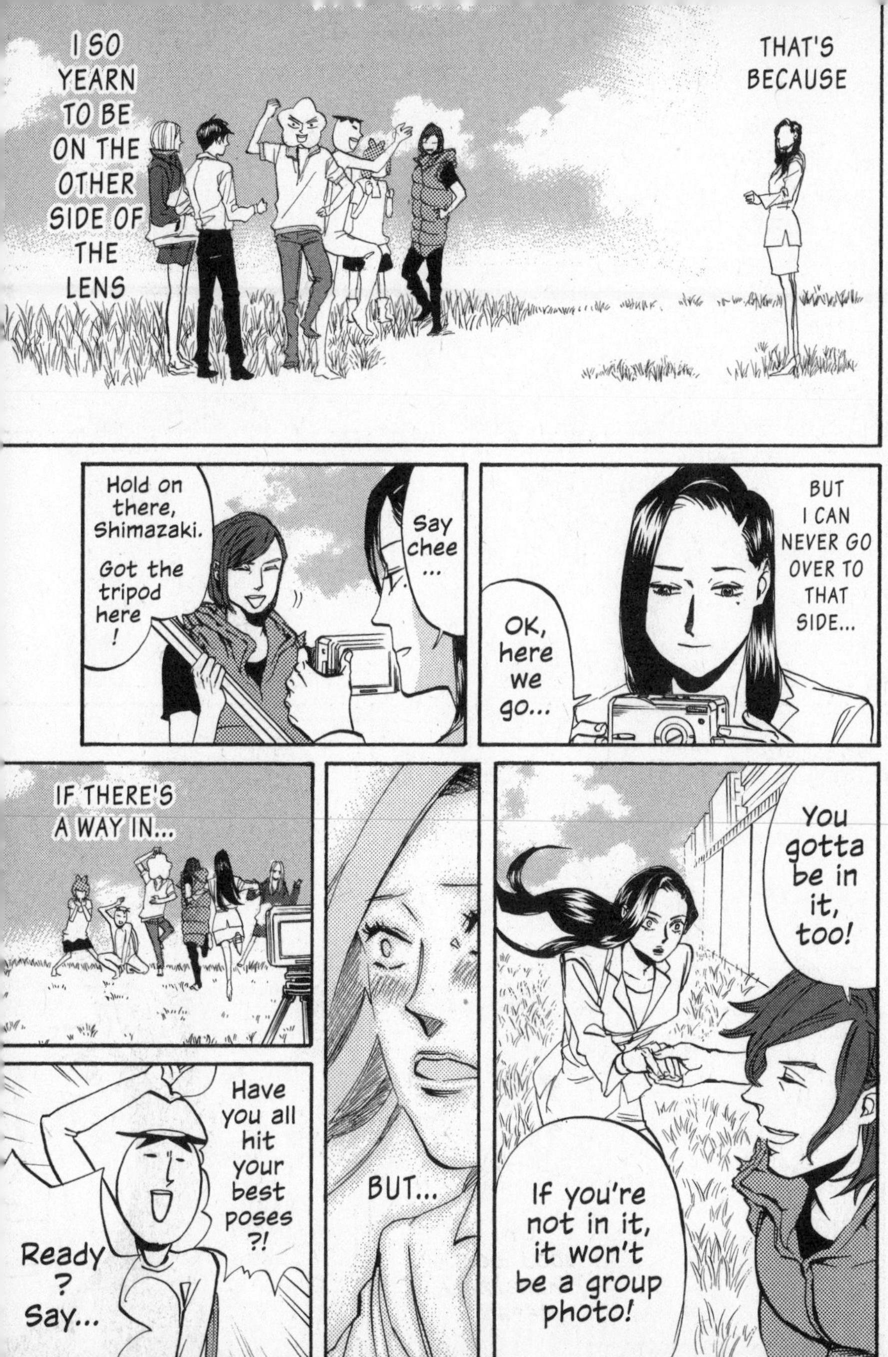
THAT'S BECAUSE
I SO YEARN TO BE ON THE OTHER SIDE OF THE LENS
BUT I CAN NEVER GO OVER TO THAT SIDE...
OK, here we go...
Say chee...
Hold on there, Shimazaki.
Got the tripod here!
You gotta be in it, too!
If you're not in it, it won't be a group photo!
BUT...
IF THERE'S A WAY IN...
Have you all hit your best poses?!
Ready? Say...

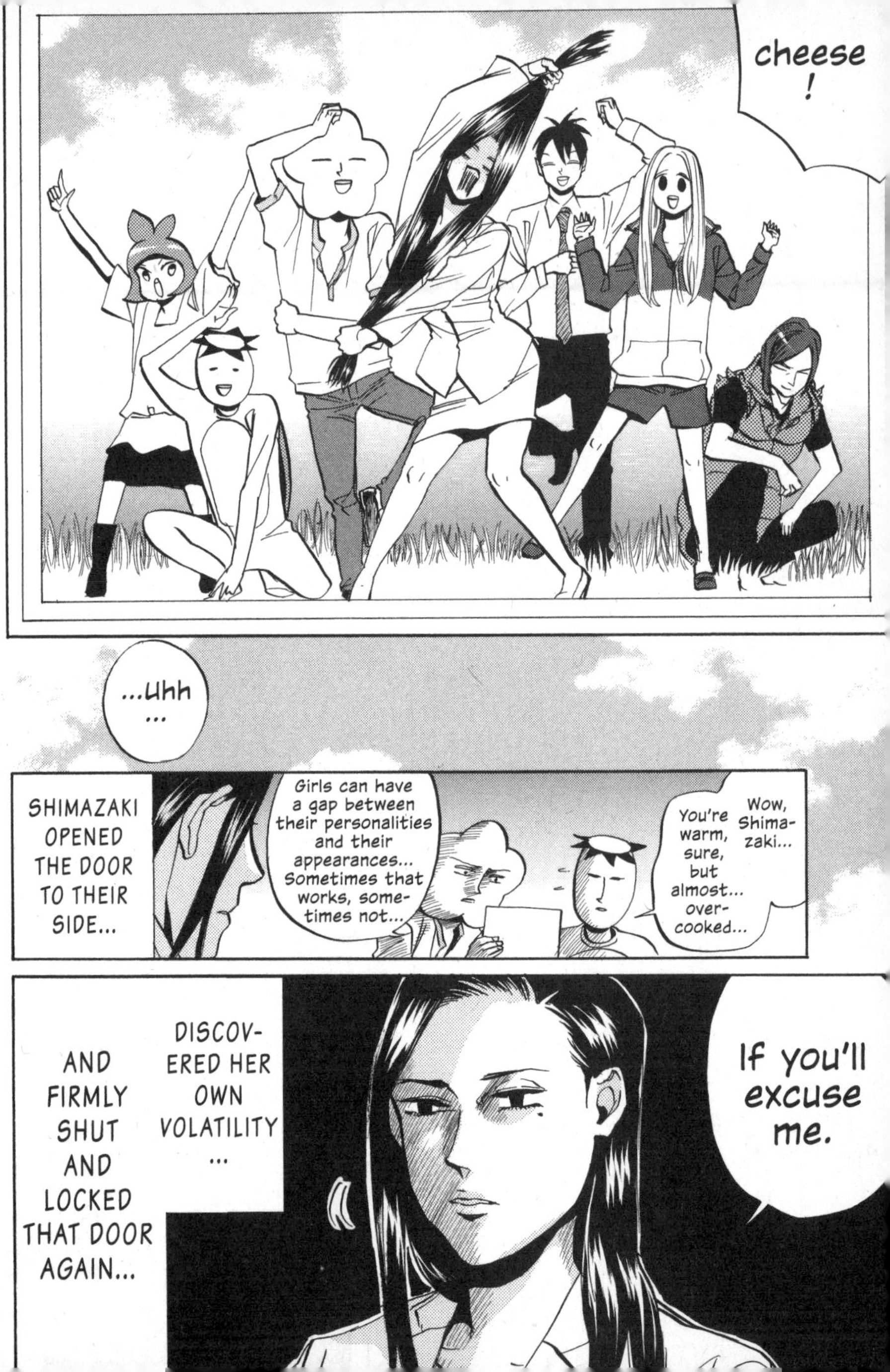
cheese !
...Uhh ...
Wow, Shimazaki... You're warm, sure, but almost... over-cooked...
Girls can have a gap between their personalities and their appearances... Sometimes that works, some-times not...
SHIMAZAKI OPENED THE DOOR TO THEIR SIDE...
If you'll excuse me.
DISCOV-ERED HER OWN VOLATILITY ...
AND FIRMLY SHUT AND LOCKED THAT DOOR AGAIN...

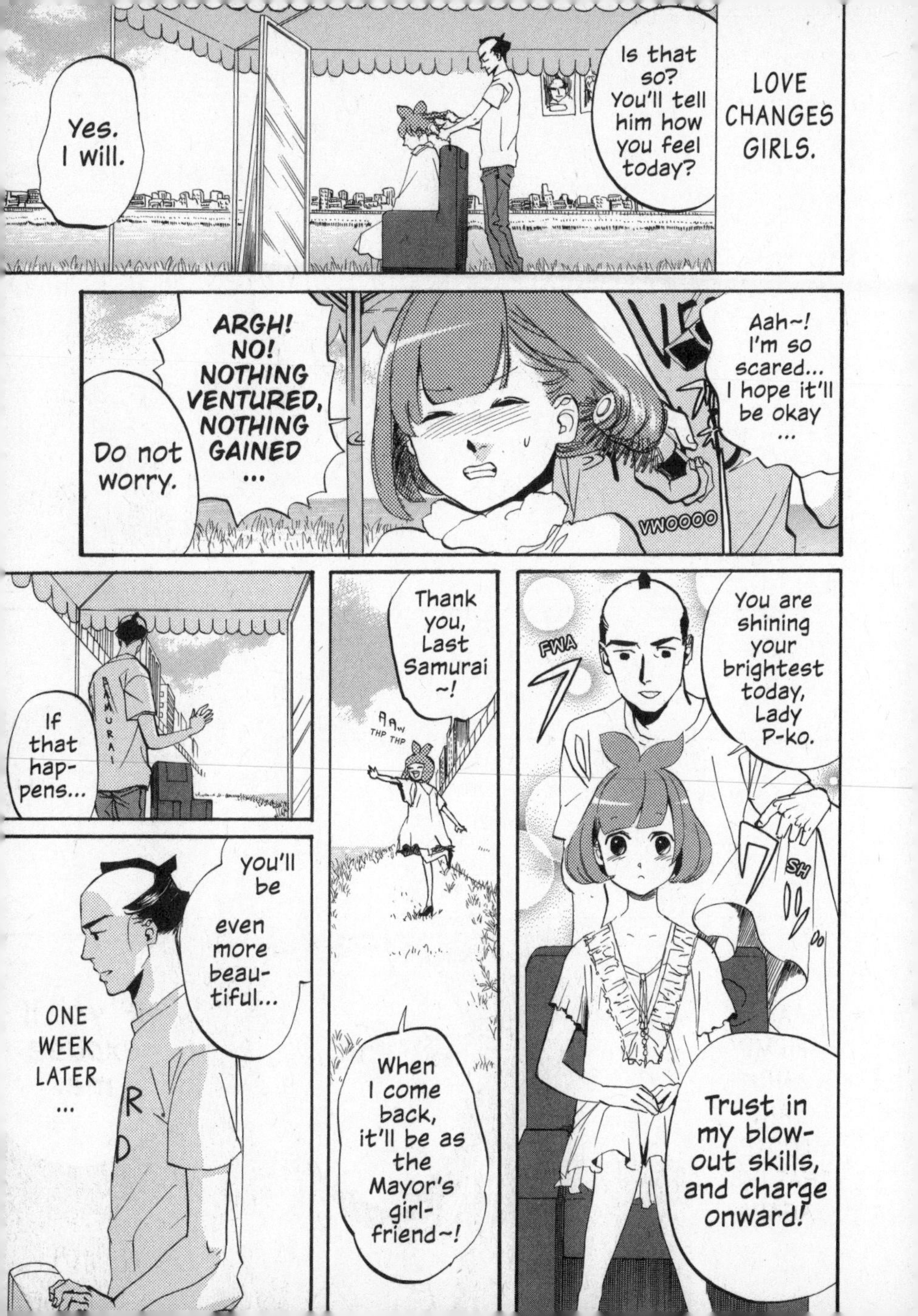
LOVE CHANGES GIRLS.
Is that so? You'll tell him how you feel today?
Yes. I will.
Aah~! I'm so scared... I hope it'll be okay ...
VWOOOO
ARGH! NO! NOTHING VENTURED, NOTHING GAINED ...
Do not worry.
You are shining your brightest today, Lady P-ko.
FWA
SH
Trust in my blow-out skills, and charge onward!
Thank you, Last Samurai ~!
THP THP
When I come back, it'll be as the Mayor's girl-friend~!
If that hap-pens...
you'll be even more beau-tiful...
ONE WEEK LATER ...

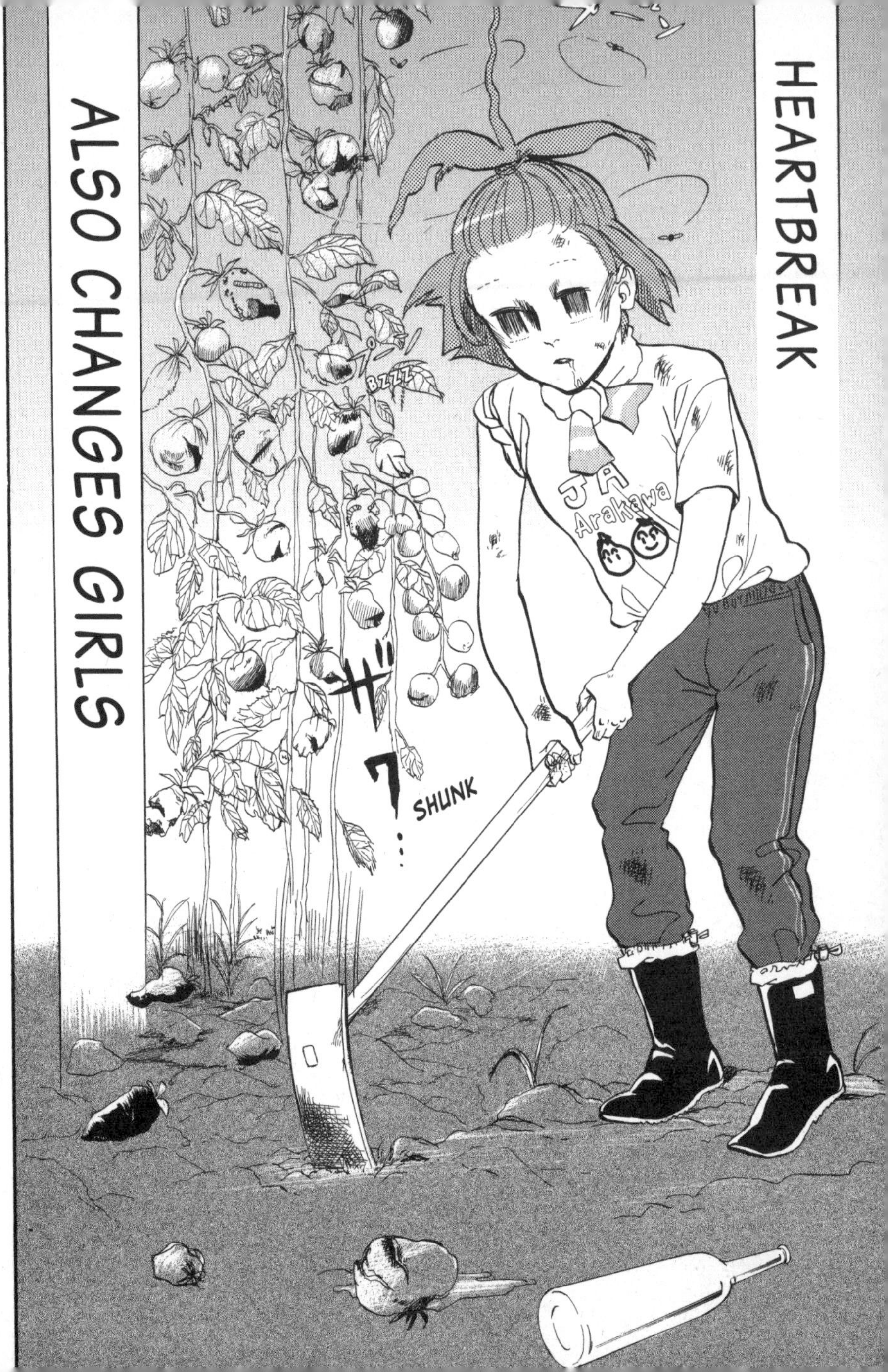
HEARTBREAK
ALSO CHANGES GIRLS
BZZZ
JA
Arakawa
SHUNK

Chapter 241: Heartbreak Farm

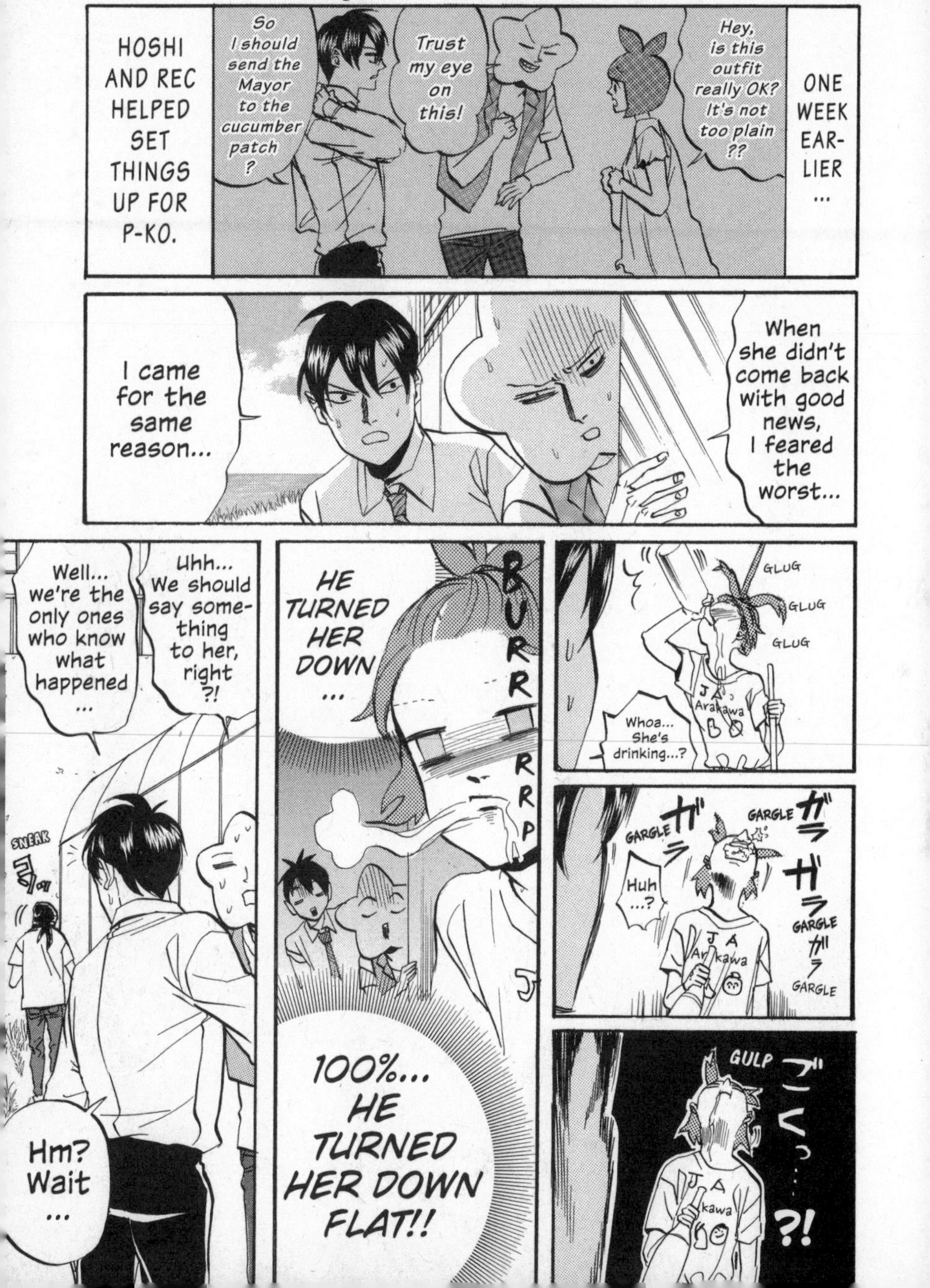

ONE WEEK EARLIER...
Hey, is this outfit really OK? It's not too plain ??
Trust my eye on this!
So I should send the Mayor to the cucumber patch ?
HOSHI AND REC HELPED SET THINGS UP FOR P-KO.
When she didn't come back with good news, I feared the worst...
I came for the same reason...
GLUG
GLUG
GLUG
Whoa... She's drinking...?
GARGLE ガラ
GARGLE ガラ
Huh ...?
ガラ
GARGLE
ガラ
GARGLE
GULP
?!
HE TURNED HER DOWN ...
BURRRRRP
100%... HE TURNED HER DOWN FLAT!!
Uhh... We should say something to her, right ?!
Well... we're the only ones who know what happened ...
SNEAK
Hm? Wait ...

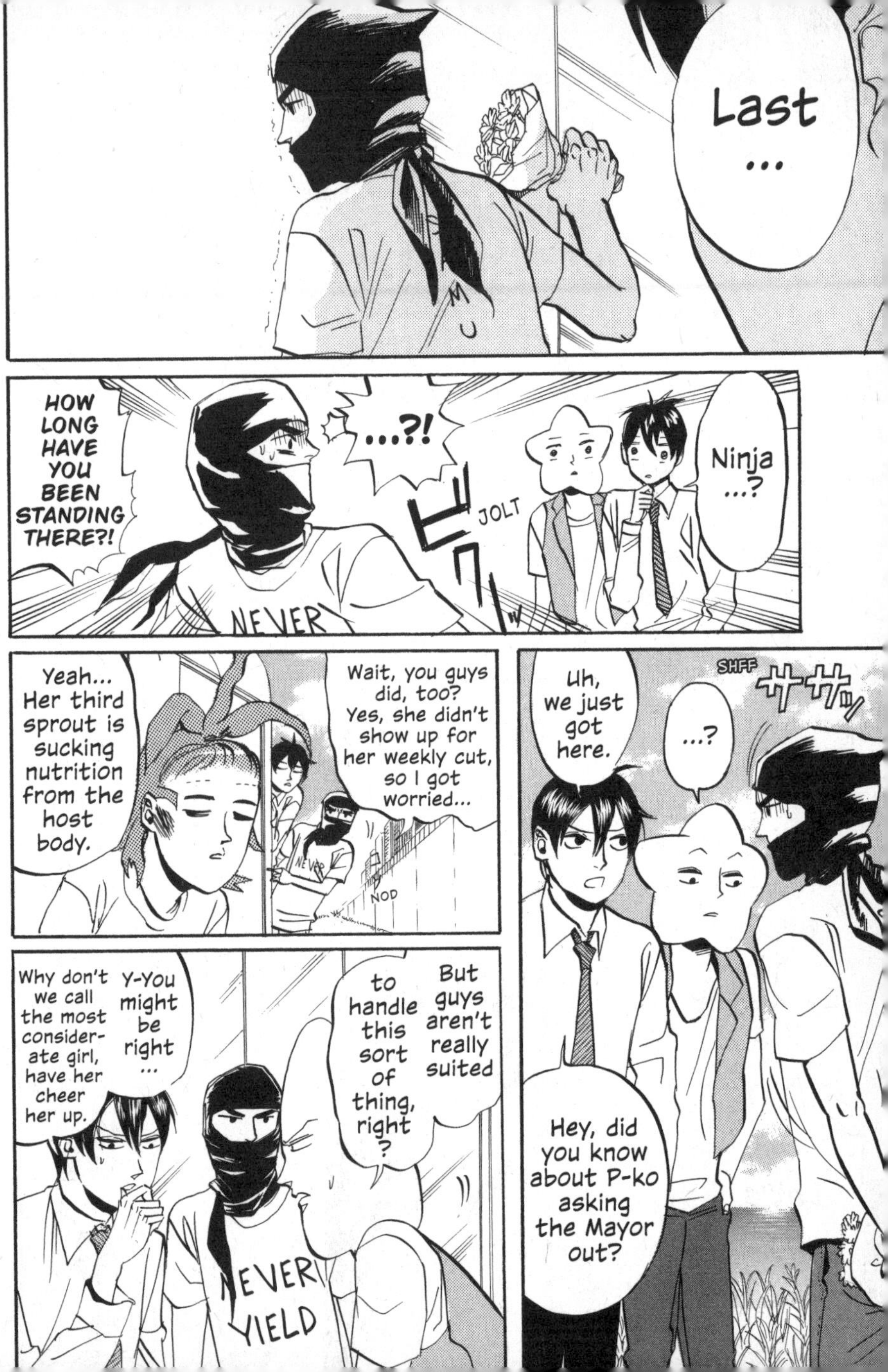

Last ...
Ninja ...?
...?!
JOLT
HOW LONG HAVE YOU BEEN STANDING THERE?!
NEVER
SHFF
Uh, we just got here.
...?
Wait, you guys did, too? Yes, she didn't show up for her weekly cut, so I got worried...
Yeah... Her third sprout is sucking nutrition from the host body.
NOD
Hey, did you know about P-ko asking the Mayor out?
But guys aren't really suited to handle this sort of thing, right?
Y-You might be right ...
Why don't we call the most consider-ate girl, have her cheer her up.
NEVER YIELD

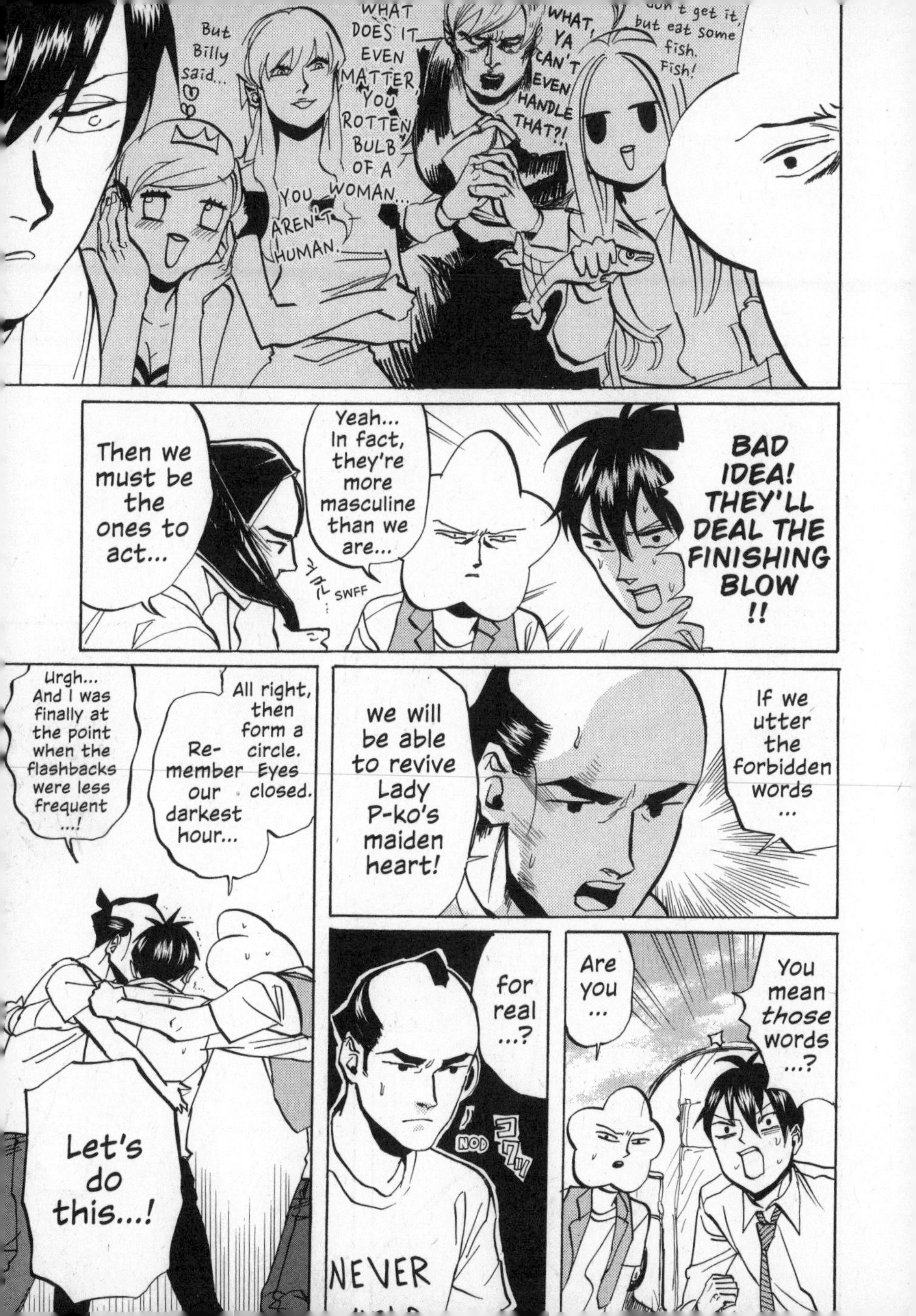

n't get it, but eat some fish. Fish!
WHAT, YA CAN'T EVEN HANDLE THAT?!
WHAT DOES IT EVEN MATTER, YOU ROTTEN BULB OF A WOMAN...
YOU AREN'T HUMAN.
But Billy said...
BAD IDEA! THEY'LL DEAL THE FINISHING BLOW !!
Yeah... In fact, they're more masculine than we are...
SWFF
Then we must be the ones to act...
If we utter the forbidden words...
we will be able to revive Lady P-ko's maiden heart!
You mean *those* words...?
Are you...
for real...?
NOD
NEVER
All right, then form a circle. Eyes closed.
Remember our darkest hour...
Urgh... And I was finally at the point when the flashbacks were less frequent...!
Let's do this...!

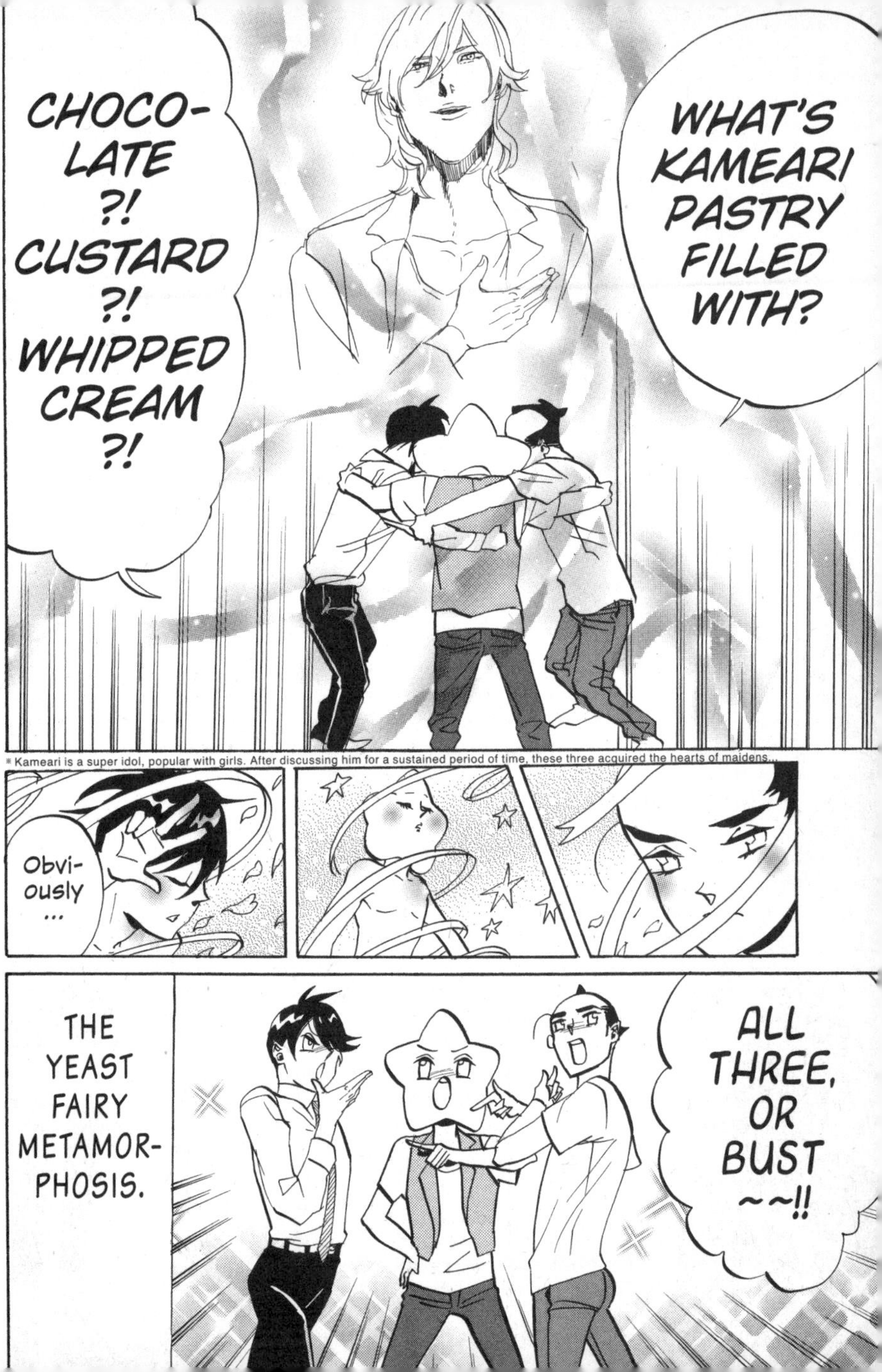
WHAT'S KAMEARI PASTRY FILLED WITH?
CHOCO-LATE ?! CUSTARD ?! WHIPPED CREAM ?!
* Kameari is a super idol, popular with girls. After discussing him for a sustained period of time, these three acquired the hearts of maidens...
Obvi-ously ...
ALL THREE, OR BUST ~~!!
THE YEAST FAIRY METAMOR-PHOSIS.

Chapter 242: Kameari Returns

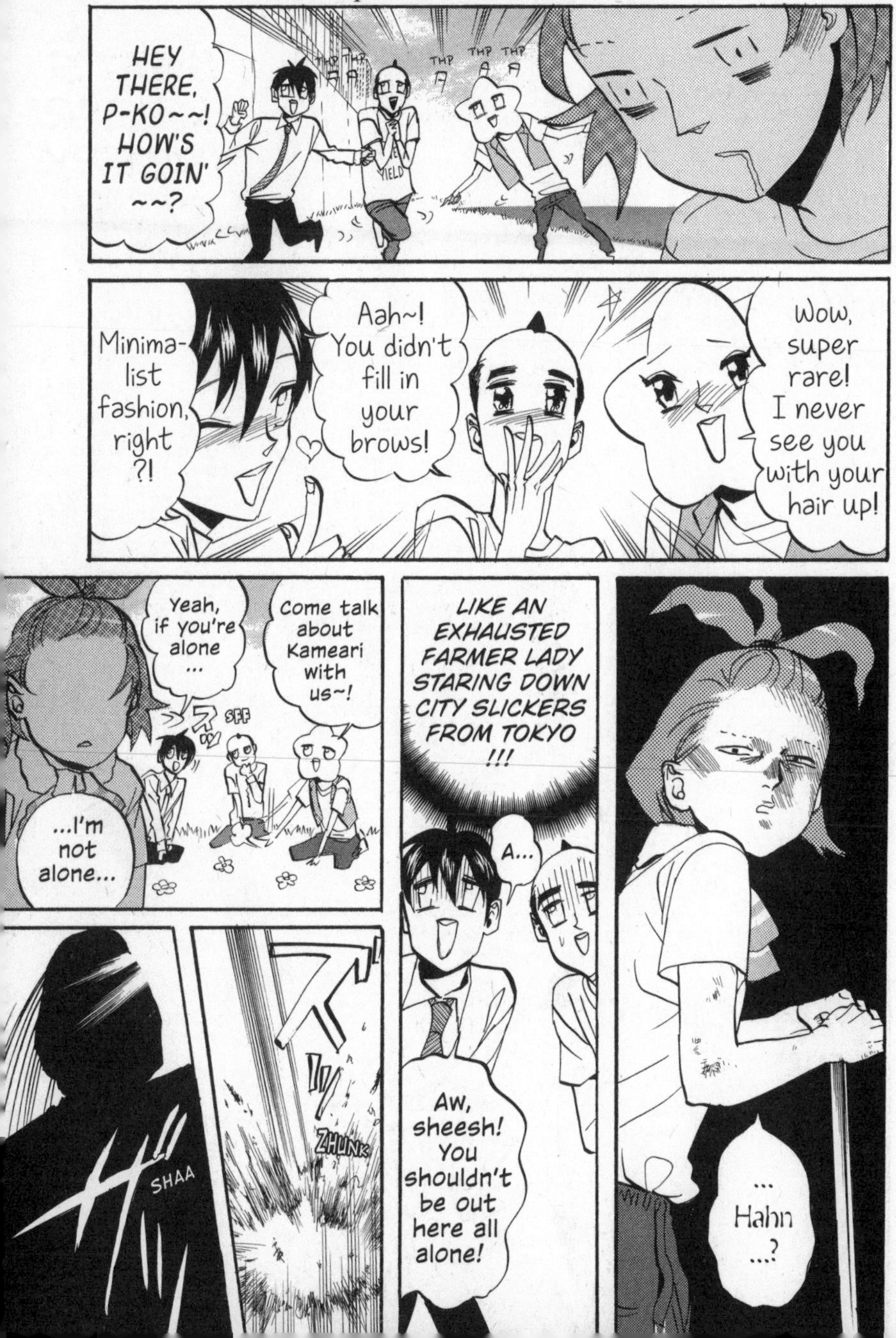
HEY THERE, P-KO~~! HOW'S IT GOIN' ~~?
THP THP
THP THP THP
Wow, super rare! I never see you with your hair up!
Aah~! You didn't fill in your brows!
Minima-list fashion, right ?!
... Hahn ...?
LIKE AN EXHAUSTED FARMER LADY STARING DOWN CITY SLICKERS FROM TOKYO !!!
A...
Aw, sheesh! You shouldn't be out here all alone!
Come talk about Kameari with us~!
Yeah, if you're alone ...
SFF
...I'm not alone...
ZHUNK
SHAA

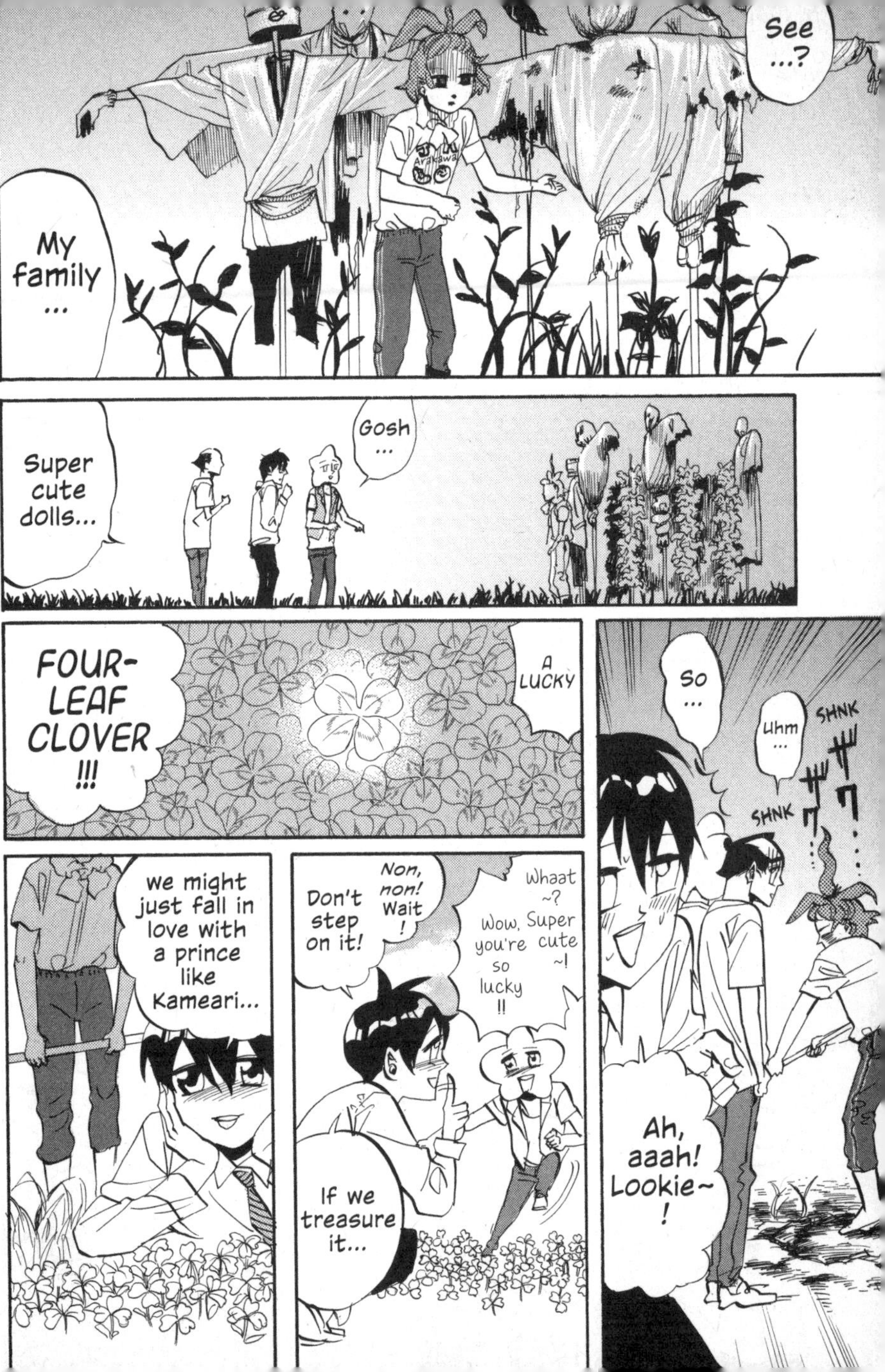

See ...?
My family ...
Gosh ...
Super cute dolls...
So ...
Uhm ...
SHNK
SHNK
Ah, aaah! Lookie~!
A LUCKY
FOUR-LEAF CLOVER !!!
Whaat ~? Super cute ~!
Wow, you're so lucky !!
Non, non! Wait !
Don't step on it!
If we treasure it...
we might just fall in love with a prince like Kameari...

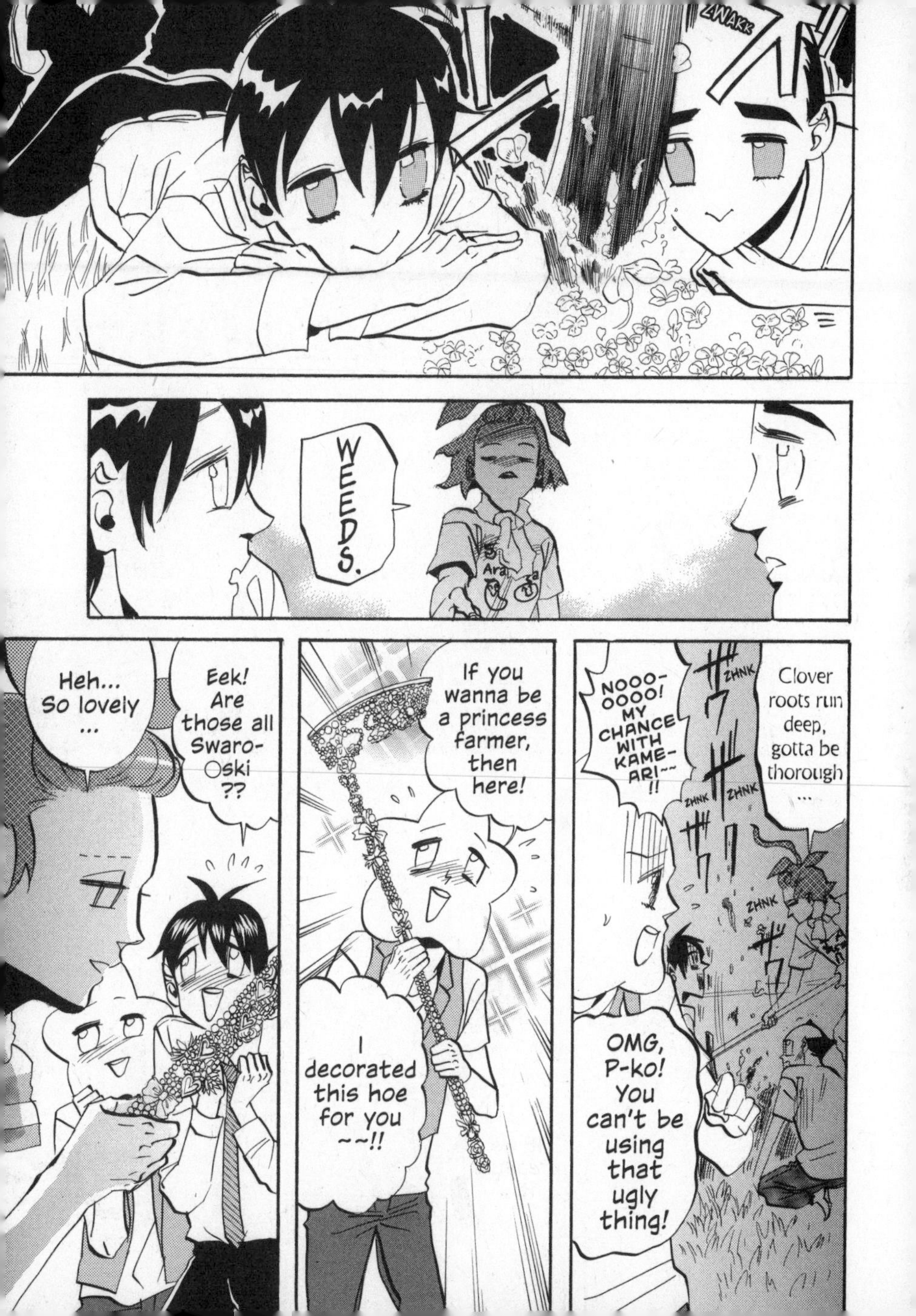
ZWAKK
WEEDS.
Clover roots run deep, gotta be thorough ...
NOOO-OOOO! MY CHANCE WITH KAME-ARI~~ !!
ZHNK
ZHNK
ZHNK
ZHNK
OMG, P-ko! You can't be using that ugly thing!
If you wanna be a princess farmer, then here!
I decorated this hoe for you ~~!!
Eek! Are those all Swaro-Oski ??
Heh... So lovely ...

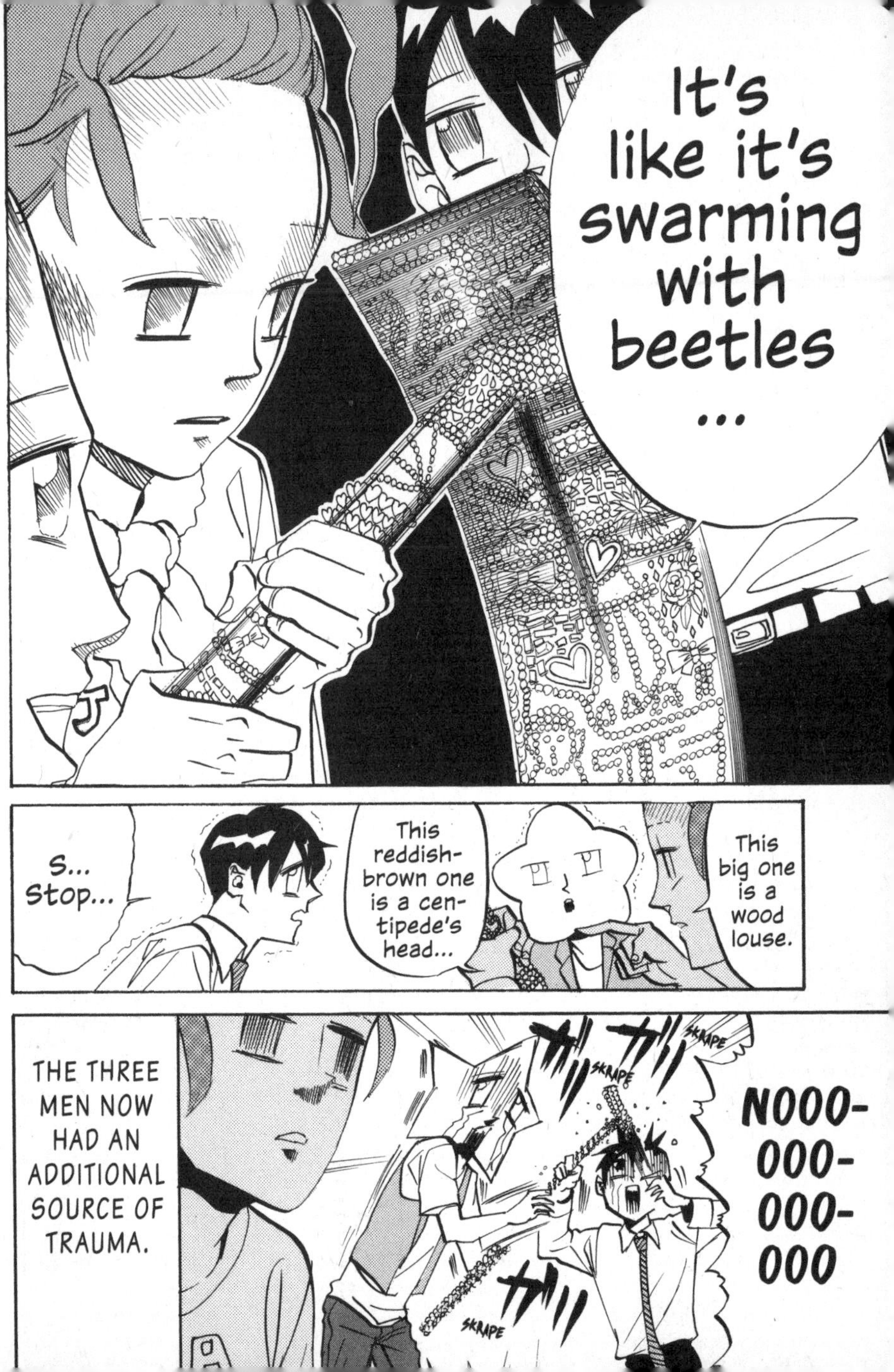
It's like it's swarming with beetles ...
This big one is a wood louse.
This reddish-brown one is a centipede's head...
S... Stop...
SKRAPE
SKRAPE
NOOO-000-000-000
THE THREE MEN NOW HAD AN ADDITIONAL SOURCE OF TRAUMA.
SKRAPE

Chapter 243: Unyielding Feelings

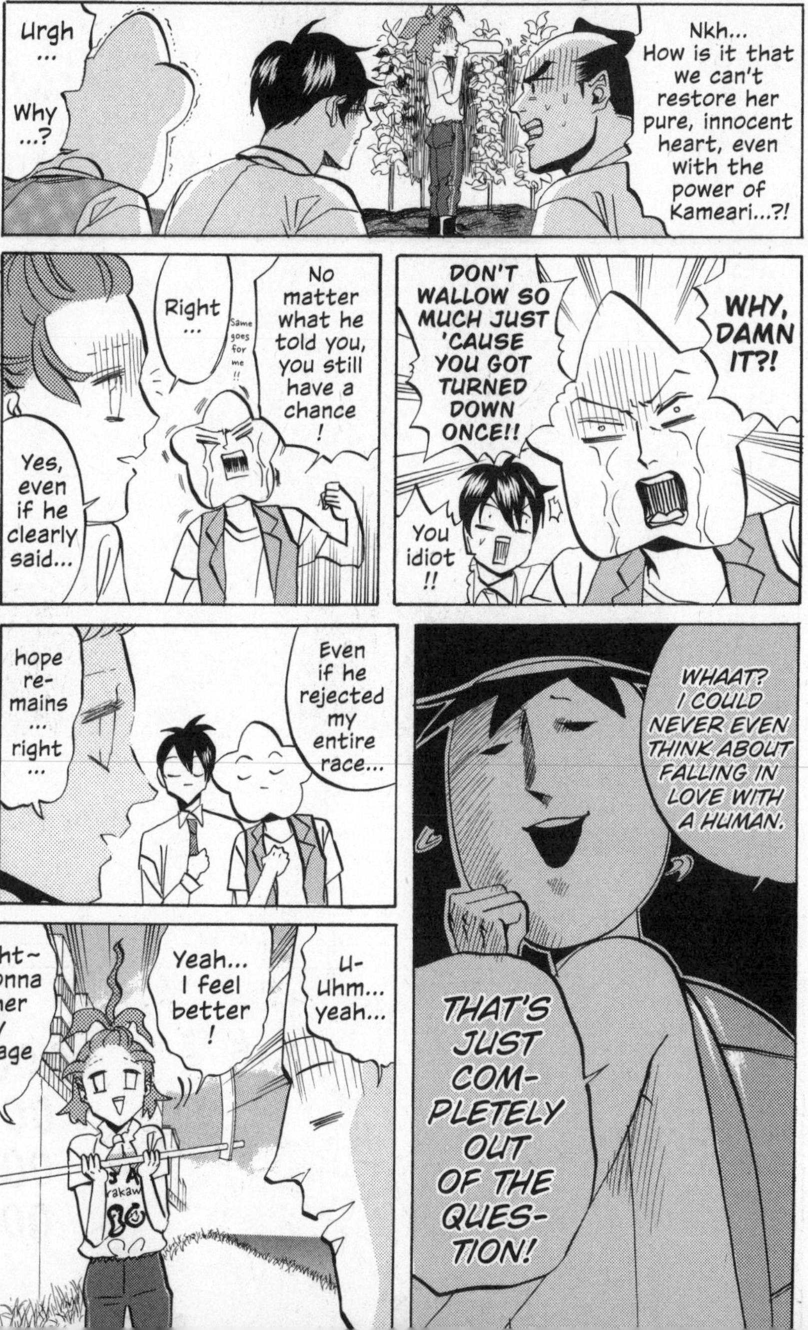
Nkh... How is it that we can't restore her pure, innocent heart, even with the power of Kameari...?!
Urgh ... Why ...?
WHY, DAMN IT?!
DON'T WALLOW SO MUCH JUST 'CAUSE YOU GOT TURNED DOWN ONCE!!
You idiot !!
No matter what he told you, you still have a chance !
Same goes for me !!
Right ...
Yes, even if he clearly said...
WHAAT? I COULD NEVER EVEN THINK ABOUT FALLING IN LOVE WITH A HUMAN.
THAT'S JUST COM-PLETELY OUT OF THE QUES-TION!
Even if he rejected my entire race...
hope re-mains ... right ...
U-Uhm... yeah...
Yeah... I feel better !
All right~ I'm gonna gather my courage ...

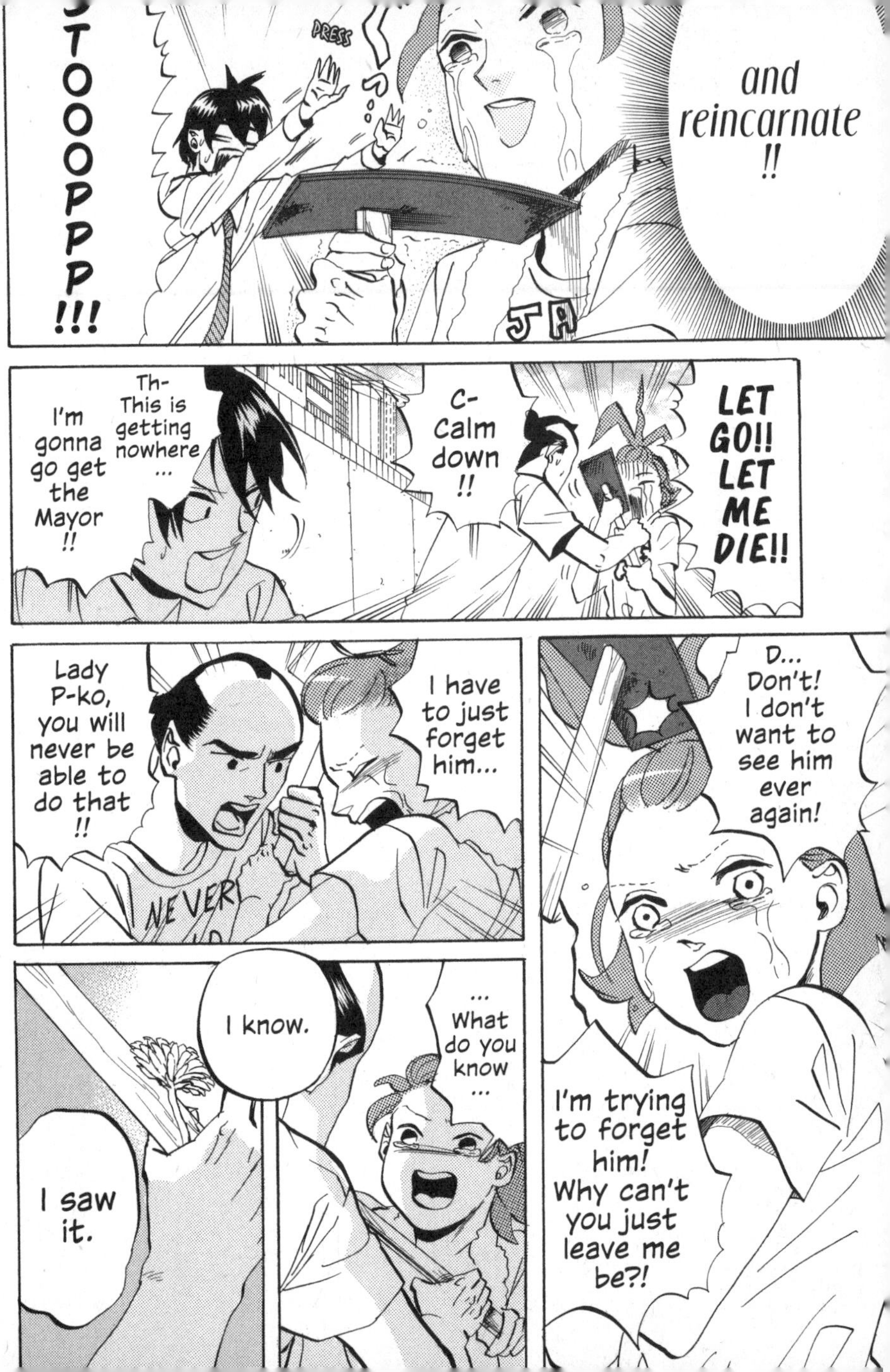
and reincarnate !!
PRESS
STOOOPPPP!!!
LET GO!! LET ME DIE!!
C- Calm down !!
Th- This is getting nowhere ...
I'm gonna go get the Mayor !!
D... Don't! I don't want to see him ever again!
I'm trying to forget him! Why can't you just leave me be?!
I have to just forget him...
Lady P-ko, you will never be able to do that !!
... What do you know ...
I know.
I saw it.

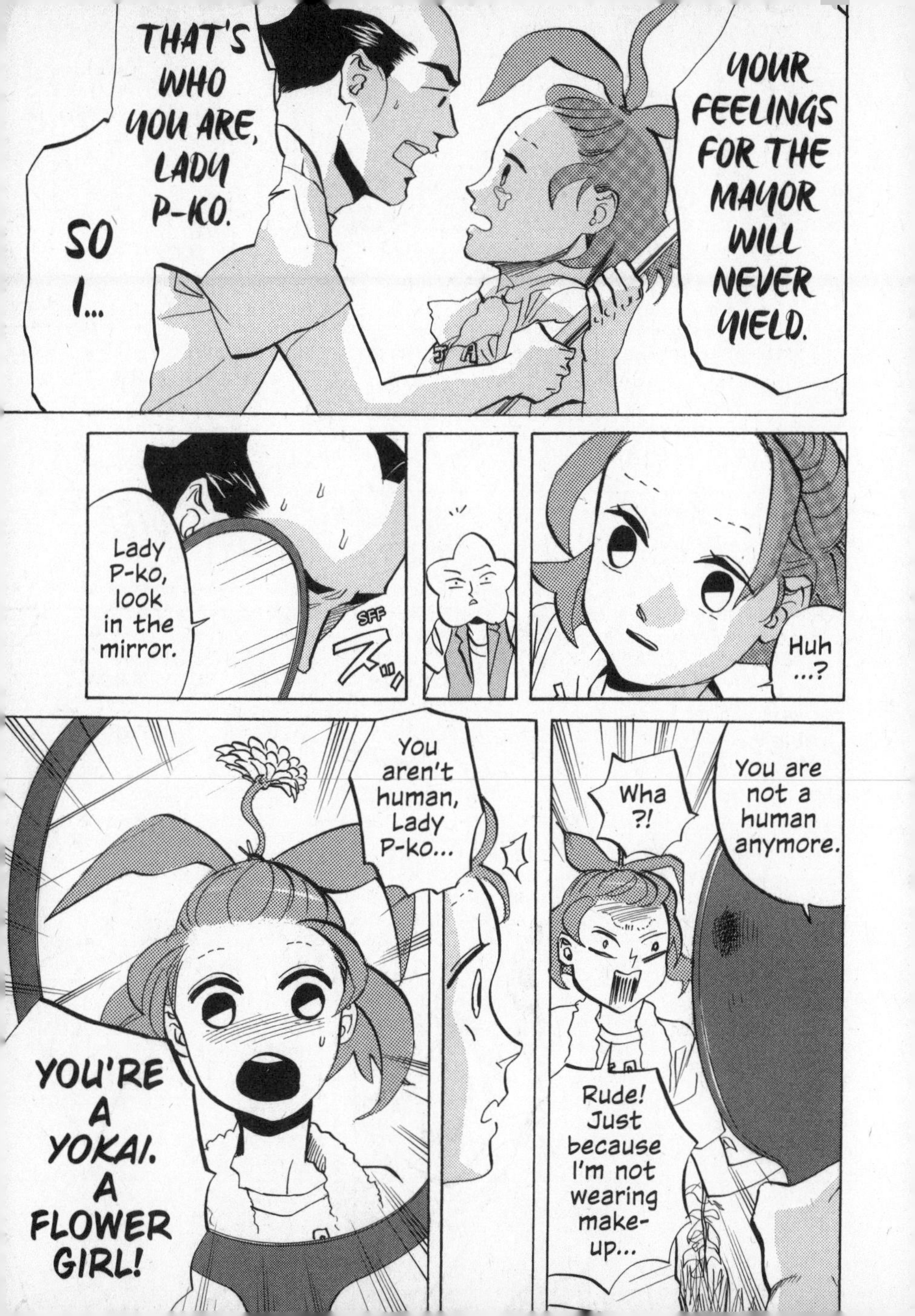
YOUR FEELINGS FOR THE MAYOR WILL NEVER YIELD.
THAT'S WHO YOU ARE, LADY P-KO.
SO I...
Huh ...?
Lady P-ko, look in the mirror.
SFF
You are not a human anymore.
Wha ?!
Rude! Just because I'm not wearing make-up...
You aren't human, Lady P-ko...
YOU'RE A YOKAI. A FLOWER GIRL!

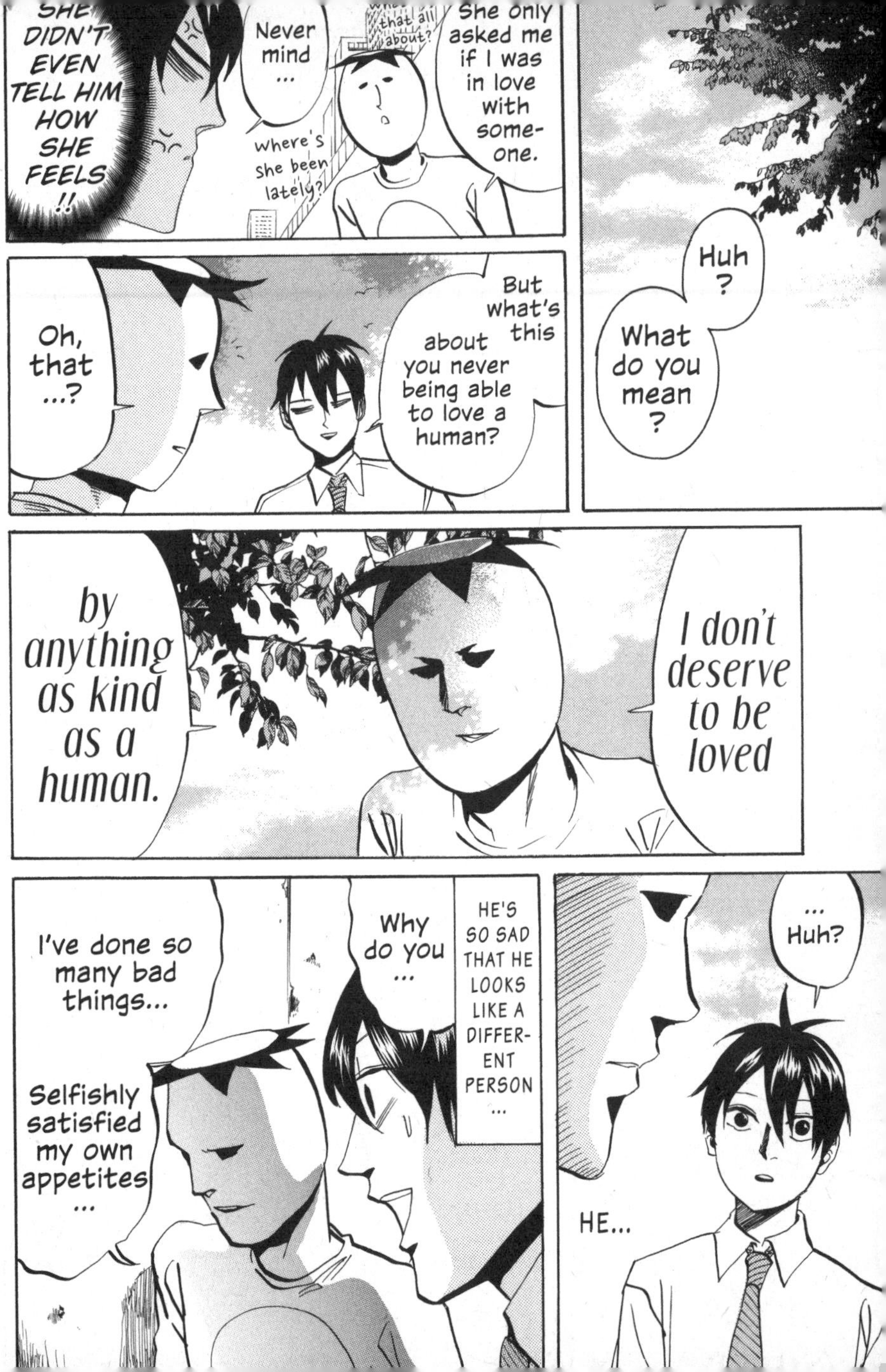
Huh?
What do you mean?
She only asked me if I was in love with someone.
what's that all about?
Where's she been lately?
Never mind ...
SHE DIDN'T EVEN TELL HIM HOW SHE FEELS!!
But what's this about you never being able to love a human?
Oh, that ...?
I don't deserve to be loved
by anything as kind as a human.
... Huh?
HE...
HE'S SO SAD THAT HE LOOKS LIKE A DIFFERENT PERSON ...
Why do you ...
I've done so many bad things...
Selfishly satisfied my own appetites ...

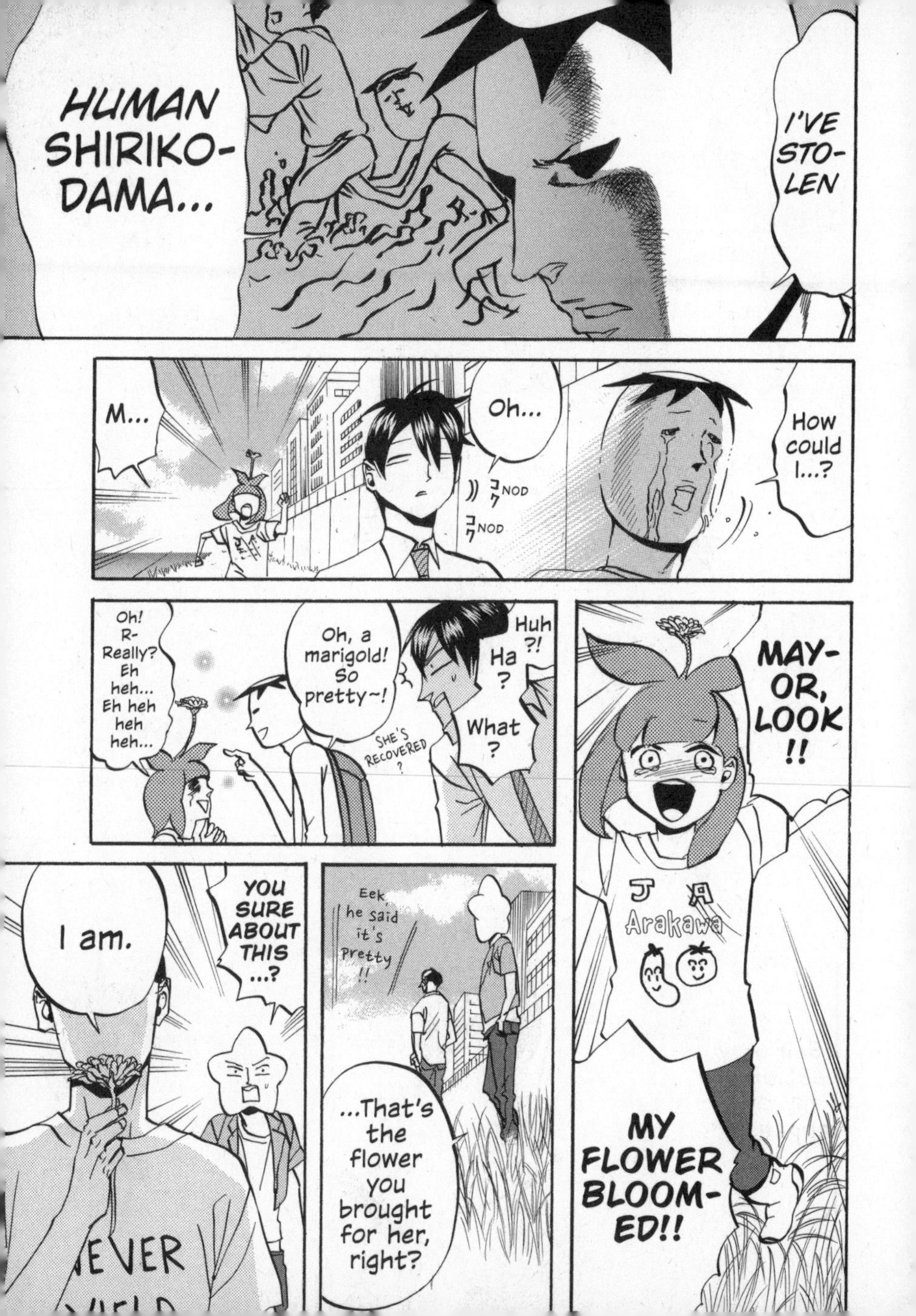
I'VE STO-LEN
HUMAN SHIRIKO-DAMA...
How could I...?
NOD
NOD
Oh...
M...
MAY-OR, LOOK!!
MY FLOWER BLOOM-ED!!
Huh?!
Ha?
What?
Oh, a marigold! So pretty~!
SHE'S RECOVERED?
Oh! R-Really? Eh heh... Eh heh heh heh...
...That's the flower you brought for her, right?
Eek, he said it's Pretty!!
YOU SURE ABOUT THIS...?
I am.

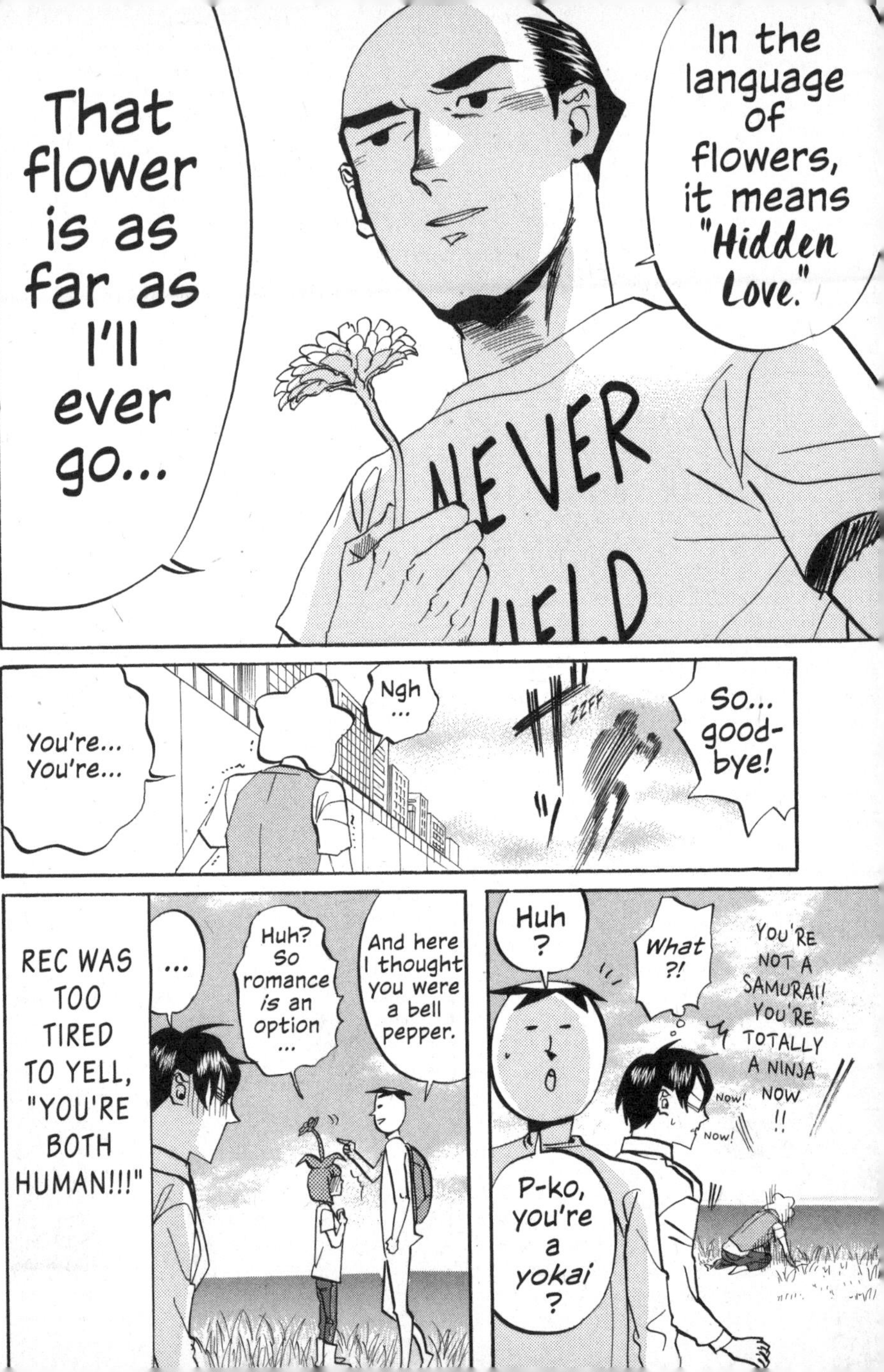
In the language of flowers, it means "Hidden Love."
That flower is as far as I'll ever go...
NEVER
So... good-bye!
ZZFF
Ngh ...
You're... You're...
YOU'RE NOT A SAMURAI! YOU'RE TOTALLY A NINJA NOW !!
What ?!
Huh ?
NOW!
NOW!
P-ko, you're a yokai ?
And here I thought you were a bell pepper.
Huh? So romance is an option ...
...
REC WAS TOO TIRED TO YELL, "YOU'RE BOTH HUMAN!!!"

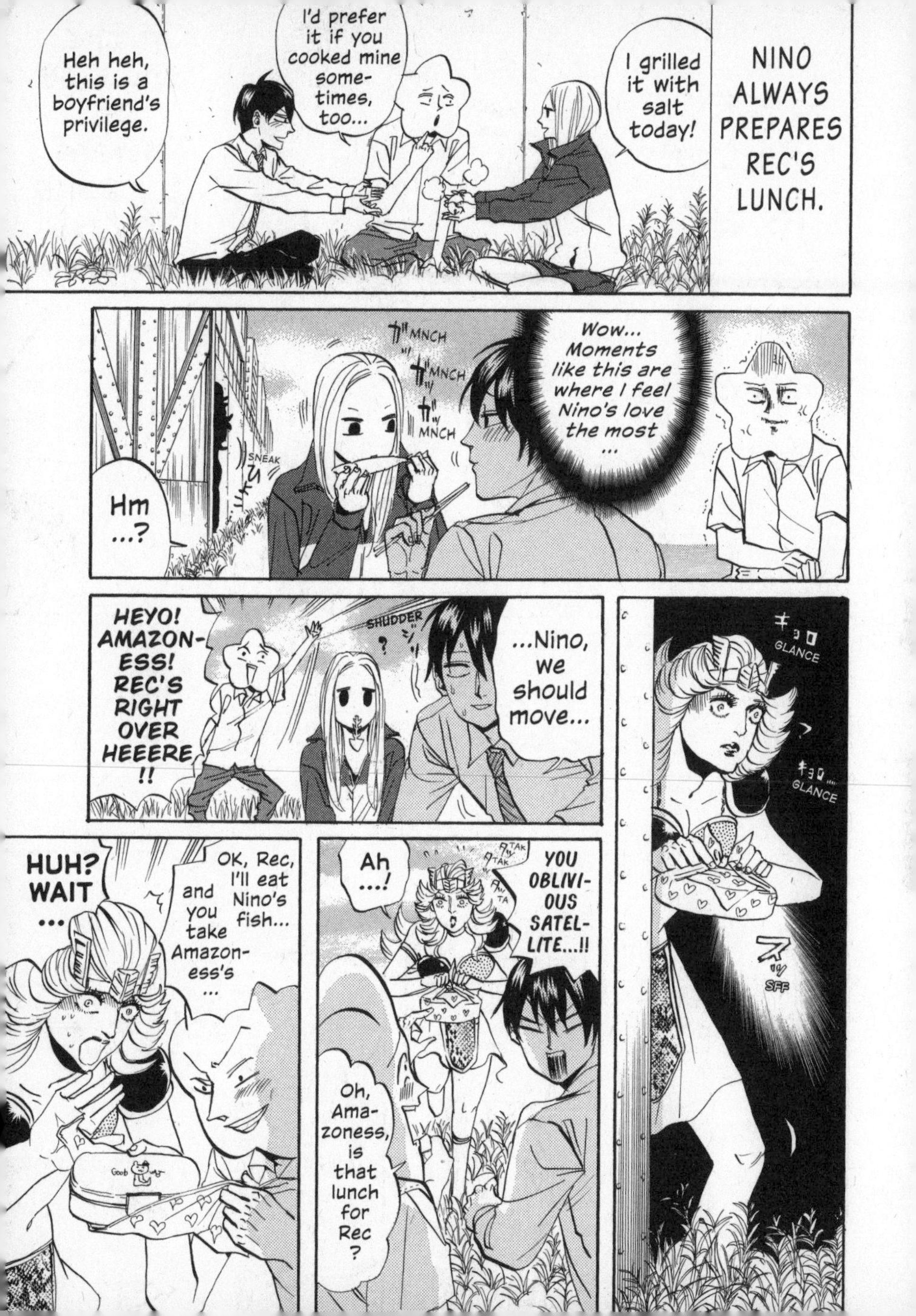

NINO ALWAYS PREPARES REC'S LUNCH.
I grilled it with salt today!
I'd prefer it if you cooked mine some-times, too...
Heh heh, this is a boyfriend's privilege.
Wow... Moments like this are where I feel Nino's love the most ...
MNCH
MNCH
MNCH
SNEAK
Hm ...?
GLANCE
GLANCE
SFF
...Nino, we should move...
SHUDDER
HEYO! AMAZON-ESS! REC'S RIGHT OVER HEEERE !!
YOU OBLIVI-OUS SATEL-LITE...!!
TAK
TAK
TA
Ah ...!
Oh, Ama-zoness, is that lunch for Rec?
OK, Rec, I'll eat Nino's fish... and you take Amazon-ess's ...
HUH? WAIT ...

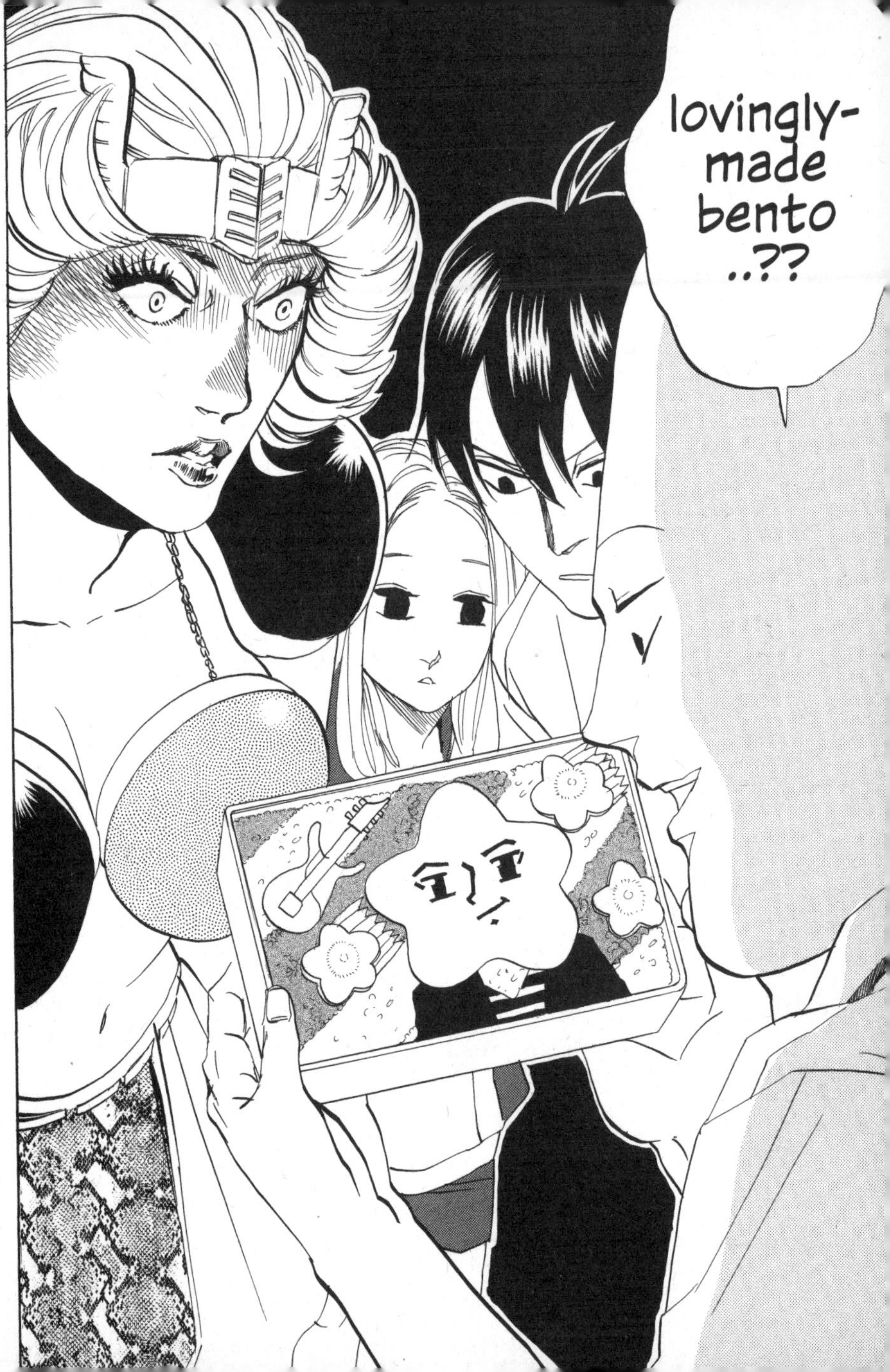
lovingly-made bento ..??

Chapter 244: Love Gift

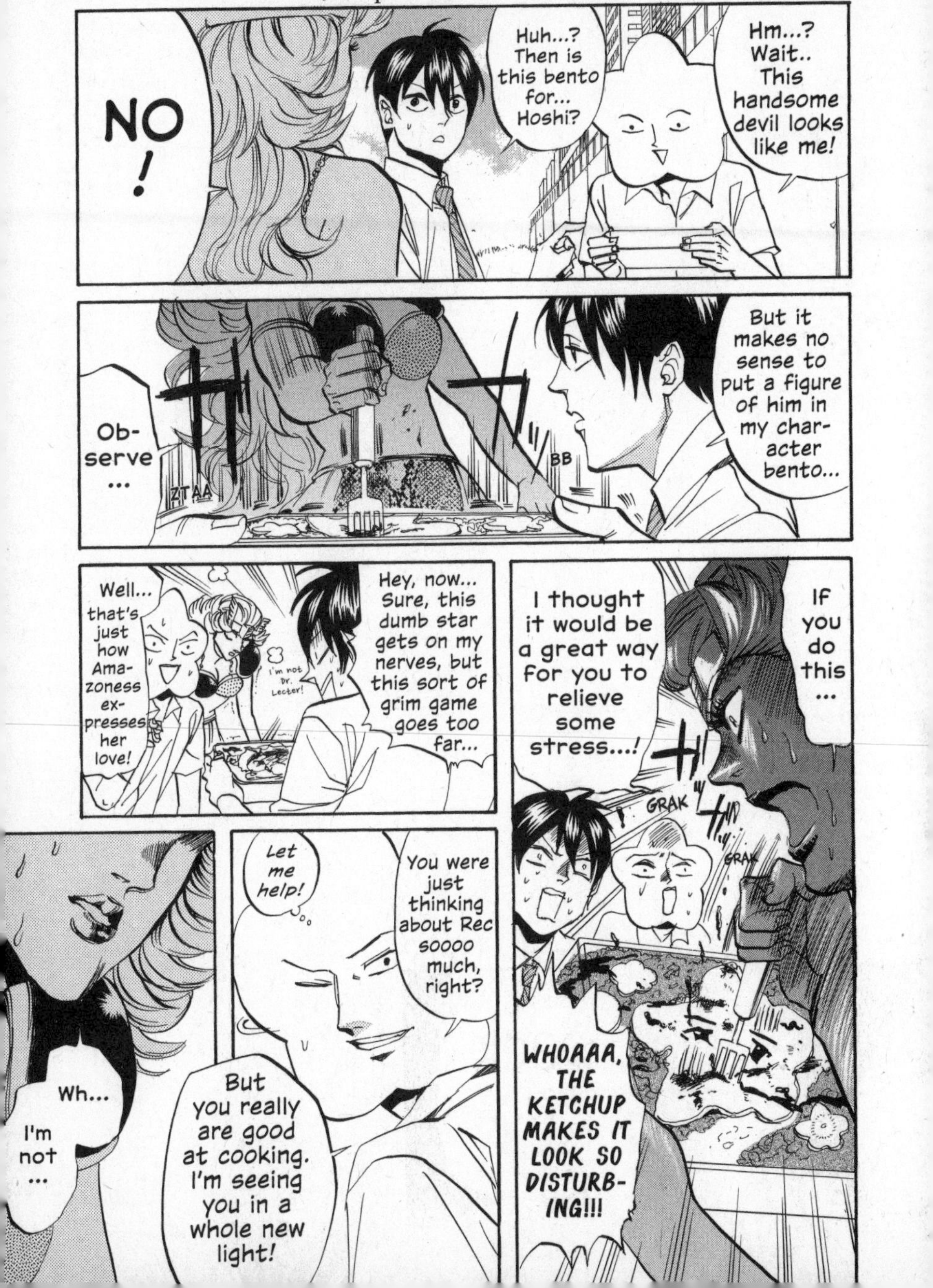
Hm...? Wait.. This handsome devil looks like me!
Huh...? Then is this bento for... Hoshi?
NO!
But it makes no sense to put a figure of him in my character bento...
BB
Observe...
ZTAA
If you do this...
I thought it would be a great way for you to relieve some stress....!
GRAK
GRAK
WHOAAA, THE KETCHUP MAKES IT LOOK SO DISTURBING!!!
Hey, now... Sure, this dumb star gets on my nerves, but this sort of grim game goes too far...
I'm not Dr. Lecter!
Well... that's just how Amazoness expresses her love!
You were just thinking about Rec soooo much, right?
Let me help!
But you really are good at cooking. I'm seeing you in a whole new light!
Wh... I'm not ...

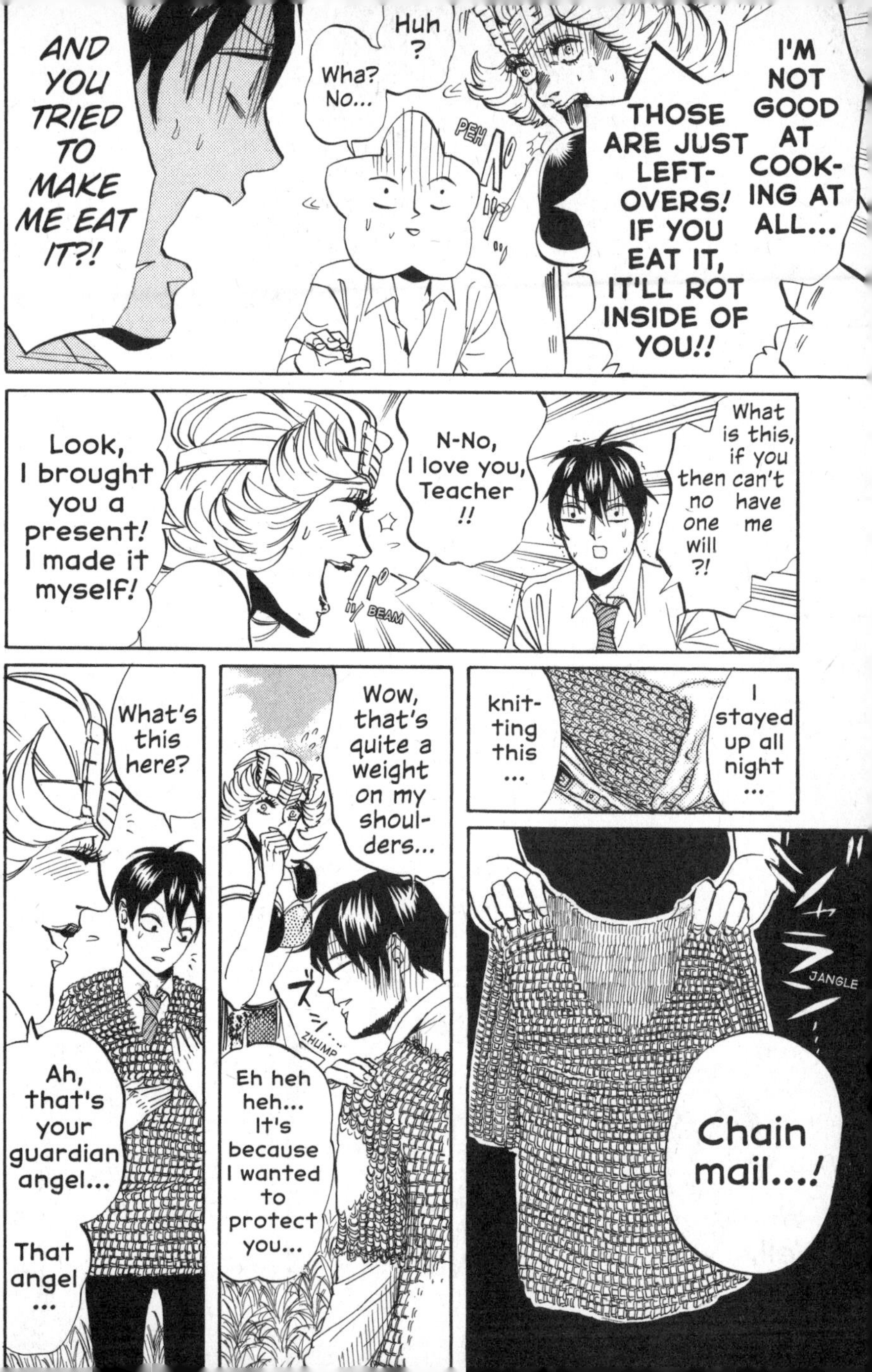
I'M NOT GOOD AT COOKING AT ALL...
THOSE ARE JUST LEFTOVERS! IF YOU EAT IT, IT'LL ROT INSIDE OF YOU!!
PEH
Huh?
Wha? No...
AND YOU TRIED TO MAKE ME EAT IT?!
What is this, if you can't have me then no one will?!
N-No, I love you, Teacher!!
BEAM
Look, I brought you a present! I made it myself!
I stayed up all night...
knitting this...
JANGLE
Chain mail...!
Wow, that's quite a weight on my shoulders...
ZHUMP
Eh heh heh... It's because I wanted to protect you...
What's this here?
Ah, that's your guardian angel...
That angel...

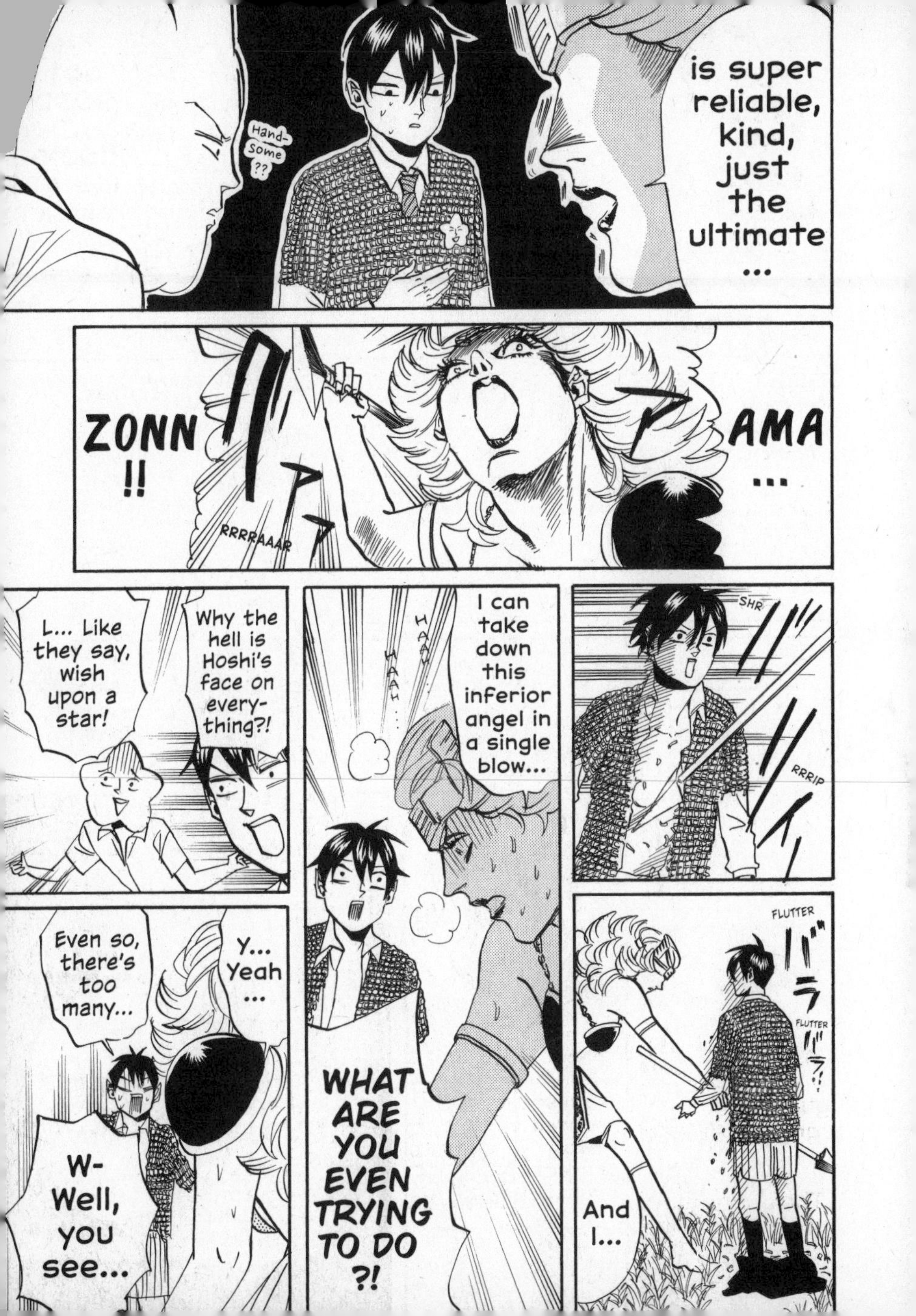

is super reliable, kind, just the ultimate ...
Hand-Some ??
AMA ...
RRRRAAAR
ZONN !!
SHR
RRRIP
FLUTTER
FLUTTER
And I...
I can take down this inferior angel in a single blow...
HAAAH...
WHAT ARE YOU EVEN TRYING TO DO ?!
Why the hell is Hoshi's face on every-thing?!
L... Like they say, wish upon a star!
Y... Yeah ...
Even so, there's too many...
W-Well, you see...

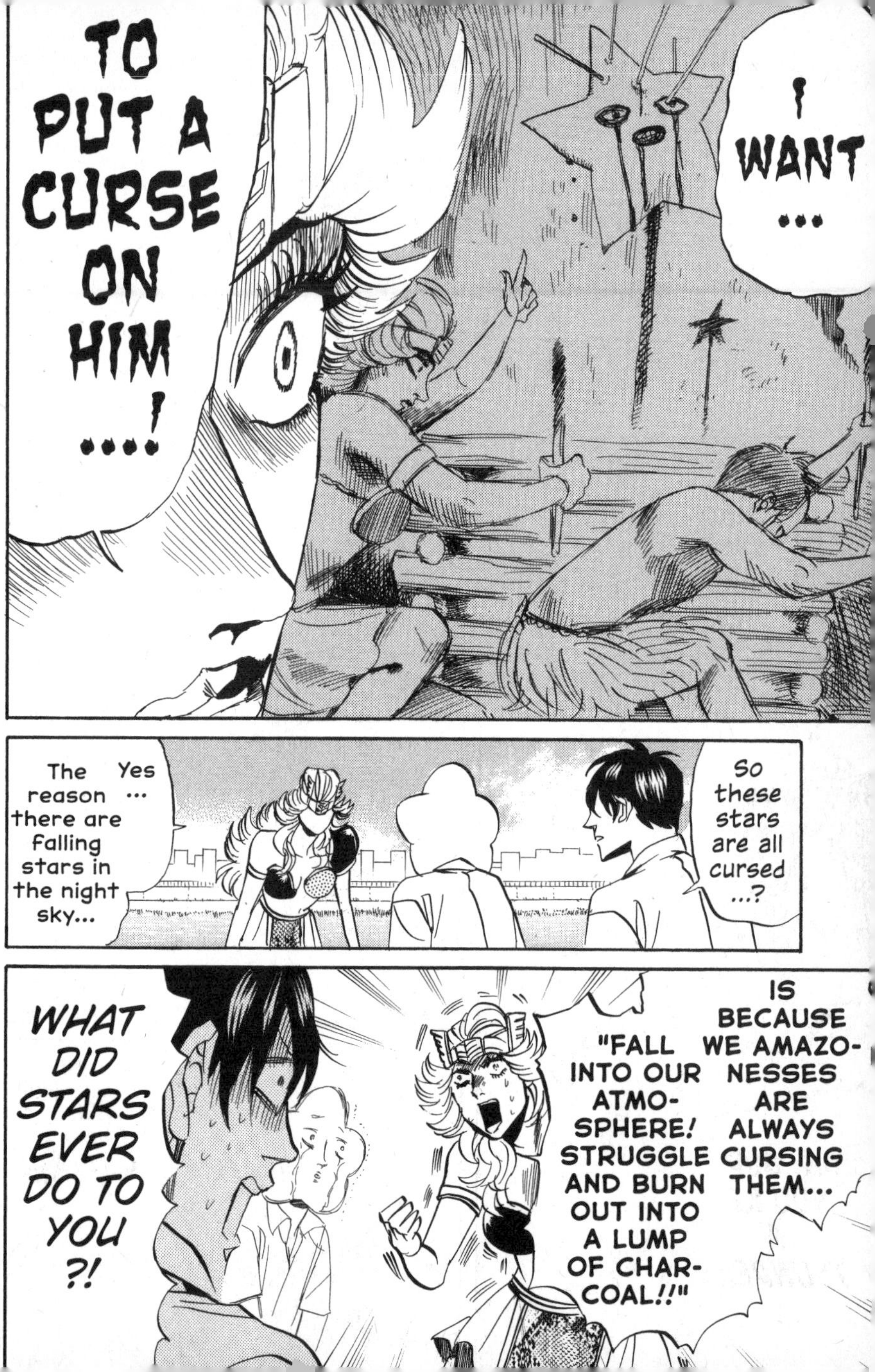
I WANT...
TO PUT A CURSE ON HIM ....!
So these stars are all cursed ...?
Yes ...
The reason there are falling stars in the night sky...
IS BECAUSE WE AMAZONESSES ARE ALWAYS CURSING THEM...
"FALL INTO OUR ATMOSPHERE! STRUGGLE AND BURN OUT INTO A LUMP OF CHARCOAL!!"
WHAT DID STARS EVER DO TO YOU?!

Chapter 245: Reason

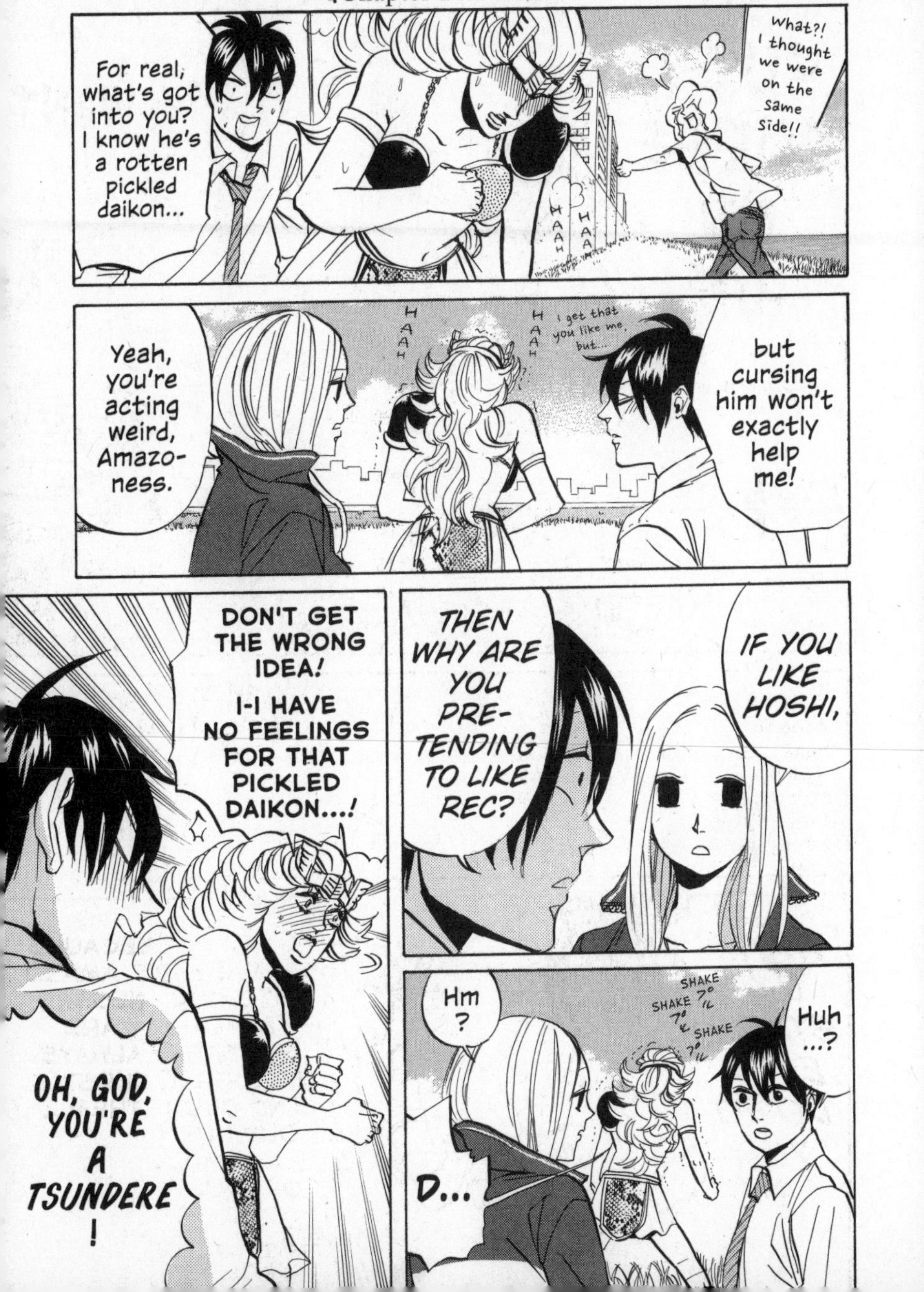

What?! I thought we were on the same side!!
HAAH HAAH
For real, what's got into you? I know he's a rotten pickled daikon...
but cursing him won't exactly help me!
I get that you like me but...
HAAH HAAH
Yeah, you're acting weird, Amazoness.
IF YOU LIKE HOSHI,
THEN WHY ARE YOU PRETENDING TO LIKE REC?
Huh ...?
SHAKE SHAKE SHAKE
Hm ?
D...
DON'T GET THE WRONG IDEA!
I-I HAVE NO FEELINGS FOR THAT PICKLED DAIKON...!
OH, GOD, YOU'RE A TSUNDERE !

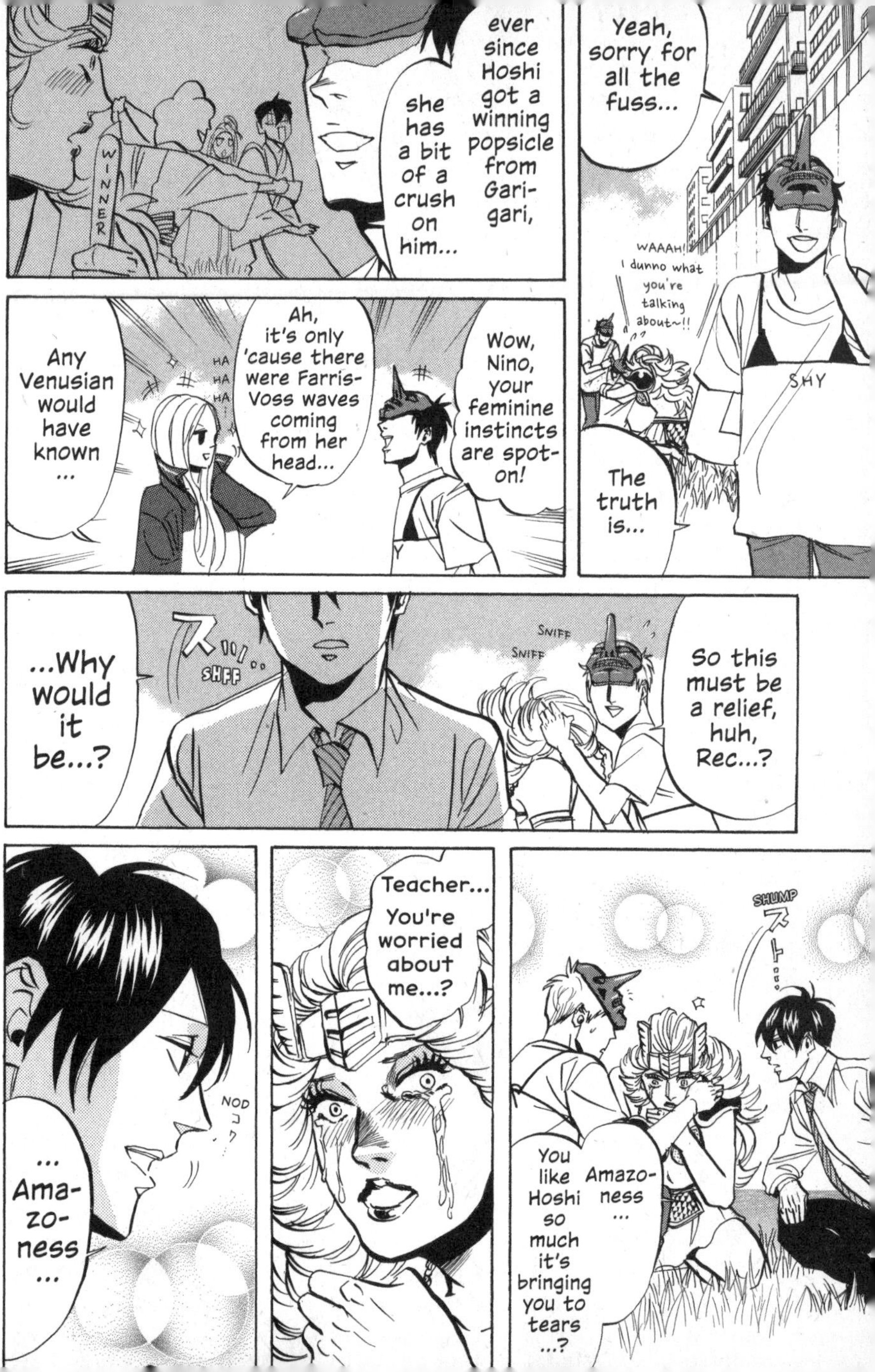

Yeah, sorry for all the fuss...
WAAAH! I dunno what you're talking about~!!
SHY
The truth is...
ever since Hoshi got a winning popsicle from Gari-gari,
she has a bit of a crush on him...
WINNER
Wow, Nino, your feminine instincts are spot-on!
Ah, it's only 'cause there were Farris-Voss waves coming from her head...
HA HA HA
Any Venusian would have known...
So this must be a relief, huh, Rec...?
SNIFF
SNIFF
SHFF
...Why would it be...?
SHUMP
You like Hoshi so much it's bringing you to tears...?
Amazoness...
Teacher... You're worried about me...?
NOD
... Amazoness ...

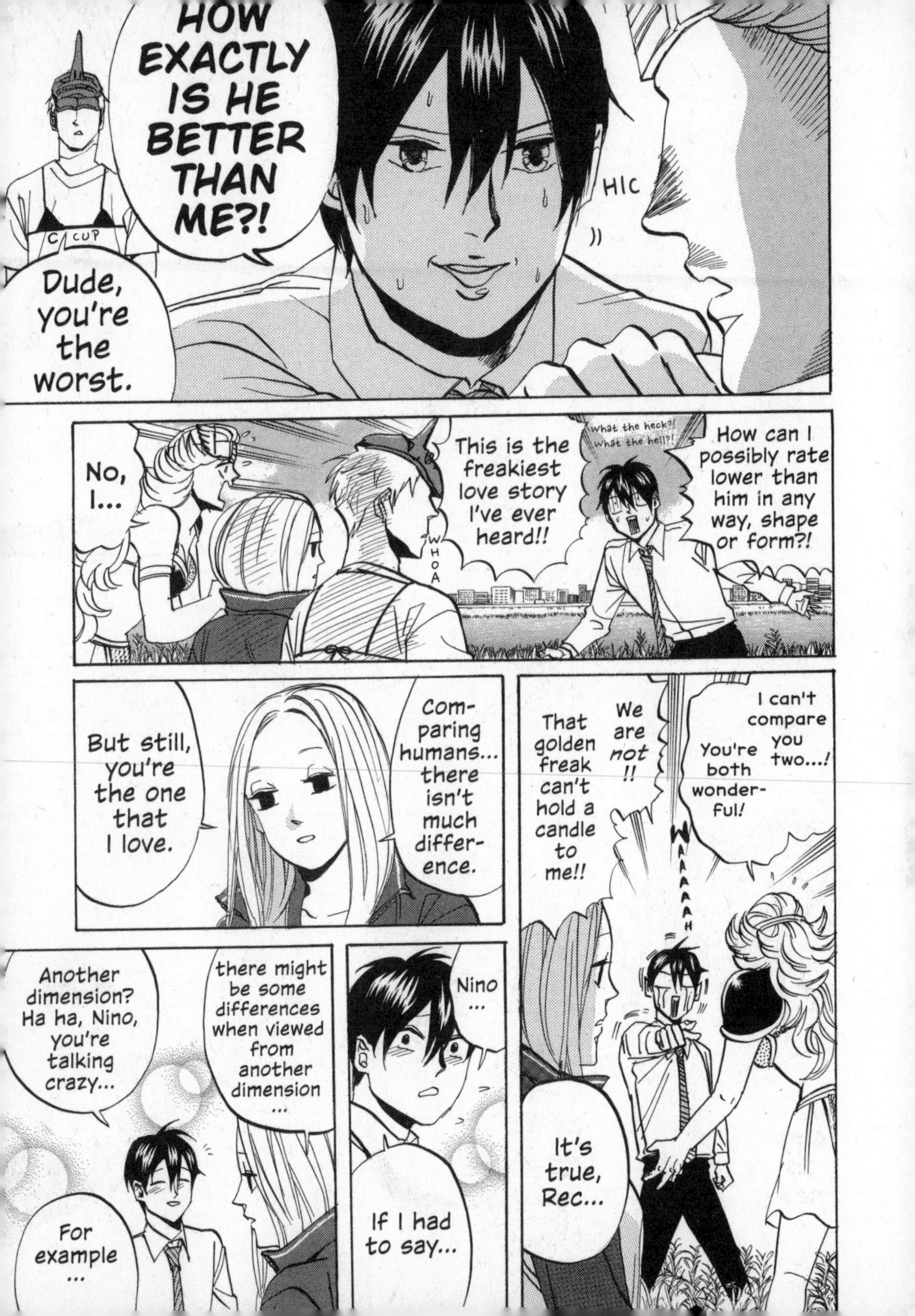
HIC
HOW EXACTLY IS HE BETTER THAN ME?!
C CUP
Dude, you're the worst.
How can I possibly rate lower than him in any way, shape or form?!
What the heck?! What the hell?!
This is the freakiest love story I've ever heard!!
WHOA
No, I...
I can't compare you two...!
You're both wonderful!
We are *not*!!
That golden freak can't hold a candle to me!!
WAAAAAH
It's true, Rec...
Com-paring humans... there isn't much differ-ence.
But still, you're the one that I love.
If I had to say...
Nino...
there might be some differences when viewed from another dimension...
Another dimension? Ha ha, Nino, you're talking crazy...
For example...

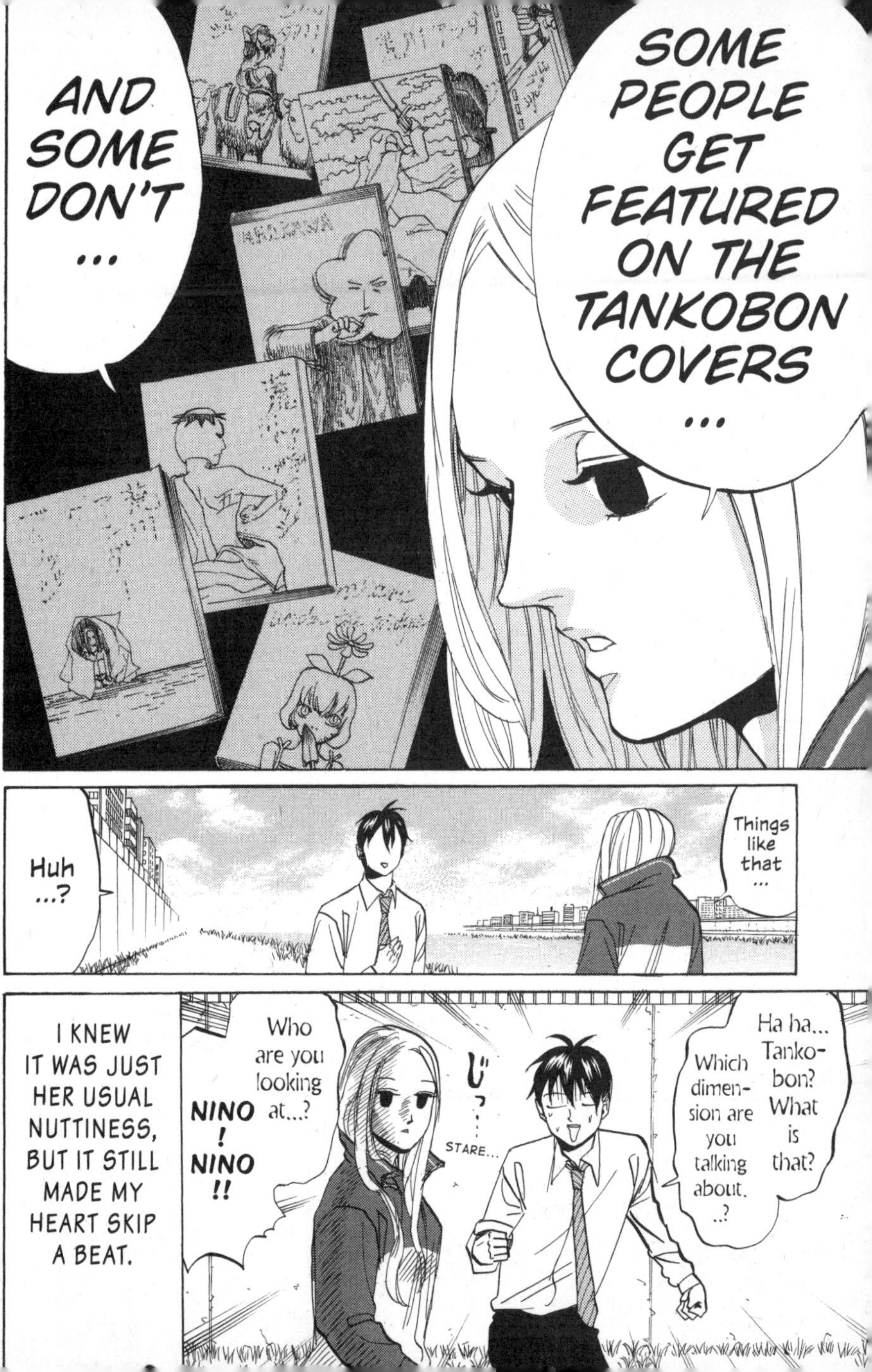
SOME PEOPLE GET FEATURED ON THE TANKOBON COVERS ...
AND SOME DON'T ...
Things like that ...
Huh ...?
Ha ha... Tankobon? What is that?
Which dimension are you talking about...?
じっ...
STARE...
Who are you looking at...?
NINO! NINO!!
I KNEW IT WAS JUST HER USUAL NUTTINESS, BUT IT STILL MADE MY HEART SKIP A BEAT.

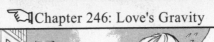

Chapter 246: Love's Gravity

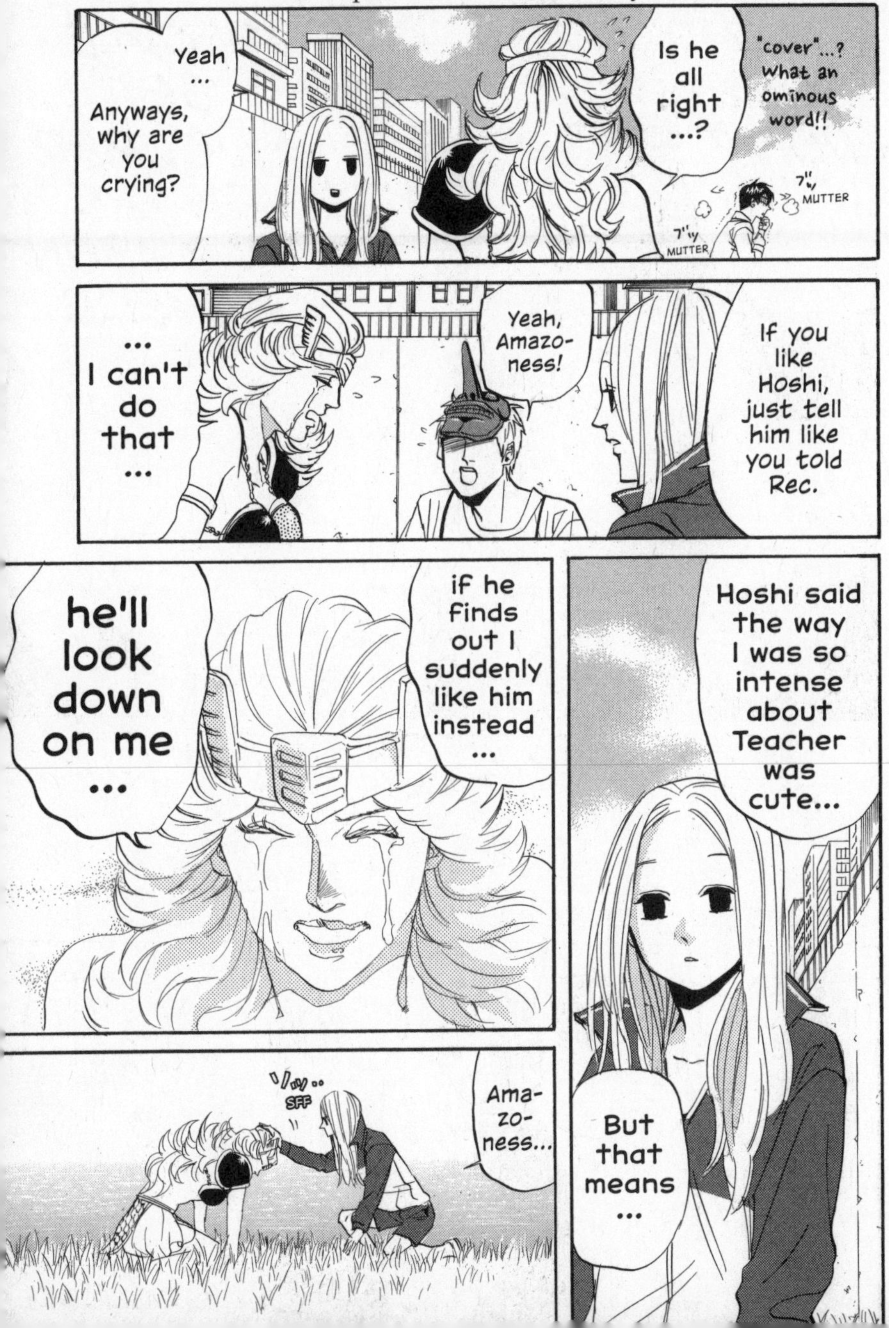
"cover"...? What an ominous word!!
Is he all right ...?
MUTTER
MUTTER
Yeah ... Anyways, why are you crying?
If you like Hoshi, just tell him like you told Rec.
Yeah, Amazoness!
... I can't do that ...
Hoshi said the way I was so intense about Teacher was cute...
But that means ...
if he finds out I suddenly like him instead ...
he'll look down on me ...
Amazoness...
SFF

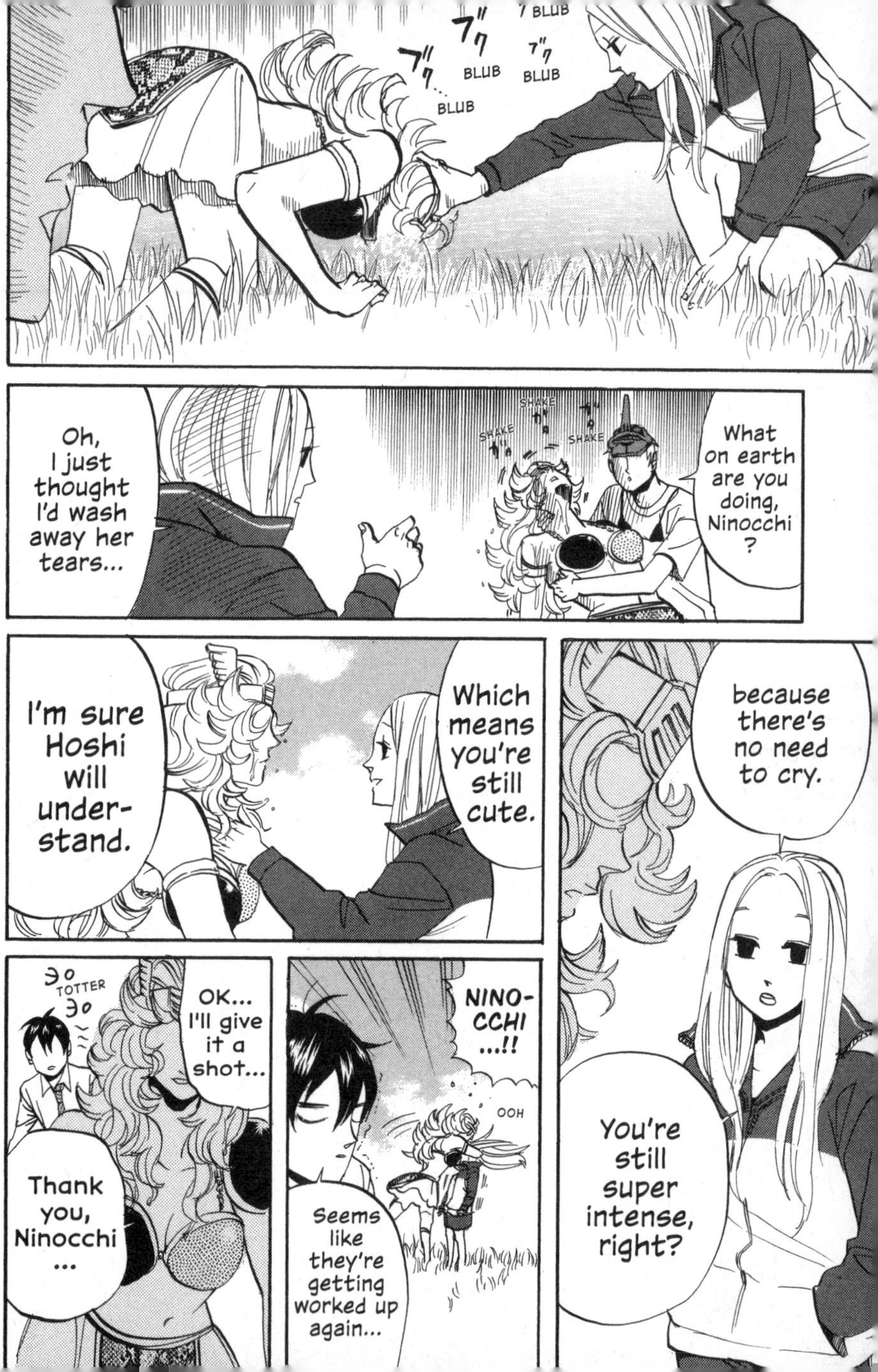

BLUB
BLUB
BLUB
BLUB
What on earth are you doing, Ninocchi?
SHAKE
SHAKE
SHAKE
Oh, I just thought I'd wash away her tears...
because there's no need to cry.
You're still super intense, right?
Which means you're still cute.
I'm sure Hoshi will understand.
NINO-CCHI...!!
OOH
Seems like they're getting worked up again...
TOTTER
OK... I'll give it a shot...
Thank you, Ninocchi...

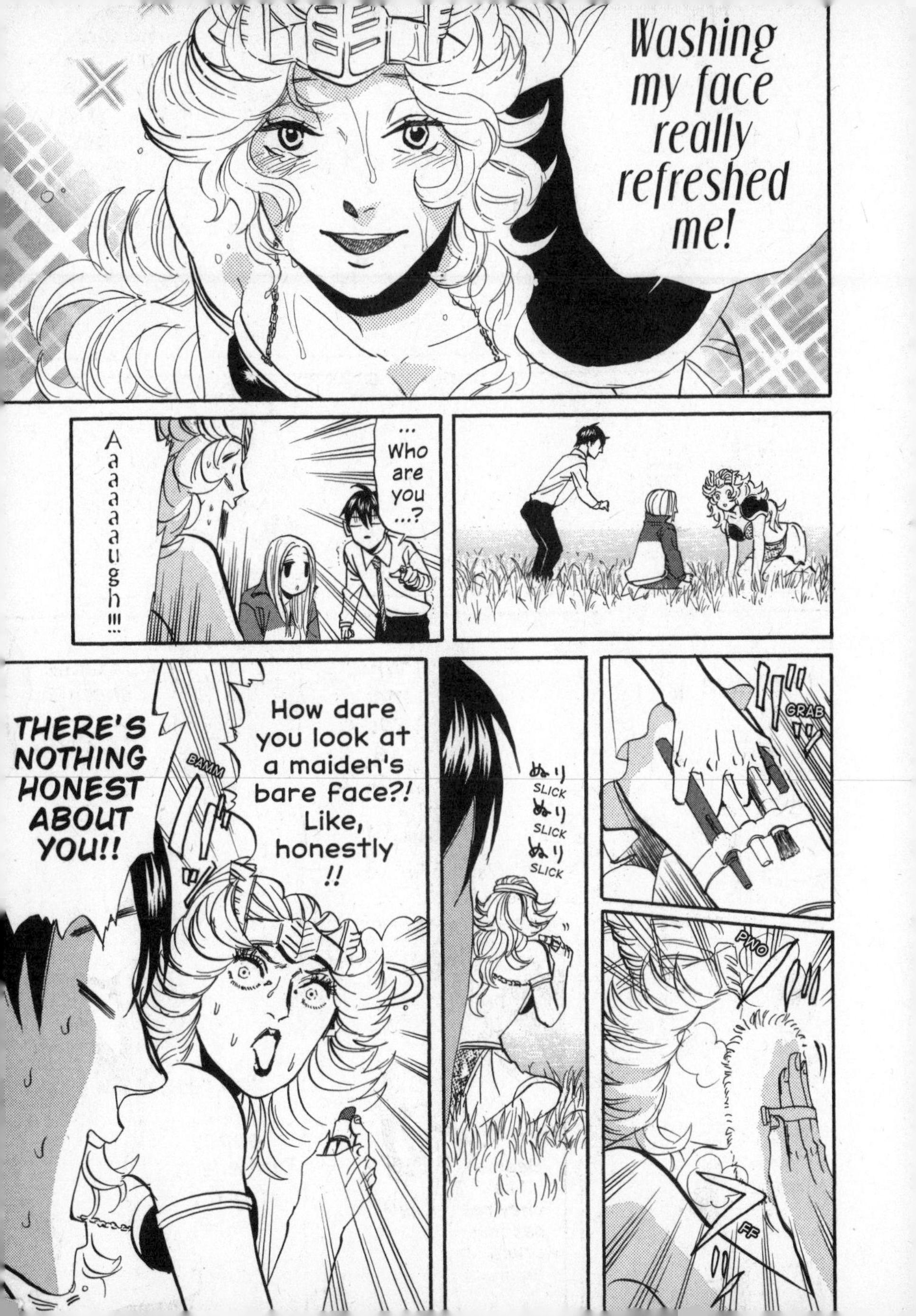
Washing my face really refreshed me!
...Who are you...?
Aaaaaaaaugh!!!
GRAB
PWO
FF
ぬり SLICK
ぬり SLICK
ぬり SLICK
How dare you look at a maiden's bare face?! Like, honestly!!
BAMM
THERE'S NOTHING HONEST ABOUT YOU!!

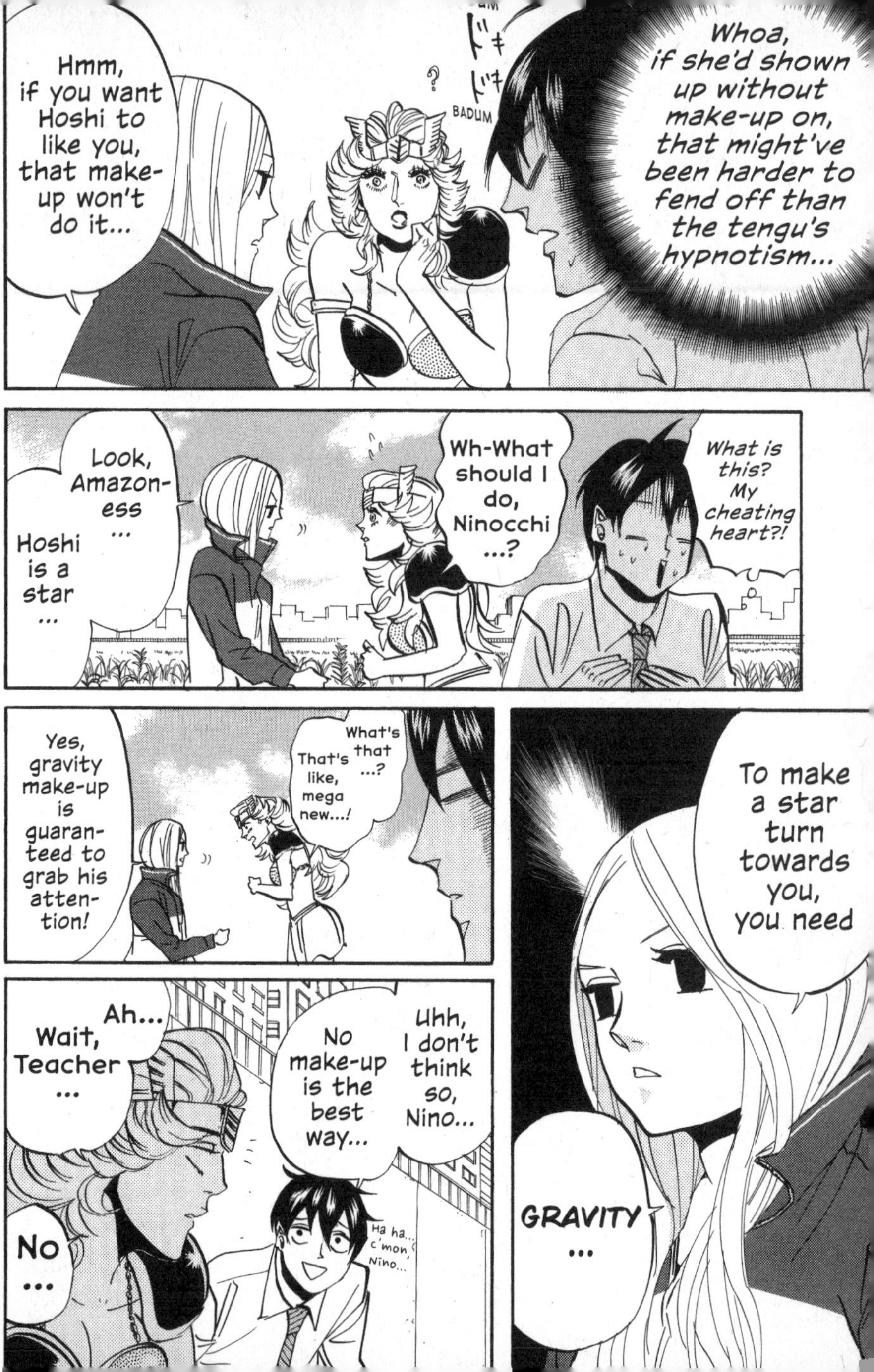
Whoa, if she'd shown up without make-up on, that might've been harder to fend off than the tengu's hypnotism...
ドキドキ
BADUM
?
Hmm, if you want Hoshi to like you, that make-up won't do it...
What is this? My cheating heart?!
Wh-What should I do, Ninocchi ...?
Look, Amazon-ess ...
Hoshi is a star ...
To make a star turn towards you, you need
GRAVITY ...
What's that ...?
That's like, mega new...!
Yes, gravity make-up is guaran-teed to grab his atten-tion!
Uhh, I don't think so, Nino...
No make-up is the best way...
Ah... Wait, Teacher ...
Ha ha... c'mon, Nino...
No ...

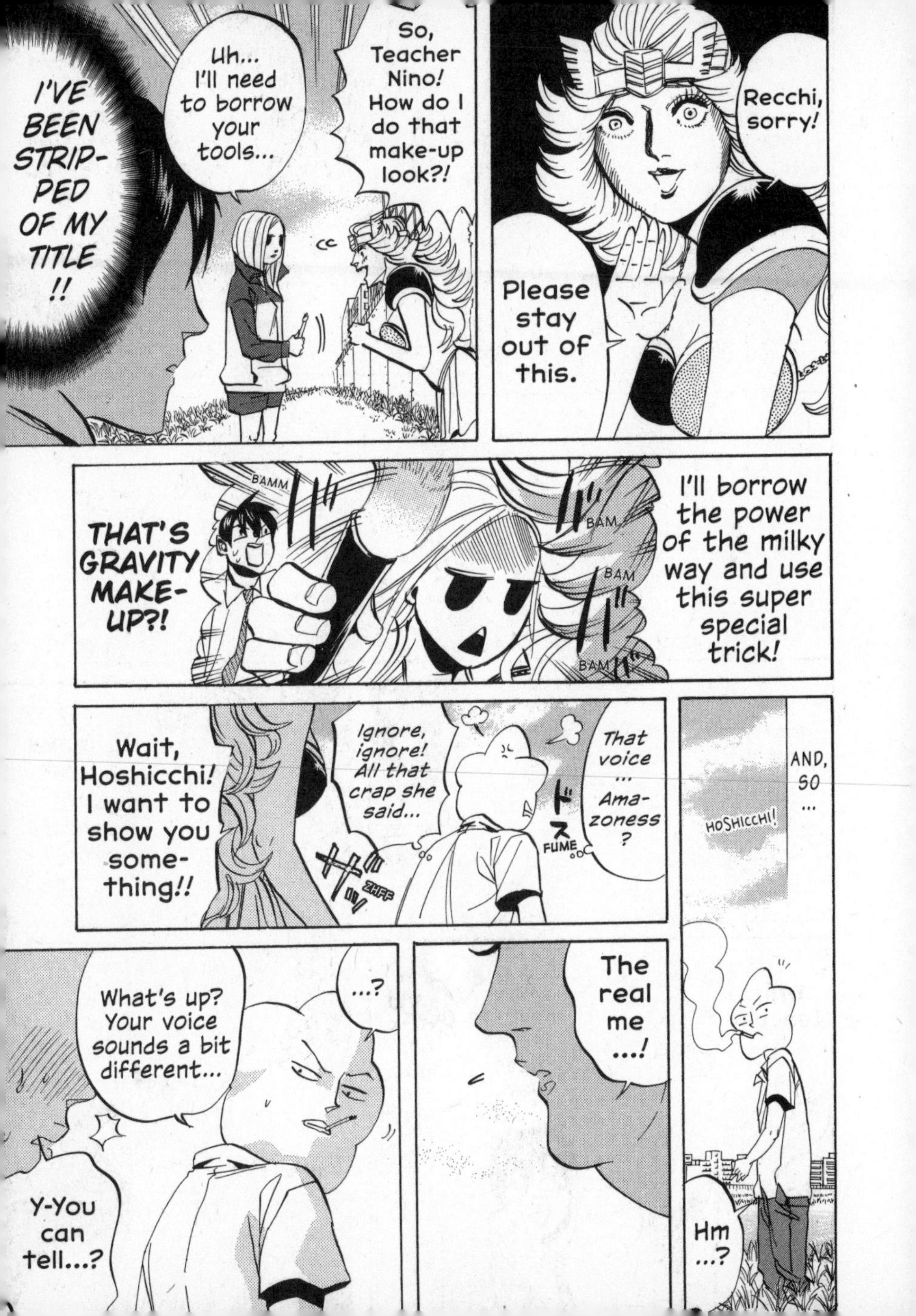
Recchi, sorry!
Please stay out of this.
So, Teacher Nino! How do I do that make-up look?!
Uh... I'll need to borrow your tools...
CC
I'VE BEEN STRIP-PED OF MY TITLE !!
I'll borrow the power of the milky way and use this super special trick!
BAMM
BAM
BAM
BAM
THAT'S GRAVITY MAKE-UP?!
AND, SO ...
HOSHICCHI!
That voice ... Ama-zoness ?
FUME
Ignore, ignore! All that crap she said...
ZHFF
Wait, Hoshicchi! I want to show you some-thing!!
Hm ...?
The real me ...!
...?
What's up? Your voice sounds a bit different...
Y-You can tell...?

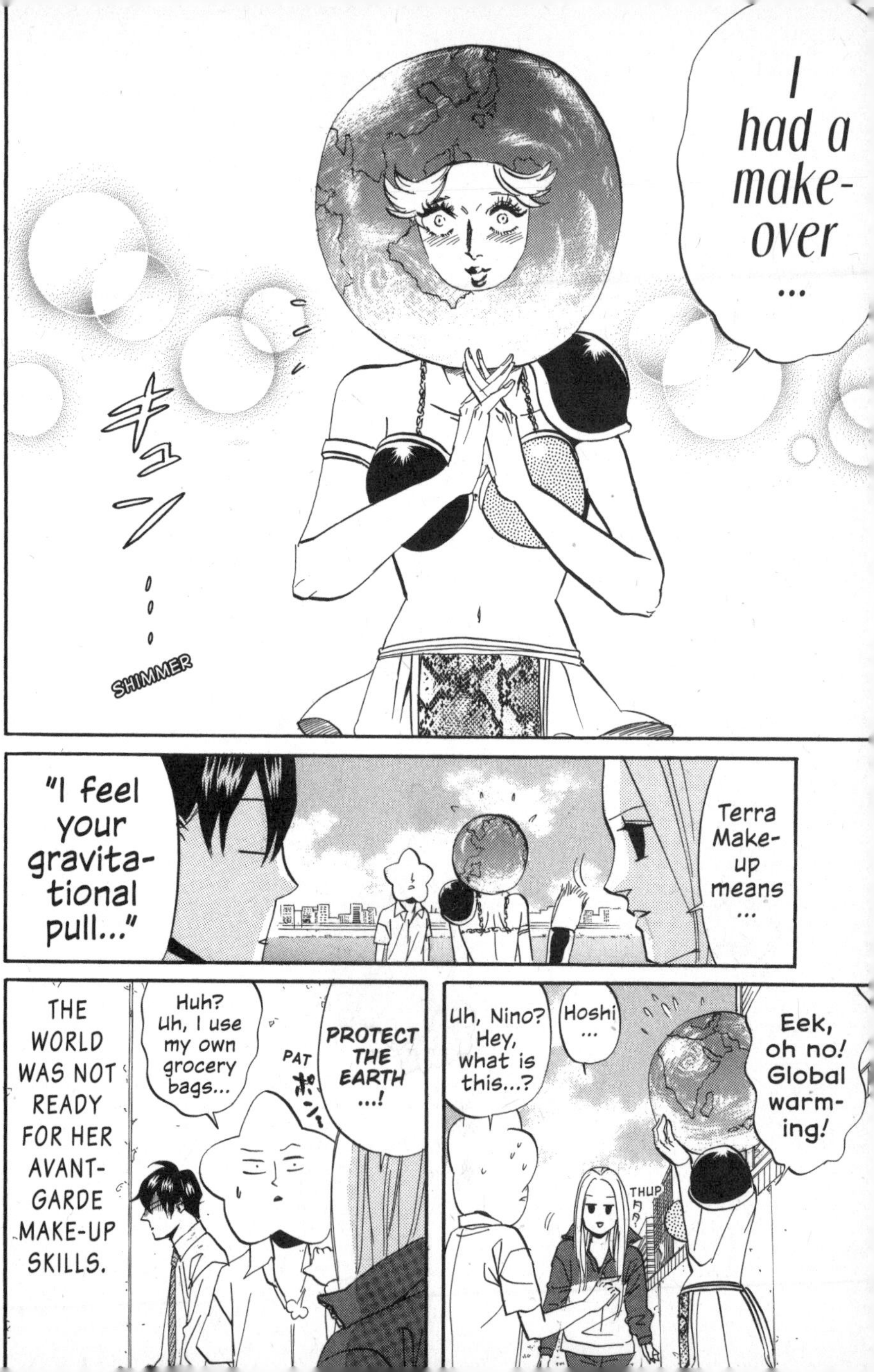
I had a make-over...
キュン
SHIMMER
Terra Make-up means...
"I feel your gravitational pull..."
Eek, oh no! Global warming!
THUP
Hoshi...
Uh, Nino? Hey, what is this...?
PROTECT THE EARTH...!
PAT
Huh? Uh, I use my own grocery bags...
THE WORLD WAS NOT READY FOR HER AVANT-GARDE MAKE-UP SKILLS.

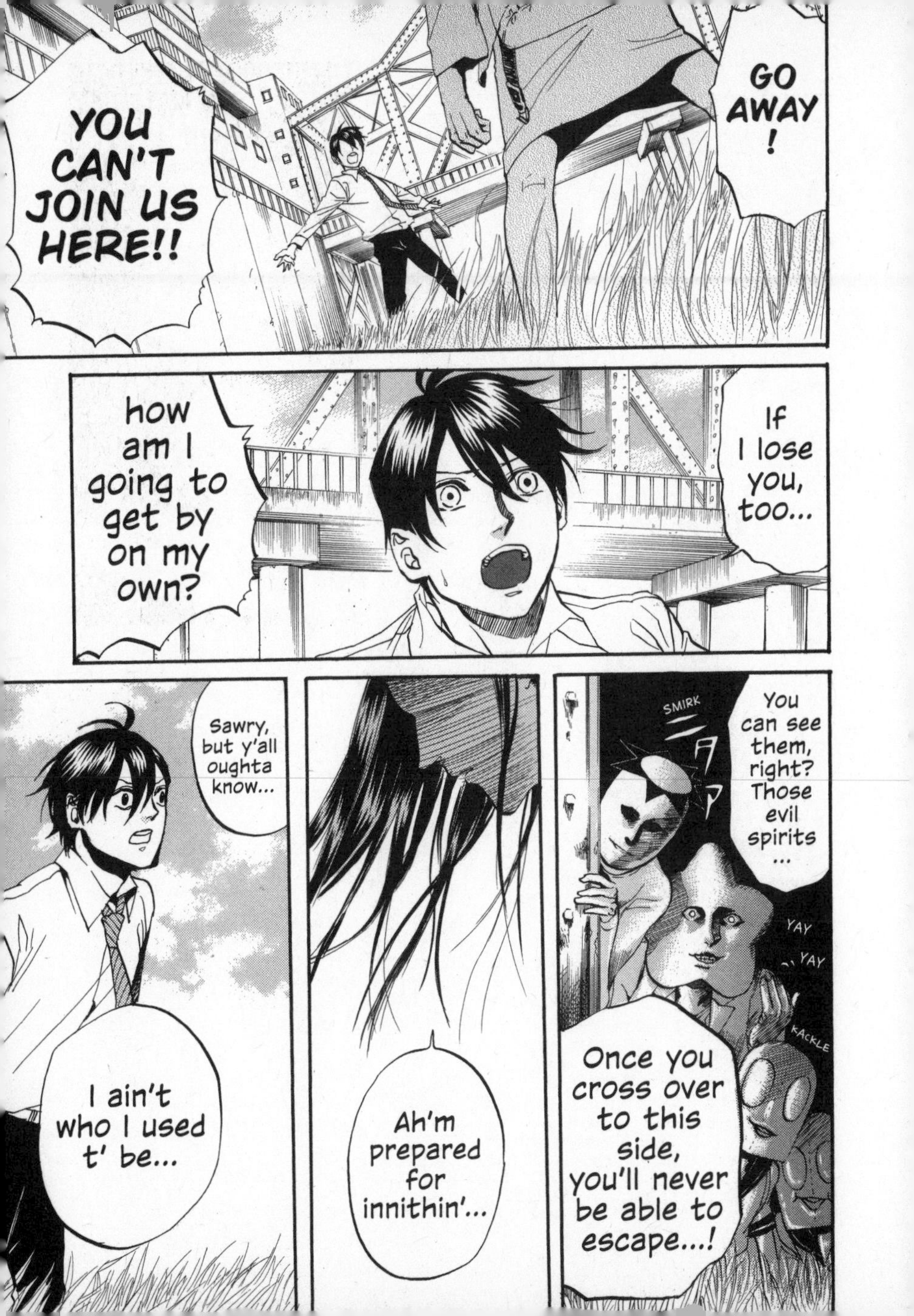
GO AWAY!
YOU CAN'T JOIN US HERE!!
If I lose you, too...
how am I going to get by on my own?
You can see them, right? Those evil spirits...
SMIRK
YAY
YAY
KACKLE
Once you cross over to this side, you'll never be able to escape...!
Ah'm prepared for innithin'...
Sawry, but y'all oughta know...
I ain't who I used t' be...

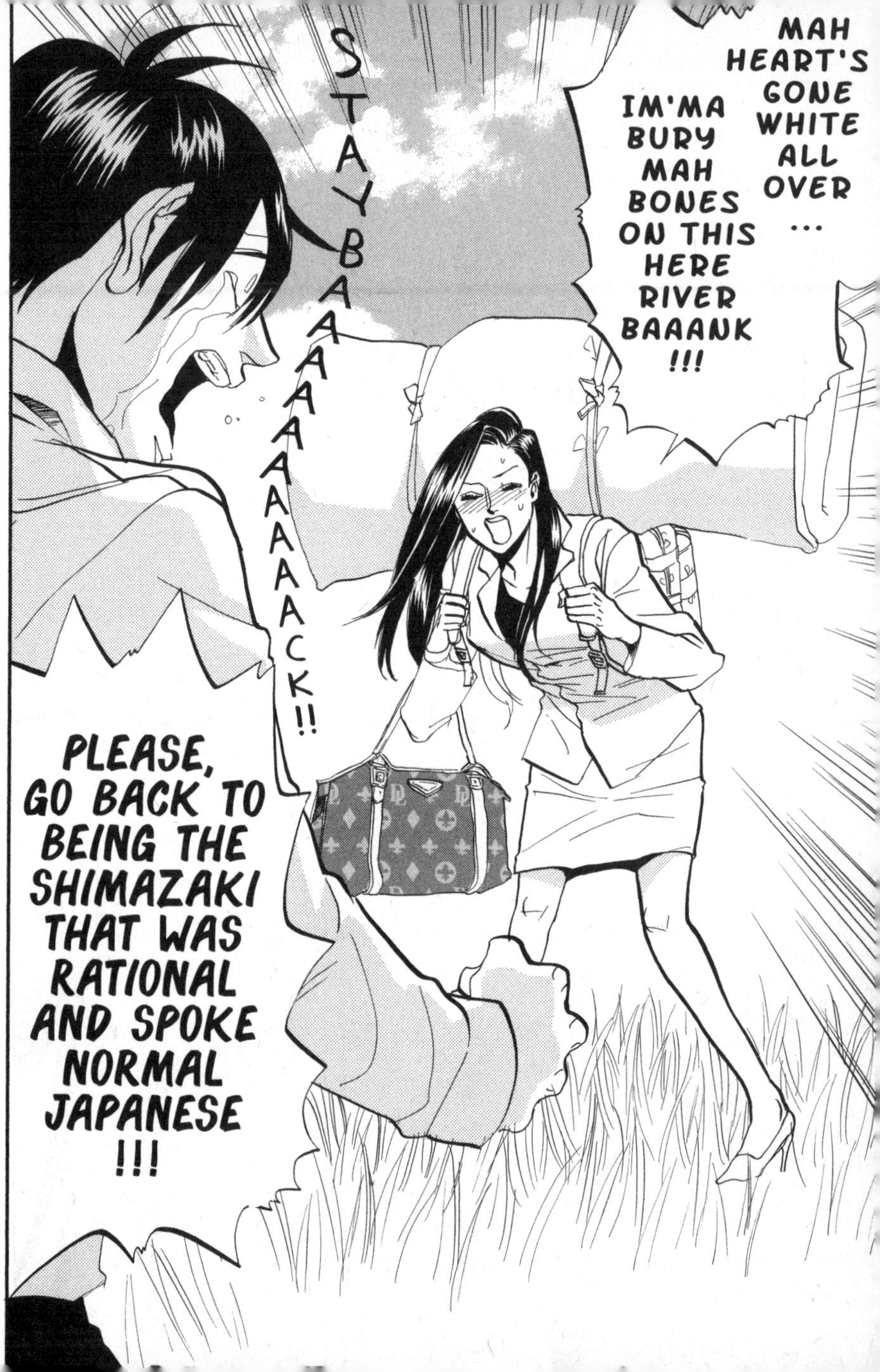
MAH HEART'S GONE WHITE ALL OVER ...
IM'MA BURY MAH BONES ON THIS HERE RIVER BAAANK !!!
STAY BAAAAAAAAAAACK!!
PLEASE, GO BACK TO BEING THE SHIMAZAKI THAT WAS RATIONAL AND SPOKE NORMAL JAPANESE !!!

Chapter 247: Moving

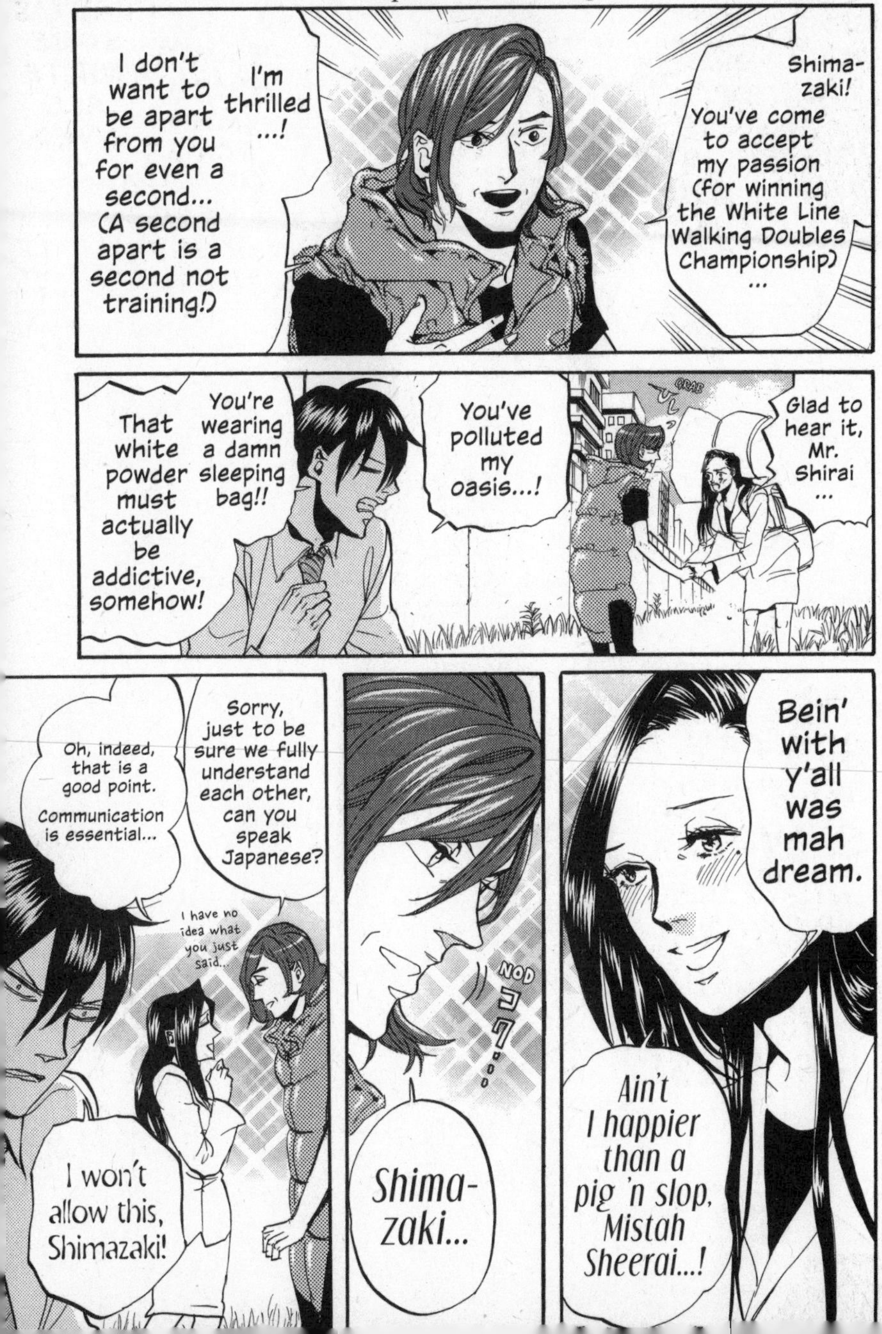

Shima-zaki! You've come to accept my passion (for winning the White Line Walking Doubles Championship) ...
I'm thrilled ...!
I don't want to be apart from you for even a second... (A second apart is a second not training!)
GRAB
Glad to hear it, Mr. Shirai ...
You've polluted my oasis...!
You're wearing a damn sleeping bag!!
That white powder must actually be addictive, somehow!
Bein' with y'all was mah dream.
Ain't I happier than a pig 'n slop, Mistah Sheerai...!
NOD
Shima-zaki...
Sorry, just to be sure we fully understand each other, can you speak Japanese?
Oh, indeed, that is a good point. Communication is essential...
I have no idea what you just said..
I won't allow this, Shimazaki!

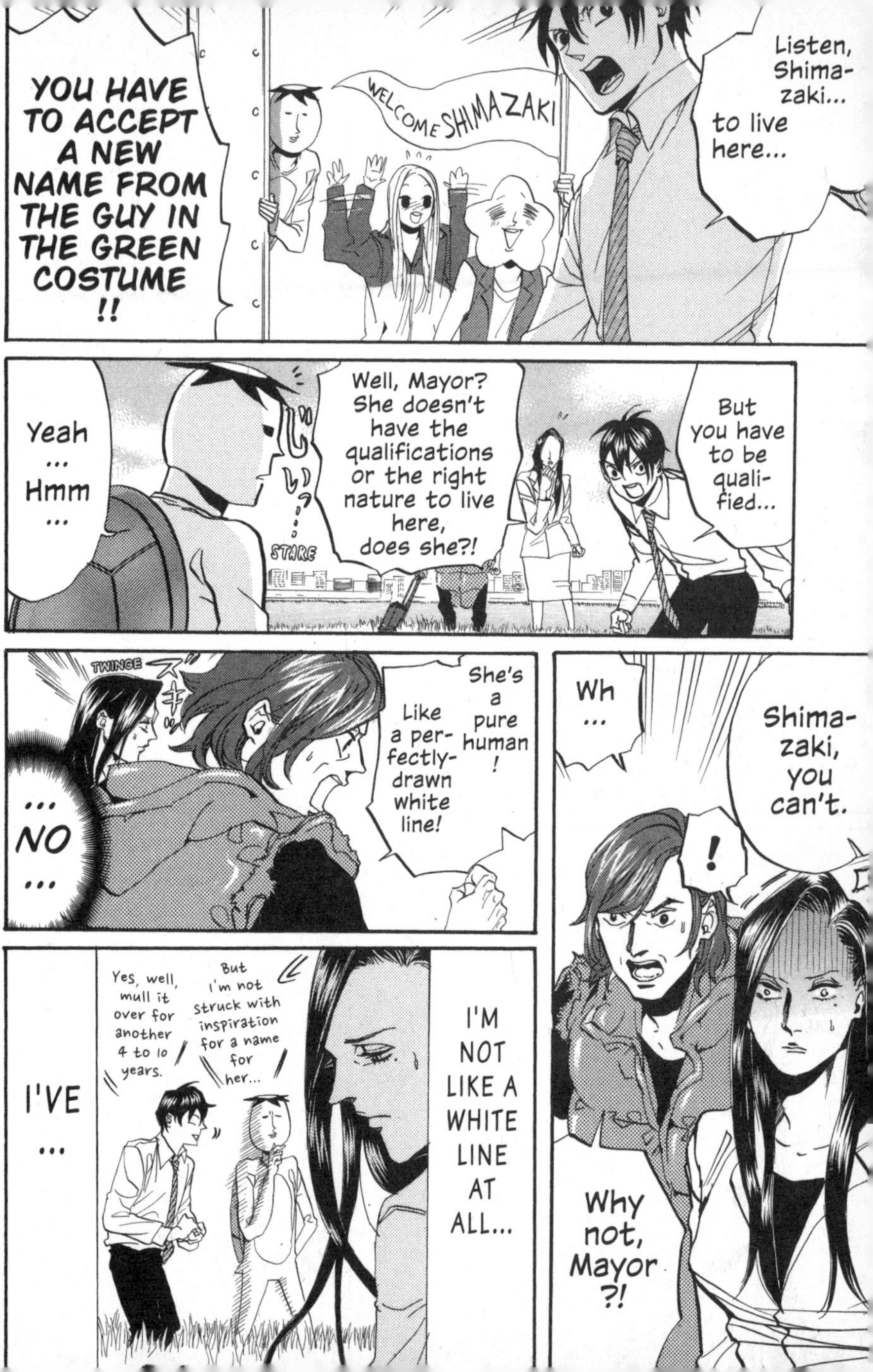

Listen, Shimazaki... to live here...
WELCOME SHIMAZAKI
YOU HAVE TO ACCEPT A NEW NAME FROM THE GUY IN THE GREEN COSTUME !!
But you have to be qualified...
Well, Mayor? She doesn't have the qualifications or the right nature to live here, does she?!
STARE
Yeah ... Hmm ...
Wh ...
Shimazaki, you can't.
!
Why not, Mayor ?!
She's a pure human!
Like a perfectly-drawn white line!
TWINGE
... NO ...
I'M NOT LIKE A WHITE LINE AT ALL...
But I'm not struck with inspiration for a name for her...
Yes, well, mull it over for another 4 to 10 years.
I'VE ...

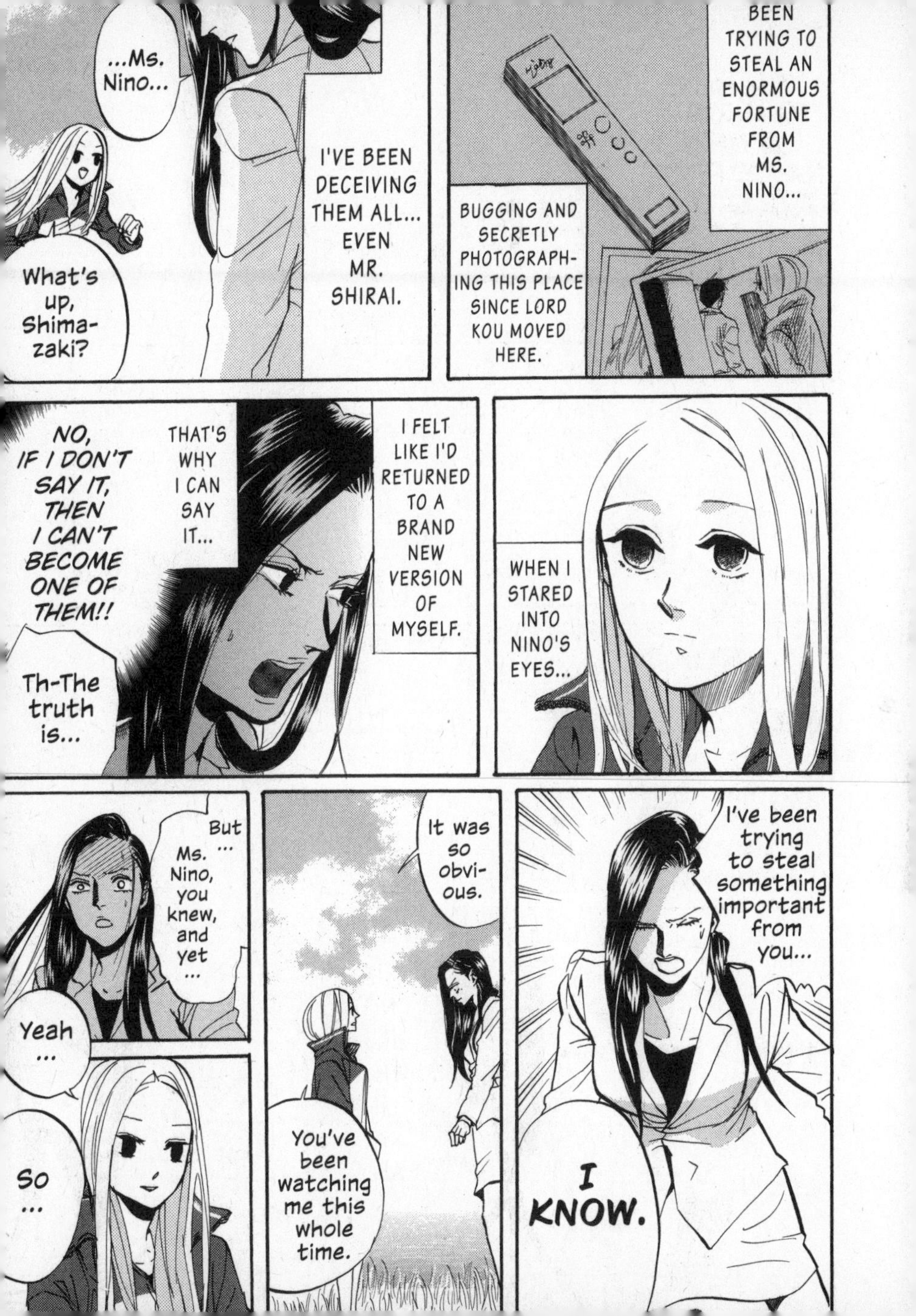
BEEN TRYING TO STEAL AN ENORMOUS FORTUNE FROM MS. NINO...
BUGGING AND SECRETLY PHOTOGRAPHING THIS PLACE SINCE LORD KOU MOVED HERE.
I'VE BEEN DECEIVING THEM ALL... EVEN MR. SHIRAI.
...Ms. Nino...
What's up, Shimazaki?
WHEN I STARED INTO NINO'S EYES...
I FELT LIKE I'D RETURNED TO A BRAND NEW VERSION OF MYSELF.
THAT'S WHY I CAN SAY IT...
NO, IF I DON'T SAY IT, THEN I CAN'T BECOME ONE OF THEM!!
Th-The truth is...
I've been trying to steal something important from you...
I KNOW.
It was so obvious.
You've been watching me this whole time.
But ... Ms. Nino, you knew, and yet ...
Yeah ...
So ...

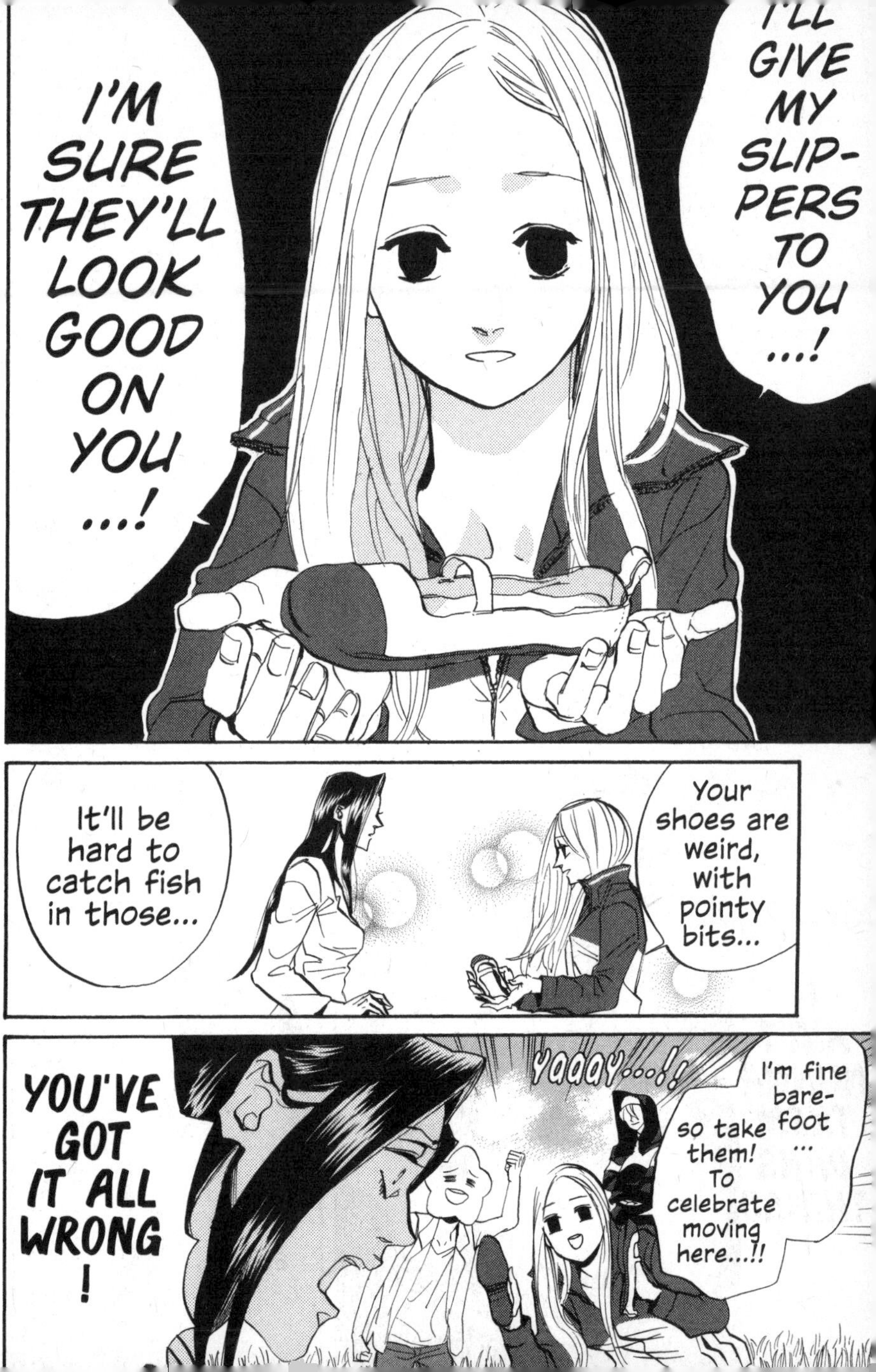
I'LL GIVE MY SLIPPERS TO YOU...!
I'M SURE THEY'LL LOOK GOOD ON YOU...!
Your shoes are weird, with pointy bits...
It'll be hard to catch fish in those...
I'm fine barefoot...
YAAAY...!!
so take them! To celebrate moving here...!!
YOU'VE GOT IT ALL WRONG!

Chapter 248: Confession II

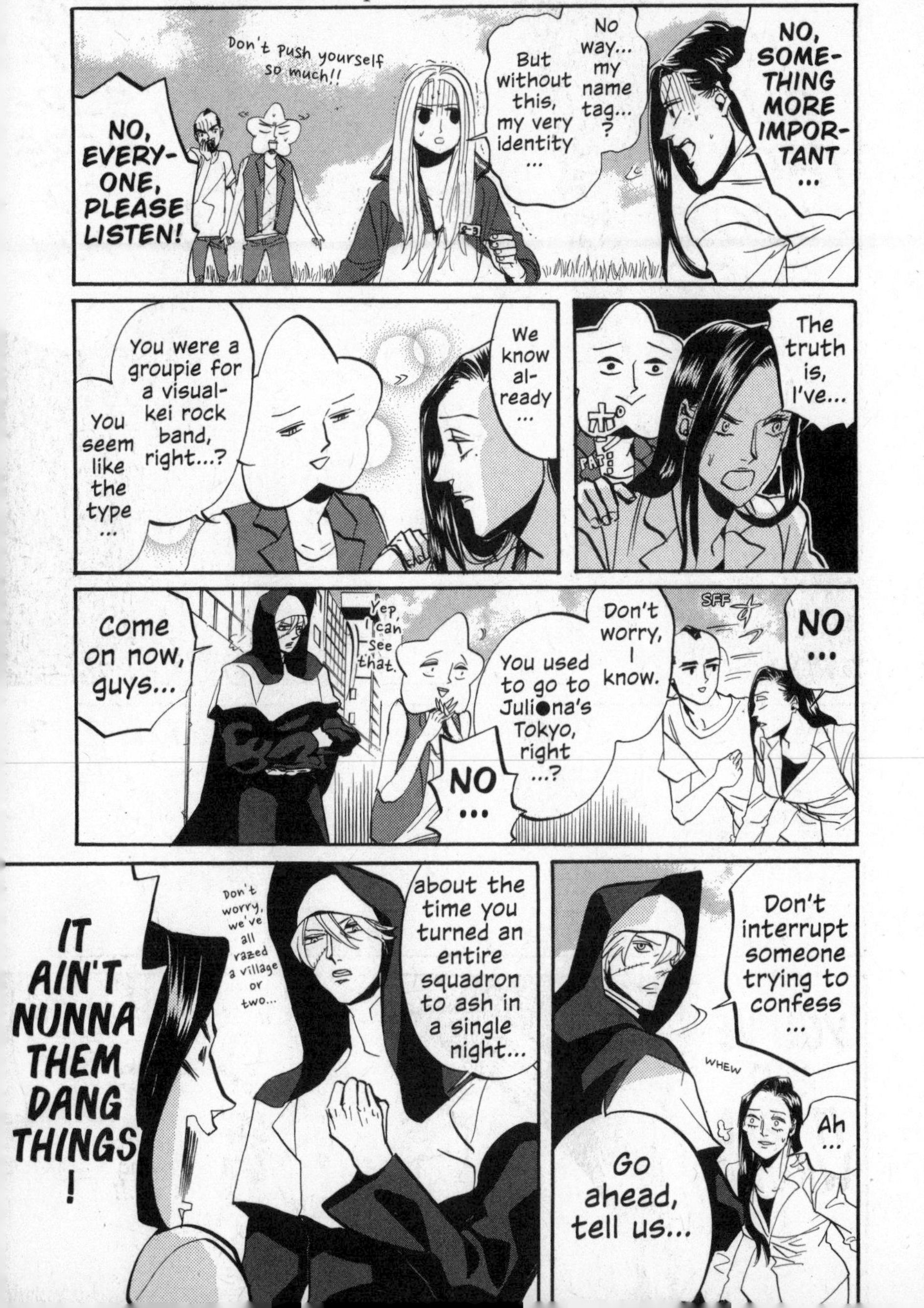
NO, SOMETHING MORE IMPORTANT...
No way... my name tag...?
But without this, my very identity...
Don't push yourself so much!!
NO, EVERYONE, PLEASE LISTEN!
The truth is, I've...
PAT
We know already...
You were a groupie for a visual-kei rock band, right...?
You seem like the type...
NO...
SFF
Don't worry, I know.
You used to go to Juli●na's Tokyo, right...?
NO...
Yep, I can see that.
Come on now, guys...
Don't interrupt someone trying to confess...
WHEW
Ah...
Go ahead, tell us...
about the time you turned an entire squadron to ash in a single night...
Don't worry, we've all razed a village or two...
IT AIN'T NUNNA THEM DANG THINGS!

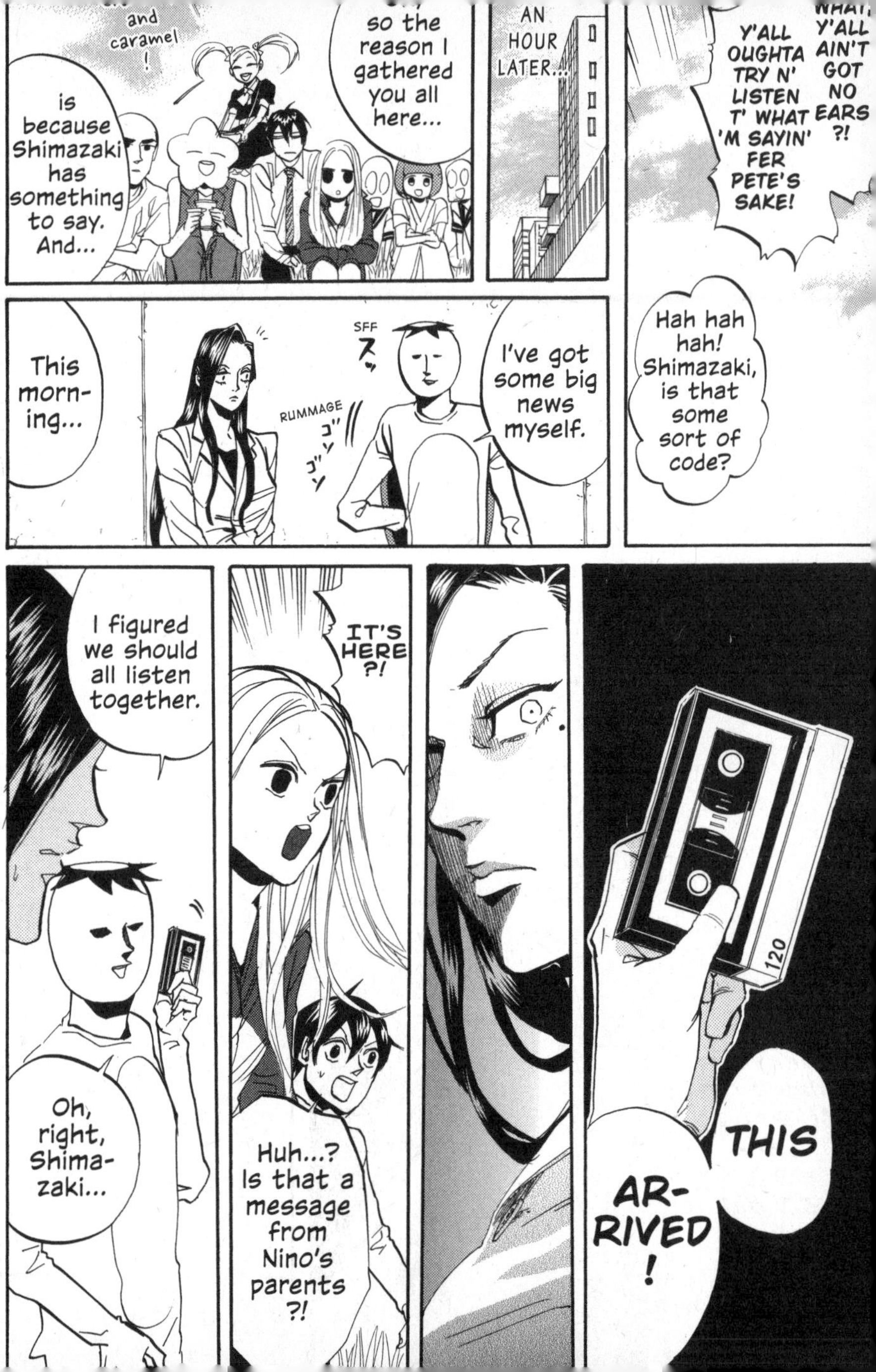

WHAT, Y'ALL AIN'T GOT NO EARS?!
Y'ALL OUGHTA TRY N' LISTEN T' WHAT 'M SAYIN' FER PETE'S SAKE!
Hah hah hah! Shimazaki, is that some sort of code?
AN HOUR LATER...
so the reason I gathered you all here...
and caramel!
is because Shimazaki has something to say. And...
I've got some big news myself.
SFF
RUMMAGE
This morning...
THIS ARRIVED!
120
IT'S HERE?!
Huh...? Is that a message from Nino's parents?!
I figured we should all listen together.
Oh, right, Shimazaki...

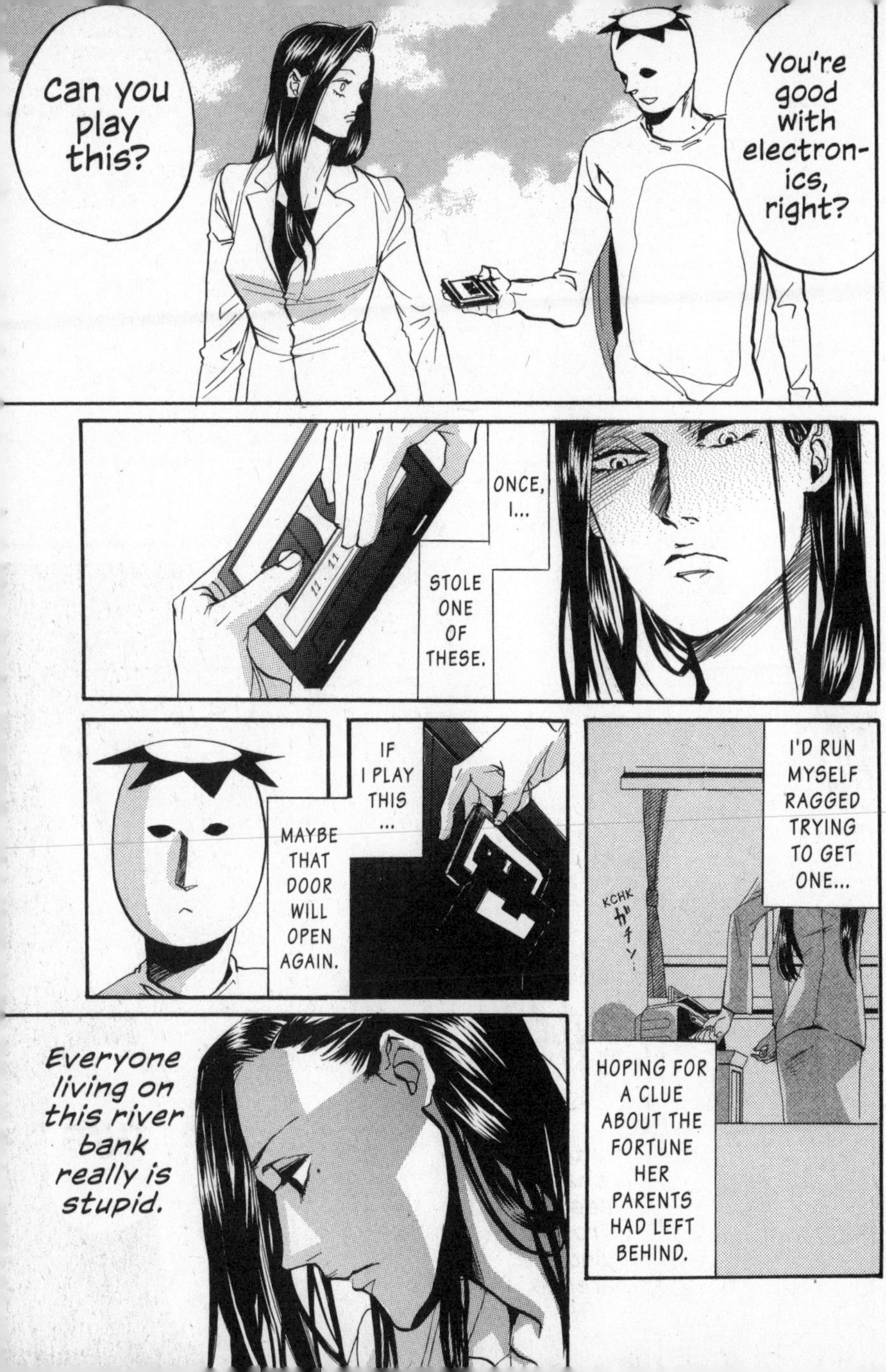
You're good with electronics, right?
Can you play this?
ONCE, I...
STOLE ONE OF THESE.
I'D RUN MYSELF RAGGED TRYING TO GET ONE...
KCHK
HOPING FOR A CLUE ABOUT THE FORTUNE HER PARENTS HAD LEFT BEHIND.
IF I PLAY THIS ...
MAYBE THAT DOOR WILL OPEN AGAIN.
Everyone living on this river bank really is stupid.

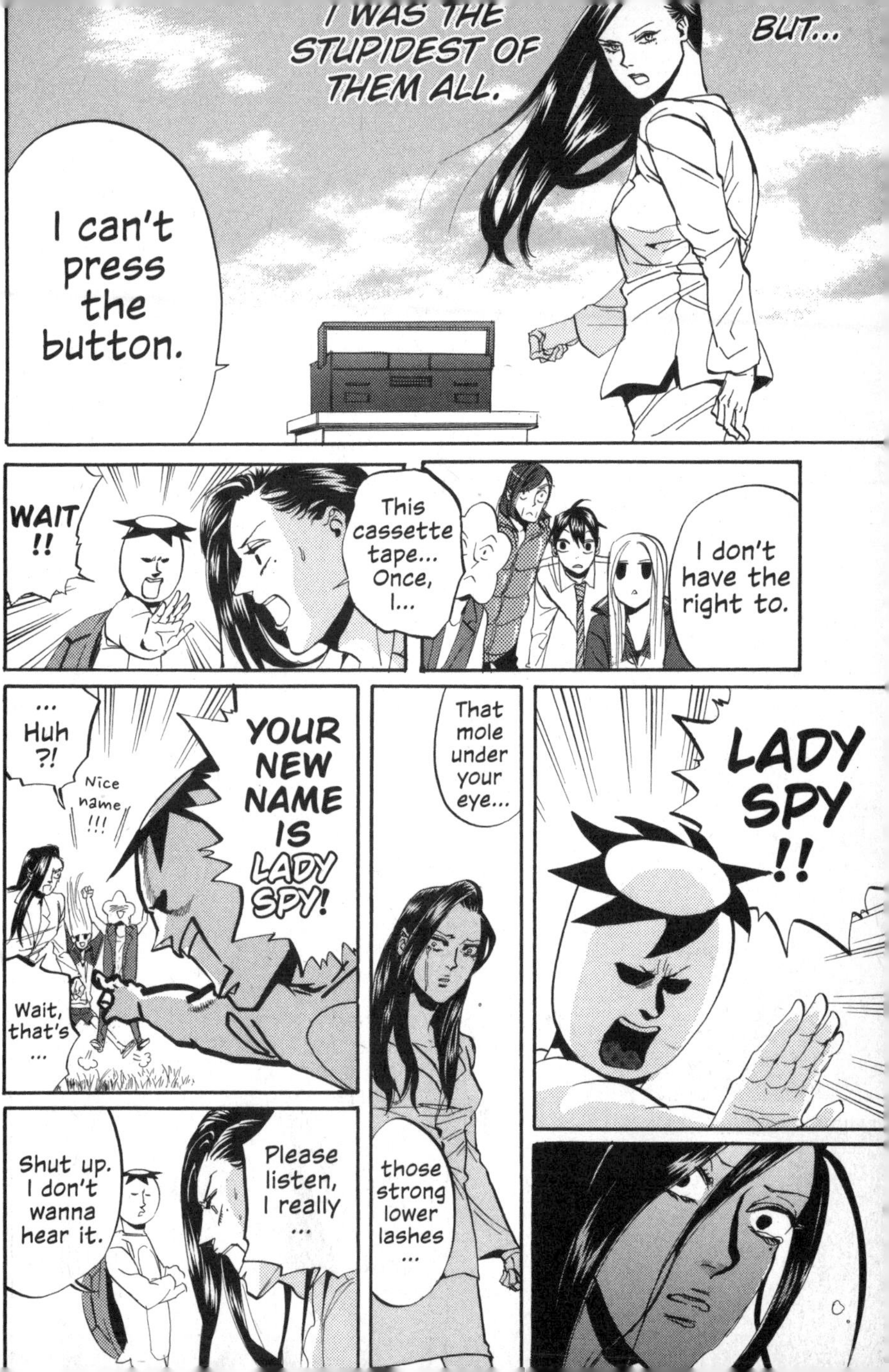
BUT...
I WAS THE STUPIDEST OF THEM ALL.
I can't press the button.
I don't have the right to.
This cassette tape... Once, I...
WAIT !!
LADY SPY !!
That mole under your eye...
those strong lower lashes ...
YOUR NEW NAME IS LADY SPY!
... Huh ?!
Nice name !!!
Wait, that's ...
Please listen, I really ...
Shut up. I don't wanna hear it.

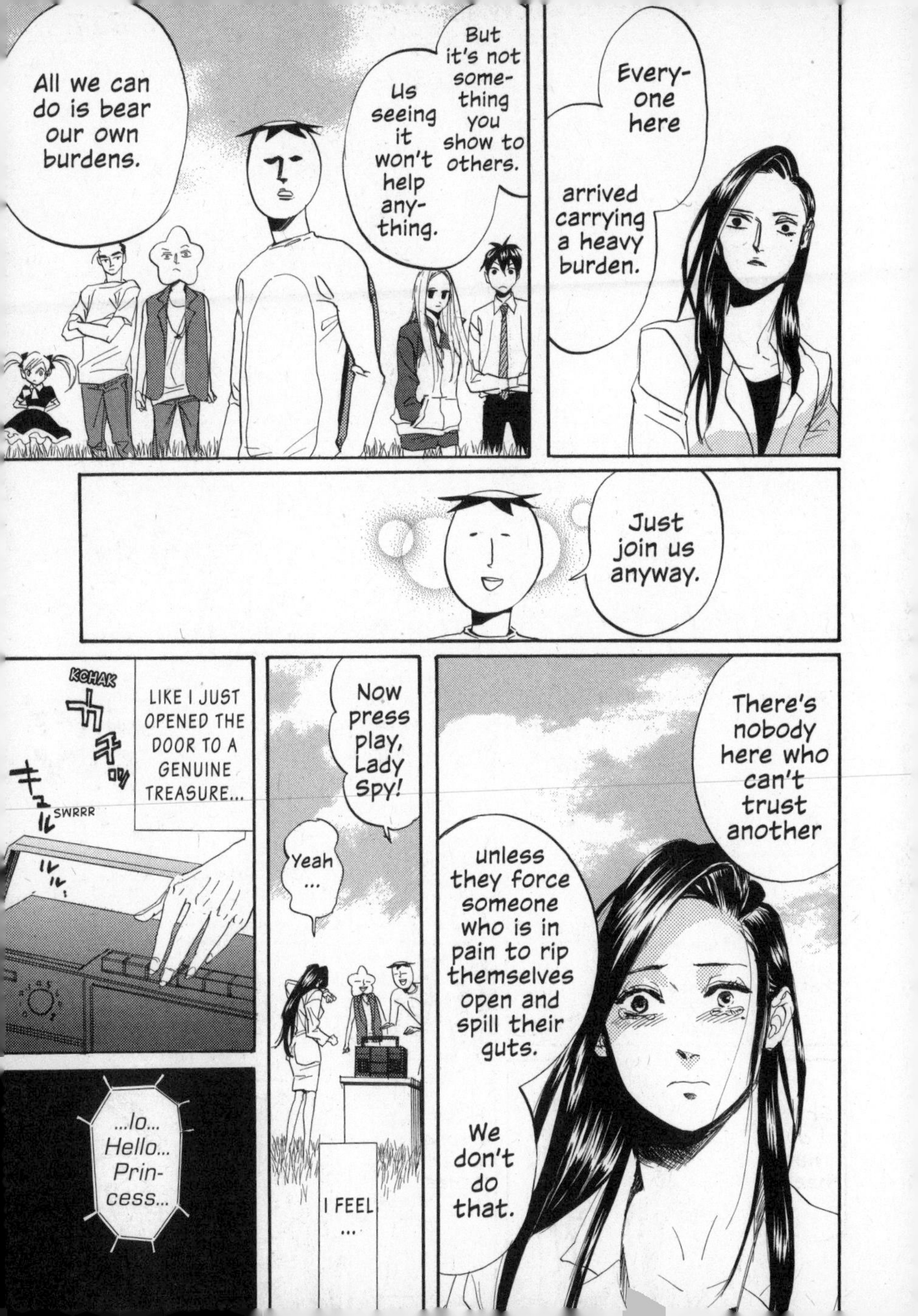
Every-one here
arrived carrying a heavy burden.
But it's not some-thing you show to others.
Us seeing it won't help any-thing.
All we can do is bear our own burdens.
Just join us anyway.
There's nobody here who can't trust another
unless they force someone who is in pain to rip themselves open and spill their guts.
We don't do that.
Now press play, Lady Spy!
Yeah ...
I FEEL ...
LIKE I JUST OPENED THE DOOR TO A GENUINE TREASURE...
KCHAK
SWRRR
...lo... Hello... Prin-cess...

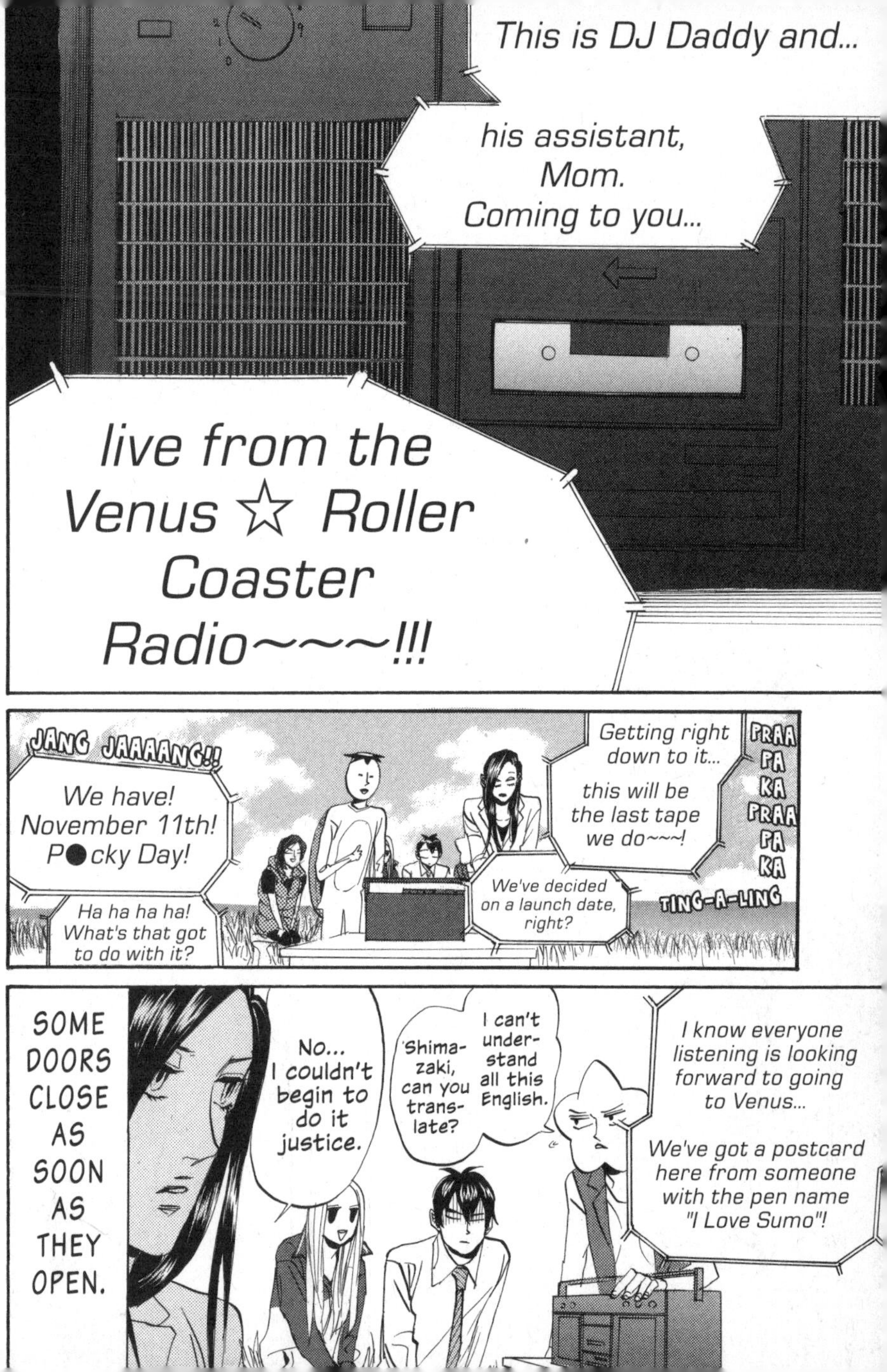
This is DJ Daddy and...
his assistant, Mom. Coming to you...
live from the Venus ☆ Roller Coaster Radio~~~!!!
PRAA PA KA PRAA PA KA
TING-A-LING
Getting right down to it...
this will be the last tape we do~~~!
We've decided on a launch date, right?
JANG JAAAANG!!
We have! November 11th! P●cky Day!
Ha ha ha ha! What's that got to do with it?
I know everyone listening is looking forward to going to Venus...
We've got a postcard here from someone with the pen name "I Love Sumo"!
I can't under-stand all this English.
'Shima-zaki, can you trans-late?
No... I couldn't begin to do it justice.
SOME DOORS CLOSE AS SOON AS THEY OPEN.

Chapter 249: Package

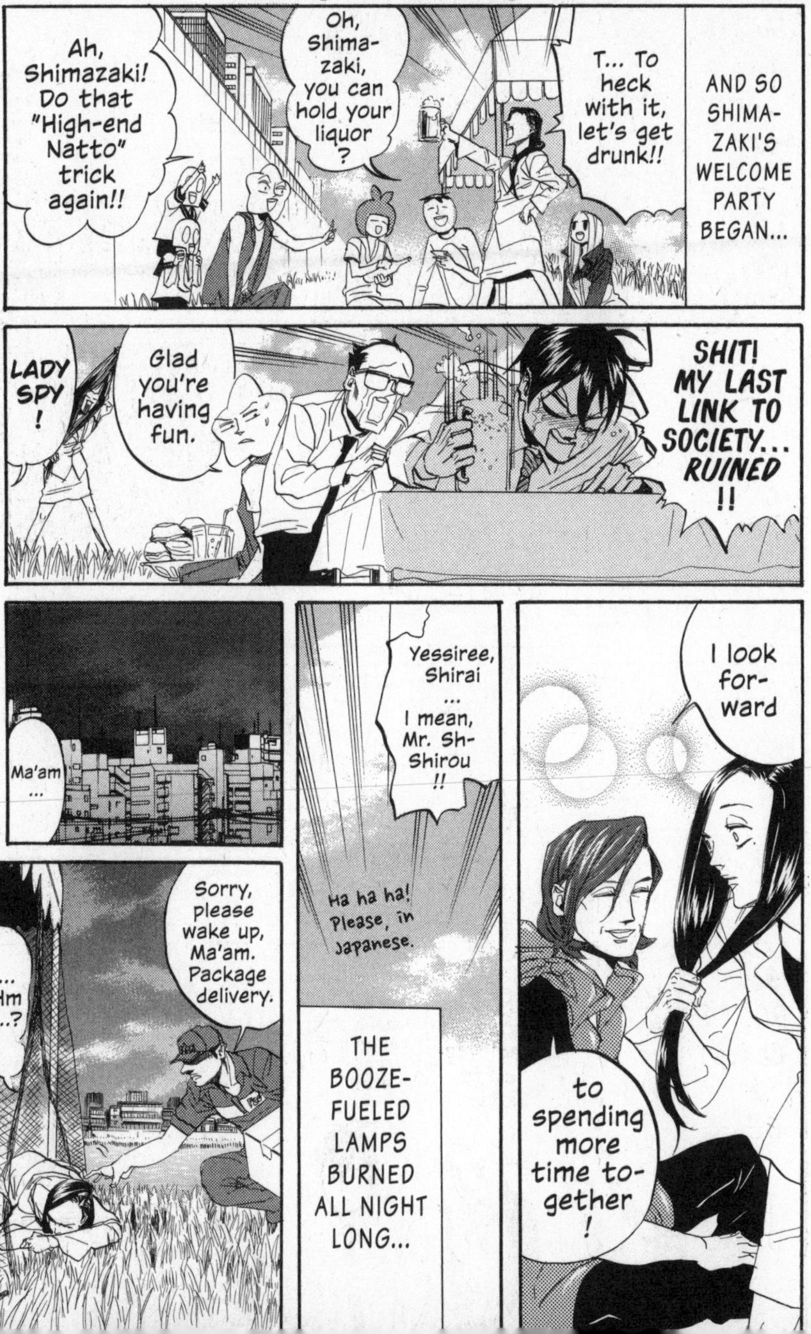
AND SO SHIMAZAKI'S WELCOME PARTY BEGAN...
T... To heck with it, let's get drunk!!
Oh, Shimazaki, you can hold your liquor?
Ah, Shimazaki! Do that "High-end Natto" trick again!!
SHIT! MY LAST LINK TO SOCIETY... RUINED!!
Glad you're having fun.
LADY SPY!
I look forward
to spending more time together!
Yessiree, Shirai... I mean, Mr. Sh-Shirou!!
Ha ha ha! Please, in Japanese.
THE BOOZE-FUELED LAMPS BURNED ALL NIGHT LONG...
Ma'am...
Sorry, please wake up, Ma'am. Package delivery.
... Hm...?

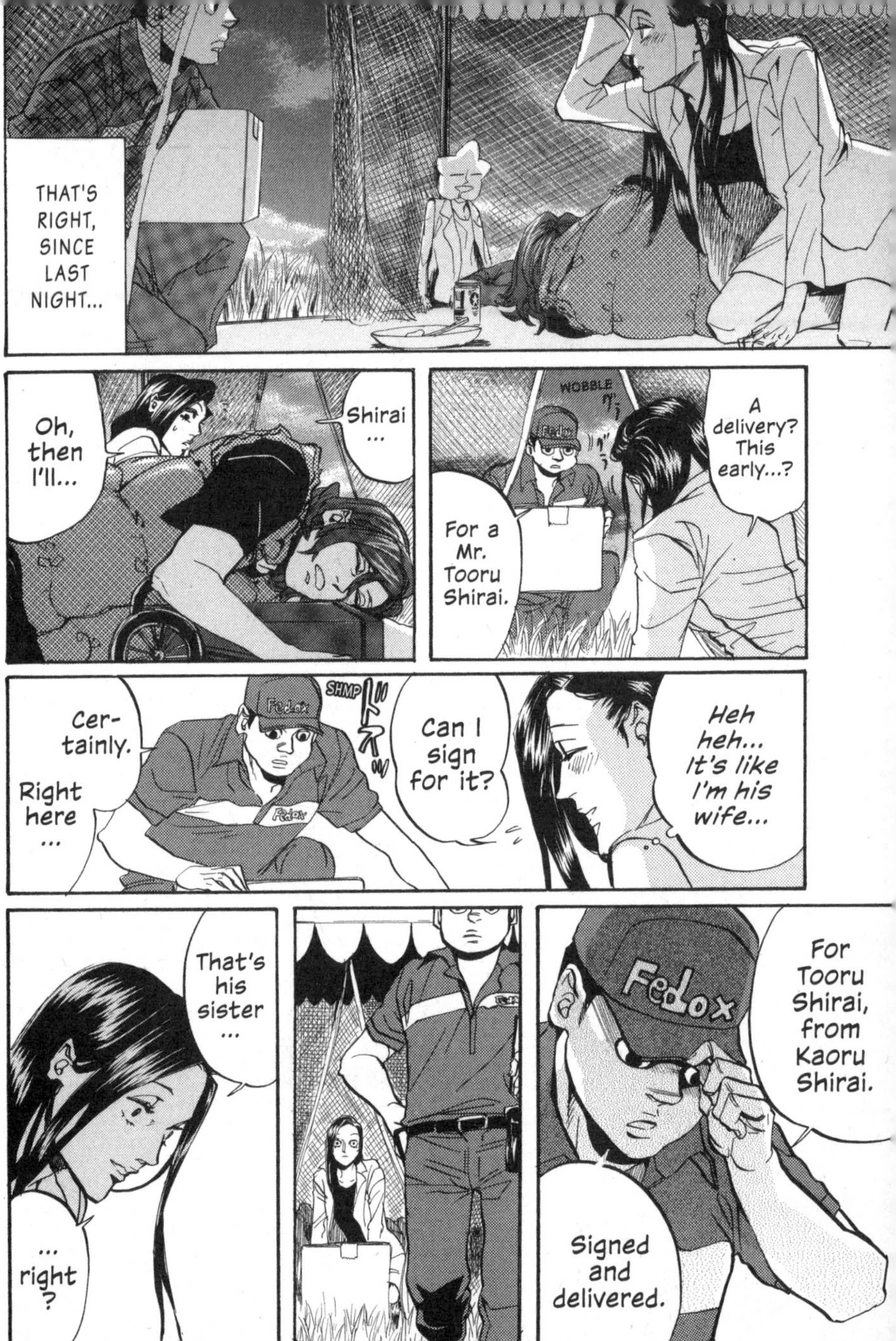
THAT'S RIGHT, SINCE LAST NIGHT...
A delivery? This early...?
WOBBLE
For a Mr. Tooru Shirai.
Shirai ...
Oh, then I'll...
Heh heh... It's like I'm his wife...
Can I sign for it?
SHMP
Cer-tainly.
Right here ...
For Tooru Shirai, from Kaoru Shirai.
Signed and delivered.
That's his sister ...
... right ?

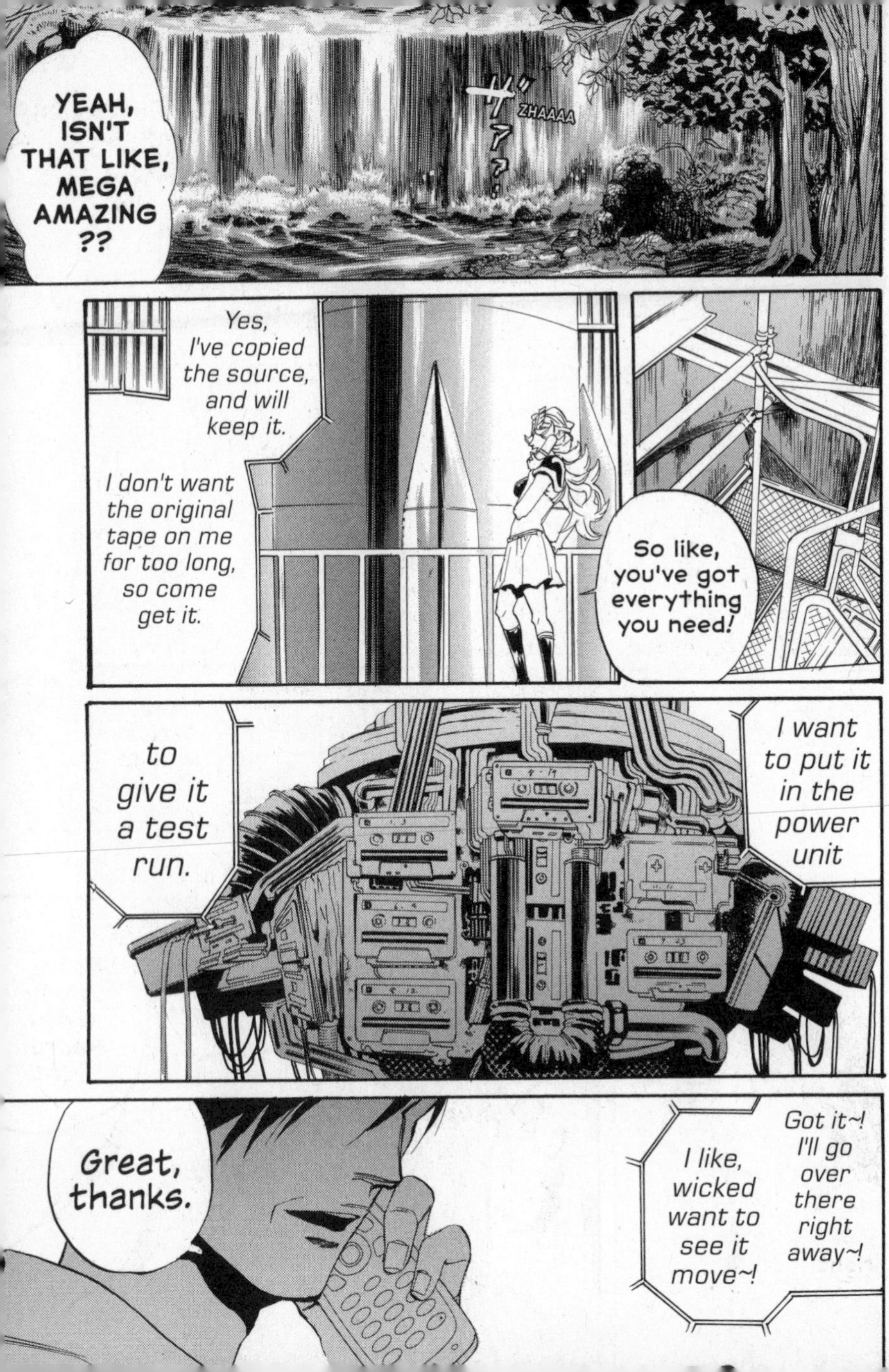
ZHAAAA
YEAH, ISN'T THAT LIKE, MEGA AMAZING ??
So like, you've got everything you need!
Yes, I've copied the source, and will keep it.
I don't want the original tape on me for too long, so come get it.
I want to put it in the power unit
to give it a test run.
Got it~! I'll go over there right away~!
I like, wicked want to see it move~!
Great, thanks.

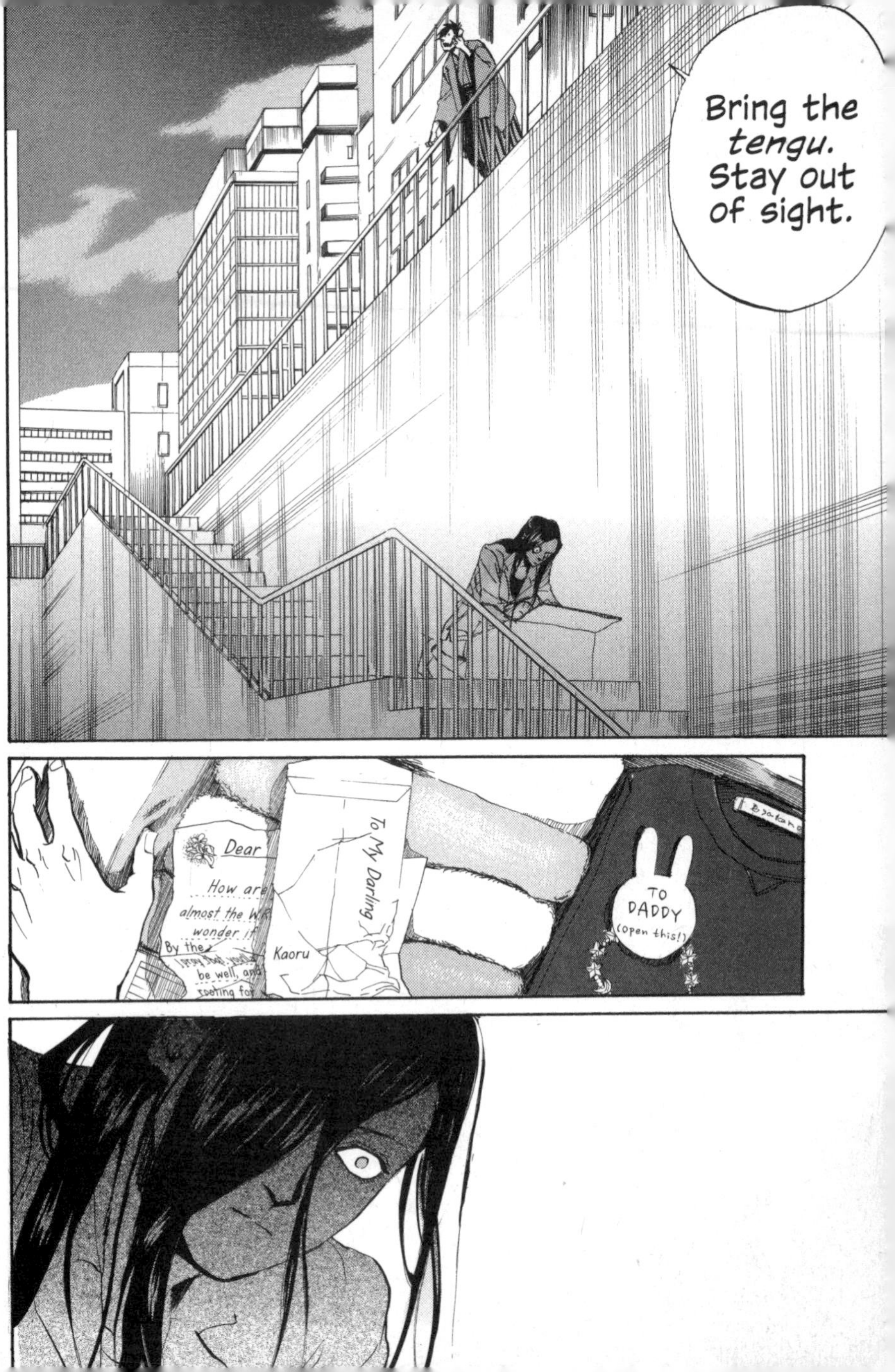
Bring the *tengu.* Stay out of sight.
Dear
How are
To My Darling
Kaoru
TO DADDY
(open this!)

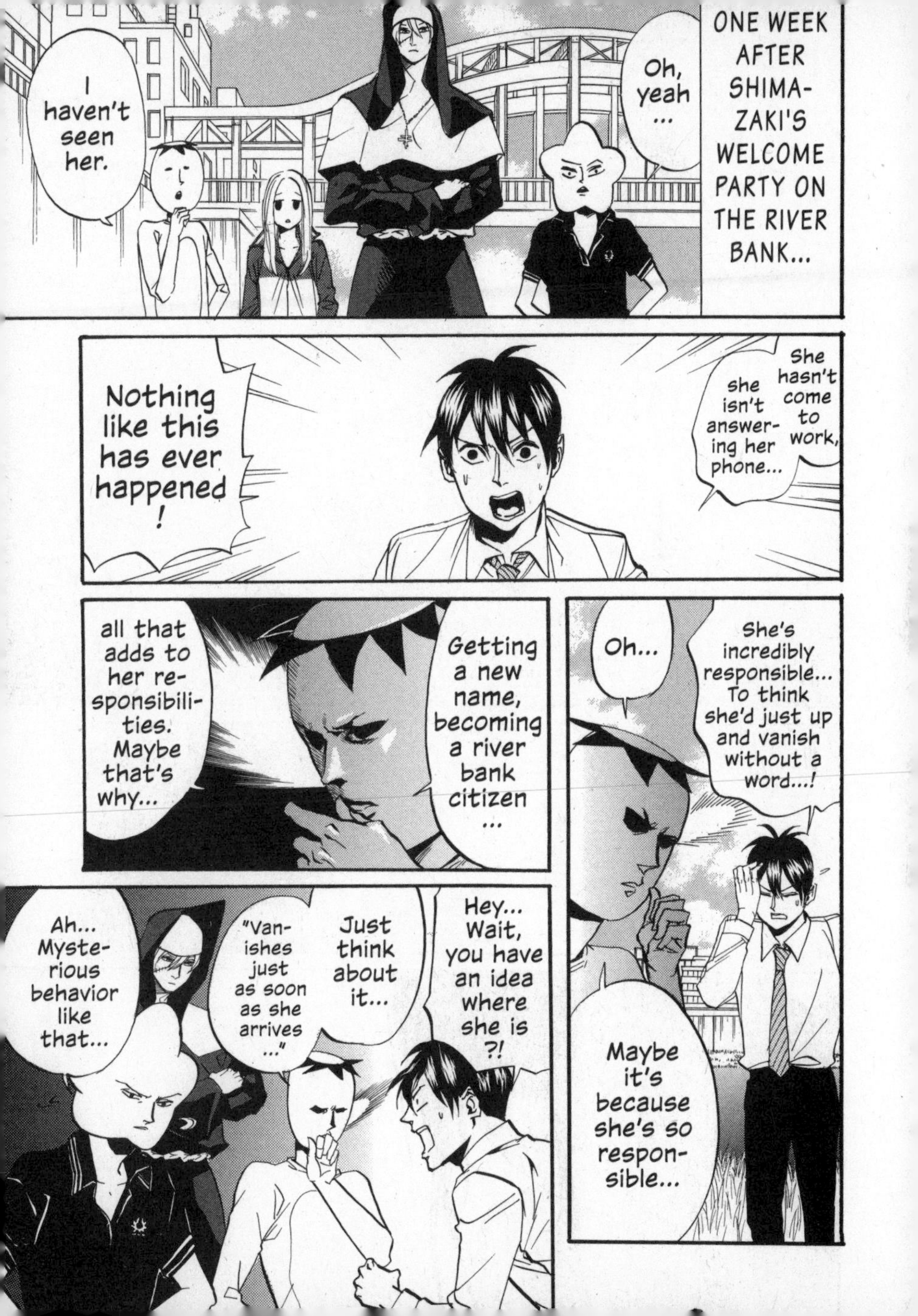
ONE WEEK AFTER SHIMAZAKI'S WELCOME PARTY ON THE RIVER BANK...
Oh, yeah ...
I haven't seen her.
She hasn't come to work, she isn't answering her phone...
Nothing like this has ever happened!
She's incredibly responsible... To think she'd just up and vanish without a word...!
Oh...
Maybe it's because she's so responsible...
Getting a new name, becoming a river bank citizen ...
all that adds to her responsibilities. Maybe that's why...
Hey... Wait, you have an idea where she is?!
Just think about it...
"Vanishes just as soon as she arrives ..."
Ah... Mysterious behavior like that...

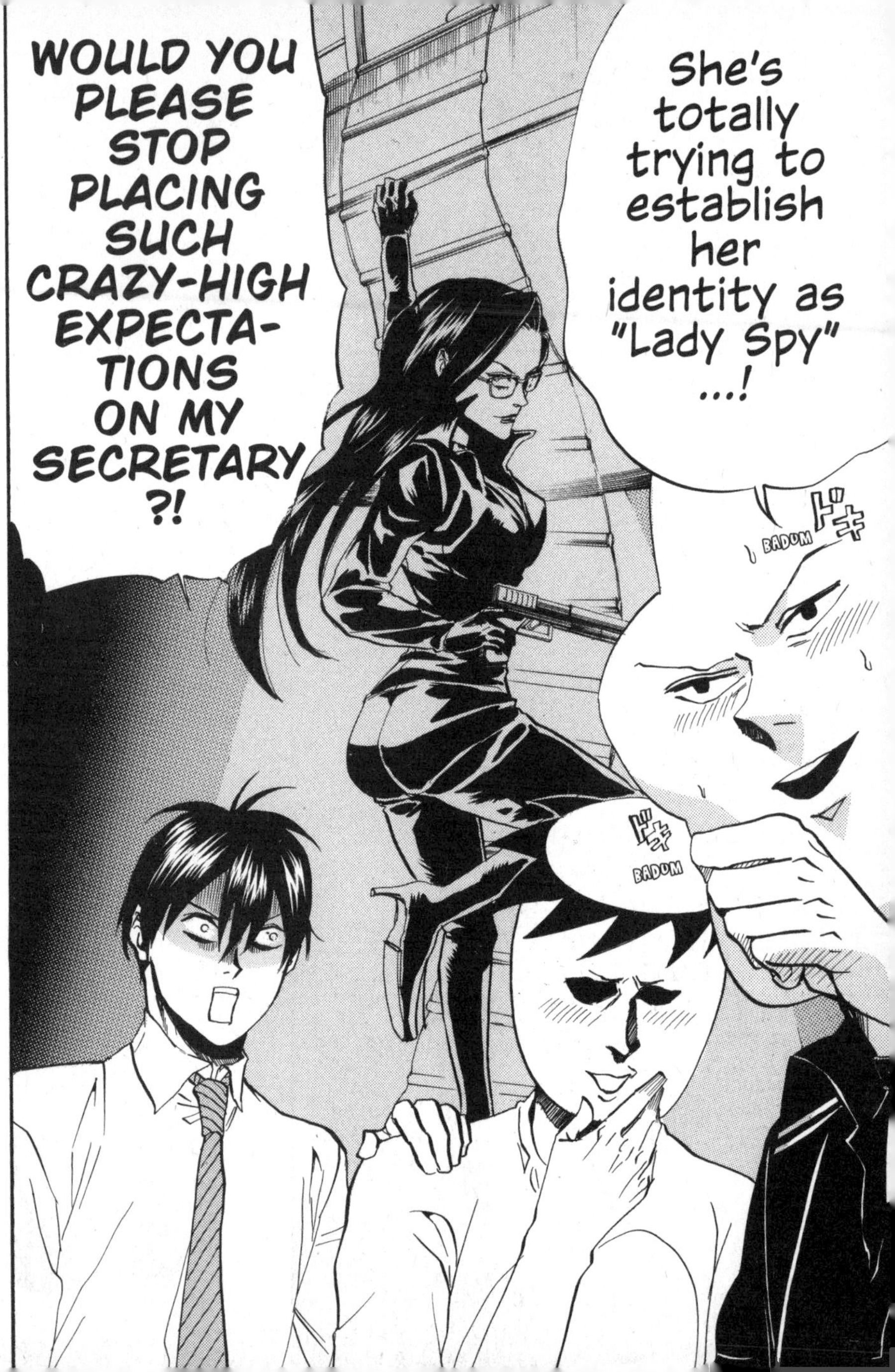

She's totally trying to establish her identity as "Lady Spy" ...!
ドキ
BADUM
ドキ
BADUM
WOULD YOU PLEASE STOP PLACING SUCH CRAZY-HIGH EXPECTA-TIONS ON MY SECRETARY ?!

Chapter 250: Establishing Identity

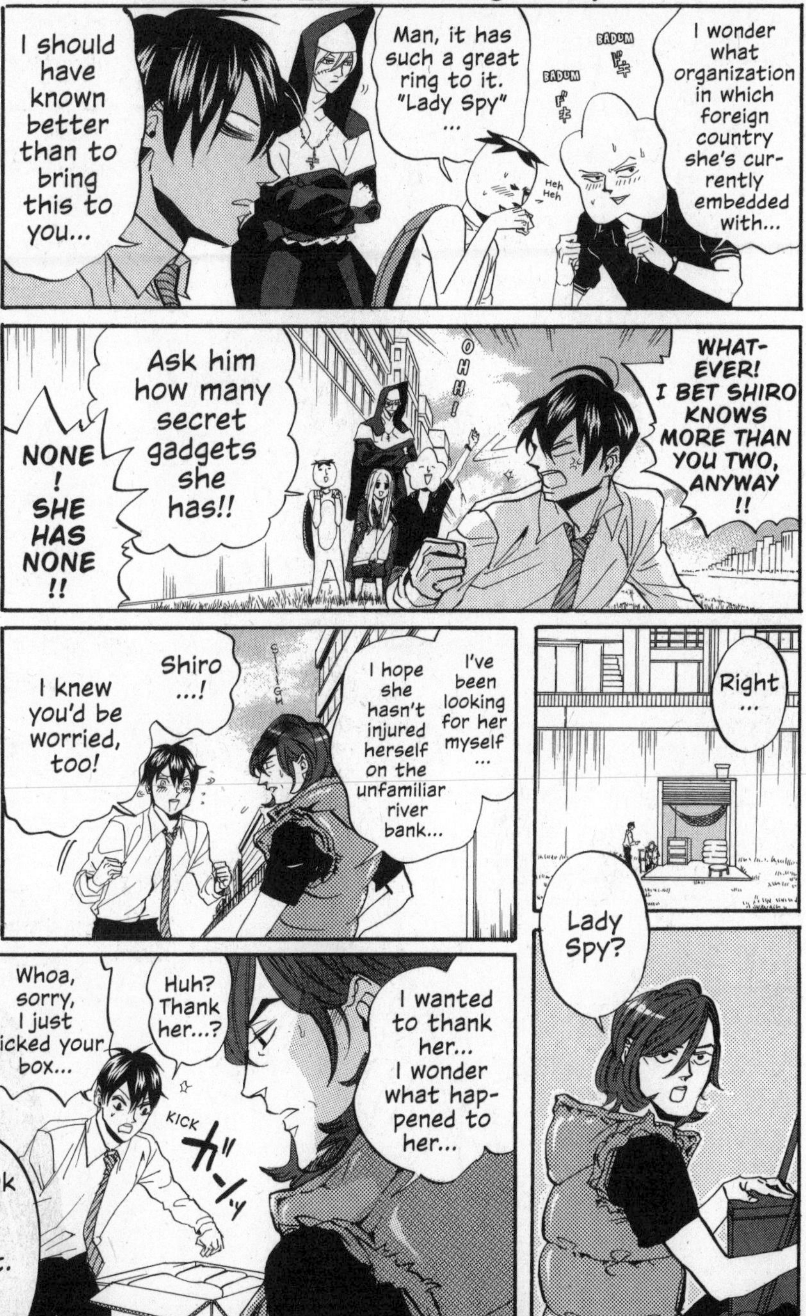

I wonder what organization in which foreign country she's currently embedded with...
BADUM
BADUM
Man, it has such a great ring to it. "Lady Spy" ...
Heh Heh
I should have known better than to bring this to you...
WHATEVER! I BET SHIRO KNOWS MORE THAN YOU TWO, ANYWAY!!
OHHHI
Ask him how many secret gadgets she has!!
NONE! SHE HAS NONE!!
Right ...
I've been looking for her myself ...
I hope she hasn't injured herself on the unfamiliar river bank...
SIGH
Shiro ...!
I knew you'd be worried, too!
Lady Spy?
I wanted to thank her... I wonder what happened to her...
Huh? Thank her...?
Whoa, sorry, I just kicked your box...
KICK
Thank her for that.

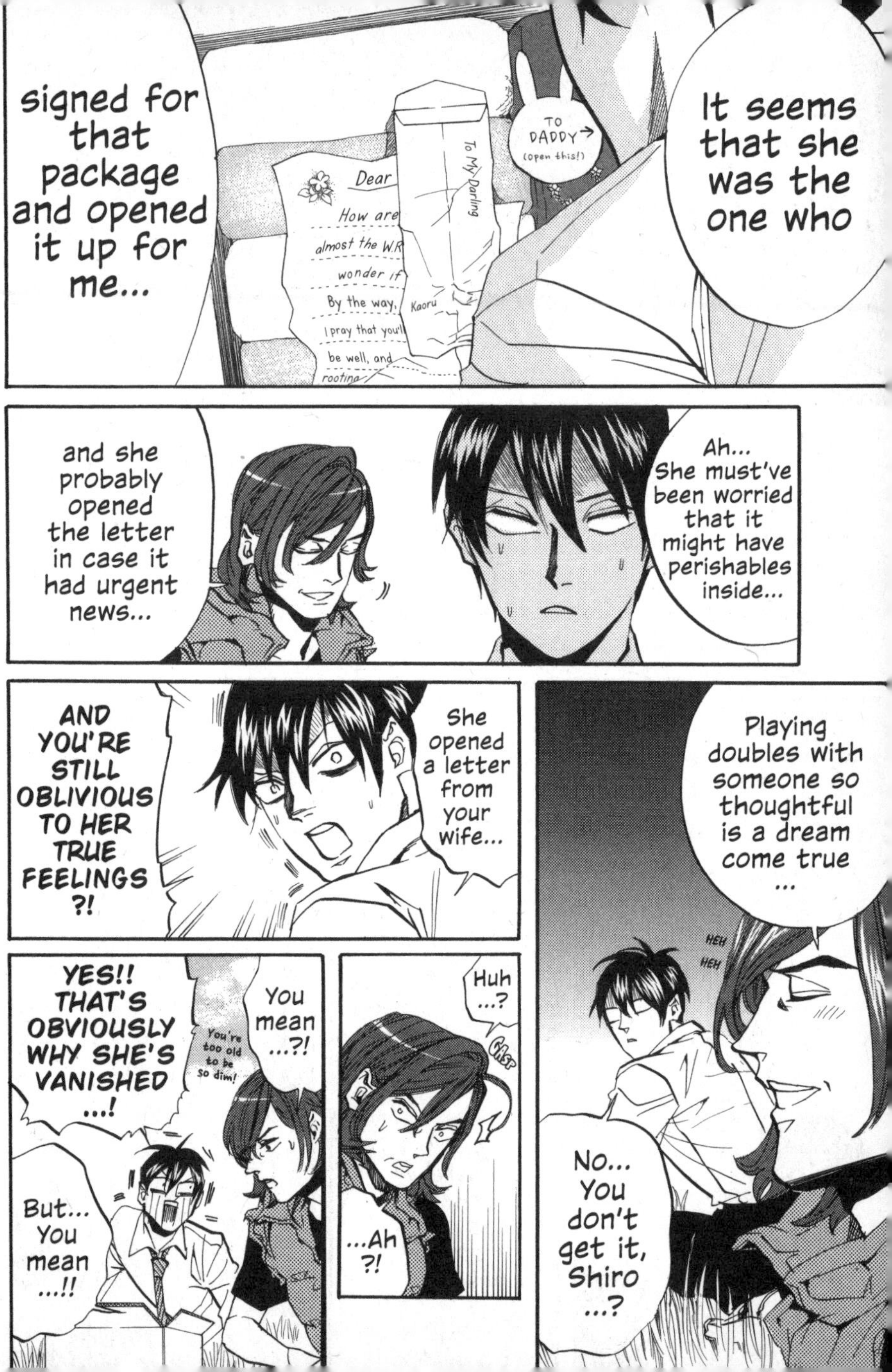
It seems that she was the one who
signed for that package and opened it up for me...
TO DADDY → (open this!)
To My Darling
Dear
How are
almost the W.R
wonder if
By the way,
Kaoru
I pray that you'l
be well, and
Ah... She must've been worried that it might have perishables inside...
and she probably opened the letter in case it had urgent news...
Playing doubles with someone so thoughtful is a dream come true ...
HEH HEH
No... You don't get it, Shiro ...?
She opened a letter from your wife...
AND YOU'RE STILL OBLIVIOUS TO HER TRUE FEELINGS ?!
Huh ...?
GASP
...Ah ?!
You mean ...?!
You're too old to be so dim!
YES!! THAT'S OBVIOUSLY WHY SHE'S VANISHED ...!
But... You mean ...!!

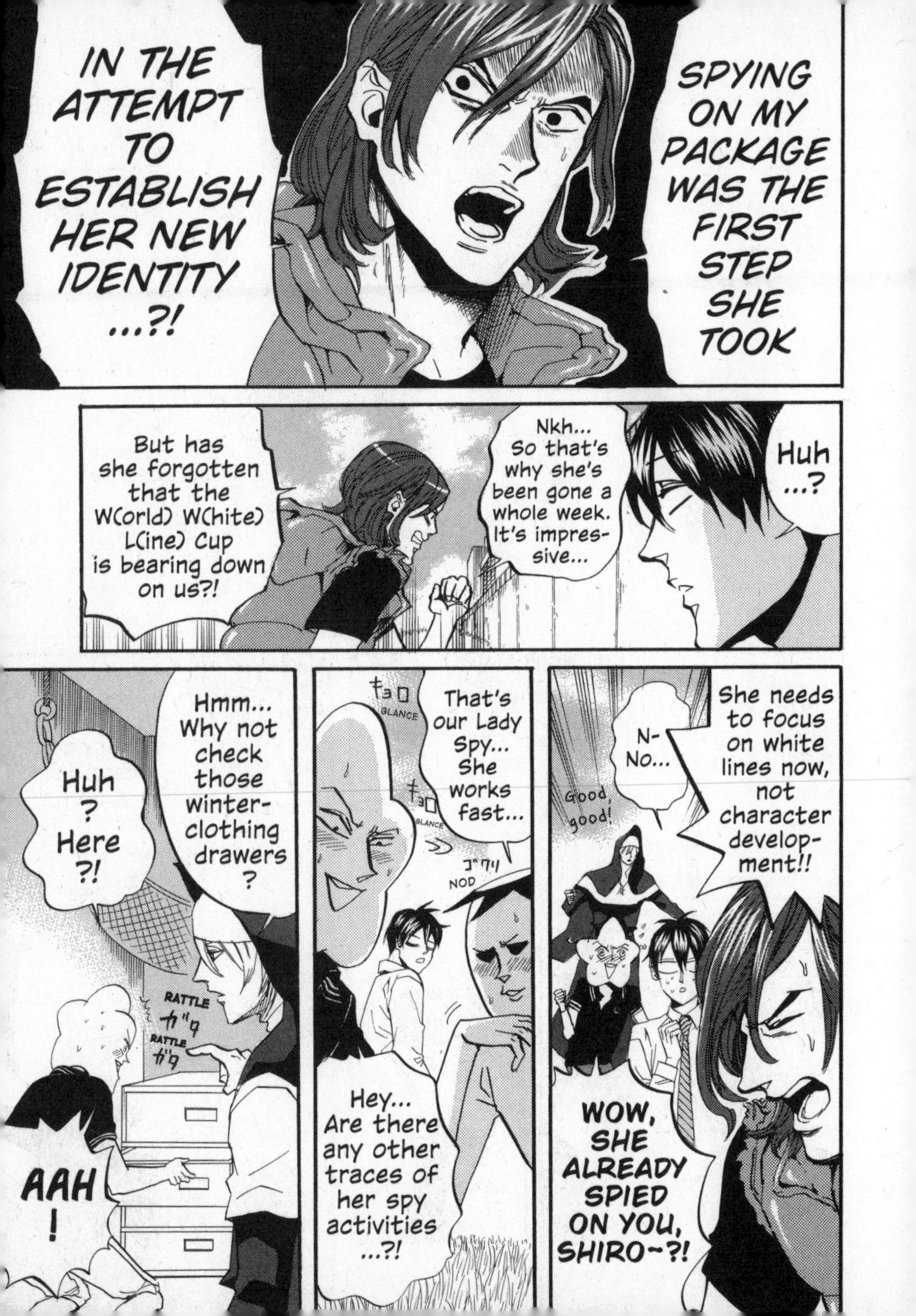
SPYING ON MY PACKAGE WAS THE FIRST STEP SHE TOOK
IN THE ATTEMPT TO ESTABLISH HER NEW IDENTITY ...?!
Huh ...?
Nkh... So that's why she's been gone a whole week. It's impressive...
But has she forgotten that the W(orld) W(hite) L(ine) Cup is bearing down on us?!
She needs to focus on white lines now, not character development!!
N- No...
Good, good!
WOW, SHE ALREADY SPIED ON YOU, SHIRO~?!
GLANCE
That's our Lady Spy... She works fast...
GLANCE
NOD
Hey... Are there any other traces of her spy activities ...?!
Hmm... Why not check those winter-clothing drawers ?
Huh ? Here ?!
RATTLE
RATTLE
AAH !

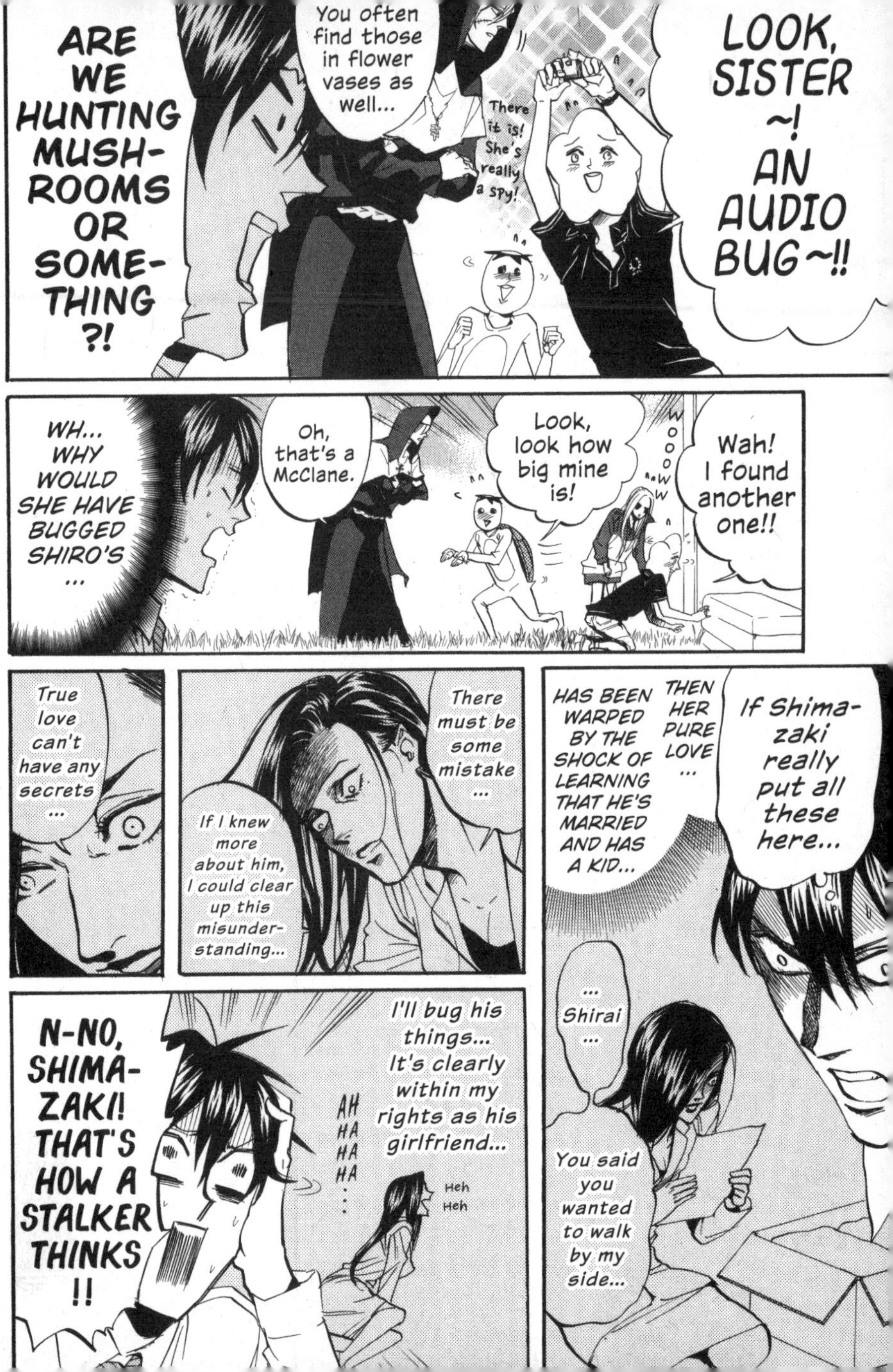
LOOK, SISTER ~! AN AUDIO BUG~!!
There it is! She's really a spy!
You often find those in flower vases as well...
ARE WE HUNTING MUSH-ROOMS OR SOME-THING?!
Wah! I found another one!!
WOOOOW
Look, look how big mine is!
Oh, that's a McClane.
WH... WHY WOULD SHE HAVE BUGGED SHIRO'S ...
If Shima-zaki really put all these here...
THEN HER PURE LOVE ...
HAS BEEN WARPED BY THE SHOCK OF LEARNING THAT HE'S MARRIED AND HAS A KID...
... Shirai ...
You said you wanted to walk by my side...
There must be some mistake ...
If I knew more about him, I could clear up this misunder-standing...
True love can't have any secrets ...
I'll bug his things... It's clearly within my rights as his girlfriend...
AH HA HA HA...
Heh Heh
N-NO, SHIMA-ZAKI! THAT'S HOW A STALKER THINKS!!

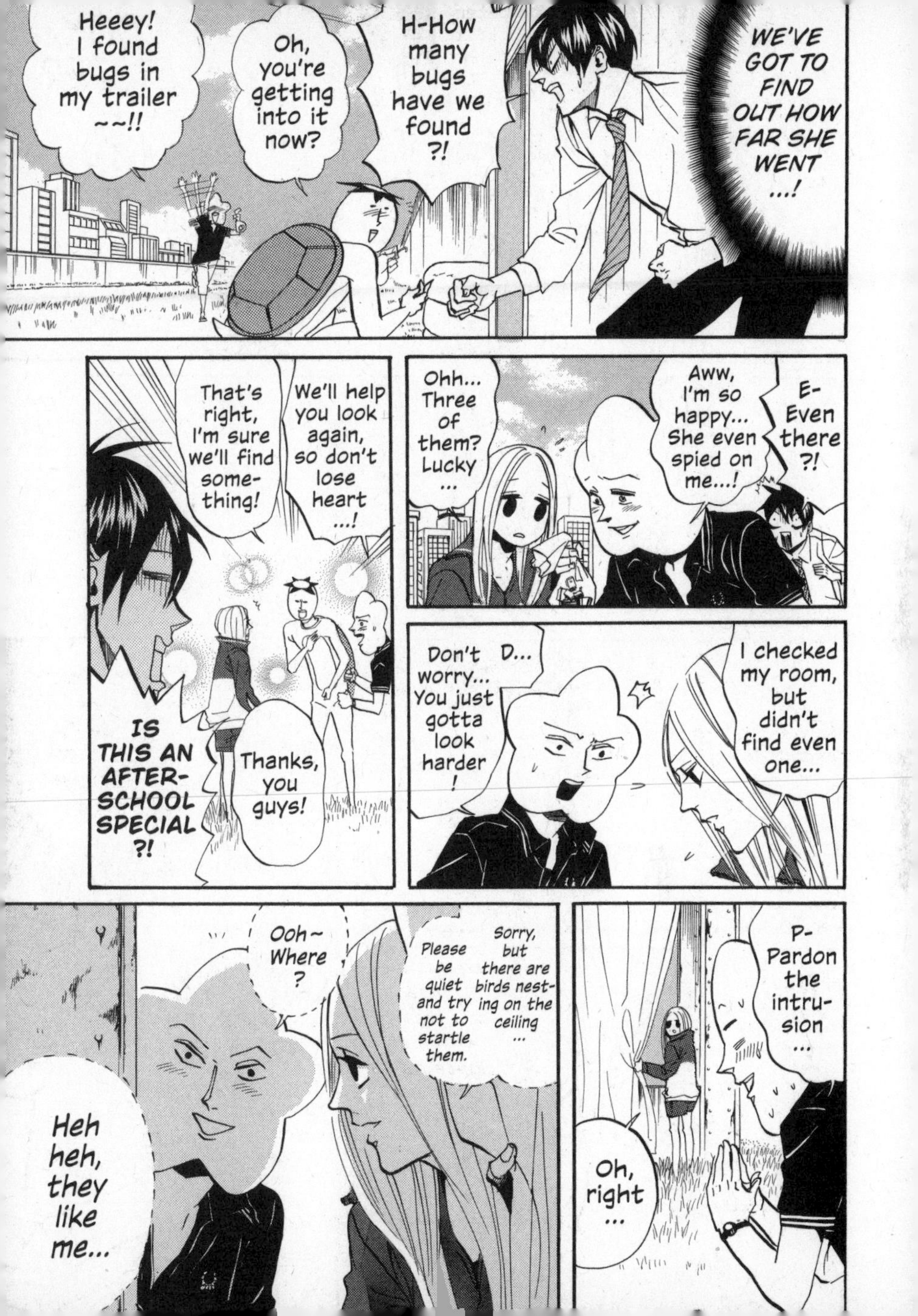
WE'VE GOT TO FIND OUT HOW FAR SHE WENT ...!
H-How many bugs have we found ?!
Oh, you're getting into it now?
Heeey! I found bugs in my trailer ~~!!
E- Even there ?!
Aww, I'm so happy... She even spied on me...!
Ohh... Three of them? Lucky ...
I checked my room, but didn't find even one...
D...
Don't worry... You just gotta look harder !
We'll help you look again, so don't lose heart ...!
That's right, I'm sure we'll find some-thing!
Thanks, you guys!
IS THIS AN AFTER-SCHOOL SPECIAL ?!
P- Pardon the intru-sion ...
Oh, right ...
Sorry, but there are birds nest-ing on the ceiling ...
Please be quiet and try not to startle them.
Ooh~ Where ?
Heh heh, they like me...

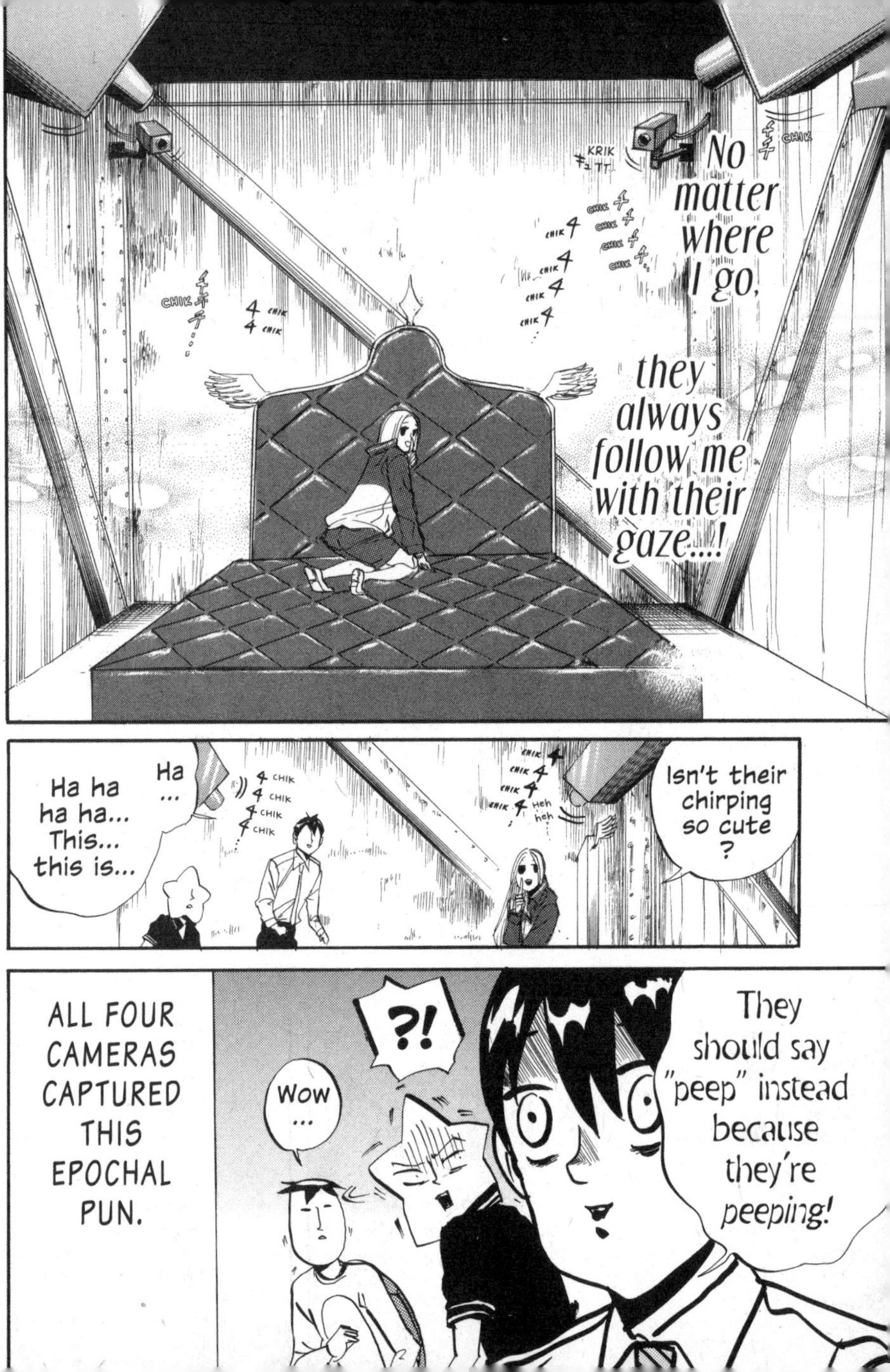
CHIK
KRIK
No matter where I go,
they always follow me with their gaze...!
CHIK CHIK CHIK CHIK
CHIK CHIK CHIK CHIK
CHIK CHIK CHIK
Isn't their chirping so cute?
CHIK CHIK CHIK CHIK
Heh heh
CHIK CHIK CHIK CHIK
Ha ...
Ha ha ha ha... This... this is...
They should say "peep" instead because they're peeping!
?!
Wow ...
ALL FOUR CAMERAS CAPTURED THIS EPOCHAL PUN.

Chapter 251: Spied-On Festival

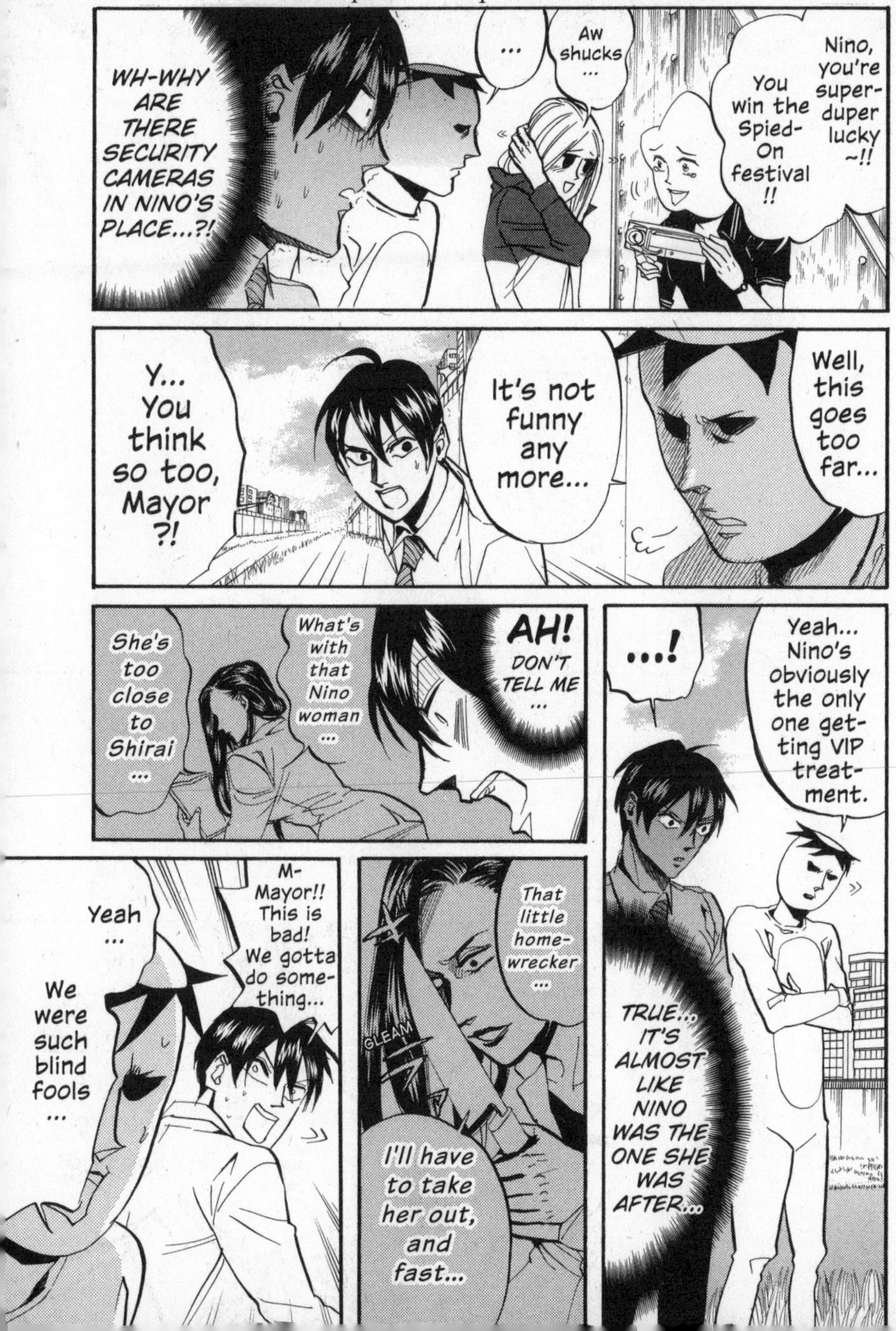
Nino, you're super-duper lucky ~!!
You win the Spied-On festival !!
Aw shucks ...
...
WH-WHY ARE THERE SECURITY CAMERAS IN NINO'S PLACE...?!
Well, this goes too far...
It's not funny any more...
Y... You think so too, Mayor ?!
Yeah... Nino's obviously the only one getting VIP treatment.
...!
TRUE... IT'S ALMOST LIKE NINO WAS THE ONE SHE WAS AFTER...
AH! DON'T TELL ME ...
What's with that Nino woman ...
She's too close to Shirai ...
That little home-wrecker ...
GLEAM
I'll have to take her out, and fast...
M-Mayor!! This is bad! We gotta do something...
Yeah ...
We were such blind fools ...

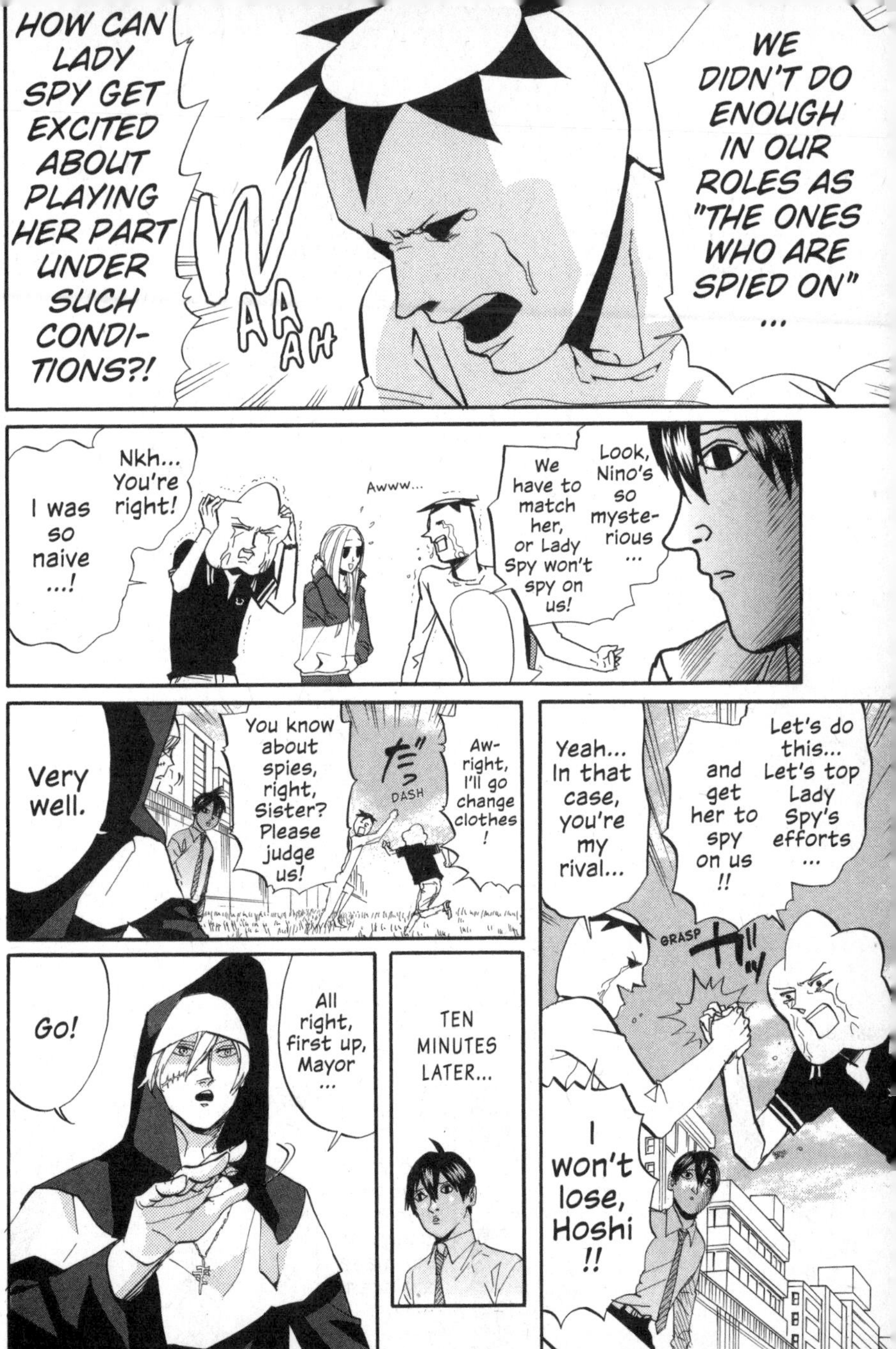
WE DIDN'T DO ENOUGH IN OUR ROLES AS "THE ONES WHO ARE SPIED ON"...
HOW CAN LADY SPY GET EXCITED ABOUT PLAYING HER PART UNDER SUCH CONDITIONS?!
WAAAH
Look, Nino's so mysterious...
We have to match her, or Lady Spy won't spy on us!
Awww...
Nkh... You're right!
I was so naive...!
Let's do this... Let's top Lady Spy's efforts...
and get her to spy on us!!
Yeah... In that case, you're my rival...
GRASP
I won't lose, Hoshi!!
Aw-right, I'll go change clothes!
DASH
You know about spies, right, Sister? Please judge us!
Very well.
TEN MINUTES LATER...
All right, first up, Mayor...
Go!

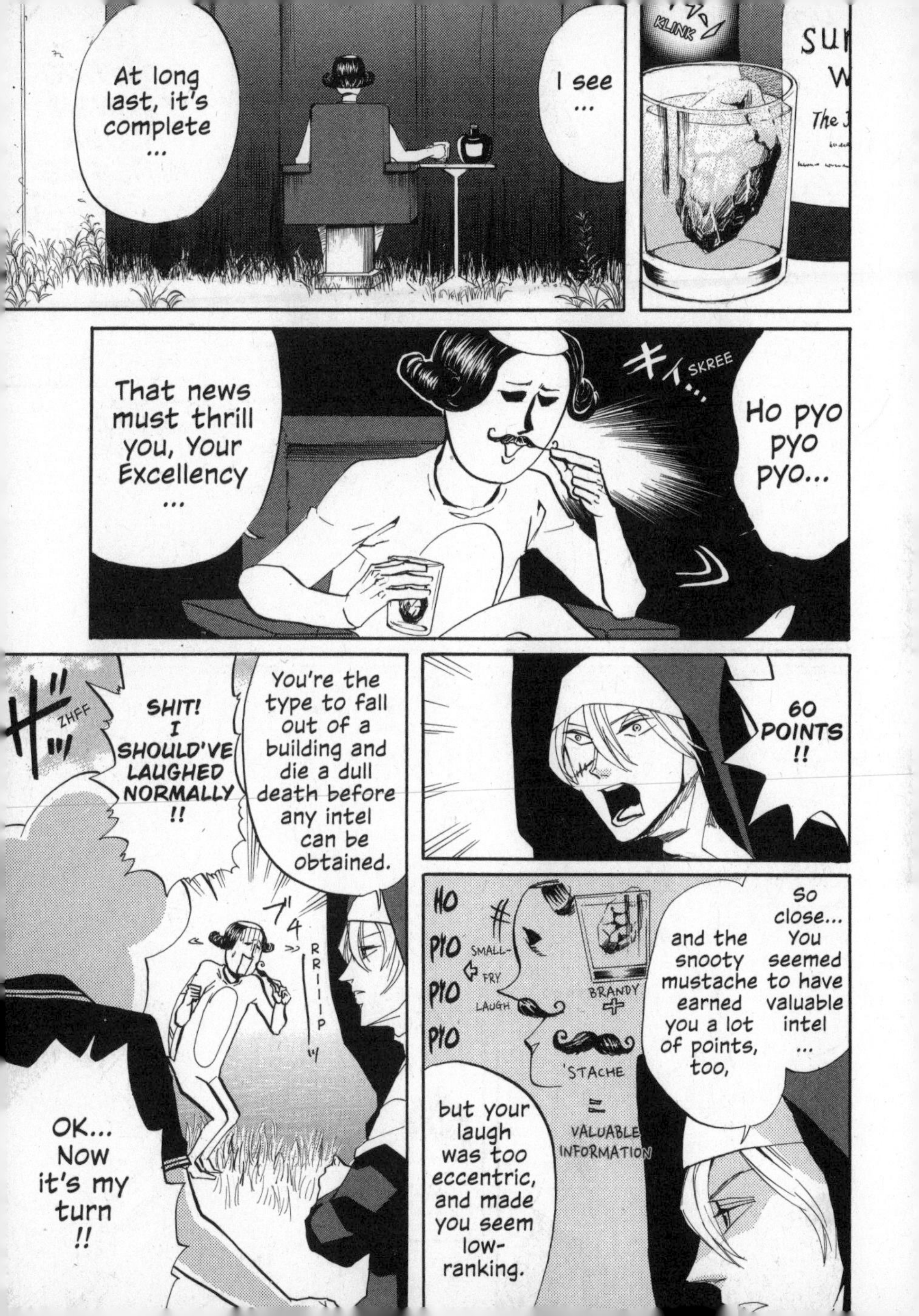
KLINK
I see ...
At long last, it's complete ...
Ho pyo pyo pyo...
SKREE
That news must thrill you, Your Excellency ...
60 POINTS !!
You're the type to fall out of a building and die a dull death before any intel can be obtained.
SHIT! I SHOULD'VE LAUGHED NORMALLY !!
ZHFF
So close... You seemed to have valuable intel ...
and the snooty mustache earned you a lot of points, too,
HO PYO PYO PYO
SMALL-FRY LAUGH
BRANDY + 'STACHE = VALUABLE INFORMATION
but your laugh was too eccentric, and made you seem low-ranking.
RRIIIP
OK... Now it's my turn !!

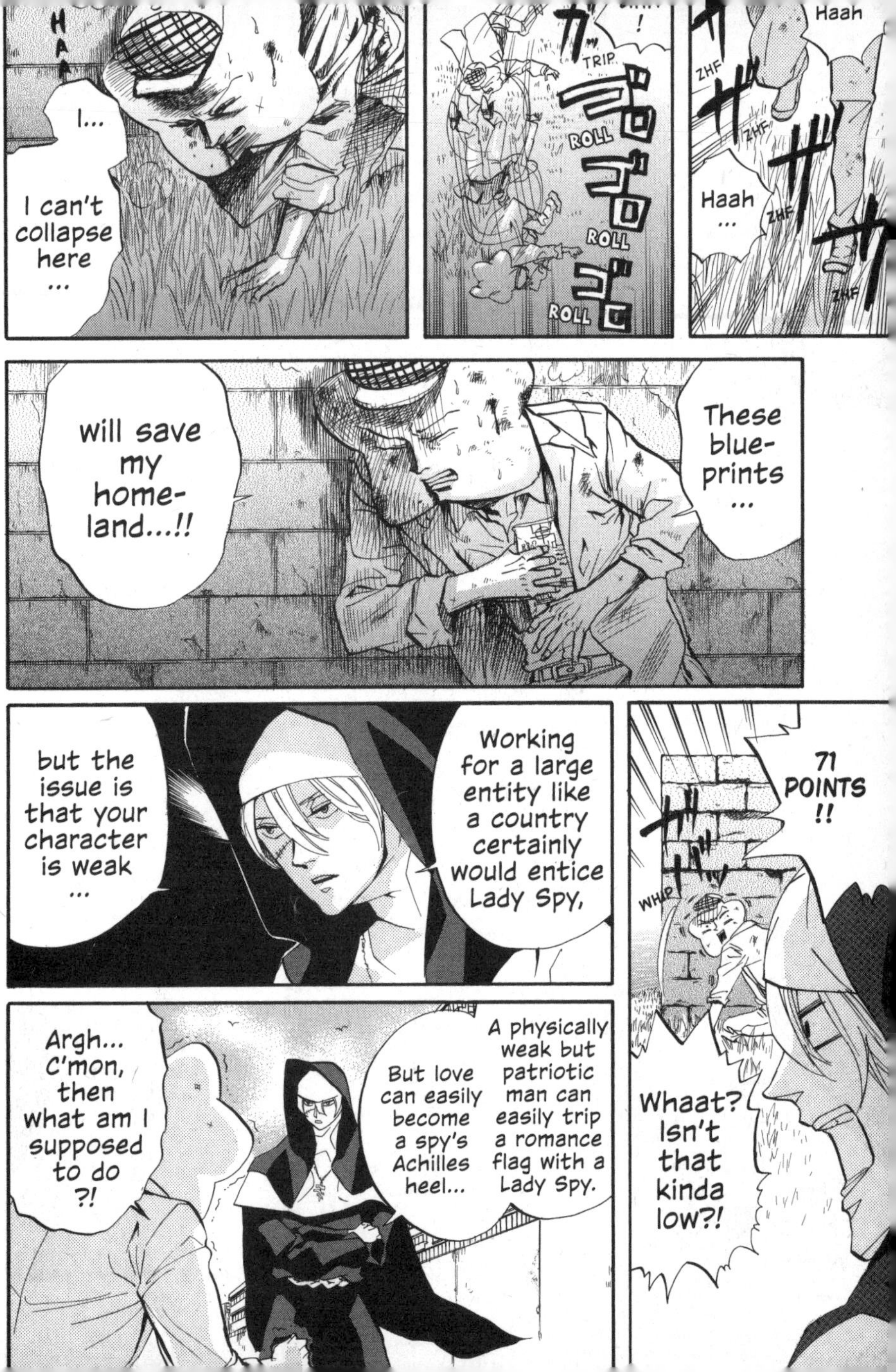
Haah
ZHF
ZHF
Haah ...
ZHF
ZHF
!
TRIP
ROLL
ROLL
ROLL
HAA
I...
I can't collapse here ...
These blue-prints ...
will save my home-land...!!
71 POINTS !!
WHIP
Whaat? Isn't that kinda low?!
Working for a large entity like a country certainly would entice Lady Spy,
but the issue is that your character is weak ...
A physically weak but patriotic man can easily trip a romance flag with a Lady Spy.
But love can easily become a spy's Achilles heel...
Argh... C'mon, then what am I supposed to do ?!

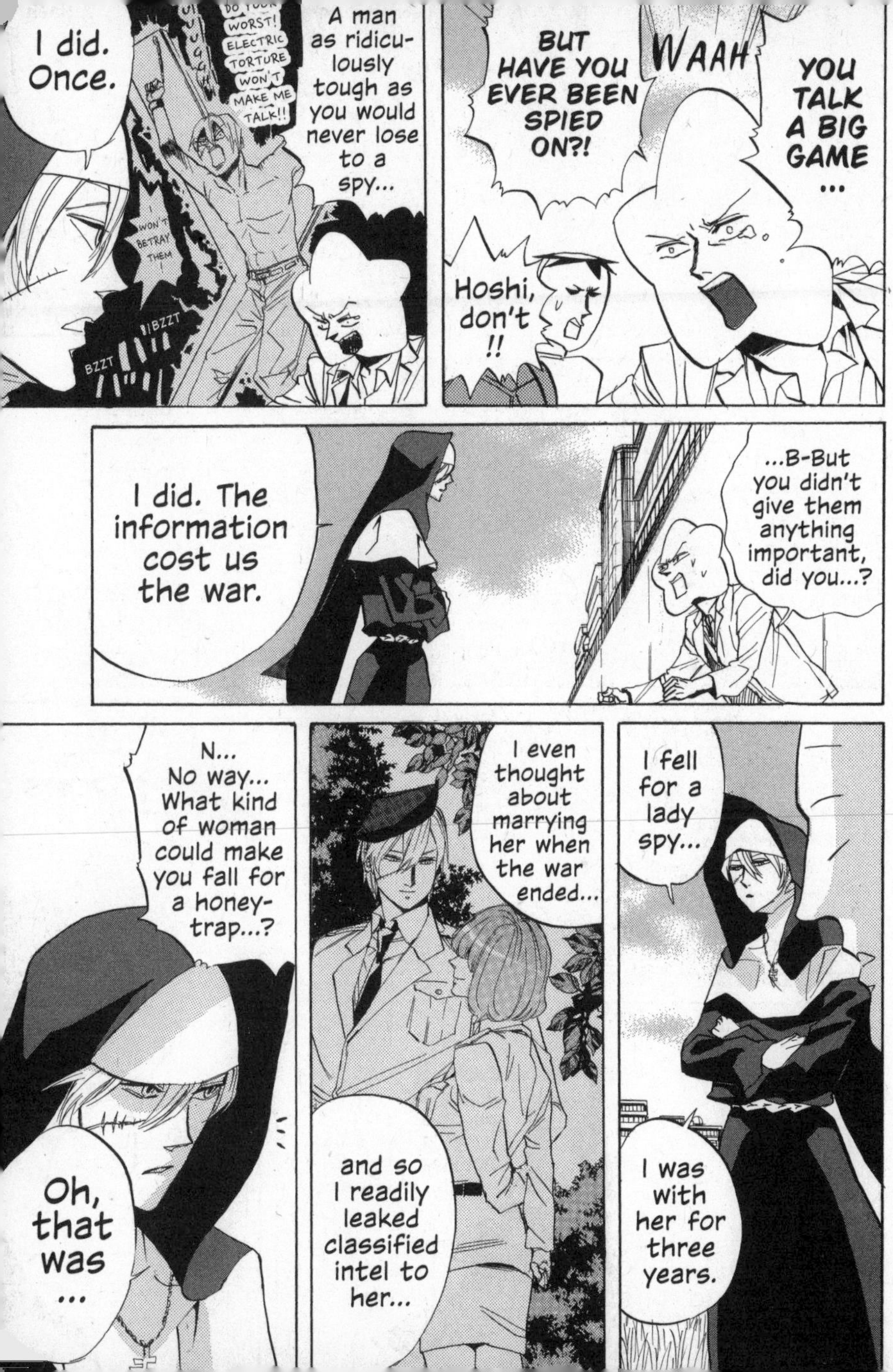
YOU TALK A BIG GAME ...
WAAH
BUT HAVE YOU EVER BEEN SPIED ON?!
Hoshi, don't !!
A man as ridicu-lously tough as you would never lose to a spy...
DO YOUR WORST! ELECTRIC TORTURE WON'T MAKE ME TALK!!
I did. Once.
I WON'T BETRAY THEM
BZZT
BZZT
...B-But you didn't give them anything important, did you...?
I did. The information cost us the war.
I fell for a lady spy...
I was with her for three years.
I even thought about marrying her when the war ended...
and so I readily leaked classified intel to her...
N... No way... What kind of woman could make you fall for a honey-trap...?
Oh, that was ...

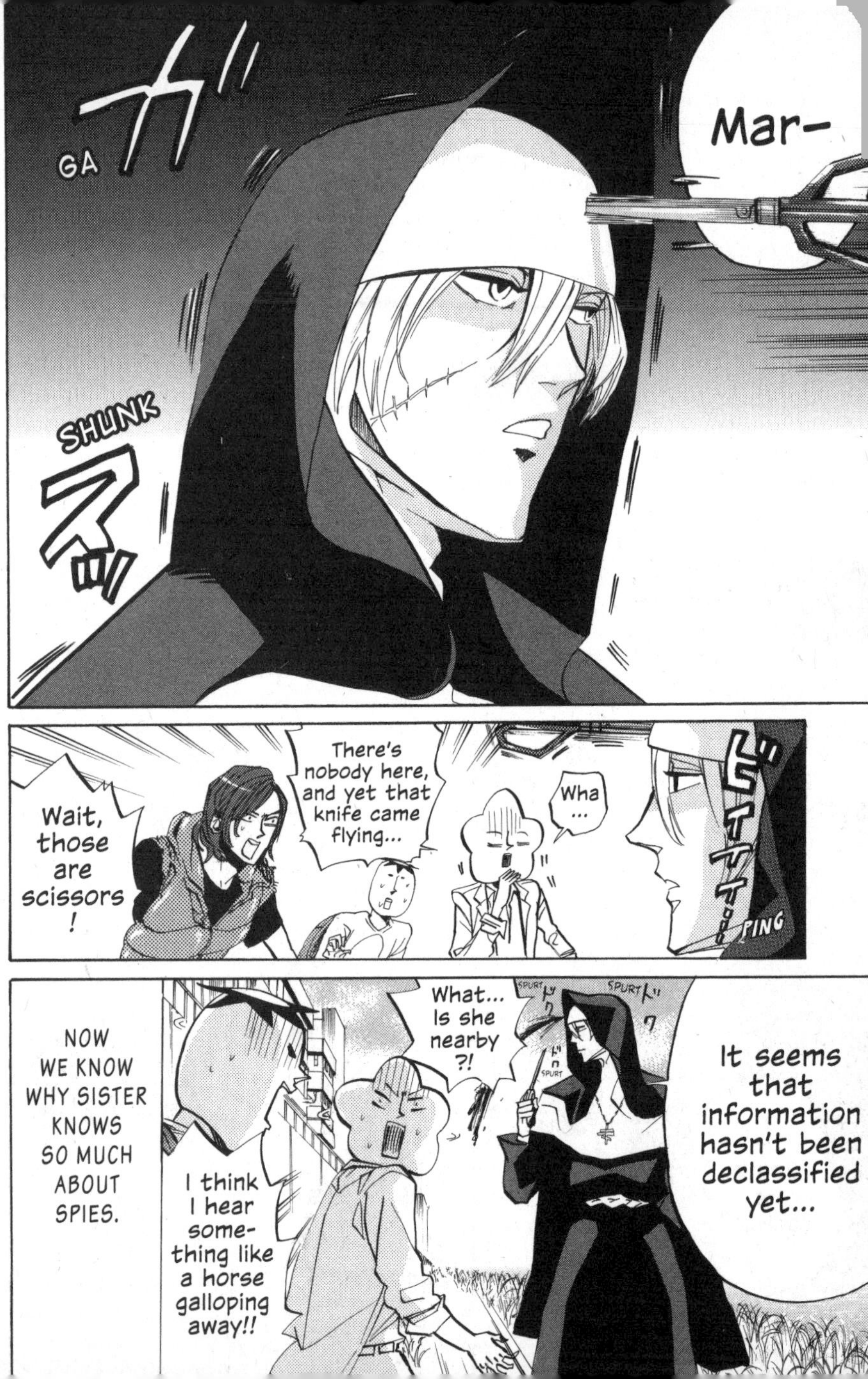
Mar-
GA
SHUNK
PING
Wha
...
There's nobody here, and yet that knife came flying...
Wait, those are scissors!
It seems that information hasn't been declassified yet...
SPURT
SPURT
SPURT
What... Is she nearby?!
I think I hear something like a horse galloping away!!
NOW WE KNOW WHY SISTER KNOWS SO MUCH ABOUT SPIES.

Chapter 252: Call and She Shall Appear...

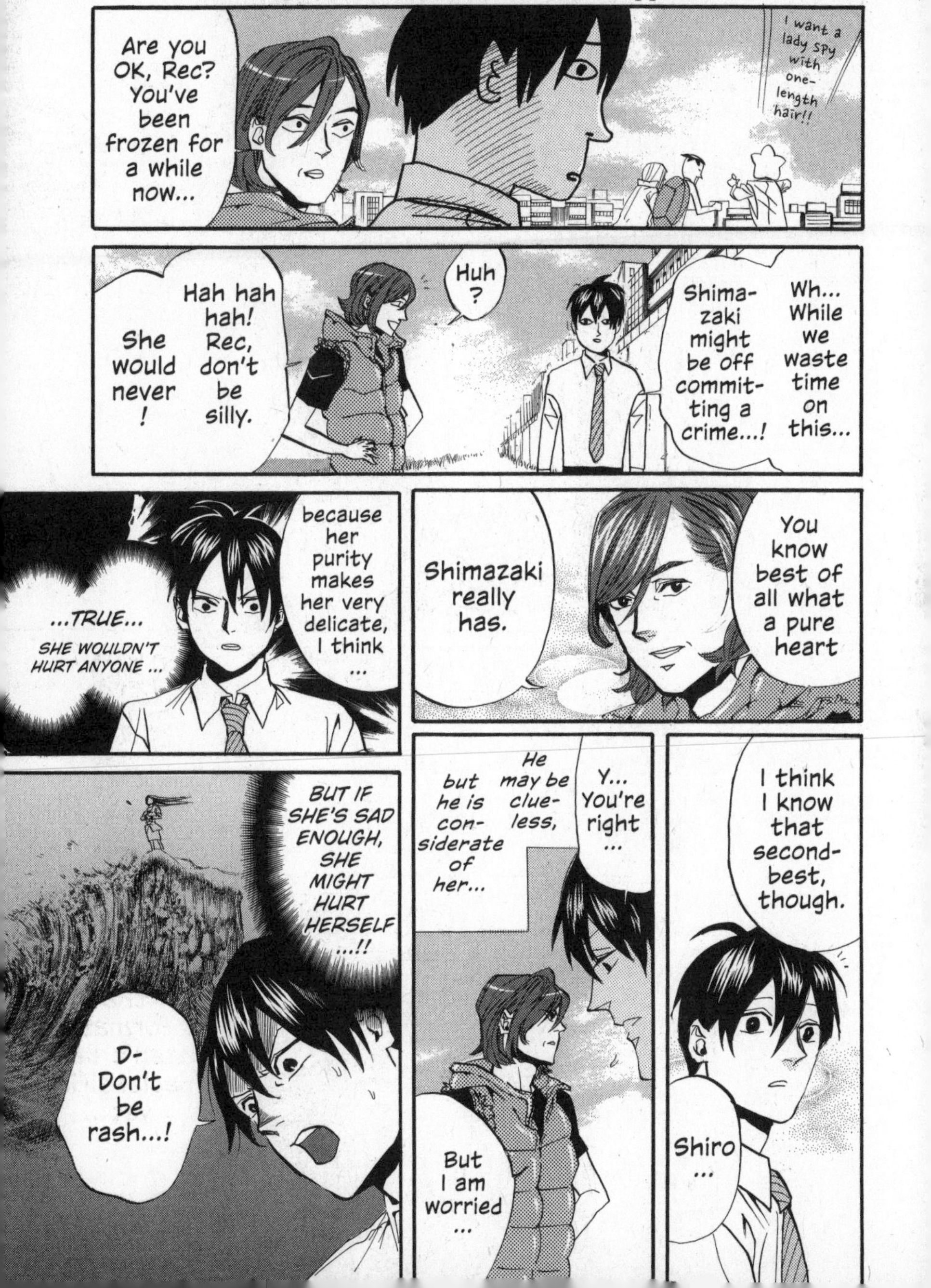
I want a lady spy with one-length hair!!
Are you OK, Rec? You've been frozen for a while now...
Wh... While we waste time on this...
Shimazaki might be off committing a crime...!
Huh?
Hah hah hah! Rec, don't be silly.
She would never!
You know best of all what a pure heart
Shimazaki really has.
because her purity makes her very delicate, I think...
...TRUE... SHE WOULDN'T HURT ANYONE ...
I think I know that second-best, though.
Shiro...
Y... You're right...
He may be clueless,
but he is considerate of her...
But I am worried...
BUT IF SHE'S SAD ENOUGH, SHE MIGHT HURT HERSELF...!!
D-Don't be rash...!

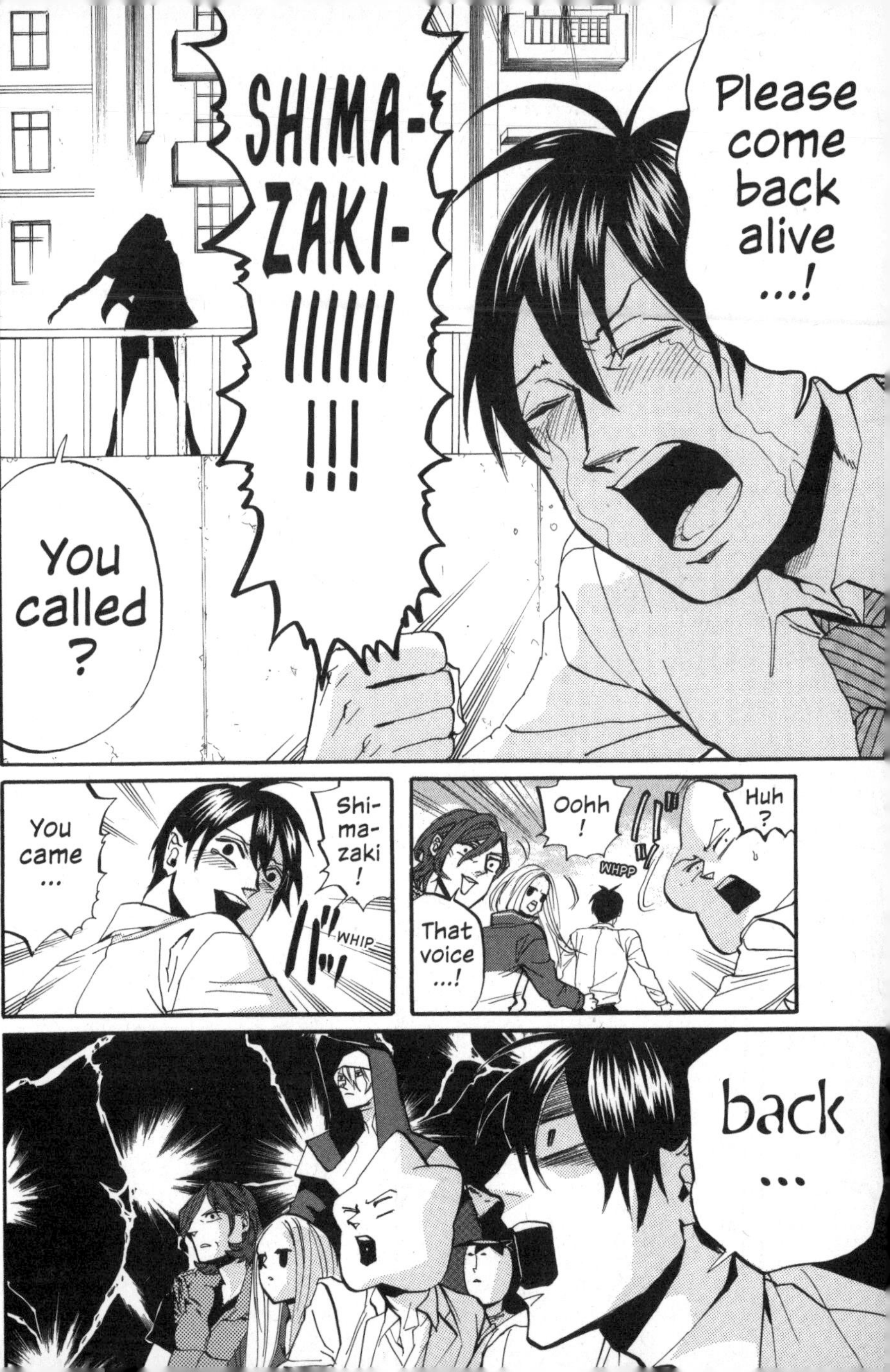
Please come back alive ...!
SHIMA-ZAKI-!!!!!!!!!!
You called ?
Huh ?
Oohh !
WHPP
That voice ...!
Shi-ma-zaki !
You came ...
WHIP
back ...

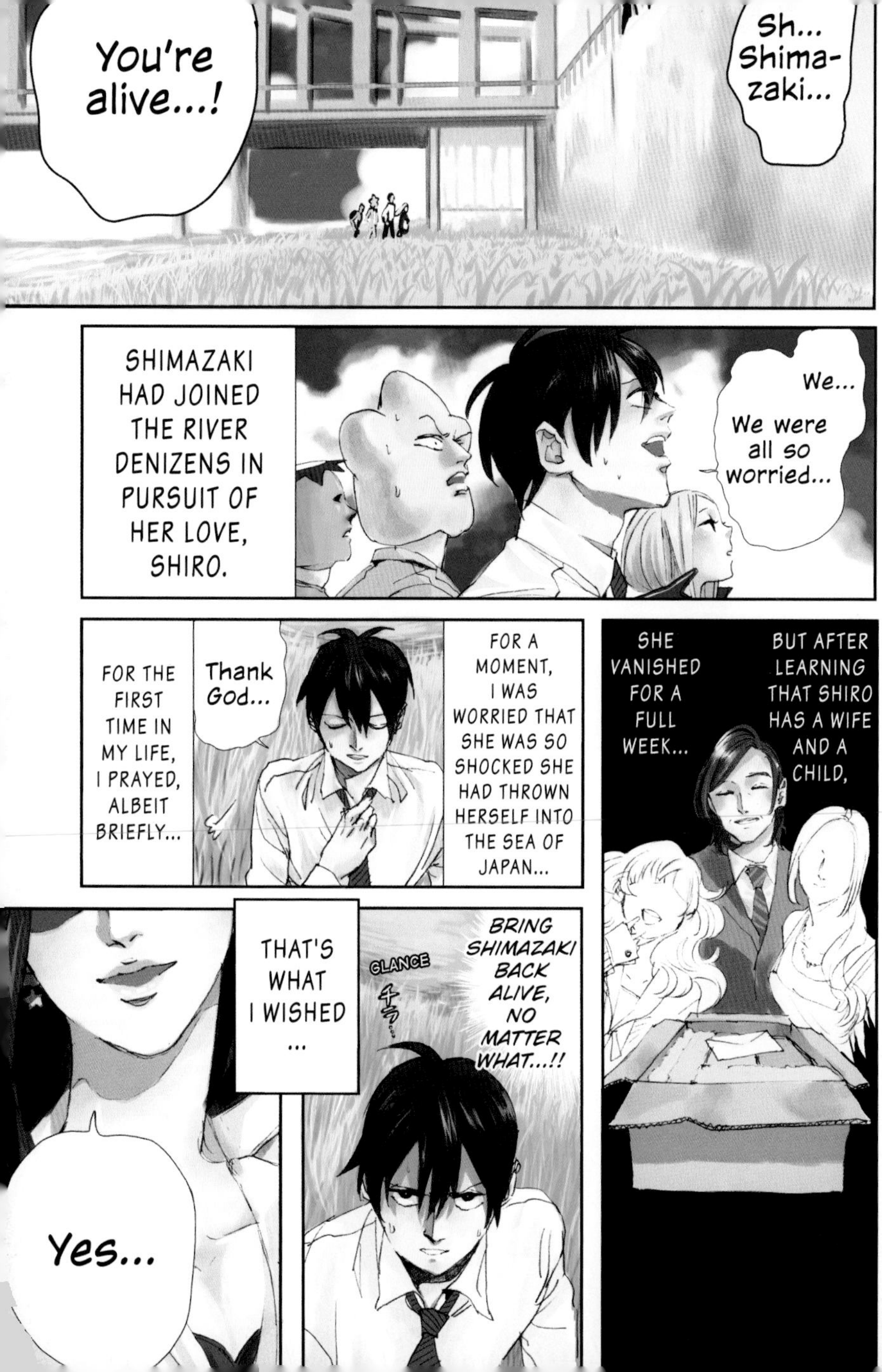
Sh... Shima-zaki...
You're alive...!
We... We were all so worried...
SHIMAZAKI HAD JOINED THE RIVER DENIZENS IN PURSUIT OF HER LOVE, SHIRO.
BUT AFTER LEARNING THAT SHIRO HAS A WIFE AND A CHILD,
SHE VANISHED FOR A FULL WEEK...
FOR A MOMENT, I WAS WORRIED THAT SHE WAS SO SHOCKED SHE HAD THROWN HERSELF INTO THE SEA OF JAPAN...
Thank God...
FOR THE FIRST TIME IN MY LIFE, I PRAYED, ALBEIT BRIEFLY...
BRING SHIMAZAKI BACK ALIVE, NO MATTER WHAT...!!
GLANCE
THAT'S WHAT I WISHED ...
Yes...

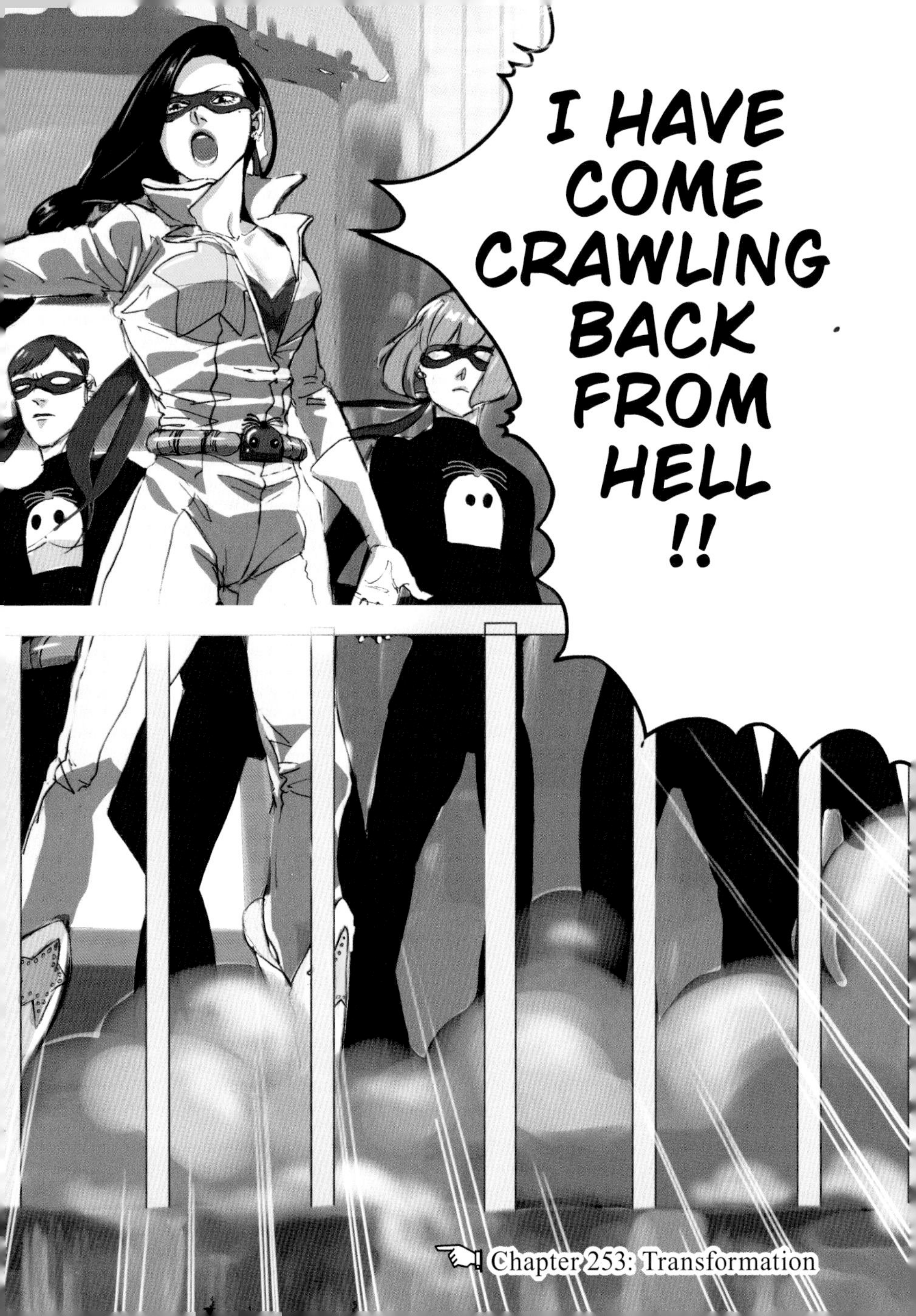
I HAVE COME CRAWLING BACK FROM HELL !!

Chapter 253: Transformation

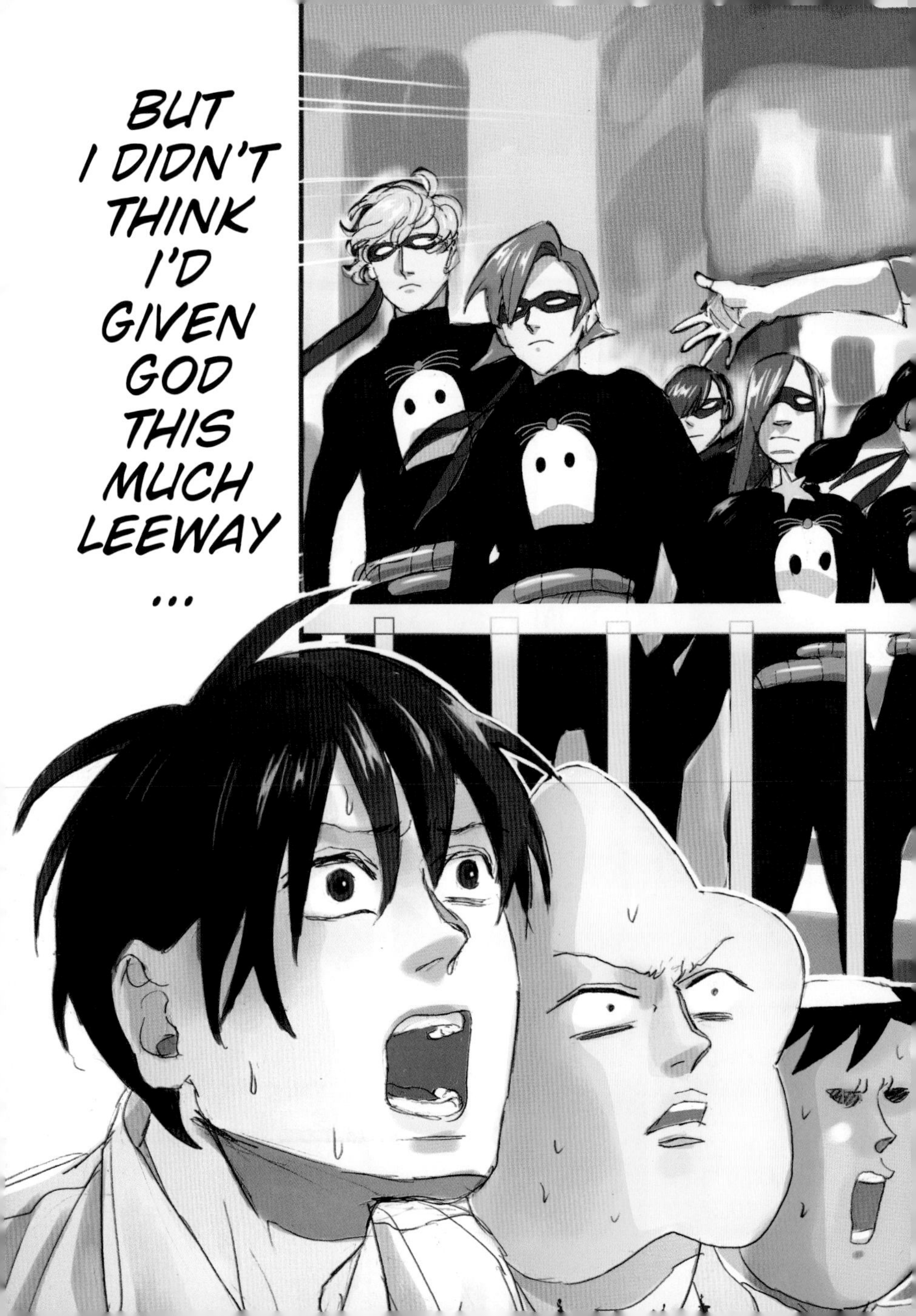
BUT I DIDN'T THINK I'D GIVEN GOD THIS MUCH LEEWAY ...

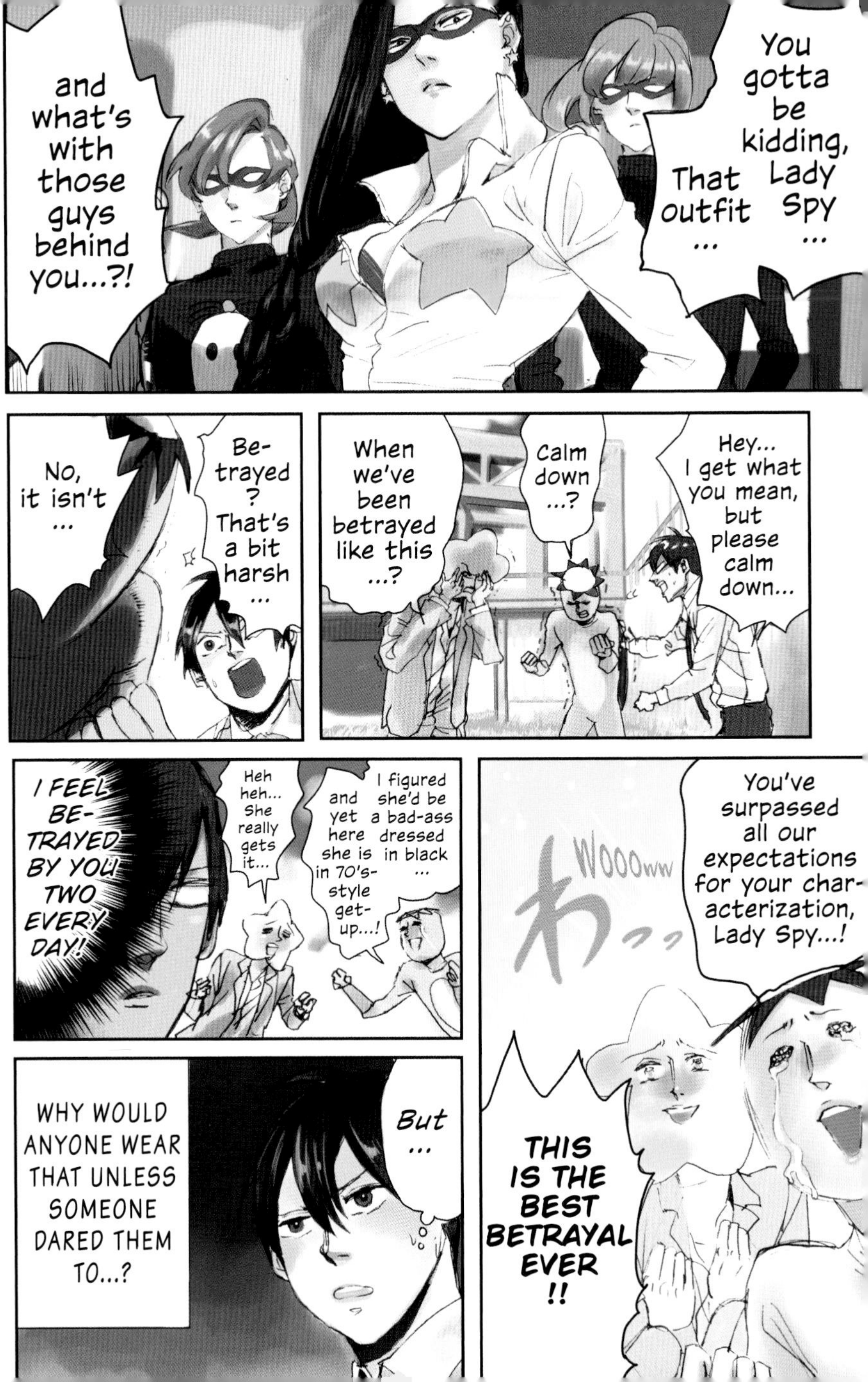
You gotta be kidding, Lady Spy...
That outfit...
and what's with those guys behind you...?!
Hey... I get what you mean, but please calm down...
Calm down...?
When we've been betrayed like this...?
Be-trayed? That's a bit harsh...
No, it isn't...
You've surpassed all our expectations for your char-acterization, Lady Spy...!
WOOOww
わっっ
THIS IS THE BEST BETRAYAL EVER!!
I figured she'd be a bad-ass dressed in black...
and yet here she is in 70's-style get-up...!
Heh heh... She really gets it...
I FEEL BE-TRAYED BY YOU TWO EVERY DAY!
But...
WHY WOULD ANYONE WEAR THAT UNLESS SOMEONE DARED THEM TO...?

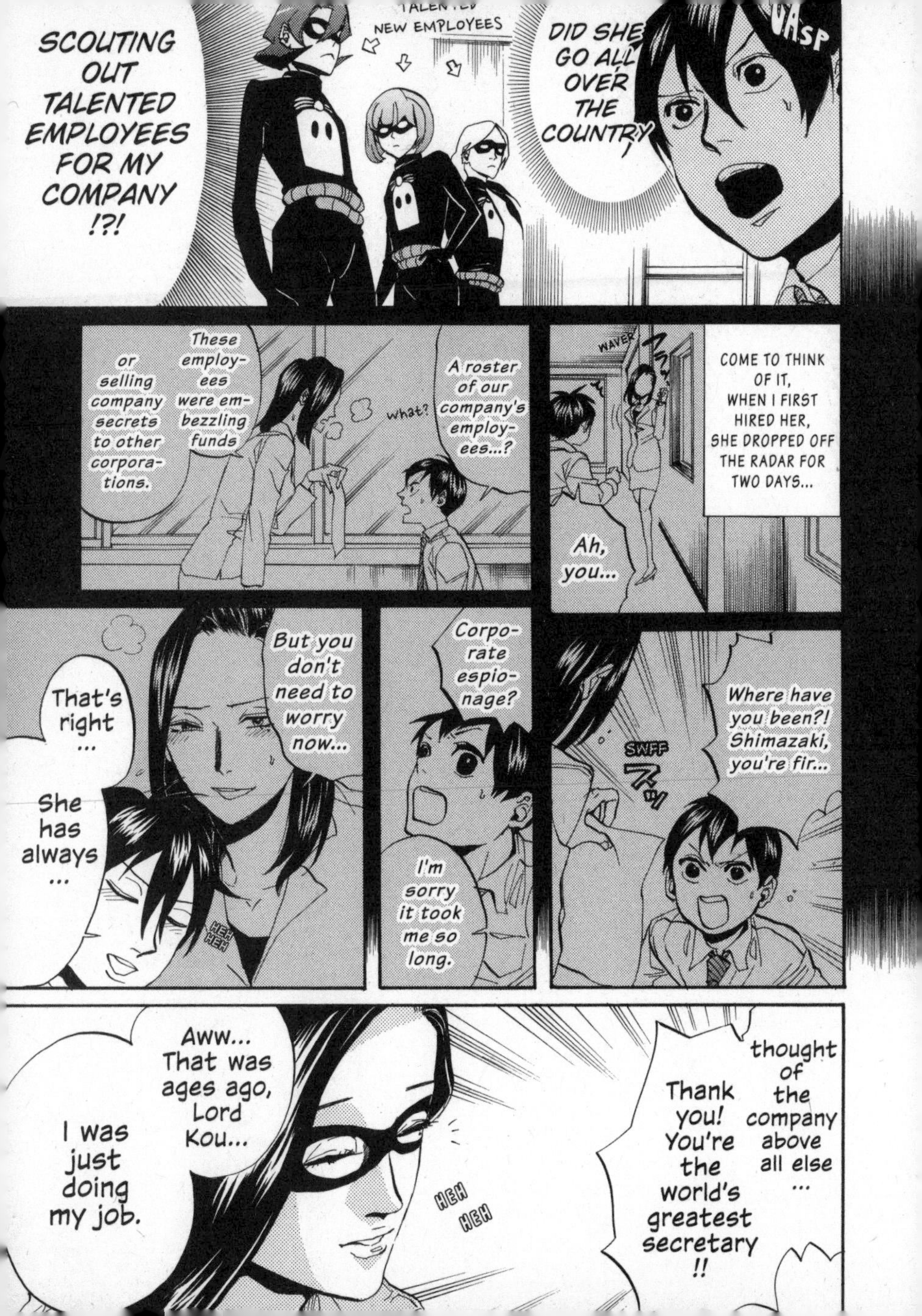
DID SHE GO ALL OVER THE COUNTRY
TALENTED NEW EMPLOYEES
SCOUTING OUT TALENTED EMPLOYEES FOR MY COMPANY !?!
COME TO THINK OF IT, WHEN I FIRST HIRED HER, SHE DROPPED OFF THE RADAR FOR TWO DAYS...
WAVER
Ah, you...
A roster of our company's employees...?
what?
These employees were embezzling funds
or selling company secrets to other corporations.
Where have you been?! Shimazaki, you're fir...
SWFF
Corporate espionage?
I'm sorry it took me so long.
But you don't need to worry now...
That's right...
She has always...
HEH HEH
thought of the company above all else...
Thank you! You're the world's greatest secretary!!
Aww... That was ages ago, Lord Kou...
I was just doing my job.
HEH HEH

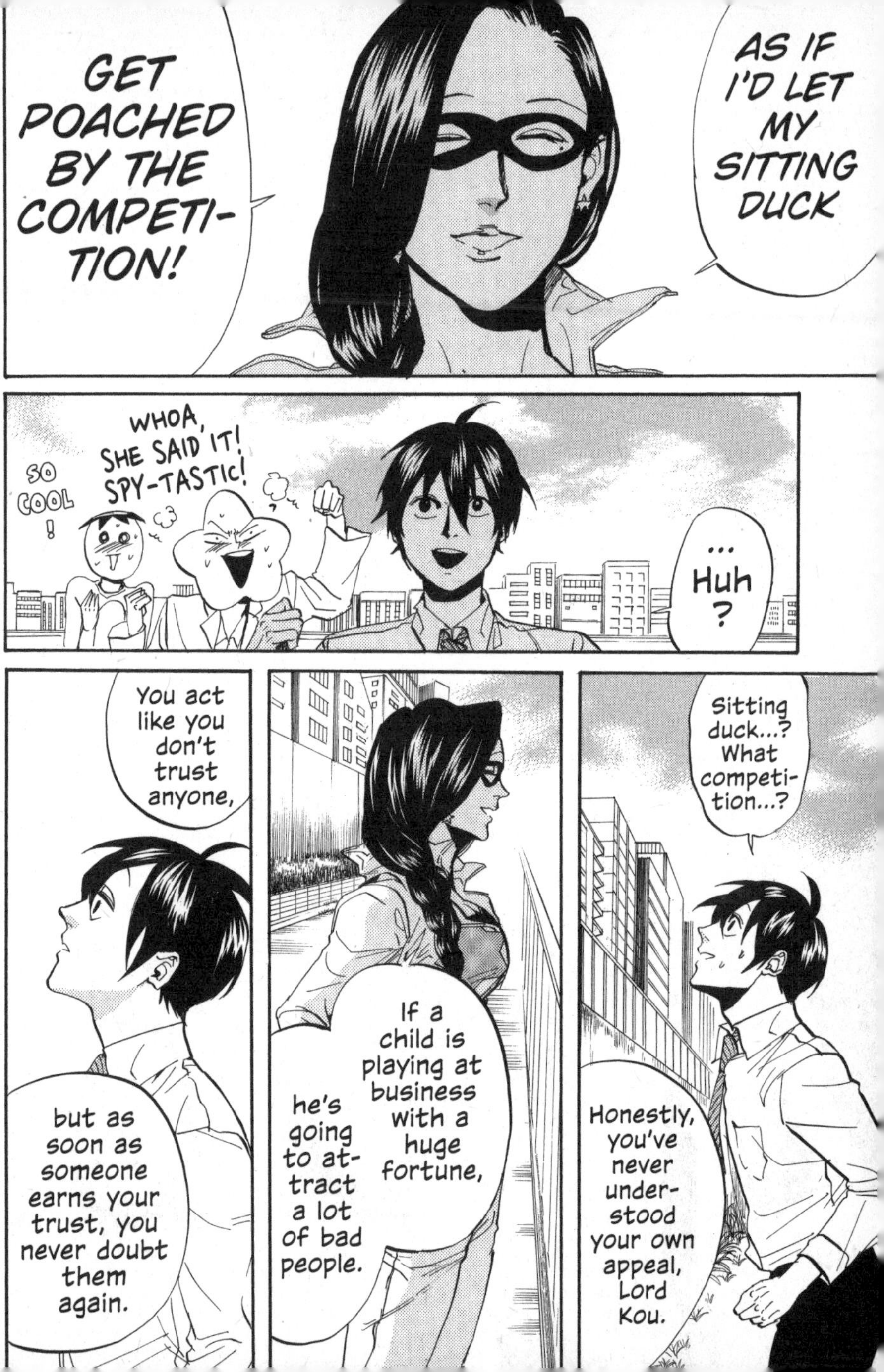
AS IF I'D LET MY SITTING DUCK
GET POACHED BY THE COMPETITION!
... Huh?
WHOA, SHE SAID IT! SPY-TASTIC!
SO COOL!
Sitting duck...? What competition...?
Honestly, you've never understood your own appeal, Lord Kou.
If a child is playing at business with a huge fortune,
he's going to attract a lot of bad people.
You act like you don't trust anyone,
but as soon as someone earns your trust, you never doubt them again.

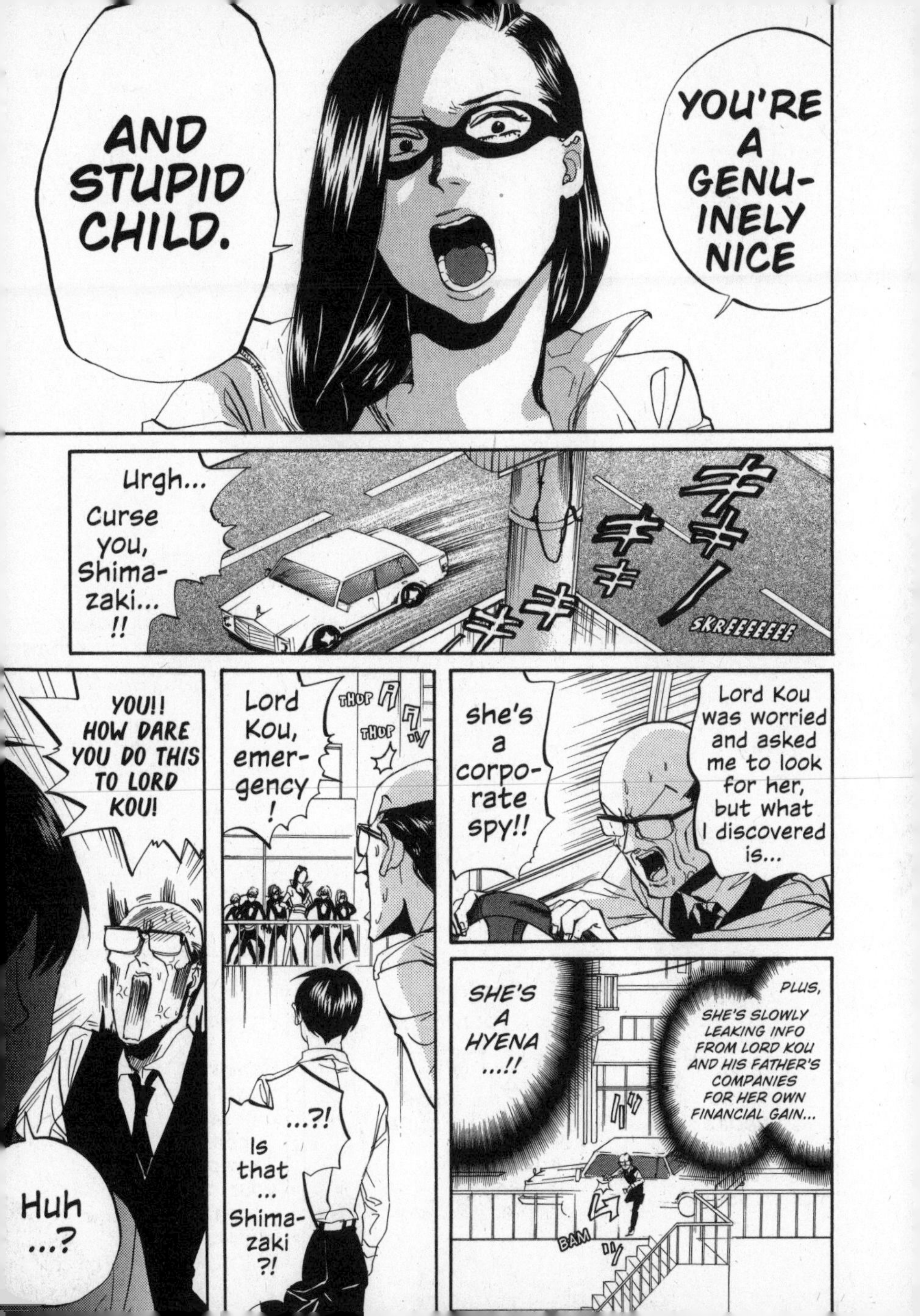
YOU'RE A GENU-INELY NICE
AND STUPID CHILD.
SKREEEEEEE
Urgh...
Curse you, Shima-zaki...!!
Lord Kou was worried and asked me to look for her, but what I discovered is...
she's a corpo-rate spy!!
PLUS,
SHE'S SLOWLY LEAKING INFO FROM LORD KOU AND HIS FATHER'S COMPANIES FOR HER OWN FINANCIAL GAIN...
SHE'S A HYENA...!!
BAM
THUP
THUP
Lord Kou, emer-gency!
...?!
Is that ... Shima-zaki ?!
YOU!! HOW DARE YOU DO THIS TO LORD KOU!
Huh ...?

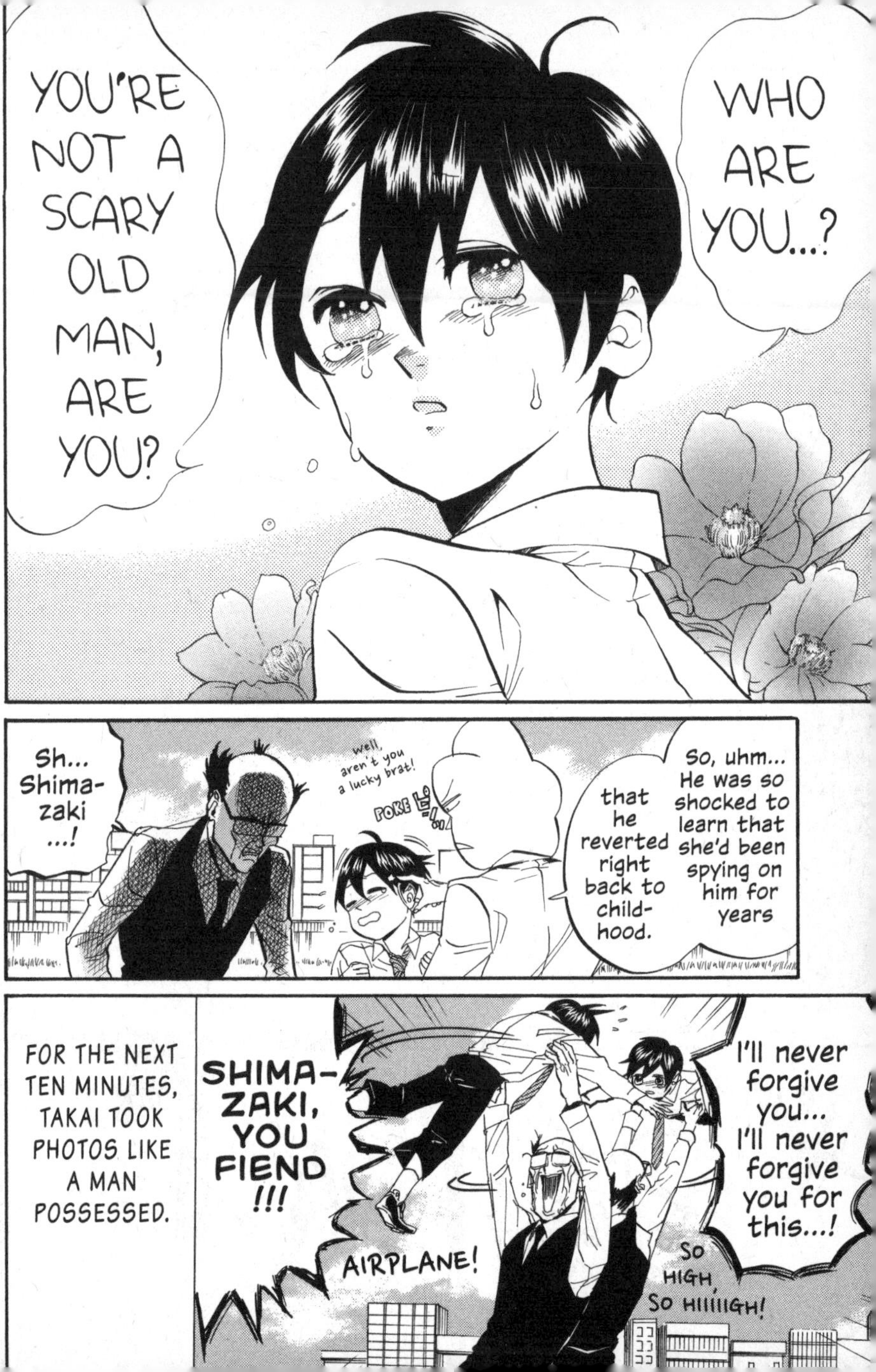
WHO ARE YOU...?
YOU'RE NOT A SCARY OLD MAN, ARE YOU?
So, uhm... He was so shocked to learn that she'd been spying on him for years
that he reverted right back to childhood.
well, aren't you a lucky brat!
POKE
Sh... Shimazaki ...!
I'll never forgive you... I'll never forgive you for this...!
SO HIGH, SO HIIIIIGH!
AIRPLANE!
SHIMAZAKI, YOU FIEND!!!
FOR THE NEXT TEN MINUTES, TAKAI TOOK PHOTOS LIKE A MAN POSSESSED.

Chapter 254: Ritual

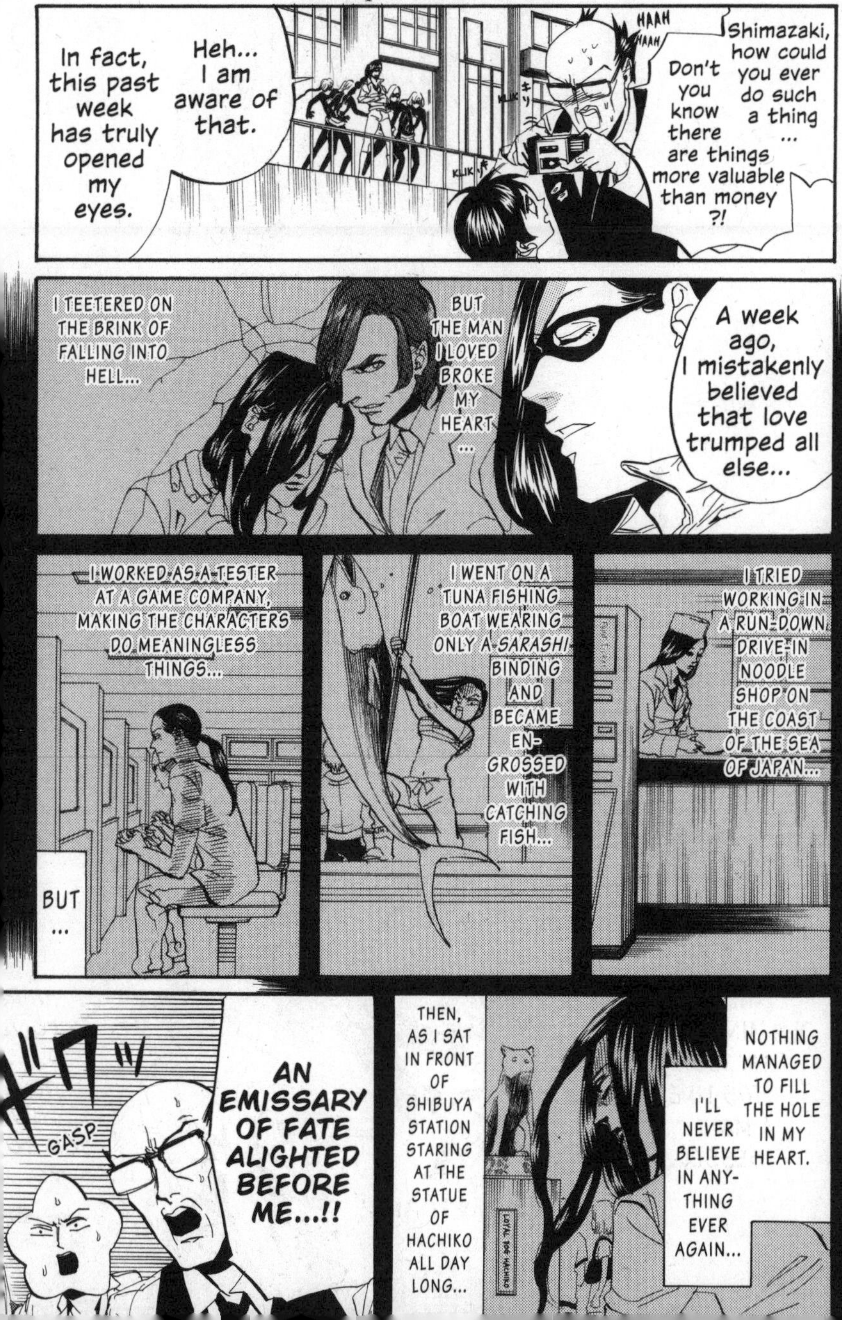
Shimazaki, how could you ever do such a thing ...
Don't you know there are things more valuable than money ?!
HAAH HAAH
KLIK
KLIK
Heh... I am aware of that.
In fact, this past week has truly opened my eyes.
A week ago, I mistakenly believed that love trumped all else...
BUT THE MAN I LOVED BROKE MY HEART ...
I TEETERED ON THE BRINK OF FALLING INTO HELL...
I TRIED WORKING IN A RUN-DOWN DRIVE-IN NOODLE SHOP ON THE COAST OF THE SEA OF JAPAN...
I WENT ON A TUNA FISHING BOAT WEARING ONLY A *SARASHI* BINDING AND BECAME EN-GROSSED WITH CATCHING FISH...
I WORKED AS A TESTER AT A GAME COMPANY, MAKING THE CHARACTERS DO MEANINGLESS THINGS...
BUT ...
NOTHING MANAGED TO FILL THE HOLE IN MY HEART.
I'LL NEVER BELIEVE IN ANY-THING EVER AGAIN...
THEN, AS I SAT IN FRONT OF SHIBUYA STATION STARING AT THE STATUE OF HACHIKO ALL DAY LONG...
AN EMISSARY OF FATE ALIGHTED BEFORE ME...!!
GASP

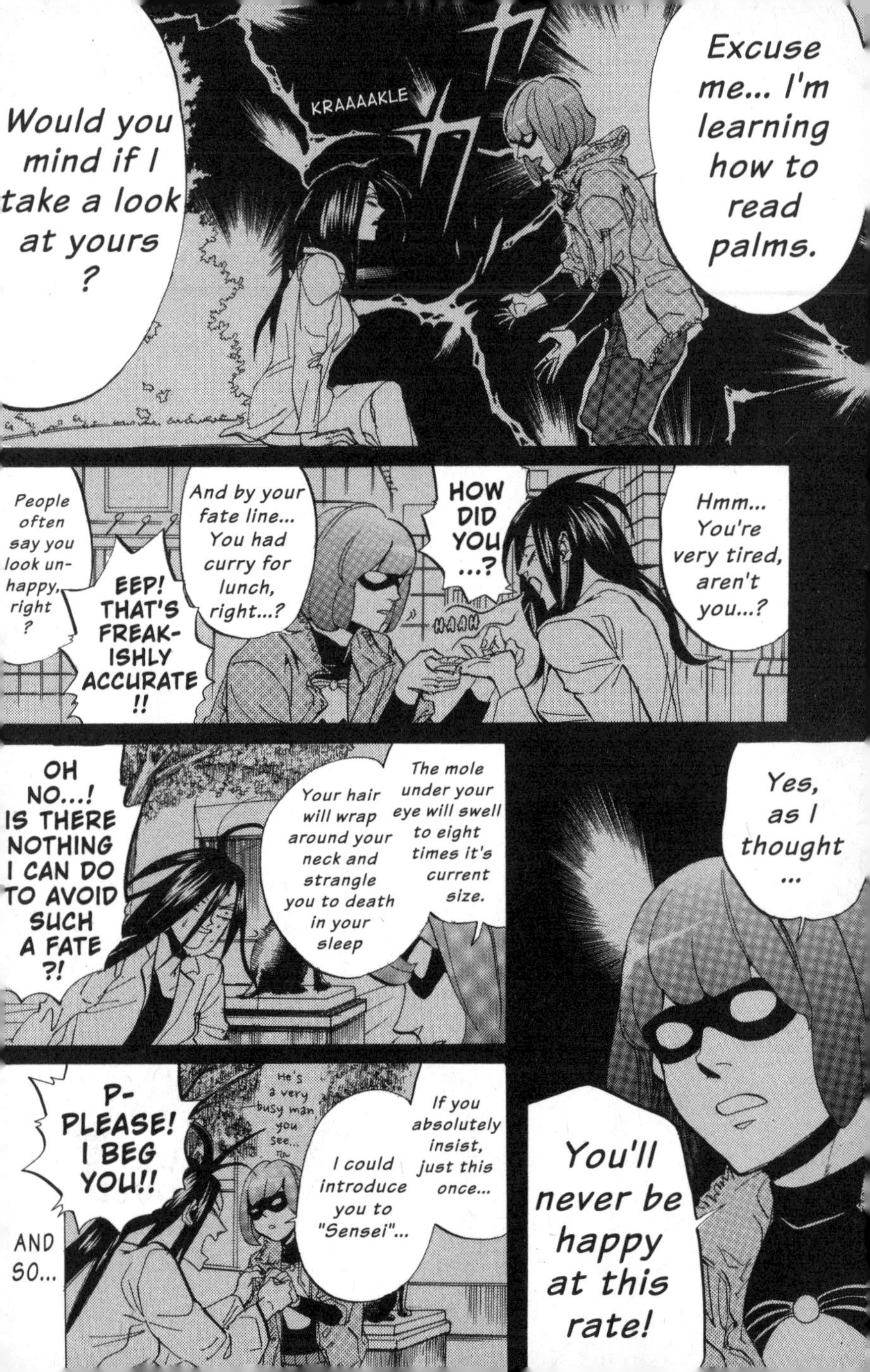
Excuse me... I'm learning how to read palms.
KRAAAAKLE
Would you mind if I take a look at yours?
Hmm... You're very tired, aren't you...?
HOW DID YOU ...?
And by your fate line... You had curry for lunch, right...?
EEP! THAT'S FREAKISHLY ACCURATE!!
People often say you look unhappy, right?
Yes, as I thought...
You'll never be happy at this rate!
The mole under your eye will swell to eight times it's current size.
Your hair will wrap around your neck and strangle you to death in your sleep
OH NO...! IS THERE NOTHING I CAN DO TO AVOID SUCH A FATE?!
If you absolutely insist, just this once...
He's a very busy man, you see...
I could introduce you to "Sensei"...
P-PLEASE! I BEG YOU!!
AND SO...

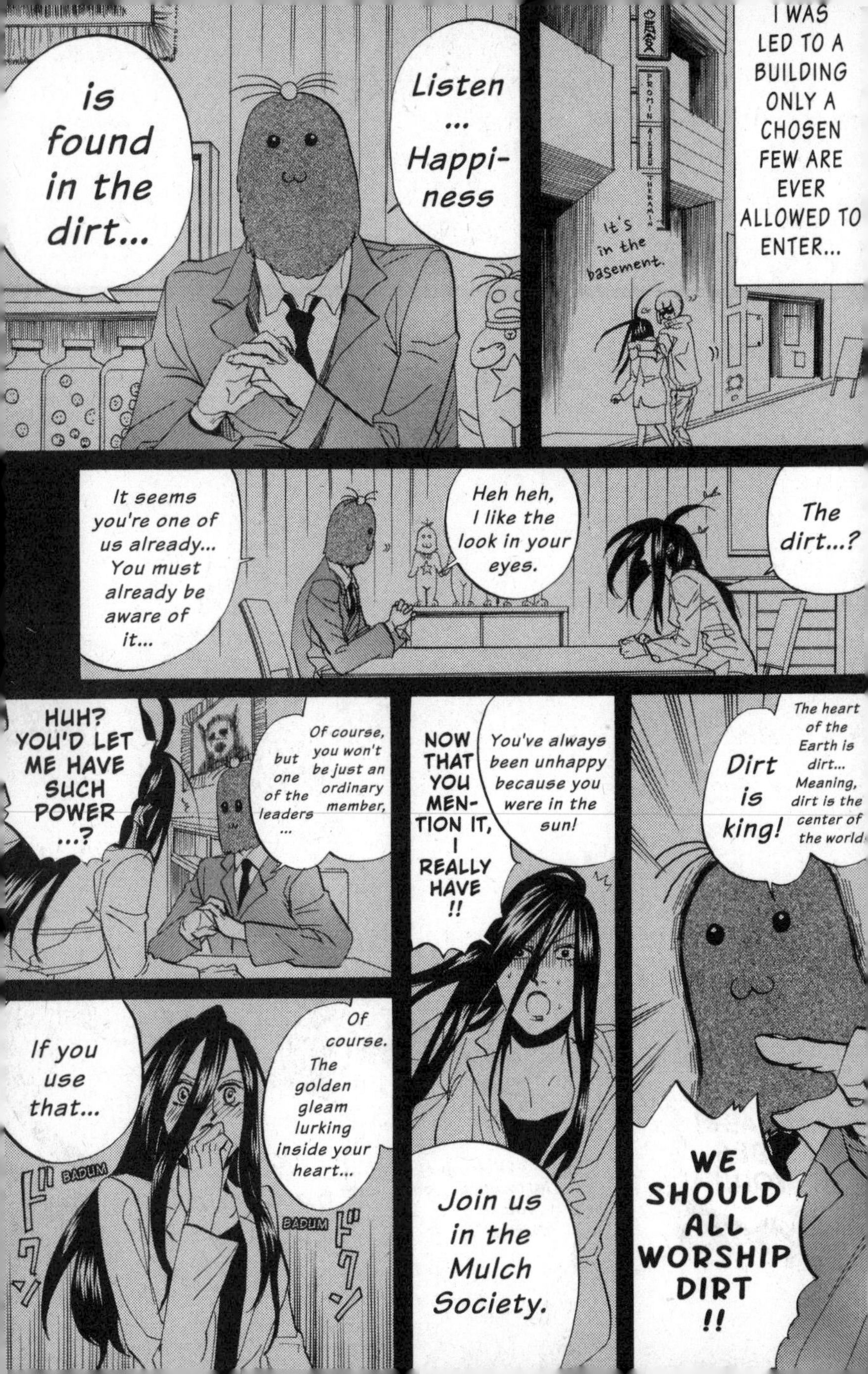
I WAS LED TO A BUILDING ONLY A CHOSEN FEW ARE EVER ALLOWED TO ENTER...
It's in the basement.
Listen... Happiness
is found in the dirt...
The dirt...?
Heh heh, I like the look in your eyes.
It seems you're one of us already... You must already be aware of it...
Dirt is king!
The heart of the Earth is dirt... Meaning, dirt is the center of the world
WE SHOULD ALL WORSHIP DIRT!!
You've always been unhappy because you were in the sun!
NOW THAT YOU MENTION IT, I REALLY HAVE!!
Join us in the Mulch Society.
Of course, you won't be just an ordinary member,
but one of the leaders...
HUH? YOU'D LET ME HAVE SUCH POWER...?
Of course. The golden gleam lurking inside your heart...
If you use that...
BADUM
BADUM

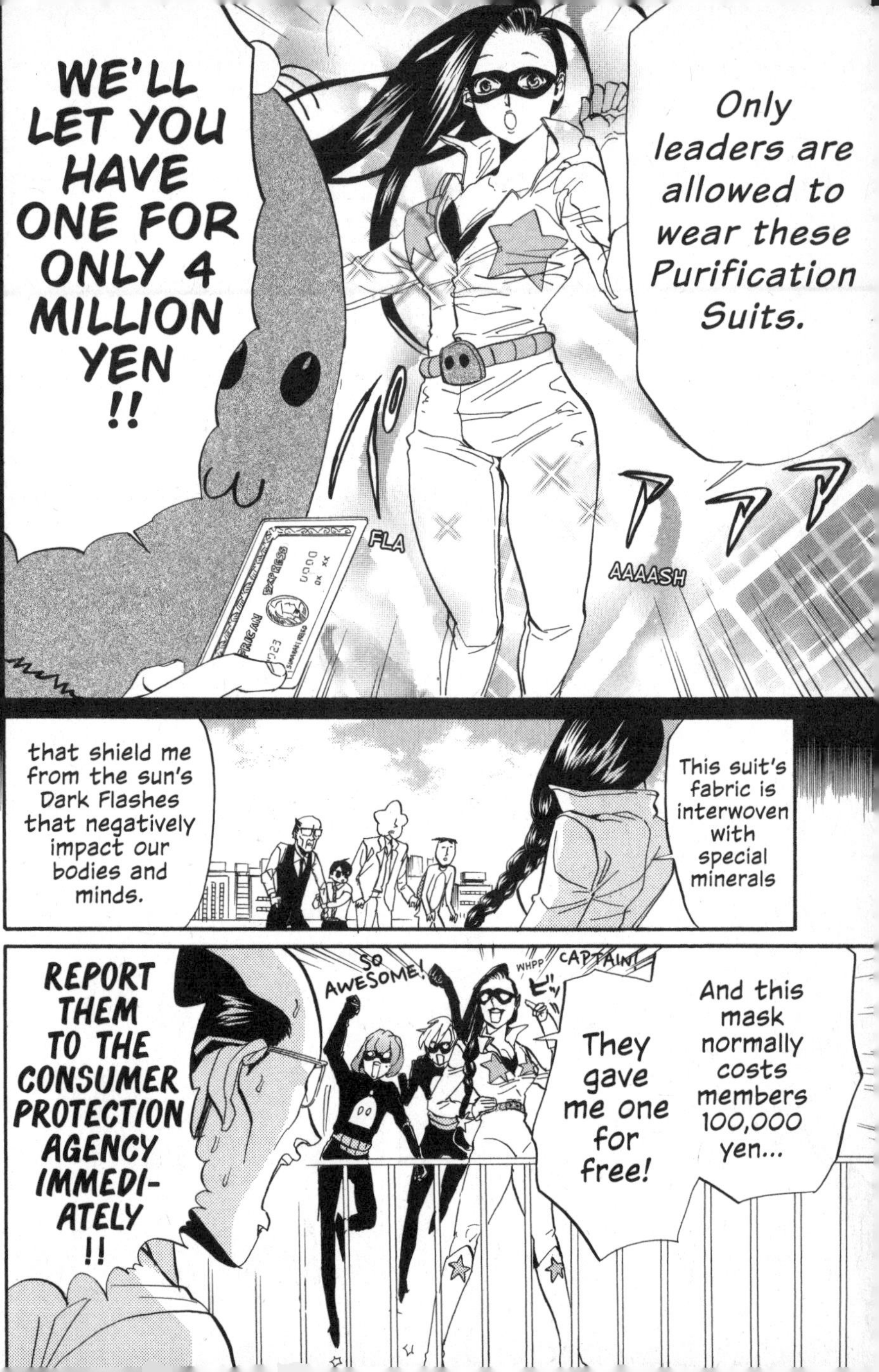
Only leaders are allowed to wear these Purification Suits.
FLA
AAAASH
WE'LL LET YOU HAVE ONE FOR ONLY 4 MILLION YEN !!
This suit's fabric is interwoven with special minerals
that shield me from the sun's Dark Flashes that negatively impact our bodies and minds.
And this mask normally costs members 100,000 yen...
They gave me one for free!
CAPTAIN!
WHPP
SO AWESOME!
REPORT THEM TO THE CONSUMER PROTECTION AGENCY IMMEDIATELY !!

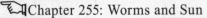

Chapter 255: Worms and Sun

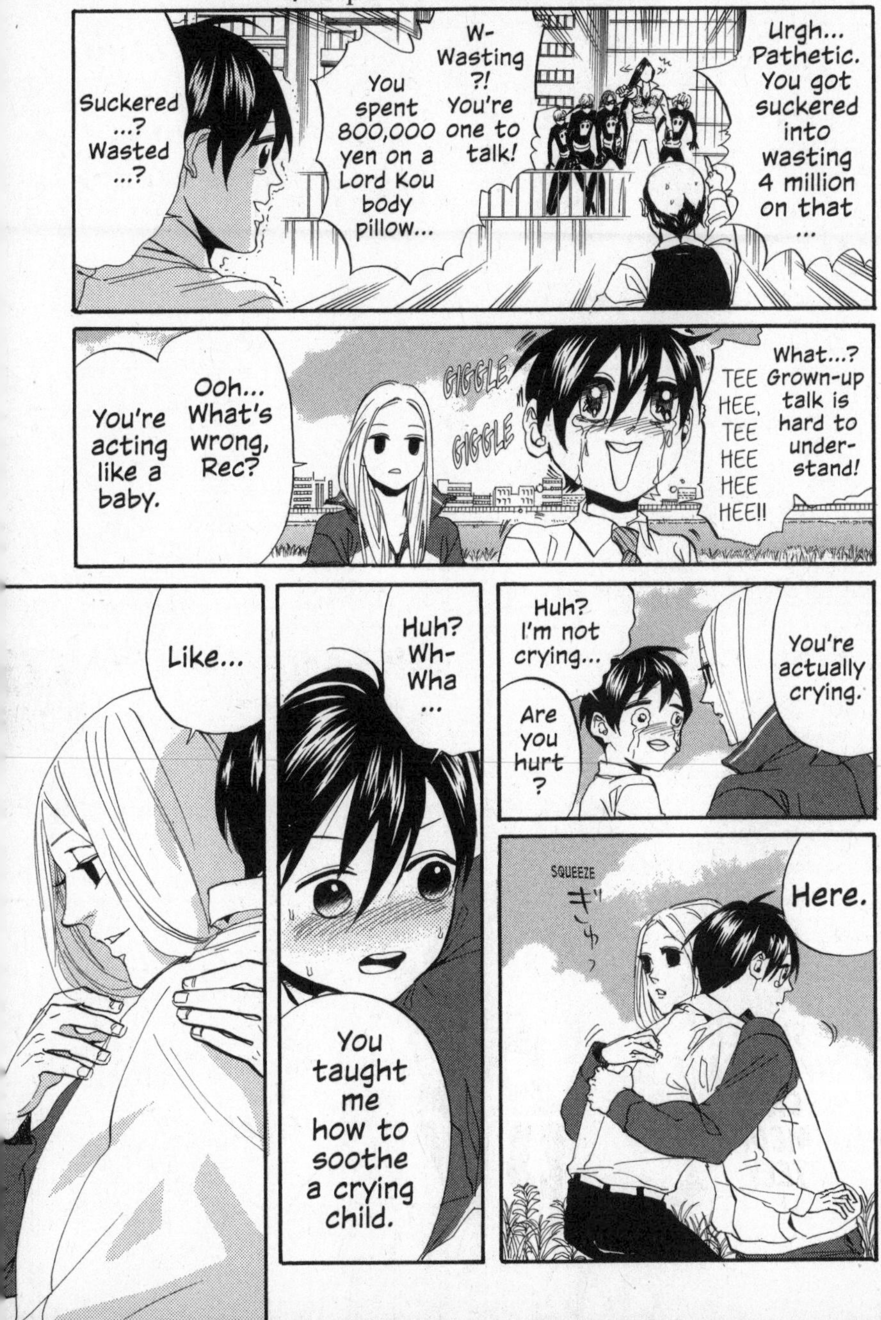
Urgh... Pathetic. You got suckered into wasting 4 million on that ...
W-Wasting?! You're one to talk!
You spent 800,000 yen on a Lord Kou body pillow...
Suckered...? Wasted...?
What...? Grown-up talk is hard to understand!
TEE HEE, TEE HEE HEE HEE!!
GIGGLE
GIGGLE
Ooh... What's wrong, Rec?
You're acting like a baby.
You're actually crying.
Huh? I'm not crying...
Are you hurt?
Here.
SQUEEZE
Huh? Wh-Wha...
You taught me how to soothe a crying child.
Like...

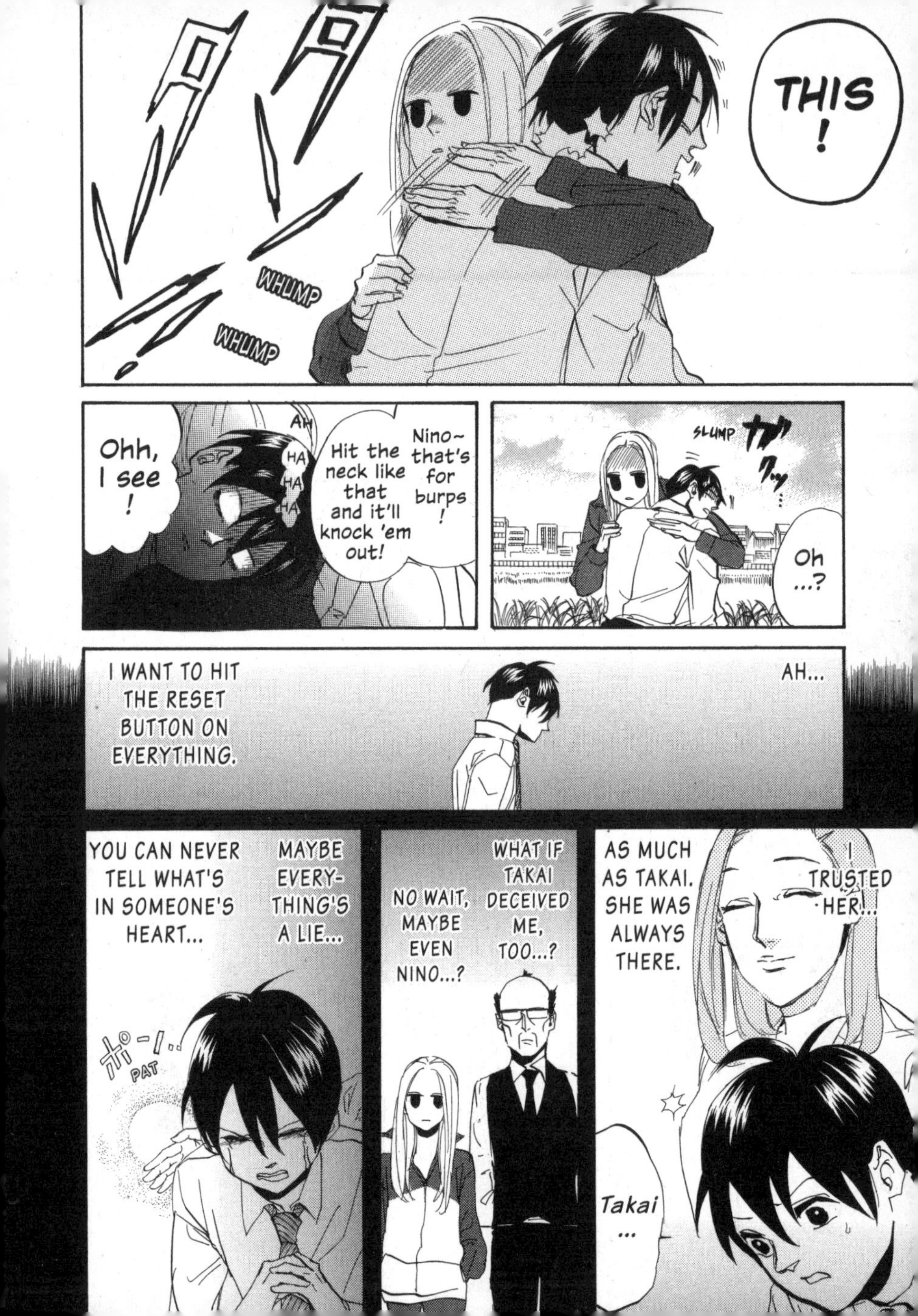
THIS!
WHUMP
WHUMP
SLUMP
Oh ...?
Nino~ that's for burps!
Hit the neck like that and it'll knock 'em out!
AH HA HA HA
Ohh, I see!
AH...
I WANT TO HIT THE RESET BUTTON ON EVERYTHING.
I TRUSTED HER...
AS MUCH AS TAKAI. SHE WAS ALWAYS THERE.
Takai ...
WHAT IF TAKAI DECEIVED ME, TOO...?
NO WAIT, MAYBE EVEN NINO...?
MAYBE EVERY-THING'S A LIE...
YOU CAN NEVER TELL WHAT'S IN SOMEONE'S HEART...
PAT

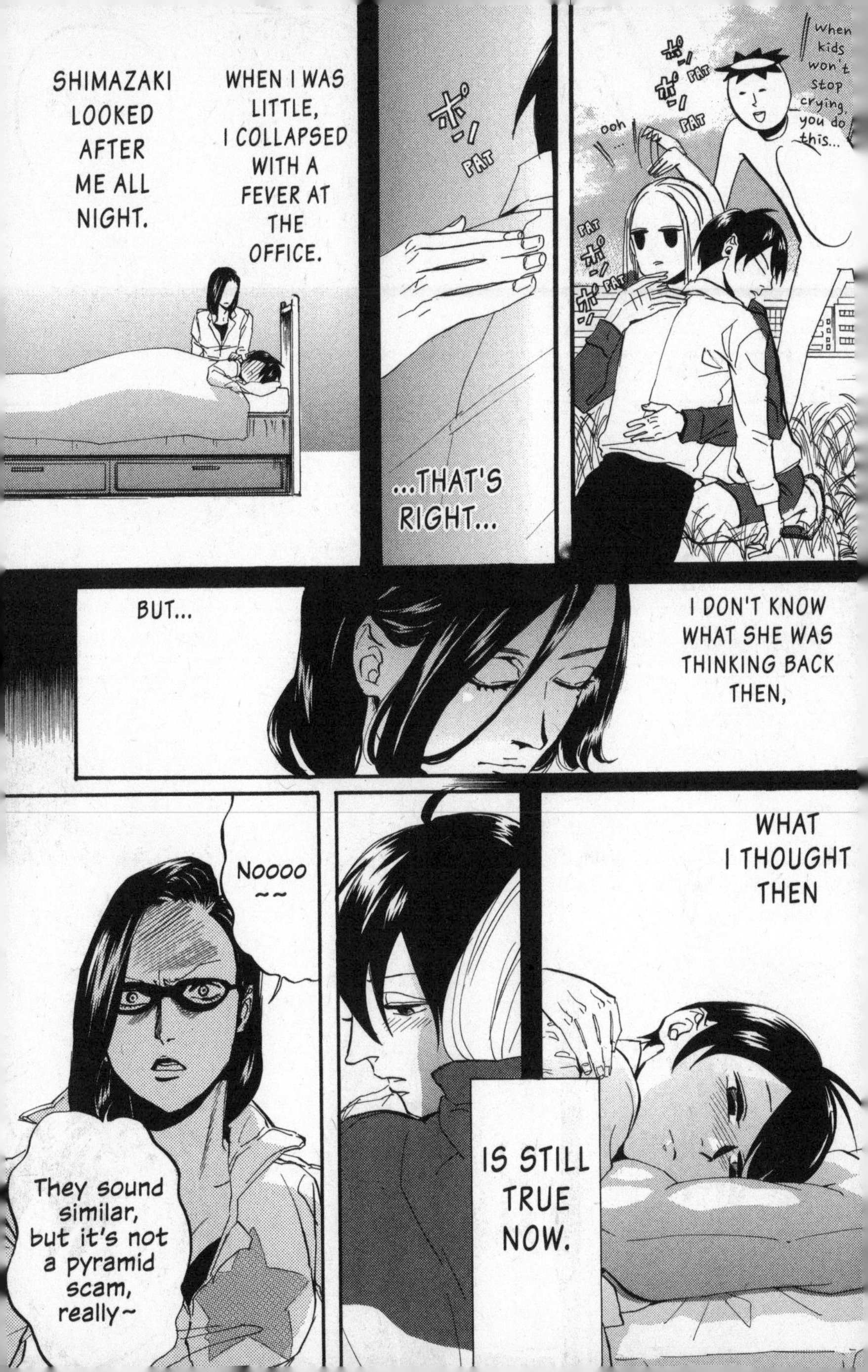
When kids won't stop crying, you do this...
ooh...
PAT
PAT
PAT
PAT
PAT
...THAT'S RIGHT...
WHEN I WAS LITTLE, I COLLAPSED WITH A FEVER AT THE OFFICE.
SHIMAZAKI LOOKED AFTER ME ALL NIGHT.
I DON'T KNOW WHAT SHE WAS THINKING BACK THEN,
BUT...
WHAT I THOUGHT THEN
IS STILL TRUE NOW.
Noooo ~~
They sound similar, but it's not a pyramid scam, really~

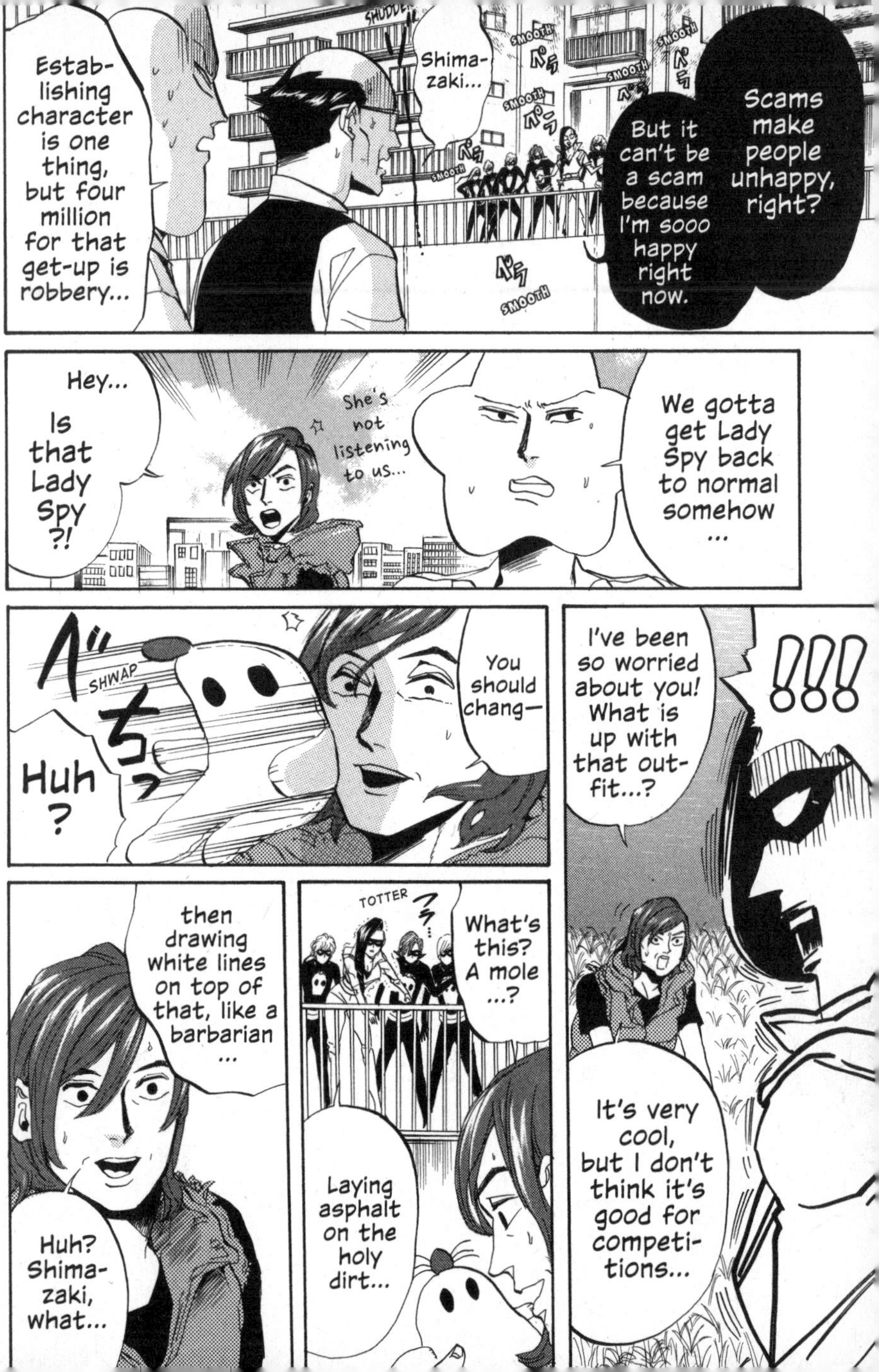
Scams make people unhappy, right?
But it can't be a scam because I'm sooo happy right now.
SMOOTH
Shima-zaki...
SHUDDER
Estab-lishing character is one thing, but four million for that get-up is robbery...
We gotta get Lady Spy back to normal somehow...
She's not listening to us...
Hey...
Is that Lady Spy?!
!!!
I've been so worried about you! What is up with that out-fit...?
It's very cool, but I don't think it's good for competi-tions...
You should chang—
SHWAP
Huh?
What's this? A mole...?
TOTTER
Laying asphalt on the holy dirt...
then drawing white lines on top of that, like a barbarian...
Huh? Shima-zaki, what...

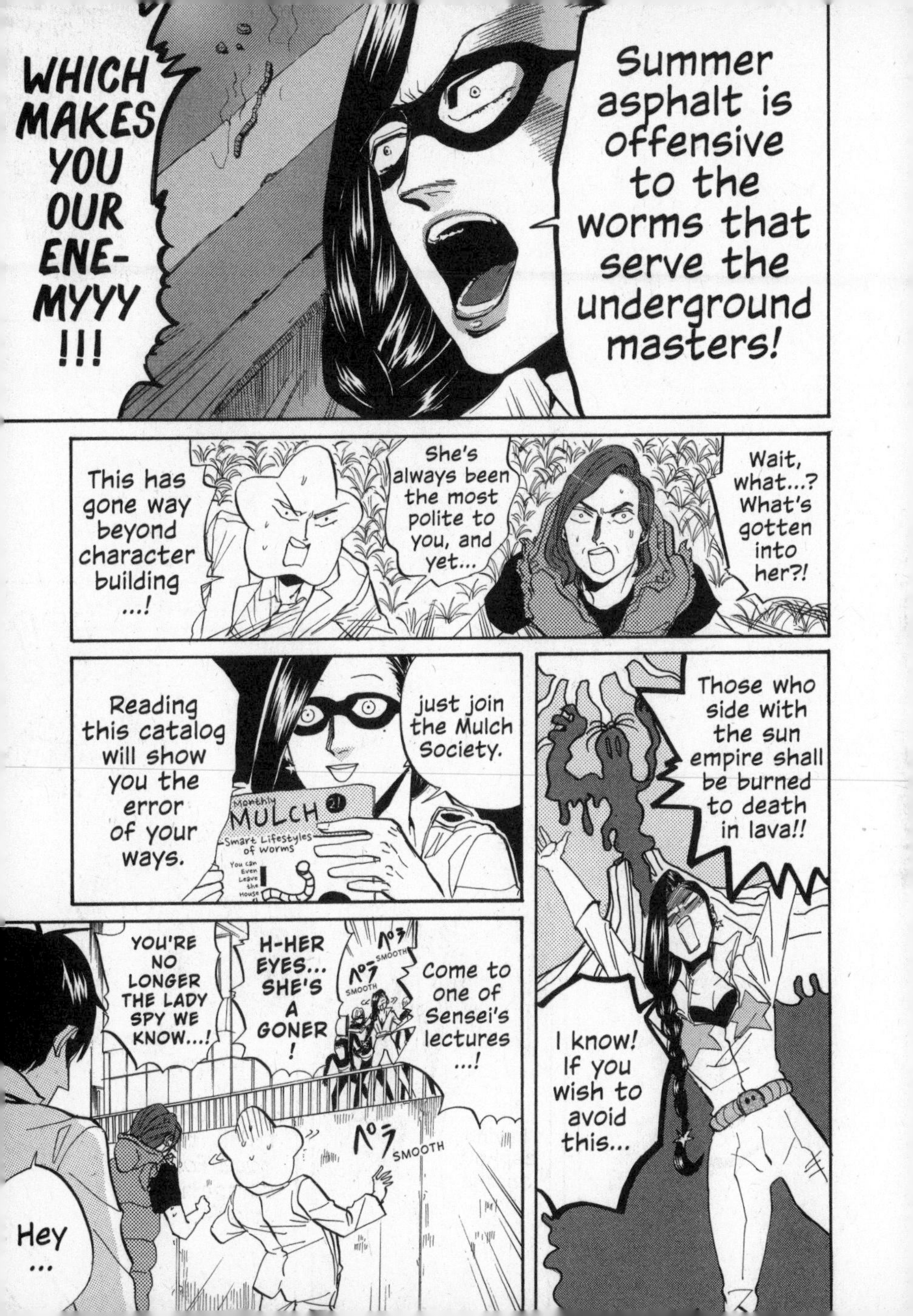
Summer asphalt is offensive to the worms that serve the underground masters!
WHICH MAKES YOU OUR ENE-MYYY!!!
Wait, what...? What's gotten into her?!
She's always been the most polite to you, and yet...
This has gone way beyond character building...!
Those who side with the sun empire shall be burned to death in lava!!
I know! If you wish to avoid this...
just join the Mulch Society.
Reading this catalog will show you the error of your ways.
Monthly MULCH 21
Smart Lifestyles of Worms
You can Even Leave the House
Come to one of Sensei's lectures...!
SMOOTH
SMOOTH
H-HER EYES... SHE'S A GONER!
YOU'RE NO LONGER THE LADY SPY WE KNOW...!
SMOOTH
Hey...

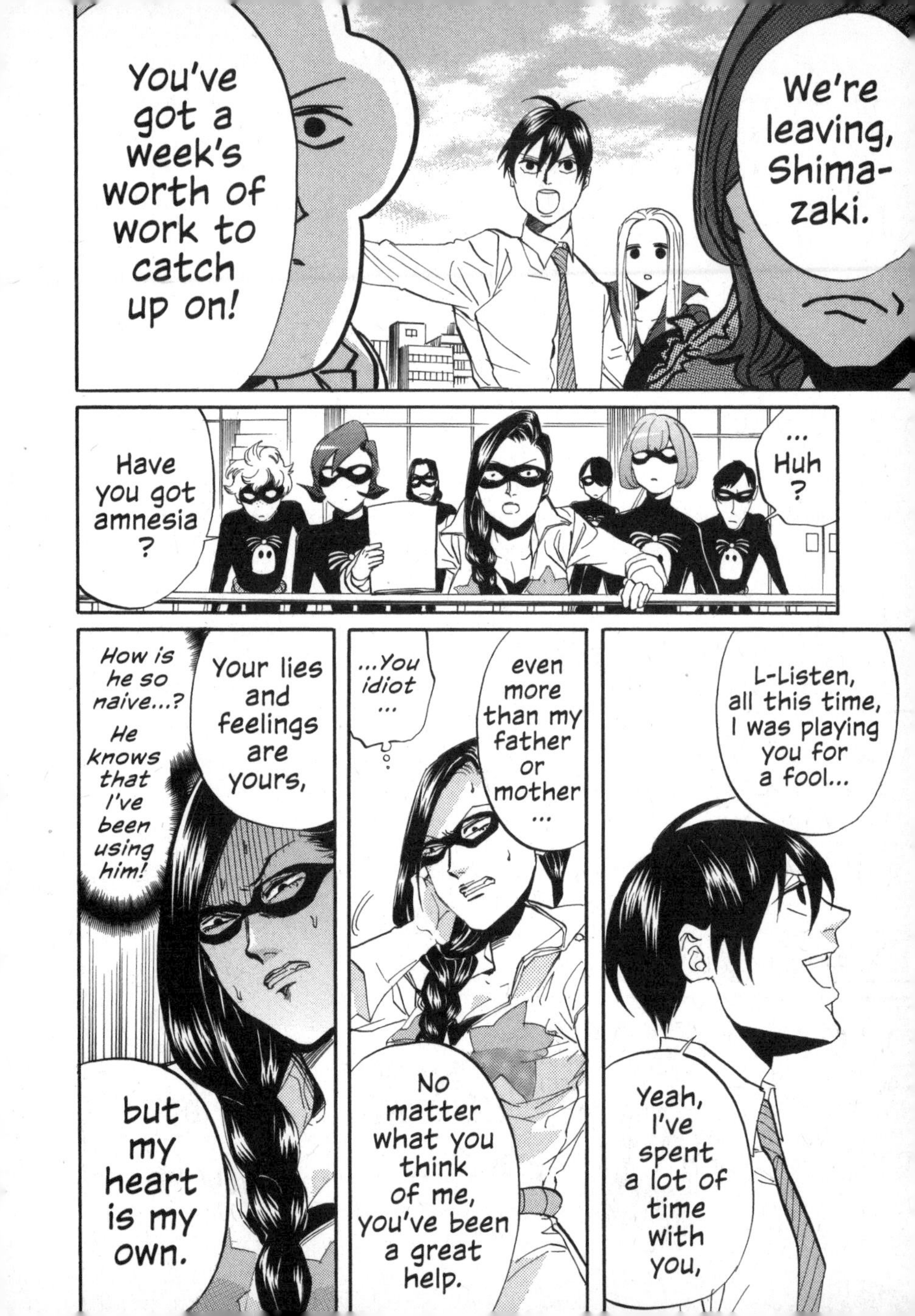
We're leaving, Shimazaki.
You've got a week's worth of work to catch up on!
... Huh?
Have you got amnesia?
L-Listen, all this time, I was playing you for a fool...
Yeah, I've spent a lot of time with you,
even more than my father or mother...
...You idiot...
No matter what you think of me, you've been a great help.
Your lies and feelings are yours,
How is he so naive...? He knows that I've been using him!
but my heart is my own.

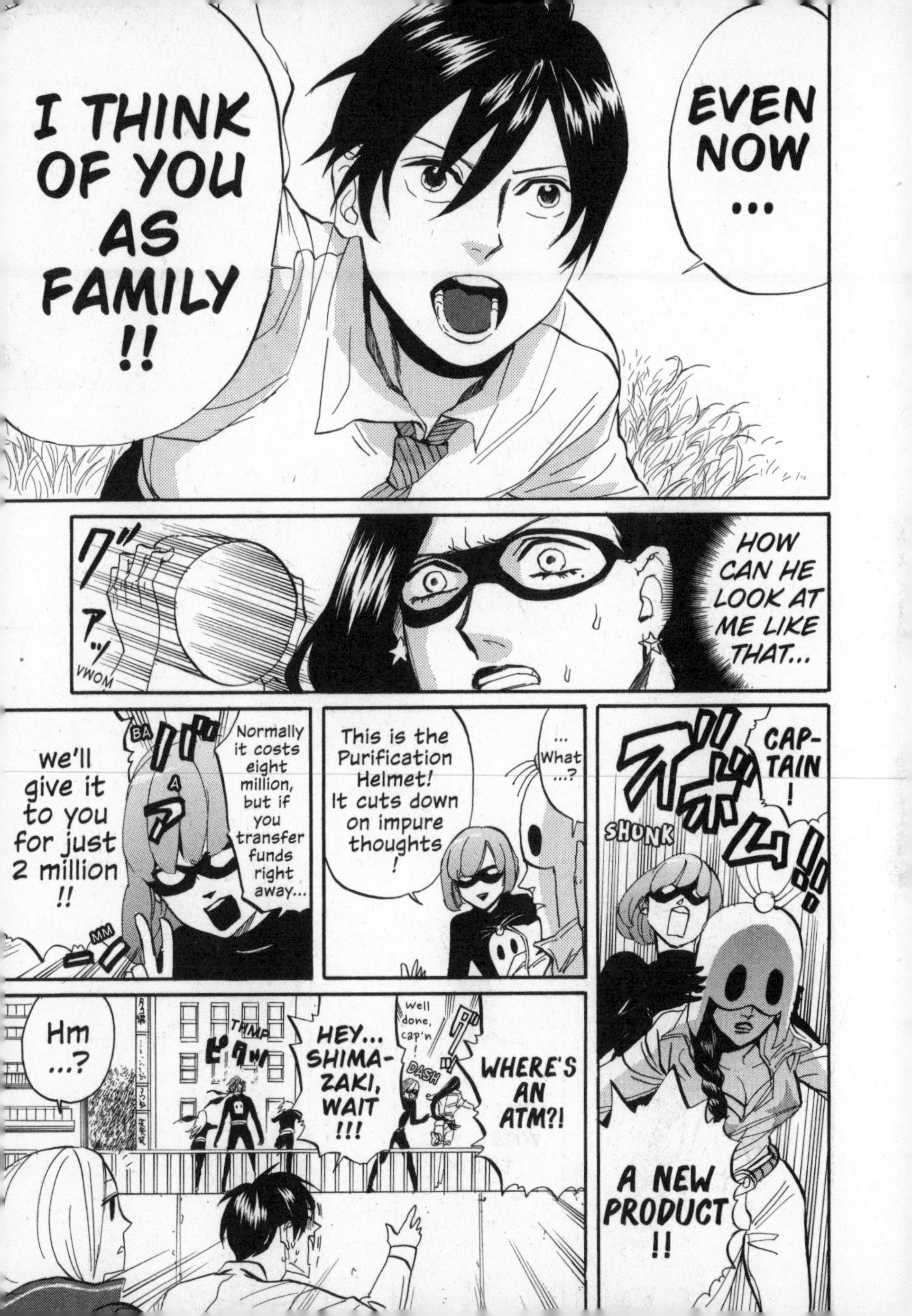
EVEN NOW ...
I THINK OF YOU AS FAMILY !!
HOW CAN HE LOOK AT ME LIKE THAT...
VWOM
CAP-TAIN !
SHUNK
A NEW PRODUCT !!
... What ...?
This is the Purification Helmet! It cuts down on impure thoughts !
BA
Normally it costs eight million, but if you transfer funds right away...
we'll give it to you for just 2 million !!
MM
WHERE'S AN ATM?!
DASH
Well done, cap'n !
HEY... SHIMA-ZAKI, WAIT !!!
THMP
Hm ...?

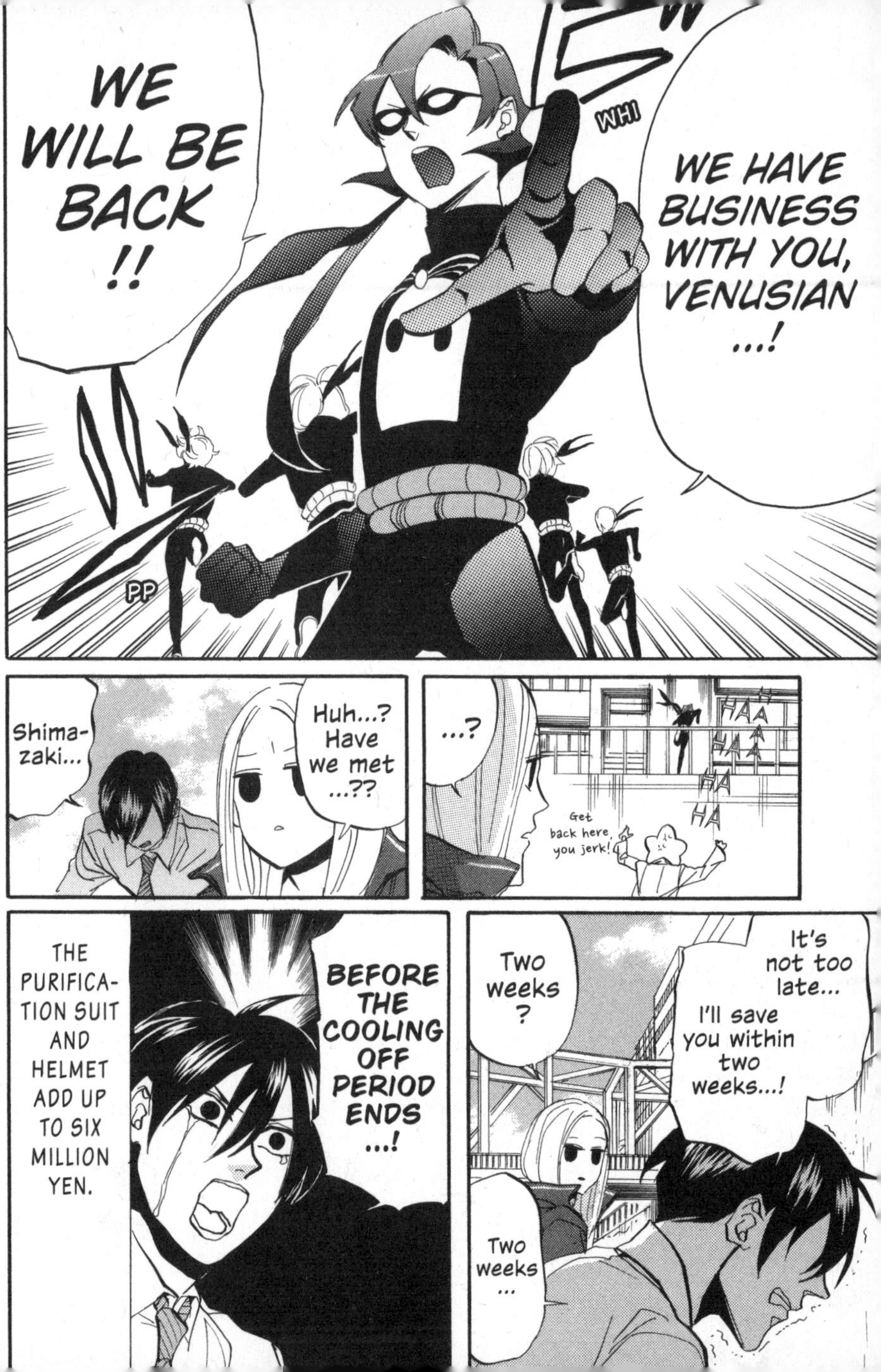
WE HAVE BUSINESS WITH YOU, VENUSIAN ...!
WHI
WE WILL BE BACK !!
PP
...?
HAA HAA HAA HA HA
Get back here you jerk!
Huh...? Have we met ...??
Shimazaki...
It's not too late...
I'll save you within two weeks...!
Two weeks ?
Two weeks ...
BEFORE THE COOLING OFF PERIOD ENDS ...!
THE PURIFICATION SUIT AND HELMET ADD UP TO SIX MILLION YEN.

AFTERWORD

Thank you for buying Arakawa volume 9!
This is the last single-digit volume!
A new world! 10, and... it's a total miracle!
I've come this far thanks to you, dear reader,
and my editors, family and friends.
And... and...

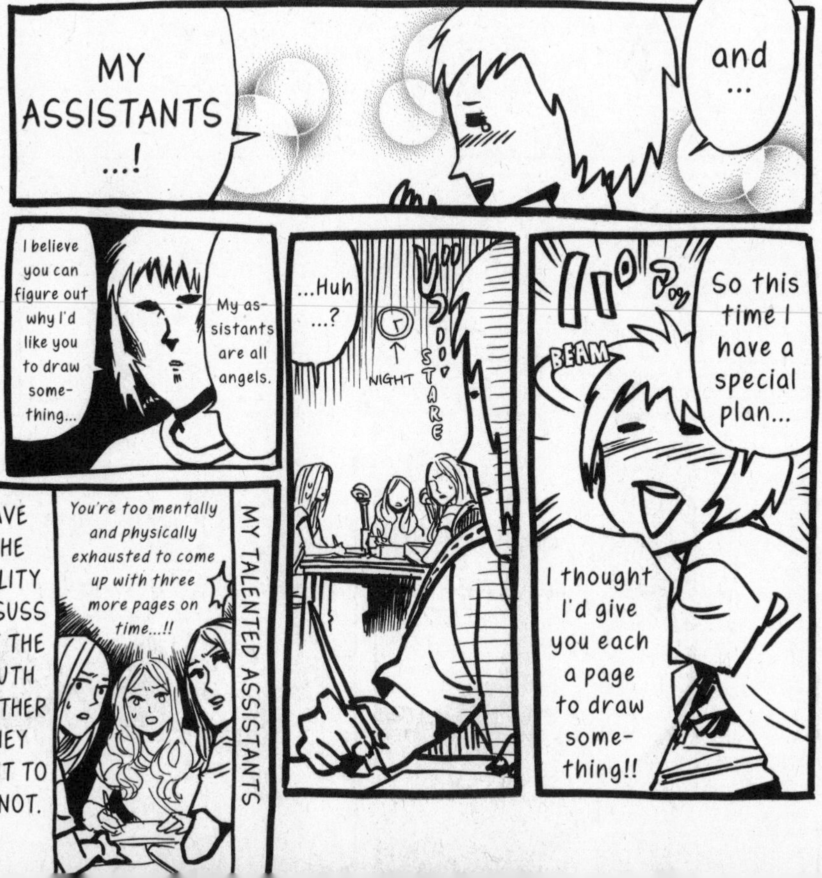

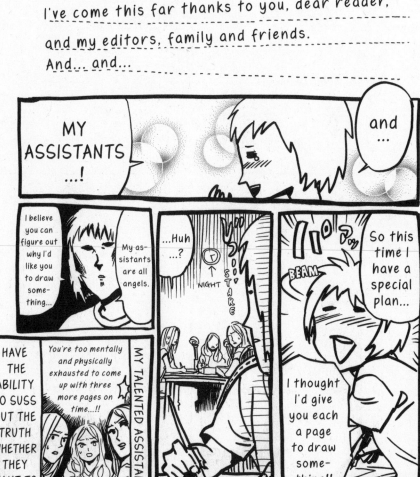

and ...
MY ASSISTANTS ...!
So this time I have a special plan...
BEAM
I thought I'd give you each a page to draw something!!
...Huh ...?
NIGHT
STARE
My assistants are all angels.
I believe you can figure out why I'd like you to draw something...
MY TALENTED ASSISTANTS
You're too mentally and physically exhausted to come up with three more pages on time...!!
HAVE THE ABILITY TO SUSS OUT THE TRUTH WHETHER THEY WANT TO OR NOT.

ASSISTANT ★ N TOMO

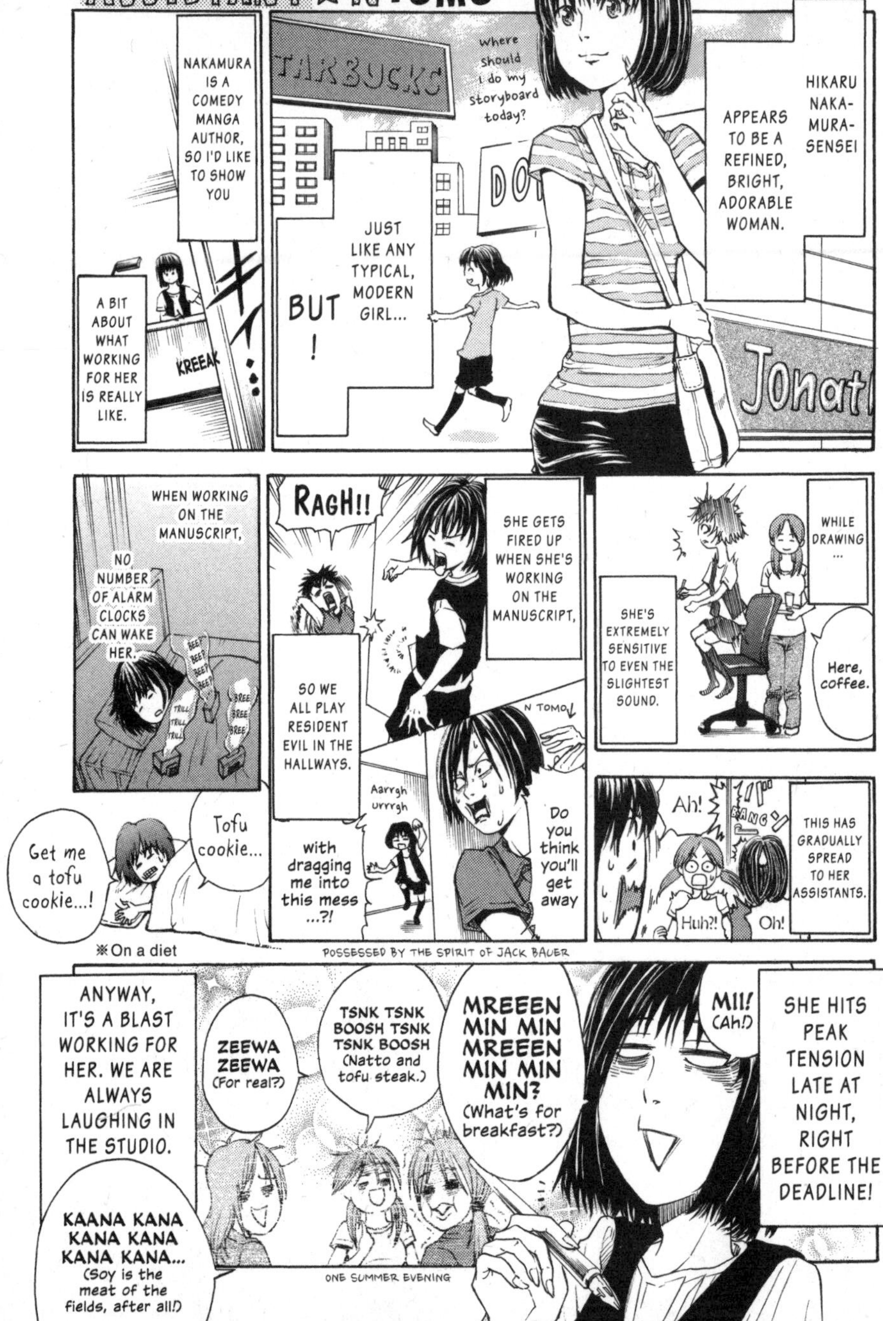

HIKARU NAKAMURA-SENSEI
APPEARS TO BE A REFINED, BRIGHT, ADORABLE WOMAN.
Jonat
Where should I do my storyboard today?
TARBUCKS
DO
JUST LIKE ANY TYPICAL, MODERN GIRL...
BUT!
NAKAMURA IS A COMEDY MANGA AUTHOR, SO I'D LIKE TO SHOW YOU
A BIT ABOUT WHAT WORKING FOR HER IS REALLY LIKE.
KREEAK
WHILE DRAWING...
SHE'S EXTREMELY SENSITIVE TO EVEN THE SLIGHTEST SOUND.
Here, coffee.
THIS HAS GRADUALLY SPREAD TO HER ASSISTANTS.
Ah!
Huh?!
Oh!
RAGH!!
SHE GETS FIRED UP WHEN SHE'S WORKING ON THE MANUSCRIPT,
SO WE ALL PLAY RESIDENT EVIL IN THE HALLWAYS.
N TOMO
Do you think you'll get away
with dragging me into this mess...?!
Aarrgh urrrgh
POSSESSED BY THE SPIRIT OF JACK BAUER
WHEN WORKING ON THE MANUSCRIPT,
NO NUMBER OF ALARM CLOCKS CAN WAKE HER.
TRILL TRILL TRILL
BREE BREE BREE
Tofu cookie...
Get me a tofu cookie...!
※On a diet
SHE HITS PEAK TENSION LATE AT NIGHT, RIGHT BEFORE THE DEADLINE!
MII! (Ah!)
MREEEN MIN MIN MREEEN MIN MIN MIN? (What's for breakfast?)
TSNK TSNK BOOSH TSNK TSNK BOOSH (Natto and tofu steak.)
ZEEWA ZEEWA (For real?)
ANYWAY, IT'S A BLAST WORKING FOR HER. WE ARE ALWAYS LAUGHING IN THE STUDIO.
KAANA KANA KANA KANA KANA KANA... (Soy is the meat of the fields, after all!)
ONE SUMMER EVENING

NAKAMURA-SENSEI'S WARM FAMILY

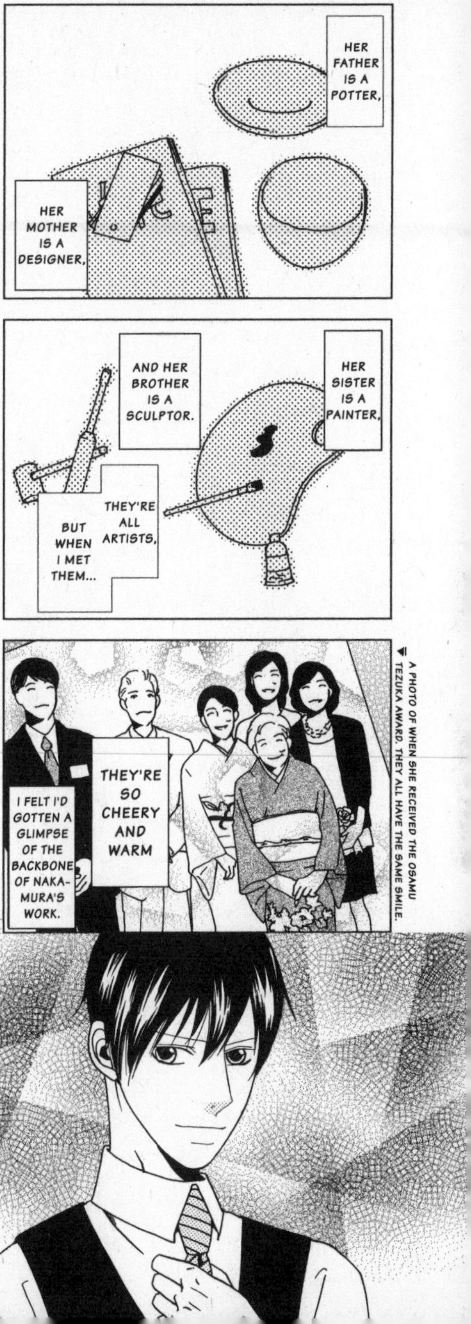
HER FATHER IS A POTTER,
HER MOTHER IS A DESIGNER,
HER SISTER IS A PAINTER,
AND HER BROTHER IS A SCULPTOR.
THEY'RE ALL ARTISTS,
BUT WHEN I MET THEM...
THEY'RE SO CHEERY AND WARM
I FELT I'D GOTTEN A GLIMPSE OF THE BACKBONE OF NAKA-MURA'S WORK.

▼A PHOTO OF WHEN SHE RECEIVED THE OSAMU TEZUKA AWARD. THEY ALL HAVE THE SAME SMILE.

NAKAMURA-SENSEI AND HER FUNNY FRIENDS

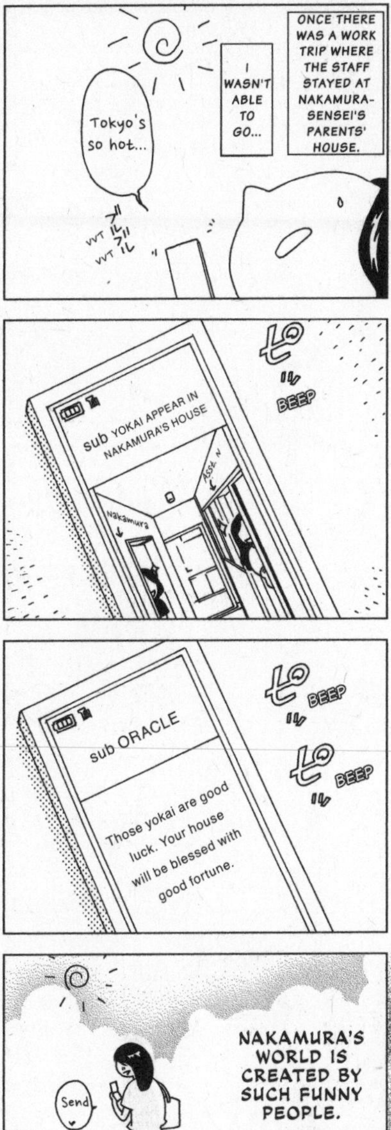
ONCE THERE WAS A WORK TRIP WHERE THE STAFF STAYED AT NAKAMURA-SENSEI'S PARENTS' HOUSE.
I WASN'T ABLE TO GO...
Tokyo's so hot...
VVT VVT
BEEP
sub YOKAI APPEAR IN NAKAMURA'S HOUSE
Nakamura
BEEP
BEEP
sub ORACLE
Those yokai are good luck. Your house will be blessed with good fortune.
Send
NAKAMURA'S WORLD IS CREATED BY SUCH FUNNY PEOPLE.

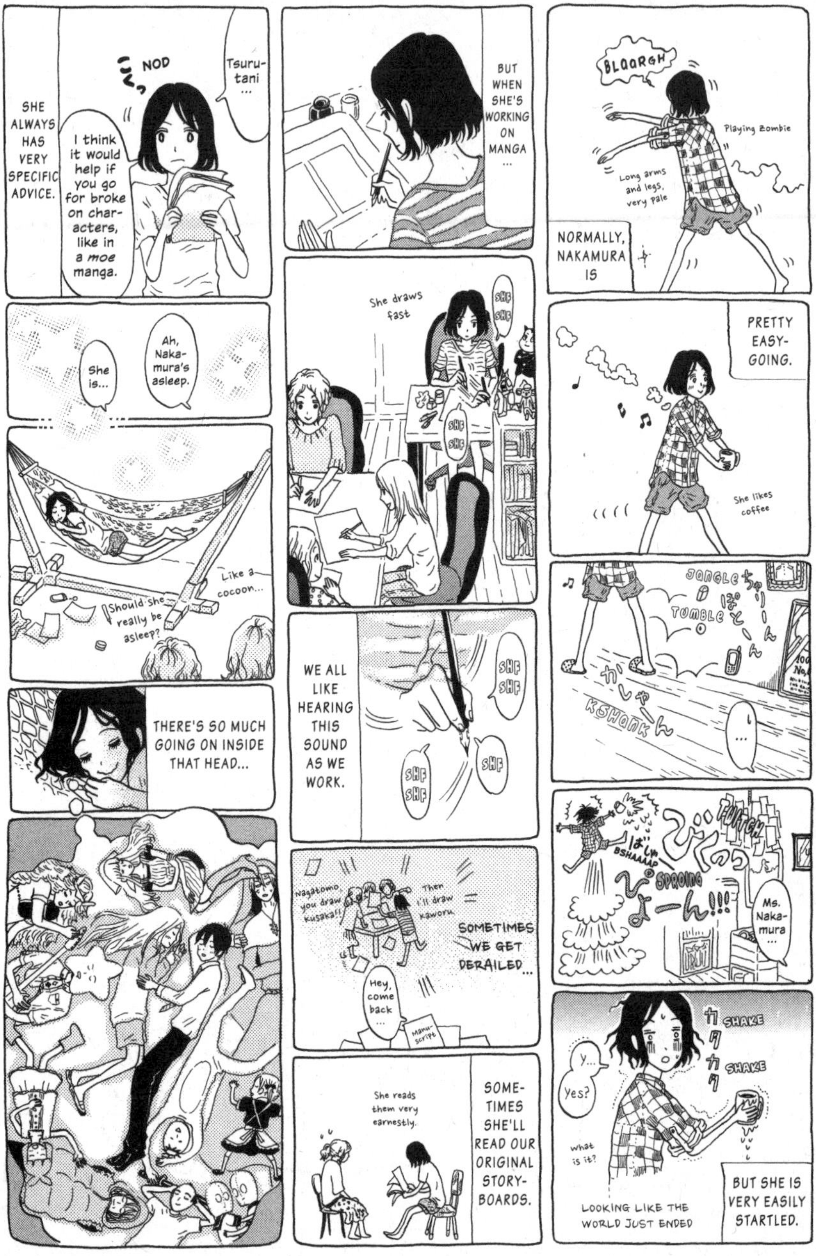
BLAARGH
Playing zombie
Long arms and legs, very pale
NORMALLY, NAKAMURA IS
PRETTY EASY-GOING.
She likes coffee
JANGLE
TUMBLE
KSHONK
...
TWITCH
BSHAAAAP
SPROING
Ms. Nakamura...
SHAKE
SHAKE
Y... yes?
what is it?
LOOKING LIKE THE WORLD JUST ENDED
BUT SHE IS VERY EASILY STARTLED.
BUT WHEN SHE'S WORKING ON MANGA...
She draws fast
SHF SHF
SHF SHF
WE ALL LIKE HEARING THIS SOUND AS WE WORK.
SHF SHF
SHF
SHF SHF
SOMETIMES WE GET DERAILED...
Then I'll draw Kaworu
Nagatomo, you draw Kusaka!!
Hey, come back...
Manuscript
SOMETIMES SHE'LL READ OUR ORIGINAL STORYBOARDS.
She reads them very earnestly.
SHE ALWAYS HAS VERY SPECIFIC ADVICE.
Tsurutani...
NOD
I think it would help if you go for broke on characters, like in a moe manga.
Ah, Nakamura's asleep.
She is...
Like a cocoon...
Should she really be asleep?
THERE'S SO MUCH GOING ON INSIDE THAT HEAD...

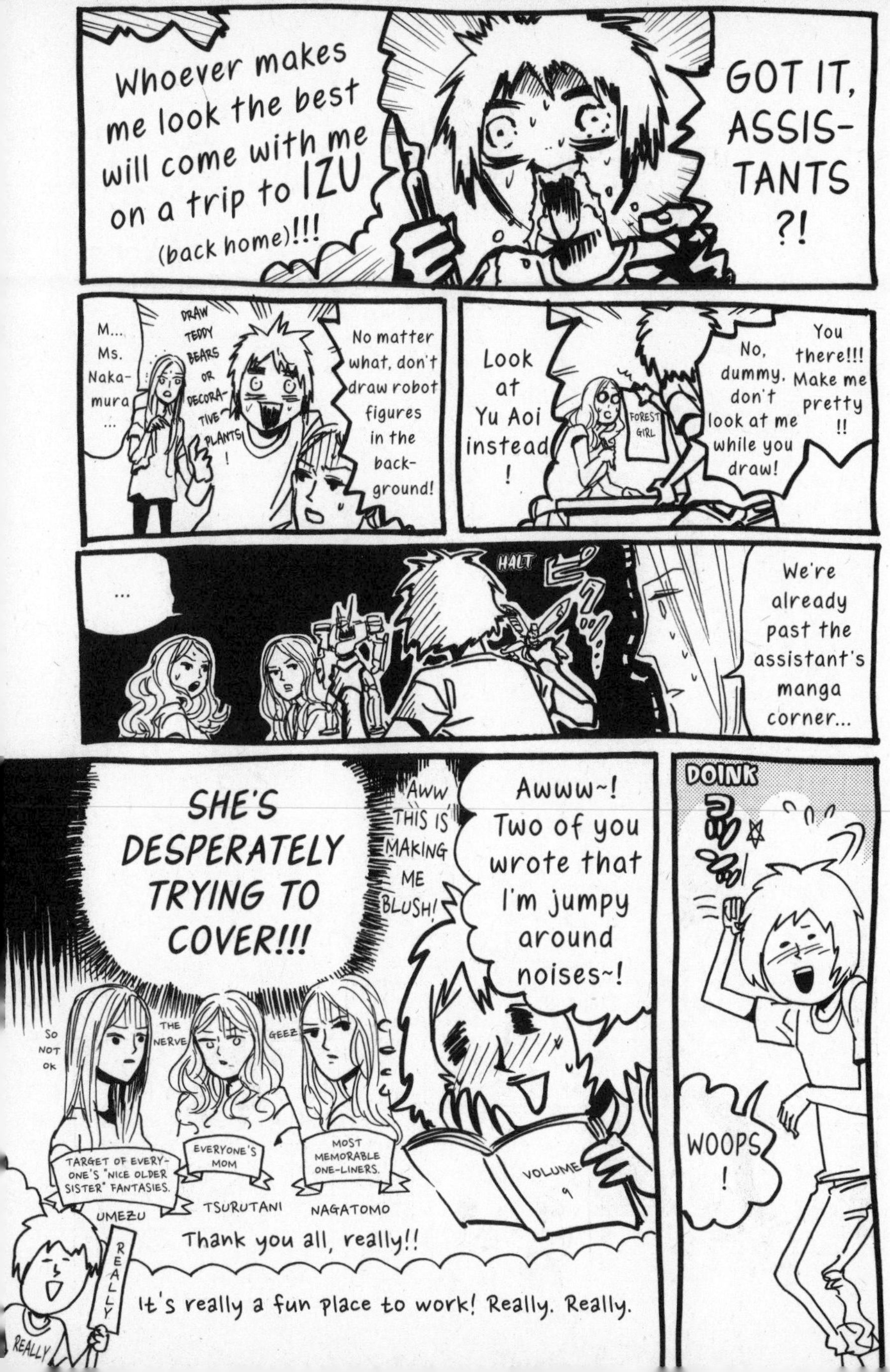
Whoever makes me look the best will come with me on a trip to IZU (back home)!!!
GOT IT, ASSIS-TANTS ?!
You there!!! Make me pretty !!
No, dummy, don't look at me while you draw!
FOREST GIRL
Look at Yu Aoi instead !
No matter what, don't draw robot figures in the back-ground!
DRAW TEDDY BEARS OR DECORA-TIVE PLANTS !
M... Ms. Naka-mura ...
We're already past the assistant's manga corner...
HALT
...
DOINK
WOOPS !
Awww~! Two of you wrote that I'm jumpy around noises~!
AWW THIS IS MAKING ME BLUSH!
SHE'S DESPERATELY TRYING TO COVER!!!
VOLUME 9
GEEZ
MOST MEMORABLE ONE-LINERS.
NAGATOMO
THE NERVE
EVERYONE'S MOM
TSURUTANI
SO NOT OK
TARGET OF EVERY-ONE'S "NICE OLDER SISTER" FANTASIES.
UMEZU
Thank you all, really!!
REALLY
It's really a fun place to work! Really. Really.
REALLY

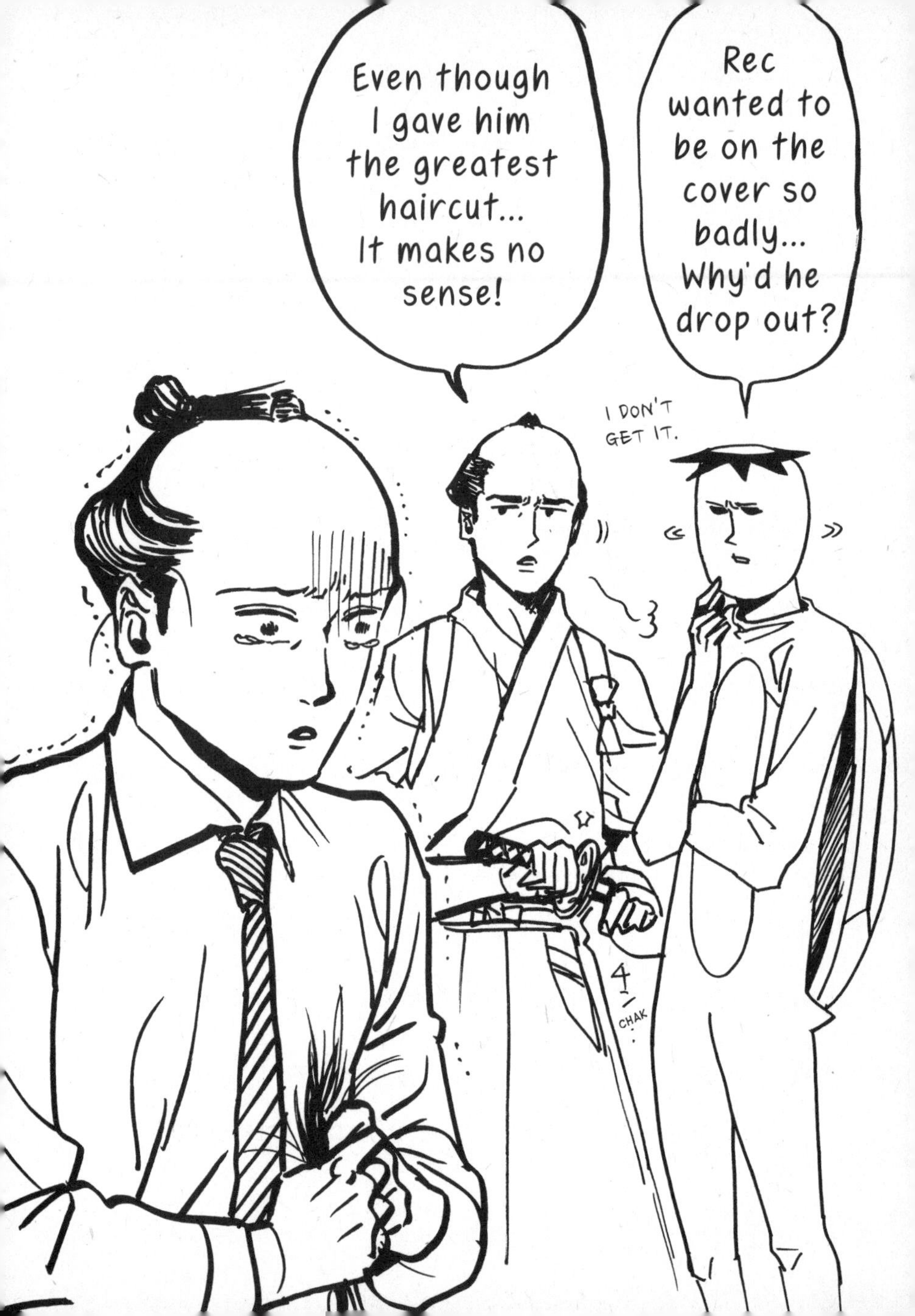
Rec wanted to be on the cover so badly... Why'd he drop out?
I DON'T GET IT.
Even though I gave him the greatest haircut... It makes no sense!
CHAK

THE ORIGINAL T-SHIRTS YOU CAN BUY
IN LAST SAMURAI'S SALON.

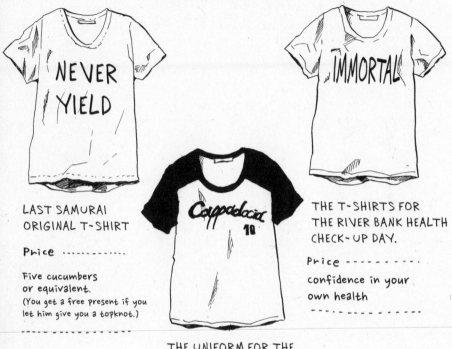

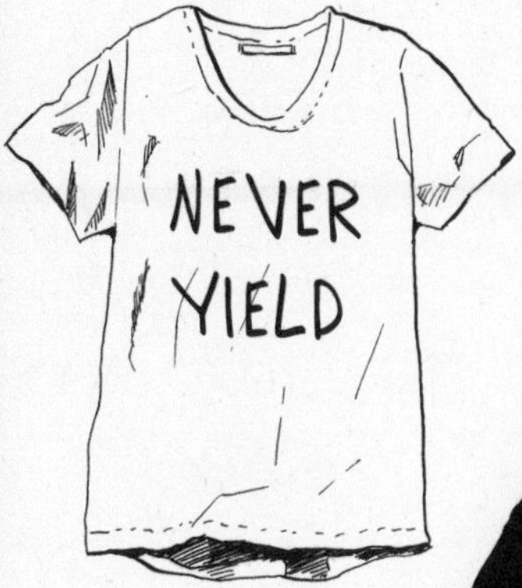
NEVER
YIELD

LAST SAMURAI
ORIGINAL T-SHIRT

Price ------------

Five cucumbers
or equivalent.
(You get a free present if you
let him give you a topknot.)

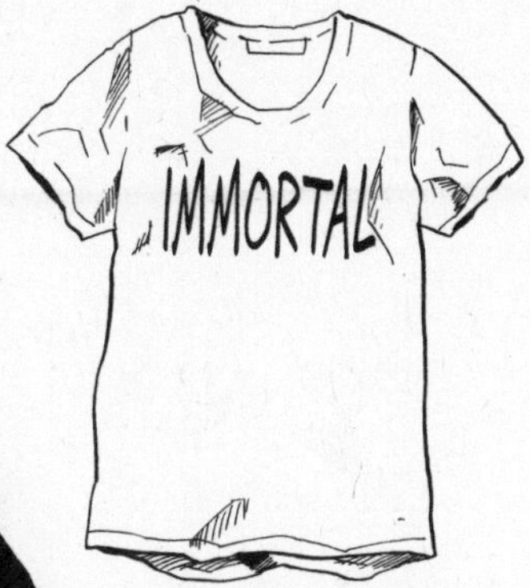
IMMORTAL

THE T-SHIRTS FOR
THE RIVER BANK HEALTH
CHECK-UP DAY.

Price ---------

confidence in your
own health

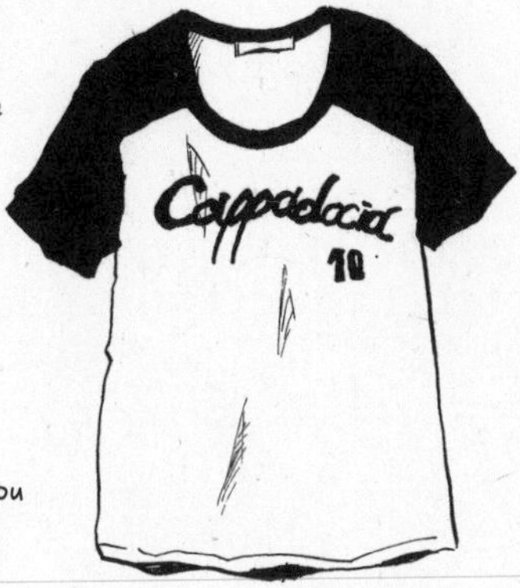
Cappadocia
10

THE UNIFORM FOR THE
RIVER BANK BASEBALL
TEAM, CAPPADOCIA.

Price -------------
Three cucumbers,
or equivalent.
(And proof of having passed the
Mayor's team recruitment test)

ALL SHIRTS COME IN XS, S, M, L, AND SISTER SIZE.

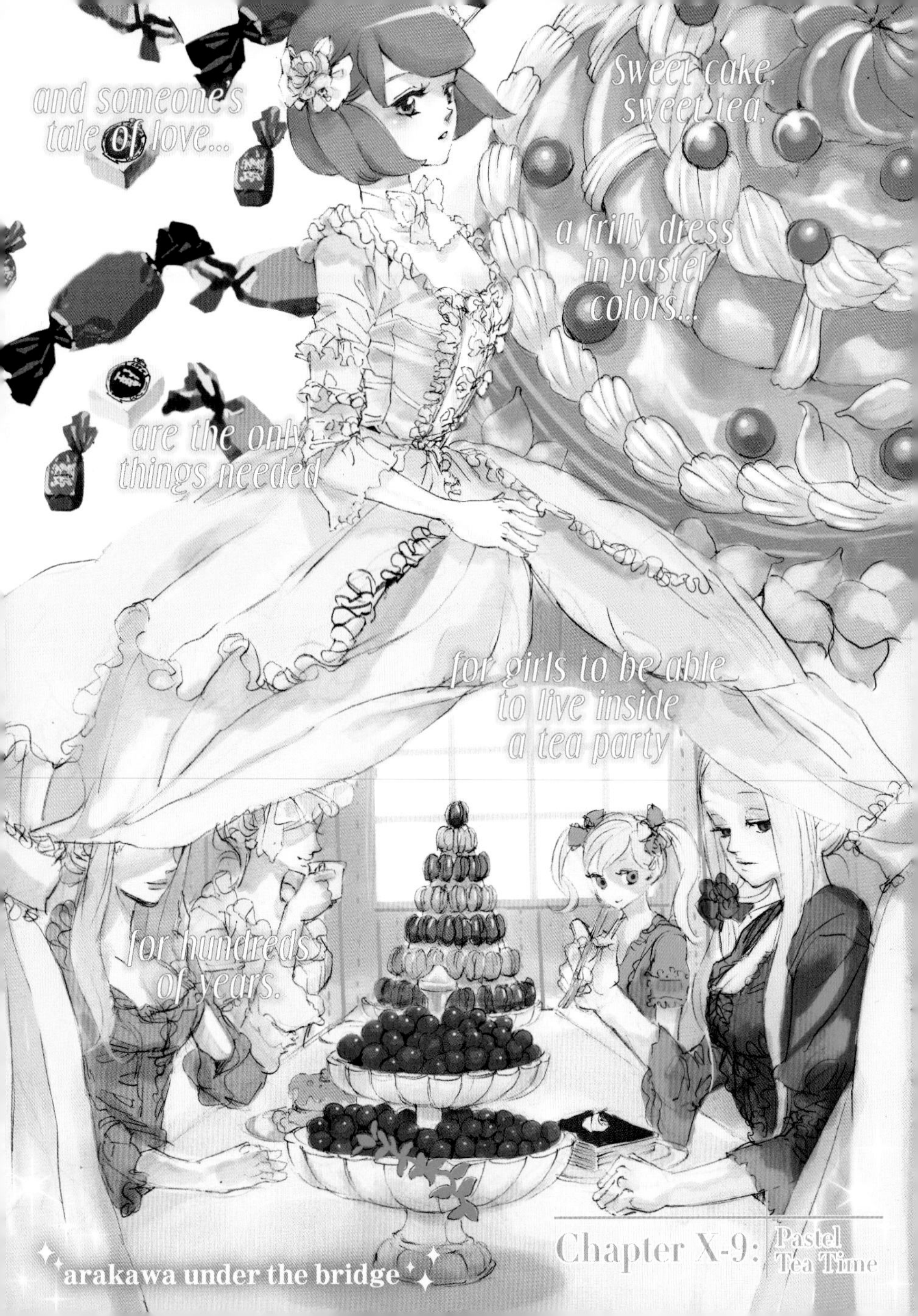
Sweet cake,
sweet tea,
a frilly dress
in pastel
colors...
and someone's
tale of love...
are the only
things needed
for girls to be able
to live inside
a tea party
for hundreds
of years.
Chapter X-9: Pastel Tea Time
arakawa under the bridge

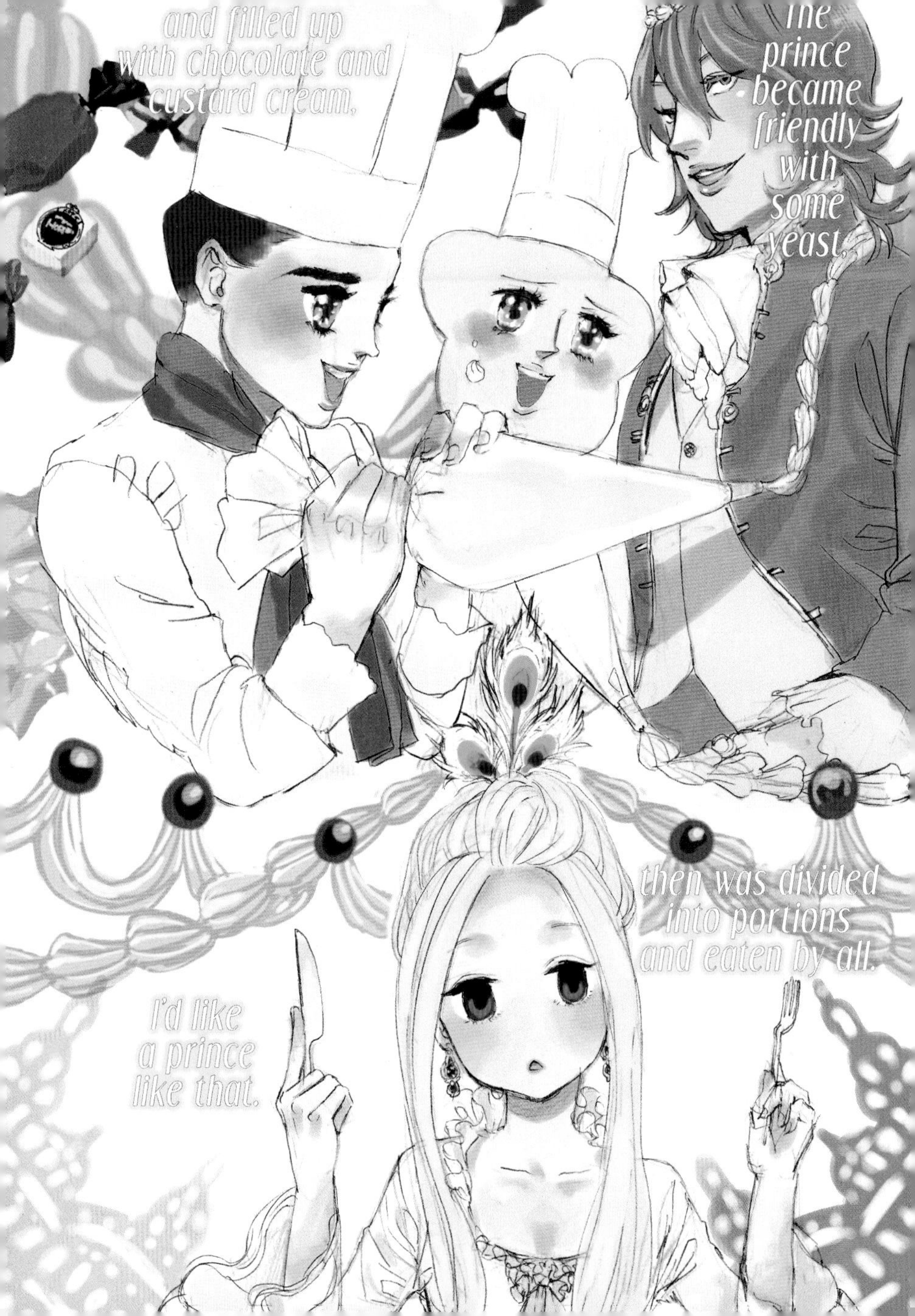
The prince became friendly with some yeast,
and filled up with chocolate and custard cream,
then was divided into portions and eaten by all.
I'd like a prince like that.

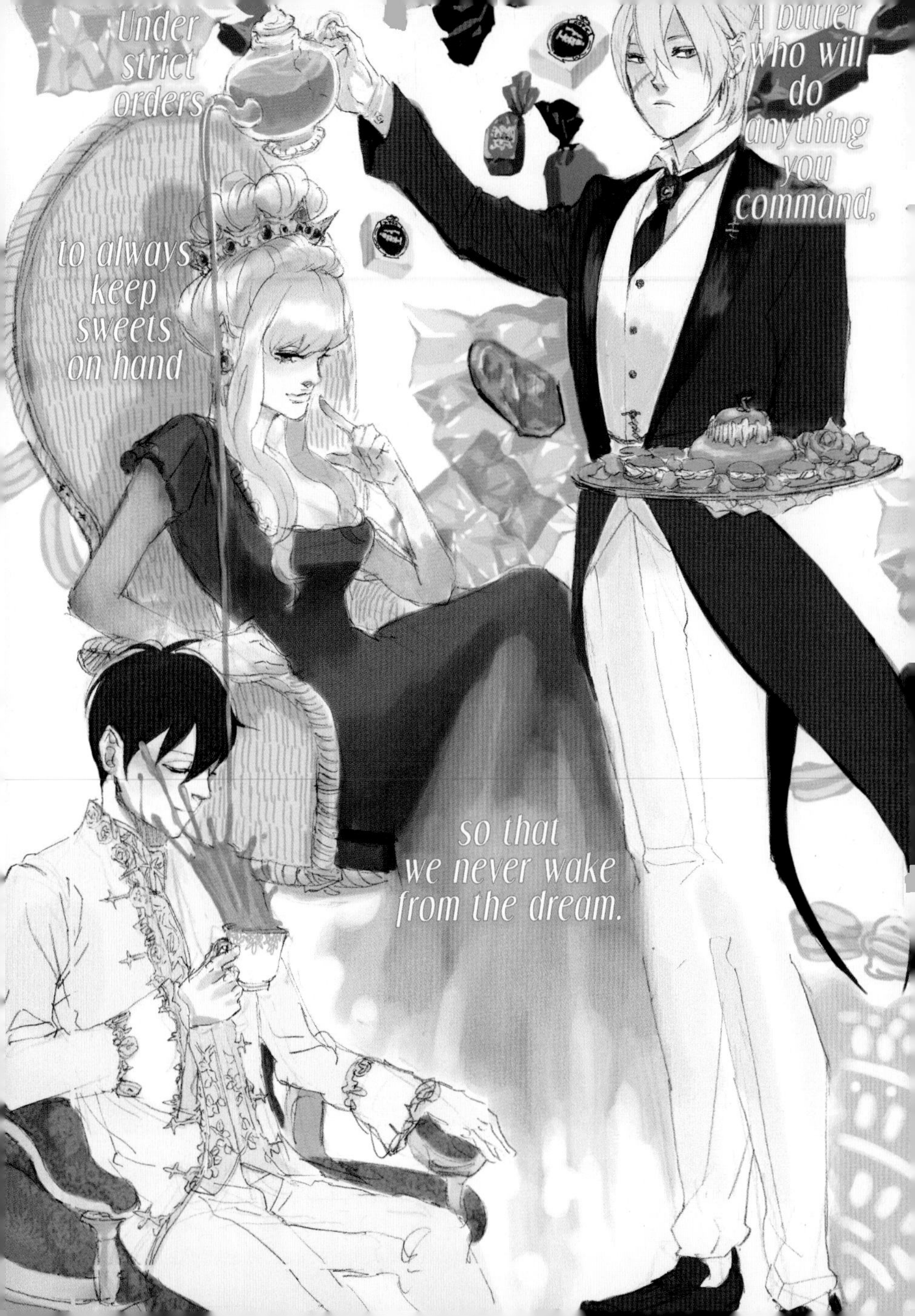
A butler who will do anything you command,
Under strict orders
to always keep sweets on hand
so that we never wake from the dream.

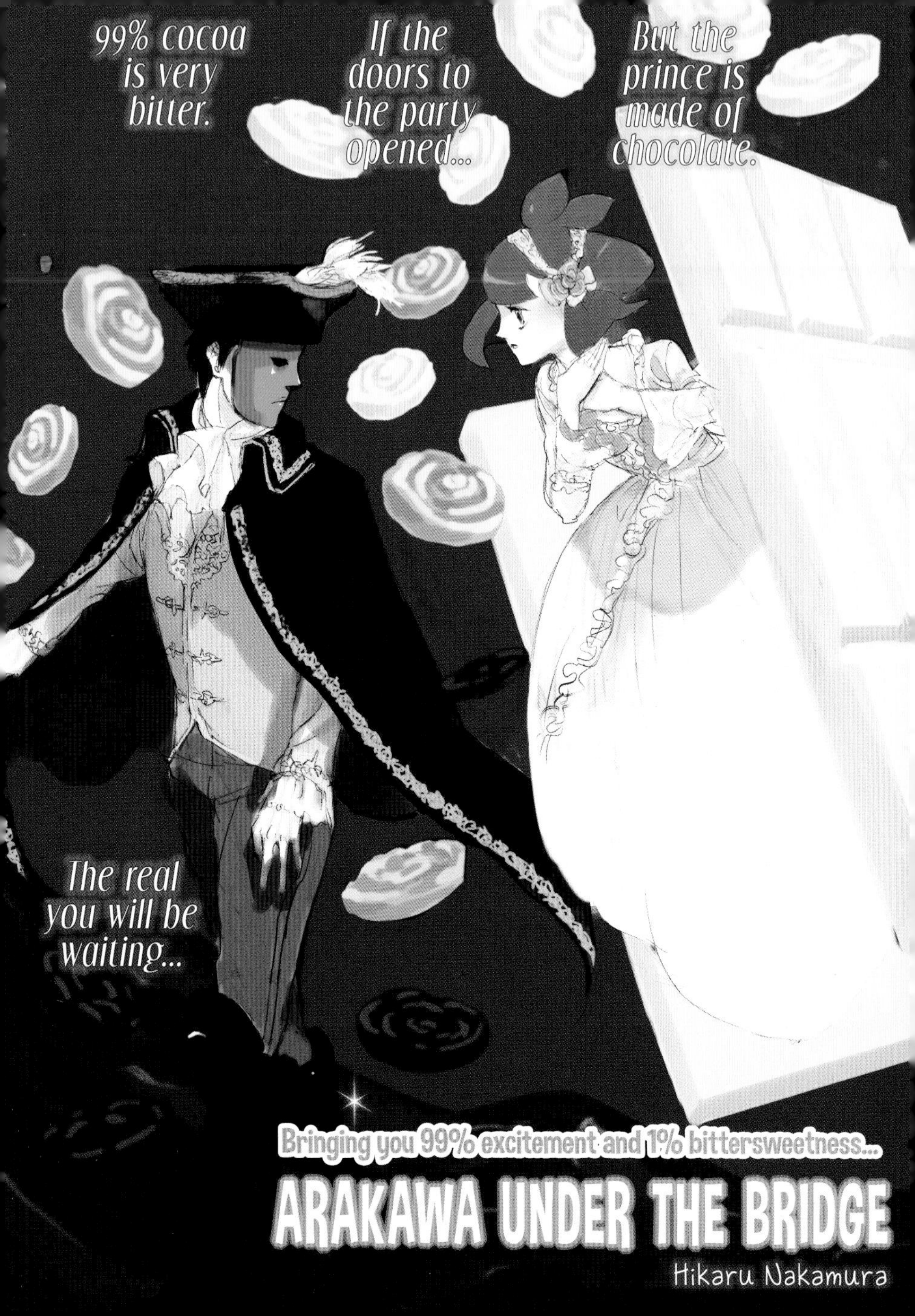

But the prince is made of chocolate.
If the doors to the party opened...
99% cocoa is very bitter.
The real you will be waiting...
Bringing you 99% excitement and 1% bittersweetness...
ARAKAWA UNDER THE BRIDGE
Hikaru Nakamura

In the middle of my work room is a fun lamp we can hang paper from. When any friends or assistants come over, I have them draw my characters. I'll get all of them drawn eventually!!

—Hikaru Nakamura

Volume 10 at last! I am so happy I could spend this much time with the people under the bridge. This photo was taken on the symbol of the Izu Plateau, Mt. Omuro, on a trip last summer with my assistants. Whoever first decided to do archery on a volcanic crater was a genius! It's a beautiful bowl-shaped mountain.

—Hikaru Nakamura

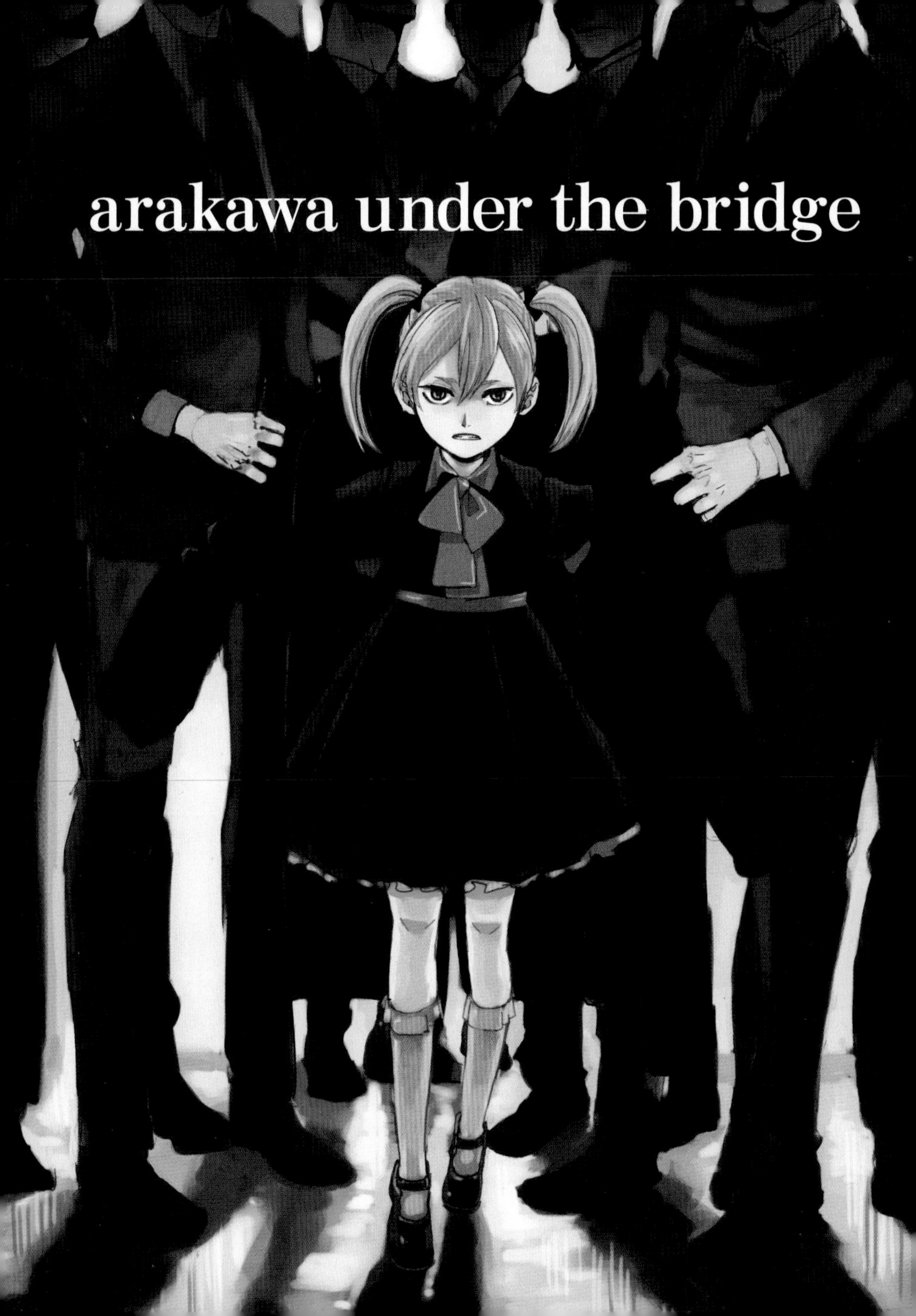
arakawa under the bridge

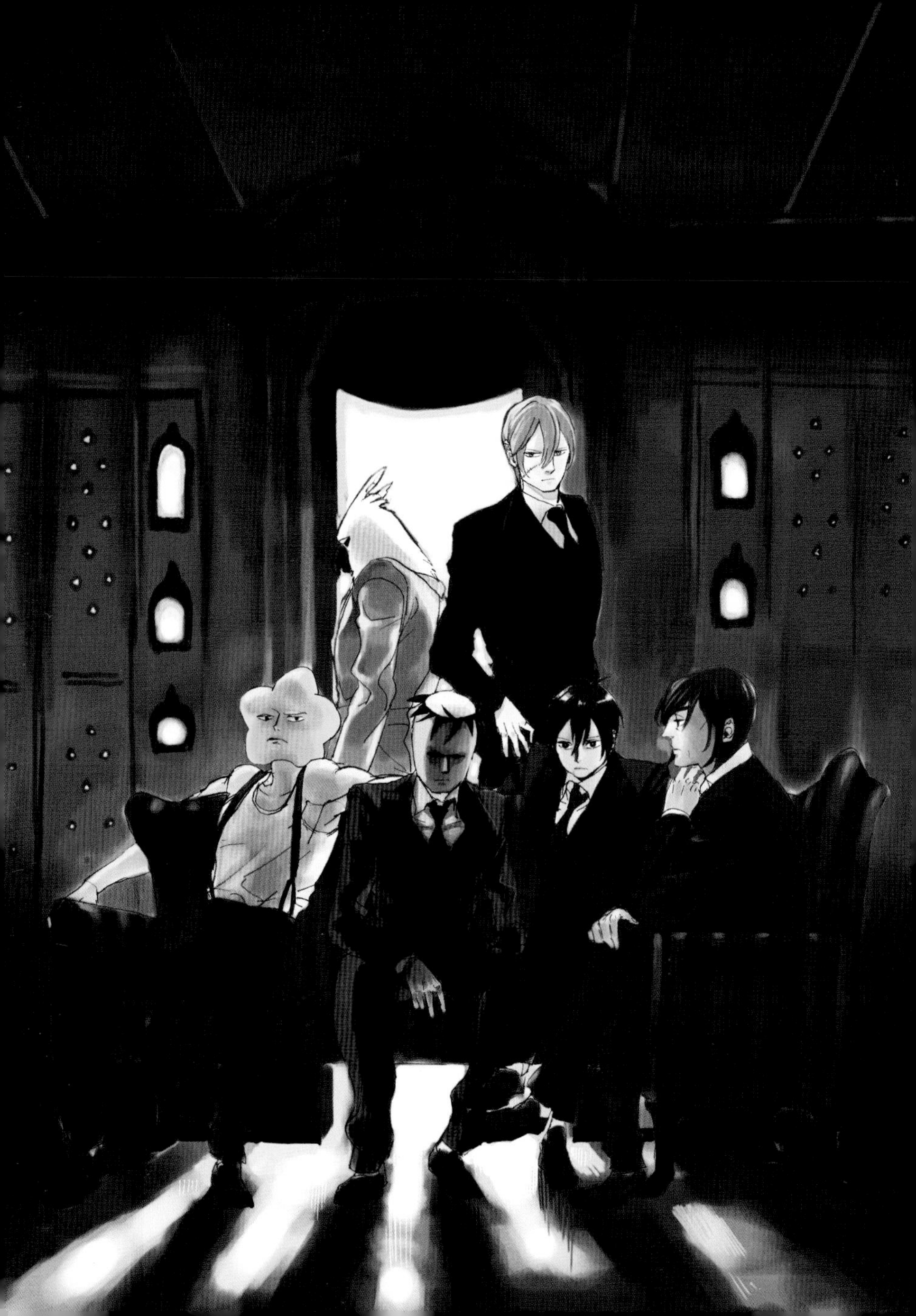

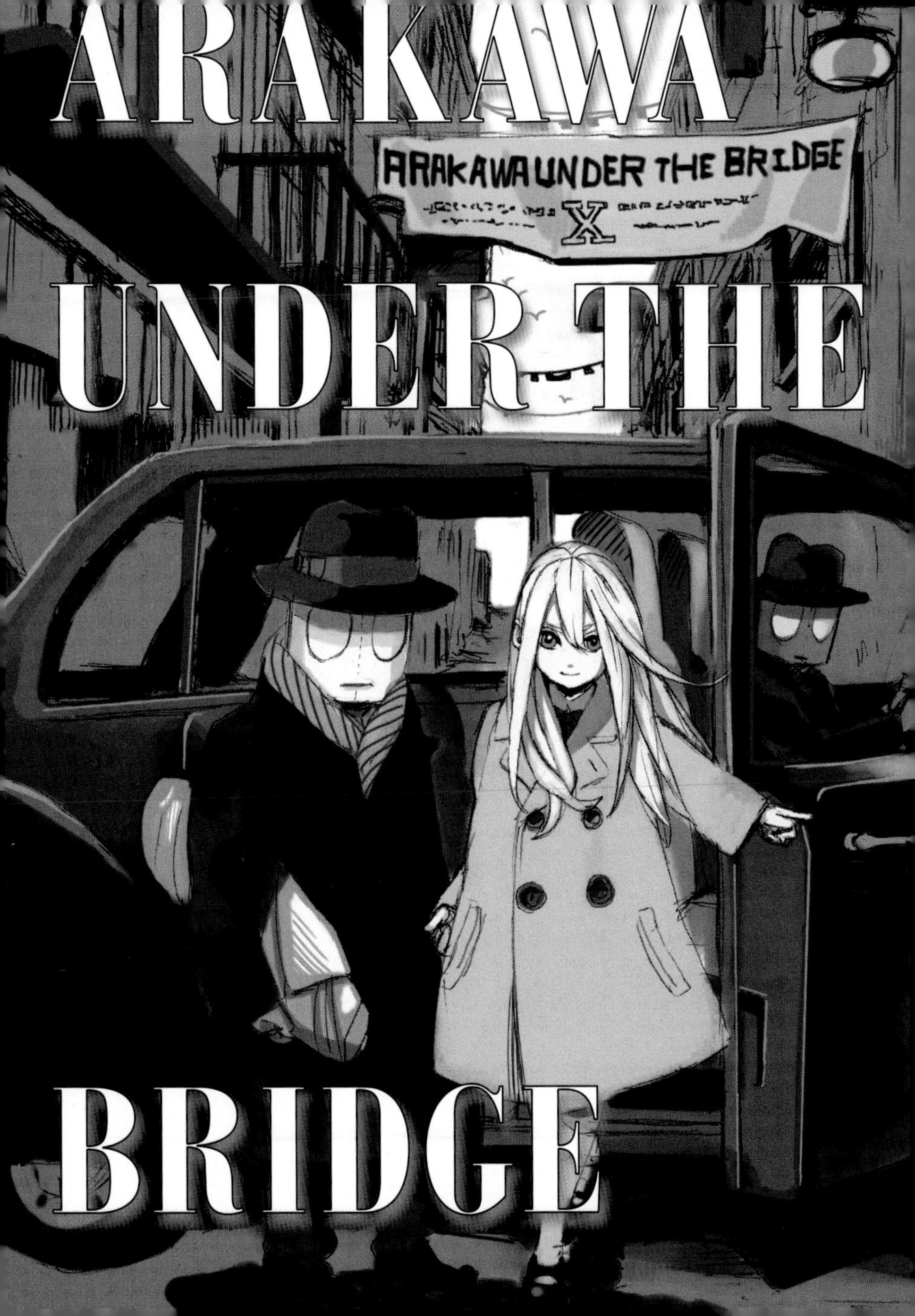
ARAKAWA UNDER THE BRIDGE
ARAKAWA UNDER THE BRIDGE
X

C O N T E N T S

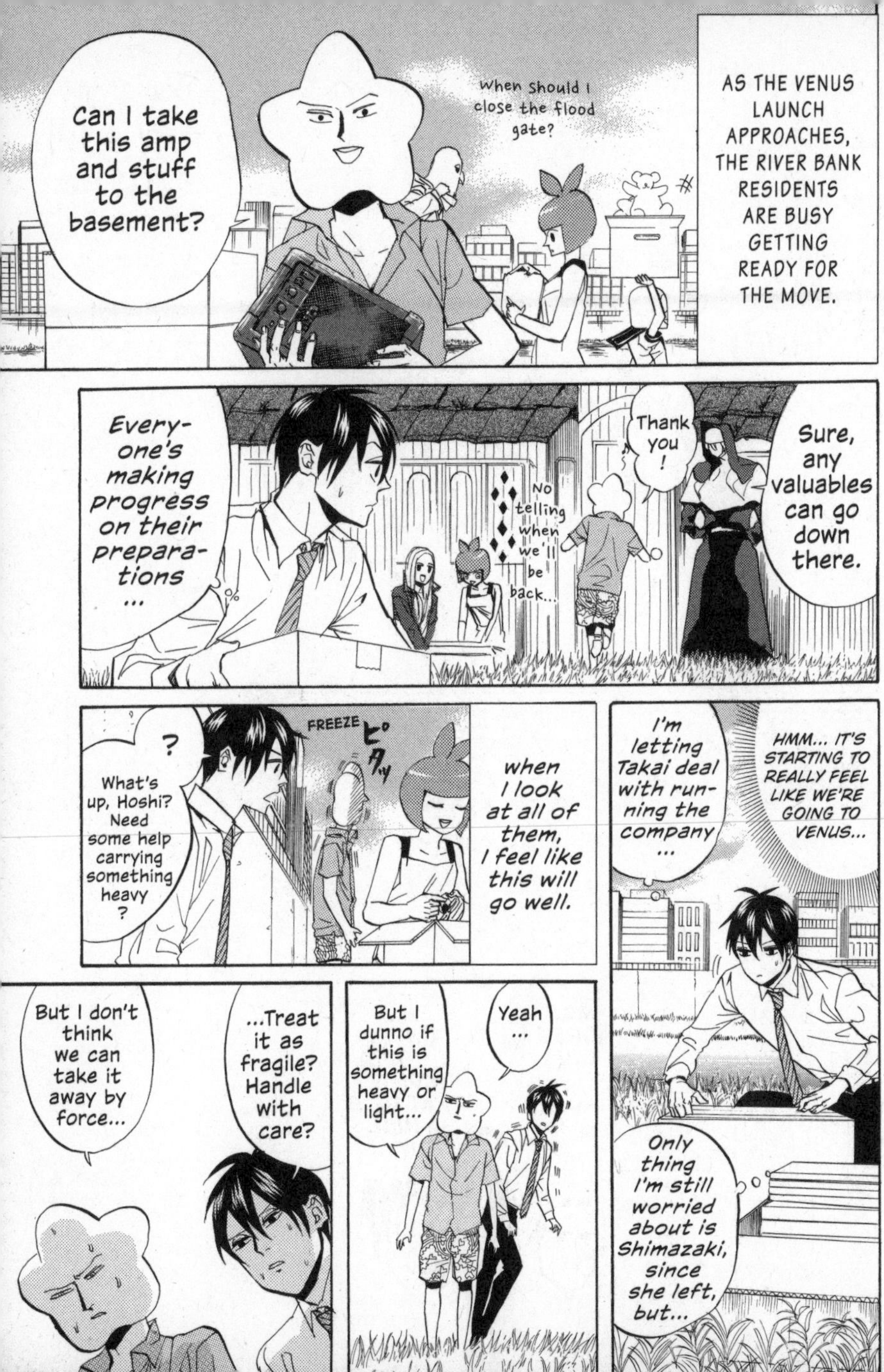
AS THE VENUS LAUNCH APPROACHES, THE RIVER BANK RESIDENTS ARE BUSY GETTING READY FOR THE MOVE.
When should I close the flood gate?
Can I take this amp and stuff to the basement?
Sure, any valuables can go down there.
Thank you!
No telling when we'll be back...
Every-one's making progress on their prepara-tions...
HMM... IT'S STARTING TO REALLY FEEL LIKE WE'RE GOING TO VENUS...
I'm letting Takai deal with run-ning the company...
Only thing I'm still worried about is Shimazaki, since she left, but...
when I look at all of them, I feel like this will go well.
FREEZE
ピタッ
?
What's up, Hoshi? Need some help carrying something heavy?
Yeah...
But I dunno if this is something heavy or light...
...Treat it as fragile? Handle with care?
But I don't think we can take it away by force...

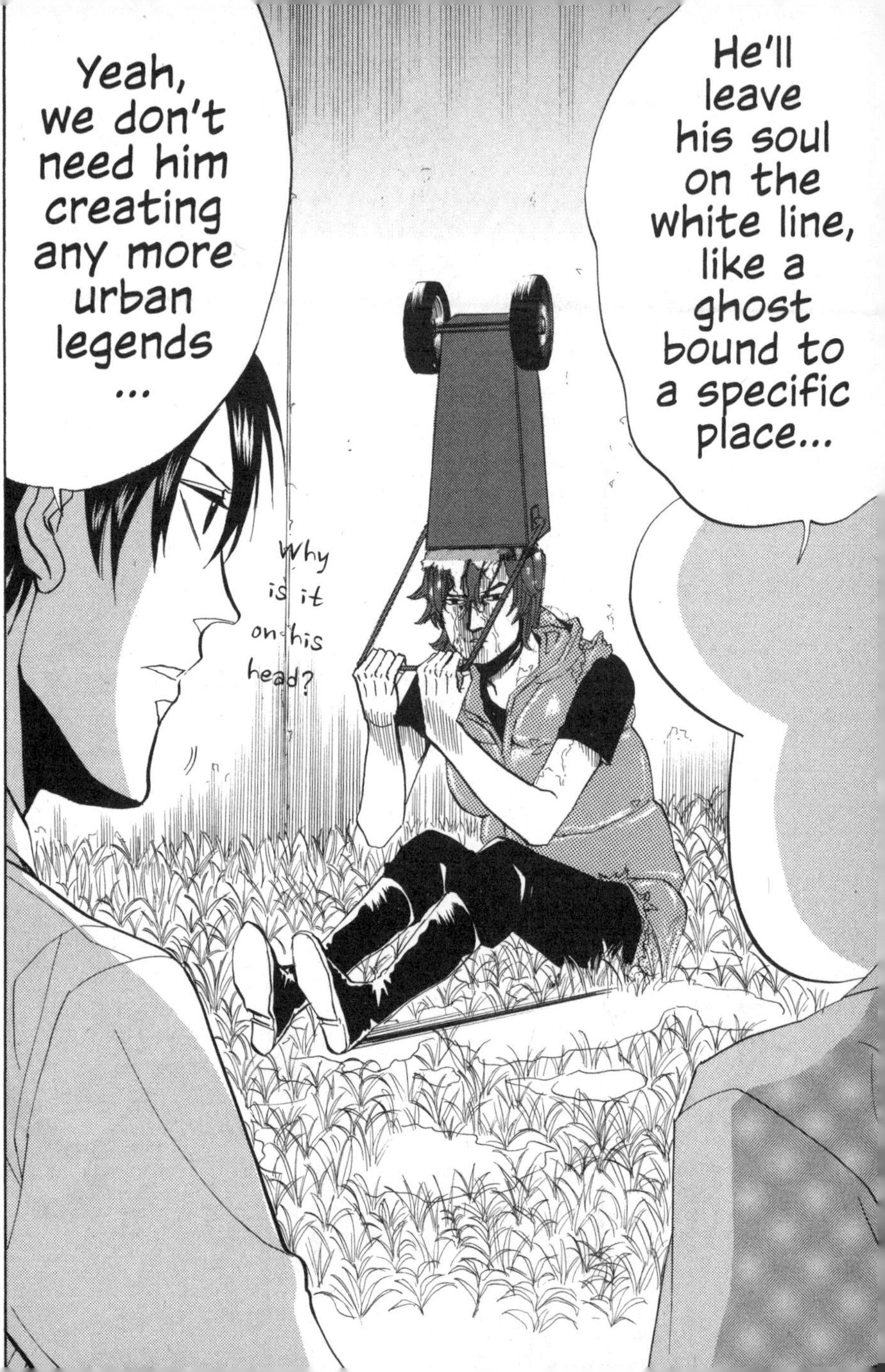
He'll leave his soul on the white line, like a ghost bound to a specific place...
Yeah, we don't need him creating any more urban legends ...
Why is it on his head?

Chapter 256: On the White Lines

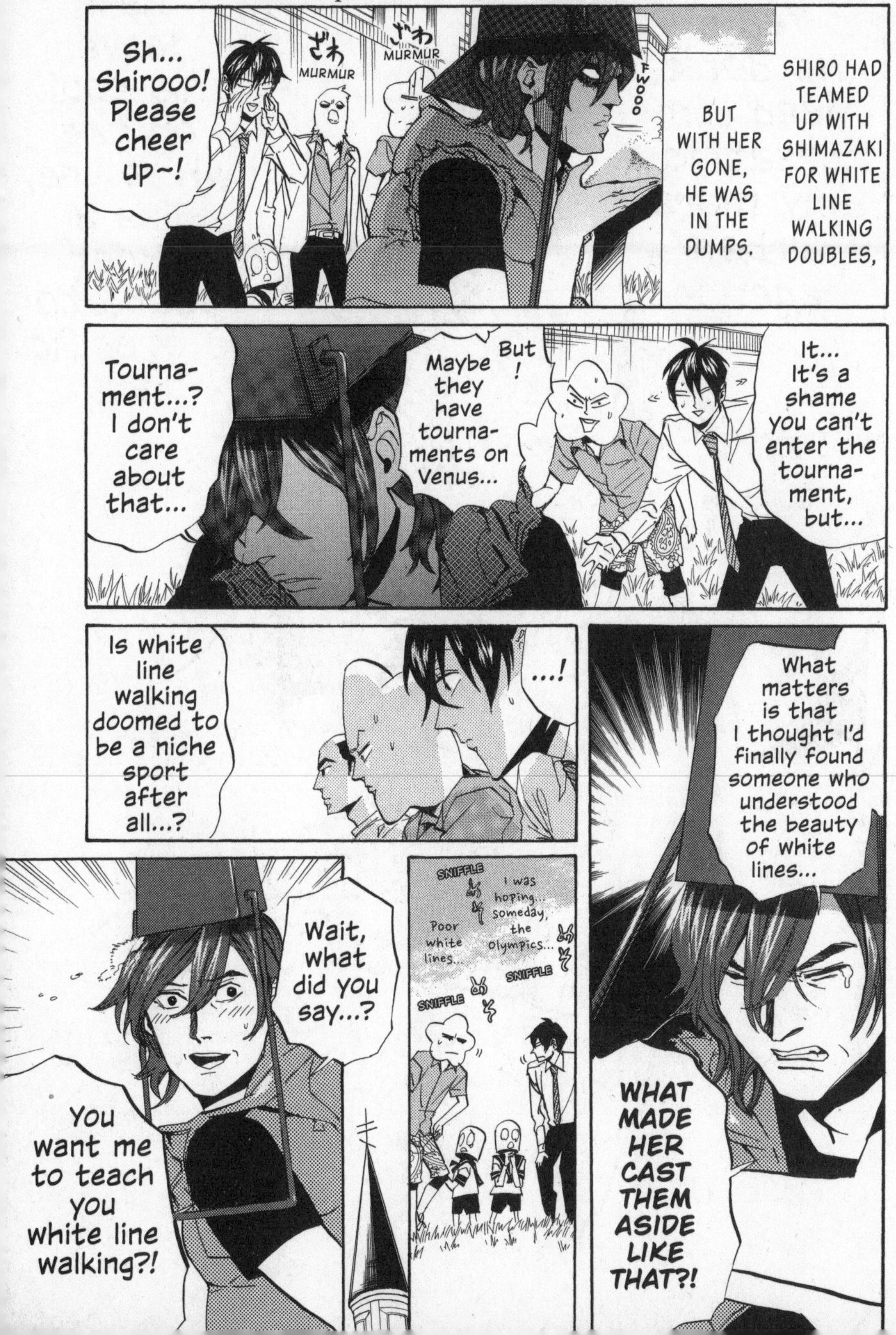
SHIRO HAD TEAMED UP WITH SHIMAZAKI FOR WHITE LINE WALKING DOUBLES,
BUT WITH HER GONE, HE WAS IN THE DUMPS.
FWOOO
ざわ MURMUR
ざわ MURMUR
Sh... Shirooo! Please cheer up~!
It... It's a shame you can't enter the tournament, but...
But!
Maybe they have tournaments on Venus...
Tournament...? I don't care about that...
What matters is that I thought I'd finally found someone who understood the beauty of white lines...
WHAT MADE HER CAST THEM ASIDE LIKE THAT?!
...!
Is white line walking doomed to be a niche sport after all...?
SNIFFLE
I was hoping... someday, the Olympics...
Poor white lines...
SNIFFLE
SNIFFLE
Wait, what did you say...?
You want me to teach you white line walking?!

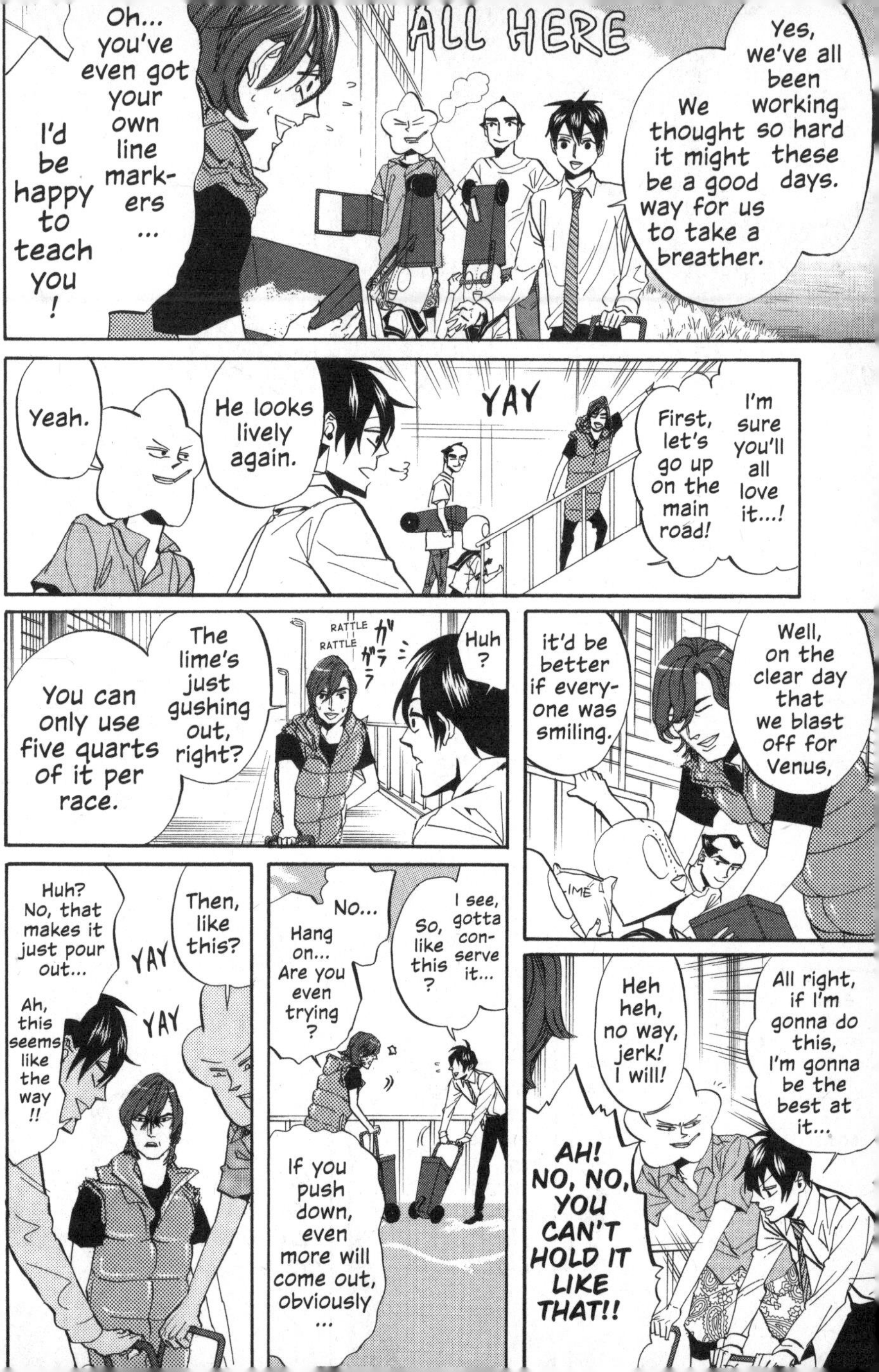

Yes, we've all been working so hard these days.
We thought it might be a good way for us to take a breather.
ALL HERE
Oh... you've even got your own line markers...
I'd be happy to teach you!
I'm sure you'll all love it...!
First, let's go up on the main road!
YAY
He looks lively again.
Yeah.
Well, on the clear day that we blast off for Venus,
it'd be better if everyone was smiling.
Huh?
RATTLE RATTLE ガラガラ
The lime's just gushing out, right?
You can only use five quarts of it per race.
All right, if I'm gonna do this, I'm gonna be the best at it...
Heh heh, no way, jerk! I will!
AH! NO, NO, YOU CAN'T HOLD IT LIKE THAT!!
I see, gotta conserve it...
So, like this?
No...
Hang on... Are you even trying?
If you push down, even more will come out, obviously...
Then, like this?
Huh? No, that makes it just pour out...
YAY
YAY
Ah, this seems like the way!!

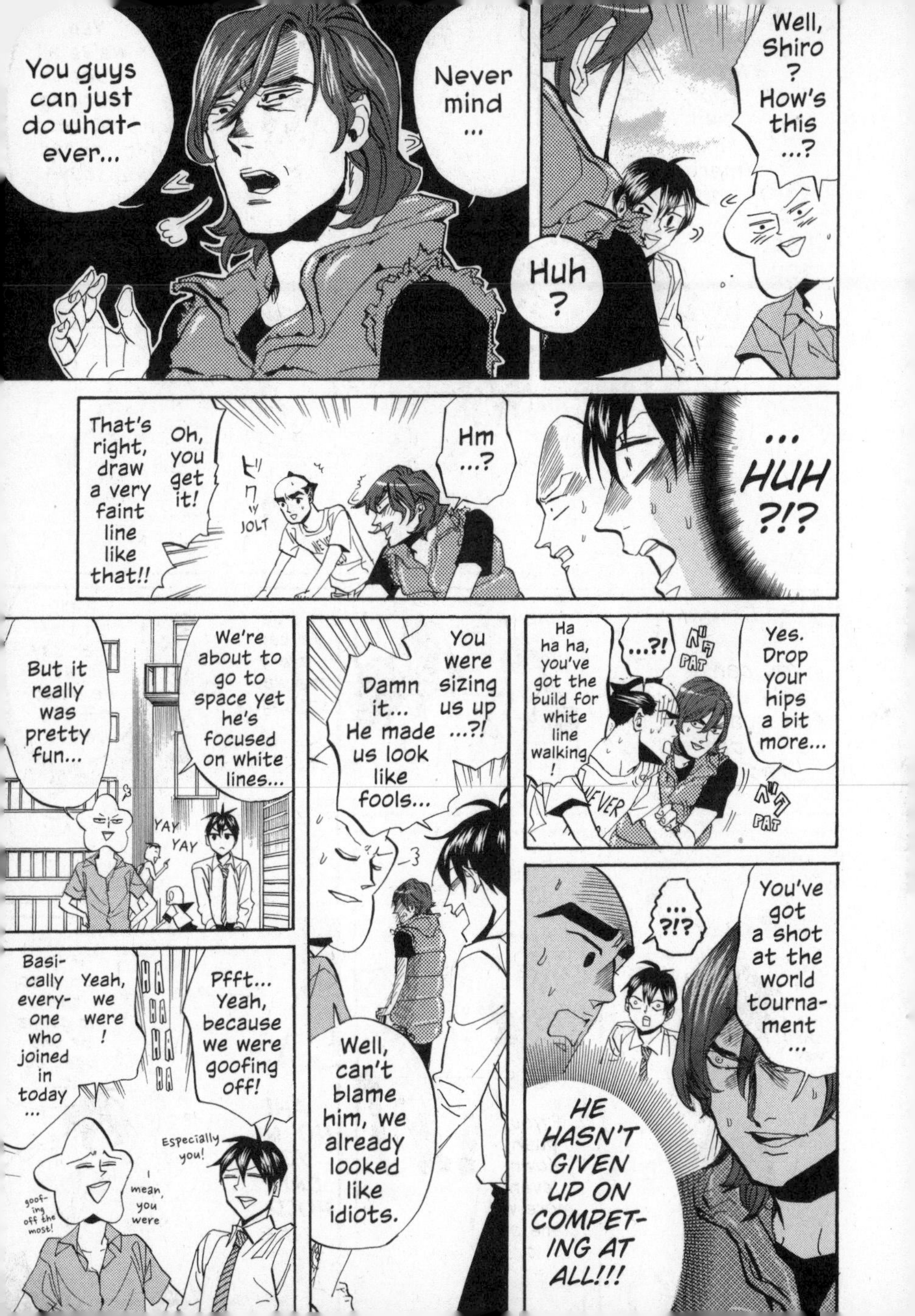

Well, Shiro? How's this...?
Huh?
Never mind...
You guys can just do whatever...
...HUH?!?
Hm...?
Oh, you get it!
That's right, draw a very faint line like that!!
JOLT
Yes. Drop your hips a bit more...
PAT
...?!
Ha ha ha, you've got the build for white line walking!
PAT
You've got a shot at the world tournament...
...?!?
HE HASN'T GIVEN UP ON COMPETING AT ALL!!!
You were sizing us up...?!
Damn it... He made us look like fools...
Well, can't blame him, we already looked like idiots.
We're about to go to space yet he's focused on white lines...
But it really was pretty fun...
YAY YAY
Pfft... Yeah, because we were goofing off!
Yeah, we were!
Basically everyone who joined in today...
HA HA HA HA HA
Especially you!
I mean, you were goofing off the most!

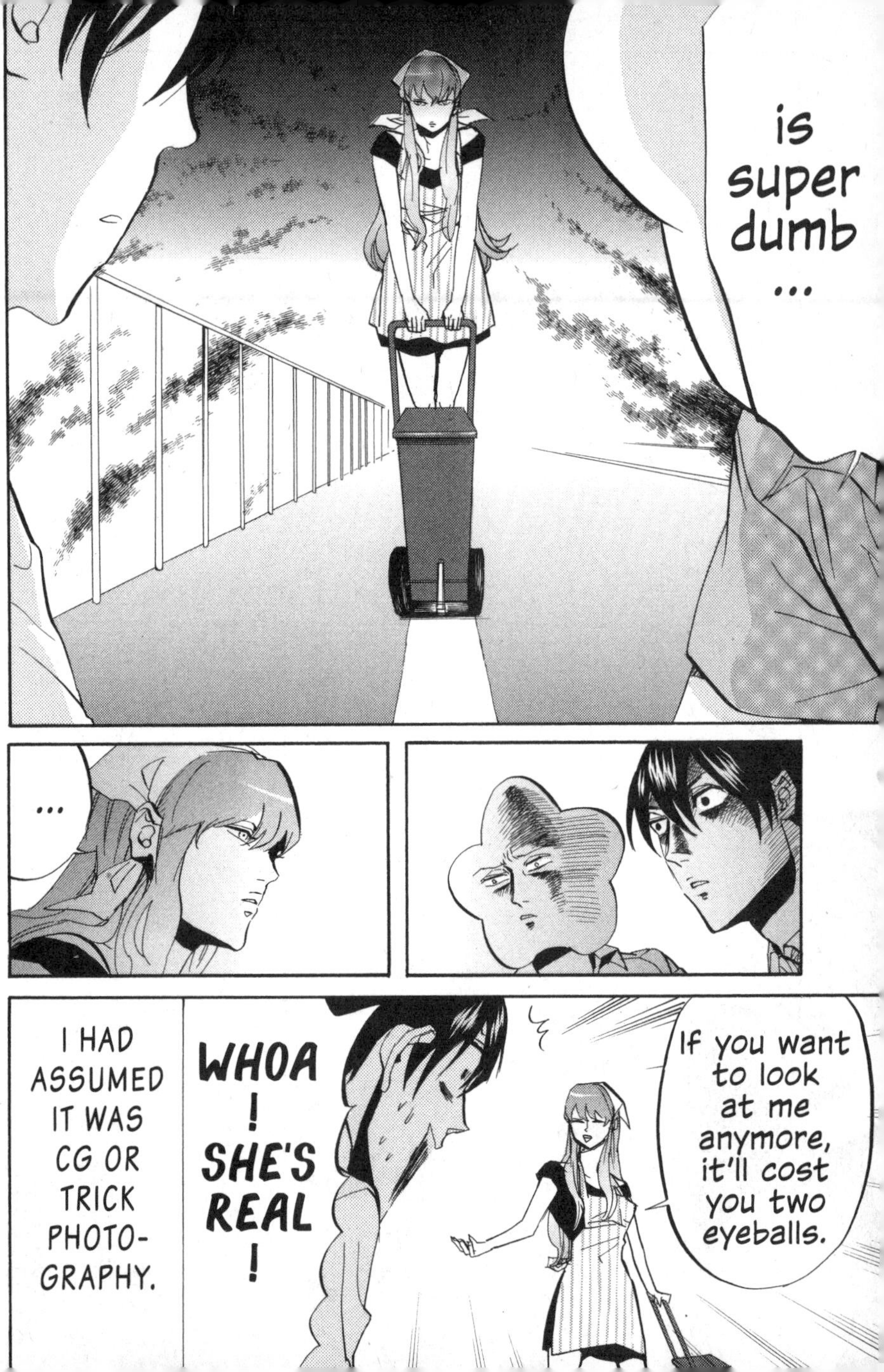
is super dumb ...
...
If you want to look at me anymore, it'll cost you two eyeballs.
WHOA! SHE'S REAL!
I HAD ASSUMED IT WAS CG OR TRICK PHOTOGRAPHY.

Chapter 257: Taking a Risk

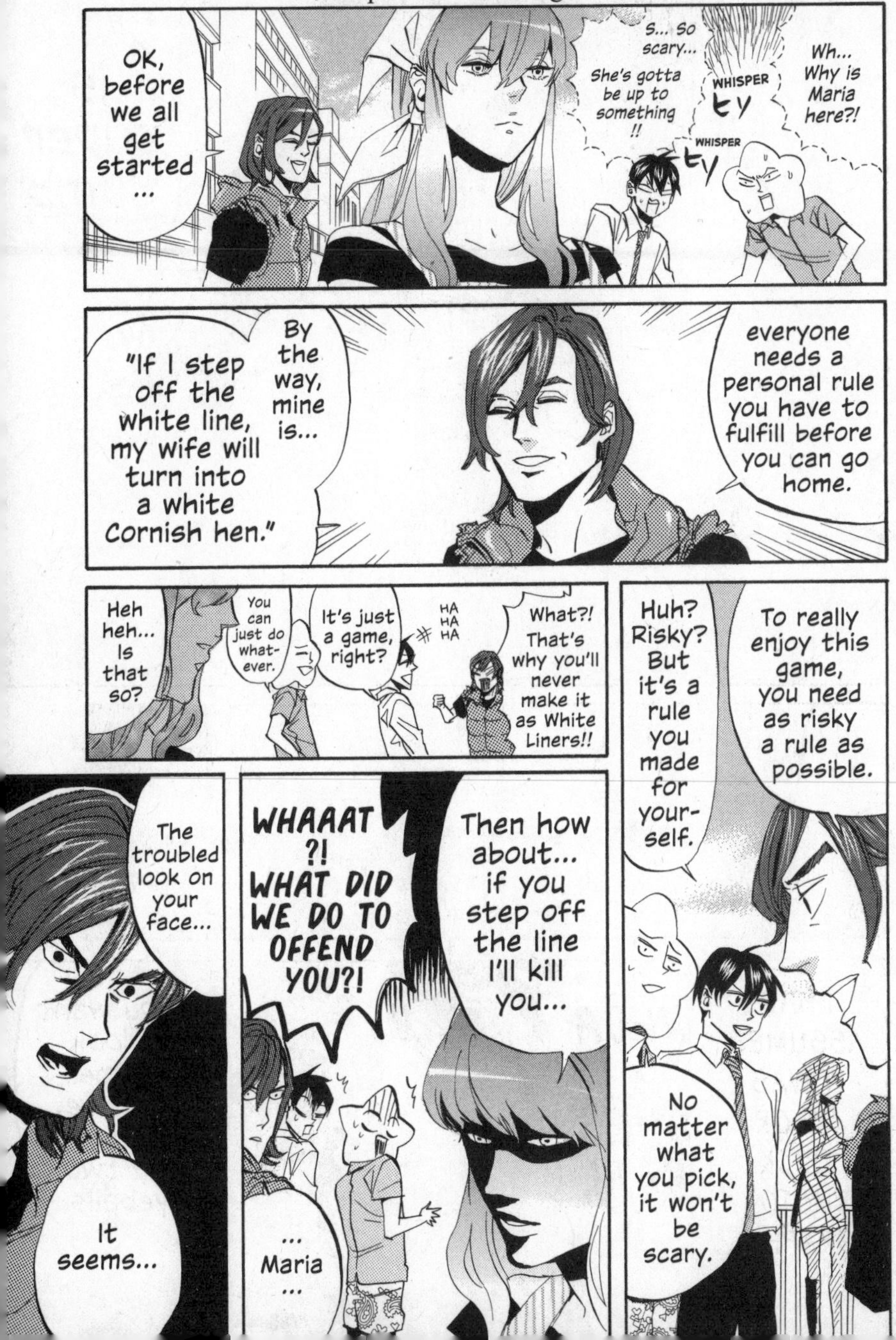
Wh... Why is Maria here?!
WHISPER
ヒソ
S... So scary...
She's gotta be up to something!!
WHISPER
ヒソ
OK, before we all get started...
everyone needs a personal rule you have to fulfill before you can go home.
By the way, mine is...
"If I step off the white line, my wife will turn into a white Cornish hen."
To really enjoy this game, you need as risky a rule as possible.
Huh? Risky? But it's a rule you made for yourself.
What?! That's why you'll never make it as White Liners!!
HA HA HA
It's just a game, right?
You can just do whatever.
Heh heh... Is that so?
No matter what you pick, it won't be scary.
Then how about... if you step off the line I'll kill you...
WHAAAT?! WHAT DID WE DO TO OFFEND YOU?!
...Maria...
The troubled look on your face...
It seems...

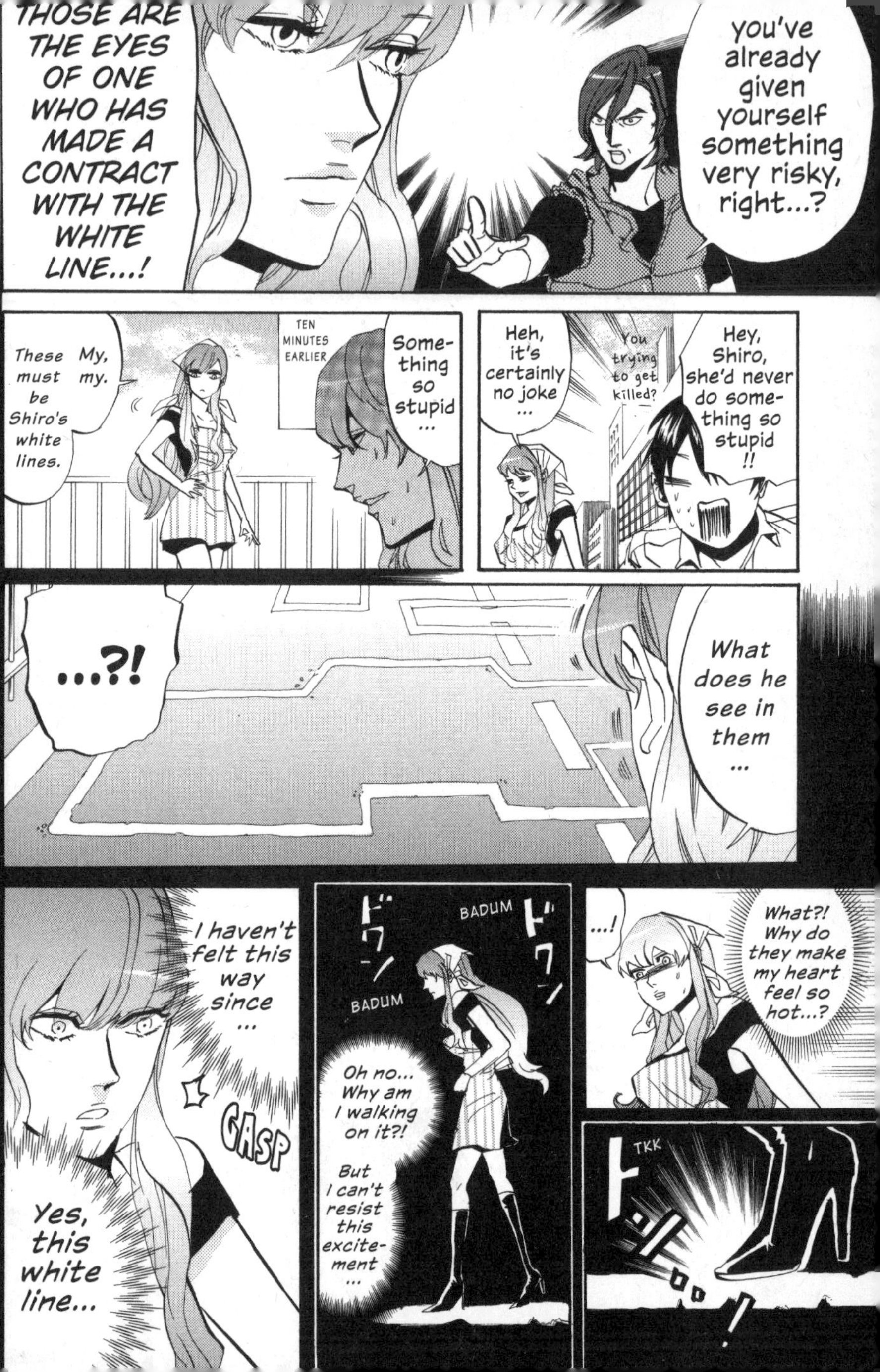
you've already given yourself something very risky, right...?
THOSE ARE THE EYES OF ONE WHO HAS MADE A CONTRACT WITH THE WHITE LINE...!
Hey, Shiro, she'd never do something so stupid!!
You trying to get killed?
Heh, it's certainly no joke...
Some-thing so stupid...
TEN MINUTES EARLIER
My, my.
These must be Shiro's white lines.
What does he see in them...
...?!
What?! Why do they make my heart feel so hot...?
...!
TKK
BADUM
BADUM
Oh no... Why am I walking on it?!
But I can't resist this excite-ment...
I haven't felt this way since...
GASP
Yes, this white line...

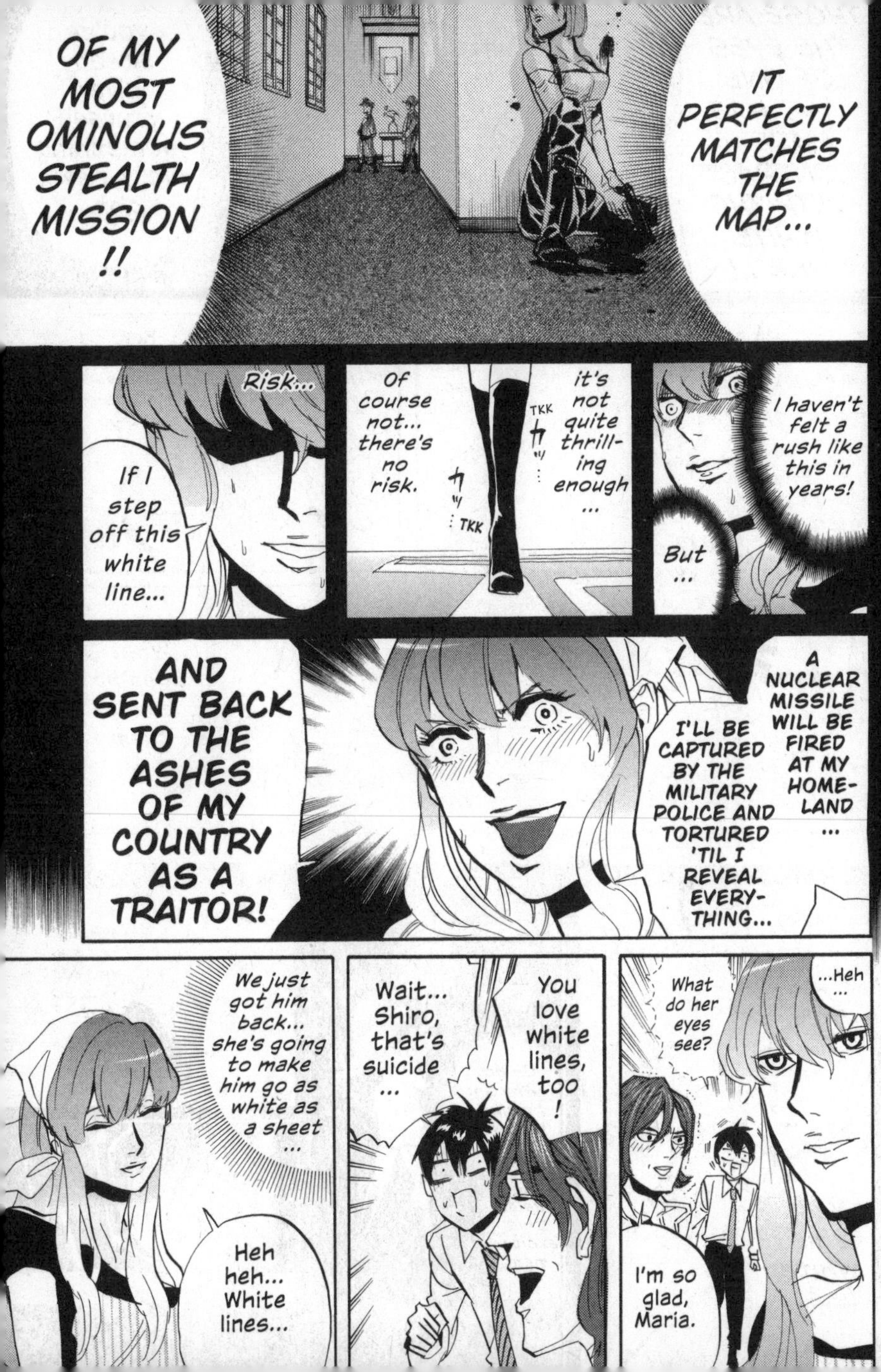
IT PERFECTLY MATCHES THE MAP...
OF MY MOST OMINOUS STEALTH MISSION !!
I haven't felt a rush like this in years!
But ...
it's not quite thrill-ing enough ...
TKK
Of course not... there's no risk.
TKK
Risk...
If I step off this white line...
A NUCLEAR MISSILE WILL BE FIRED AT MY HOME-LAND ...
I'LL BE CAPTURED BY THE MILITARY POLICE AND TORTURED 'TIL I REVEAL EVERY-THING...
AND SENT BACK TO THE ASHES OF MY COUNTRY AS A TRAITOR!
...Heh ...
What do her eyes see?
I'm so glad, Maria.
You love white lines, too!
Wait... Shiro, that's suicide ...
We just got him back... she's going to make him go as white as a sheet ...
Heh heh... White lines...

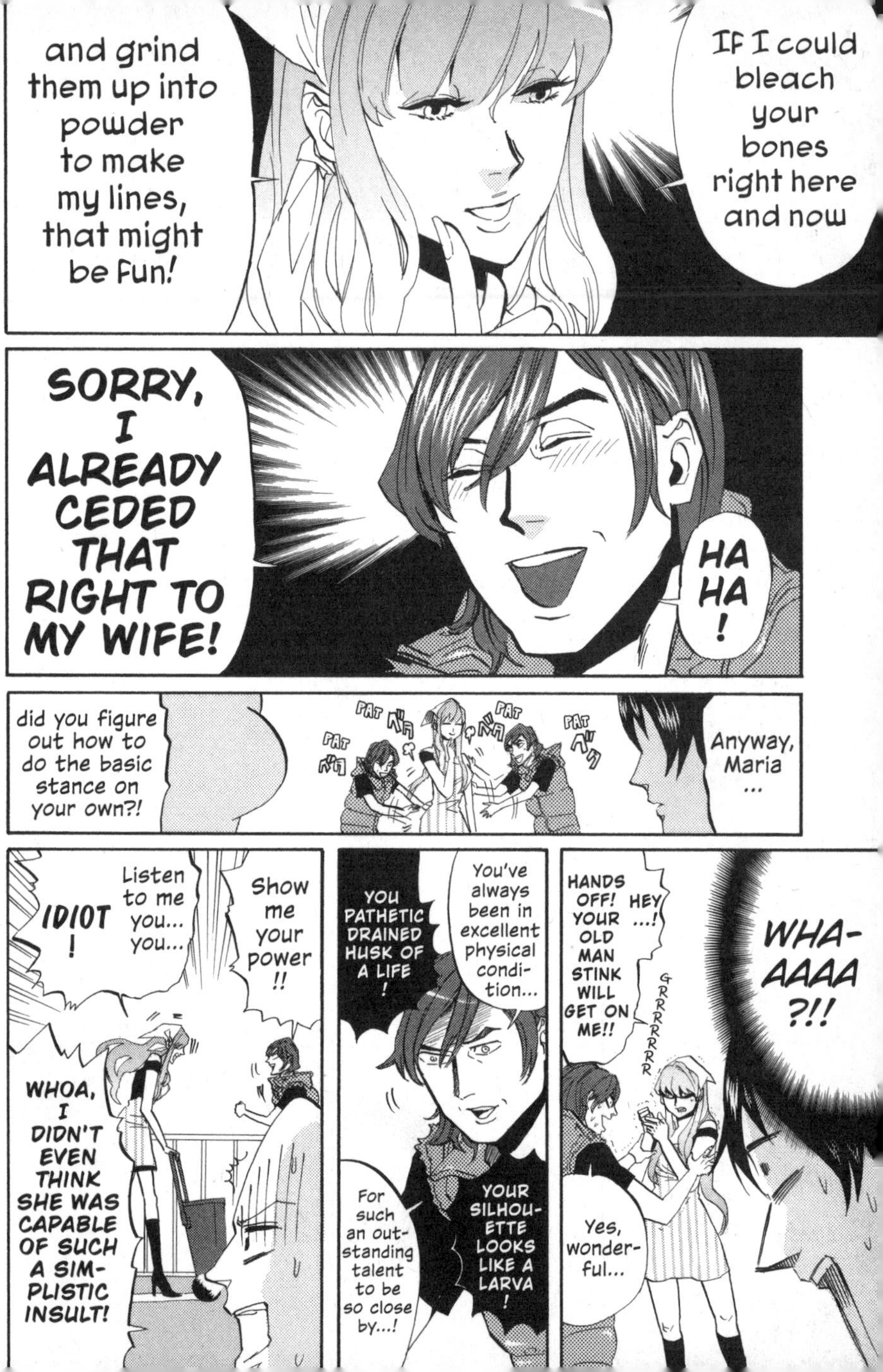

If I could bleach your bones right here and now
and grind them up into powder to make my lines, that might be fun!
HA HA!
SORRY, I ALREADY CEDED THAT RIGHT TO MY WIFE!
Anyway, Maria ...
PAT PAT PAT PAT
did you figure out how to do the basic stance on your own?!
WHA-AAAA?!!
HEY ...!
HANDS OFF! YOUR OLD MAN STINK WILL GET ON ME!!
GRRRRRRR
Yes, wonder-ful...
You've always been in excellent physical condi-tion...
YOU PATHETIC DRAINED HUSK OF A LIFE!
For such an out-standing talent to be so close by...!
YOUR SILHOU-ETTE LOOKS LIKE A LARVA!
Show me your power!!
Listen to me you... you...
IDIOT!
WHOA, I DIDN'T EVEN THINK SHE WAS CAPABLE OF SUCH A SIM-PLISTIC INSULT!

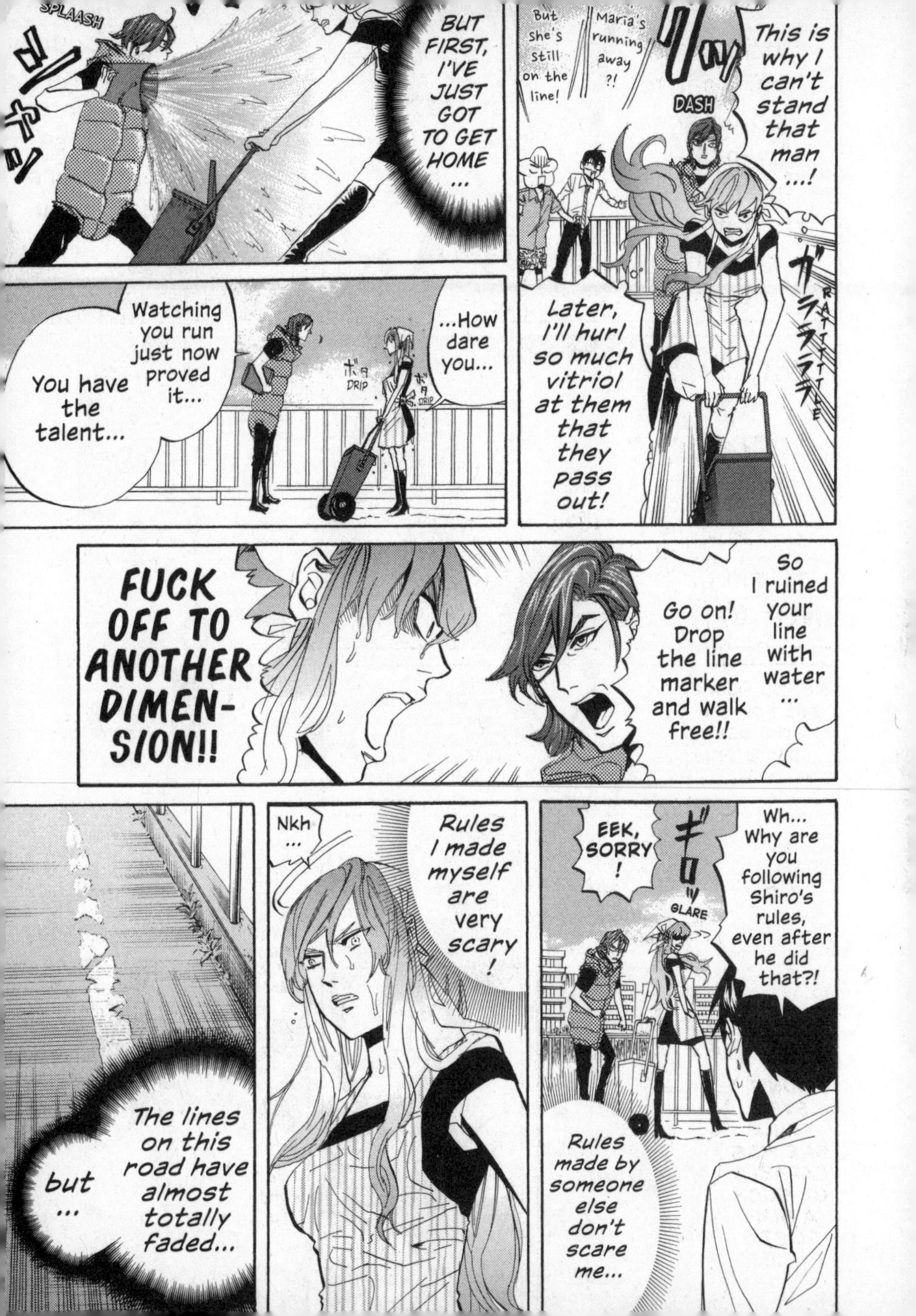
This is why I can't stand that man...!
Maria's running away ?!
But she's still on the line!
DASH
RATTTTLE
Later, I'll hurl so much vitriol at them that they pass out!
BUT FIRST, I'VE JUST GOT TO GET HOME ...
SPLAASH
...How dare you...
DRIP
DRIP
Watching you run just now proved it...
You have the talent...
So I ruined your line with water ...
Go on! Drop the line marker and walk free!!
FUCK OFF TO ANOTHER DIMENSION!!
Wh... Why are you following Shiro's rules, even after he did that?!
EEK, SORRY!
GLARE
Rules made by someone else don't scare me...
Rules I made myself are very scary!
Nkh ...
The lines on this road have almost totally faded...
but ...

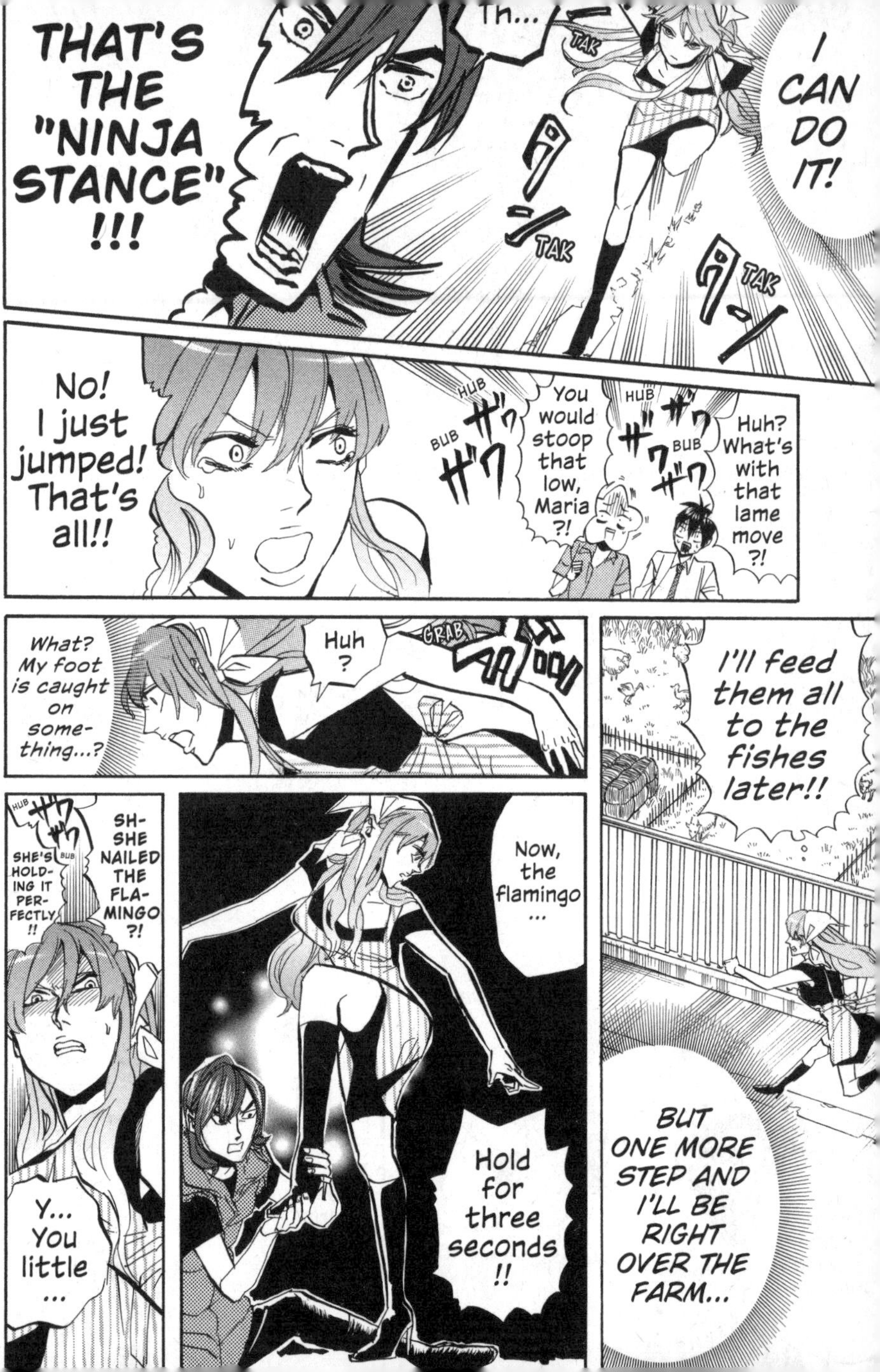
I CAN DO IT!
TAK
TAK
TAK
Th...
THAT'S THE "NINJA STANCE"!!!
Huh? What's with that lame move?!
HUB
BUB
You would stoop that low, Maria?!
HUB
BUB
No! I just jumped! That's all!!
I'll feed them all to the fishes later!!
BUT ONE MORE STEP AND I'LL BE RIGHT OVER THE FARM...
GRAB
Huh?
What? My foot is caught on something...?
Now, the flamingo...
Hold for three seconds!!
SH-SHE NAILED THE FLAMINGO?!
SHE'S HOLDING IT PERFECTLY!!
HUB
BUB
Y... You little...

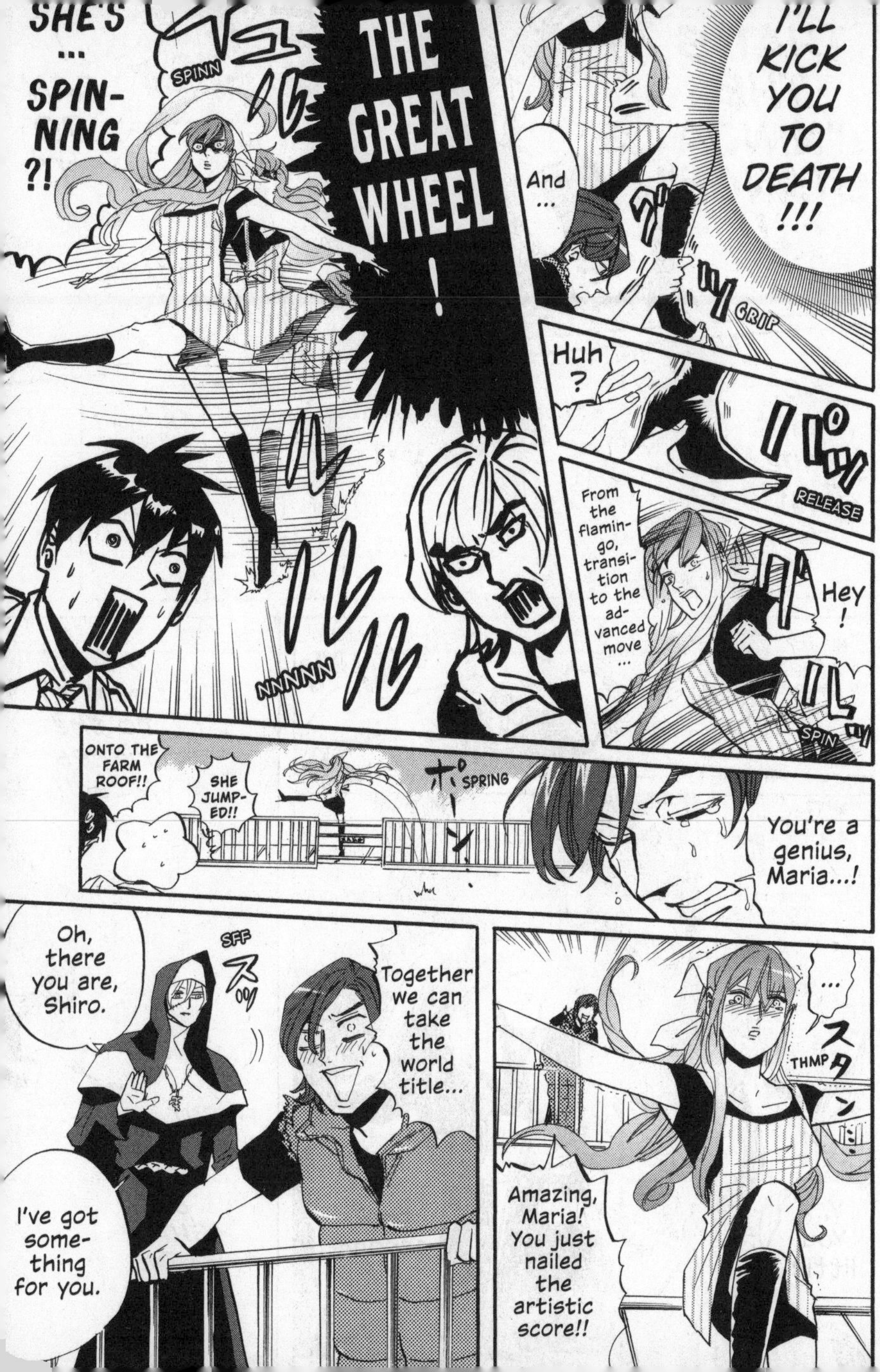
I'LL KICK YOU TO DEATH!!!
And...
GRIP
Huh?
RELEASE
From the flamingo, transition to the advanced move...
Hey!
SPIN
SHE'S... SPINNING?!
SPINN
THE GREAT WHEEL!
NNNNN
You're a genius, Maria...!
SPRING
SHE JUMPED!!
ONTO THE FARM ROOF!!
...
THMP
Amazing, Maria! You just nailed the artistic score!!
Together we can take the world title...
Oh, there you are, Shiro.
SFF
I've got something for you.

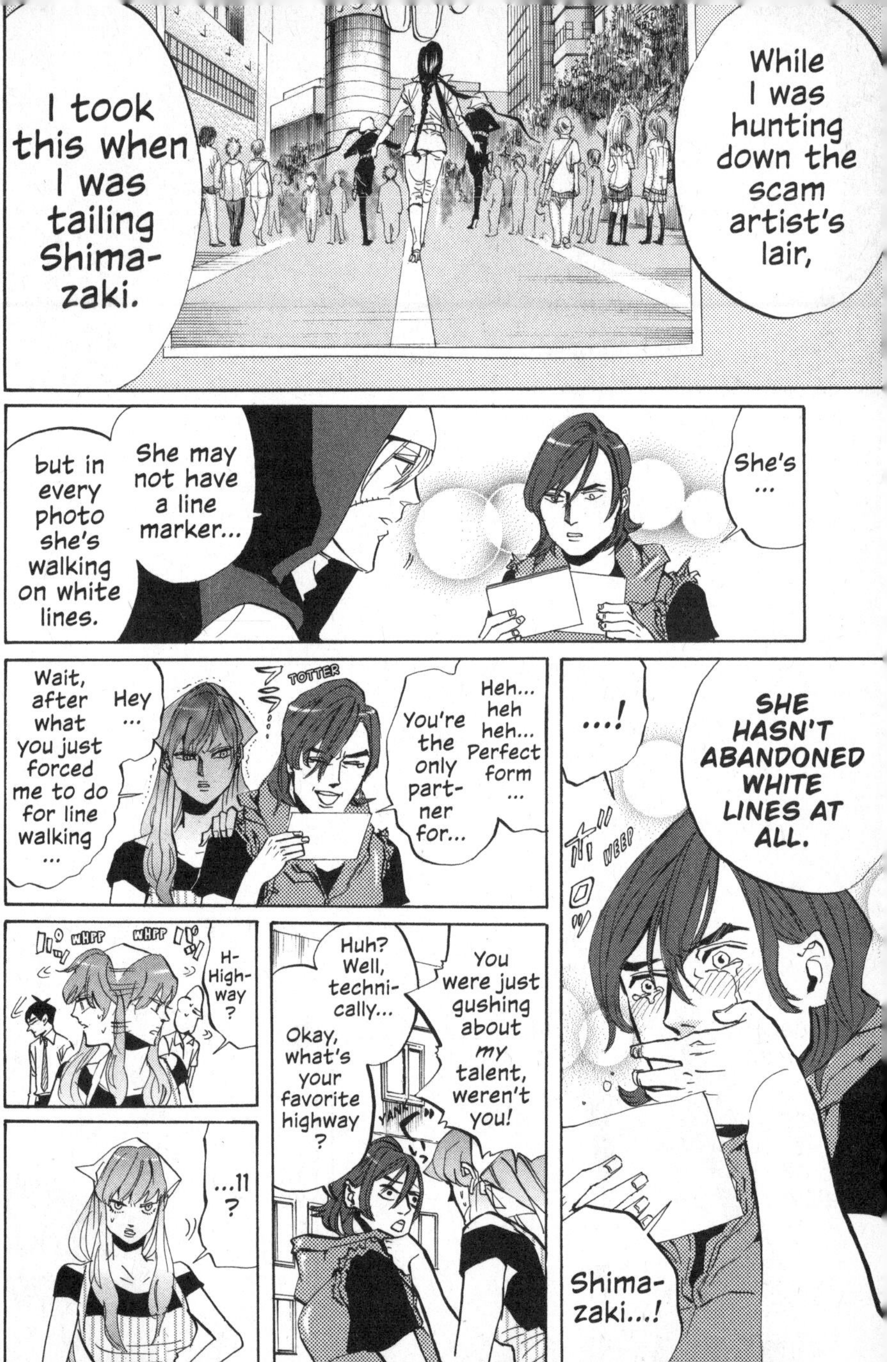
While I was hunting down the scam artist's lair,
I took this when I was tailing Shima-zaki.
She's...
She may not have a line marker...
but in every photo she's walking on white lines.
SHE HASN'T ABANDONED WHITE LINES AT ALL.
...!
WEEP
Shima-zaki...!
Heh... heh heh... Perfect form...
You're the only part-ner for...
TOTTER
Hey...
Wait, after what you just forced me to do for line walking...
You were just gushing about *my* talent, weren't you!
Huh? Well, techni-cally...
Okay, what's your favorite highway?
YANK
H-High-way?
WHPP
WHPP
...11?

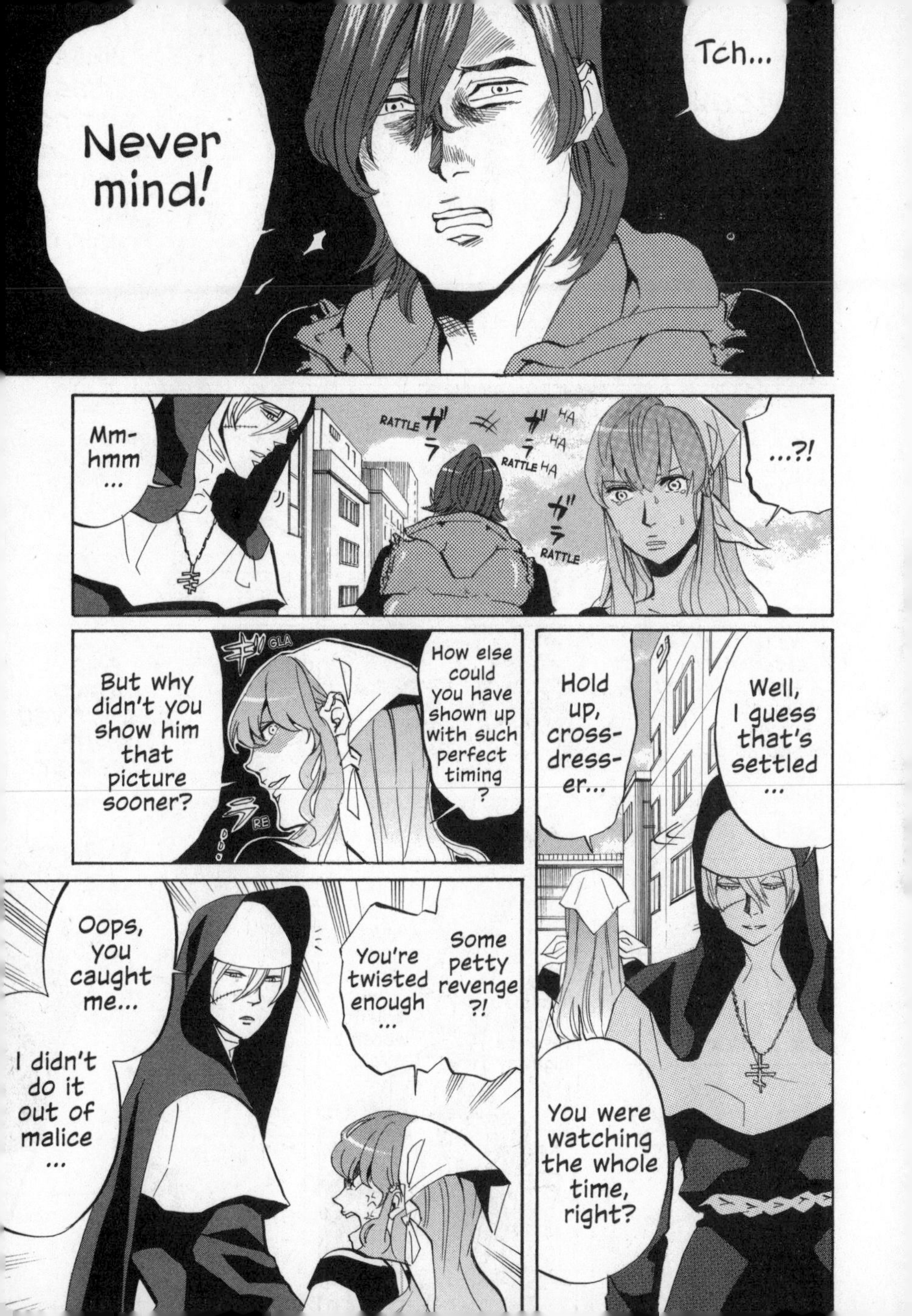

Tch...
Never mind!
...?!
RATTLE
HA
HA
RATTLE HA
RATTLE
Mm-hmm ...
Well, I guess that's settled ...
Hold up, cross-dresser...
You were watching the whole time, right?
How else could you have shown up with such perfect timing ?
GLA
RE
But why didn't you show him that picture sooner?
Some petty revenge ?!
You're twisted enough ...
Oops, you caught me...
I didn't do it out of malice ...

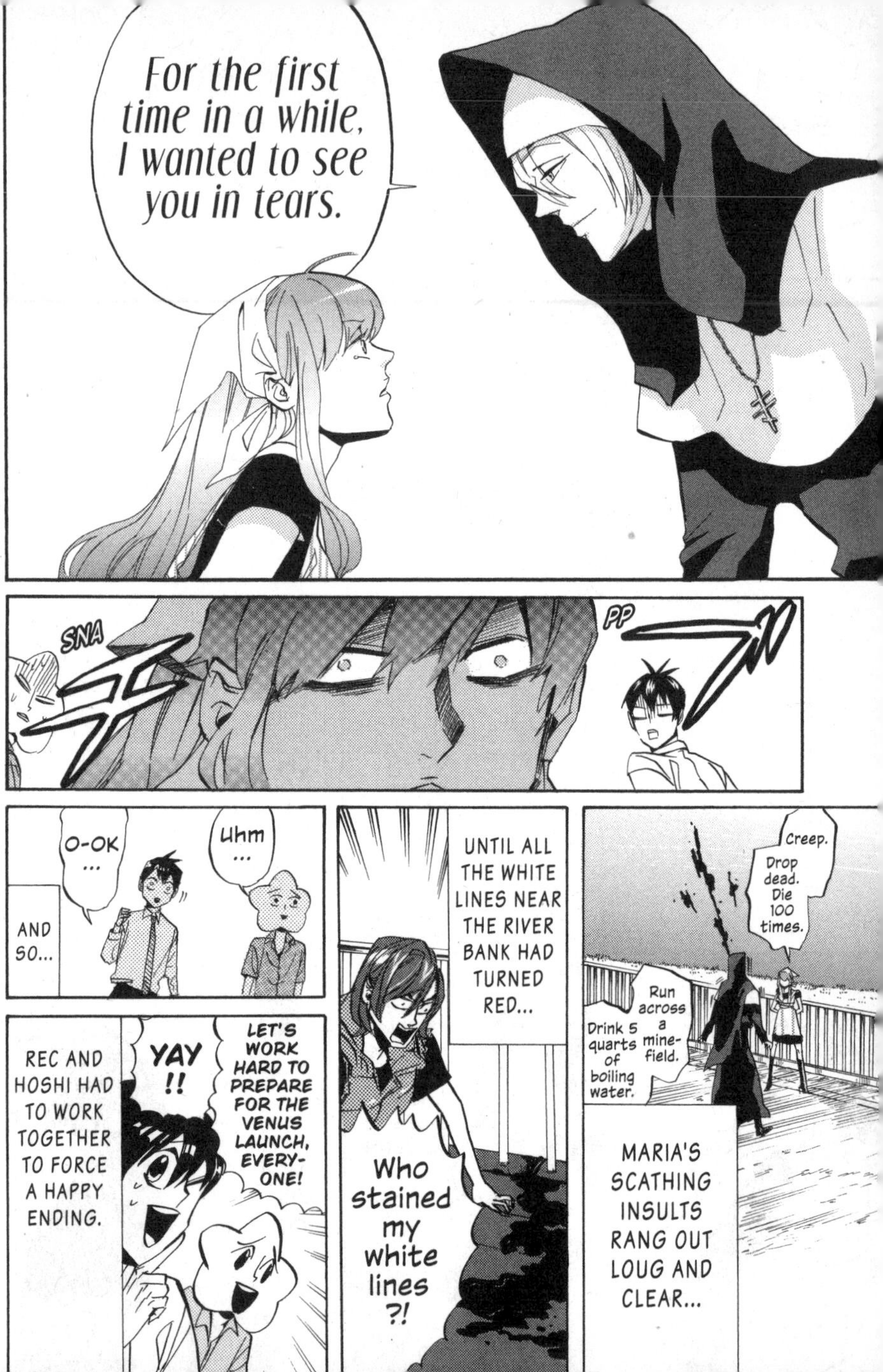
For the first time in a while, I wanted to see you in tears.
SNA
PP
Creep.
Drop dead.
Die 100 times.
Run across a minefield.
Drink 5 quarts of boiling water.
MARIA'S SCATHING INSULTS RANG OUT LOUG AND CLEAR...
UNTIL ALL THE WHITE LINES NEAR THE RIVER BANK HAD TURNED RED...
Who stained my white lines?!
Uhm ...
O-OK ...
AND SO...
LET'S WORK HARD TO PREPARE FOR THE VENUS LAUNCH, EVERY-ONE!
YAY !!
REC AND HOSHI HAD TO WORK TOGETHER TO FORCE A HAPPY ENDING.

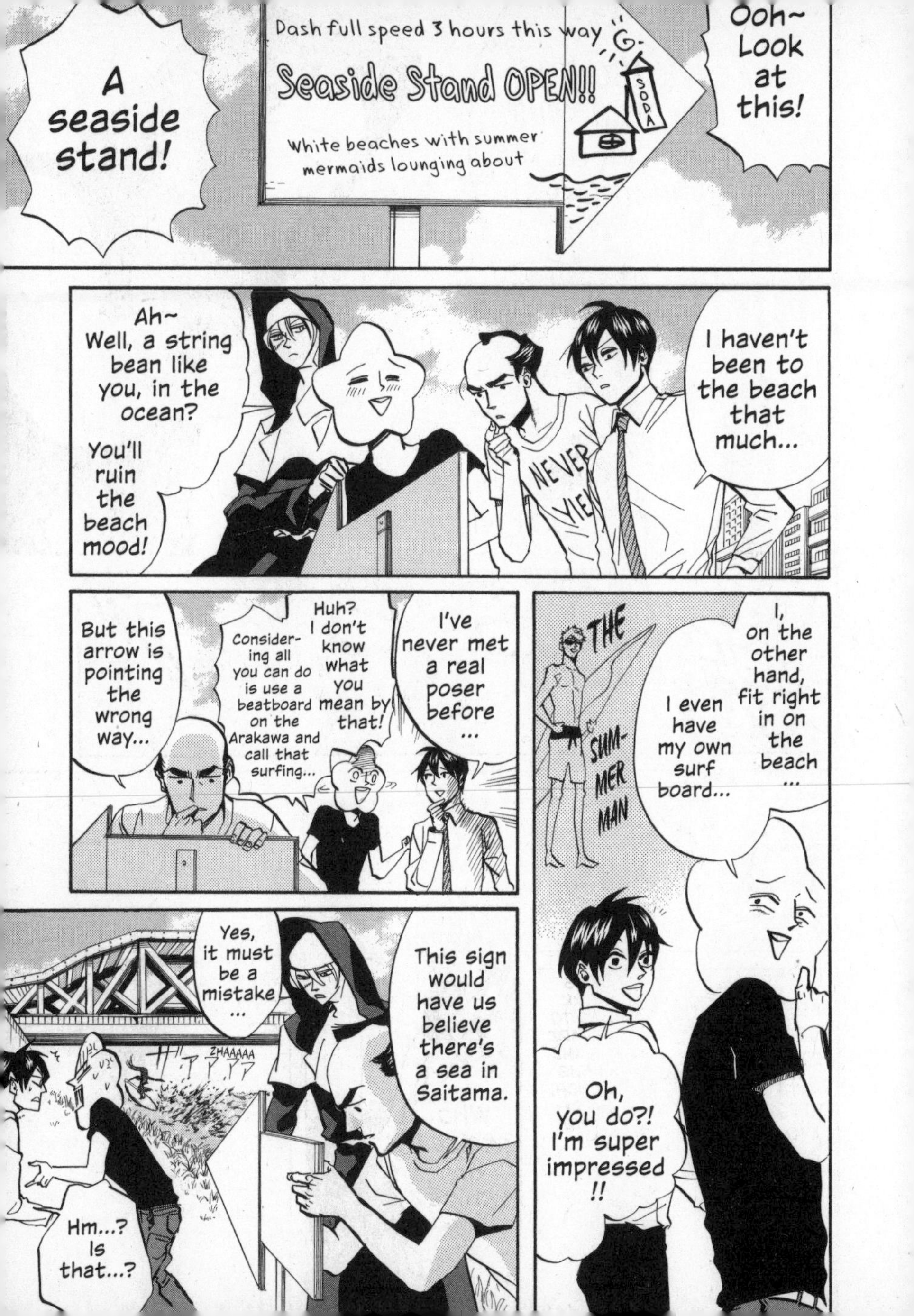
Ooh~ Look at this!
Dash full speed 3 hours this way
Seaside Stand OPEN!!
SODA
White beaches with summer mermaids lounging about
A seaside stand!
I haven't been to the beach that much...
Ah~ Well, a string bean like you, in the ocean?
You'll ruin the beach mood!
NEVER YIE
I, on the other hand, fit right in on the beach...
I even have my own surf board...
THE SUMMER MAN
Oh, you do?! I'm super impressed!!
I've never met a real poser before...
Huh? I don't know what you mean by that!
Considering all you can do is use a beatboard on the Arakawa and call that surfing...
But this arrow is pointing the wrong way...
This sign would have us believe there's a sea in Saitama.
Yes, it must be a mistake...
ZHAAAAA
Hm...? Is that...?

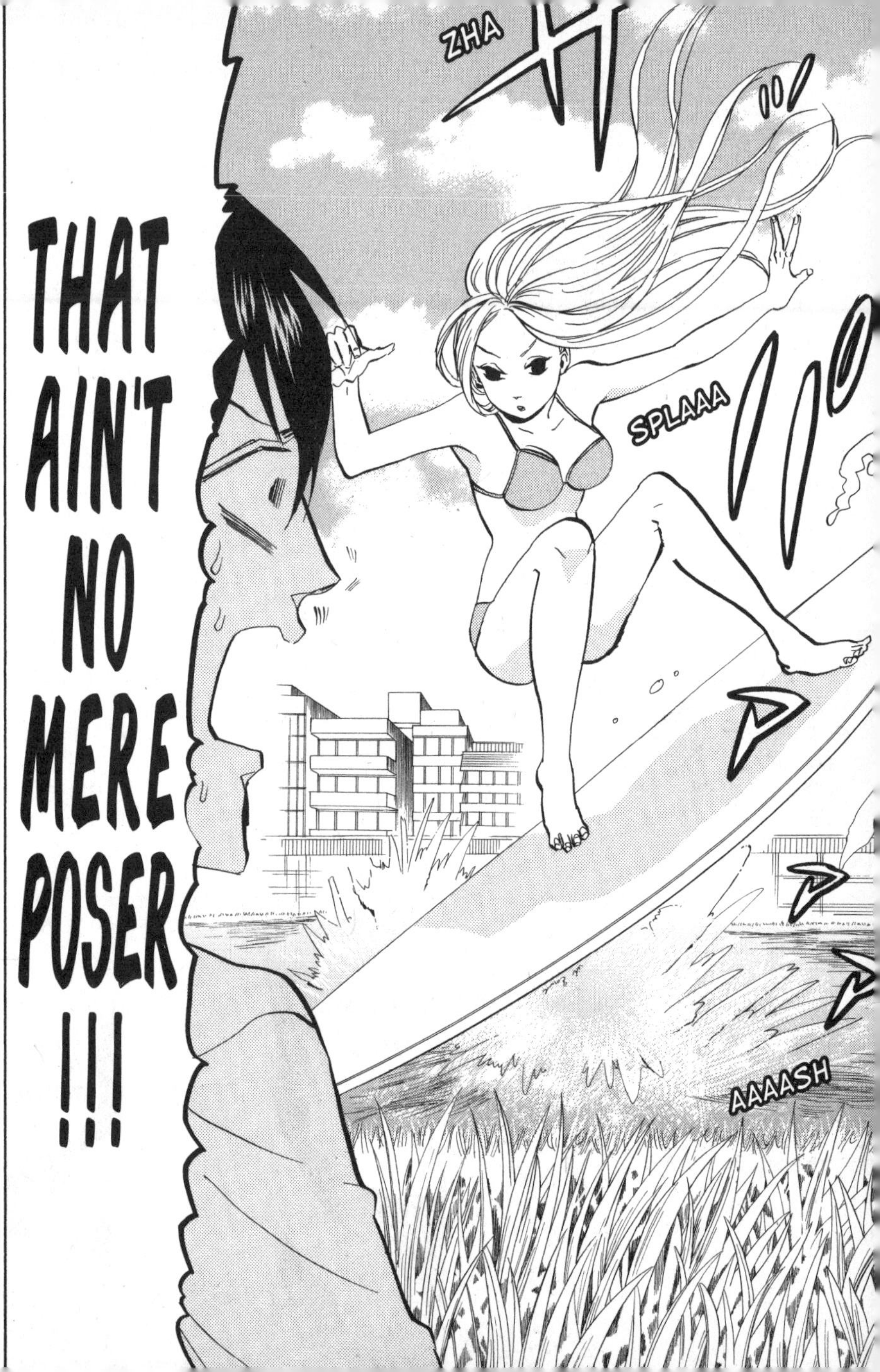
ZHA
SPLAAA
AAAASH
THAT AIN'T NO MERE POSER!!!

Chapter 258: Seaside Stand

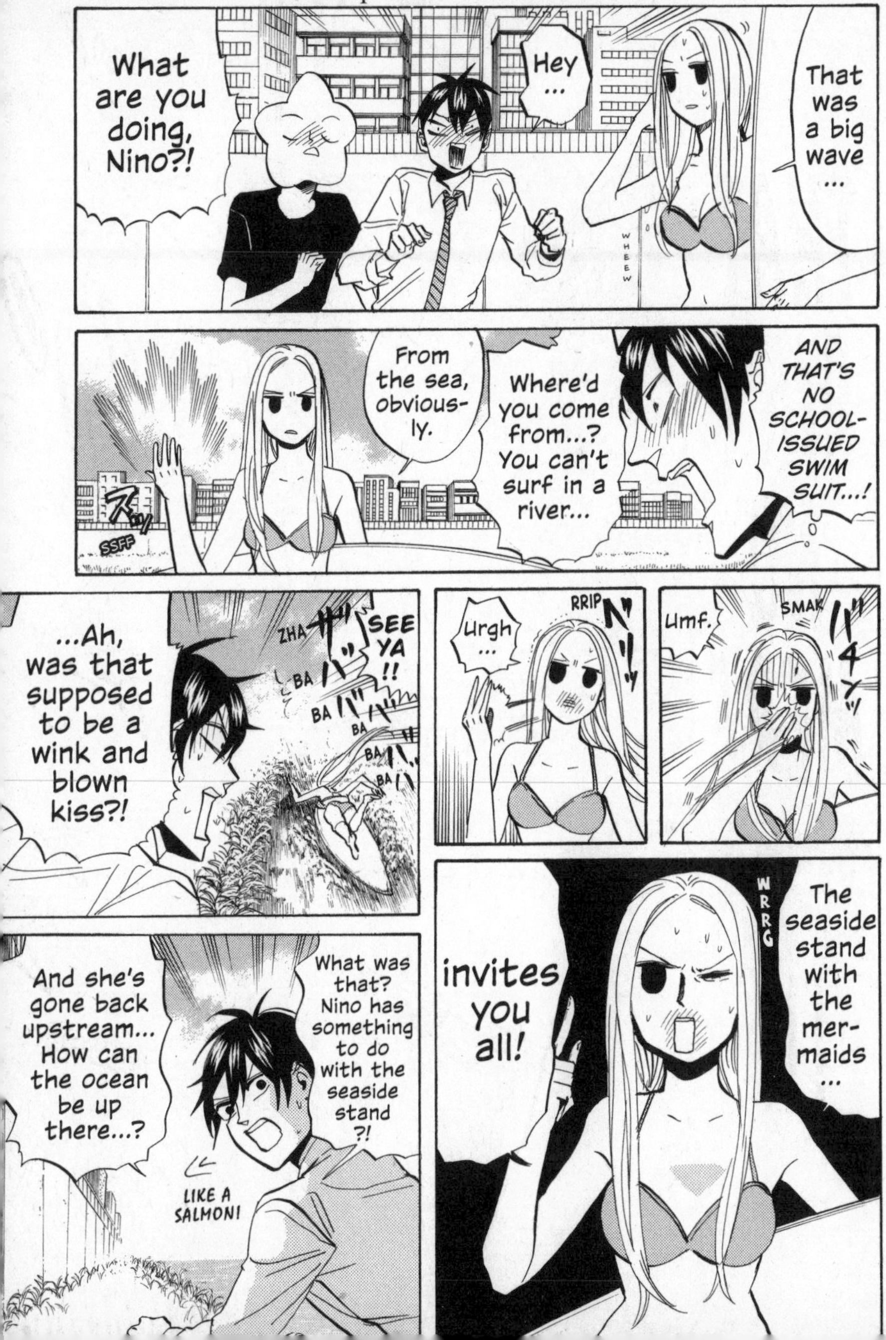
That was a big wave ...
WHEEEW
Hey ...
What are you doing, Nino?!
AND THAT'S NO SCHOOL-ISSUED SWIM SUIT...!
Where'd you come from...? You can't surf in a river...
From the sea, obviously.
SSFF
SMAK
Umf.
RRIP
Urgh ...
SEE YA !!
ZHA
BA
BA
BA
BA
BA
...Ah, was that supposed to be a wink and blown kiss?!
The seaside stand with the mermaids ...
WRRG
invites you all!
What was that? Nino has something to do with the seaside stand ?!
And she's gone back upstream... How can the ocean be up there...?
LIKE A SALMON!

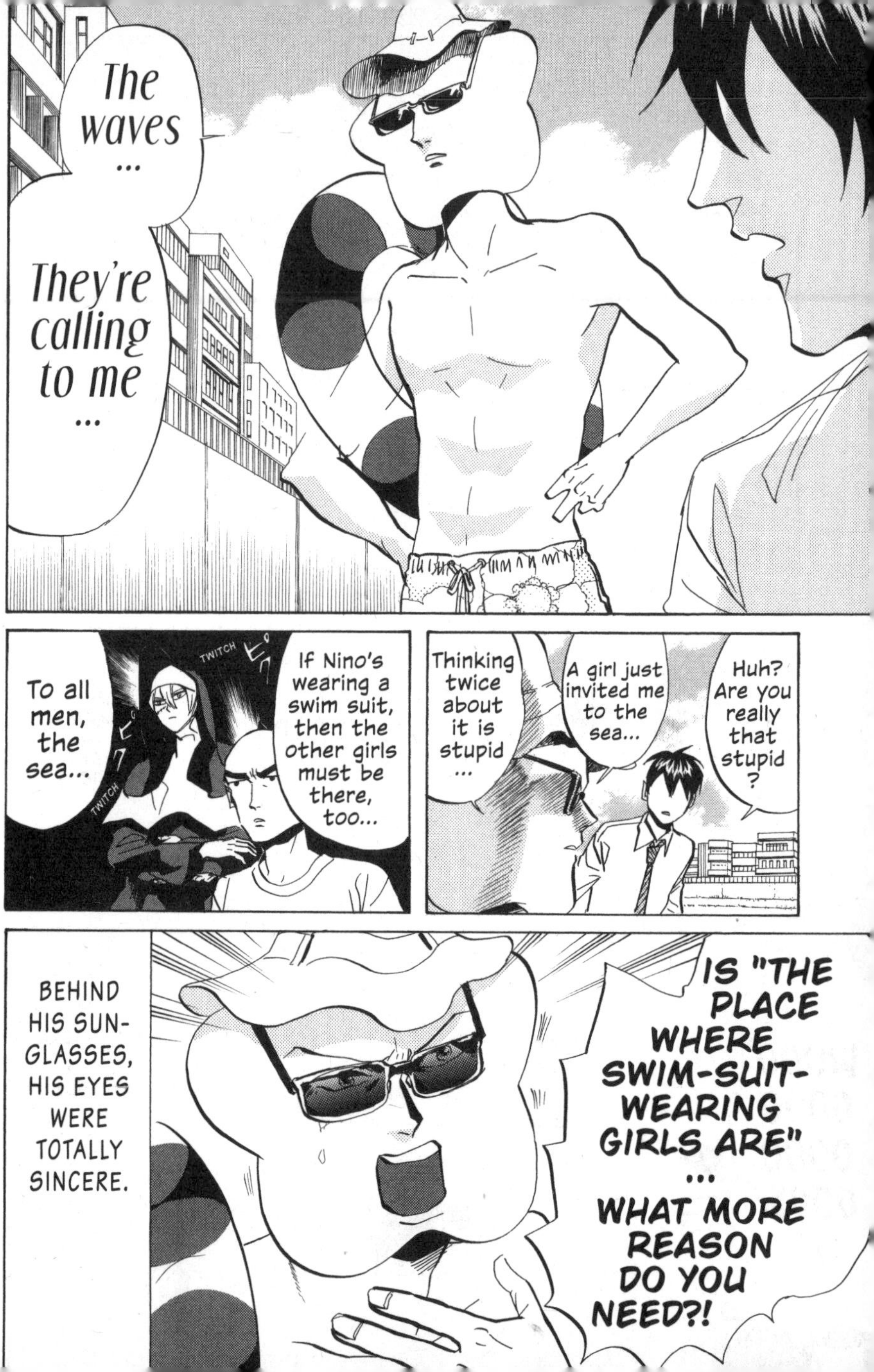
The waves ...
They're calling to me ...
Huh? Are you really that stupid?
A girl just invited me to the sea...
Thinking twice about it is stupid ...
If Nino's wearing a swim suit, then the other girls must be there, too...
TWITCH
To all men, the sea...
TWITCH
IS "THE PLACE WHERE SWIM-SUIT-WEARING GIRLS ARE" ... WHAT MORE REASON DO YOU NEED?!
BEHIND HIS SUN-GLASSES, HIS EYES WERE TOTALLY SINCERE.

Chapter 259: Dry Run

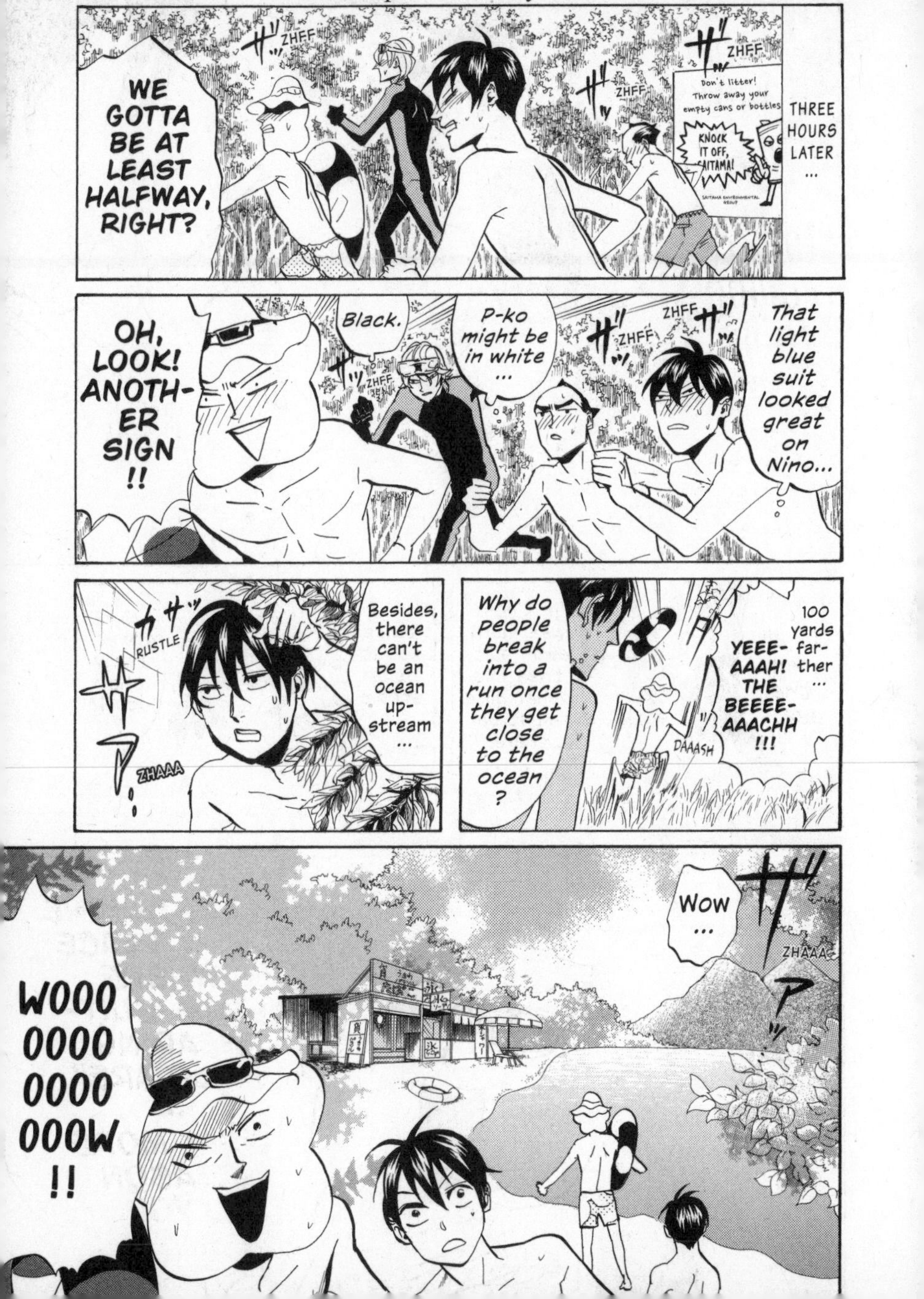
THREE HOURS LATER ...
ZHFF
Don't litter! Throw away your empty cans or bottles
KNOCK IT OFF, SAITAMA!
SAITAMA ENVIRONMENTAL GROUP
ZHFF
ZHFF
WE GOTTA BE AT LEAST HALFWAY, RIGHT?
That light blue suit looked great on Nino...
ZHFF
ZHFF
P-ko might be in white ...
Black.
ZHFF
OH, LOOK! ANOTHER SIGN !!
100 yards farther ...
YEEE-AAAH! THE BEEEE-AAACHH !!!
DAAASH
Why do people break into a run once they get close to the ocean ?
Besides, there can't be an ocean upstream ...
RUSTLE
ZHAAA
Wow ...
ZHAAA
WOOO0000000000000OOOW !!

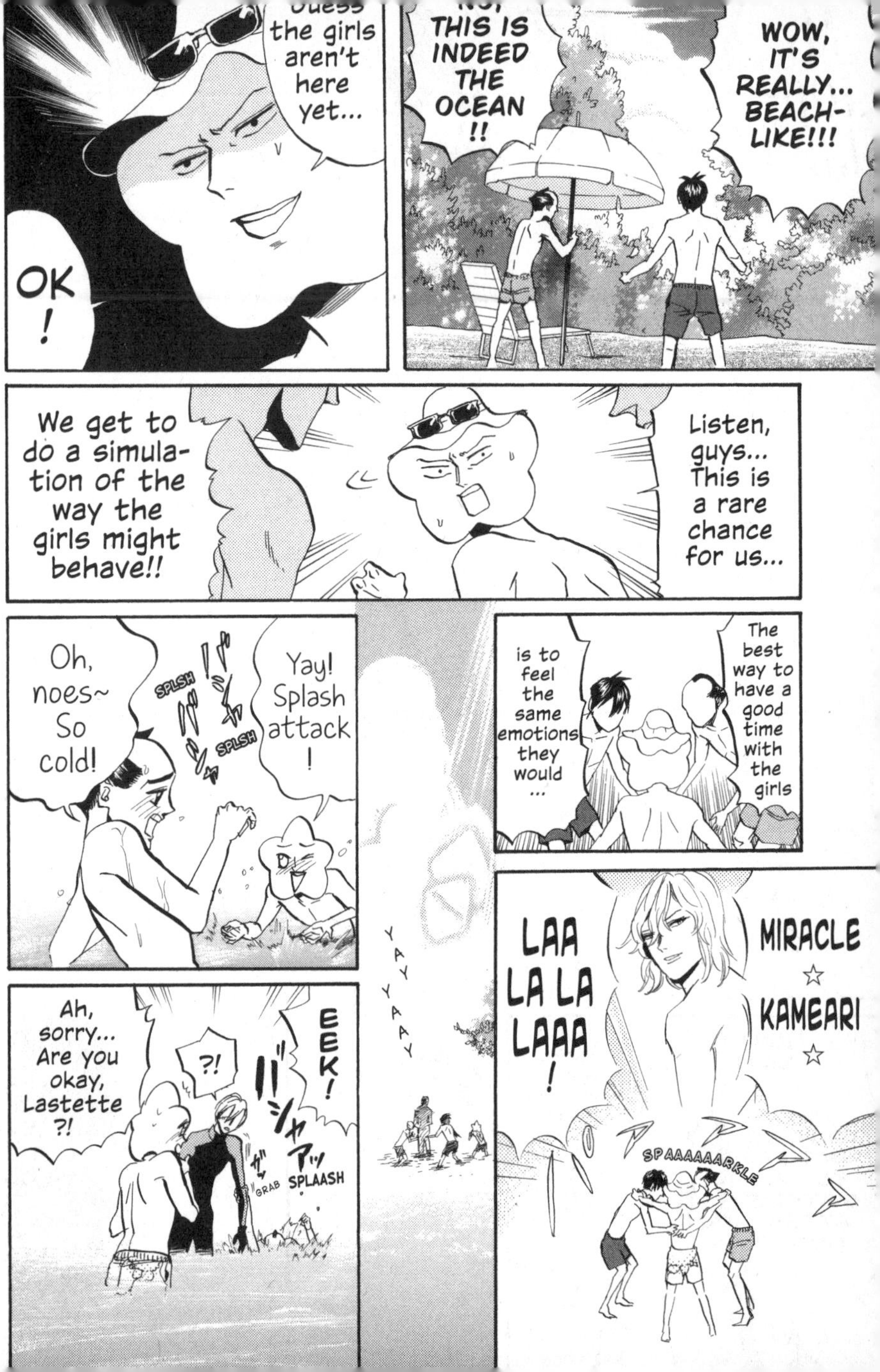
WOW, IT'S REALLY... BEACH-LIKE!!!
THIS IS INDEED THE OCEAN !!
the girls aren't here yet...
OK !
Listen, guys... This is a rare chance for us...
We get to do a simulation of the way the girls might behave!!
The best way to have a good time with the girls
is to feel the same emotions they would ...
Yay! Splash attack !
SPLSH
SPLSH
Oh, noes~ So cold!
MIRACLE ☆ KAMEARI ☆
LAA LA LA LAAA !
SPAAAAAARKLE
YAY YAAAY
EEK!
SPLAASH
GRAB
?!
Ah, sorry... Are you okay, Lastette ?!

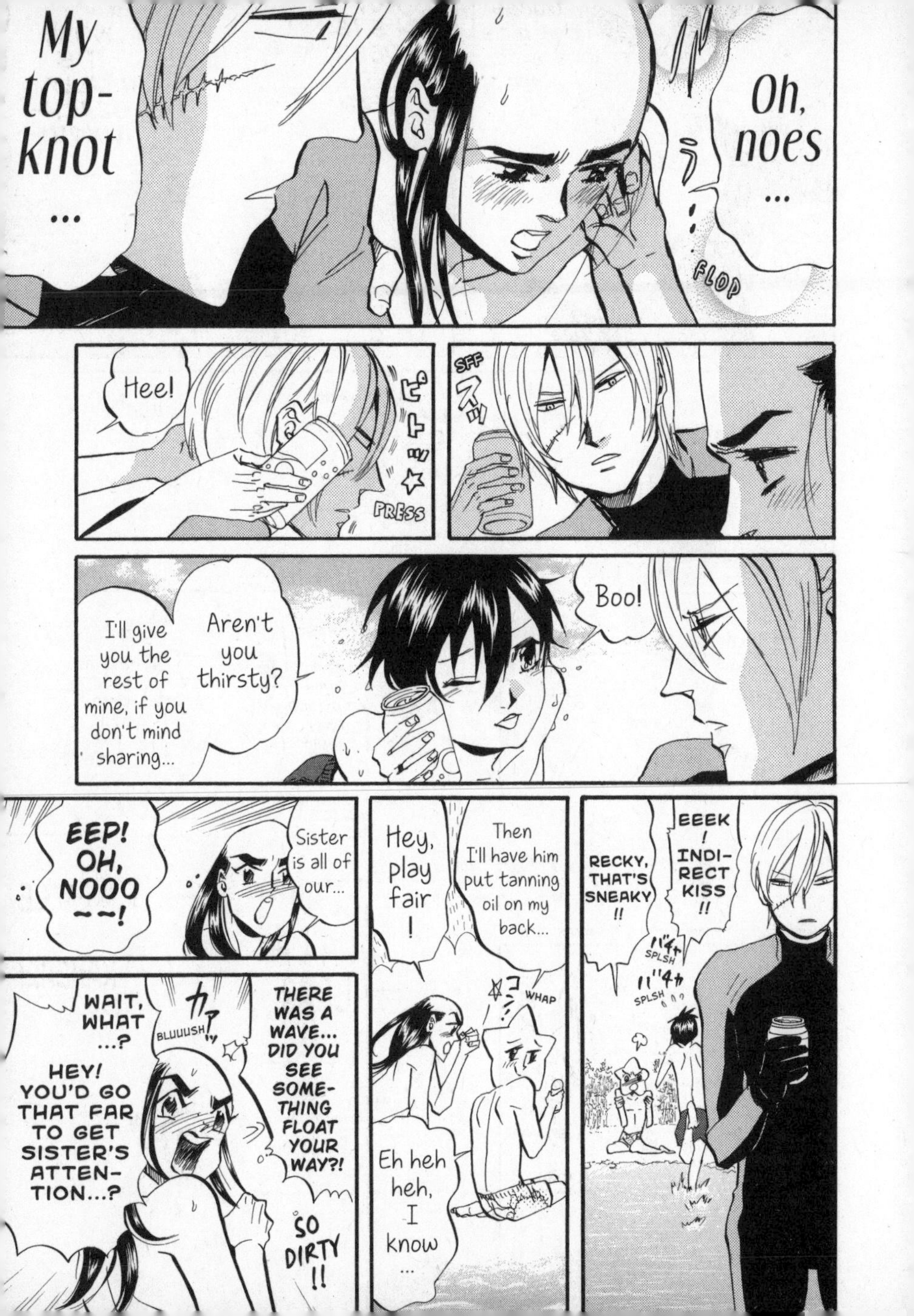
Oh, noes ...
FLOP
My top-knot ...
SFF
Hee!
PRESS
Boo!
Aren't you thirsty?
I'll give you the rest of mine, if you don't mind sharing...
EEEK! INDIRECT KISS !!
RECKY, THAT'S SNEAKY !!
SPLSH
SPLSH
Then I'll have him put tanning oil on my back...
Hey, play fair !
WHAP
Eh heh heh, I know ...
Sister is all of our...
EEP! OH, NOOO ~~!
THERE WAS A WAVE... DID YOU SEE SOMETHING FLOAT YOUR WAY?!
BLUUUSH
WAIT, WHAT ...?
HEY! YOU'D GO THAT FAR TO GET SISTER'S ATTENTION...?
SO DIRTY !!

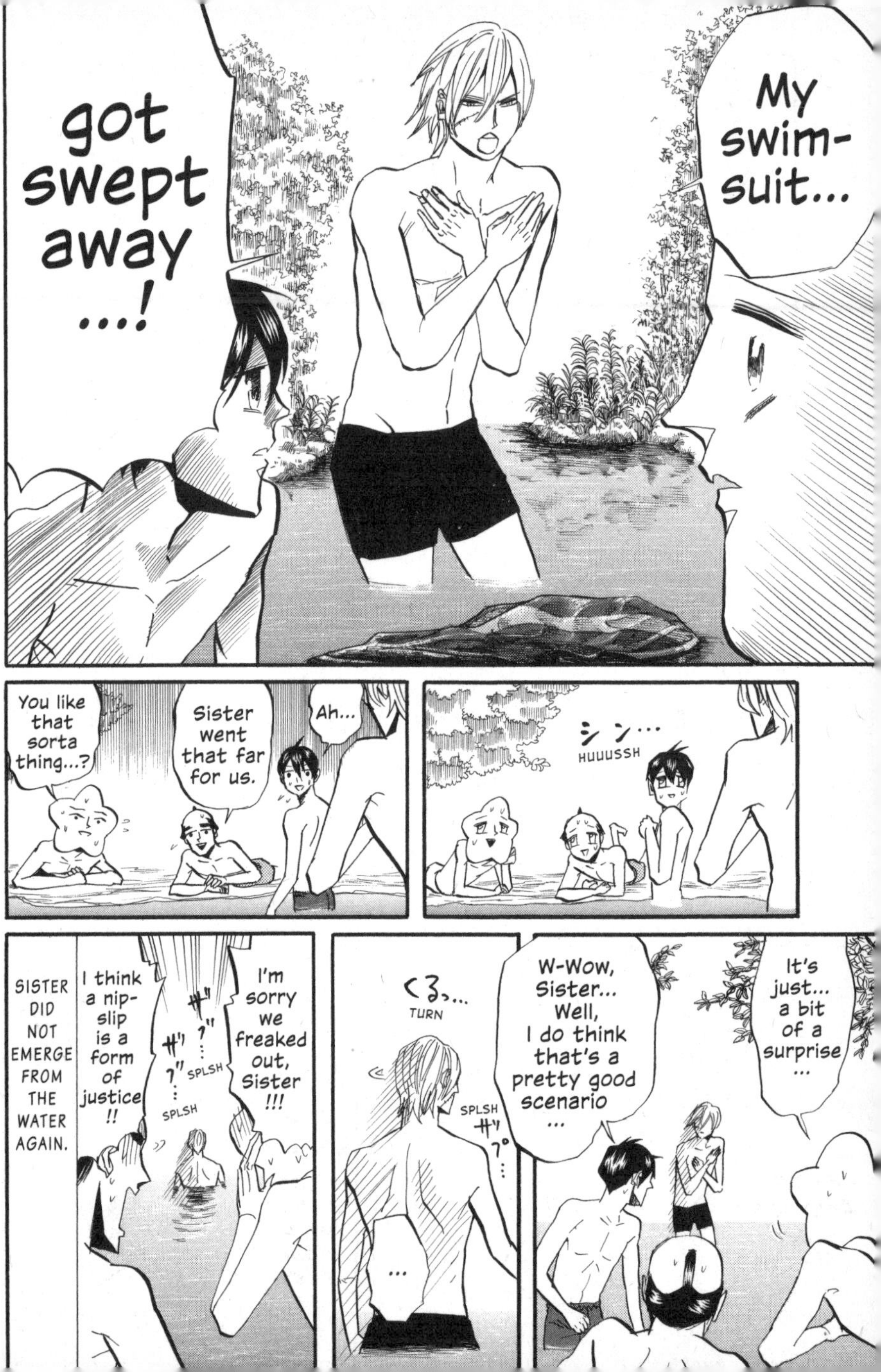
My swim-suit...
got swept away ...!
シン…
HUUUSSH
Ah...
Sister went that far for us.
You like that sorta thing...?
It's just... a bit of a surprise ...
W-Wow, Sister... Well, I do think that's a pretty good scenario ...
くるっ…
TURN
ザプ…
SPLSH
...
I'm sorry we freaked out, Sister !!!
ザブ…
SPLSH
ザブ…
SPLSH
I think a nip-slip is a form of justice !!
SISTER DID NOT EMERGE FROM THE WATER AGAIN.

Chapter 260: Lifesaver

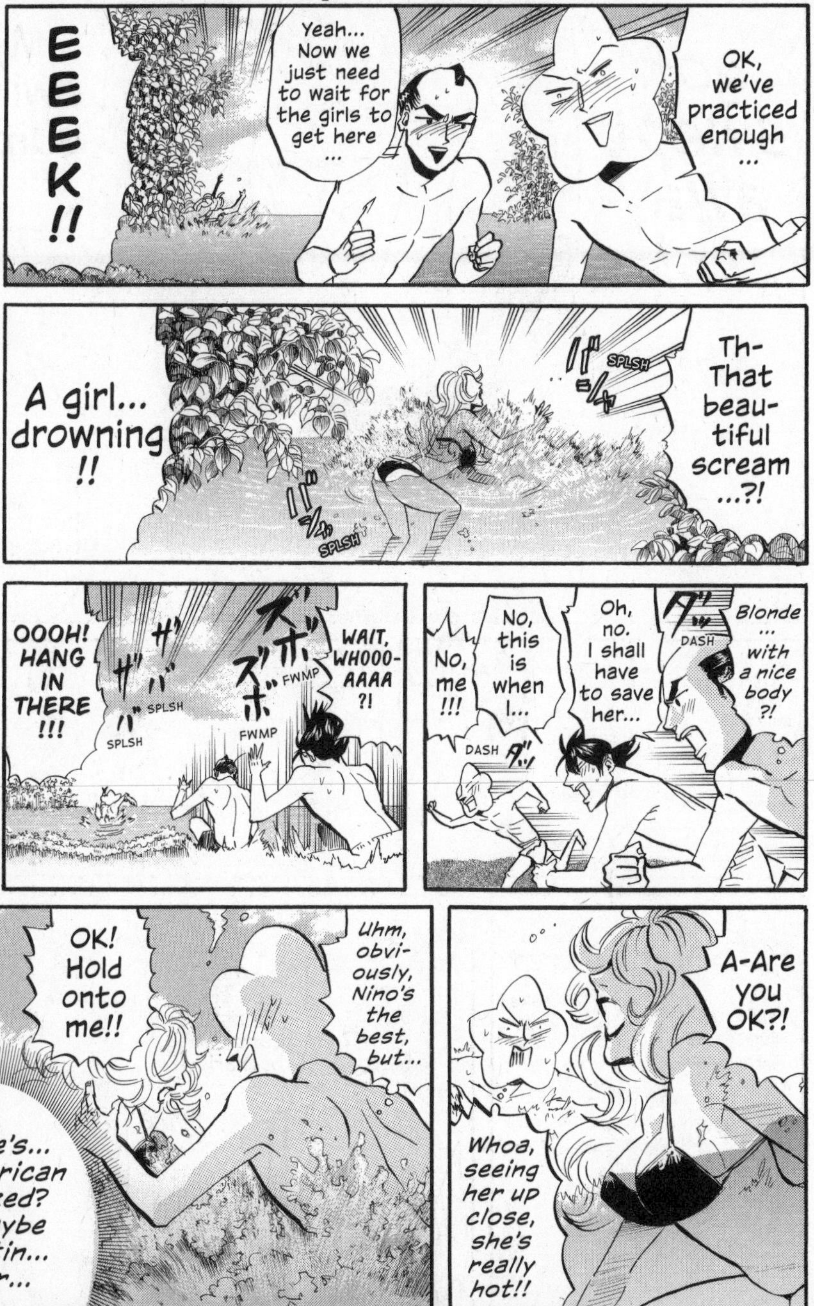

OK, we've practiced enough ...
Yeah... Now we just need to wait for the girls to get here ...
EEEK!!
Th- That beau-tiful scream ...?!
SPLSH
A girl... drowning !!
SPLSH
Blonde ... with a nice body ?!
DASH
Oh, no. I shall have to save her...
No, this is when I...
No, me !!!
DASH
WAIT, WHOOO-AAAA ?!
FWMP
FWMP
OOOH! HANG IN THERE !!!
SPLSH
SPLSH
A-Are you OK?!
Whoa, seeing her up close, she's really hot!!
Uhm, obvi-ously, Nino's the best, but...
OK! Hold onto me!!
She's... American sized? Maybe Latin... or...

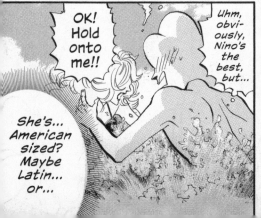

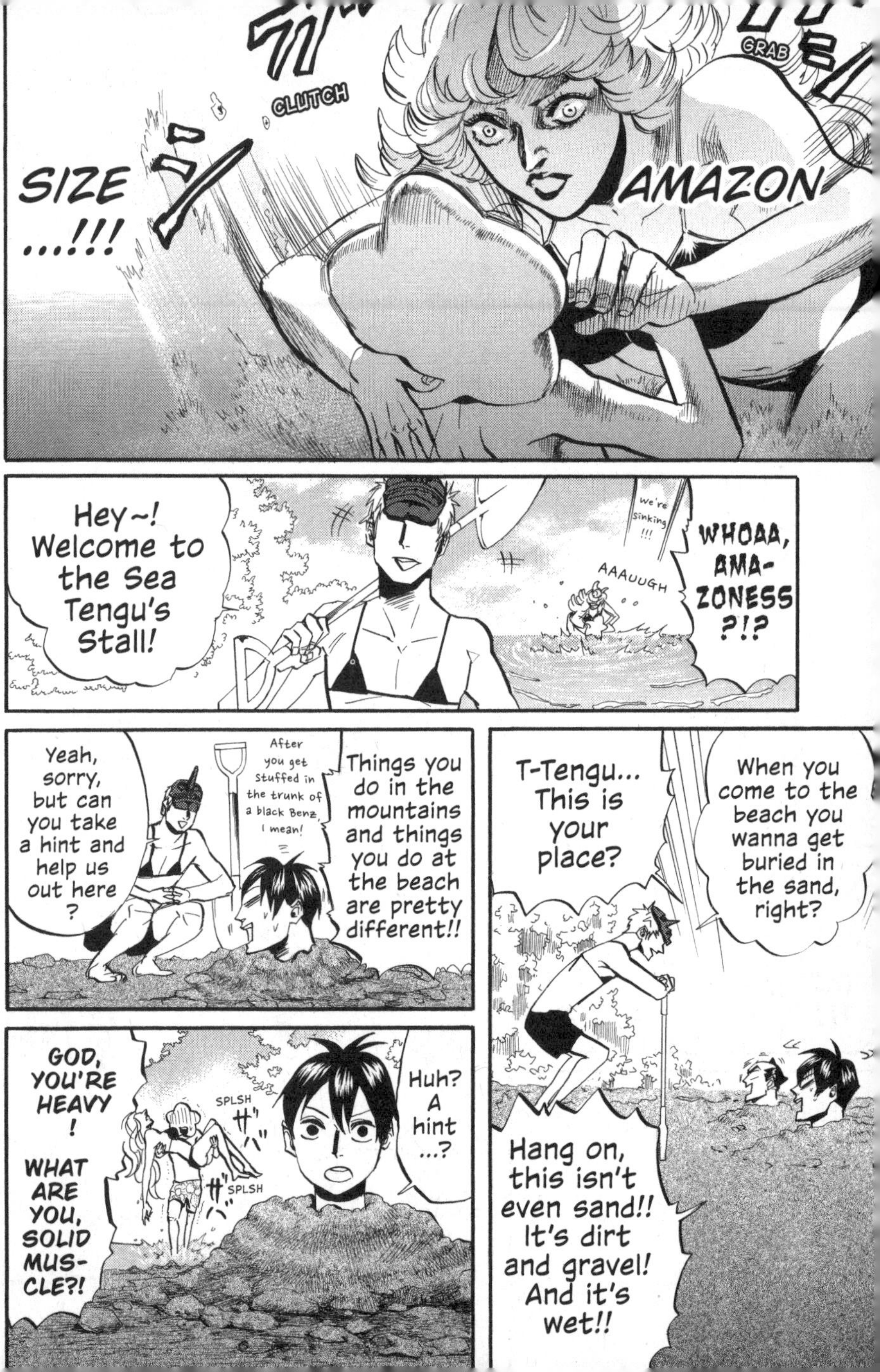
GRAB
AMAZON
CLUTCH
SIZE ...!!!
WHOAA, AMA-ZONESS ?!?
we're sinking !!!
AAAUUGH
Hey~! Welcome to the Sea Tengu's Stall!
When you come to the beach you wanna get buried in the sand, right?
T-Tengu... This is your place?
Hang on, this isn't even sand!! It's dirt and gravel! And it's wet!!
Things you do in the mountains and things you do at the beach are pretty different!!
After you get stuffed in the trunk of a black Benz, I mean!
Yeah, sorry, but can you take a hint and help us out here ?
Huh? A hint ...?
SPLSH
SPLSH
GOD, YOU'RE HEAVY !
WHAT ARE YOU, SOLID MUS-CLE?!

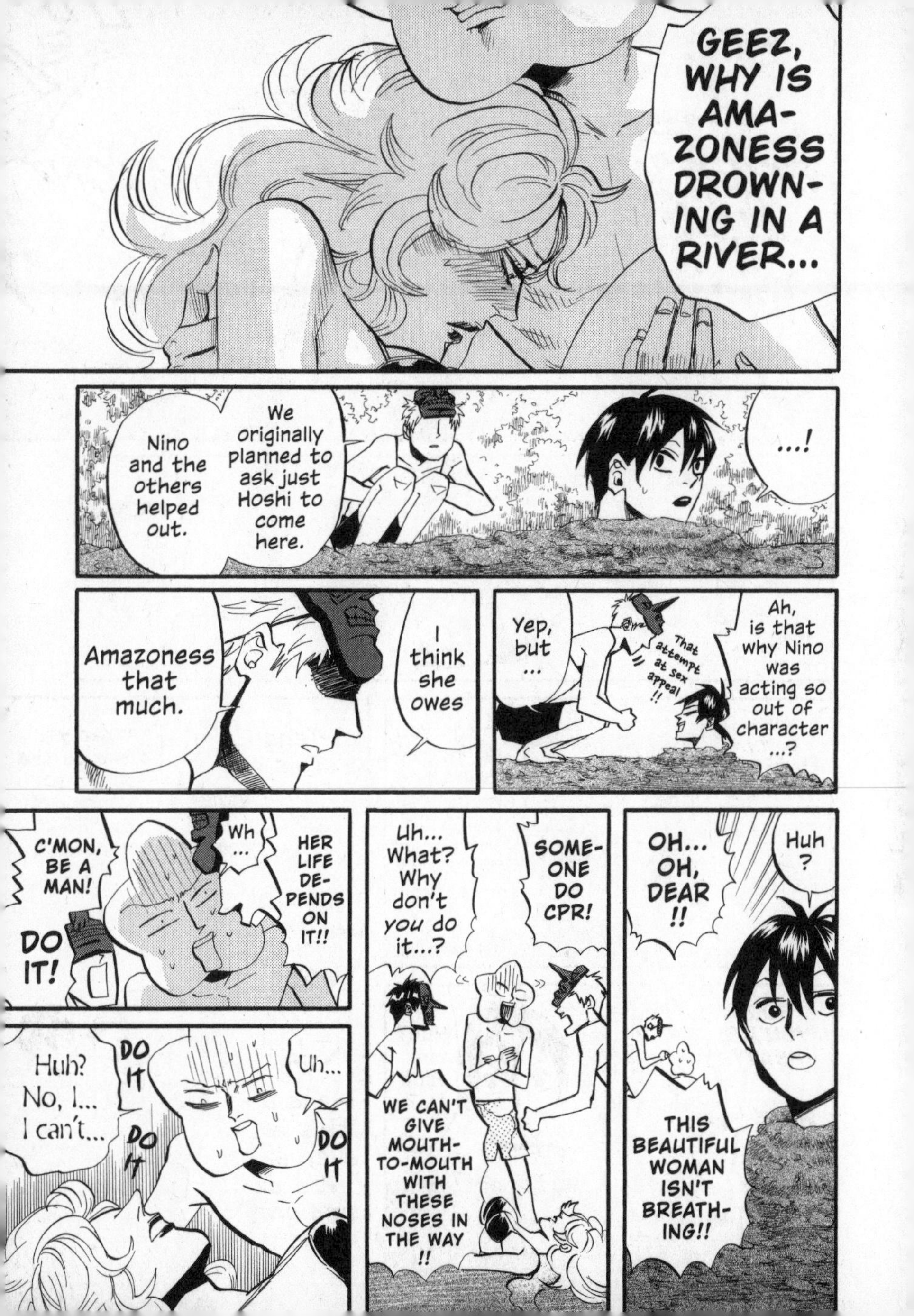
GEEZ, WHY IS AMAZONESS DROWNING IN A RIVER...
...!
We originally planned to ask just Hoshi to come here.
Nino and the others helped out.
Ah, is that why Nino was acting so out of character...?
That attempt at sex appeal!!
Yep, but...
I think she owes
Amazoness that much.
Huh?
OH... OH, DEAR!!
THIS BEAUTIFUL WOMAN ISN'T BREATHING!!
SOMEONE DO CPR!
Uh... What? Why don't you do it...?
WE CAN'T GIVE MOUTH-TO-MOUTH WITH THESE NOSES IN THE WAY!!
HER LIFE DEPENDS ON IT!!
Wh...
C'MON, BE A MAN!
DO IT!
Uh...
DO IT
DO IT
DO IT
Huh? No, I... I can't...

HER EYES ARE WIDE OPEN ...!

Not when

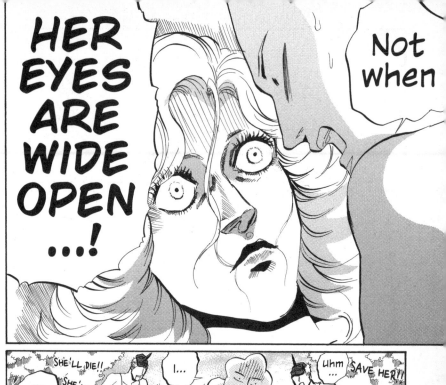

SHE'LL DIE!!

SHE'LL DIE!!

No, I can't ...

I...

Uhm ...

SAVE HER!!

SAVE HER!!

THIS BEACH-SIDE MEMORY WOULD CERTAINLY NEVER BE FORGOTTEN.

AAAAIEEEE!

GWA AAA AAA AAA GGG GHH

...

PRESS

Uh ...

Here.

Chapter 261: Parting Words

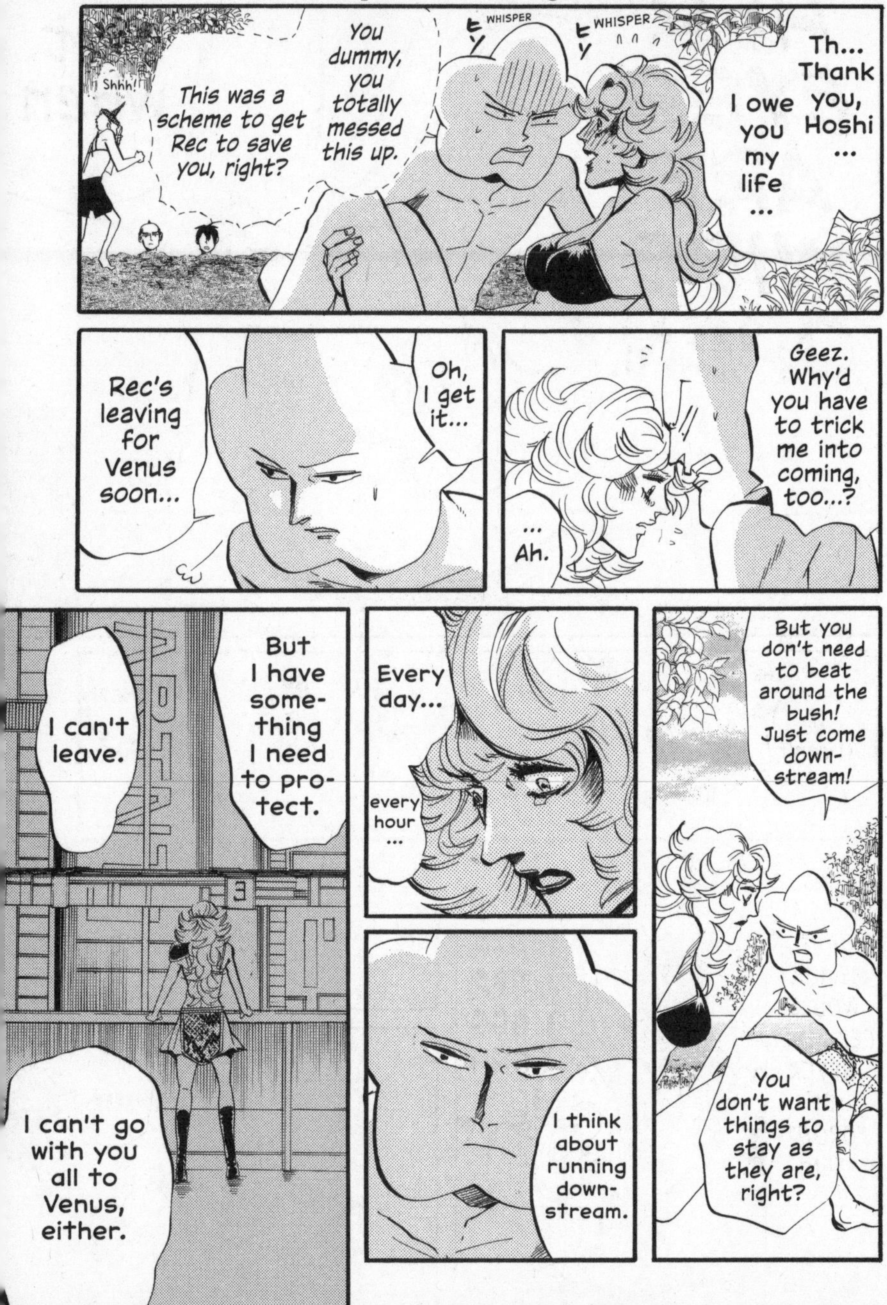

Th... Thank you, Hoshi...
I owe you my life...
ヒソ WHISPER
ヒソ WHISPER
You dummy, you totally messed this up.
This was a scheme to get Rec to save you, right?
Shhh!
Geez. Why'd you have to trick me into coming, too...?
... Ah.
Oh, I get it...
Rec's leaving for Venus soon...
But you don't need to beat around the bush! Just come downstream!
You don't want things to stay as they are, right?
Every day...
every hour...
I think about running downstream.
But I have something I need to protect.
I can't leave.
I can't go with you all to Venus, either.

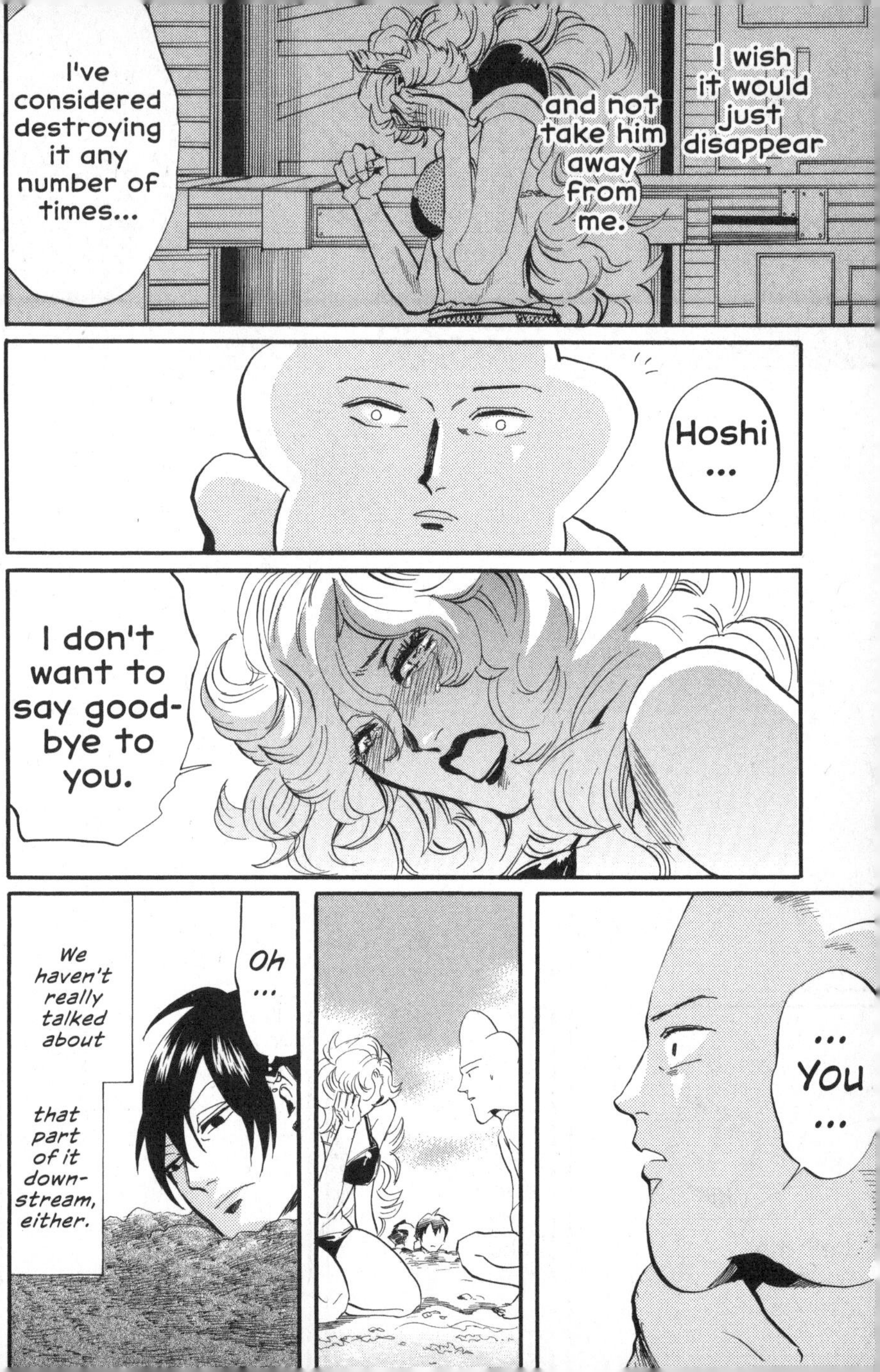
I wish it would just disappear
and not take him away from me.
I've considered destroying it any number of times...
Hoshi ...
I don't want to say good-bye to you.
... You ...
Oh ...
We haven't really talked about
that part of it down-stream, either.

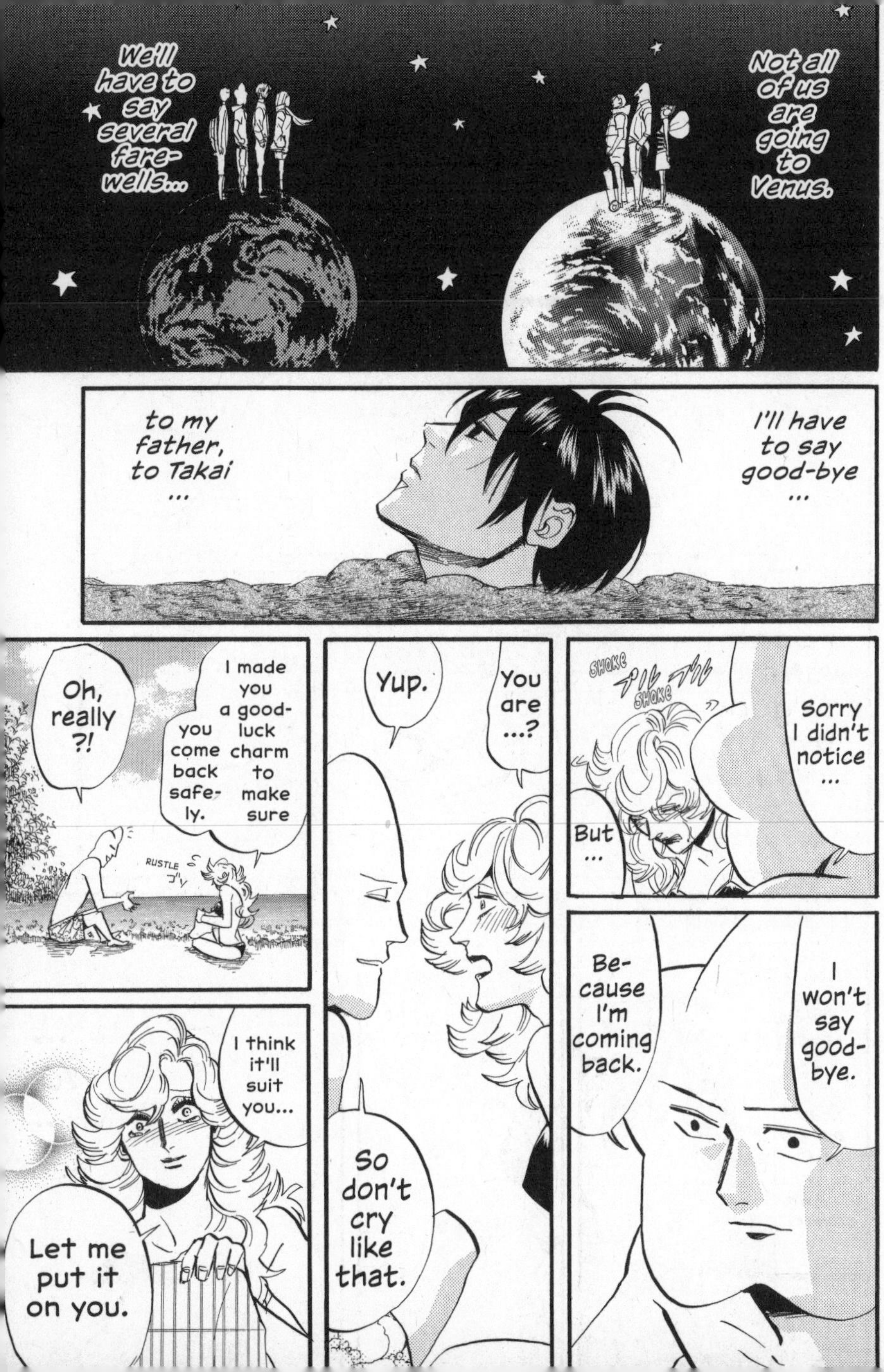

Not all of us are going to Venus.
We'll have to say several farewells...
I'll have to say good-bye ...
to my father, to Takai ...
SHAKE SHAKE
Sorry I didn't notice ...
But ...
I won't say good-bye.
Because I'm coming back.
You are ...?
Yup.
So don't cry like that.
I made you a good-luck charm to make sure you come back safely.
Oh, really?!
RUSTLE
I think it'll suit you...
Let me put it on you.

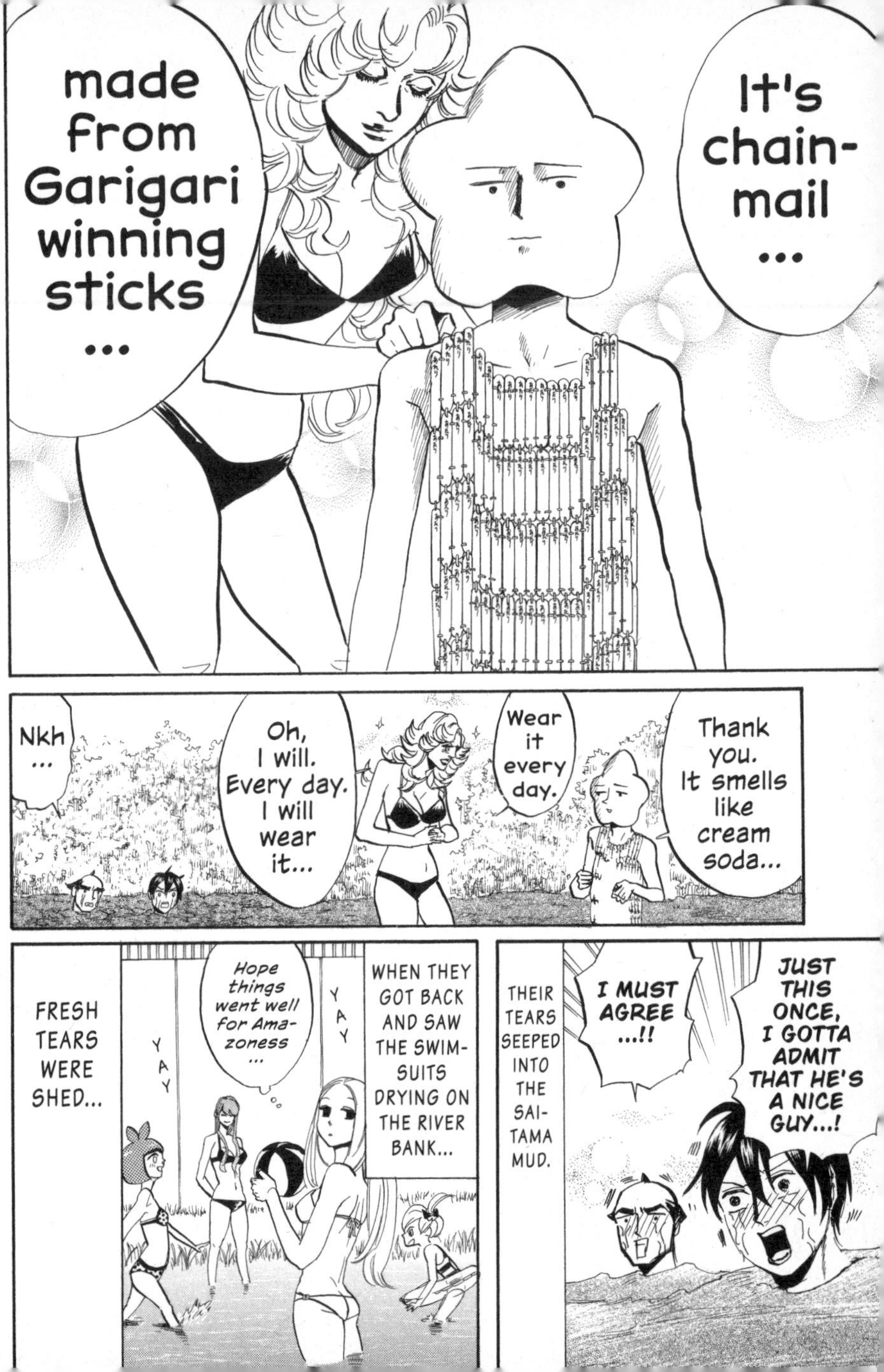
It's chain-mail...
made from Garigari winning sticks...
Thank you. It smells like cream soda...
Wear it every day.
Oh, I will. Every day. I will wear it...
Nkh...
JUST THIS ONCE, I GOTTA ADMIT THAT HE'S A NICE GUY...!
I MUST AGREE...!!
THEIR TEARS SEEPED INTO THE SAI-TAMA MUD.
WHEN THEY GOT BACK AND SAW THE SWIM-SUITS DRYING ON THE RIVER BANK...
YAY
Hope things went well for Ama-zoness...
YAY
FRESH TEARS WERE SHED...

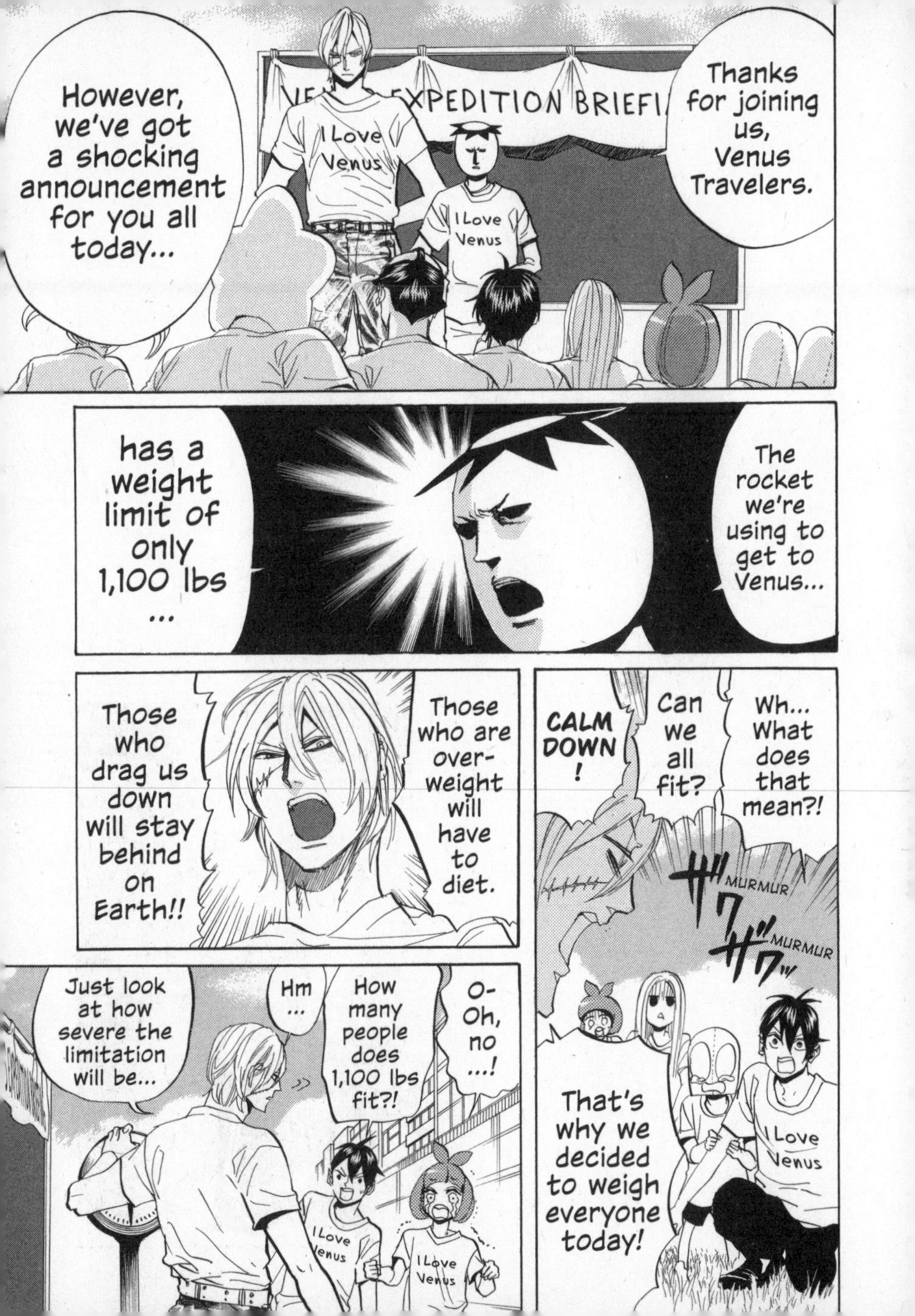
Thanks for joining us, Venus Travelers.
However, we've got a shocking announcement for you all today...
I Love Venus
I Love Venus
The rocket we're using to get to Venus...
has a weight limit of only 1,100 lbs ...
Wh... What does that mean?!
Can we all fit?
CALM DOWN!
MURMUR
MURMUR
I Love Venus
That's why we decided to weigh everyone today!
Those who are over-weight will have to diet.
Those who drag us down will stay behind on Earth!!
O-Oh, no ...!
How many people does 1,100 lbs fit?!
Hm ...
Just look at how severe the limitation will be...
I Love Venus
I Love Venus

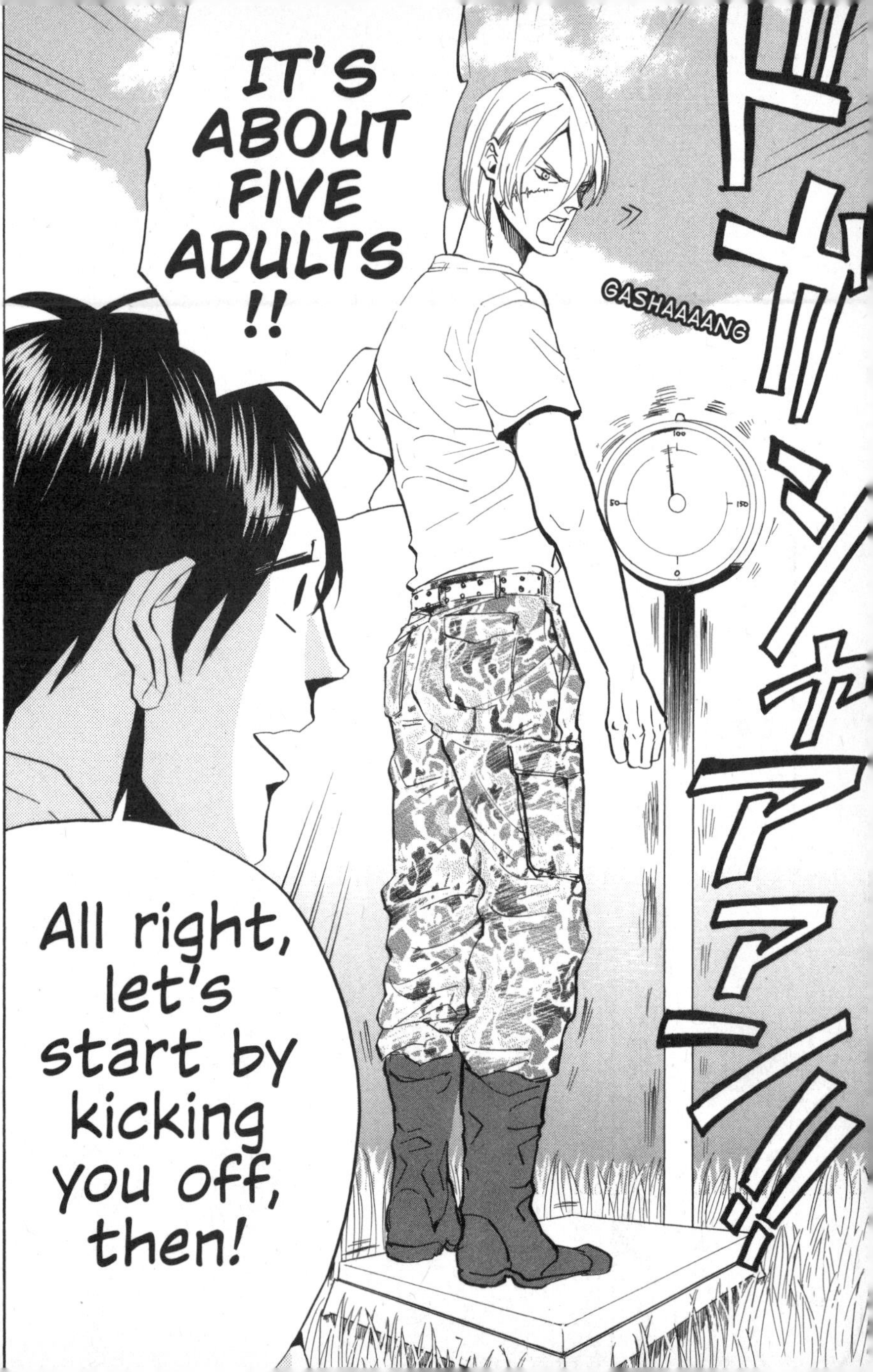
ドガッシャアアアン!!
GASHAAAAANG
IT'S ABOUT FIVE ADULTS!!
All right, let's start by kicking you off, then!

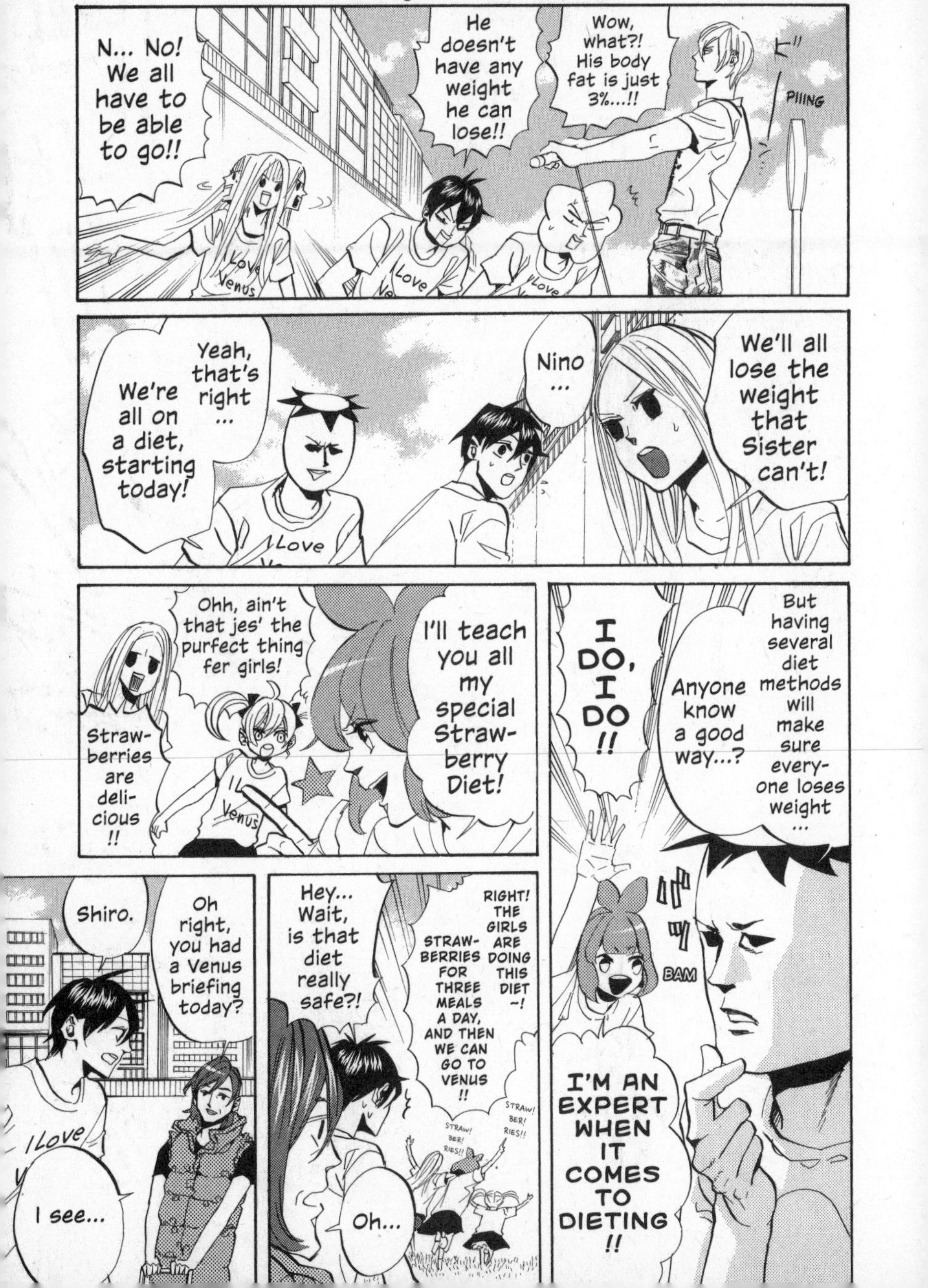
PIIING
Wow, what?! His body fat is just 3%...!!
He doesn't have any weight he can lose!!
N... No! We all have to be able to go!!
We'll all lose the weight that Sister can't!
Nino ...
Yeah, that's right ...
We're all on a diet, starting today!
But having several diet methods will make sure everyone loses weight ...
Anyone know a good way...?
I DO, I DO !!
BAM
I'M AN EXPERT WHEN IT COMES TO DIETING !!
I'll teach you all my special Straw-berry Diet!
Ohh, ain't that jes' the purfect thing fer girls!
Straw-berries are deli-cious !!
Hey... Wait, is that diet really safe?!
RIGHT! THE GIRLS ARE DOING THIS DIET ~!
STRAW-BERRIES FOR THREE MEALS A DAY, AND THEN WE CAN GO TO VENUS !!
STRAW! BER! RIES!!
STRAW! BER! RIES!!
Oh...
Oh right, you had a Venus briefing today?
Shiro.
I see...

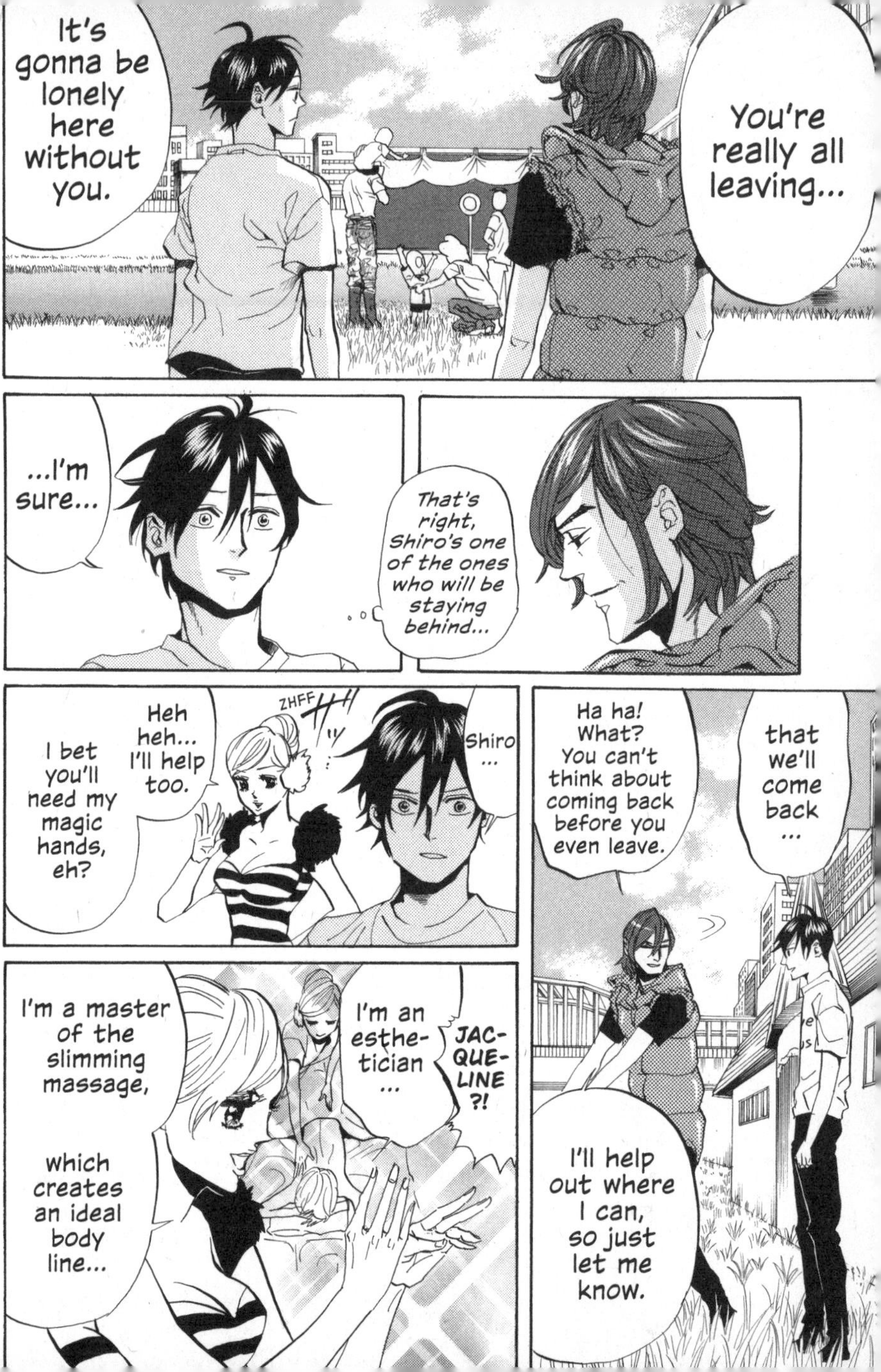
You're really all leaving...
It's gonna be lonely here without you.
...I'm sure...
That's right, Shiro's one of the ones who will be staying behind...
that we'll come back...
Ha ha! What? You can't think about coming back before you even leave.
I'll help out where I can, so just let me know.
Shiro...
ZHFF
Heh heh... I'll help too.
I bet you'll need my magic hands, eh?
JACQUELINE?!
I'm an esthetician...
I'm a master of the slimming massage,
which creates an ideal body line...

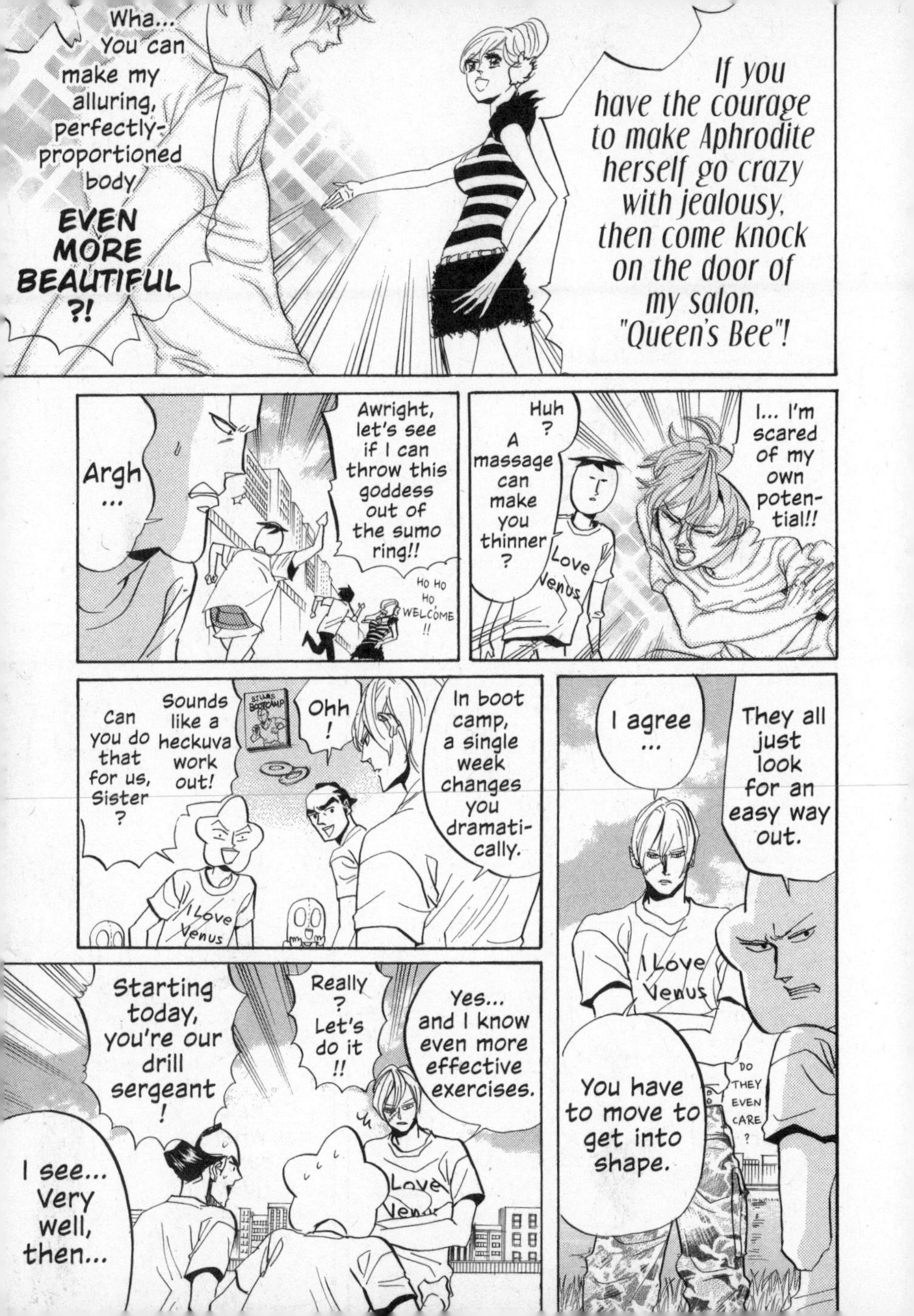
If you have the courage to make Aphrodite herself go crazy with jealousy, then come knock on the door of my salon, "Queen's Bee"!
Wha... You can make my alluring, perfectly-proportioned body
EVEN MORE BEAUTIFUL ?!
I... I'm scared of my own poten-tial!!
Huh? A massage can make you thinner?
Awright, let's see if I can throw this goddess out of the sumo ring!!
Argh...
HO HO HO, WELCOME!!
They all just look for an easy way out.
I agree...
DO THEY EVEN CARE?
You have to move to get into shape.
In boot camp, a single week changes you dramati-cally.
Ohh!
Sounds like a heckuva work out!
Can you do that for us, Sister?
Yes... and I know even more effective exercises.
Really? Let's do it!!
Starting today, you're our drill sergeant!
I see... Very well, then...

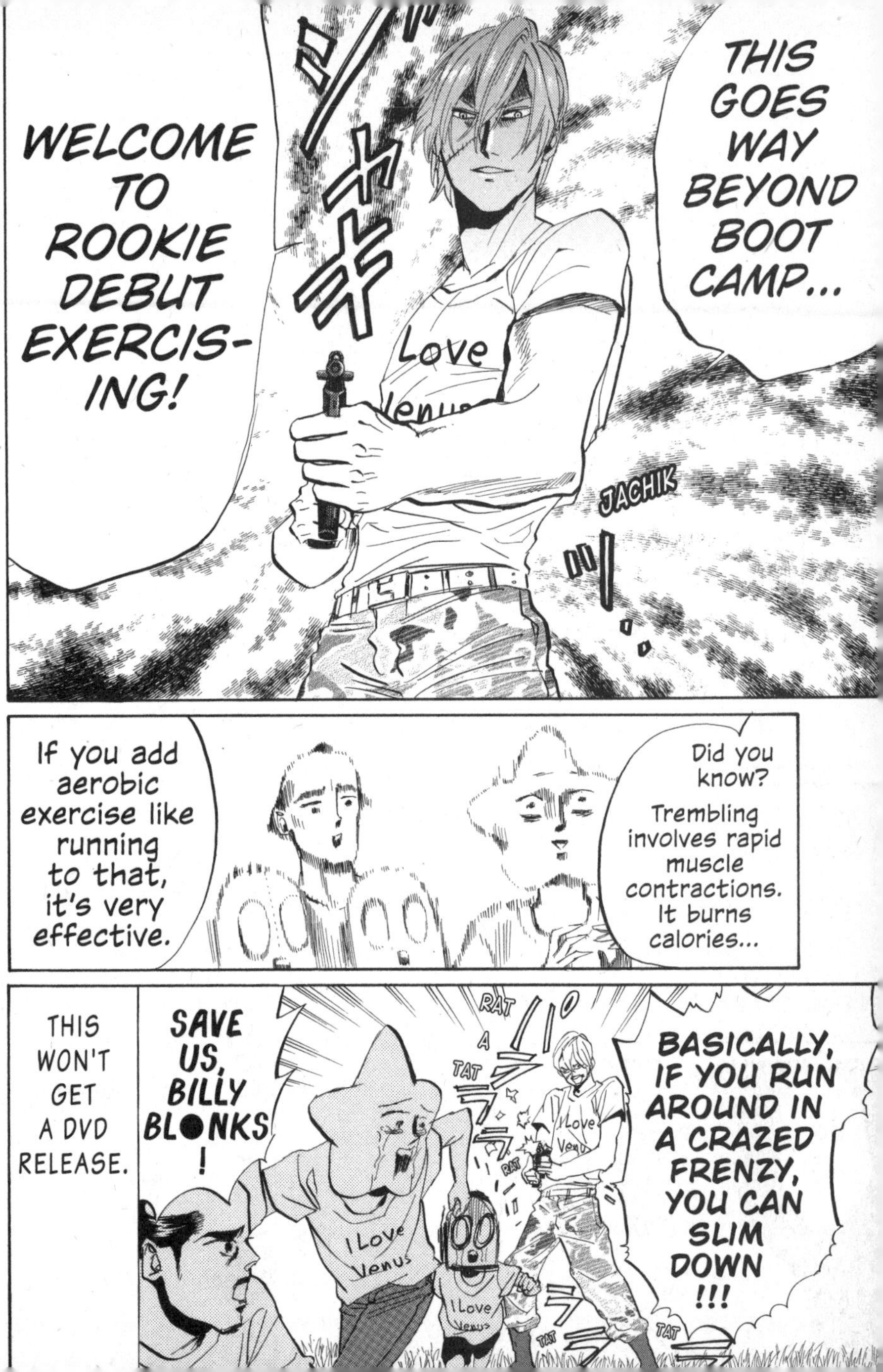
THIS GOES WAY BEYOND BOOT CAMP...
WELCOME TO ROOKIE DEBUT EXERCIS-ING!
JACHIK
Did you know? Trembling involves rapid muscle contractions. It burns calories...
If you add aerobic exercise like running to that, it's very effective.
BASICALLY, IF YOU RUN AROUND IN A CRAZED FRENZY, YOU CAN SLIM DOWN!!!
RAT A TAT
RAT
TAT
TAT
SAVE US, BILLY BL●NKS!
THIS WON'T GET A DVD RELEASE.

Chapter 263: One Other Goal

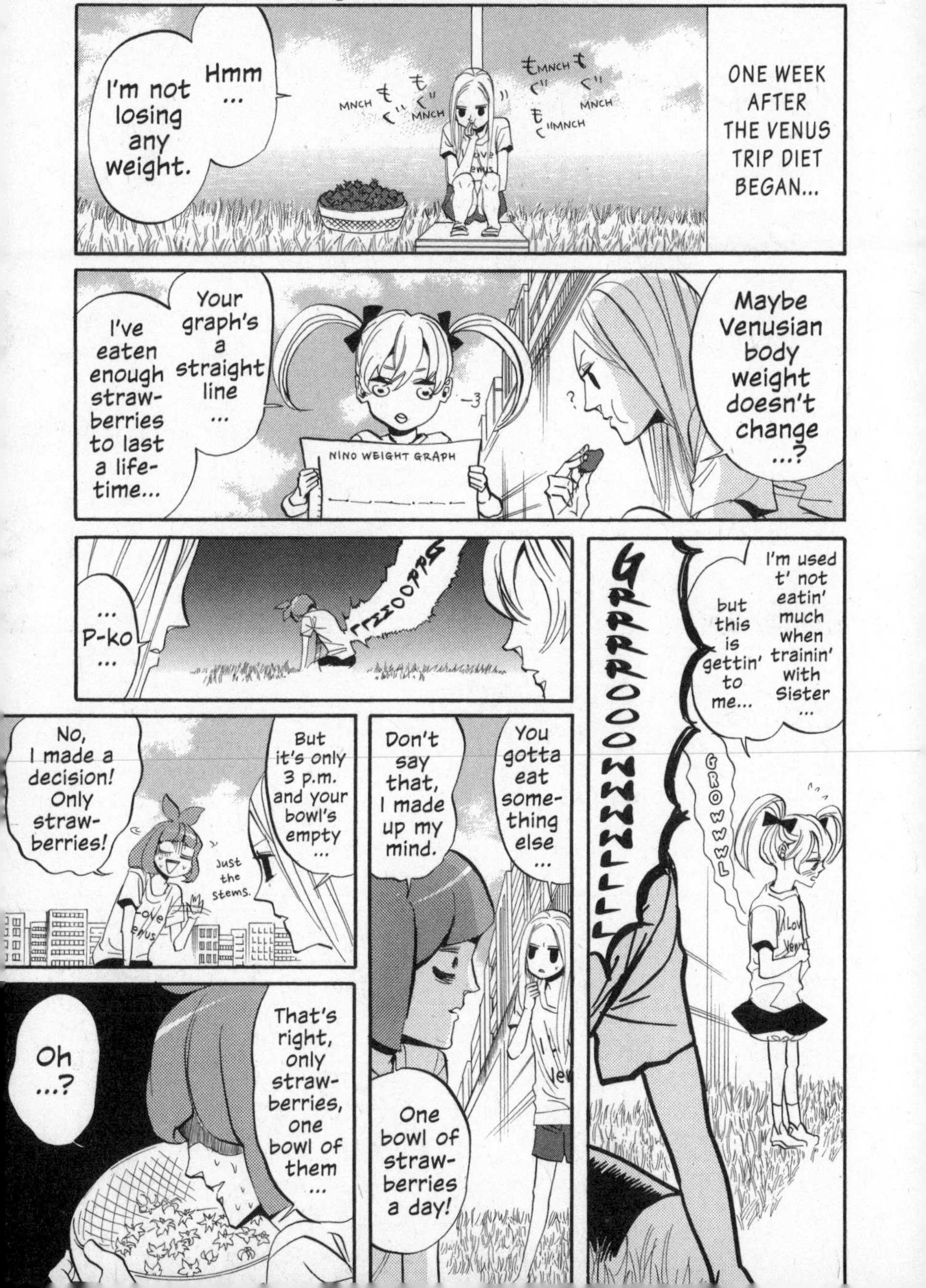
ONE WEEK AFTER THE VENUS TRIP DIET BEGAN...
MNCH MNCH MNCH MNCH MNCH
Hmm ...
I'm not losing any weight.
Maybe Venusian body weight doesn't change ...?
Your graph's a straight line ...
I've eaten enough straw-berries to last a life-time...
NINO WEIGHT GRAPH
GRRRROOOWWWLLLL
I'm used t' not eatin' much when trainin' with Sister ...
but this is gettin' to me...
GROWWL
... P-ko ...
You gotta eat some-thing else ...
Don't say that, I made up my mind.
But it's only 3 p.m. and your bowl's empty ...
No, I made a decision! Only straw-berries!
Just the stems.
One bowl of straw-berries a day!
That's right, only straw-berries, one bowl of them ...
Oh ...?

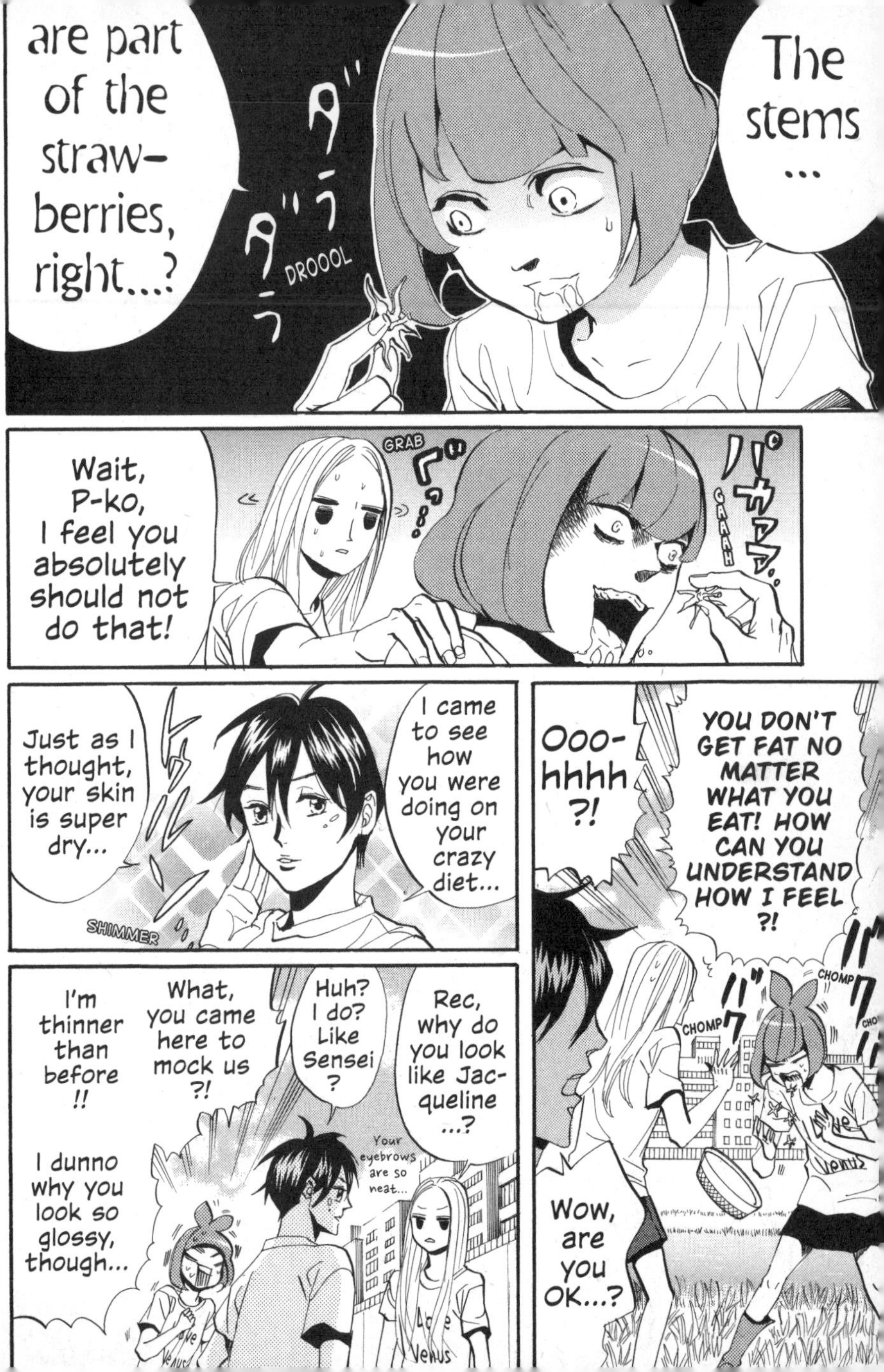
The stems...
are part of the straw-berries, right...?
DROOOL
GRAB
GAAAH
Wait, P-ko, I feel you absolutely should not do that!
YOU DON'T GET FAT NO MATTER WHAT YOU EAT! HOW CAN YOU UNDERSTAND HOW I FEEL?!
Ooo-hhhh?!
CHOMP
CHOMP
Wow, are you OK...?
I came to see how you were doing on your crazy diet...
Just as I thought, your skin is super dry...
SHIMMER
Rec, why do you look like Jac-queline...?
Huh? I do? Like Sensei?
What, you came here to mock us?!
I'm thinner than before!!
Your eyebrows are so neat...
I dunno why you look so glossy, though...

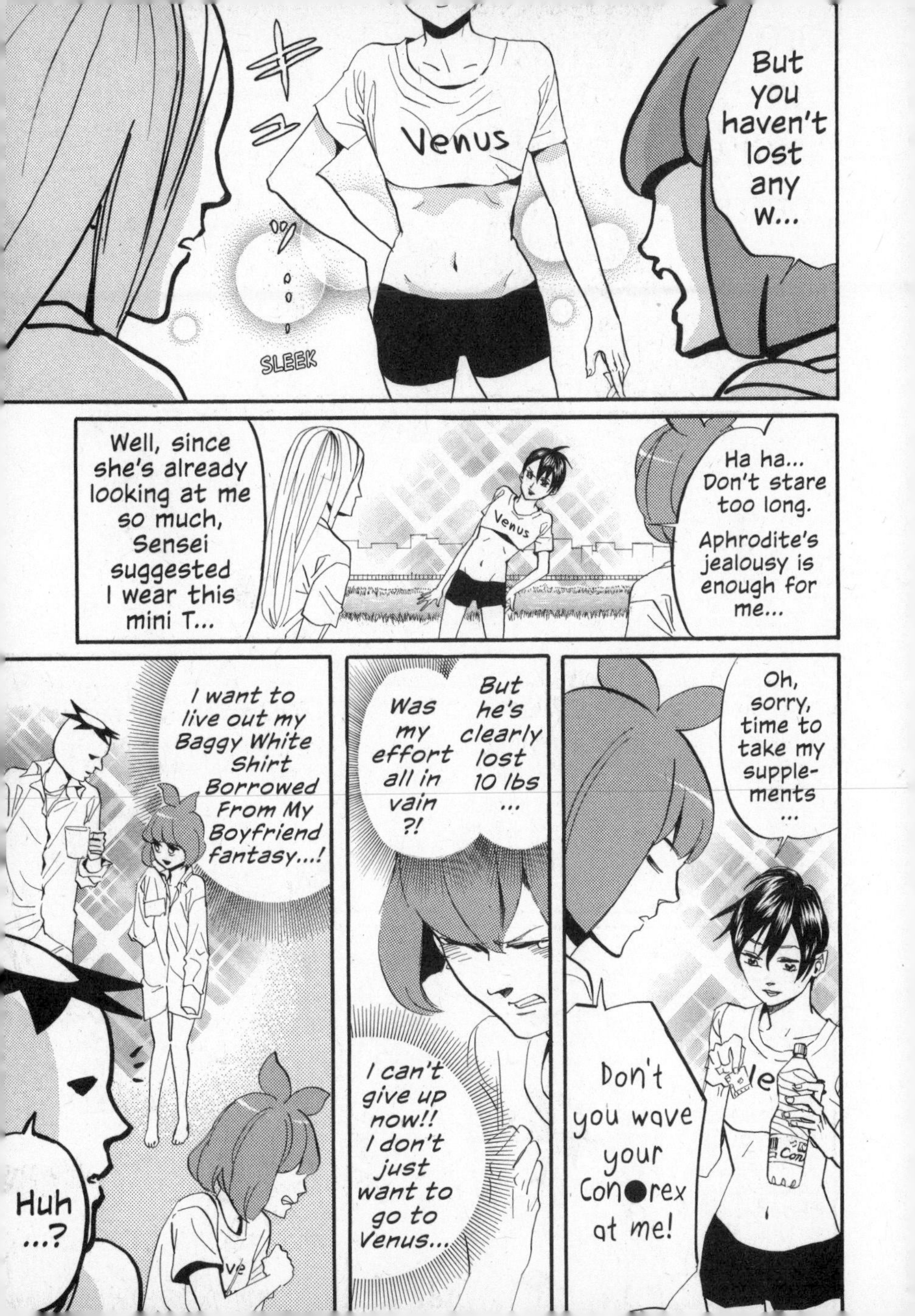
But you haven't lost any w...
SLEEK
Ha ha... Don't stare too long.
Aphrodite's jealousy is enough for me...
Well, since she's already looking at me so much, Sensei suggested I wear this mini T...
Oh, sorry, time to take my supple-ments...
Don't you wave your Con●rex at me!
But he's clearly lost 10 lbs...
Was my effort all in vain?!
I can't give up now!! I don't just want to go to Venus...
I want to live out my Baggy White Shirt Borrowed From My Boyfriend fantasy...!
Huh...?

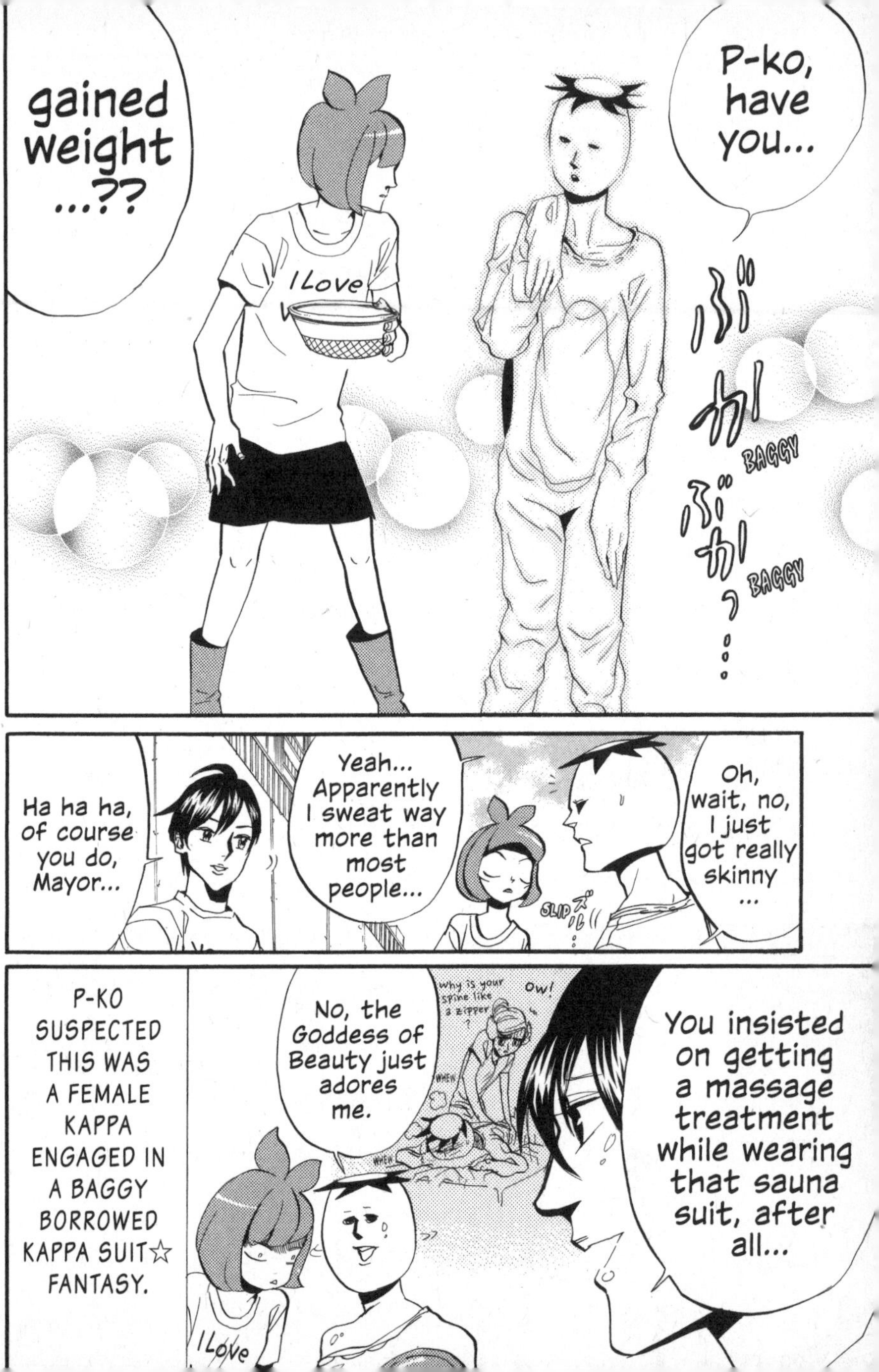
P-ko, have you...
ぶかぶかっ...
BAGGY
BAGGY
gained weight ...??
I Love
Oh, wait, no, I just got really skinny ...
SLIP
ズル
Yeah... Apparently I sweat way more than most people...
Ha ha ha, of course you do, Mayor...
You insisted on getting a massage treatment while wearing that sauna suit, after all...
Ow!
why is your spine like a zipper ?
WHEW
WHEW
No, the Goddess of Beauty just adores me.
P-KO SUSPECTED THIS WAS A FEMALE KAPPA ENGAGED IN A BAGGY BORROWED KAPPA SUIT☆ FANTASY.
I Love

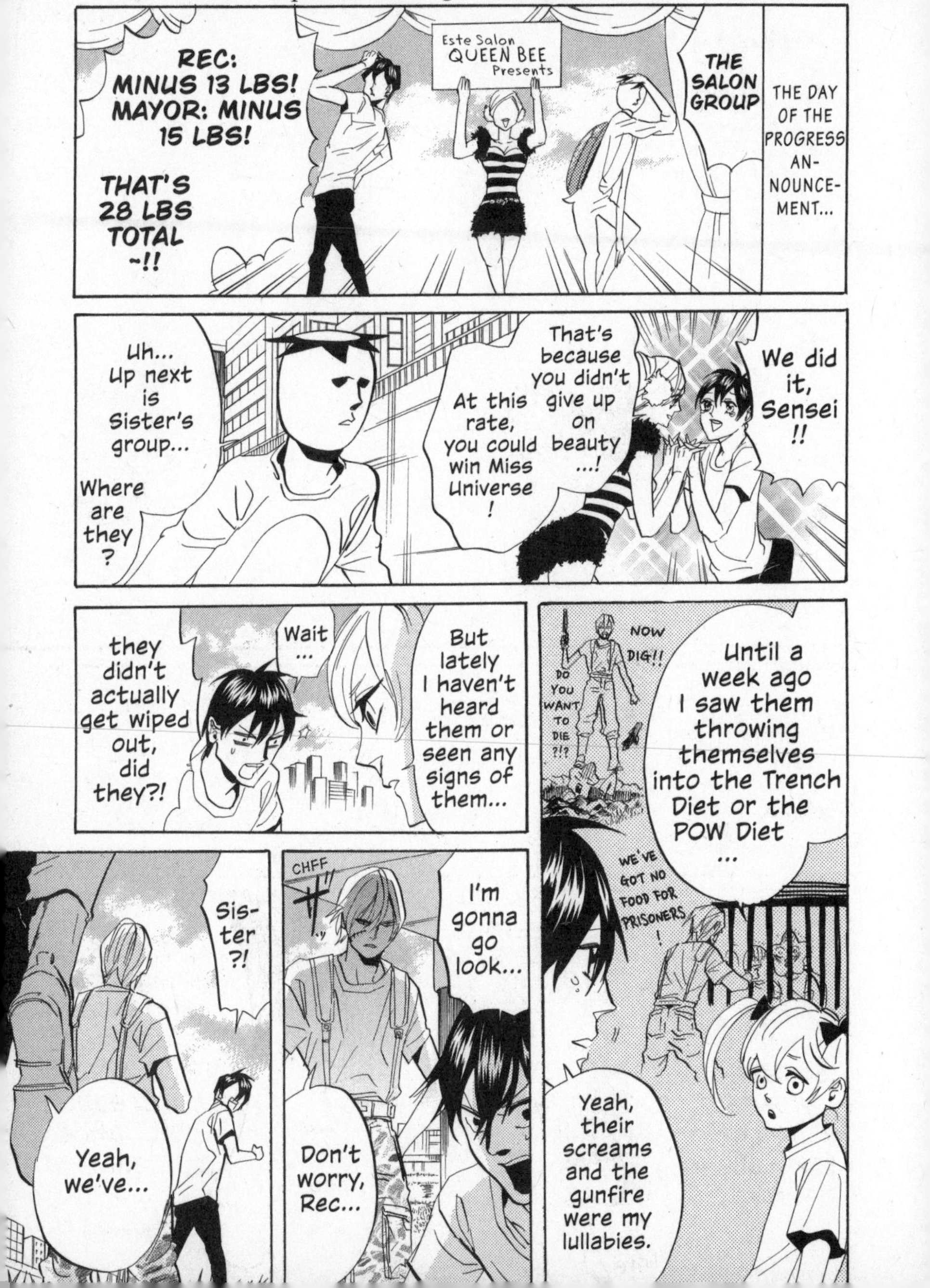
THE DAY OF THE PROGRESS AN-NOUNCE-MENT...
THE SALON GROUP
Este Salon QUEEN BEE Presents
REC: MINUS 13 LBS! MAYOR: MINUS 15 LBS!
THAT'S 28 LBS TOTAL ~!!
We did it, Sensei !!
That's because you didn't give up on beauty ...!
At this rate, you could win Miss Universe !
Uh... Up next is Sister's group...
Where are they ?
Until a week ago I saw them throwing themselves into the Trench Diet or the POW Diet ...
NOW DIG!!
DO YOU WANT TO DIE ?!?
WE'VE GOT NO FOOD FOR PRISONERS !
Yeah, their screams and the gunfire were my lullabies.
But lately I haven't heard them or seen any signs of them...
Wait ...
they didn't actually get wiped out, did they?!
CHFF
I'm gonna go look...
Don't worry, Rec...
Sis-ter ?!
Yeah, we've...

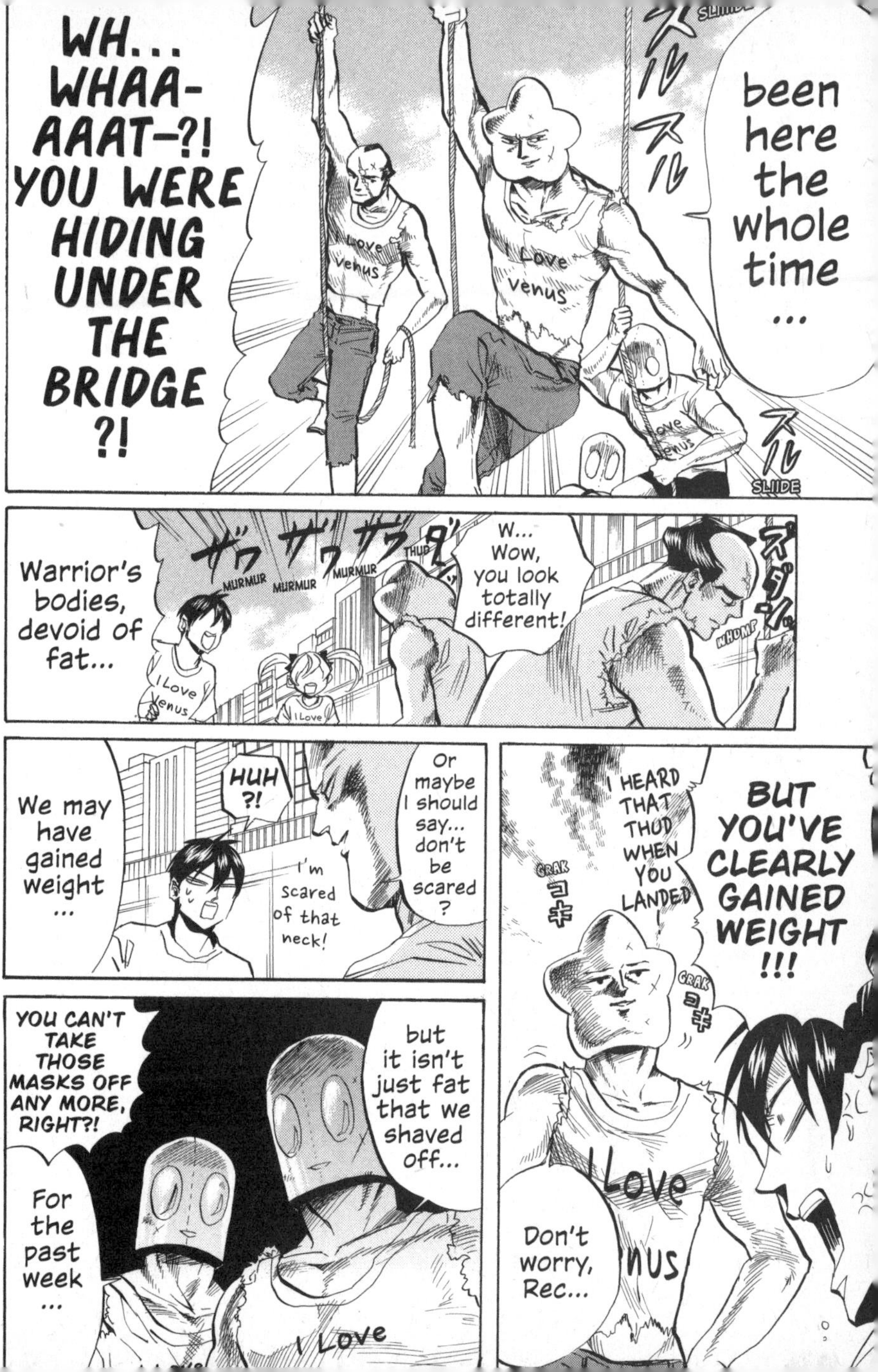
SLIIDE
been here the whole time ...
WH... WHAA-AAAT-?! YOU WERE HIDING UNDER THE BRIDGE ?!
SLIIDE
WHUMP
W... Wow, you look totally different!
THUD
MURMUR
MURMUR
MURMUR
Warrior's bodies, devoid of fat...
BUT YOU'VE CLEARLY GAINED WEIGHT !!!
I HEARD THAT THUD WHEN YOU LANDED!
GRAK
GRAK
Don't worry, Rec...
Or maybe I should say... don't be scared?
HUH ?!
I'm scared of that neck!
We may have gained weight ...
but it isn't just fat that we shaved off...
YOU CAN'T TAKE THOSE MASKS OFF ANY MORE, RIGHT?!
For the past week ...

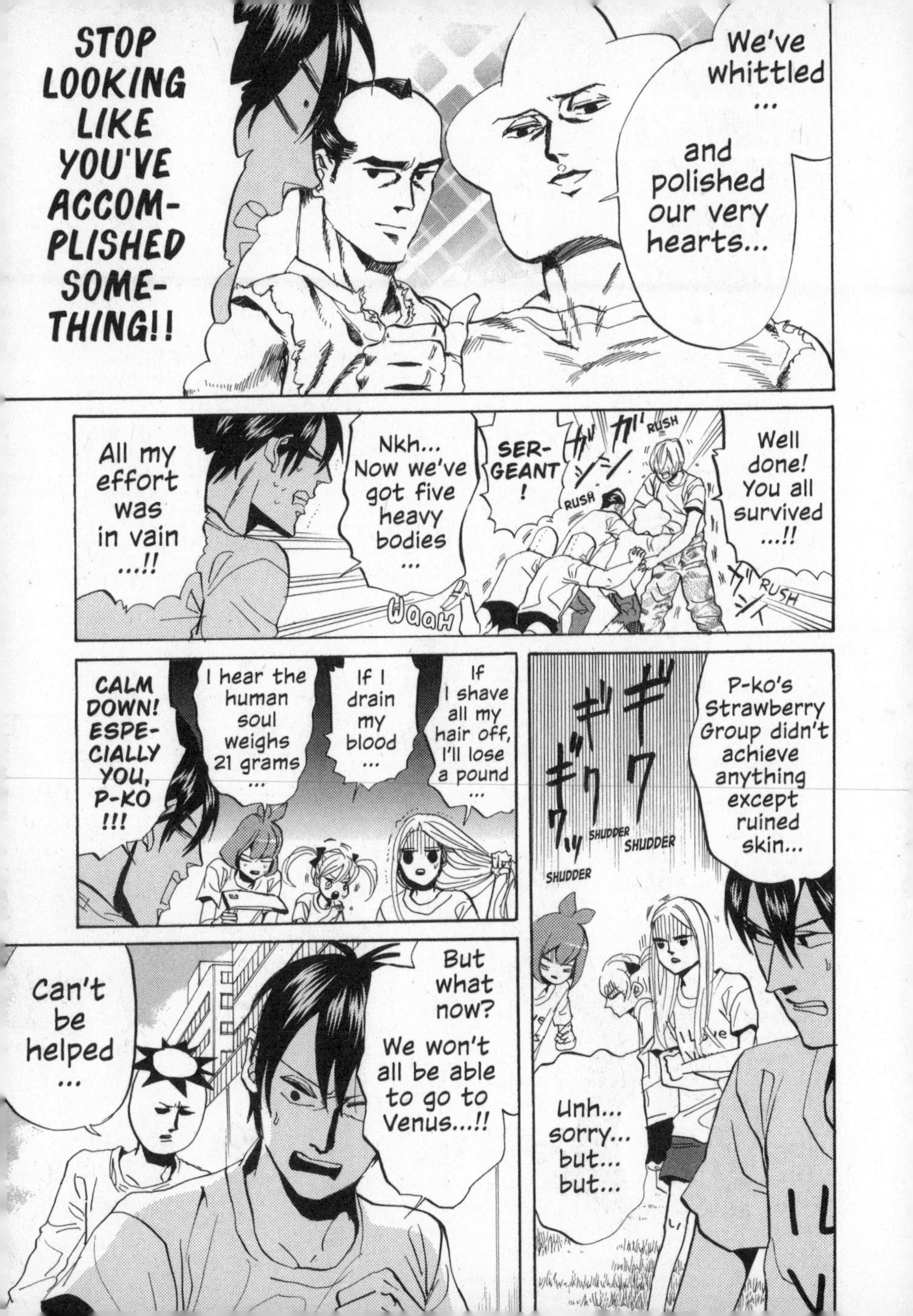

We've whittled ... and polished our very hearts...
STOP LOOKING LIKE YOU'VE ACCOMPLISHED SOMETHING!!
Well done! You all survived ...!!
RUSH
RUSH
RUSH
SERGEANT!
Nkh... Now we've got five heavy bodies ...
All my effort was in vain ...!!
WAAAH
P-ko's Strawberry Group didn't achieve anything except ruined skin...
SHUDDER
SHUDDER
SHUDDER
Unh... sorry... but... but...
If I shave all my hair off, I'll lose a pound ...
If I drain my blood ...
I hear the human soul weighs 21 grams ...
CALM DOWN! ESPECIALLY YOU, P-KO!!!
But what now? We won't all be able to go to Venus...!!
Can't be helped ...

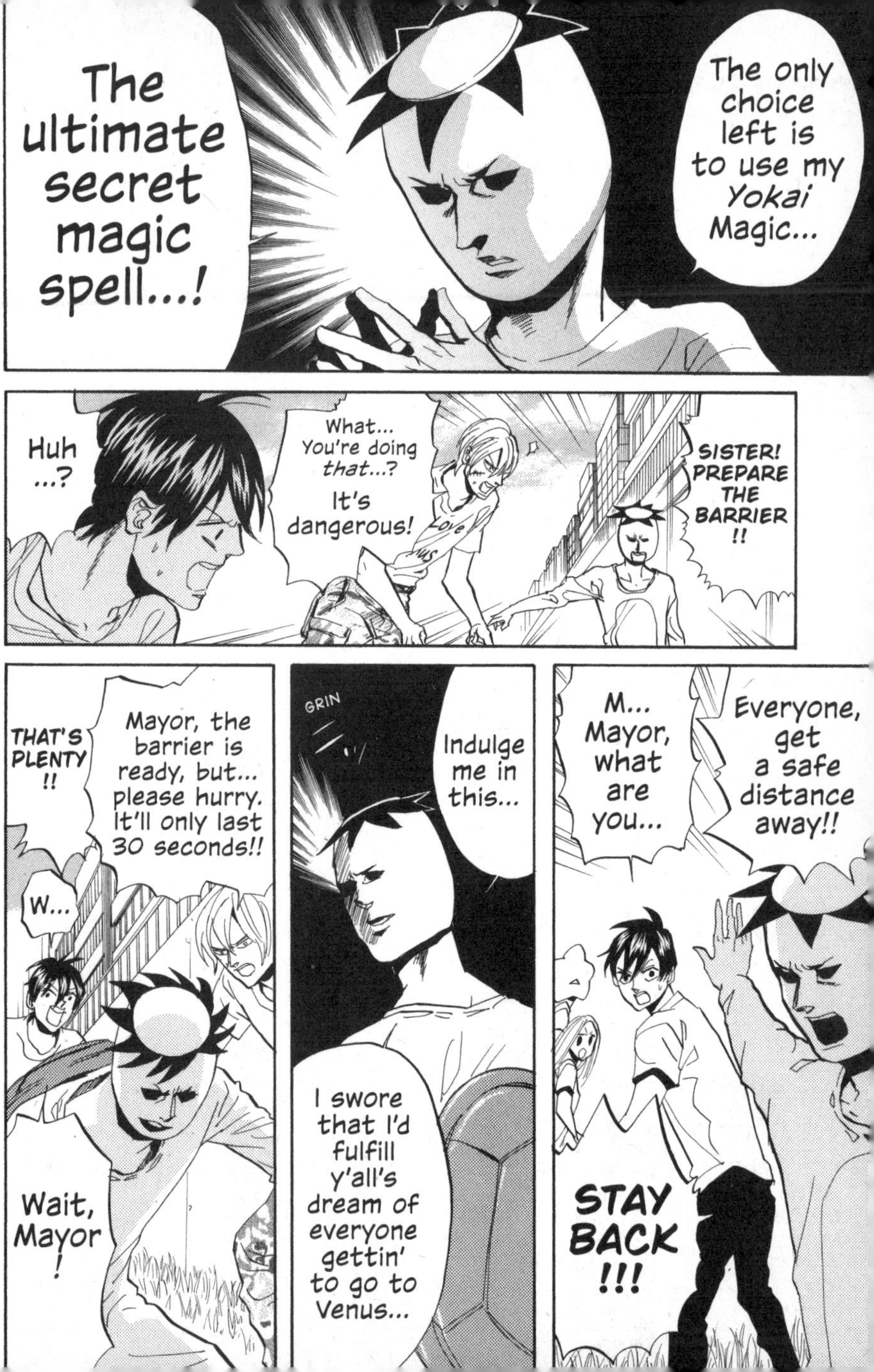
The only choice left is to use my *Yokai* Magic...
The ultimate secret magic spell...!
SISTER! PREPARE THE BARRIER!!
What... You're doing *that*...?
It's dangerous!
Huh ...?
Everyone, get a safe distance away!!
M... Mayor, what are you...
STAY BACK!!!
GRIN
Indulge me in this...
I swore that I'd fulfill y'all's dream of everyone gettin' to go to Venus...
Mayor, the barrier is ready, but... please hurry. It'll only last 30 seconds!!
THAT'S PLENTY!!
W...
Wait, Mayor!

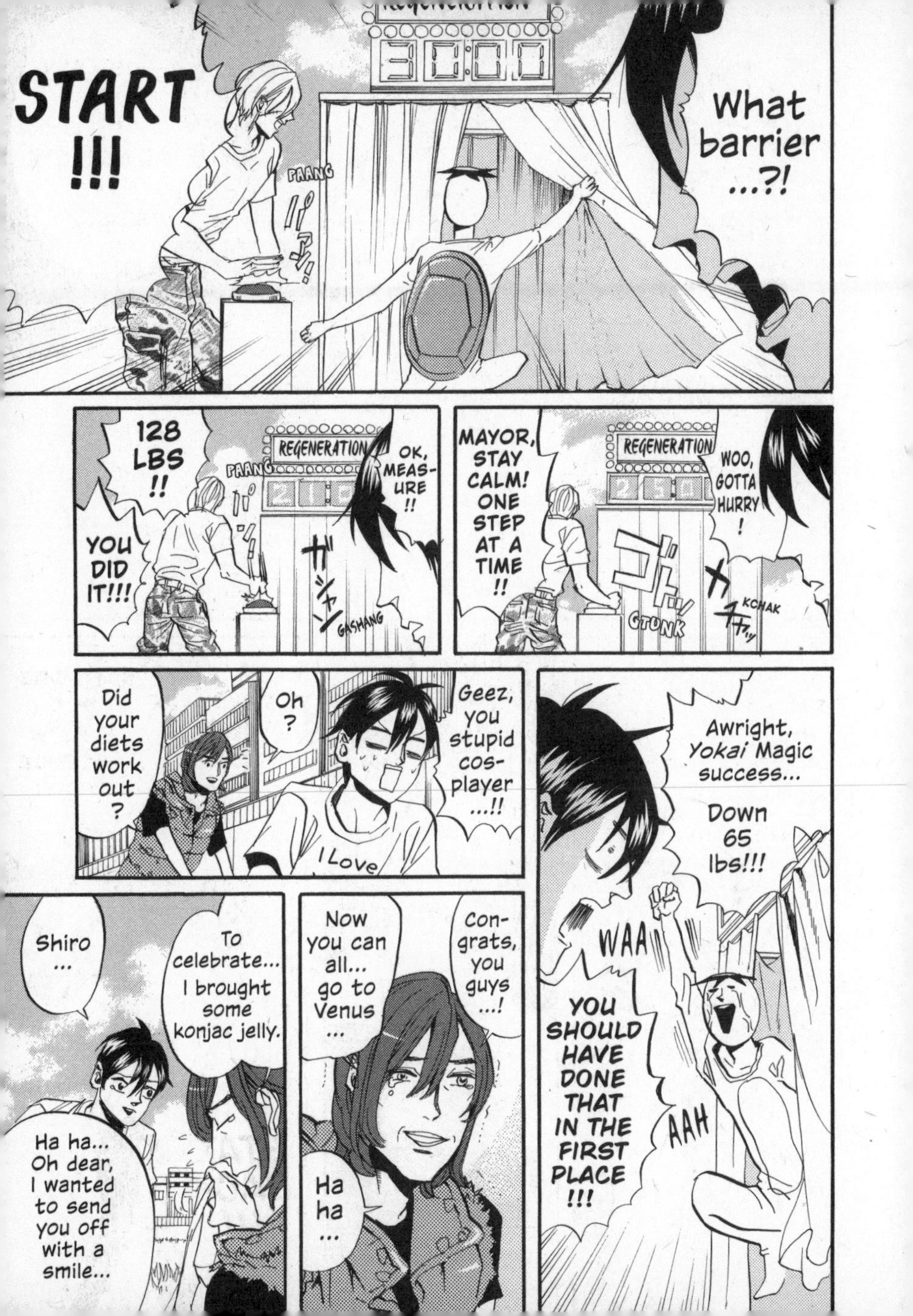

What barrier ...?!
PAANG
START !!!
WOO, GOTTA HURRY!
REGENERATION
MAYOR, STAY CALM! ONE STEP AT A TIME!!
KCHAK
GTUNK
OK, MEASURE!!
REGENERATION
128 LBS!!
PAANG
YOU DID IT!!!
GASHANG
Awright, Yokai Magic success...
Down 65 lbs!!!
WAA
YOU SHOULD HAVE DONE THAT IN THE FIRST PLACE!!!
AAH
Geez, you stupid cos-player...!!
Oh?
Did your diets work out?
I Love
Con-grats, you guys...!
Now you can all... go to Venus...
Ha ha...
To celebrate... I brought some konjac jelly.
Shiro...
Ha ha... Oh dear, I wanted to send you off with a smile...

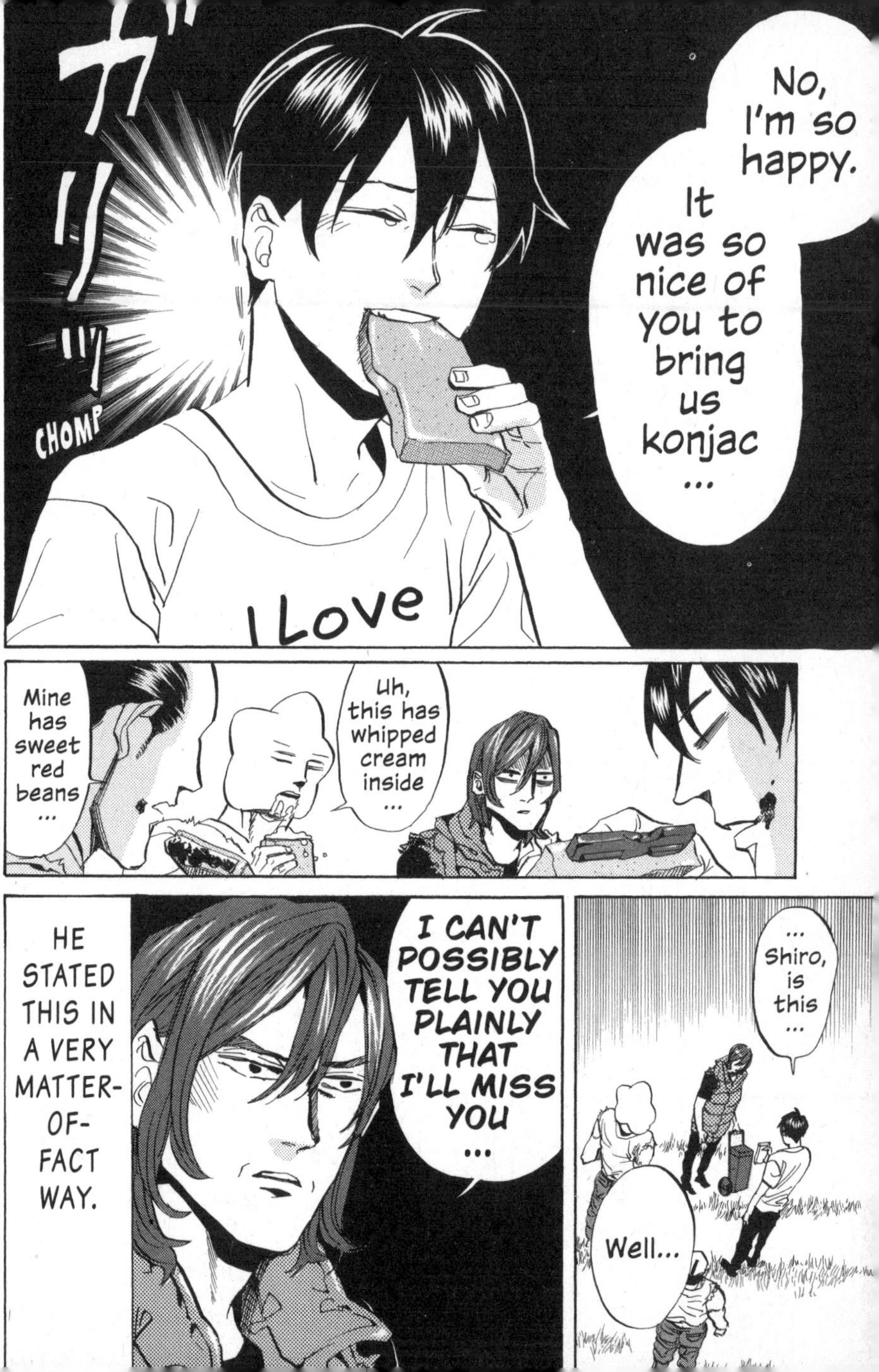
No, I'm so happy. It was so nice of you to bring us konjac...
CHOMP
I Love
Uh, this has whipped cream inside...
Mine has sweet red beans...
...Shiro, is this...
Well...
I CAN'T POSSIBLY TELL YOU PLAINLY THAT I'LL MISS YOU...
HE STATED THIS IN A VERY MATTER-OF-FACT WAY.

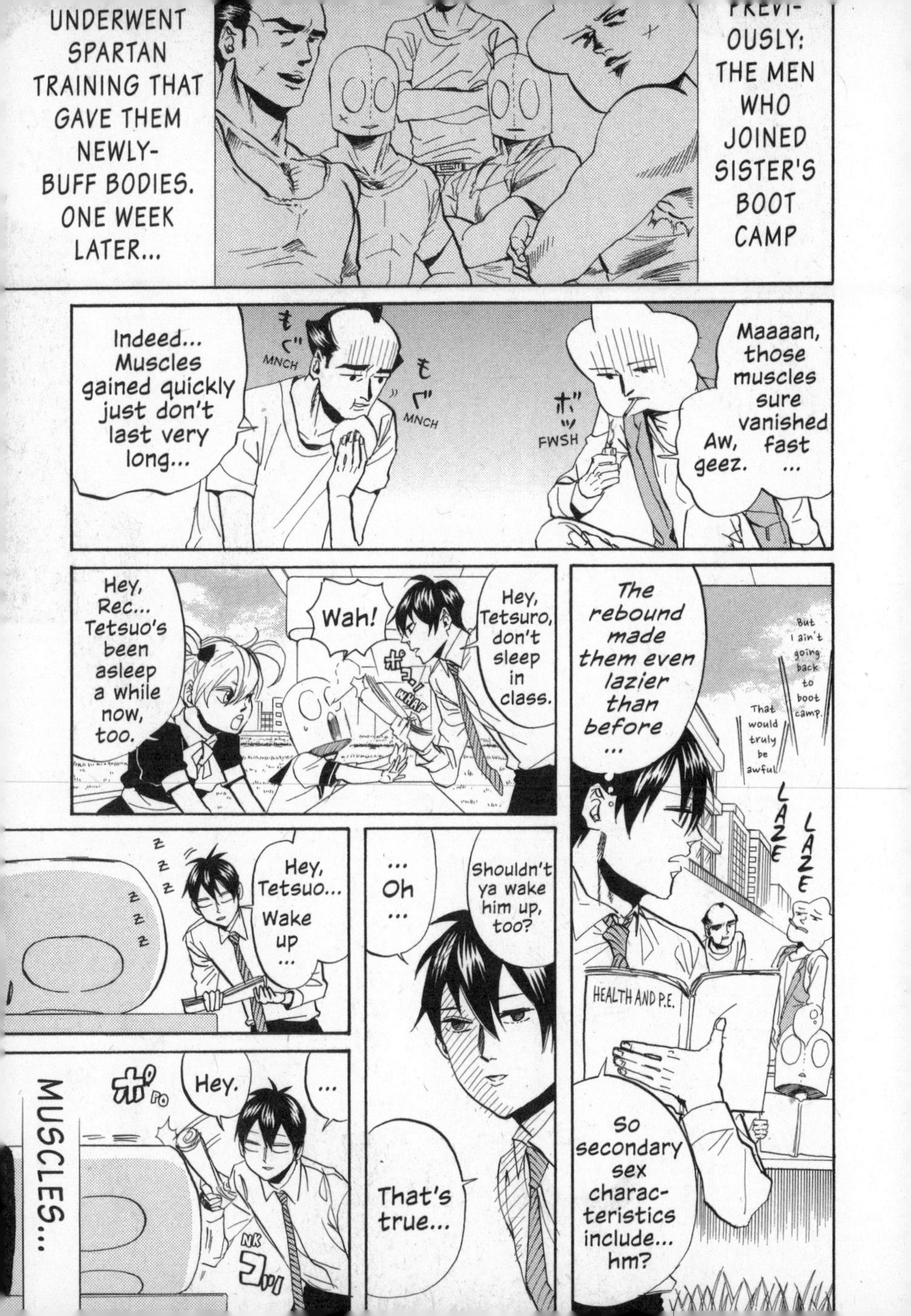
PREVI-OUSLY: THE MEN WHO JOINED SISTER'S BOOT CAMP
UNDERWENT SPARTAN TRAINING THAT GAVE THEM NEWLY-BUFF BODIES. ONE WEEK LATER...
Maaaan, those muscles sure vanished fast...
Aw, geez.
FWSH
MNCH
MNCH
Indeed... Muscles gained quickly just don't last very long...
The rebound made them even lazier than before...
But I ain't going back to boot camp.
That would truly be awful
LAZE
LAZE
HEALTH AND P.E.
So secondary sex characteristics include... hm?
Hey, Tetsuro, don't sleep in class.
Wah!
WHAP
Hey, Rec... Tetsuo's been asleep a while now, too.
Shouldn't ya wake him up, too?
... Oh ...
That's true...
Hey, Tetsuo... Wake up...
...
Hey.
PO
NK
MUSCLES...

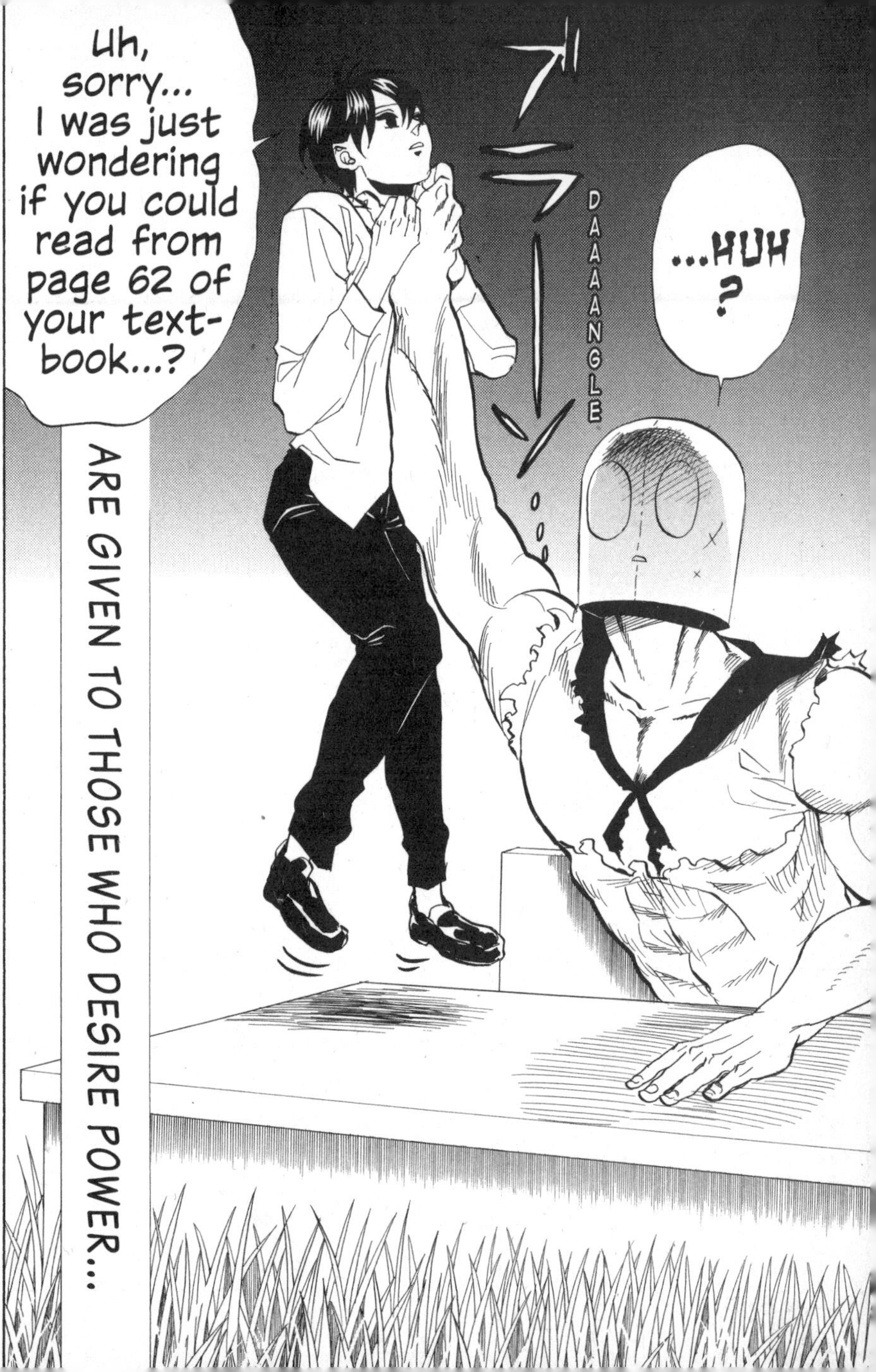
...HUH?
DAAAANGLE
Uh, sorry... I was just wondering if you could read from page 62 of your text-book...?
ARE GIVEN TO THOSE WHO DESIRE POWER...

Chapter 265: Muscle

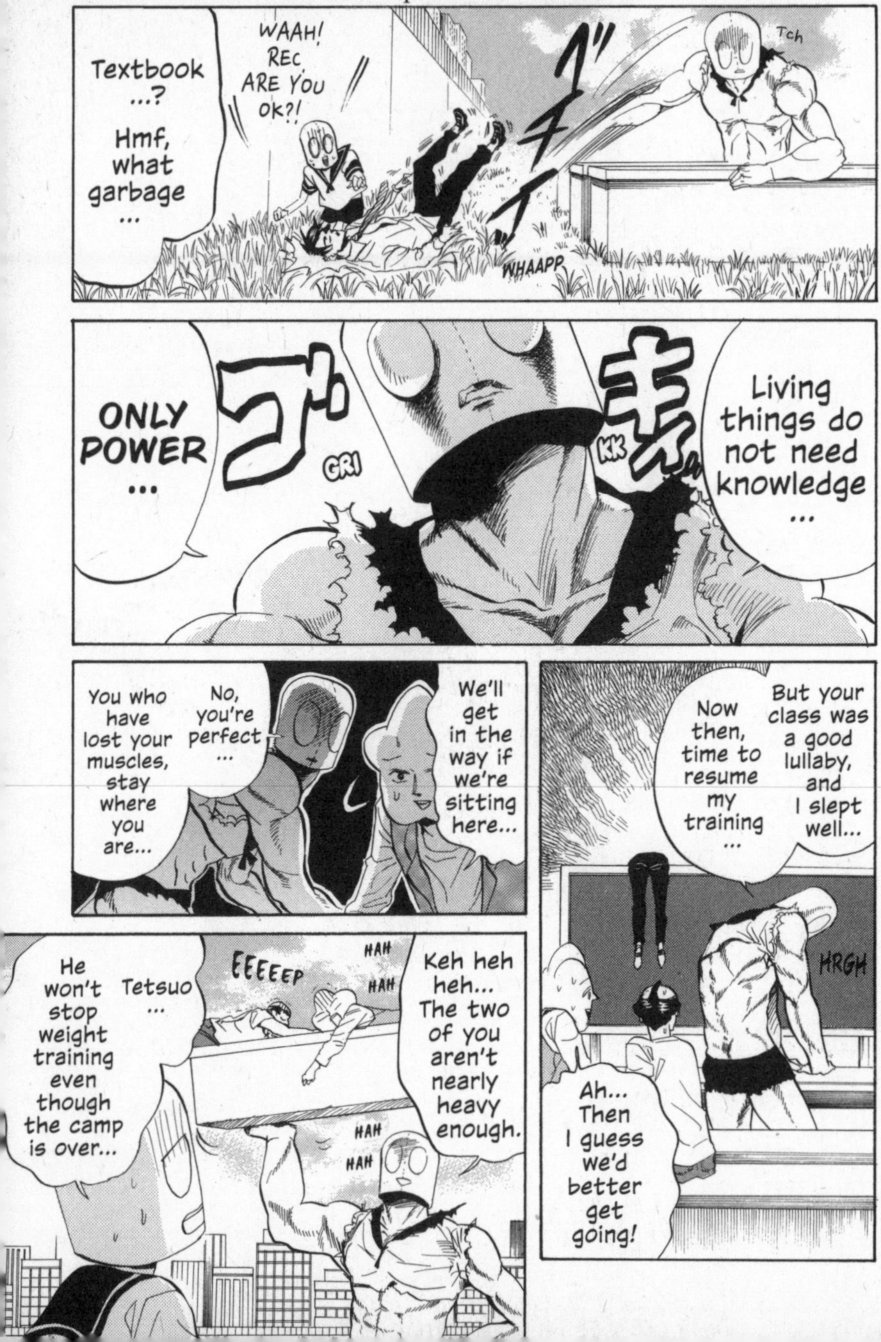
Tch
WAAH! REC ARE YOU OK?!
Textbook ...? Hmf, what garbage ...
WHAAPP
Living things do not need knowledge ...
KK
GRI
ONLY POWER ...
But your class was a good lullaby, and I slept well...
Now then, time to resume my training ...
HRGH
Ah... Then I guess we'd better get going!
We'll get in the way if we're sitting here...
No, you're perfect ...
You who have lost your muscles, stay where you are...
Keh heh heh... The two of you aren't nearly heavy enough.
HAH
HAH
EEEEEP
Tetsuo ...
He won't stop weight training even though the camp is over...
HAH
HAH

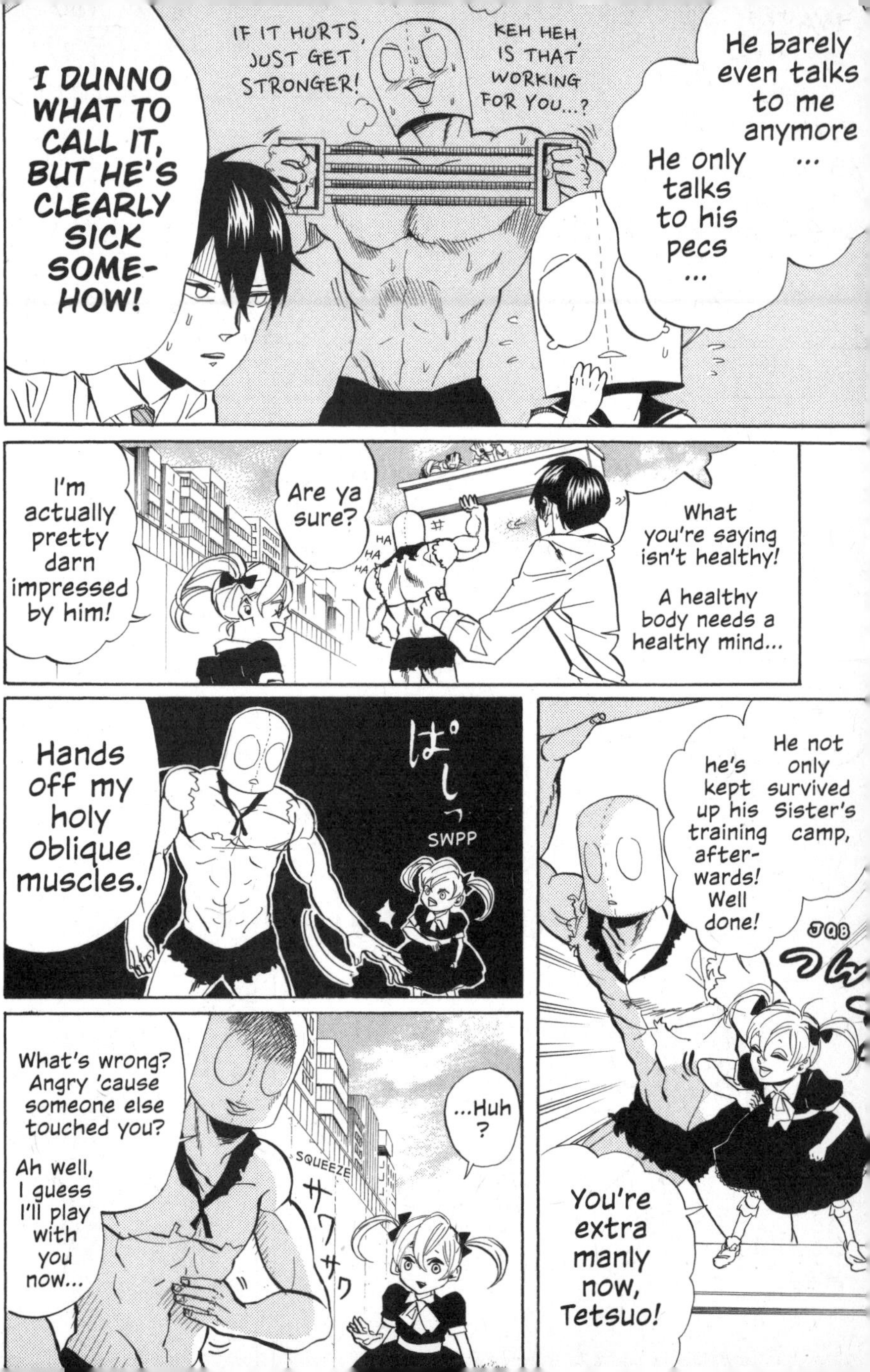
He barely even talks to me anymore...
He only talks to his pecs...
KEH HEH, IS THAT WORKING FOR YOU...?
IF IT HURTS, JUST GET STRONGER!
I DUNNO WHAT TO CALL IT, BUT HE'S CLEARLY SICK SOME-HOW!
What you're saying isn't healthy!
A healthy body needs a healthy mind...
HA HA HA
Are ya sure?
I'm actually pretty darn impressed by him!
He not only survived Sister's camp, he's kept up his training after-wards! Well done!
JAB
You're extra manly now, Tetsuo!
ぱしっ
SWPP
Hands off my holy oblique muscles.
...Huh?
SQUEEZE
サワサワ
What's wrong? Angry 'cause someone else touched you?
Ah well, I guess I'll play with you now...

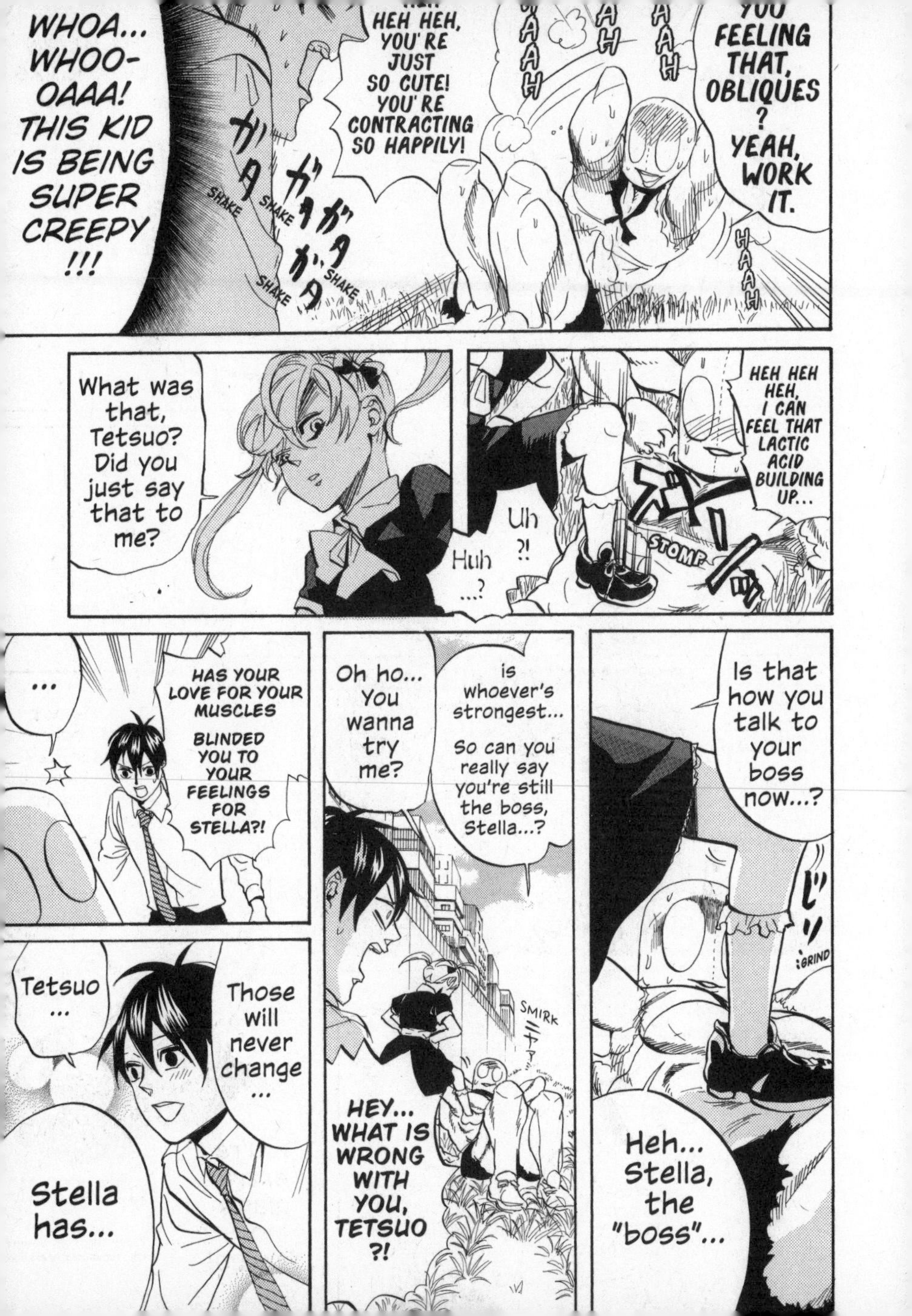
YOU FEELING THAT, OBLIQUES? YEAH, WORK IT.
HAAAH
AAH
AAH
HAAAH
HEH HEH, YOU'RE JUST SO CUTE! YOU'RE CONTRACTING SO HAPPILY!
SHAKE
SHAKE
SHAKE
SHAKE
WHOA... WHOO-OAAA! THIS KID IS BEING SUPER CREEPY!!!
HEH HEH HEH, I CAN FEEL THAT LACTIC ACID BUILDING UP...
STOMP
Uh?!
Huh...?
What was that, Tetsuo? Did you just say that to me?
Is that how you talk to your boss now...?
GRIND
Heh... Stella, the "boss"...
is whoever's strongest...
So can you really say you're still the boss, Stella...?
Oh ho... You wanna try me?
SMIRK
HEY... WHAT IS WRONG WITH YOU, TETSUO?!
HAS YOUR LOVE FOR YOUR MUSCLES BLINDED YOU TO YOUR FEELINGS FOR STELLA?!
...
Those will never change...
Tetsuo...
Stella has...

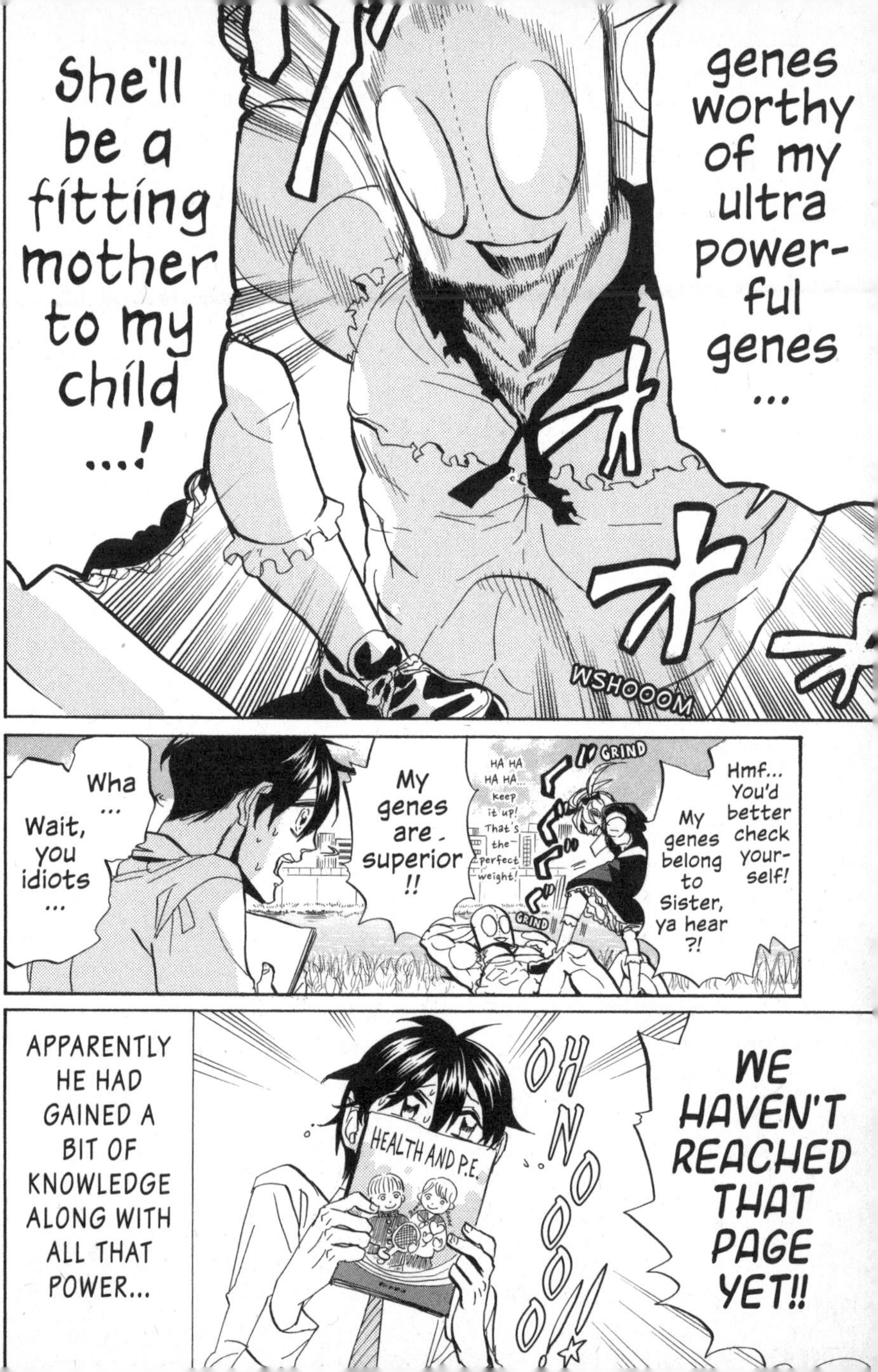
genes worthy of my ultra power-ful genes ...
She'll be a fitting mother to my child ...!
WSHOOOM
Hmf... You'd better check your-self!
My genes belong to Sister, ya hear ?!
GRIND
HA HA HA HA... keep it up! That's the perfect weight!
GRIND
My genes are superior !!
Wha ... Wait, you idiots ...
WE HAVEN'T REACHED THAT PAGE YET!!
OH NOOOOO!!
HEALTH AND P.E.
APPARENTLY HE HAD GAINED A BIT OF KNOWLEDGE ALONG WITH ALL THAT POWER...

Chapter 266: Conquest

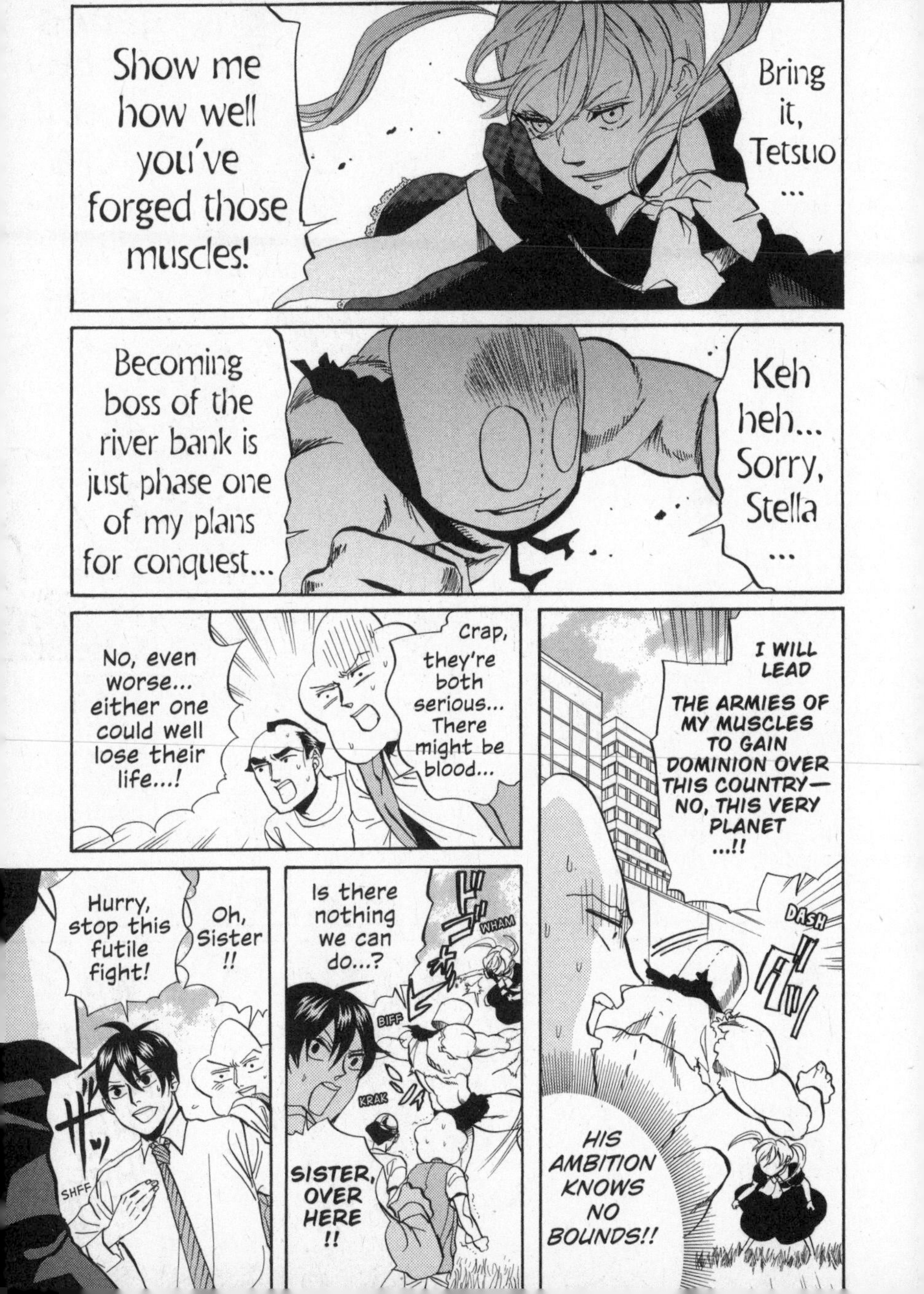

Bring it, Tetsuo ...
Show me how well you've forged those muscles!
Keh heh... Sorry, Stella ...
Becoming boss of the river bank is just phase one of my plans for conquest...
I WILL LEAD THE ARMIES OF MY MUSCLES TO GAIN DOMINION OVER THIS COUNTRY—NO, THIS VERY PLANET ...!!
DASH
HIS AMBITION KNOWS NO BOUNDS!!
Crap, they're both serious... There might be blood...
No, even worse... either one could well lose their life...!
Is there nothing we can do...?
WHAM
BIFF
KRAK
SISTER, OVER HERE !!
Oh, Sister !!
Hurry, stop this futile fight!
SHFF

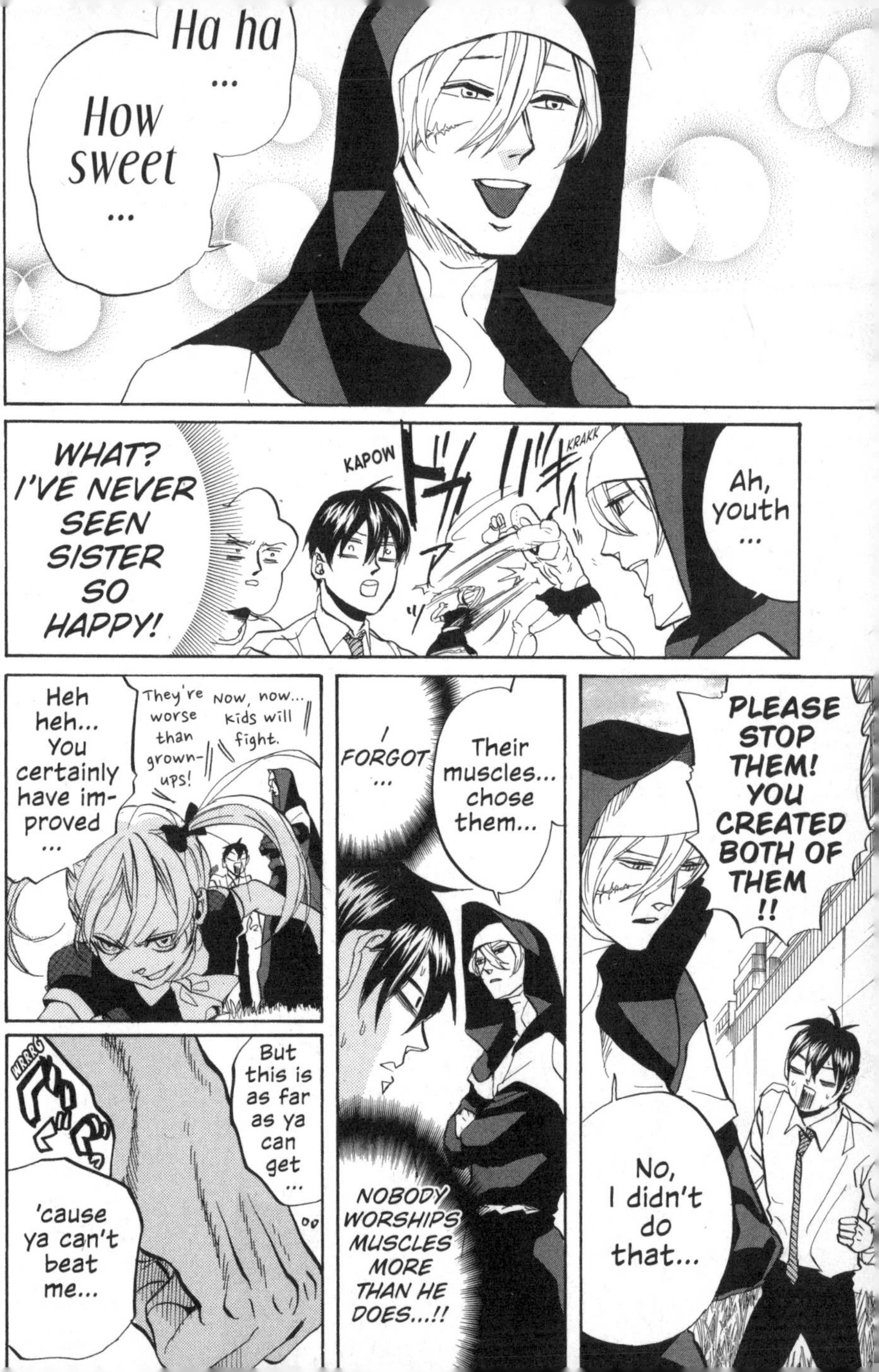
Ha ha ... How sweet ...
Ah, youth ...
KRAKK
KAPOW
WHAT? I'VE NEVER SEEN SISTER SO HAPPY!
PLEASE STOP THEM! YOU CREATED BOTH OF THEM !!
No, I didn't do that...
Their muscles... chose them...
I FORGOT ...
NOBODY WORSHIPS MUSCLES MORE THAN HE DOES...!!
Now, now... kids will fight.
They're worse than grown-ups!
Heh heh... You certainly have improved ...
WRRRG
But this is as far as ya can get ...
'cause ya can't beat me...

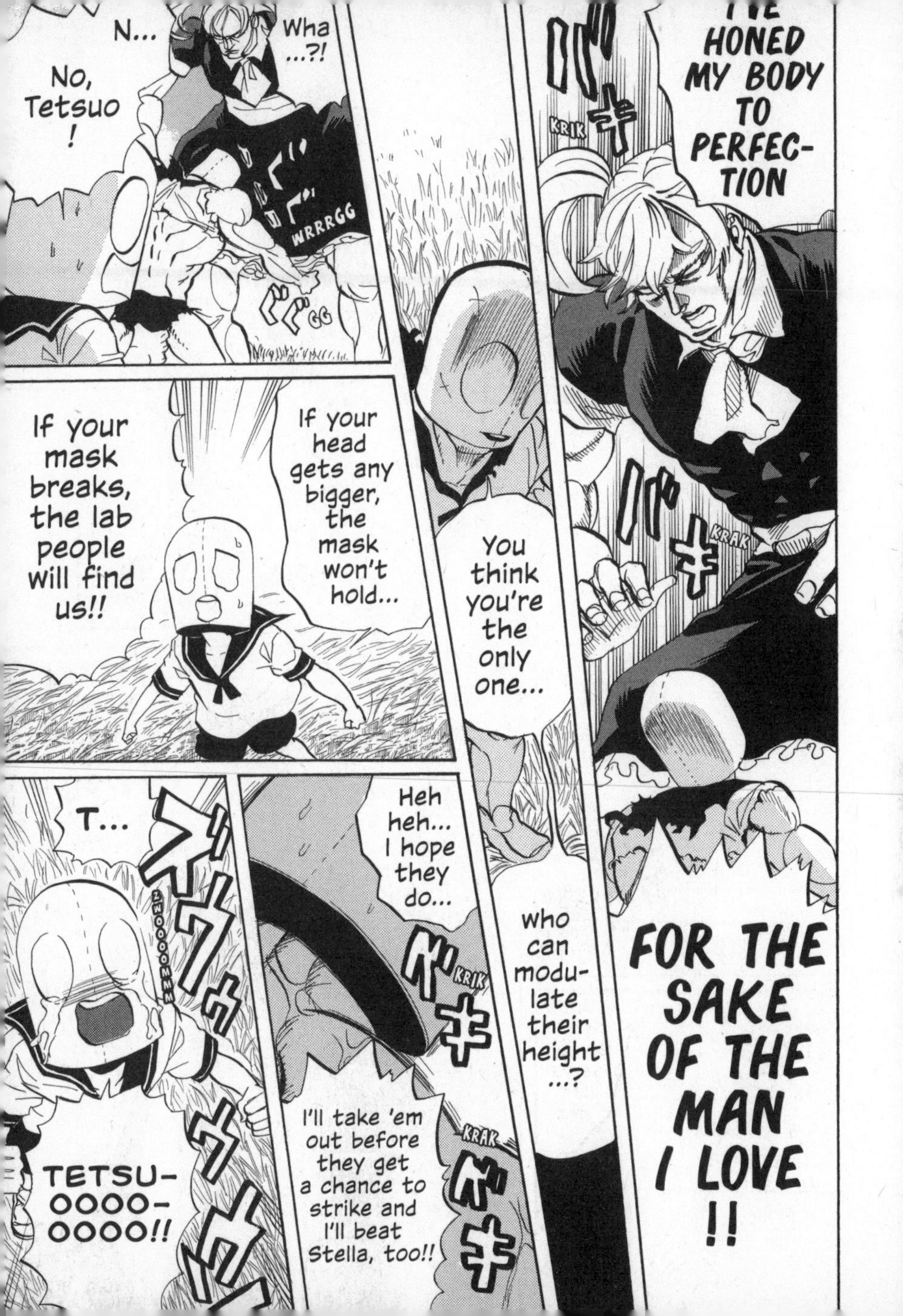

HONED MY BODY TO PERFECTION
KRIK
KRAK
FOR THE SAKE OF THE MAN I LOVE !!
You think you're the only one...
who can modulate their height ...?
Heh heh... I hope they do...
KRIK
I'll take 'em out before they get a chance to strike and I'll beat Stella, too!!
KRAK
Wha ...?!
N...
No, Tetsuo !
WRRRGG
GG
If your head gets any bigger, the mask won't hold...
If your mask breaks, the lab people will find us!!
T...
ZWOOOOMM
TETSU-OOOO-OOOO!!

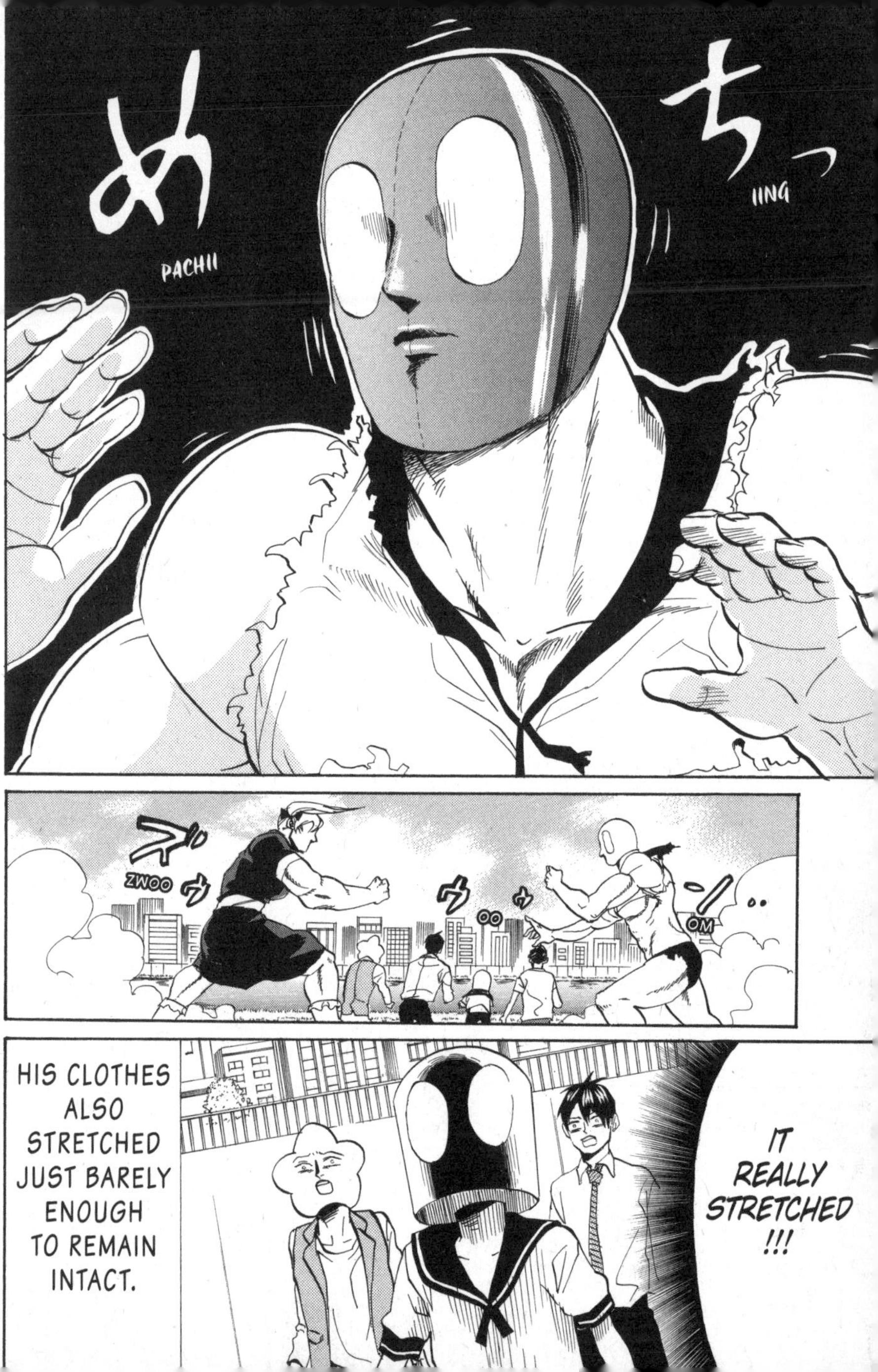
ちっ
IING
め
PACHII
ズ
ZWOO
ゥ
ゥ
OO
ッ
OM
IT REALLY STRETCHED!!!
HIS CLOTHES ALSO STRETCHED JUST BARELY ENOUGH TO REMAIN INTACT.

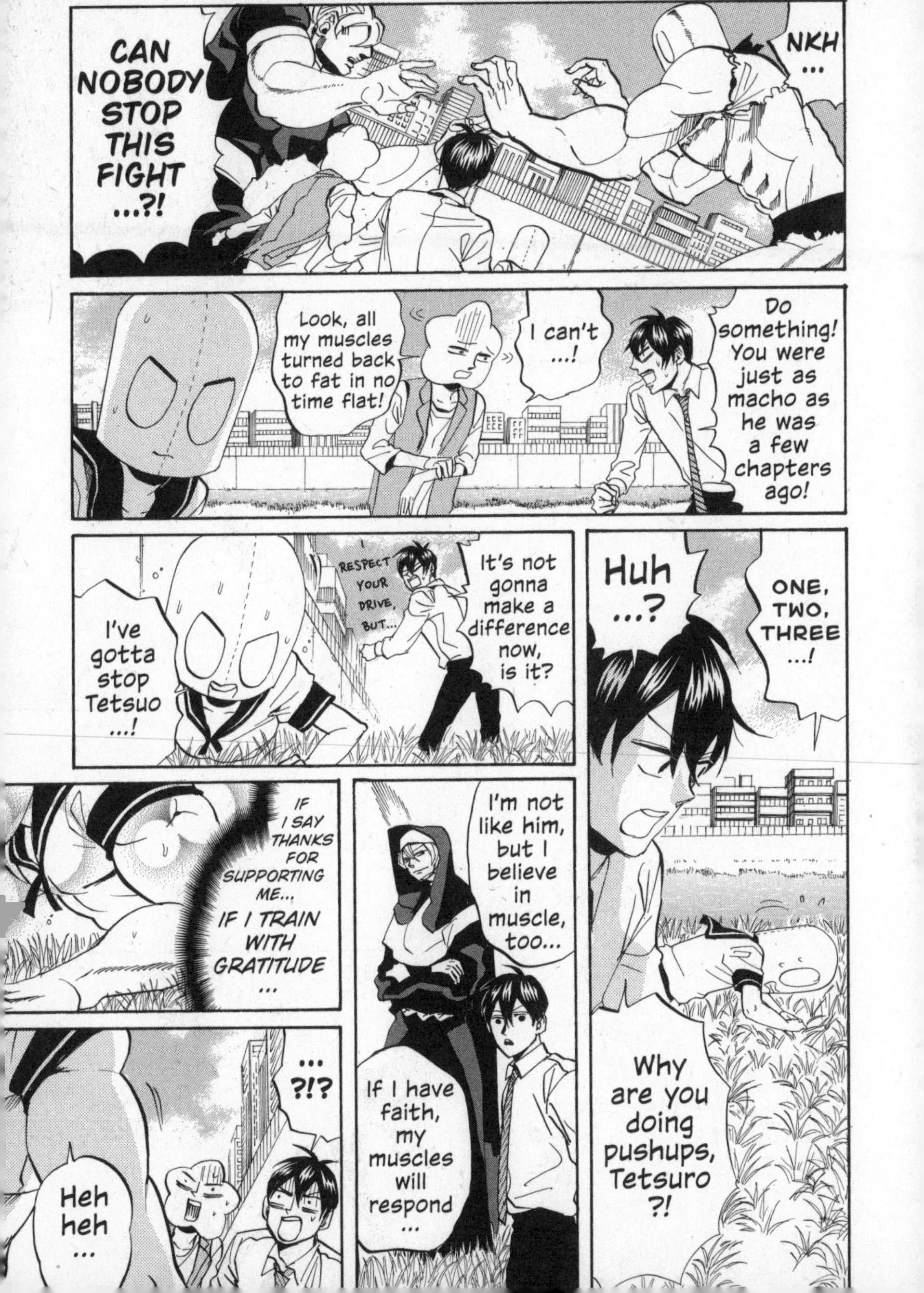
NKH ...
CAN NOBODY STOP THIS FIGHT ...?!
Do something! You were just as macho as he was a few chapters ago!
I can't ...!
Look, all my muscles turned back to fat in no time flat!
ONE, TWO, THREE ...!
Huh ...?
Why are you doing pushups, Tetsuro ?!
It's not gonna make a difference now, is it?
I RESPECT YOUR DRIVE, BUT...
I've gotta stop Tetsuo ...!
I'm not like him, but I believe in muscle, too...
If I have faith, my muscles will respond ...
IF I SAY THANKS FOR SUPPORTING ME... IF I TRAIN WITH GRATITUDE ...
... ?!?
Heh heh ...

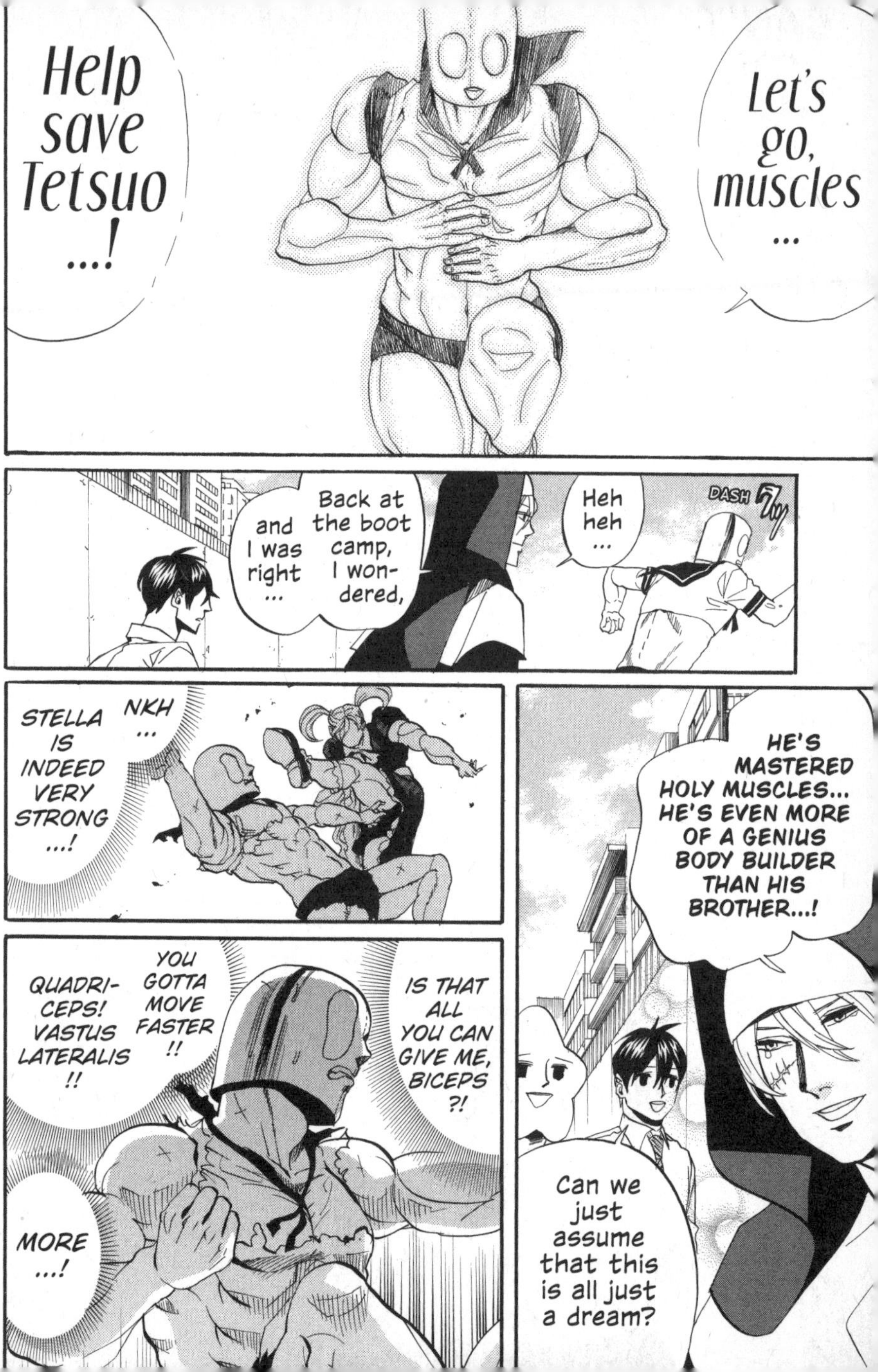
Let's go, muscles ...
Help save Tetsuo ...!
DASH
Heh heh ...
Back at the boot camp, I wondered,
and I was right ...
HE'S MASTERED HOLY MUSCLES... HE'S EVEN MORE OF A GENIUS BODY BUILDER THAN HIS BROTHER...!
Can we just assume that this is all just a dream?
NKH ...
STELLA IS INDEED VERY STRONG ...!
IS THAT ALL YOU CAN GIVE ME, BICEPS ?!
YOU GOTTA MOVE FASTER !!
QUADRI-CEPS! VASTUS LATERALIS !!
MORE ...!

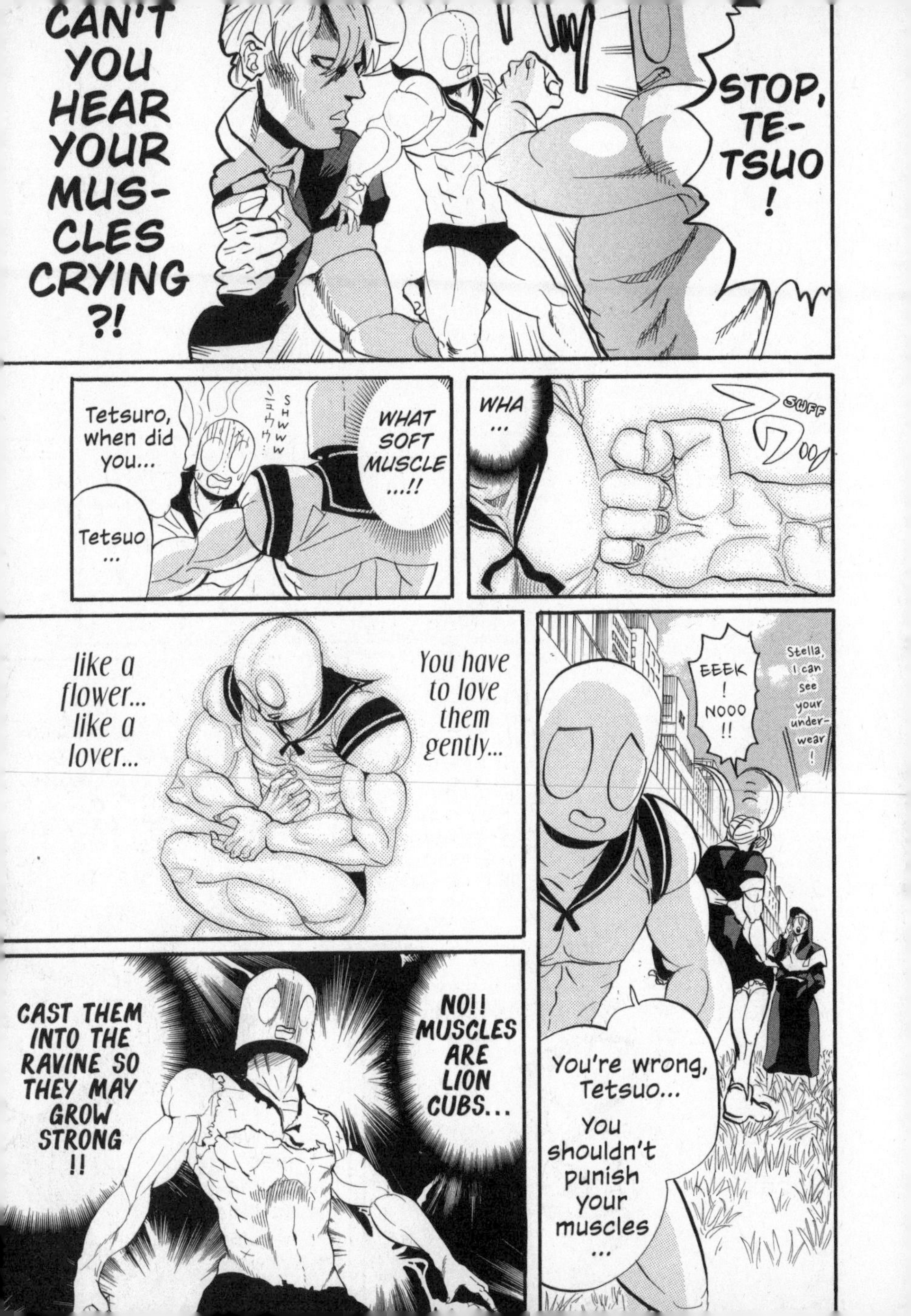
STOP, TE-TSUO!
CAN'T YOU HEAR YOUR MUS-CLES CRYING?!
SWFF
WHA...
SHWWW
WHAT SOFT MUSCLE...!!
Tetsuro, when did you...
Tetsuo...
Stella, I can see your under-wear!
EEEK! NOOO!!
You're wrong, Tetsuo...
You shouldn't punish your muscles...
You have to love them gently...
like a flower... like a lover...
NO!! MUSCLES ARE LION CUBS...
CAST THEM INTO THE RAVINE SO THEY MAY GROW STRONG!!

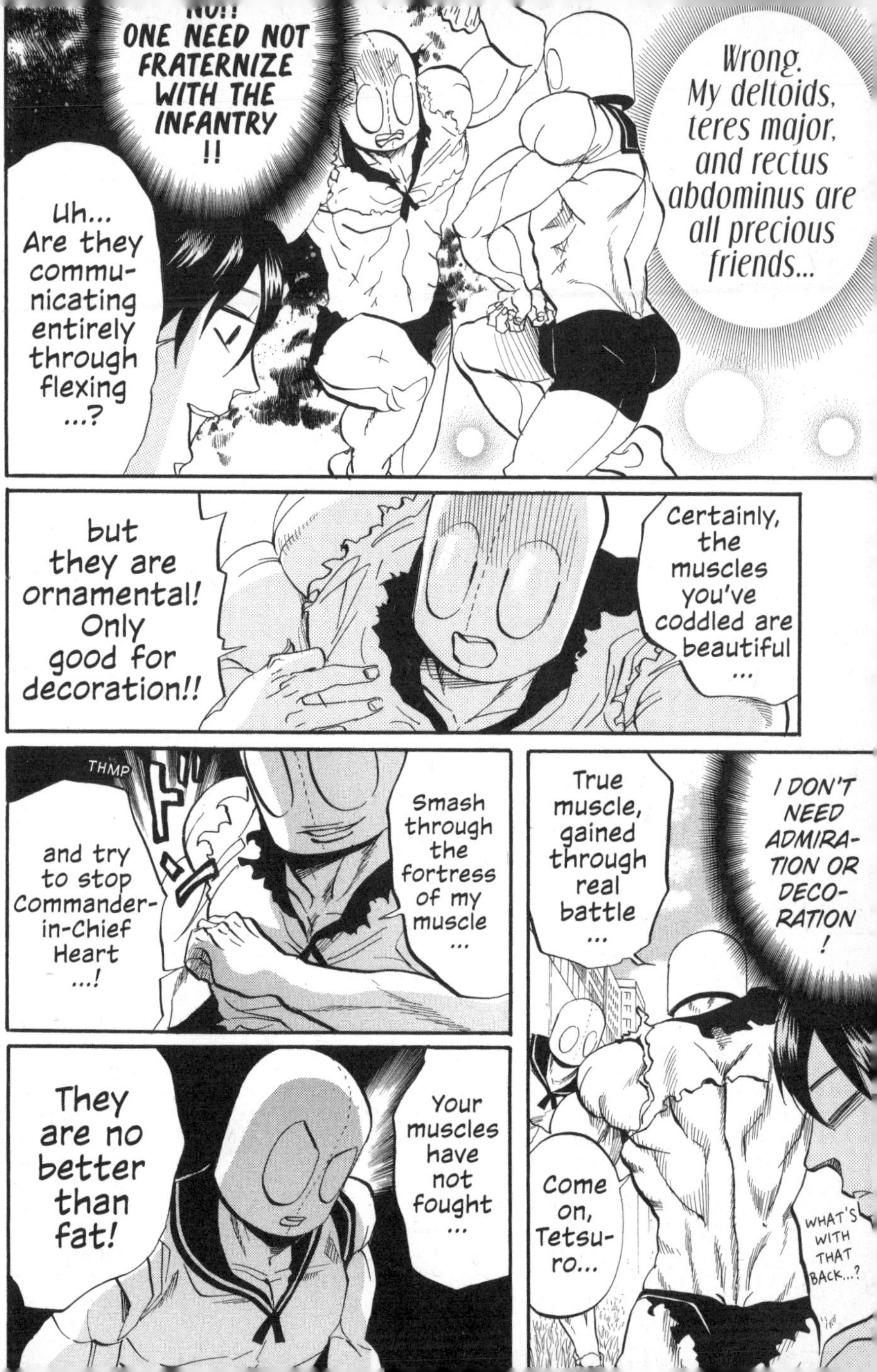
Wrong. My deltoids, teres major, and rectus abdominus are all precious friends...
ONE NEED NOT FRATERNIZE WITH THE INFANTRY !!
Uh... Are they commu-nicating entirely through flexing ...?
Certainly, the muscles you've coddled are beautiful ...
but they are ornamental! Only good for decoration!!
I DON'T NEED ADMIRA-TION OR DECO-RATION !
True muscle, gained through real battle ...
Come on, Tetsu-ro...
WHAT'S WITH THAT BACK...?
THMP
Smash through the fortress of my muscle ...
and try to stop Commander-in-Chief Heart ...!
Your muscles have not fought ...
They are no better than fat!

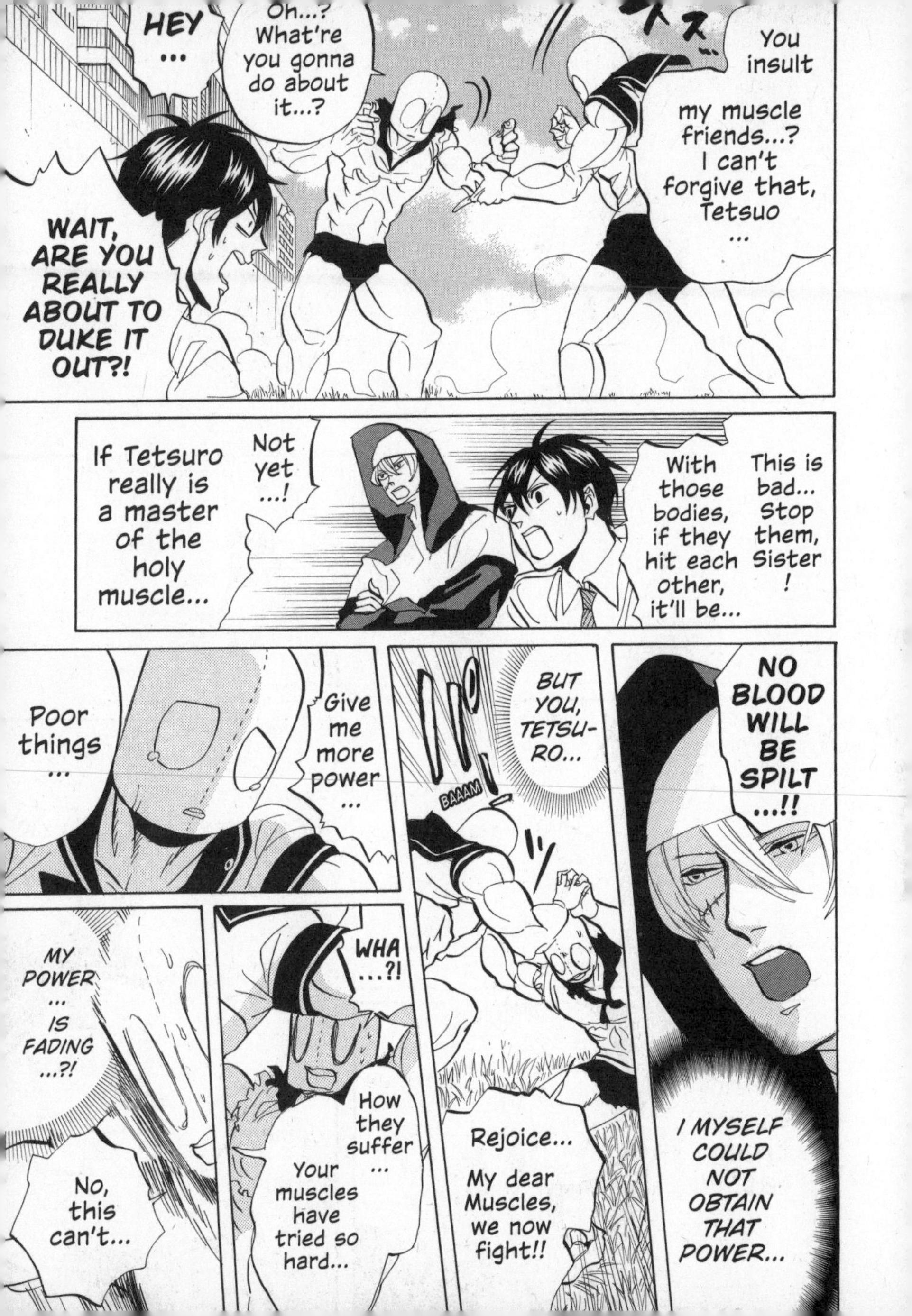

You insult my muscle friends...? I can't forgive that, Tetsuo ...
Oh...? What're you gonna do about it...?
HEY ...
WAIT, ARE YOU REALLY ABOUT TO DUKE IT OUT?!
This is bad... Stop them, Sister !
With those bodies, if they hit each other, it'll be...
Not yet ...!
If Tetsuro really is a master of the holy muscle...
NO BLOOD WILL BE SPILT ...!!
I MYSELF COULD NOT OBTAIN THAT POWER...
BUT YOU, TETSU-RO...
BAAAM
Rejoice...
My dear Muscles, we now fight!!
Give me more power ...
Poor things ...
WHA ...?!
How they suffer ...
Your muscles have tried so hard...
MY POWER ... IS FADING ...?!
No, this can't...

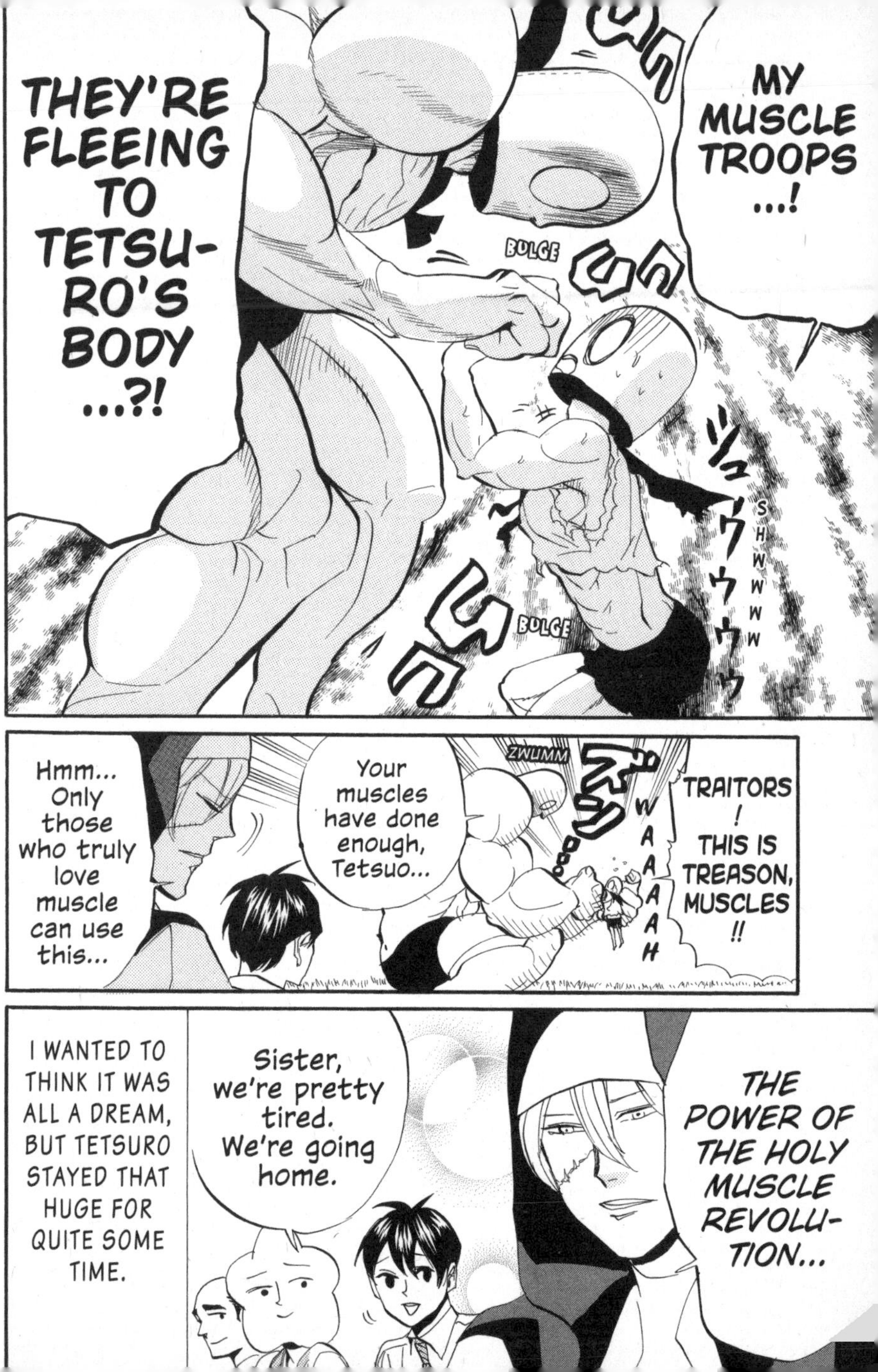
MY MUSCLE TROOPS ...!
BULGE
SHWWWWW
BULGE
THEY'RE FLEEING TO TETSU-RO'S BODY ...?!
TRAITORS! THIS IS TREASON, MUSCLES!!
WAAAAAH
ZWUMM
Your muscles have done enough, Tetsuo...
Hmm... Only those who truly love muscle can use this...
THE POWER OF THE HOLY MUSCLE REVOLU-TION...
Sister, we're pretty tired. We're going home.
I WANTED TO THINK IT WAS ALL A DREAM, BUT TETSURO STAYED THAT HUGE FOR QUITE SOME TIME.

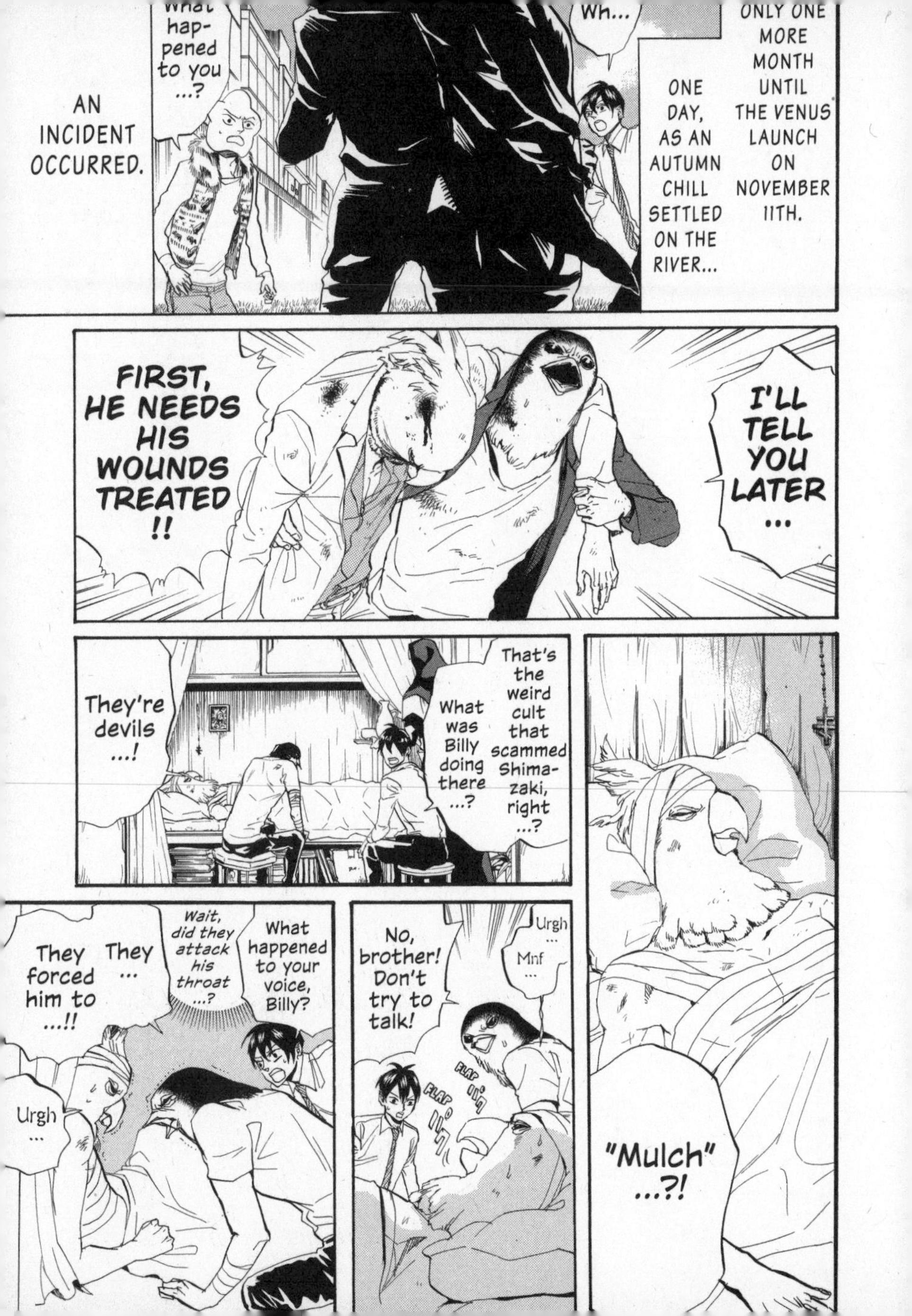
ONLY ONE MORE MONTH UNTIL THE VENUS LAUNCH ON NOVEMBER 11TH.
ONE DAY, AS AN AUTUMN CHILL SETTLED ON THE RIVER...
Wh...
What hap-pened to you ...?
AN INCIDENT OCCURRED.
I'LL TELL YOU LATER ...
FIRST, HE NEEDS HIS WOUNDS TREATED !!
"Mulch" ...?!
That's the weird cult that scammed Shima-zaki, right ...?
What was Billy doing there ...?
They're devils ...!
Urgh ...
Mnf ...
No, brother! Don't try to talk!
FLAP
FLAP
What happened to your voice, Billy?
Wait, did they attack his throat ...?
They ...
They forced him to ...!!
Urgh ...

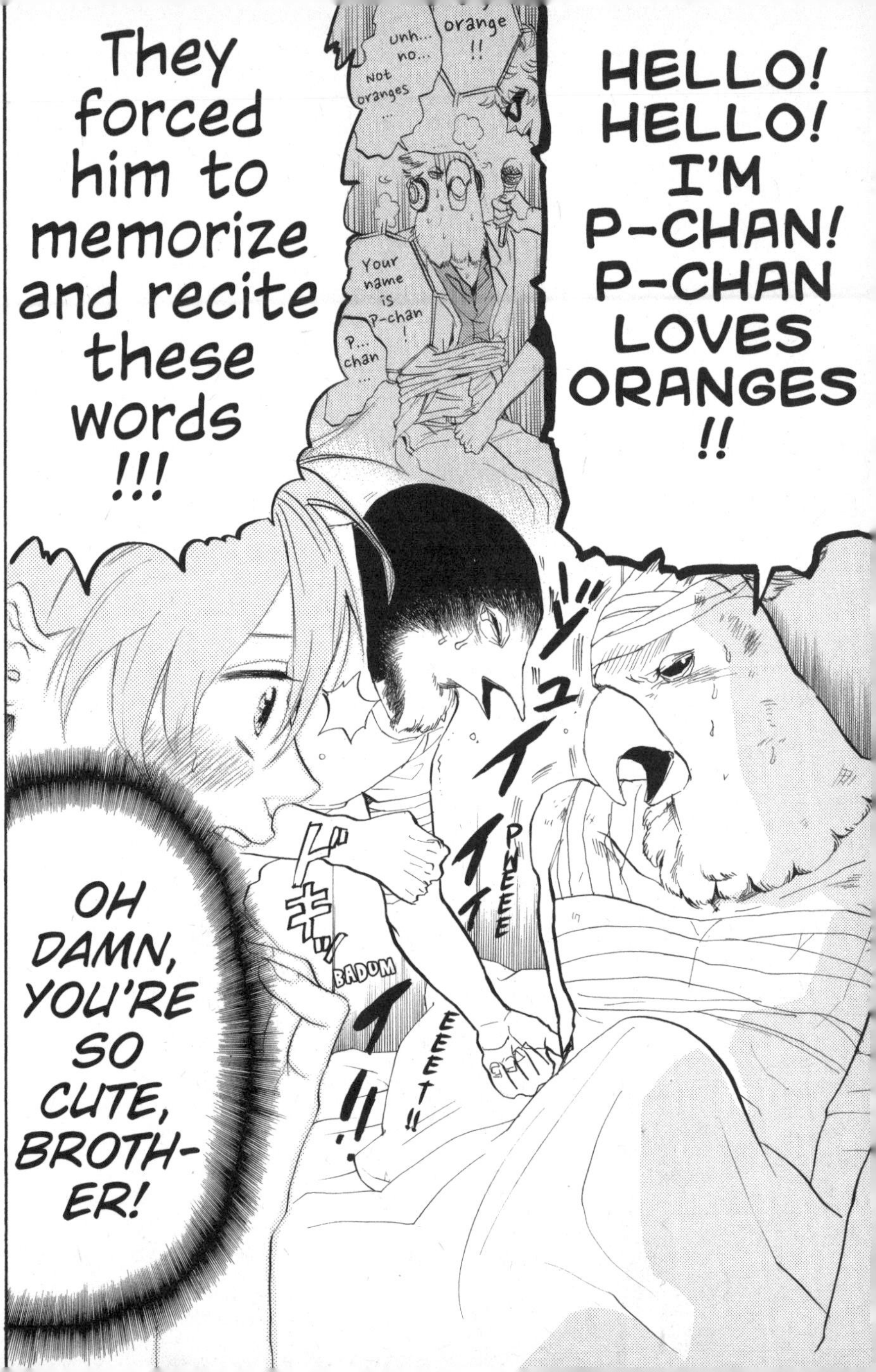
HELLO! HELLO! I'M P-CHAN! P-CHAN LOVES ORANGES !!
orange !!
unh... no... Not oranges ...
Your name is P-chan !
P... chan ...
They forced him to memorize and recite these words !!!
PWEEE EEEET !!
BADUM
OH DAMN, YOU'RE SO CUTE, BROTH-ER!

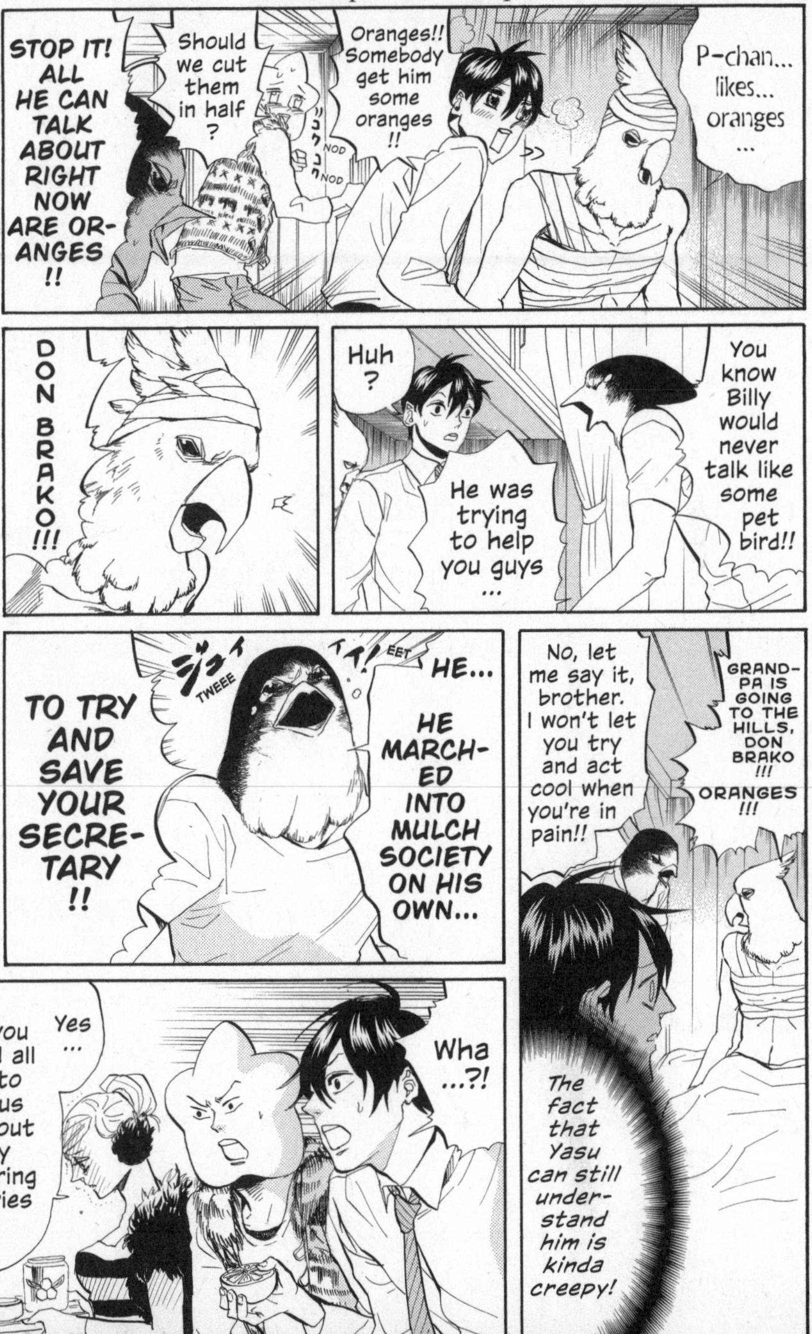
P-chan... likes... oranges ...
Oranges!! Somebody get him some oranges !!
Should we cut them in half ?
NOD
NOD
STOP IT! ALL HE CAN TALK ABOUT RIGHT NOW ARE OR-ANGES !!
You know Billy would never talk like some pet bird!!
Huh ?
He was trying to help you guys ...
DON BRAKO!!!
No, let me say it, brother. I won't let you try and act cool when you're in pain!!
GRAND-PA IS GOING TO THE HILLS, DON BRAKO !!! ORANGES !!!
The fact that Yasu can still under-stand him is kinda creepy!
EET
TWEEE
HE...
HE MARCH-ED INTO MULCH SOCIETY ON HIS OWN...
TO TRY AND SAVE YOUR SECRE-TARY !!
Wha ...?!
Yes ...
So you could all go to Venus without any lingering worries ...

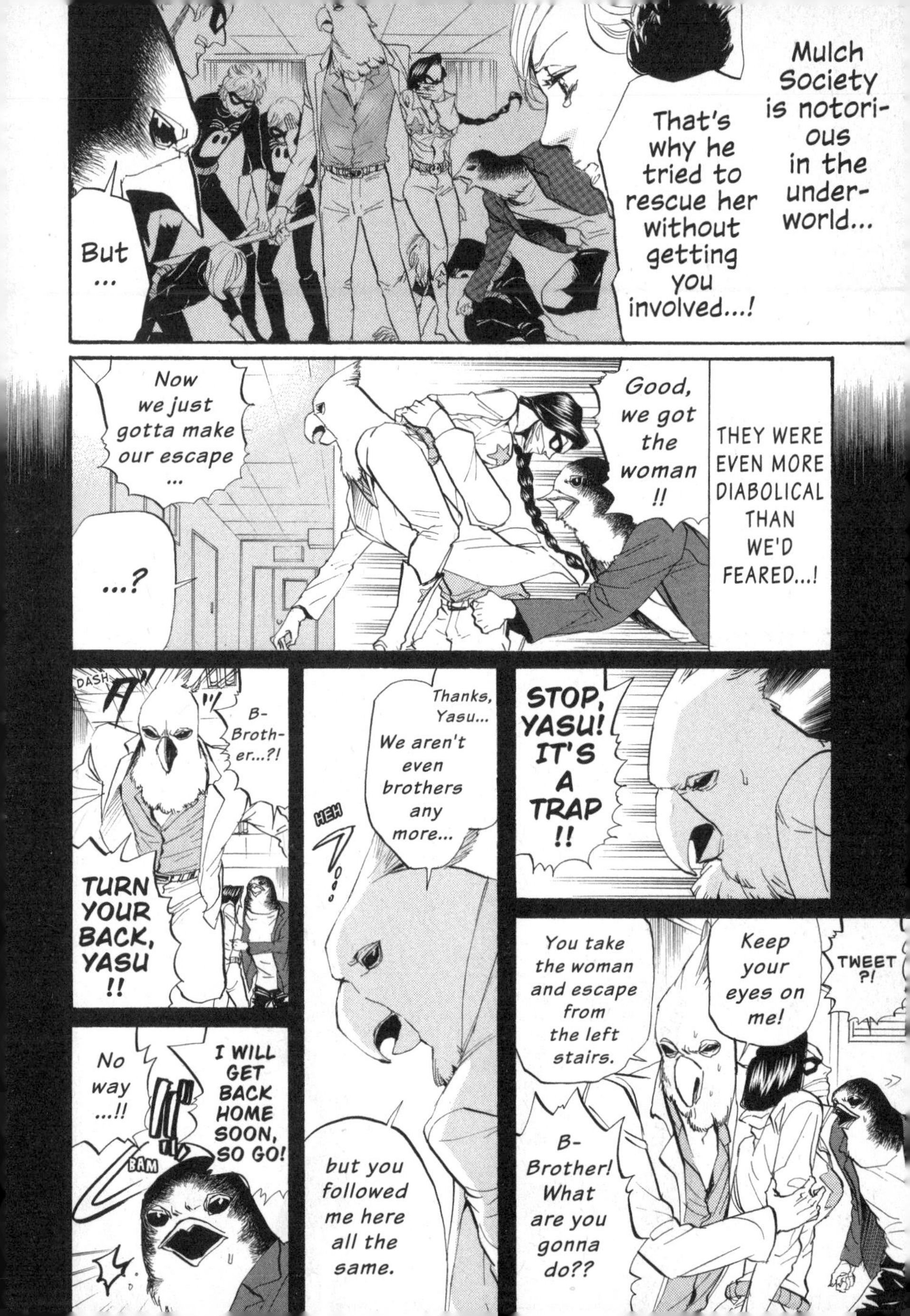
Mulch Society is notorious in the underworld...
That's why he tried to rescue her without getting you involved...!
But ...
THEY WERE EVEN MORE DIABOLICAL THAN WE'D FEARED...!
Good, we got the woman !!
Now we just gotta make our escape ...
...?
STOP, YASU! IT'S A TRAP !!
TWEET ?!
Keep your eyes on me!
You take the woman and escape from the left stairs.
B-Brother! What are you gonna do??
Thanks, Yasu...
We aren't even brothers any more...
HEH
but you followed me here all the same.
DASH
B-Brother...?!
TURN YOUR BACK, YASU !!
I WILL GET BACK HOME SOON, SO GO!
No way ...!!
BAM

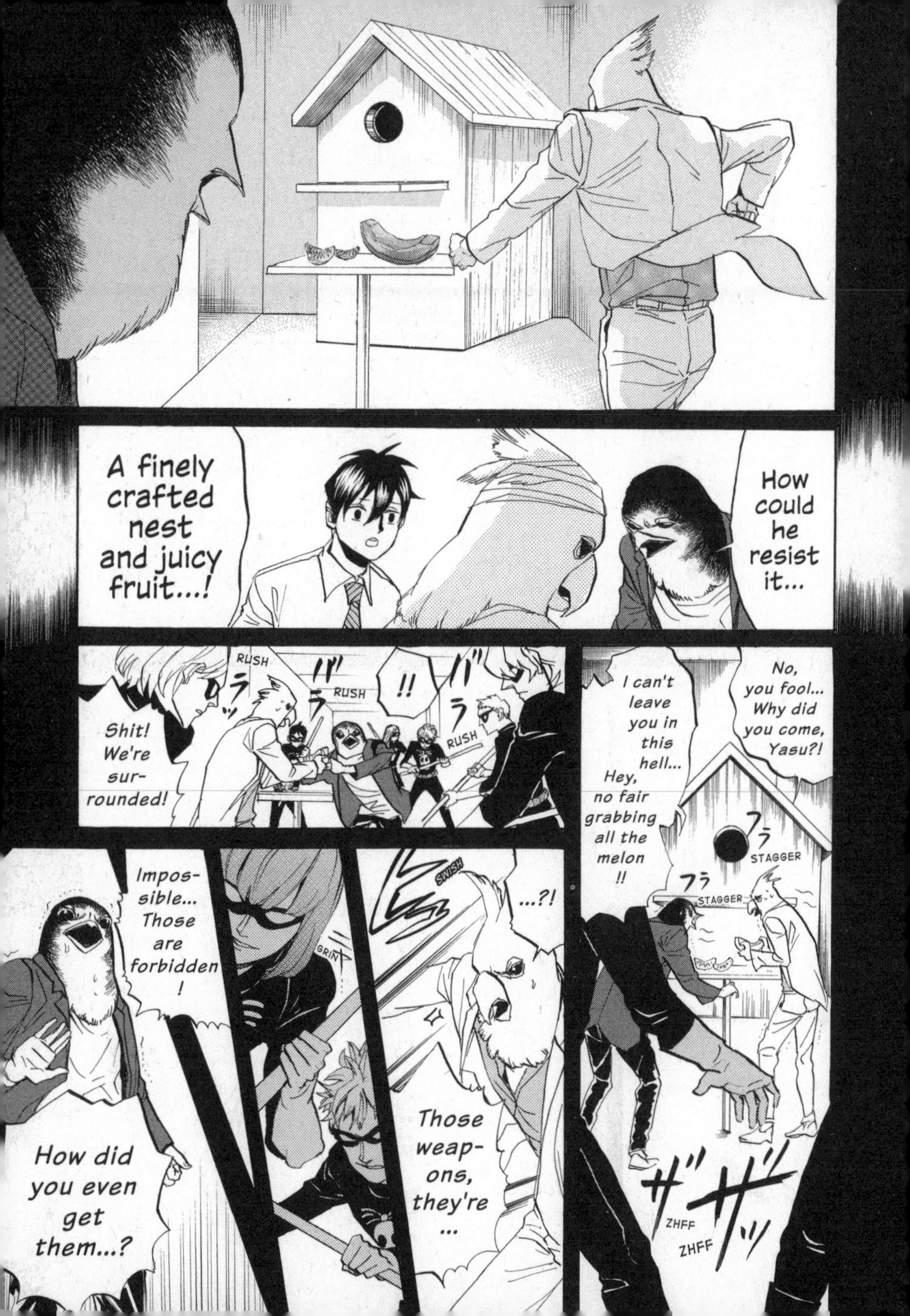
How could he resist it...
A finely crafted nest and juicy fruit...!
No, you fool... Why did you come, Yasu?!
I can't leave you in this hell...
Hey, no fair grabbing all the melon !!
フラ STAGGER
フラ STAGGER
ザザッ
ZHFF
ZHFF
ラ RUSH
!!
バラ RUSH
バラッ RUSH
Shit! We're sur-rounded!
...?!
SWISH
Those weap-ons, they're ...
GRIN
Impos-sible... Those are forbidden !
How did you even get them...?

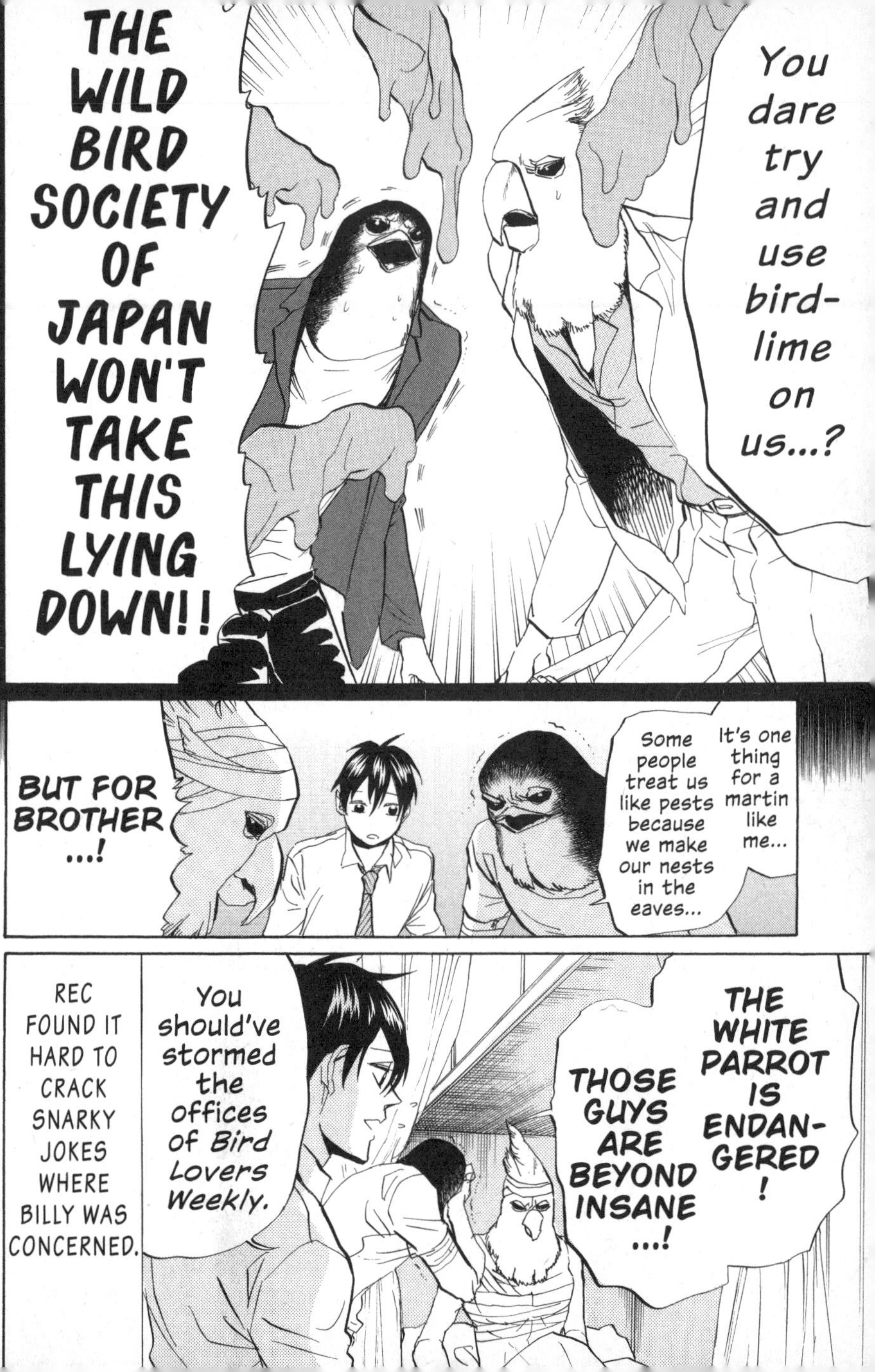
You dare try and use bird-lime on us...?
THE WILD BIRD SOCIETY OF JAPAN WON'T TAKE THIS LYING DOWN!!
It's one thing for a martin like me...
Some people treat us like pests because we make our nests in the eaves...
BUT FOR BROTHER ...!
THE WHITE PARROT IS ENDANGERED!
THOSE GUYS ARE BEYOND INSANE ...!
You should've stormed the offices of *Bird Lovers Weekly*.
REC FOUND IT HARD TO CRACK SNARKY JOKES WHERE BILLY WAS CONCERNED.

Chapter 269: Torture

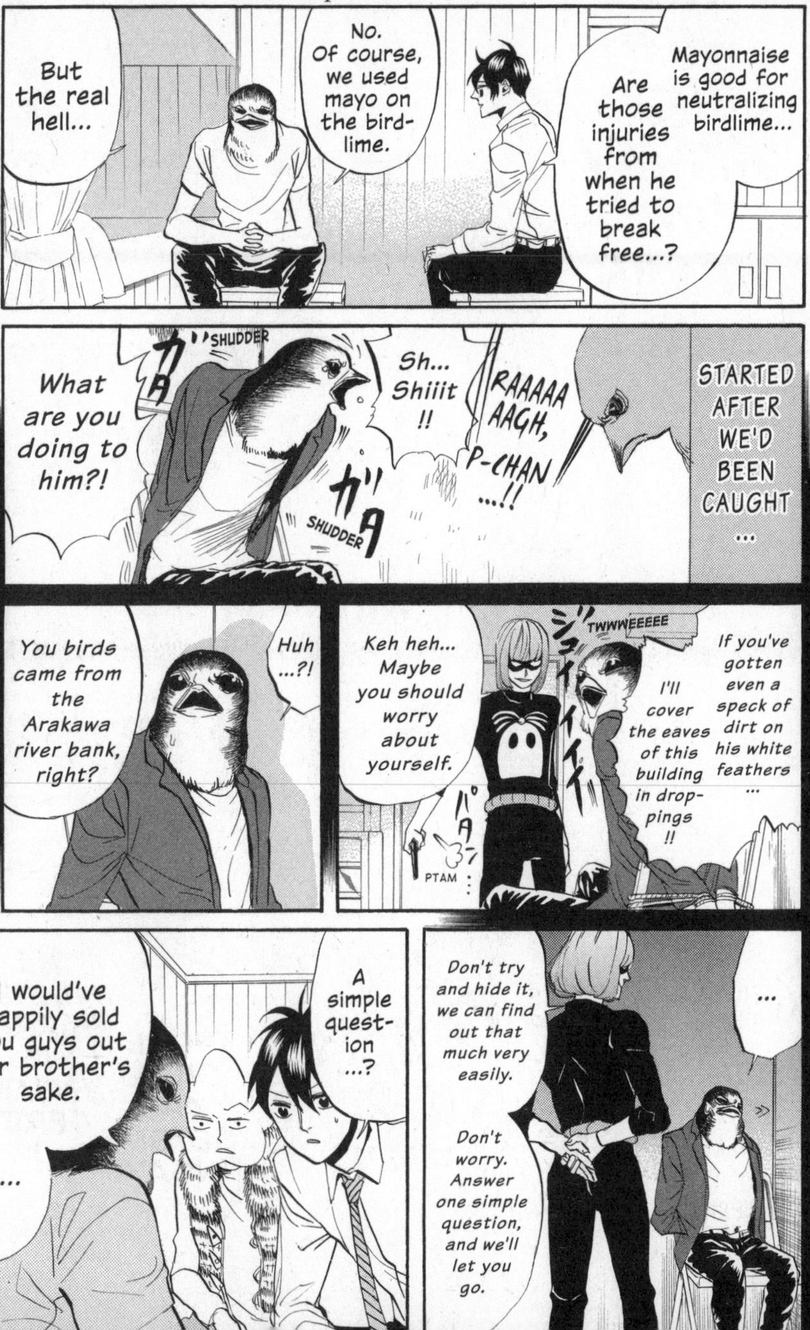
Mayonnaise is good for neutralizing birdlime...
Are those injuries from when he tried to break free...?
No. Of course, we used mayo on the bird-lime.
But the real hell...
STARTED AFTER WE'D BEEN CAUGHT ...
RAAAAAAAGH, P-CHAN ...!!
Sh... Shiiit !!
SHUDDER
What are you doing to him?!
SHUDDER
If you've gotten even a speck of dirt on his white feathers ...
I'll cover the eaves of this building in drop-pings !!
TWWWEEEEE
Keh heh... Maybe you should worry about yourself.
PTAM
Huh ...?!
You birds came from the Arakawa river bank, right?
...
Don't try and hide it, we can find out that much very easily.
Don't worry. Answer one simple question, and we'll let you go.
A simple quest-ion ...?
I would've happily sold you guys out for brother's sake.
But...

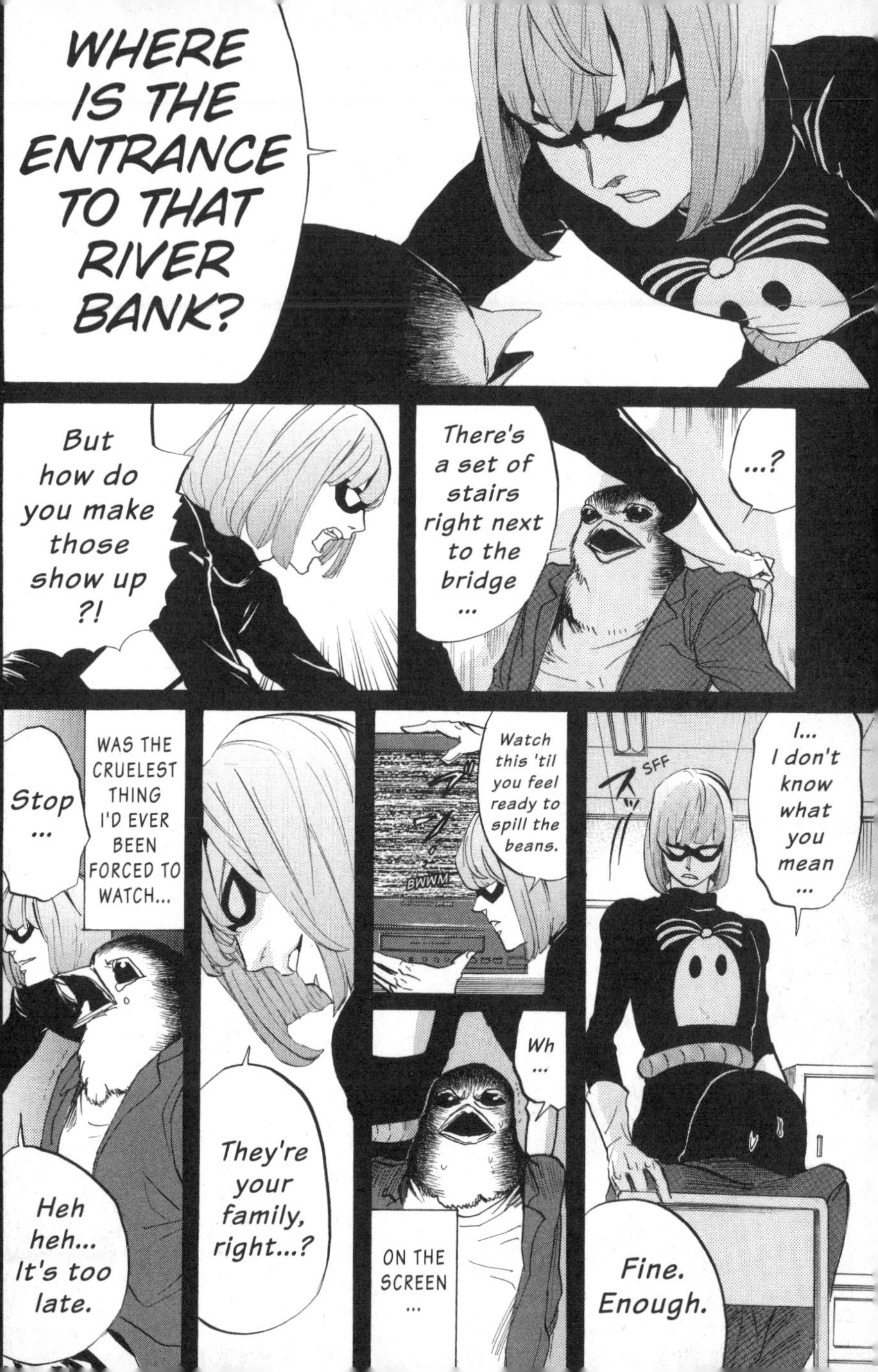
WHERE IS THE ENTRANCE TO THAT RIVER BANK?
...?
There's a set of stairs right next to the bridge ...
But how do you make those show up ?!
I... I don't know what you mean ...
SFF
Fine. Enough.
Watch this 'til you feel ready to spill the beans.
BWWM
Wh ...
ON THE SCREEN ...
They're your family, right...?
WAS THE CRUELEST THING I'D EVER BEEN FORCED TO WATCH...
Stop ...
Heh heh... It's too late.

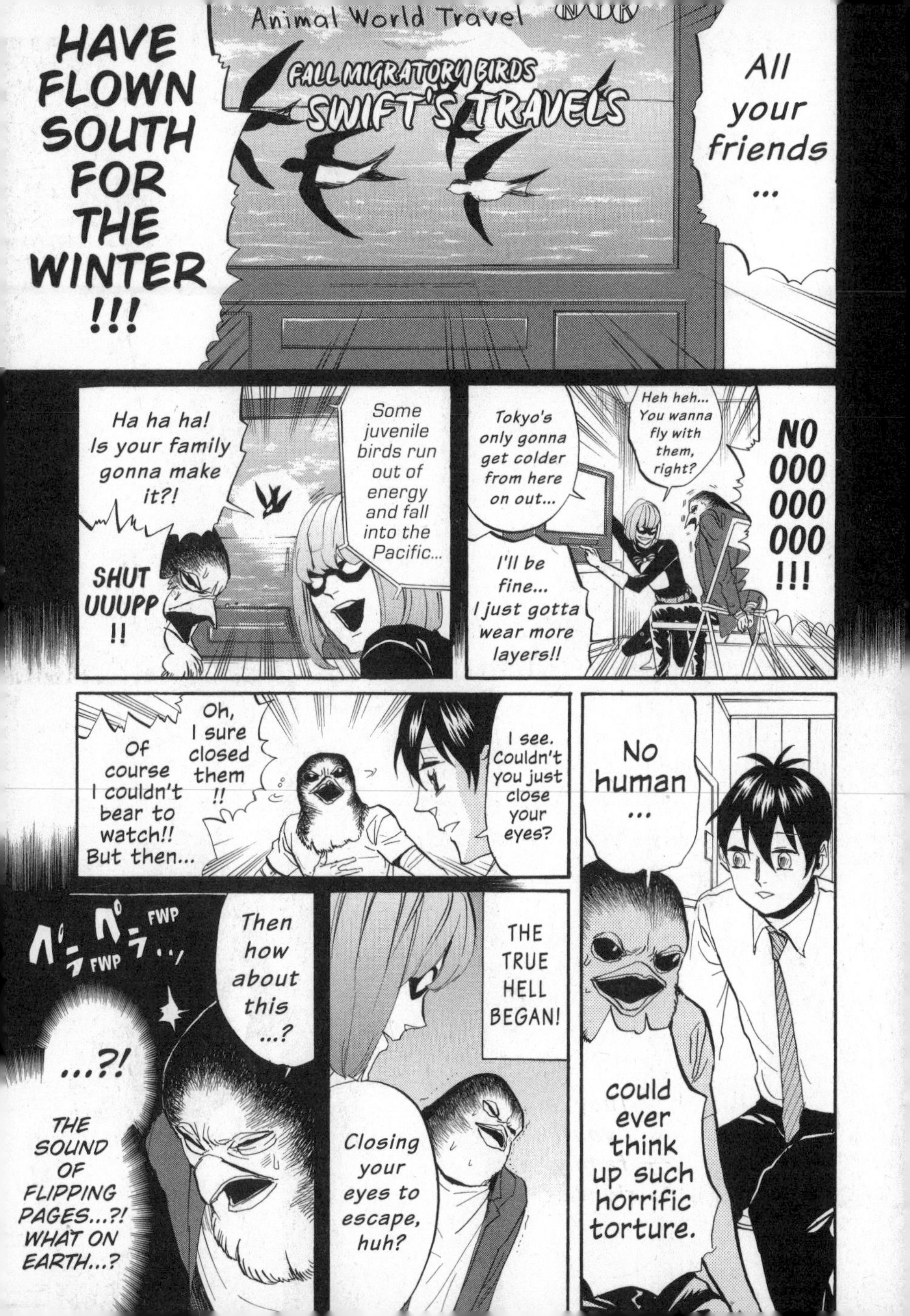
All your friends ...
Animal World Travel
FALL MIGRATORY BIRDS
SWIFT'S TRAVELS
HAVE FLOWN SOUTH FOR THE WINTER !!!
NO OOO OOO OOO !!!
Heh heh... You wanna fly with them, right?
Tokyo's only gonna get colder from here on out...
I'll be fine... I just gotta wear more layers!!
Some juvenile birds run out of energy and fall into the Pacific...
Ha ha ha! Is your family gonna make it?!
SHUT UUUPP !!
No human ...
could ever think up such horrific torture.
I see. Couldn't you just close your eyes?
Oh, I sure closed them !!
Of course I couldn't bear to watch!! But then...
THE TRUE HELL BEGAN!
Then how about this ...?
Closing your eyes to escape, huh?
FWP
FWP
...?!
THE SOUND OF FLIPPING PAGES...?! WHAT ON EARTH...?

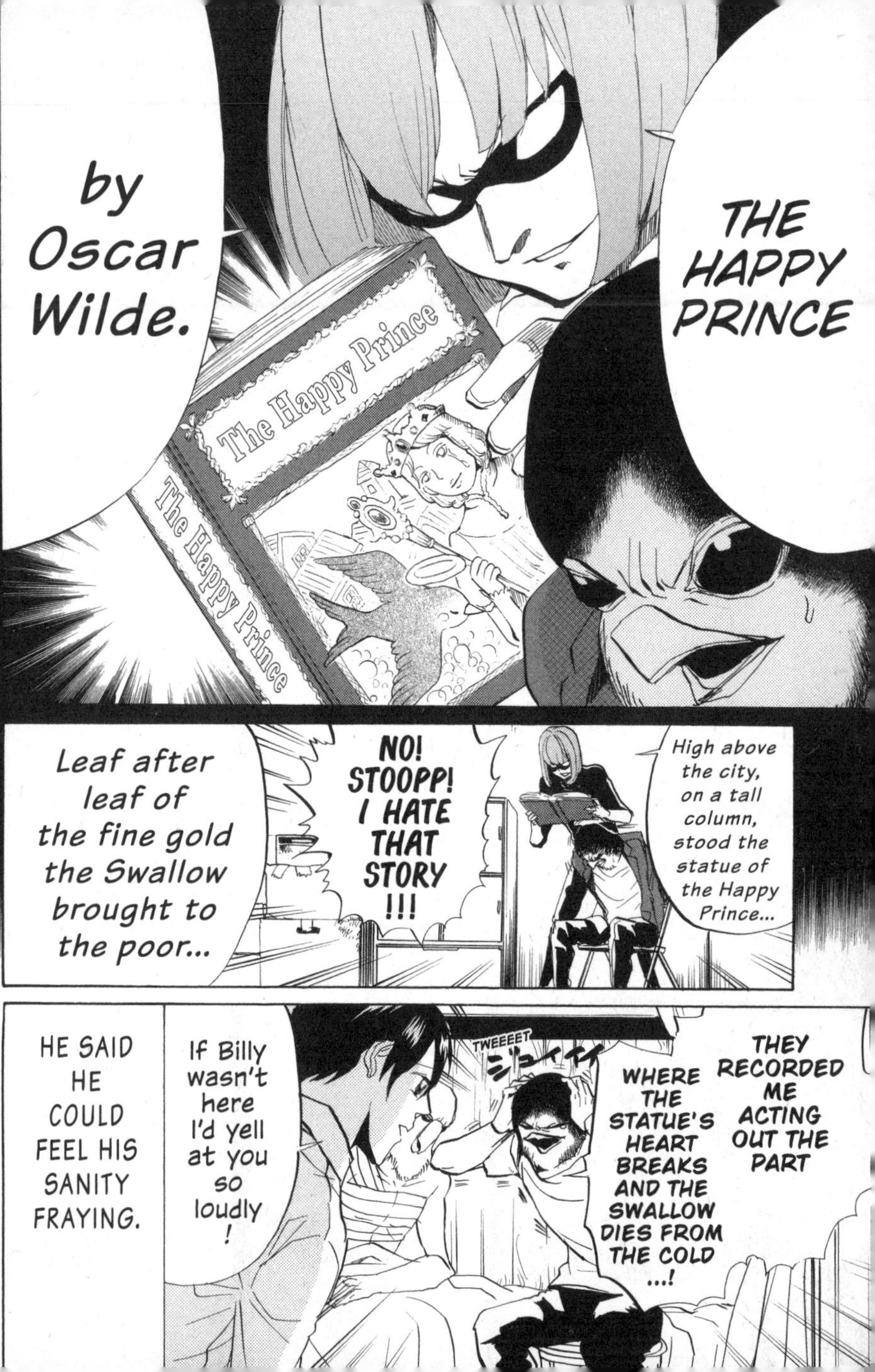
THE HAPPY PRINCE
by Oscar Wilde.
The Happy Prince
The Happy Prince
High above the city, on a tall column, stood the statue of the Happy Prince...
NO! STOOPP! I HATE THAT STORY !!!
Leaf after leaf of the fine gold the Swallow brought to the poor...
THEY RECORDED ME ACTING OUT THE PART
WHERE THE STATUE'S HEART BREAKS AND THE SWALLOW DIES FROM THE COLD ...!
TWEEEET
If Billy wasn't here I'd yell at you so loudly !
HE SAID HE COULD FEEL HIS SANITY FRAYING.

Chapter 270: Escape

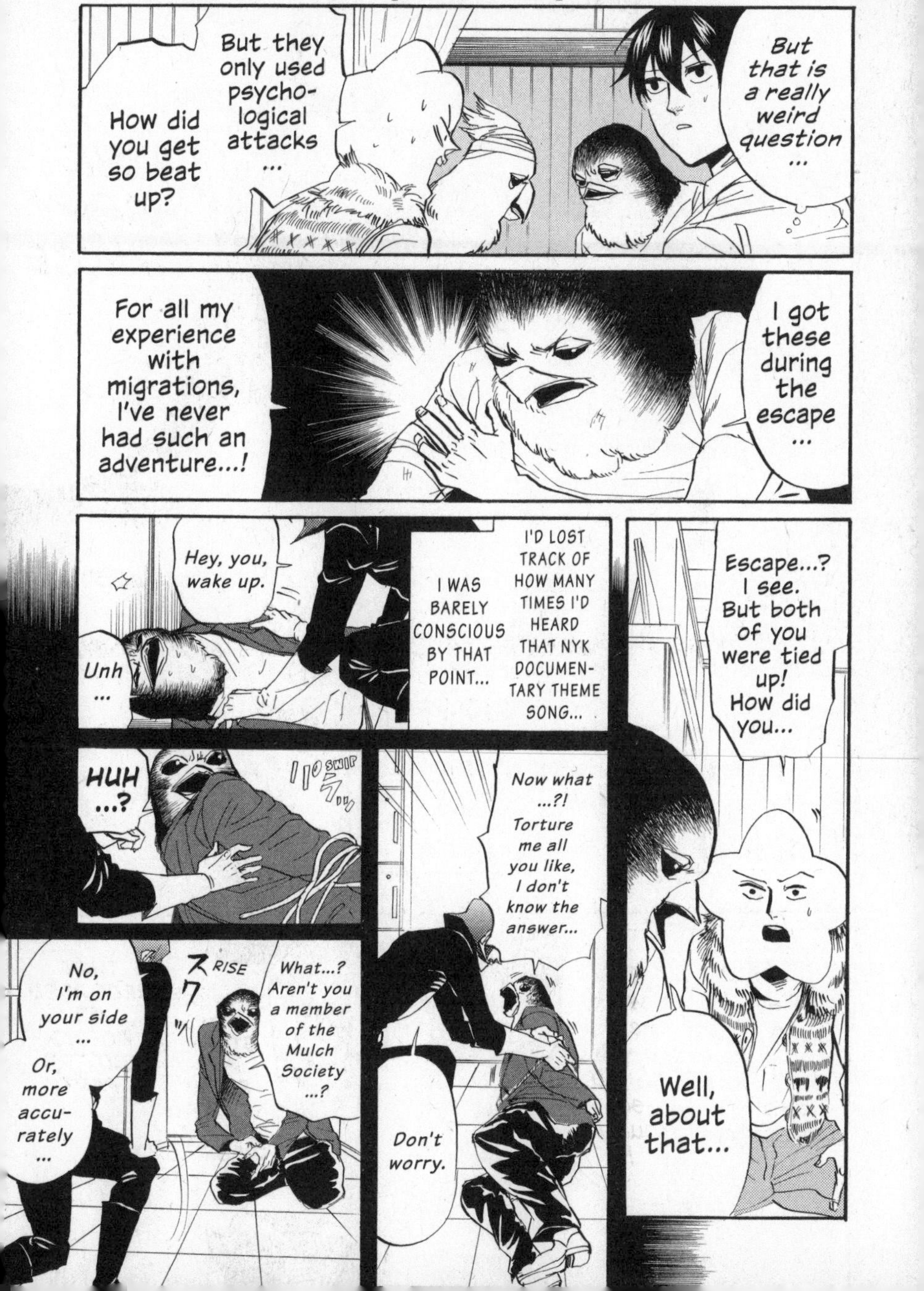
But that is a really weird question ...
But they only used psycho-logical attacks ...
How did you get so beat up?
I got these during the escape ...
For all my experience with migrations, I've never had such an adventure...!
Escape...? I see. But both of you were tied up! How did you...
Well, about that...
I'D LOST TRACK OF HOW MANY TIMES I'D HEARD THAT NYK DOCUMEN-TARY THEME SONG...
I WAS BARELY CONSCIOUS BY THAT POINT...
Hey, you, wake up.
Unh ...
Now what ...?! Torture me all you like, I don't know the answer...
Don't worry.
SWIP
HUH ...?
RISE
What...? Aren't you a member of the Mulch Society ...?
No, I'm on your side ...
Or, more accu-rately ...

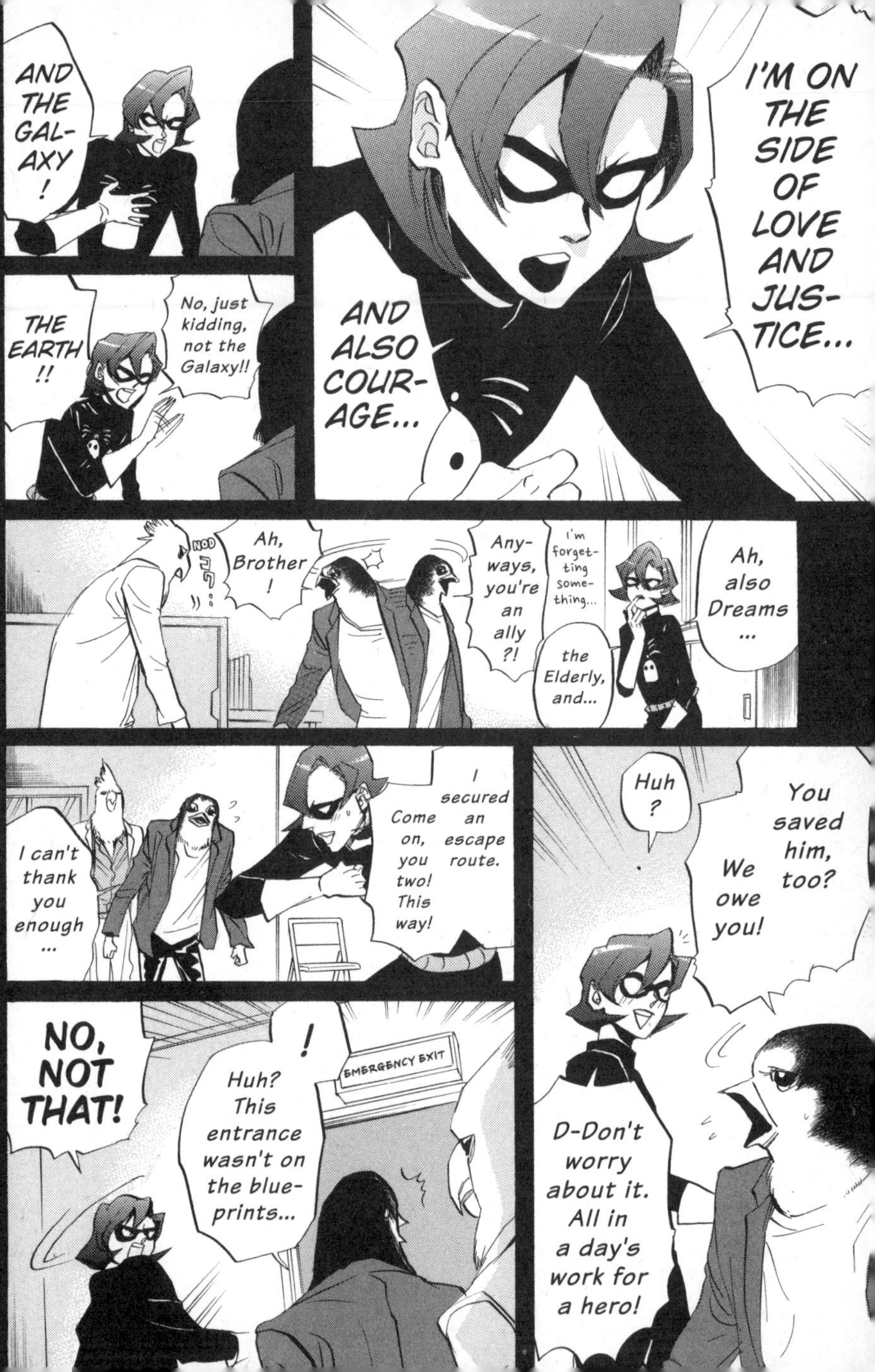
I'M ON THE SIDE OF LOVE AND JUSTICE...
AND ALSO COURAGE...
AND THE GALAXY!
No, just kidding, not the Galaxy!!
THE EARTH!!
Ah, also Dreams...
I'm forgetting something...
the Elderly, and...
Anyways, you're an ally?!
Ah, Brother!
NOD
You saved him, too?
We owe you!
Huh?
D-Don't worry about it. All in a day's work for a hero!
I secured an escape route.
Come on, you two! This way!
I can't thank you enough...
!
Huh? This entrance wasn't on the blueprints...
EMERGENCY EXIT
NO, NOT THAT!

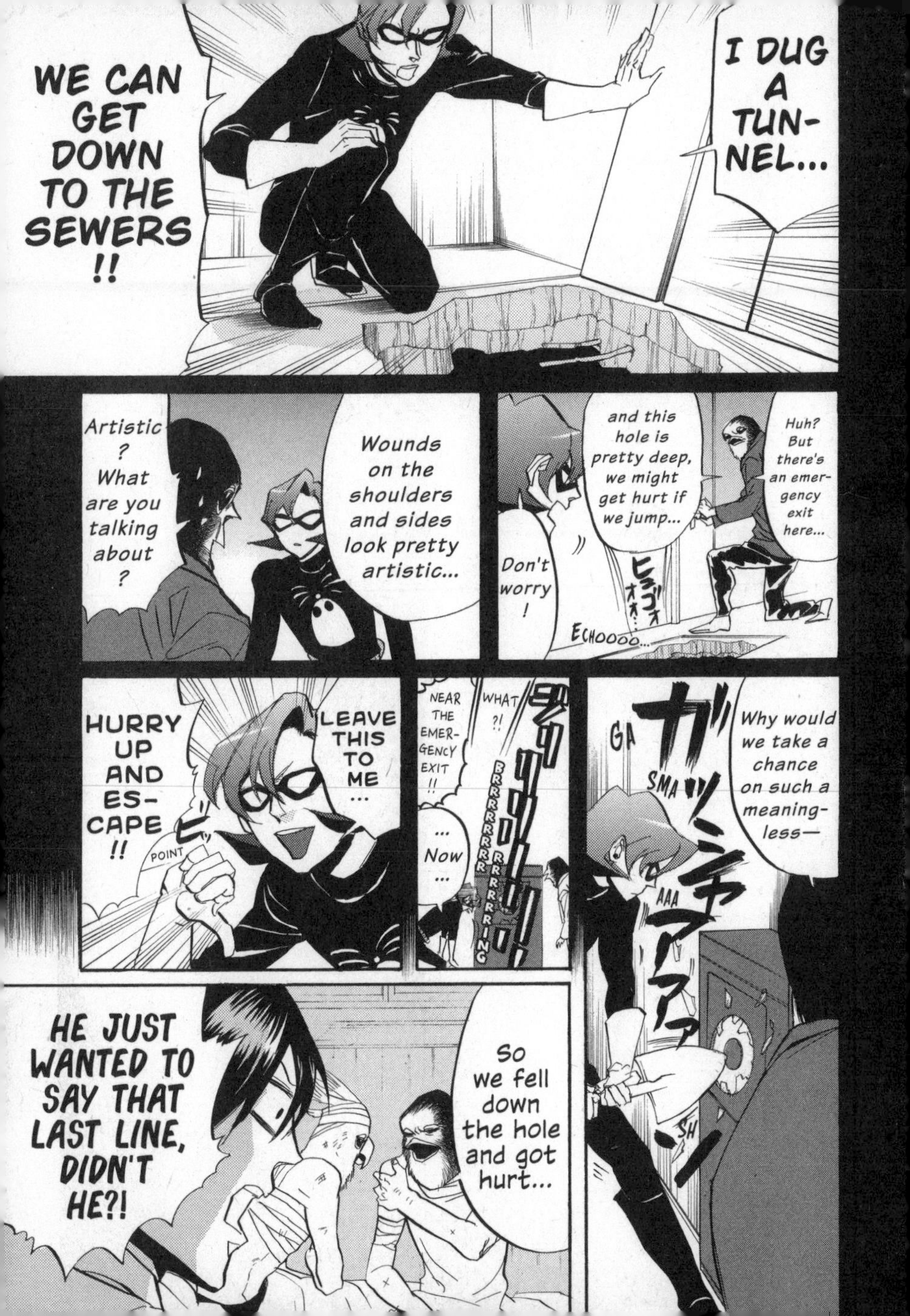
I DUG A TUNNEL...
WE CAN GET DOWN TO THE SEWERS!!
Huh? But there's an emergency exit here...
and this hole is pretty deep, we might get hurt if we jump...
Don't worry!
ECHOOOO...
Wounds on the shoulders and sides look pretty artistic...
Artistic? What are you talking about?
Why would we take a chance on such a meaningless—
GA
SMA
AAA
SH
WHAT?!
NEAR THE EMERGENCY EXIT!!
BRRRRRRRRRRRRRRRRING
... Now ...
LEAVE THIS TO ME...
HURRY UP AND ESCAPE!!
POINT
So we fell down the hole and got hurt...
HE JUST WANTED TO SAY THAT LAST LINE, DIDN'T HE?!

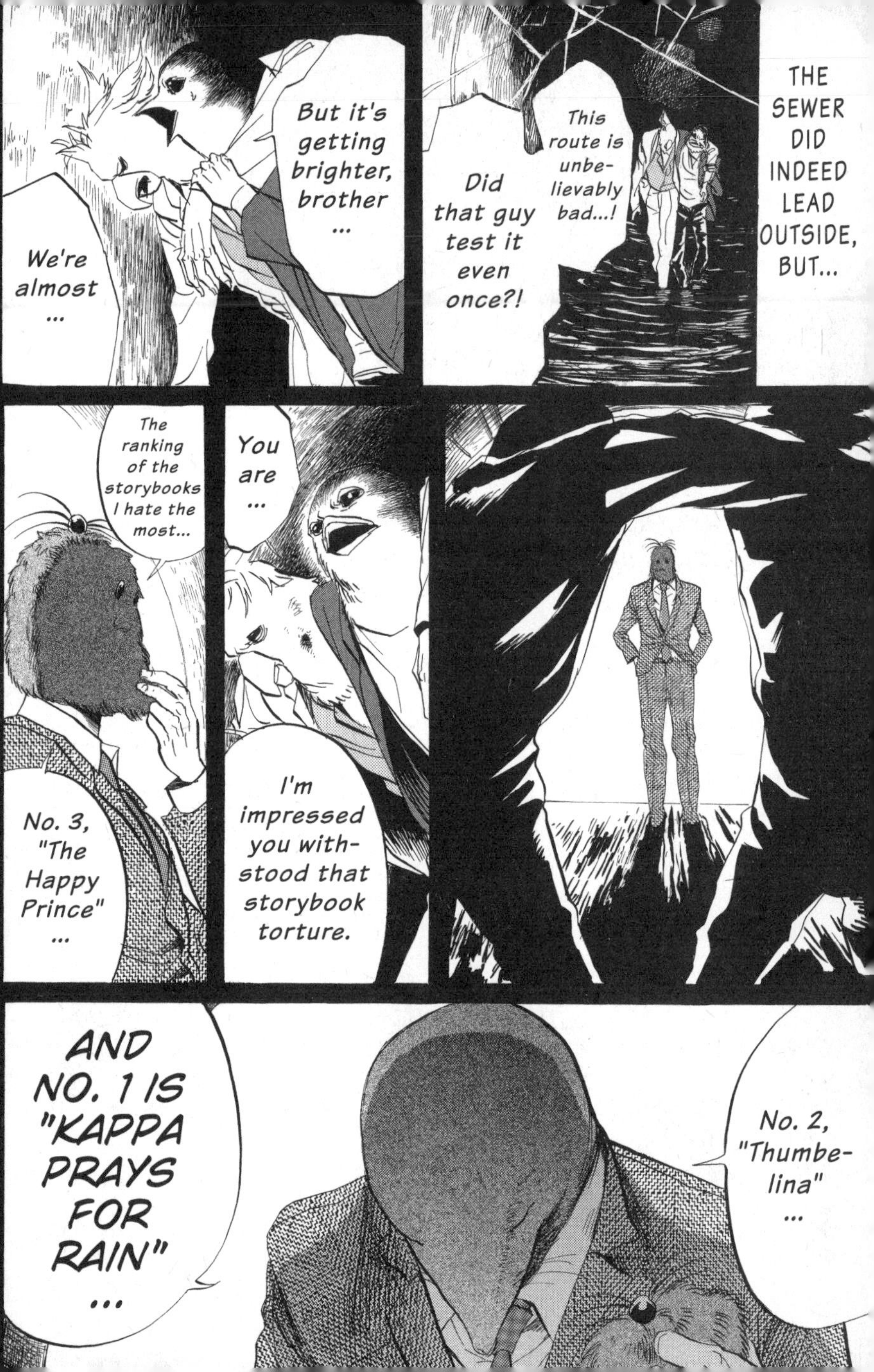
THE SEWER DID INDEED LEAD OUTSIDE, BUT...
This route is unbe-lievably bad...!
Did that guy test it even once?!
But it's getting brighter, brother ...
We're almost ...
You are ...
I'm impressed you with-stood that storybook torture.
The ranking of the storybooks I hate the most...
No. 3, "The Happy Prince" ...
No. 2, "Thumbe-lina" ...
AND NO. 1 IS "KAPPA PRAYS FOR RAIN" ...

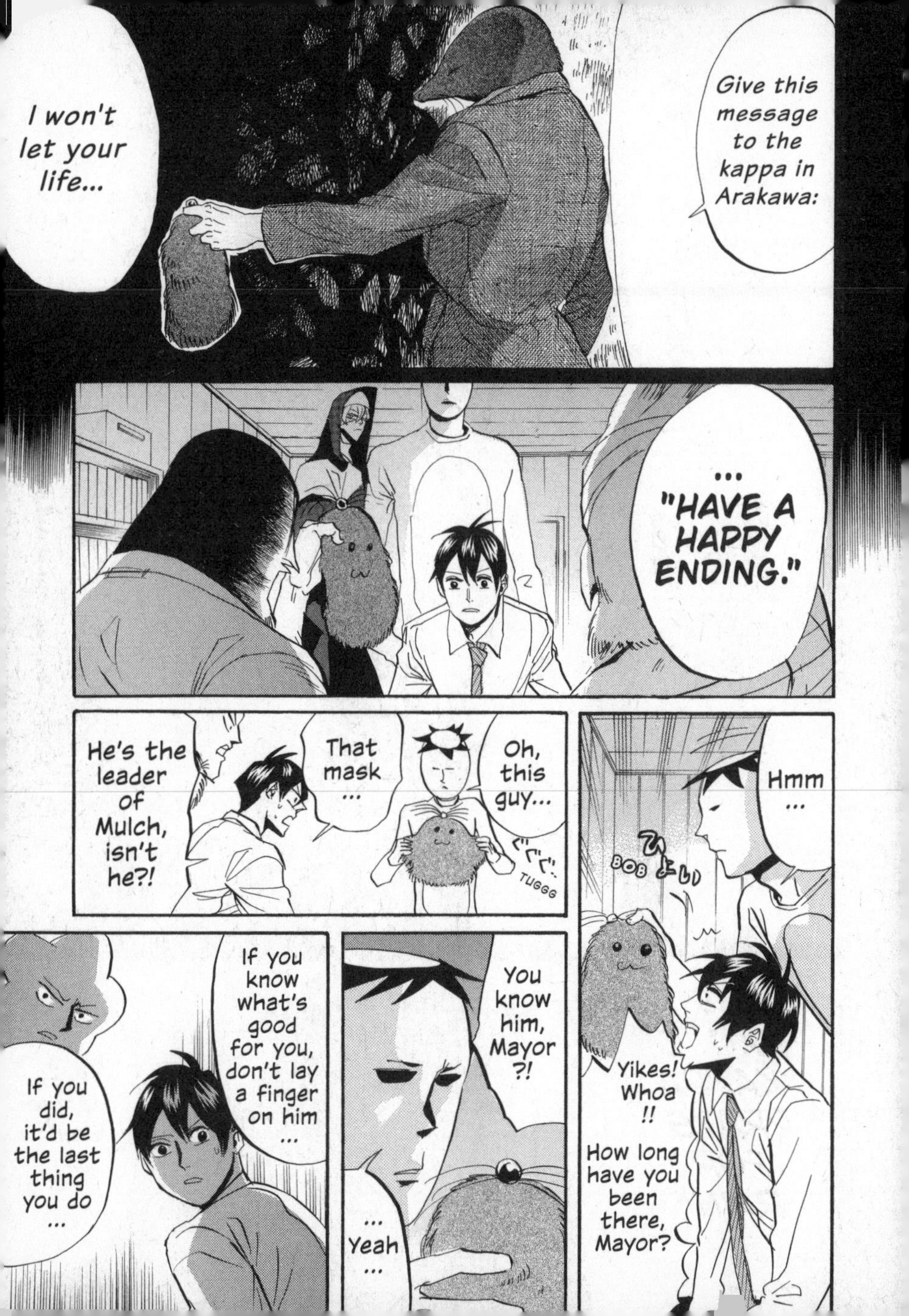
Give this message to the kappa in Arakawa:
I won't let your life...
... "HAVE A HAPPY ENDING."
Hmm ...
BOB
Yikes! Whoa !!
How long have you been there, Mayor?
Oh, this guy...
TUGGG
That mask ...
He's the leader of Mulch, isn't he?!
You know him, Mayor ?!
... Yeah ...
If you know what's good for you, don't lay a finger on him ...
If you did, it'd be the last thing you do ...

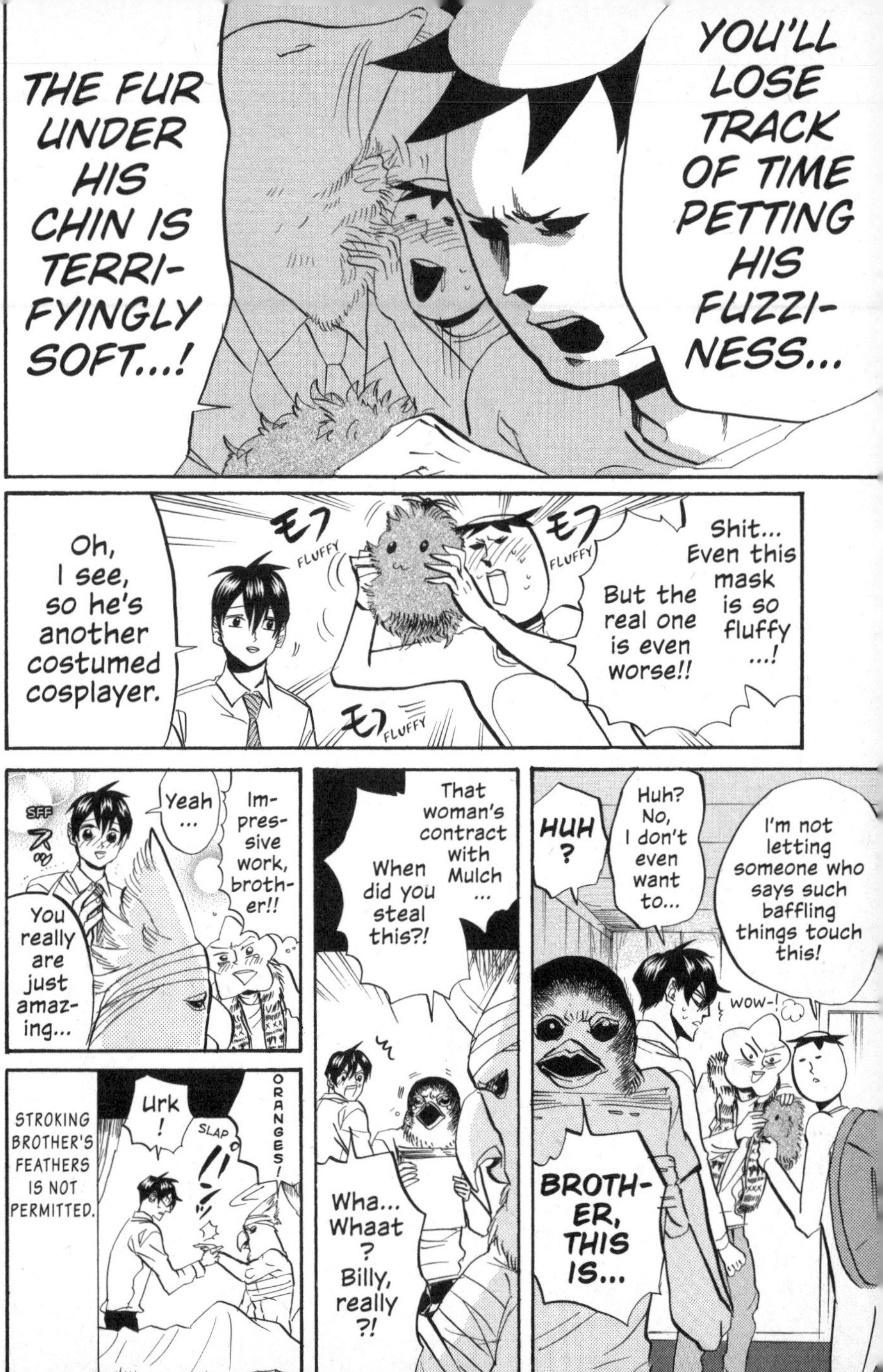
YOU'LL LOSE TRACK OF TIME PETTING HIS FUZZINESS...
THE FUR UNDER HIS CHIN IS TERRIFYINGLY SOFT...!
Shit... Even this mask is so fluffy...!
But the real one is even worse!!
モフ FLUFFY
モフ FLUFFY
Oh, I see, so he's another costumed cosplayer.
モフ FLUFFY
I'm not letting someone who says such baffling things touch this!
Huh? No, I don't even want to...
HUH?
WOW-!
BROTHER, THIS IS...
That woman's contract with Mulch...
When did you steal this?!
Wha... Whaat? Billy, really?!
Im-pressive work, brother!!
Yeah...
SFF
You really are just amazing...
ORANGES!
Urk!
SLAP
STROKING BROTHER'S FEATHERS IS NOT PERMITTED.

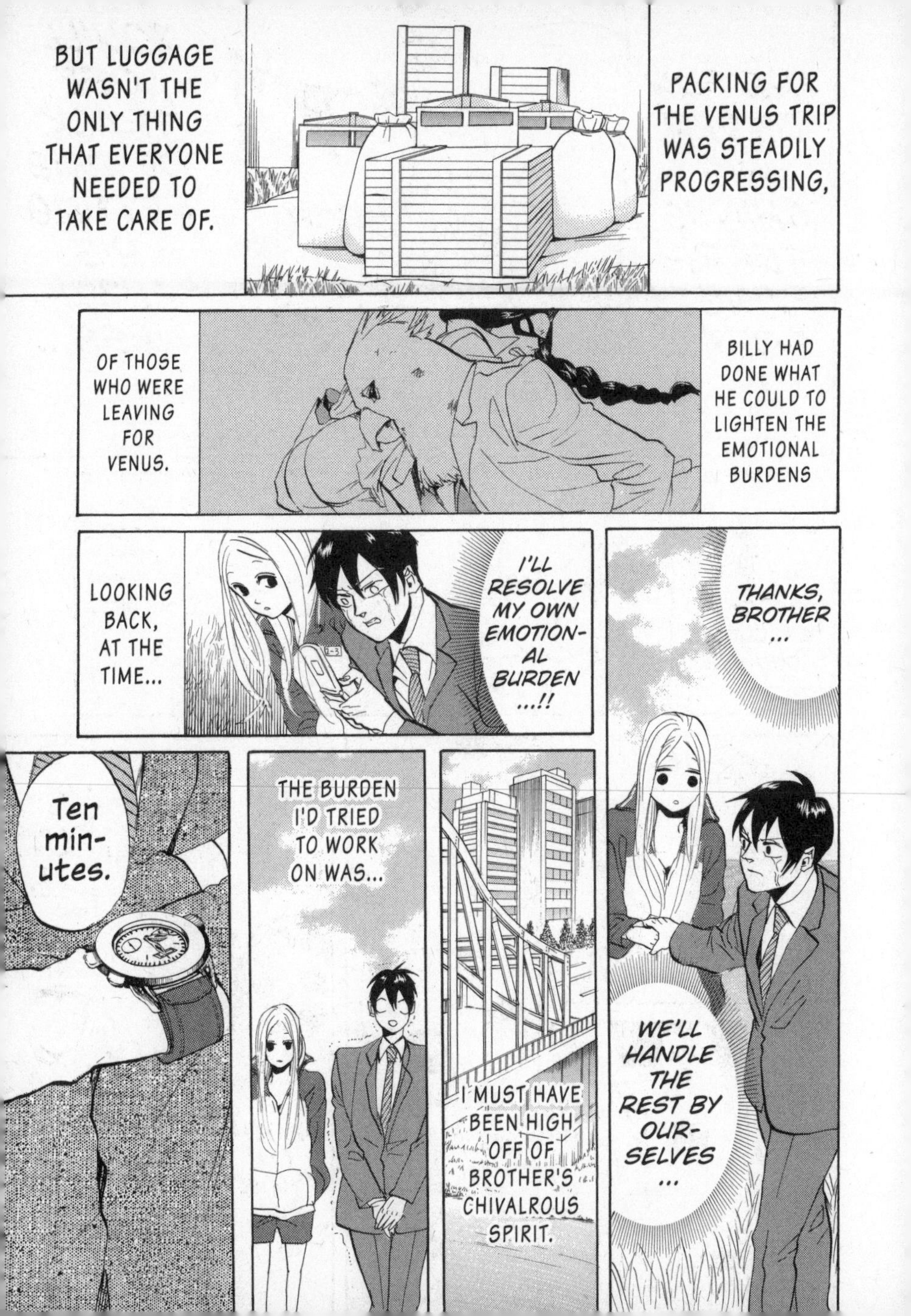
PACKING FOR THE VENUS TRIP WAS STEADILY PROGRESSING,
BUT LUGGAGE WASN'T THE ONLY THING THAT EVERYONE NEEDED TO TAKE CARE OF.
BILLY HAD DONE WHAT HE COULD TO LIGHTEN THE EMOTIONAL BURDENS
OF THOSE WHO WERE LEAVING FOR VENUS.
THANKS, BROTHER ...
WE'LL HANDLE THE REST BY OUR-SELVES ...
I'LL RESOLVE MY OWN EMOTION-AL BURDEN ...!!
LOOKING BACK, AT THE TIME...
I MUST HAVE BEEN HIGH OFF OF BROTHER'S CHIVALROUS SPIRIT.
THE BURDEN I'D TRIED TO WORK ON WAS...
Ten min-utes.

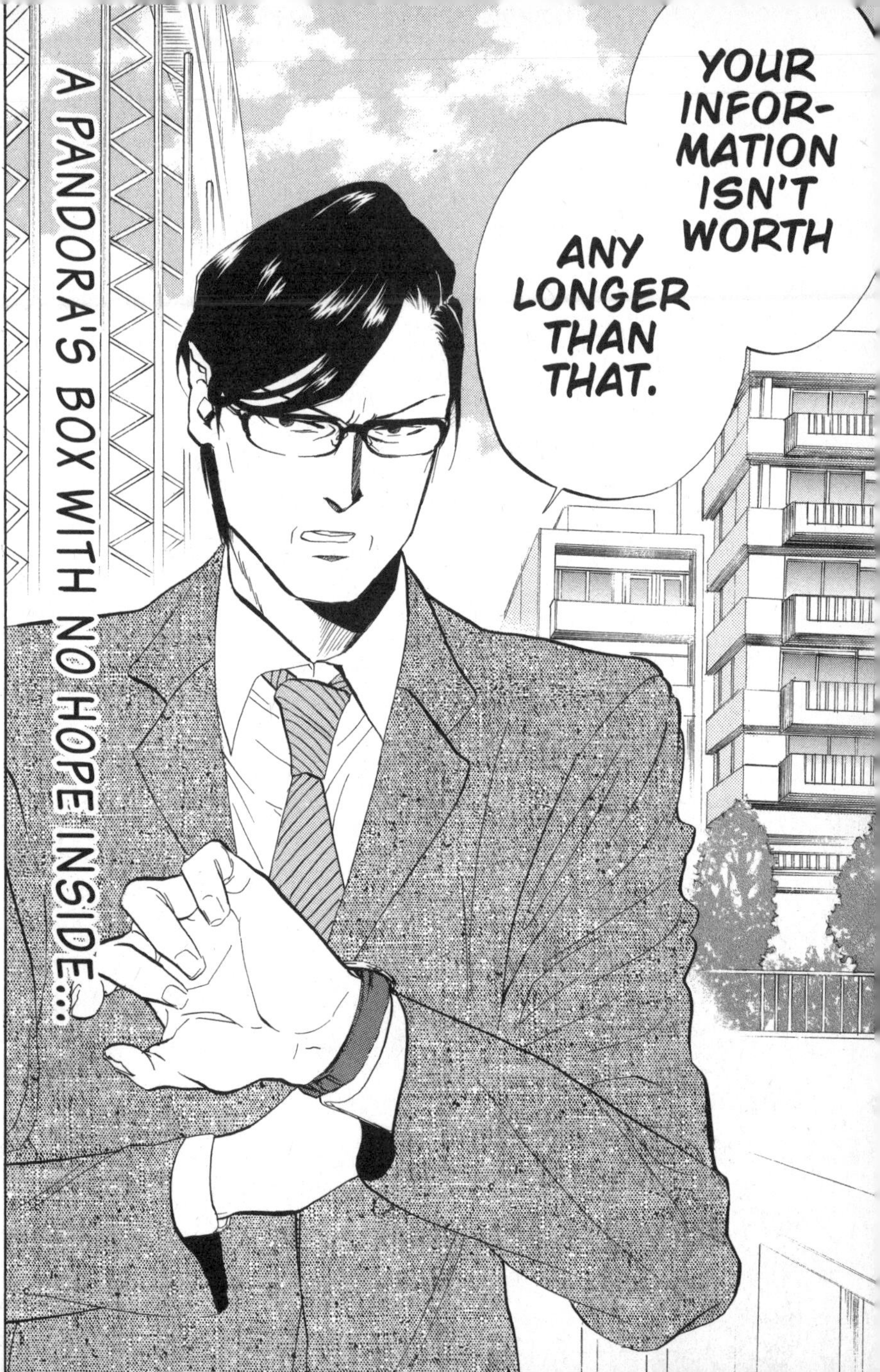
YOUR INFOR-MATION ISN'T WORTH ANY LONGER THAN THAT.
A PANDORA'S BOX WITH NO HOPE INSIDE...

Chapter 271: Courage

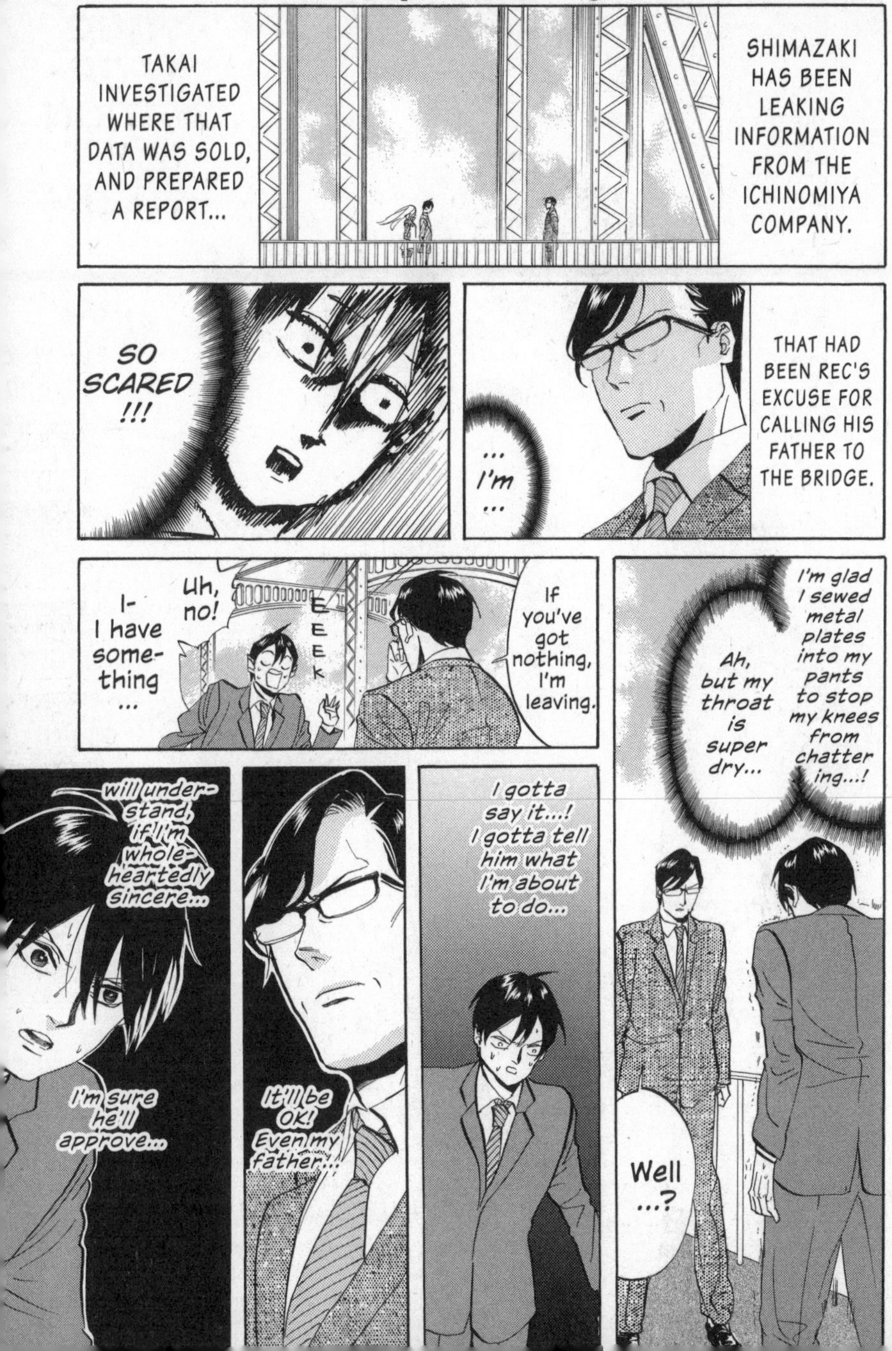
SHIMAZAKI HAS BEEN LEAKING INFORMATION FROM THE ICHINOMIYA COMPANY.
TAKAI INVESTIGATED WHERE THAT DATA WAS SOLD, AND PREPARED A REPORT...
THAT HAD BEEN REC'S EXCUSE FOR CALLING HIS FATHER TO THE BRIDGE.
... I'm ...
SO SCARED !!!
I'm glad I sewed metal plates into my pants to stop my knees from chattering...!
Ah, but my throat is super dry...
Well ...?
If you've got nothing, I'm leaving.
Uh, no!
EEEK
I- I have something ...
I gotta say it...! I gotta tell him what I'm about to do...
It'll be OK! Even my father...
will understand, if I'm wholeheartedly sincere...
I'm sure he'll approve...

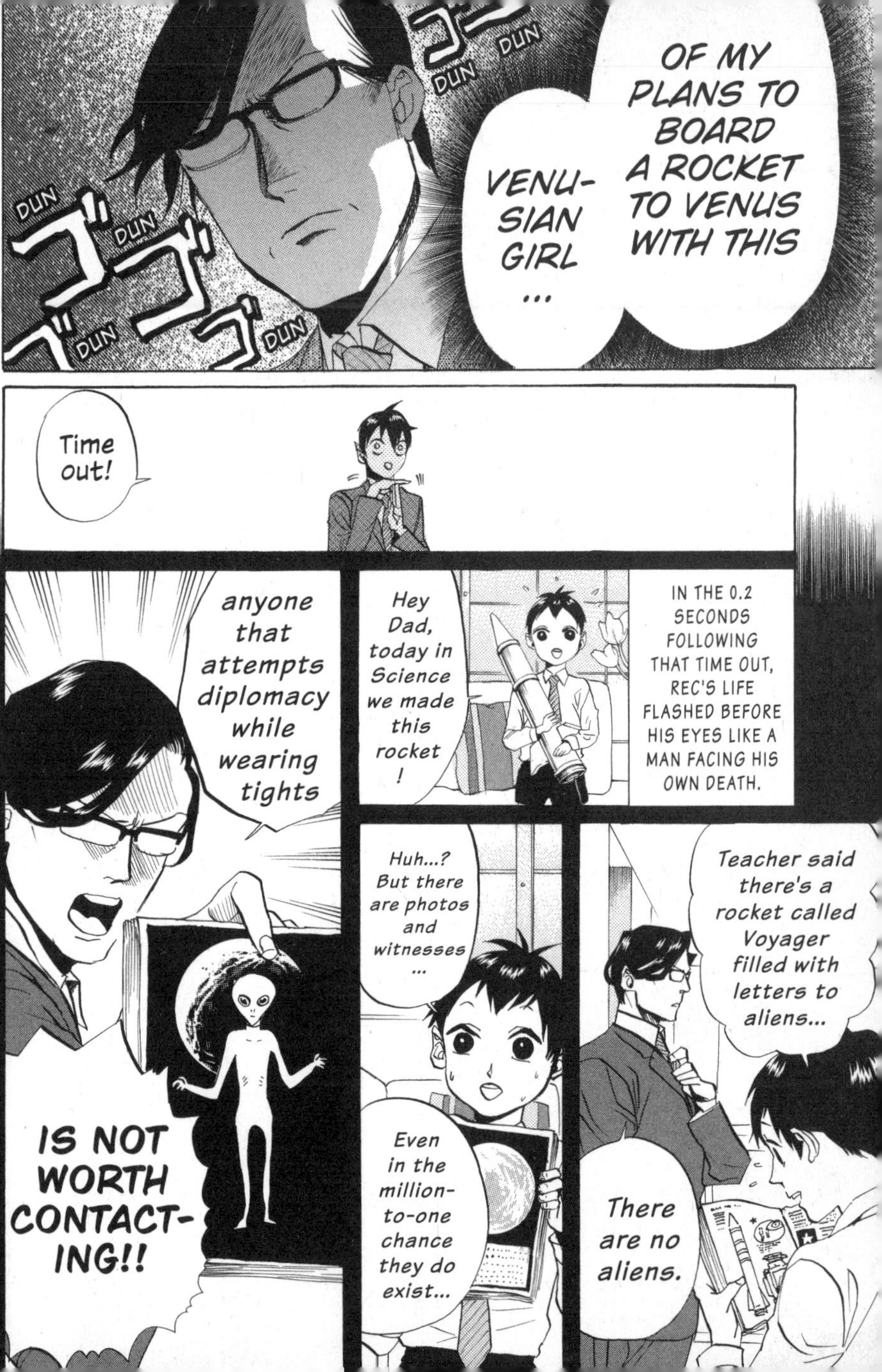
DUN DUN
OF MY PLANS TO BOARD A ROCKET TO VENUS WITH THIS
VENU-SIAN GIRL ...
DUN DUN DUN DUN
Time out!
IN THE 0.2 SECONDS FOLLOWING THAT TIME OUT, REC'S LIFE FLASHED BEFORE HIS EYES LIKE A MAN FACING HIS OWN DEATH.
Hey Dad, today in Science we made this rocket!
Teacher said there's a rocket called Voyager filled with letters to aliens...
There are no aliens.
Huh...? But there are photos and witnesses ...
Even in the million-to-one chance they do exist...
anyone that attempts diplomacy while wearing tights
IS NOT WORTH CONTACT-ING!!

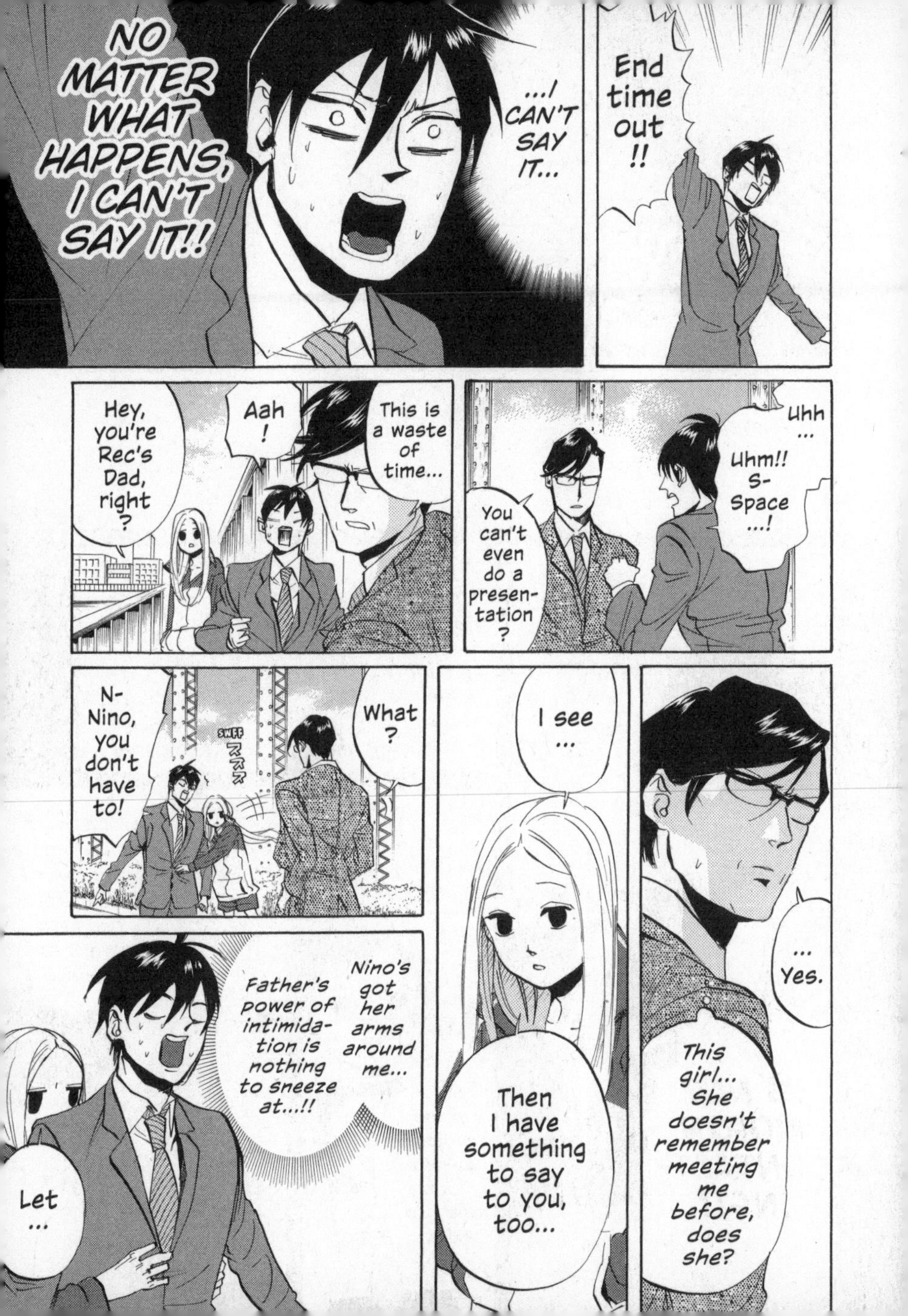
End time out !!
...I CAN'T SAY IT...
NO MATTER WHAT HAPPENS, I CAN'T SAY IT!!
Uhh ...
Uhm!! S-Space ...!
You can't even do a presentation?
This is a waste of time...
Aah !
Hey, you're Rec's Dad, right ?
... Yes.
This girl... She doesn't remember meeting me before, does she?
I see ...
Then I have something to say to you, too...
What ?
N-Nino, you don't have to!
SWFF
スス
Nino's got her arms around me...
Father's power of intimidation is nothing to sneeze at...!!
Let ...

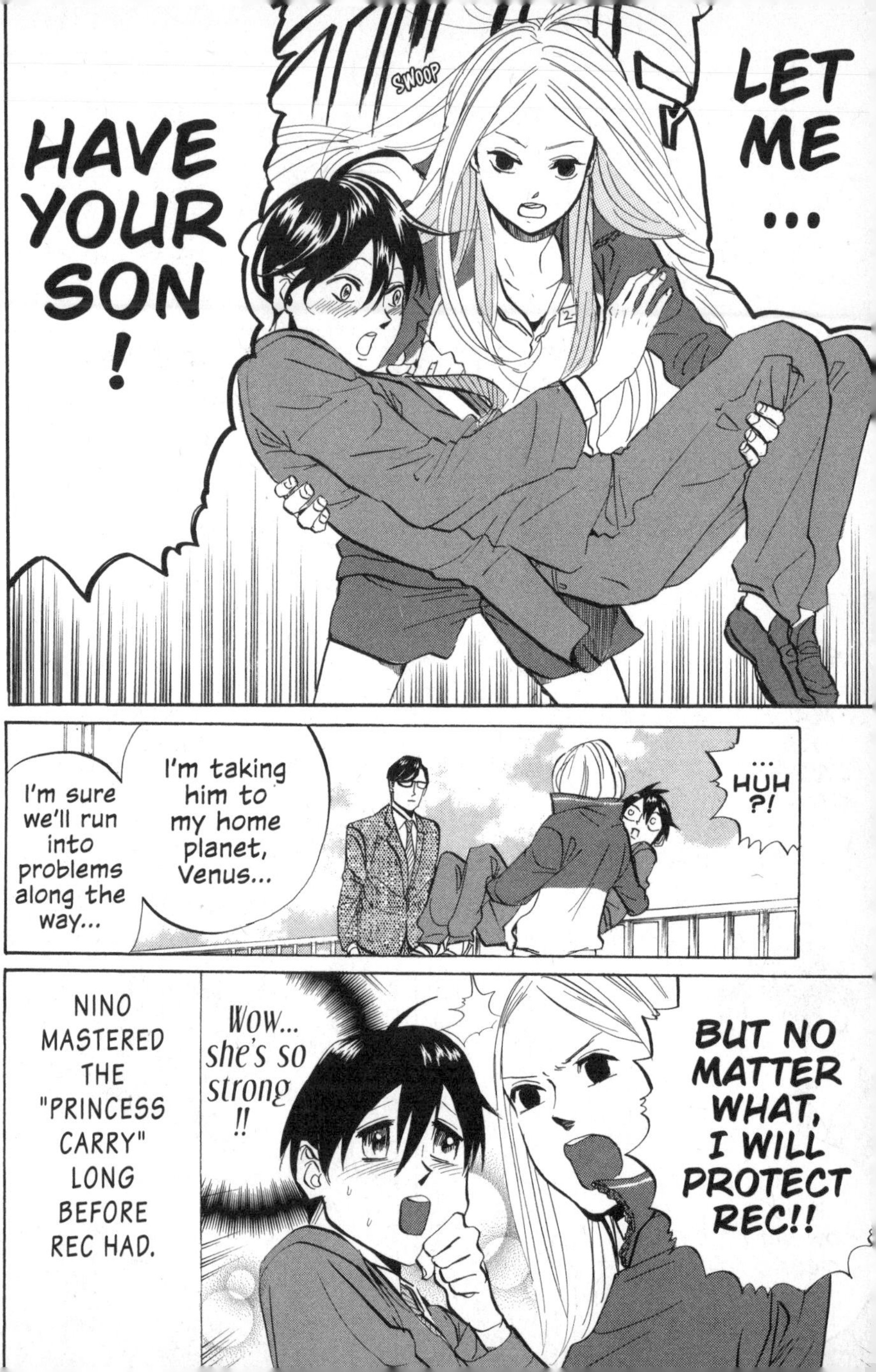
LET ME ...
SWOOP
HAVE YOUR SON !
... HUH ?!
I'm taking him to my home planet, Venus...
I'm sure we'll run into problems along the way...
BUT NO MATTER WHAT, I WILL PROTECT REC!!
Wow... she's so strong !!
NINO MASTERED THE "PRINCESS CARRY" LONG BEFORE REC HAD.

Chapter 272: Bulldoze

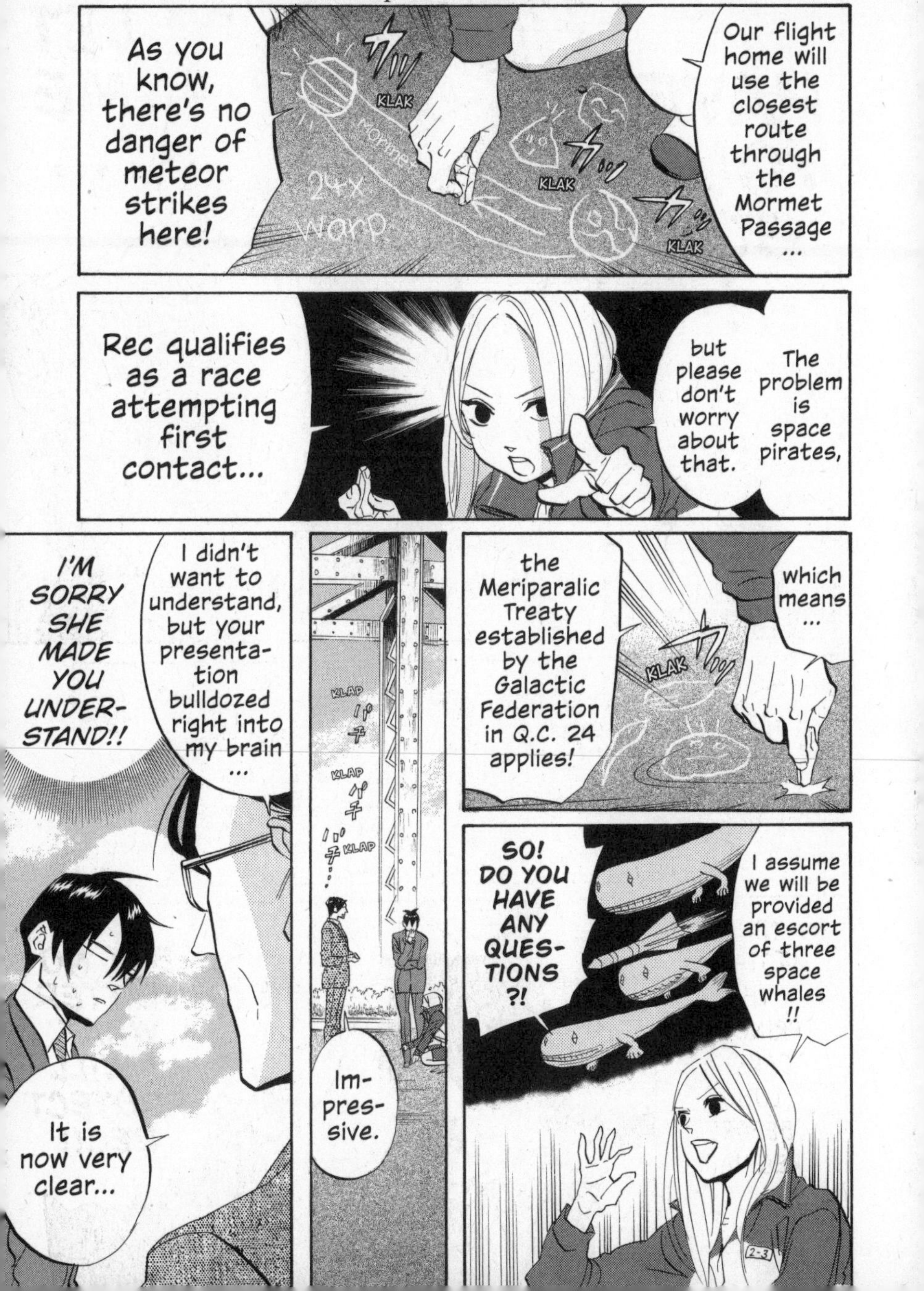
Our flight home will use the closest route through the Mormet Passage ...
KLAK
KLAK
KLAK
Mormet
24x warp
As you know, there's no danger of meteor strikes here!
The problem is space pirates,
but please don't worry about that.
Rec qualifies as a race attempting first contact...
which means ...
KLAK
the Meriparalic Treaty established by the Galactic Federation in Q.C. 24 applies!
I assume we will be provided an escort of three space whales !!
SO! DO YOU HAVE ANY QUES-TIONS ?!
KLAP
KLAP
KLAP
Im-pres-sive.
I didn't want to understand, but your presenta-tion bulldozed right into my brain ...
I'M SORRY SHE MADE YOU UNDER-STAND!!
It is now very clear...

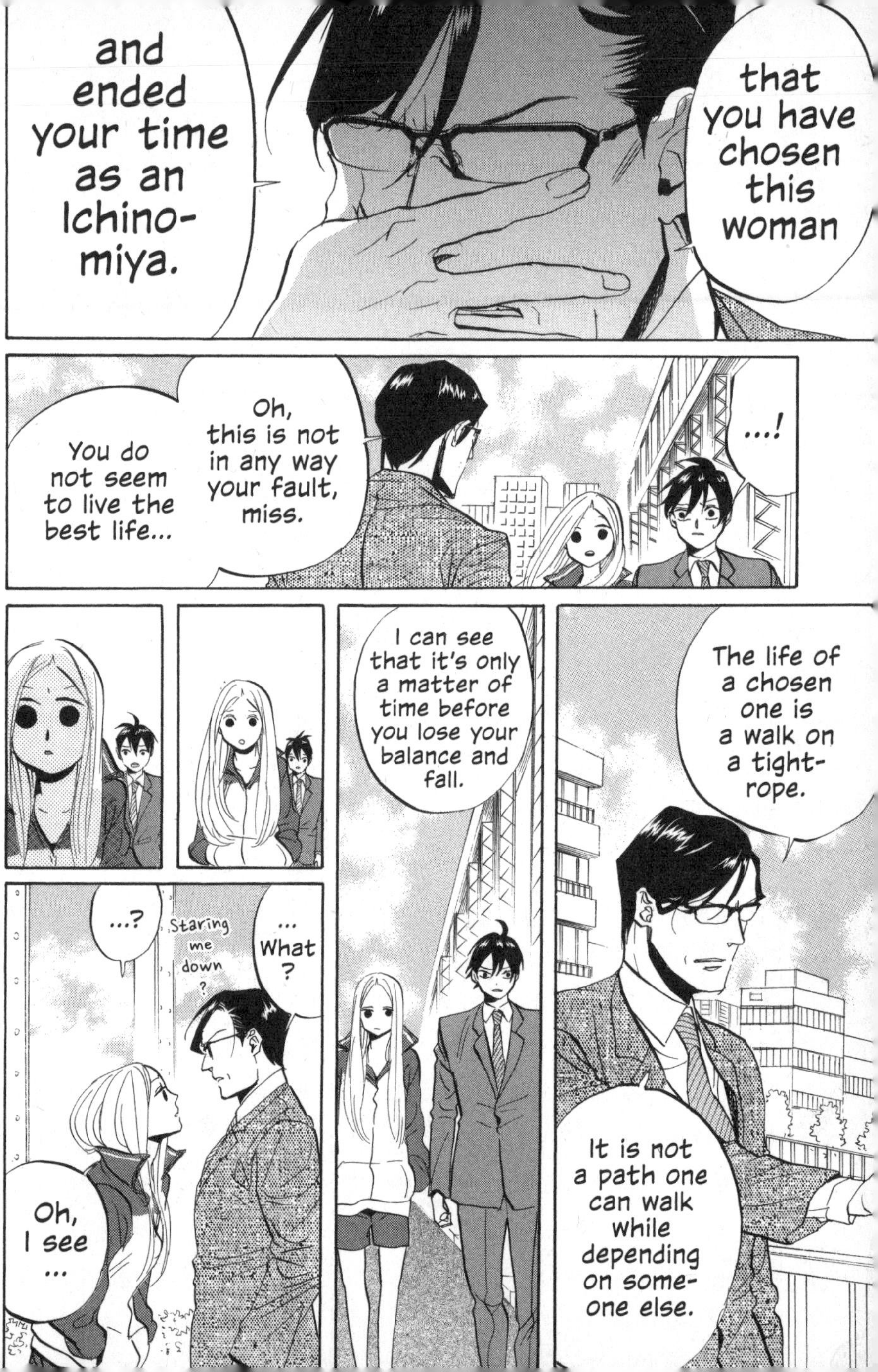
that you have chosen this woman
and ended your time as an Ichino-miya.
...!
Oh, this is not in any way your fault, miss.
You do not seem to live the best life...
The life of a chosen one is a walk on a tight-rope.
It is not a path one can walk while depending on some-one else.
I can see that it's only a matter of time before you lose your balance and fall.
... What ?
Staring me down ?
...?
Oh, I see ...

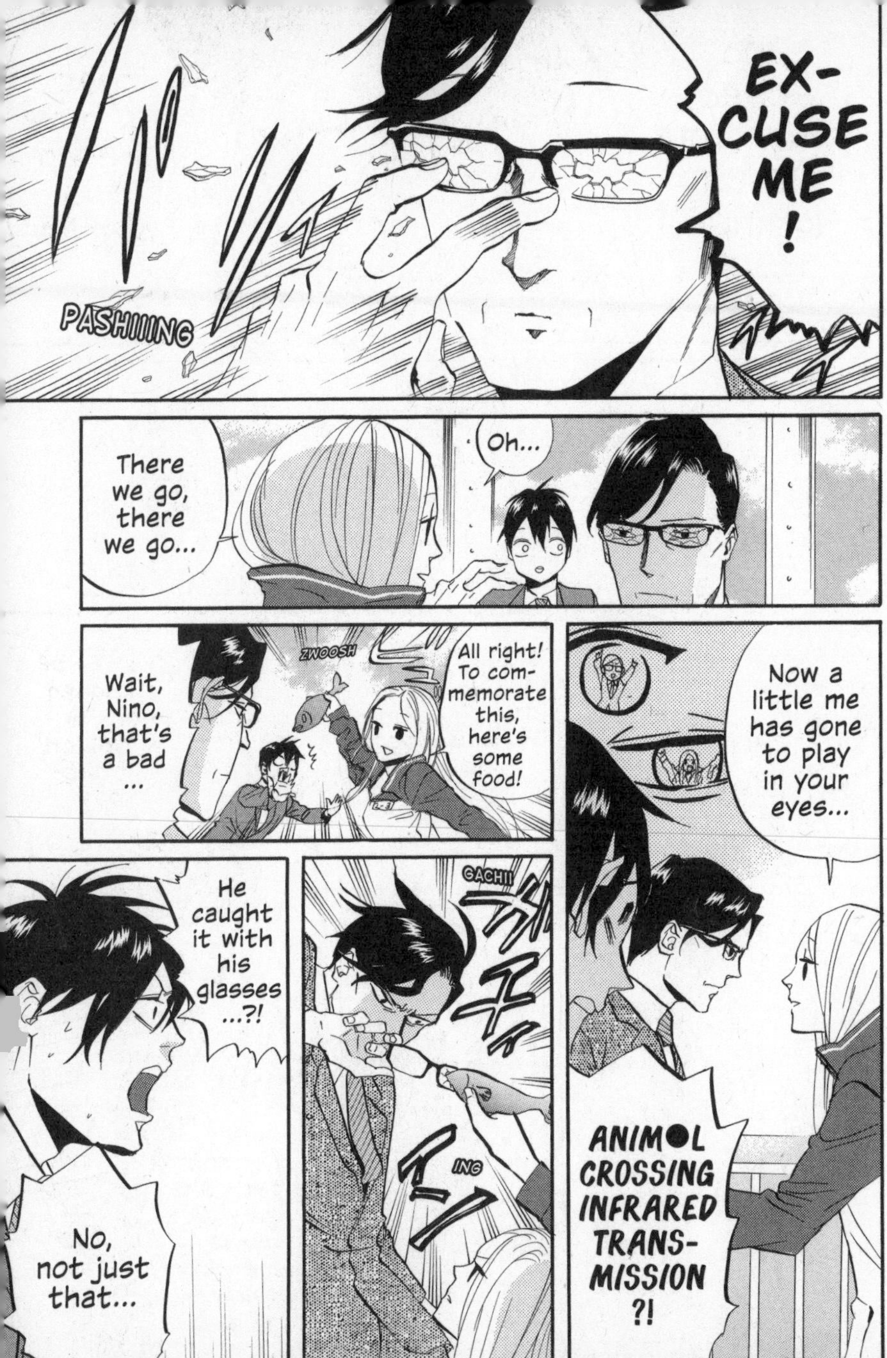
EX-CUSE ME!
PASHIIIING
Oh...
There we go, there we go...
Now a little me has gone to play in your eyes...
ANIMOL CROSSING INFRARED TRANSMISSION?!
All right! To commemorate this, here's some food!
ZWOOSH
Wait, Nino, that's a bad ...
GACHII
ING
He caught it with his glasses ...?!
No, not just that...

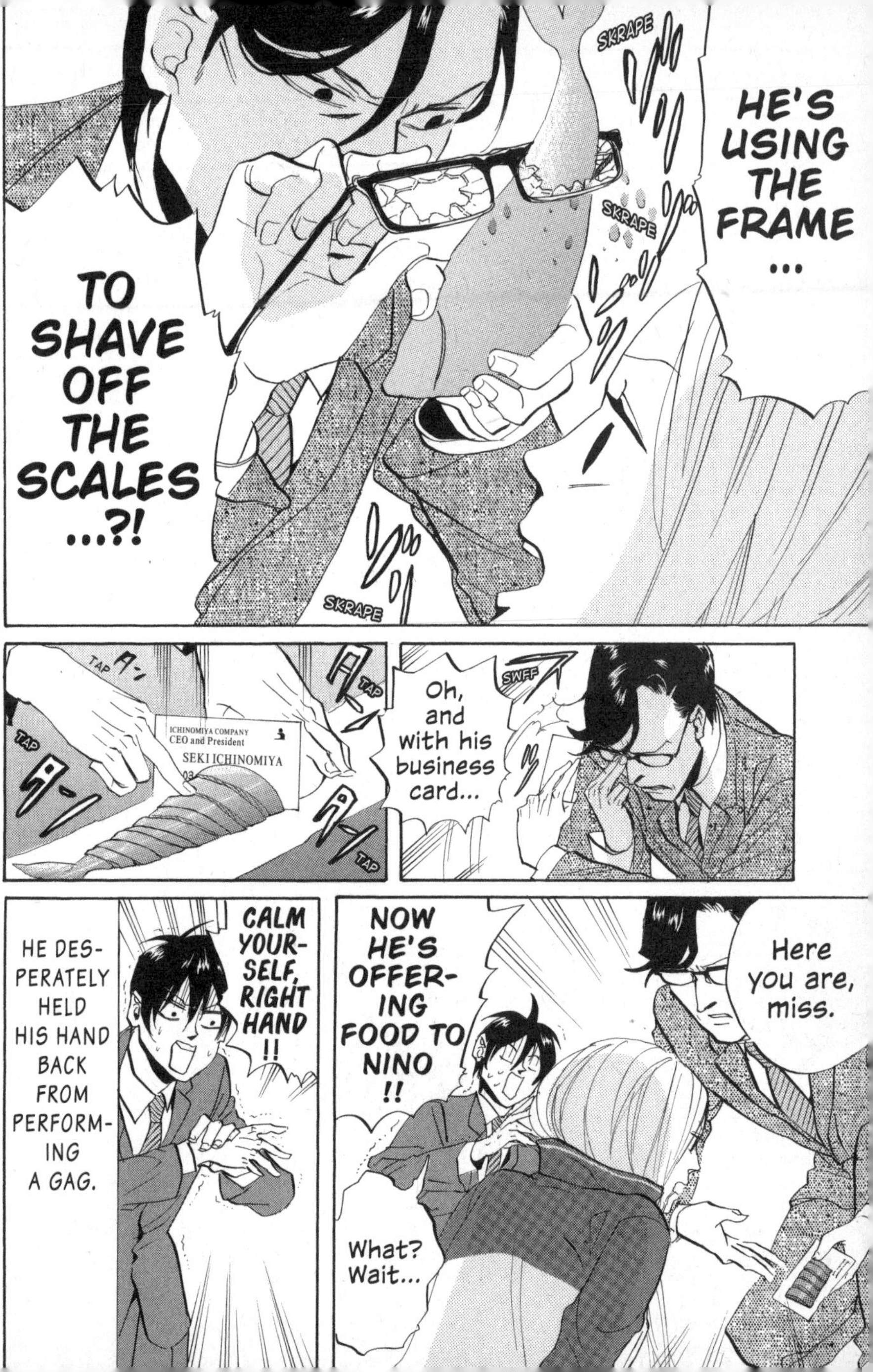
SKRAPE
HE'S USING THE FRAME ...
SKRAPE
TO SHAVE OFF THE SCALES ...?!
SKRAPE
SWFF
Oh, and with his business card...
TAP
TAP
ICHINOMIYA COMPANY
CEO and President
SEKI ICHINOMIYA
TAP
TAP
Here you are, miss.
NOW HE'S OFFERING FOOD TO NINO !!
What? Wait...
CALM YOURSELF, RIGHT HAND !!
HE DESPERATELY HELD HIS HAND BACK FROM PERFORMING A GAG.

Chapter 273: Settlement

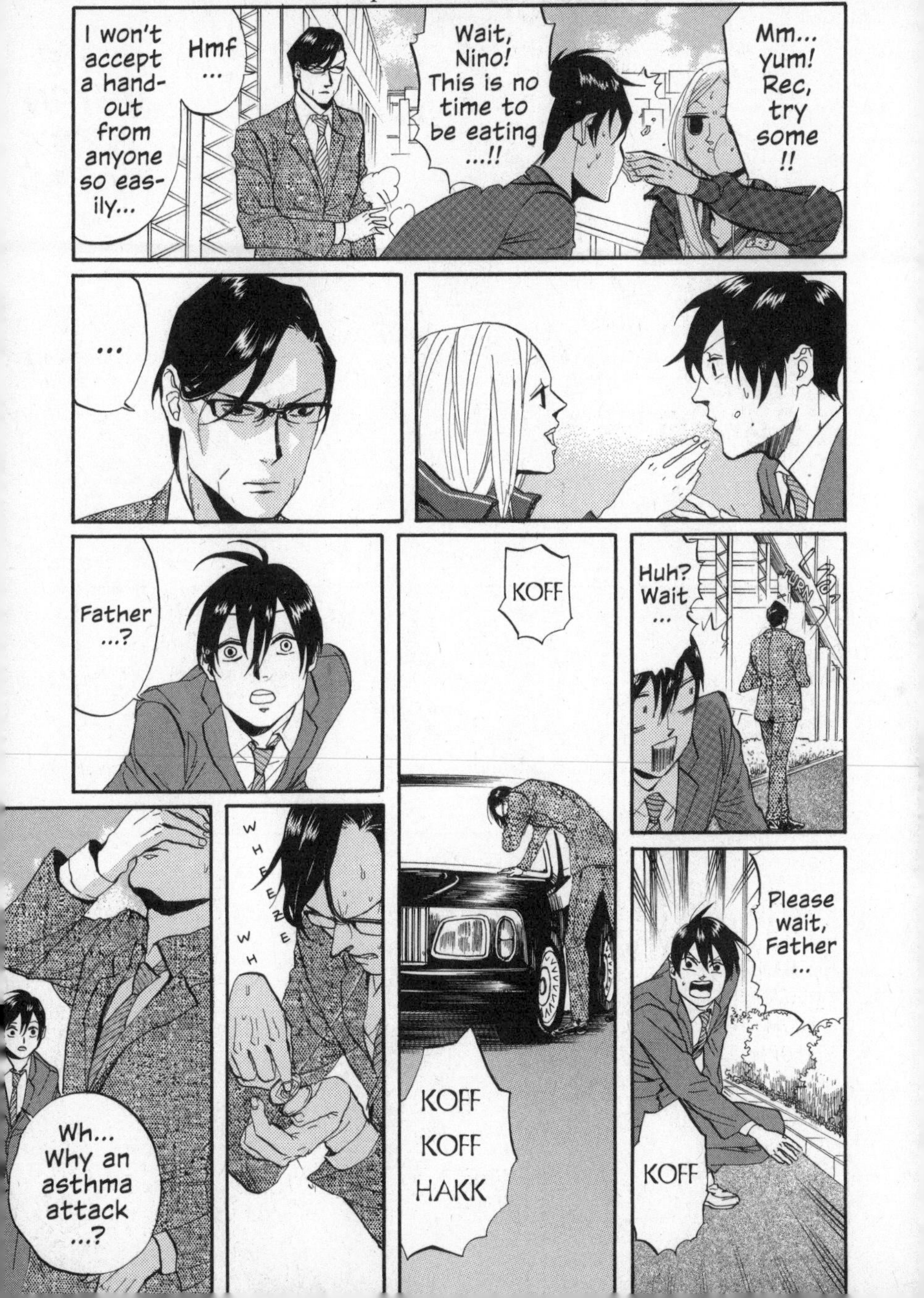
Mm... yum! Rec, try some !!
Wait, Nino! This is no time to be eating ...!!
Hmf ...
I won't accept a hand-out from anyone so easily...
...
Huh? Wait ...
TURN
Please wait, Father ...
KOFF
KOFF
KOFF KOFF HAKK
Father ...?
Wh... Why an asthma attack ...?

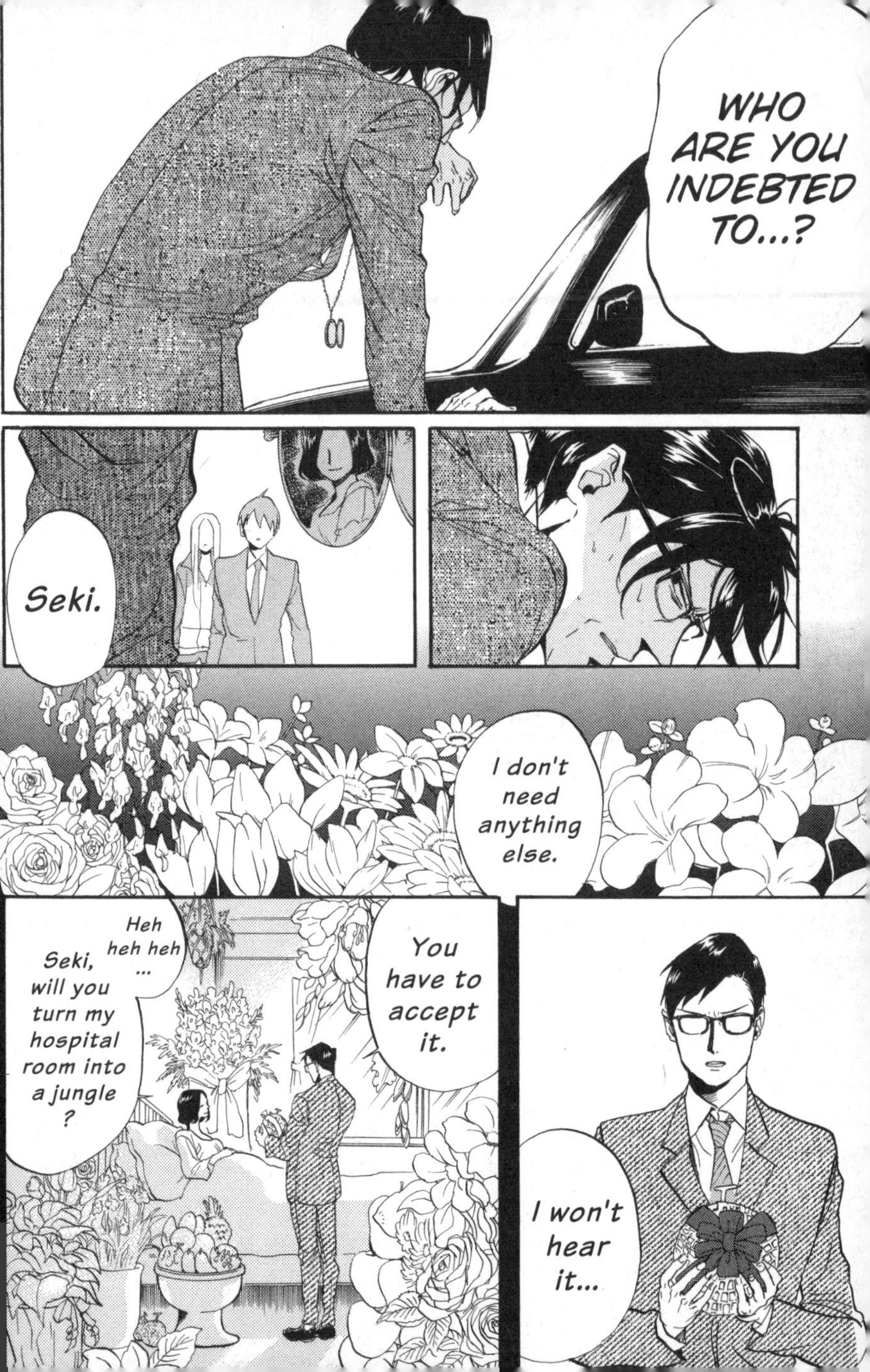
WHO ARE YOU INDEBTED TO...?
Seki.
I don't need anything else.
I won't hear it...
You have to accept it.
Heh heh heh ...
Seki, will you turn my hospital room into a jungle ?

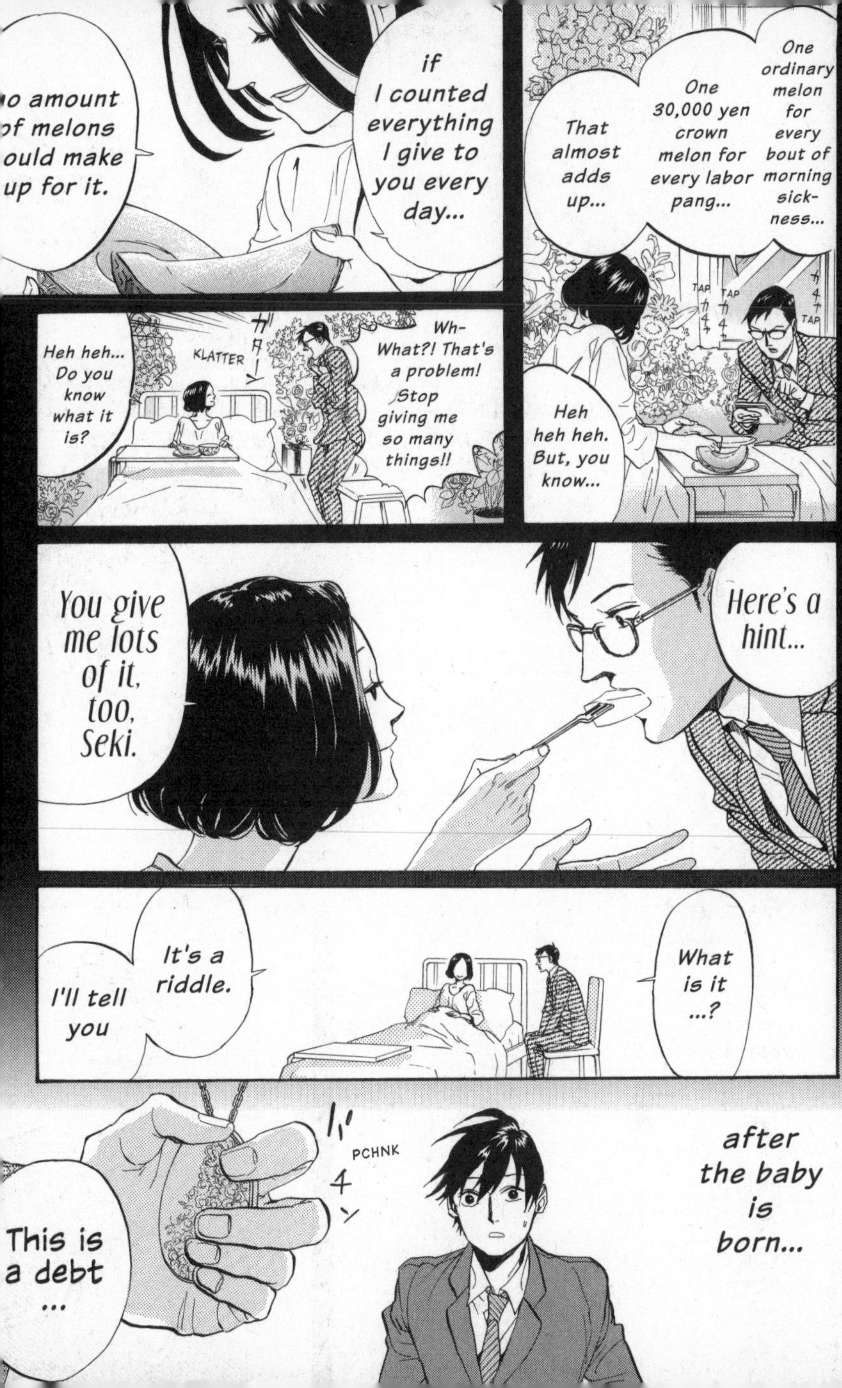
One ordinary melon for every bout of morning sickness...
One 30,000 yen crown melon for every labor pang...
That almost adds up...
TAP TAP TAP
Heh heh heh. But, you know...
if I counted everything I give to you every day...
o amount of melons ould make up for it.
Wh- What?! That's a problem! Stop giving me so many things!!
KLATTER
Heh heh... Do you know what it is?
Here's a hint...
You give me lots of it, too, Seki.
What is it ...?
It's a riddle.
I'll tell you
after the baby is born...
PCHNK
This is a debt ...

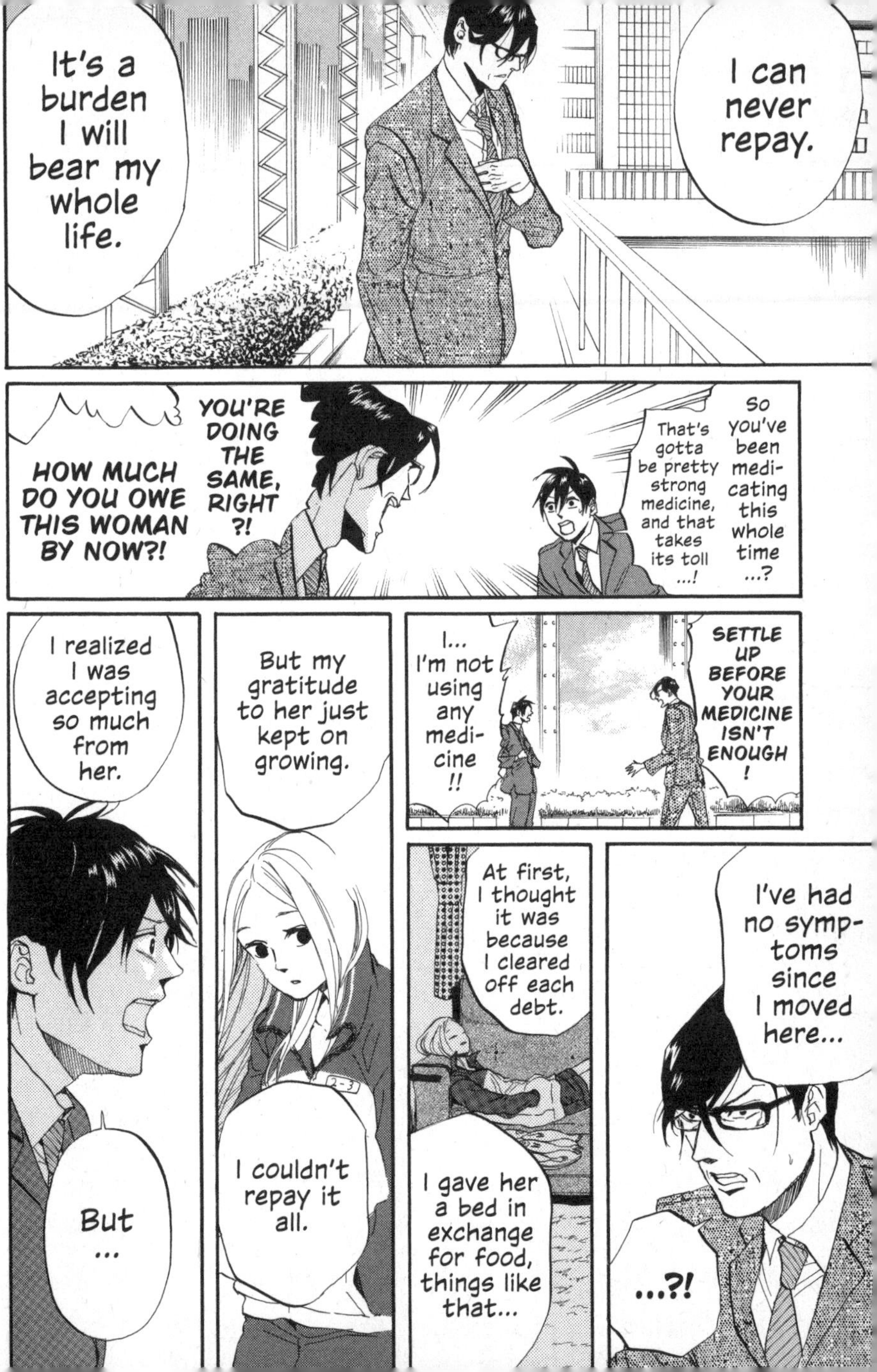

I can never repay.
It's a burden I will bear my whole life.
So you've been medi-cating this whole time ...?
That's gotta be pretty strong medicine, and that takes its toll ...!
YOU'RE DOING THE SAME, RIGHT ?!
HOW MUCH DO YOU OWE THIS WOMAN BY NOW?!
SETTLE UP BEFORE YOUR MEDICINE ISN'T ENOUGH !
I... I'm not using any medi-cine !!
I've had no symp-toms since I moved here...
...?!
At first, I thought it was because I cleared off each debt.
I gave her a bed in exchange for food, things like that...
But my gratitude to her just kept on growing.
I couldn't repay it all.
I realized I was accepting so much from her.
But ...

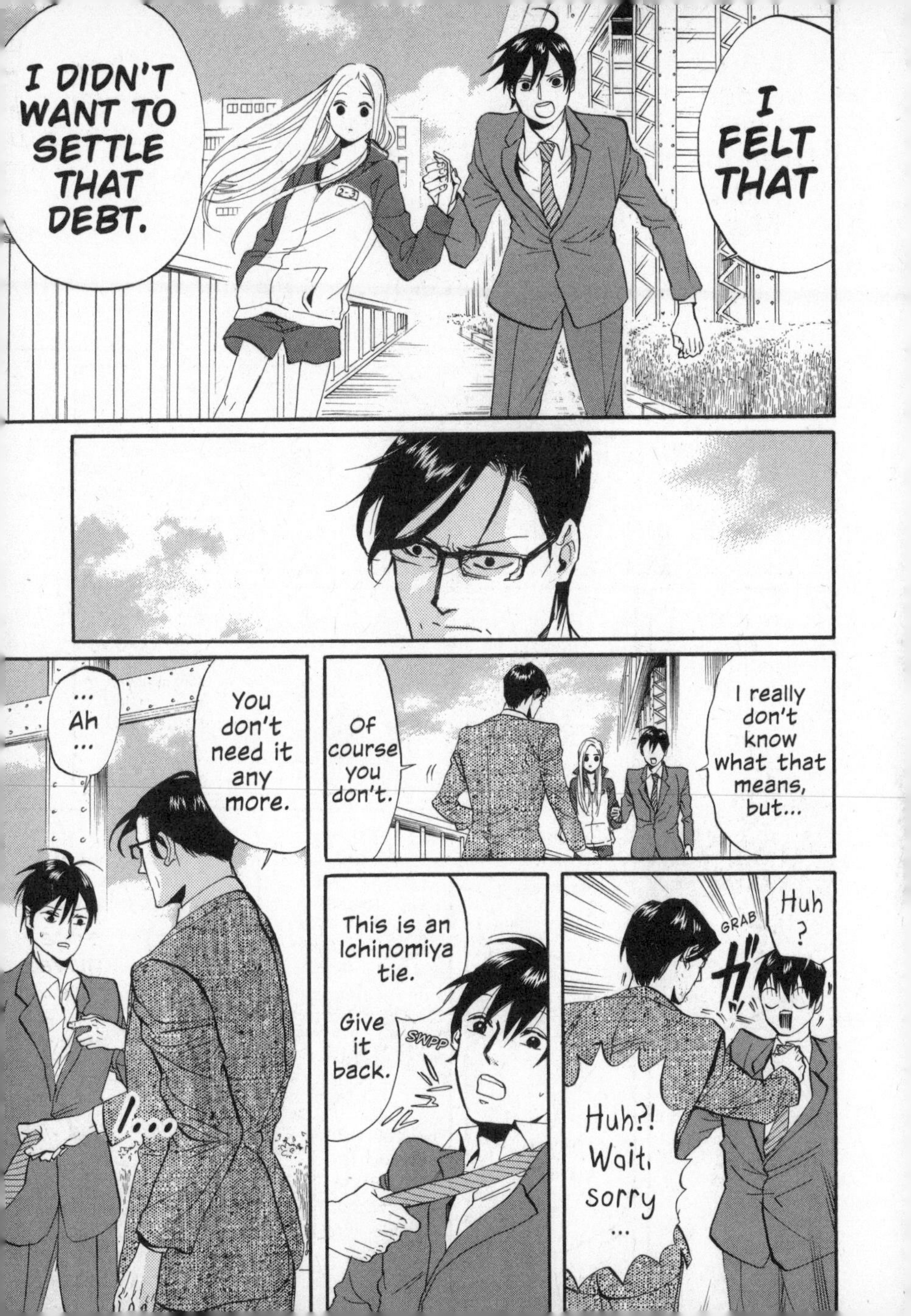
I FELT THAT
I DIDN'T WANT TO SETTLE THAT DEBT.
I really don't know what that means, but...
Of course you don't.
Huh ?
GRAB
ガ
Huh?! Wait, sorry ...
This is an Ichinomiya tie.
Give it back.
SWPP
You don't need it any more.
... Ah ...
I...

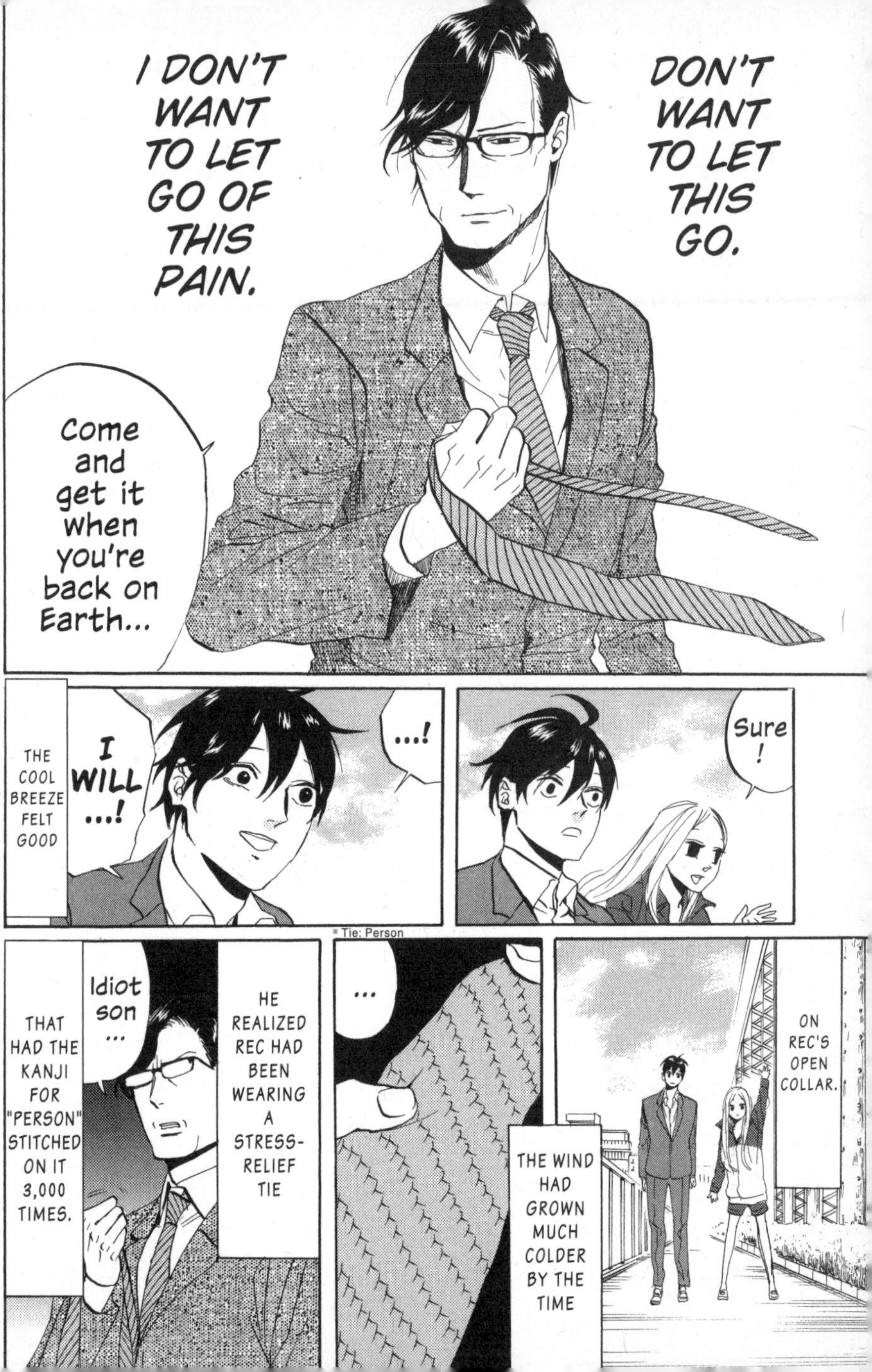
DON'T WANT TO LET THIS GO.
I DON'T WANT TO LET GO OF THIS PAIN.
Come and get it when you're back on Earth...
Sure!
...!
I WILL ...!
THE COOL BREEZE FELT GOOD
ON REC'S OPEN COLLAR.
THE WIND HAD GROWN MUCH COLDER BY THE TIME
...
HE REALIZED REC HAD BEEN WEARING A STRESS-RELIEF TIE
Idiot son ...
THAT HAD THE KANJI FOR "PERSON" STITCHED ON IT 3,000 TIMES.
* Tie: Person

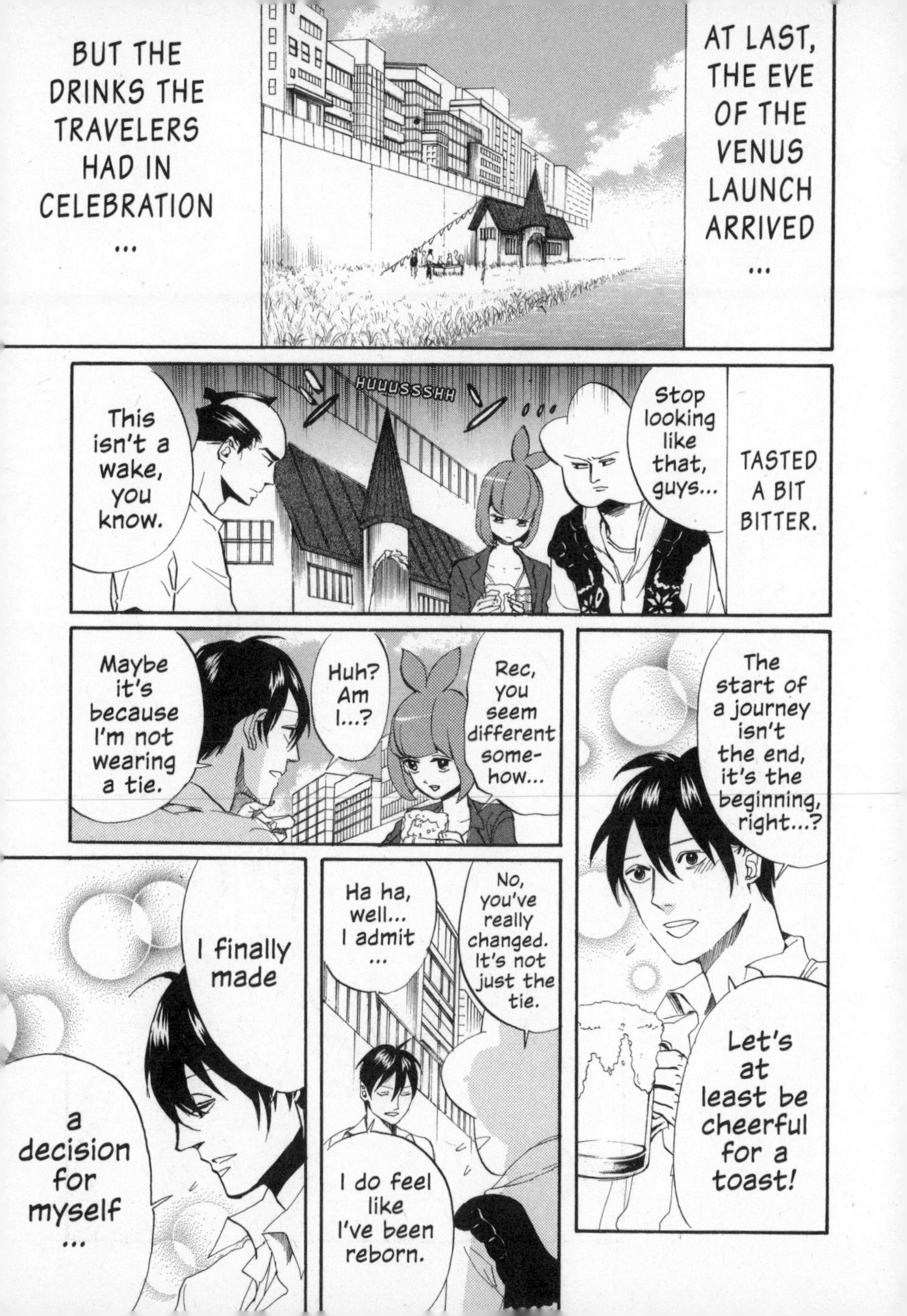
AT LAST, THE EVE OF THE VENUS LAUNCH ARRIVED ...
BUT THE DRINKS THE TRAVELERS HAD IN CELEBRATION ...
TASTED A BIT BITTER.
Stop looking like that, guys...
HUUUSSSHH
This isn't a wake, you know.
The start of a journey isn't the end, it's the beginning, right...?
Let's at least be cheerful for a toast!
Rec, you seem different some-how...
Huh? Am I...?
Maybe it's because I'm not wearing a tie.
No, you've really changed. It's not just the tie.
Ha ha, well... I admit ...
I do feel like I've been reborn.
I finally made
a decision for myself ...

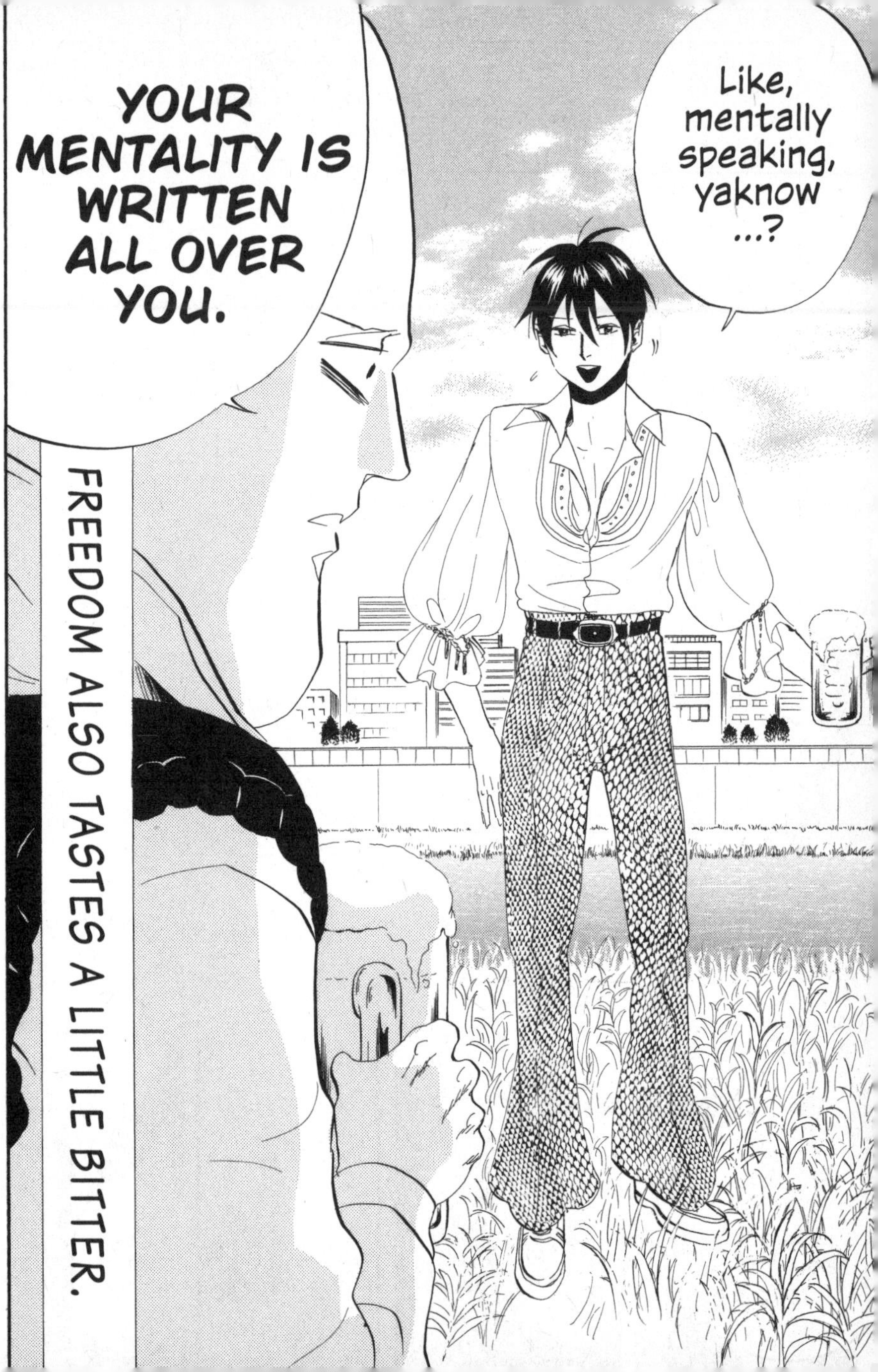
Like, mentally speaking, yaknow ...?
YOUR MENTALITY IS WRITTEN ALL OVER YOU.
FREEDOM ALSO TASTES A LITTLE BITTER.

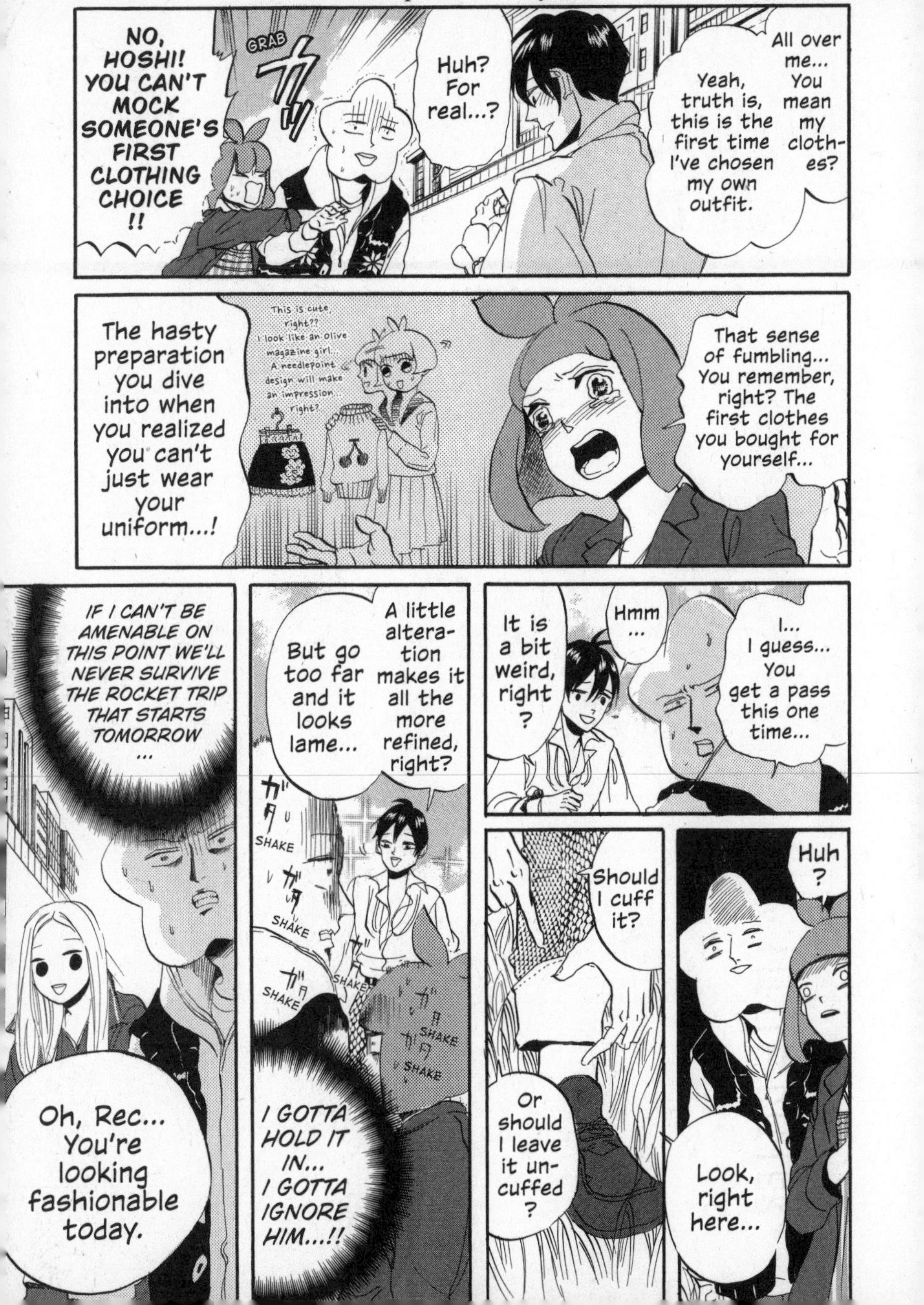
All over me... You mean my clothes?
Yeah, truth is, this is the first time I've chosen my own outfit.
Huh? For real...?
GRAB
NO, HOSHI! YOU CAN'T MOCK SOMEONE'S FIRST CLOTHING CHOICE !!
That sense of fumbling... You remember, right? The first clothes you bought for yourself...
This is cute, right?? I look like an Olive magazine girl... A needlepoint design will make an impression... right?
The hasty preparation you dive into when you realized you can't just wear your uniform...!
I... I guess... You get a pass this one time...
Hmm ...
It is a bit weird, right ?
Huh ?
Look, right here...
Should I cuff it?
Or should I leave it uncuffed ?
A little alteration makes it all the more refined, right?
But go too far and it looks lame...
SHAKE
SHAKE
SHAKE
SHAKE
SHAKE
SHAKE
I GOTTA HOLD IT IN... I GOTTA IGNORE HIM...!!
IF I CAN'T BE AMENABLE ON THIS POINT WE'LL NEVER SURVIVE THE ROCKET TRIP THAT STARTS TOMORROW ...
Oh, Rec... You're looking fashionable today.

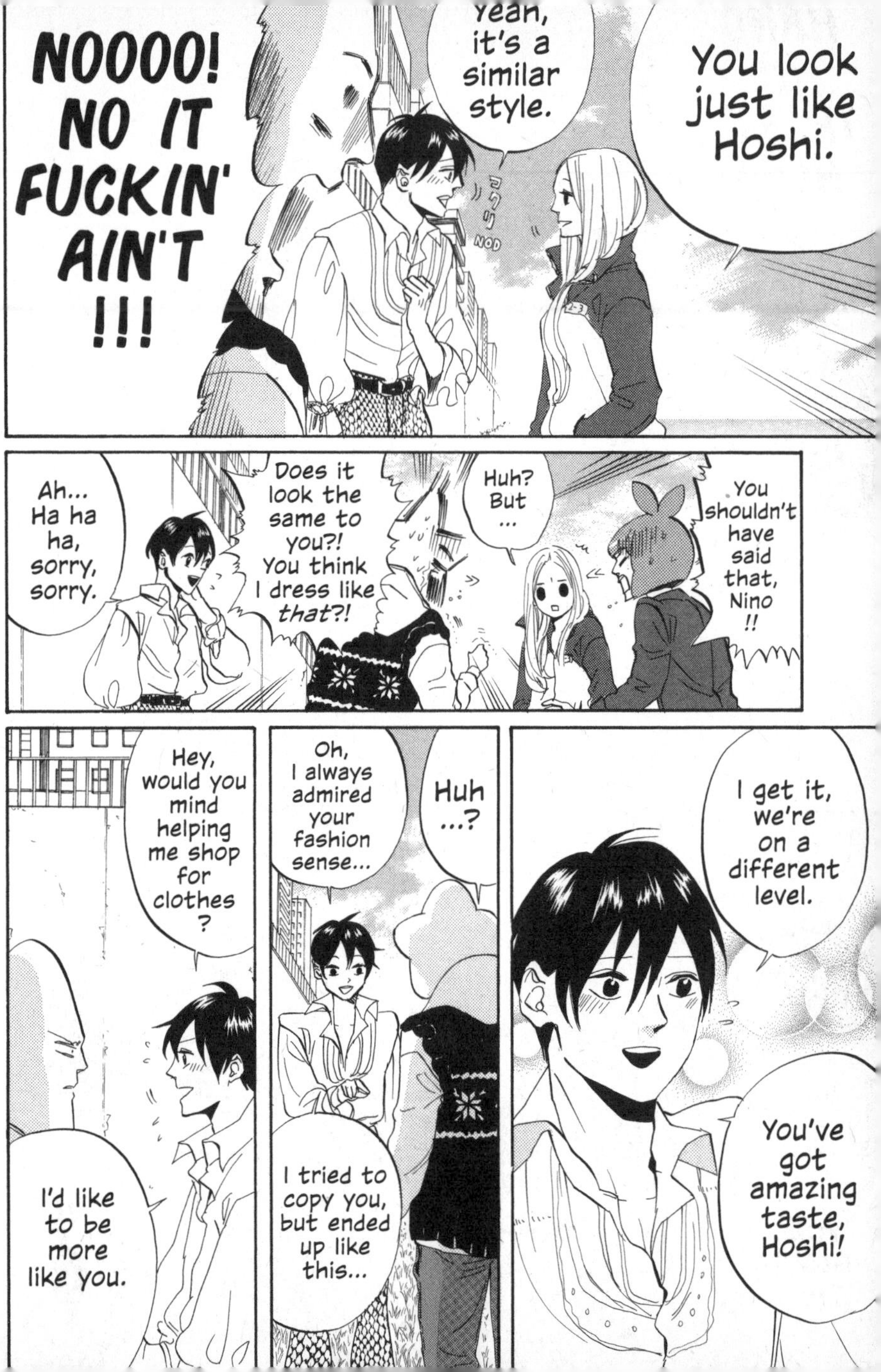
You look just like Hoshi.
Yeah, it's a similar style.
コクリ NOD
NOOOO! NO IT FUCKIN' AIN'T !!!
You shouldn't have said that, Nino !!
Huh? But ...
Does it look the same to you?! You think I dress like *that*?!
Ah... Ha ha ha, sorry, sorry.
I get it, we're on a different level.
You've got amazing taste, Hoshi!
Huh ...?
Oh, I always admired your fashion sense...
I tried to copy you, but ended up like this...
Hey, would you mind helping me shop for clothes ?
I'd like to be more like you.

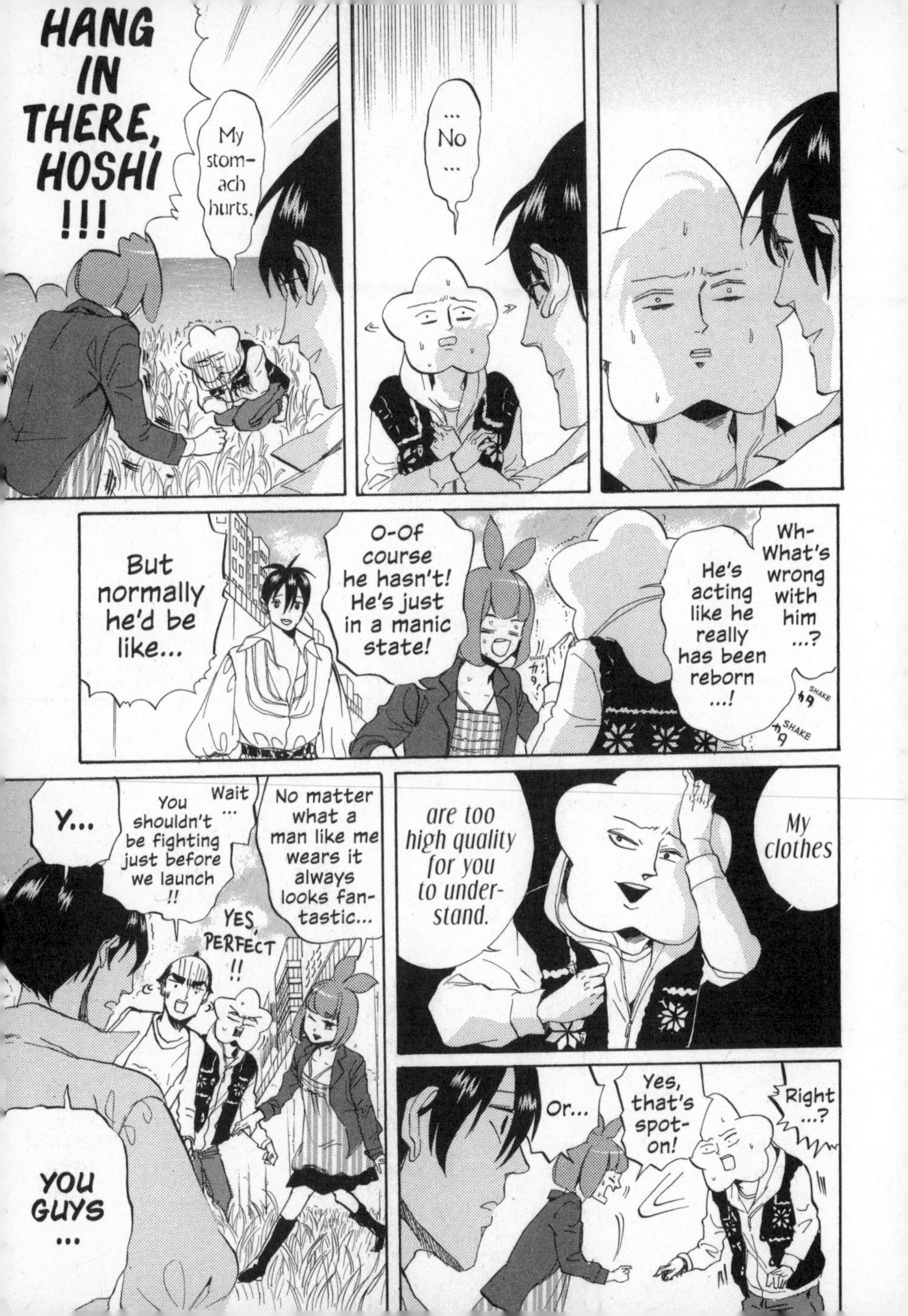
... No ...
My stomach hurts.
HANG IN THERE, HOSHI!!!
Wh-What's wrong with him...?
He's acting like he really has been reborn...!
SHAKE SHAKE
O-Of course he hasn't! He's just in a manic state!
SHAKE
But normally he'd be like...
My clothes
are too high quality for you to understand.
Right...?
Yes, that's spot-on!
Or...
No matter what a man like me wears it always looks fantastic...
YES, PERFECT!!
Wait...
You shouldn't be fighting just before we launch!!
Y...
YOU GUYS...

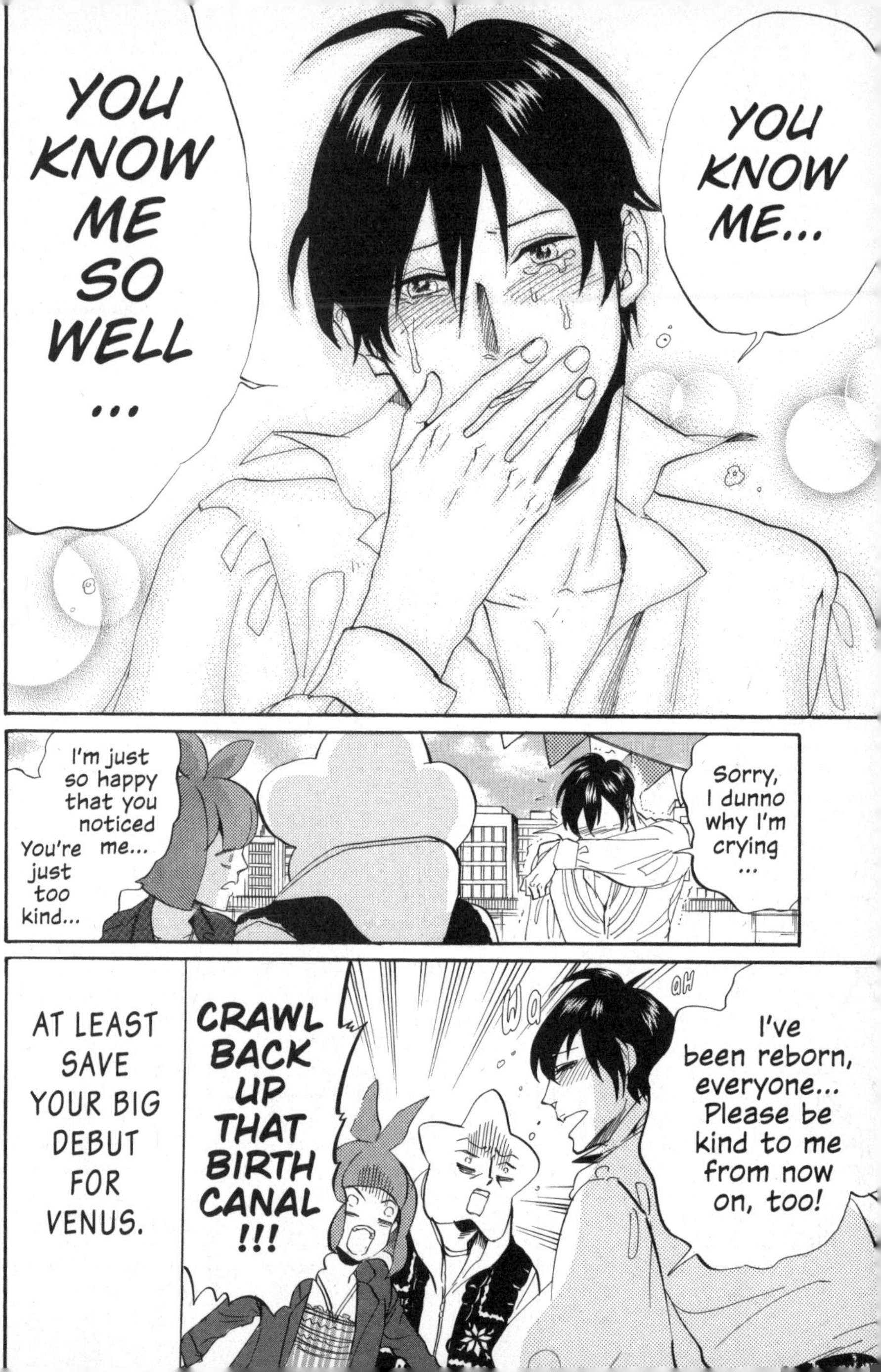
YOU KNOW ME...
YOU KNOW ME SO WELL ...
Sorry, I dunno why I'm crying ...
I'm just so happy that you noticed me...
You're just too kind...
I've been reborn, everyone... Please be kind to me from now on, too!
WA AH
CRAWL BACK UP THAT BIRTH CANAL !!!
AT LEAST SAVE YOUR BIG DEBUT FOR VENUS.

Chapter 275: Goodbye Party

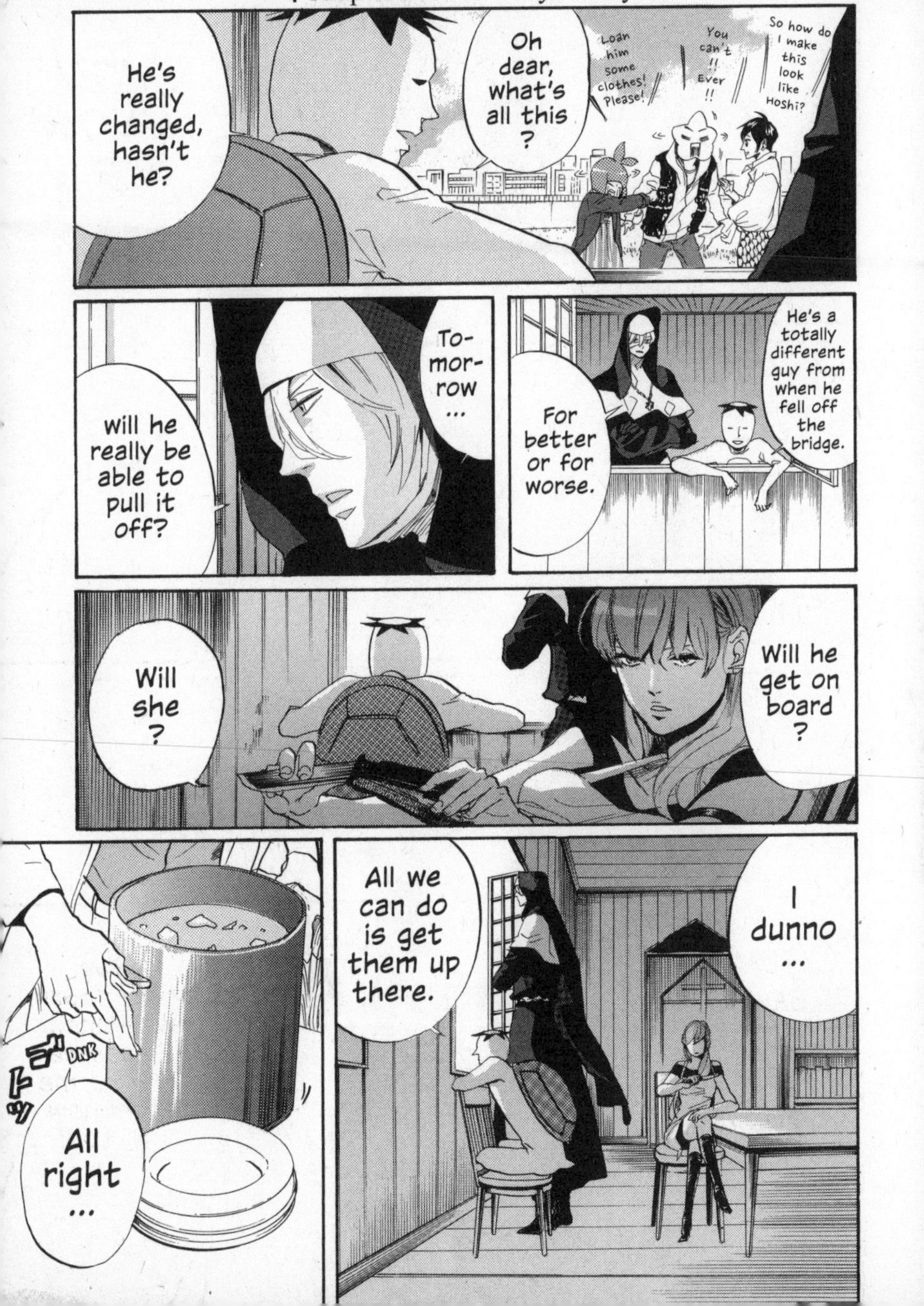

So how do I make this look like Hoshi?
You can't!! Ever!!
Loan him some clothes! Please!
Oh dear, what's all this?
He's really changed, hasn't he?
He's a totally different guy from when he fell off the bridge.
For better or for worse.
To-morrow...
will he really be able to pull it off?
Will he get on board?
Will she?
I dunno...
All we can do is get them up there.
DNK
All right...

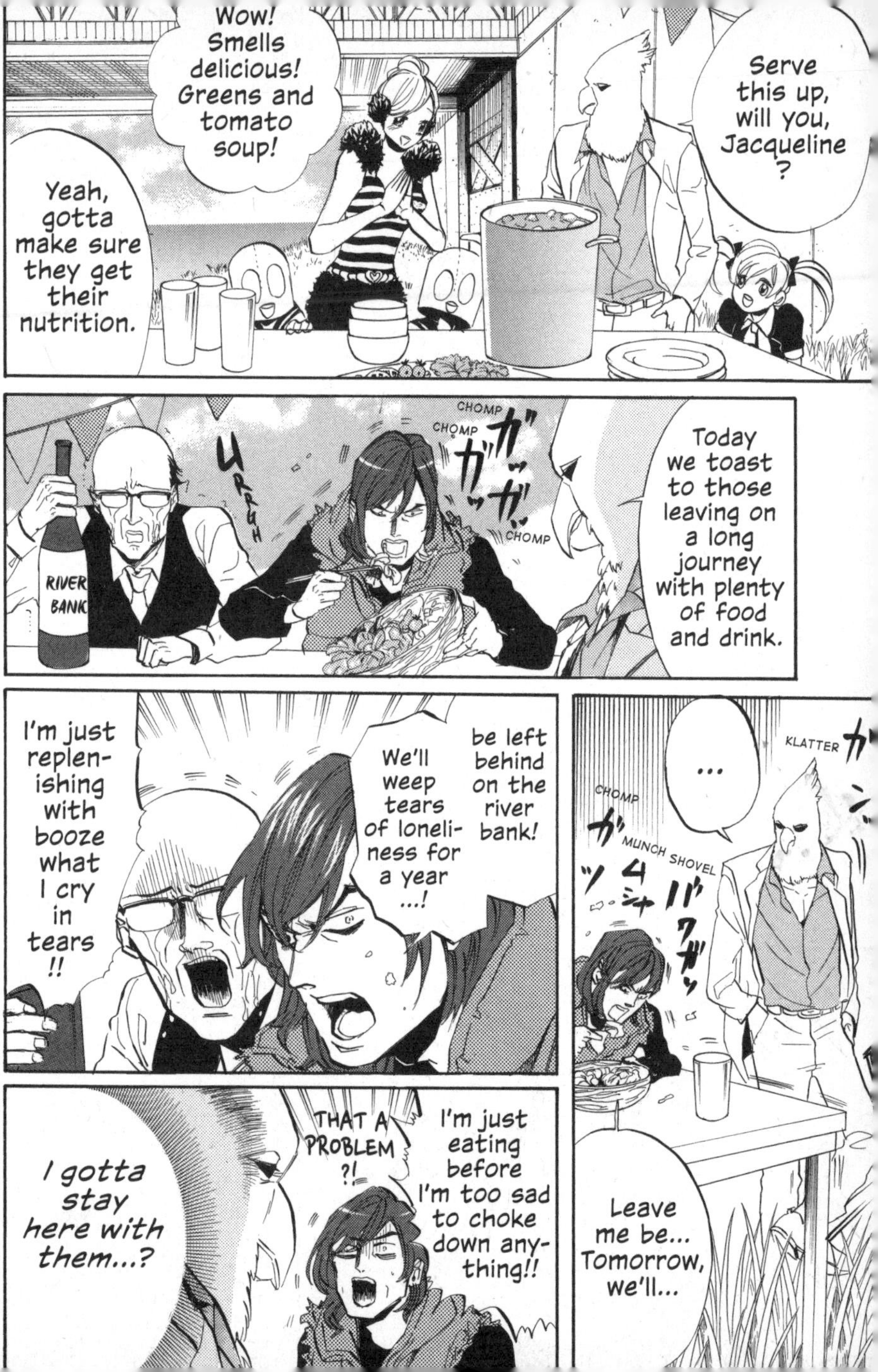
Serve this up, will you, Jacqueline?
Wow! Smells delicious! Greens and tomato soup!
Yeah, gotta make sure they get their nutrition.
Today we toast to those leaving on a long journey with plenty of food and drink.
CHOMP
CHOMP
CHOMP
URRGH
RIVER BANK
KLATTER
...
CHOMP
MUNCH SHOVEL
be left behind on the river bank!
We'll weep tears of loneli-ness for a year ...!
I'm just replen-ishing with booze what I cry in tears!!
Leave me be... Tomorrow, we'll...
I'm just eating before I'm too sad to choke down any-thing!!
THAT A PROBLEM ?!
I gotta stay here with them...?

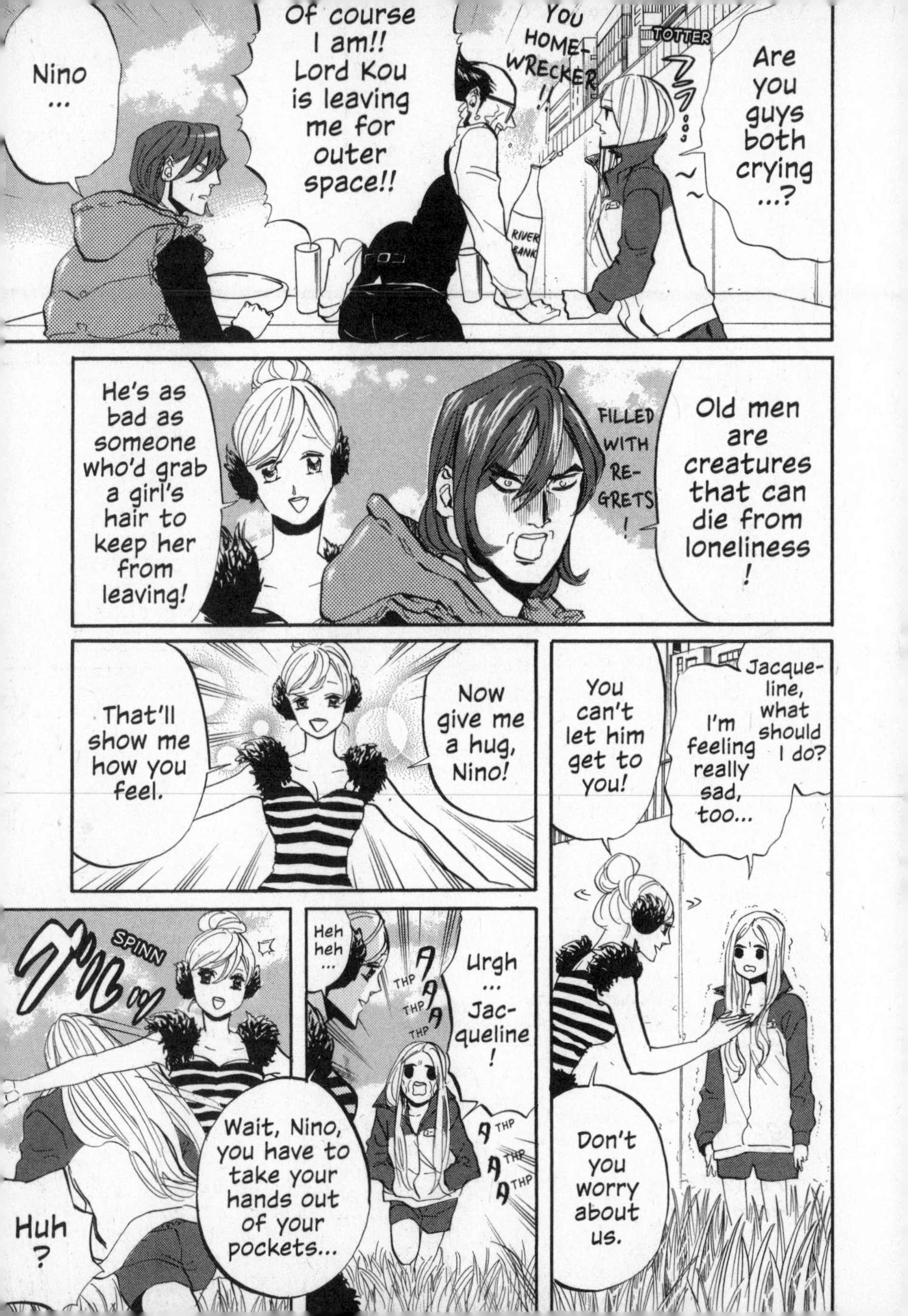
Are you guys both crying ...?
TOTTER
YOU HOME-WRECKER!!
Of course I am!! Lord Kou is leaving me for outer space!!
RIVER BANK
Nino ...
Old men are creatures that can die from loneliness!
FILLED WITH RE-GRETS!
He's as bad as someone who'd grab a girl's hair to keep her from leaving!
Jacque-line, what should I do?
I'm feeling really sad, too...
You can't let him get to you!
Don't you worry about us.
Now give me a hug, Nino!
That'll show me how you feel.
Urgh ... Jac-queline!
Heh heh ...
THP THP THP
Wait, Nino, you have to take your hands out of your pockets...
THP THP THP
SPINN
Huh?

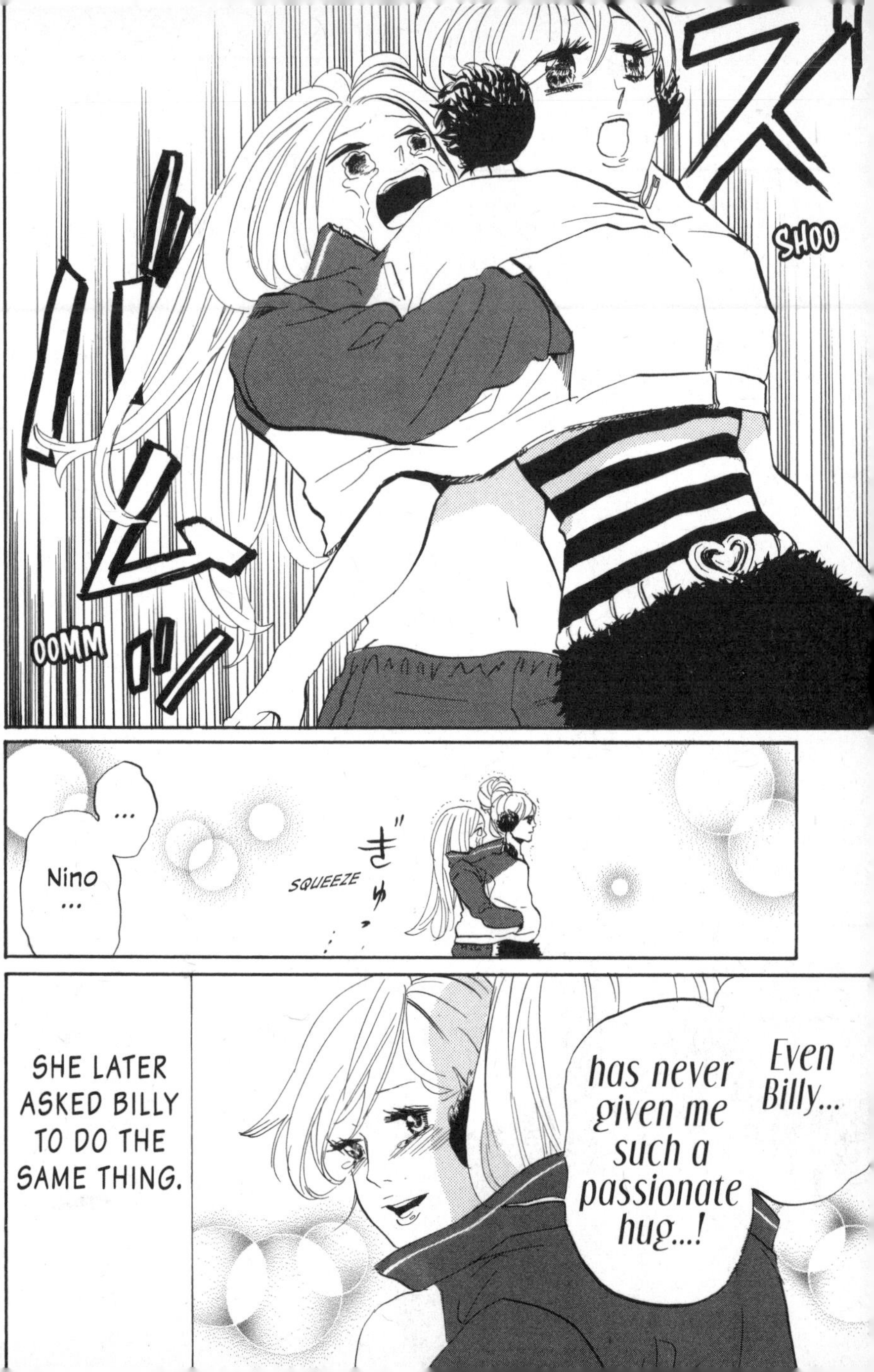
SHOO
OOMM
SQUEEZE
ぎゅ
... Nino ...
Even Billy...
has never given me such a passionate hug...!
SHE LATER ASKED BILLY TO DO THE SAME THING.

Chapter 276: Secret

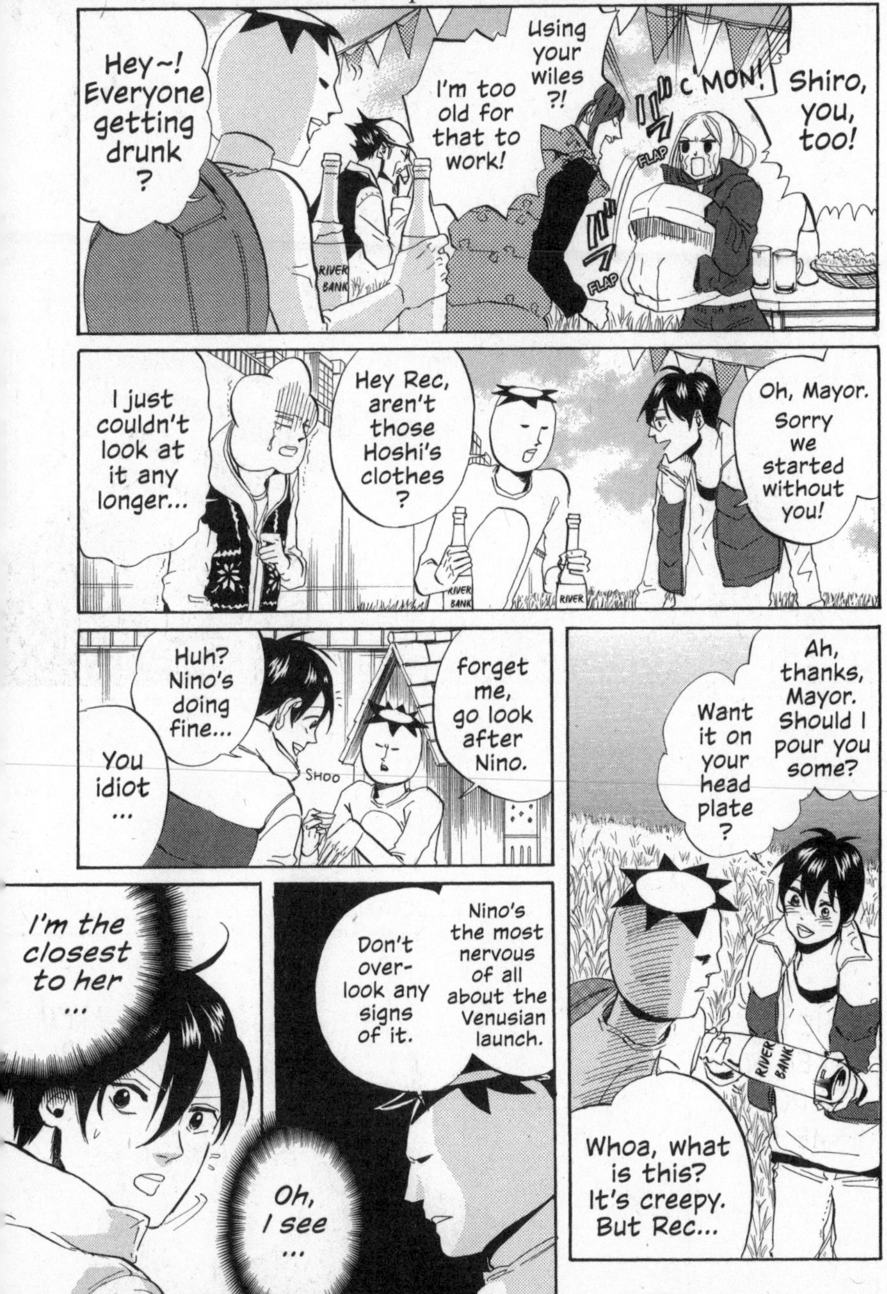
Shiro, you, too!
C'MON!
FLAP
FLAP
Using your wiles?!
I'm too old for that to work!
Hey~! Everyone getting drunk?
RIVER BANK
Oh, Mayor. Sorry we started without you!
Hey Rec, aren't those Hoshi's clothes?
I just couldn't look at it any longer...
RIVER BANK
RIVER
Ah, thanks, Mayor. Should I pour you some?
Want it on your head plate?
RIVER BANK
Whoa, what is this? It's creepy. But Rec...
forget me, go look after Nino.
Huh? Nino's doing fine...
SHOO
You idiot ...
Nino's the most nervous of all about the Venusian launch.
Don't over-look any signs of it.
Oh, I see ...
I'm the closest to her ...

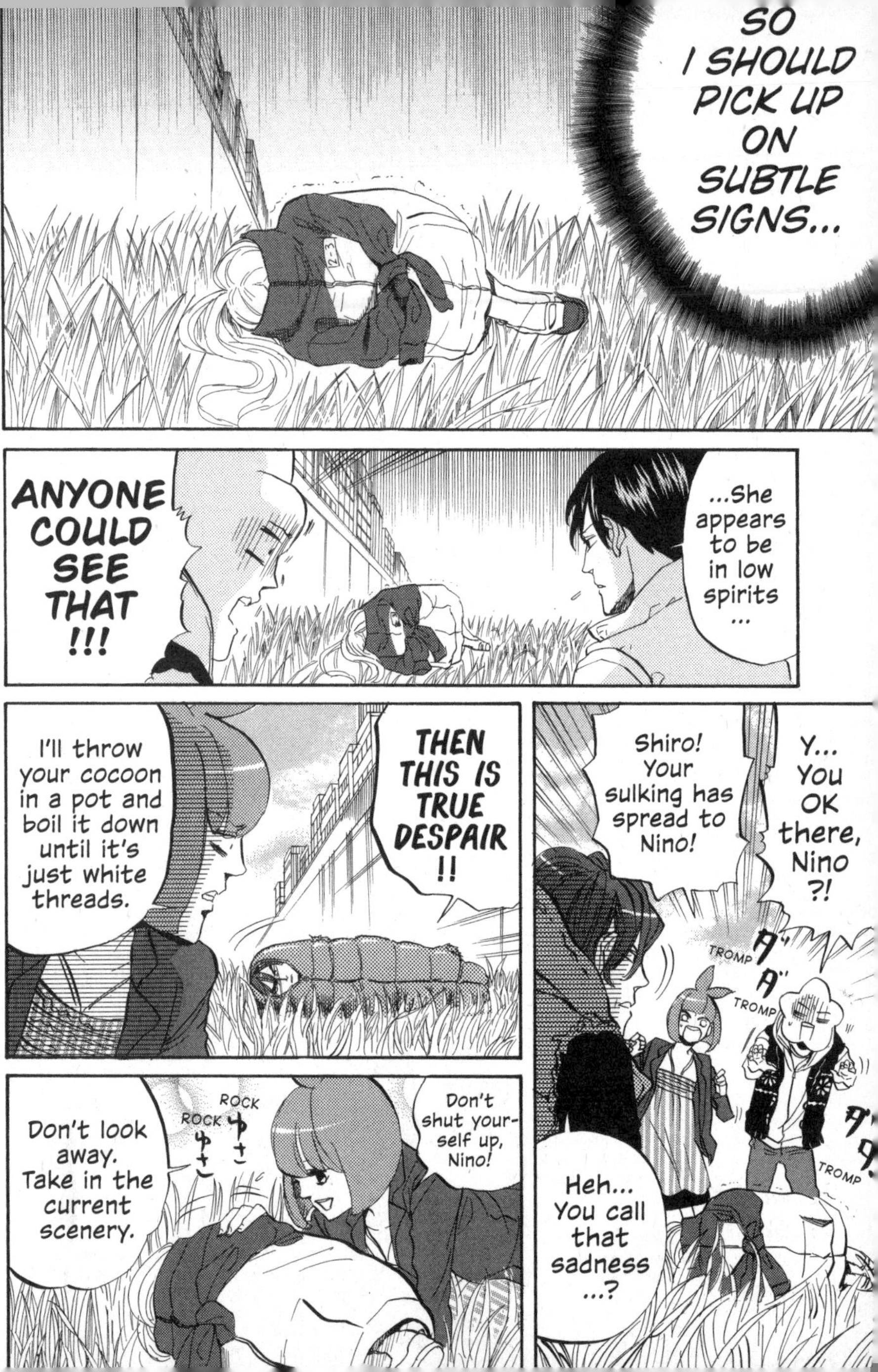
SO I SHOULD PICK UP ON SUBTLE SIGNS...
...She appears to be in low spirits ...
ANYONE COULD SEE THAT !!!
Y... You OK there, Nino ?!
Shiro! Your sulking has spread to Nino!
TROMP
TROMP
TROMP
Heh... You call that sadness ...?
THEN THIS IS TRUE DESPAIR !!
I'll throw your cocoon in a pot and boil it down until it's just white threads.
Don't shut your-self up, Nino!
ROCK
ROCK
Don't look away. Take in the current scenery.

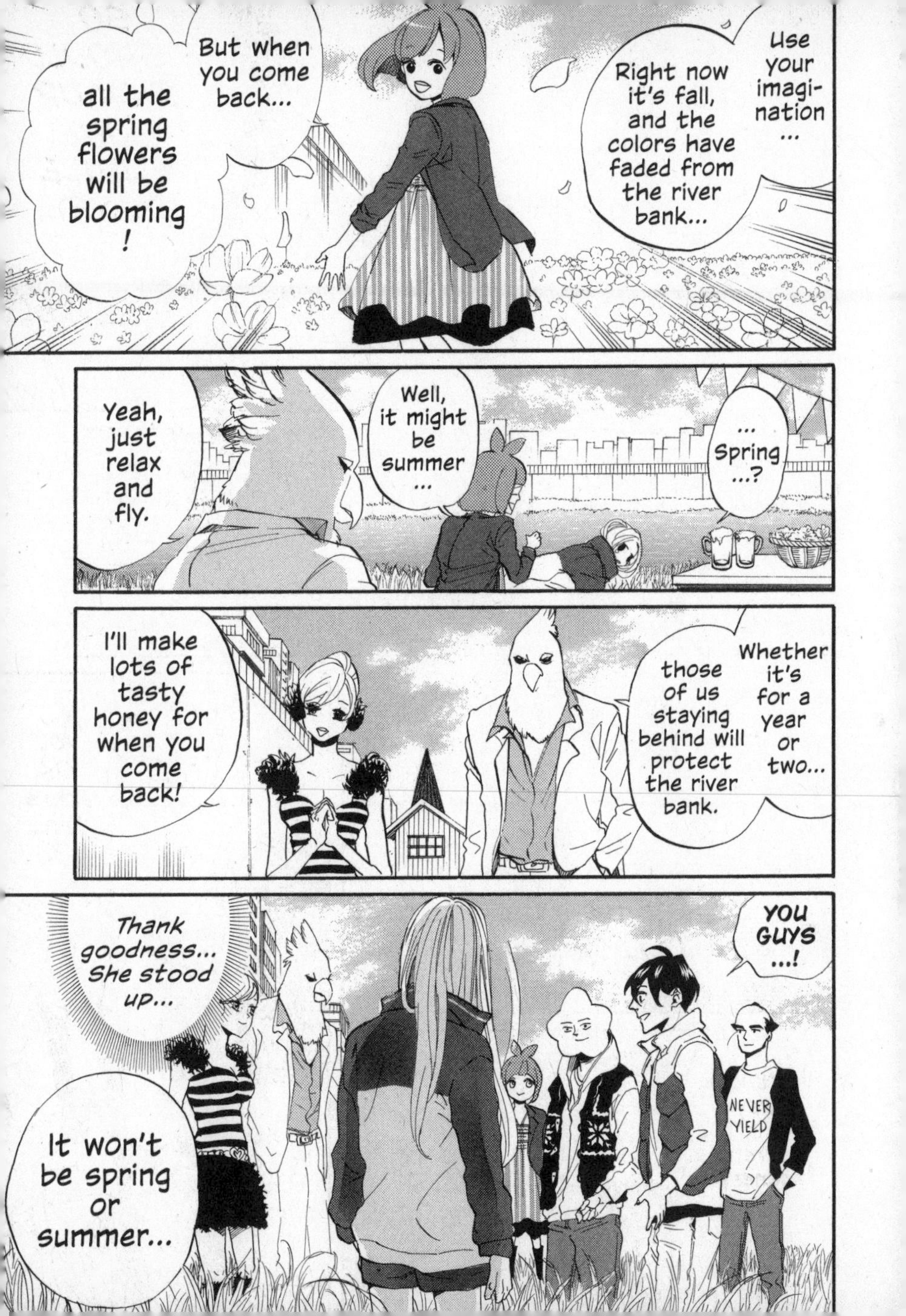
Use your imagination...
Right now it's fall, and the colors have faded from the river bank...
But when you come back...
all the spring flowers will be blooming!
...Spring...?
Well, it might be summer...
Yeah, just relax and fly.
Whether it's for a year or two...
those of us staying behind will protect the river bank.
I'll make lots of tasty honey for when you come back!
YOU GUYS ...!
NEVER YIELD
Thank goodness... She stood up...
It won't be spring or summer...

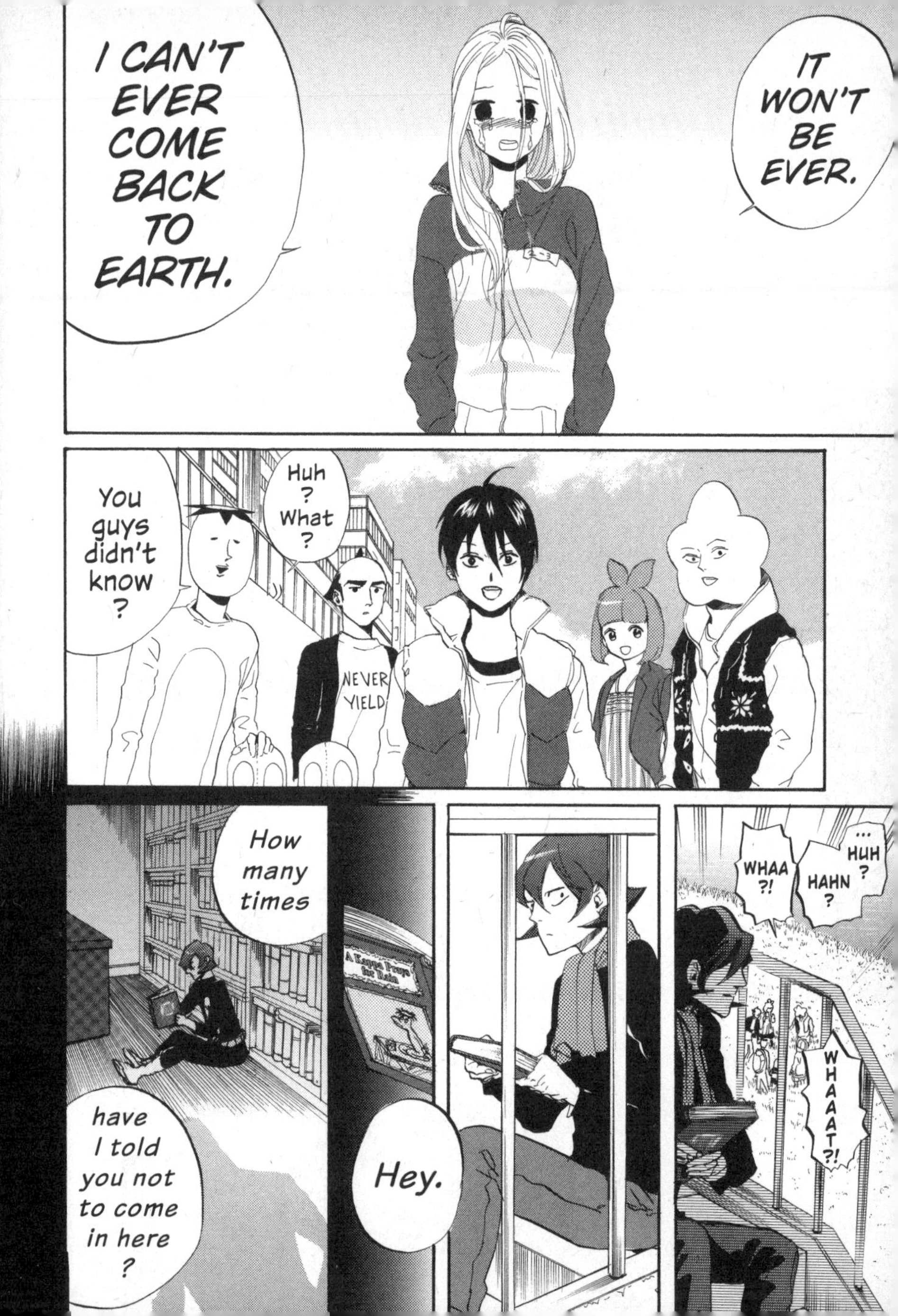
IT WON'T BE EVER.
I CAN'T EVER COME BACK TO EARTH.
Huh? What?
You guys didn't know?
NEVER YIELD
...HUH?
HAHN?
WHAA?!
WHAAAAT?!
Hey.
How many times
have I told you not to come in here?

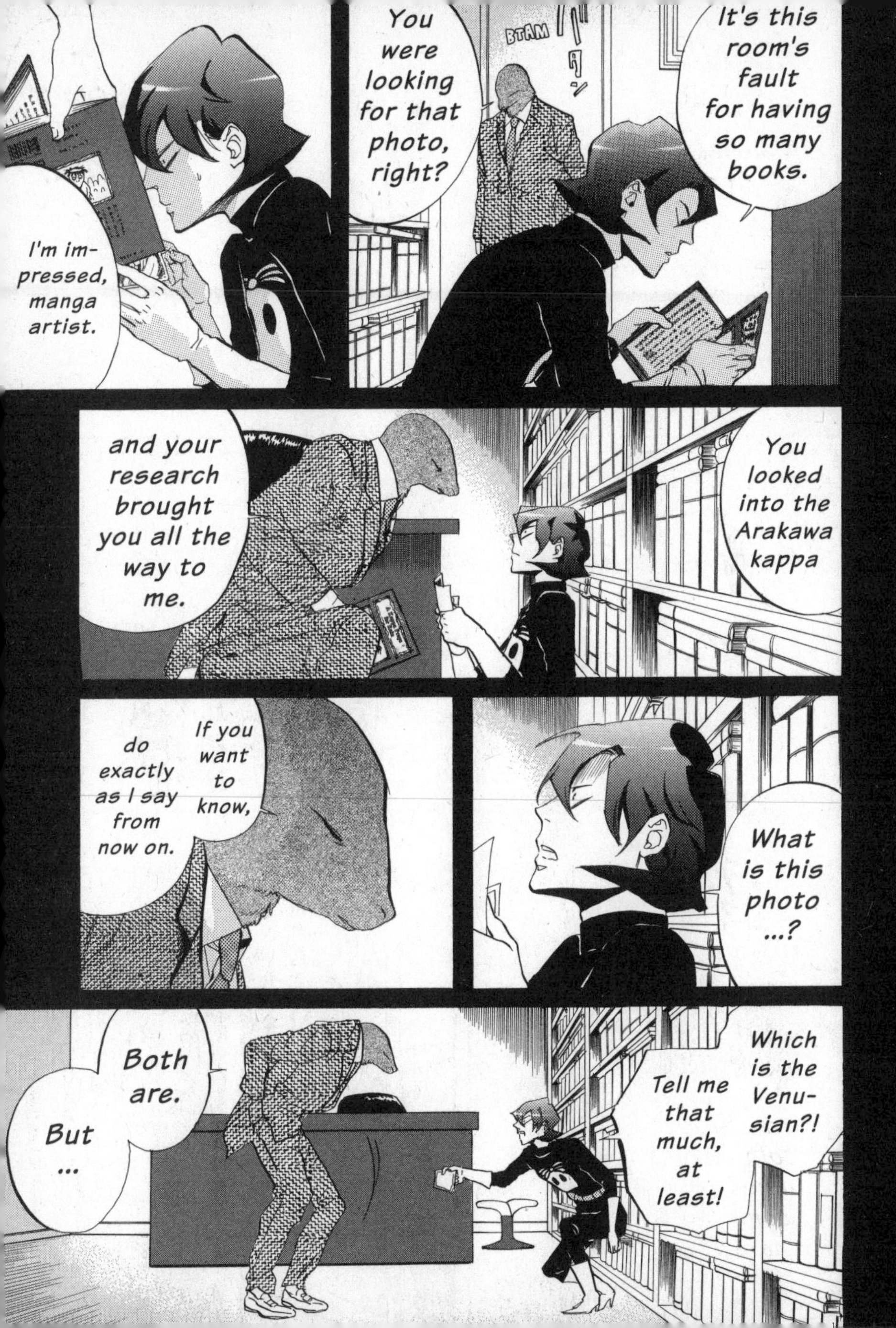
It's this room's fault for having so many books.
BTAM
You were looking for that photo, right?
I'm impressed, manga artist.
You looked into the Arakawa kappa
and your research brought you all the way to me.
What is this photo ...?
If you want to know,
do exactly as I say from now on.
Which is the Venusian?!
Tell me that much, at least!
Both are.
But ...

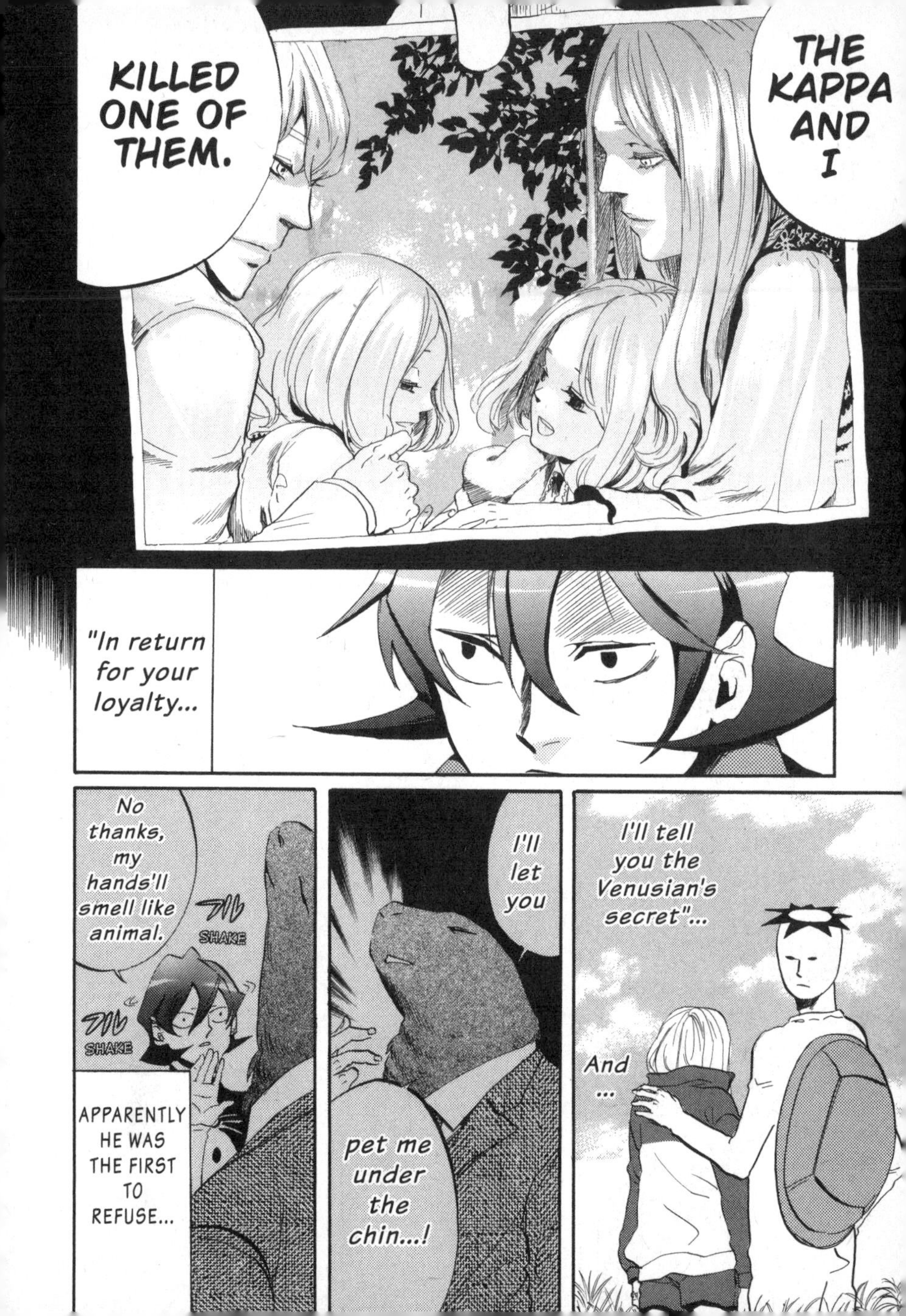
THE KAPPA AND I
KILLED ONE OF THEM.
"In return for your loyalty...
I'll tell you the Venusian's secret"...
And ...
I'll let you
pet me under the chin...!
No thanks, my hands'll smell like animal.
SHAKE
SHAKE
APPARENTLY HE WAS THE FIRST TO REFUSE...

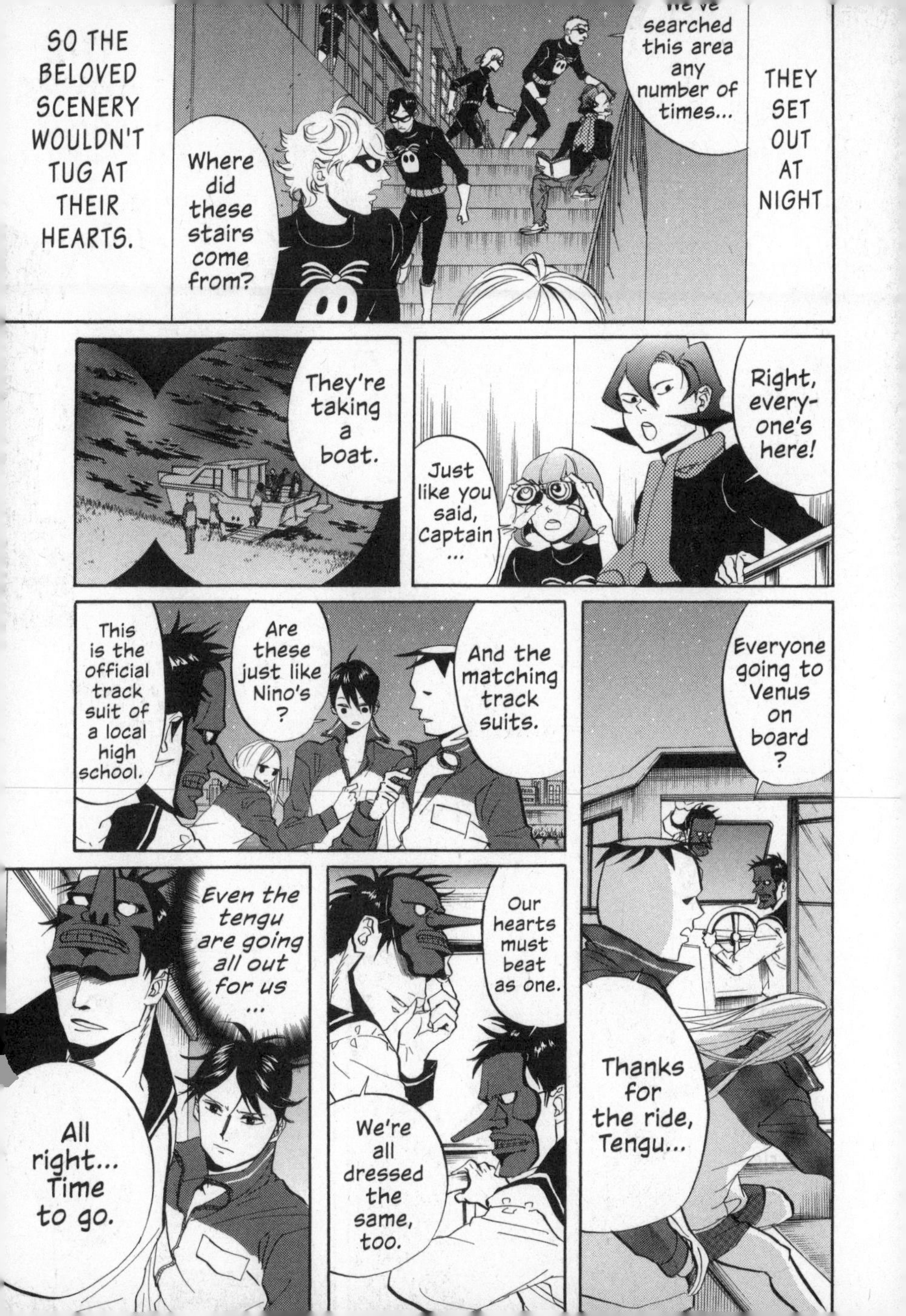
THEY SET OUT AT NIGHT
We've searched this area any number of times...
Where did these stairs come from?
SO THE BELOVED SCENERY WOULDN'T TUG AT THEIR HEARTS.
Right, every-one's here!
Just like you said, Captain...
They're taking a boat.
Everyone going to Venus on board?
Thanks for the ride, Tengu...
And the matching track suits.
Are these just like Nino's?
This is the official track suit of a local high school.
Our hearts must beat as one.
We're all dressed the same, too.
Even the tengu are going all out for us...
All right... Time to go.

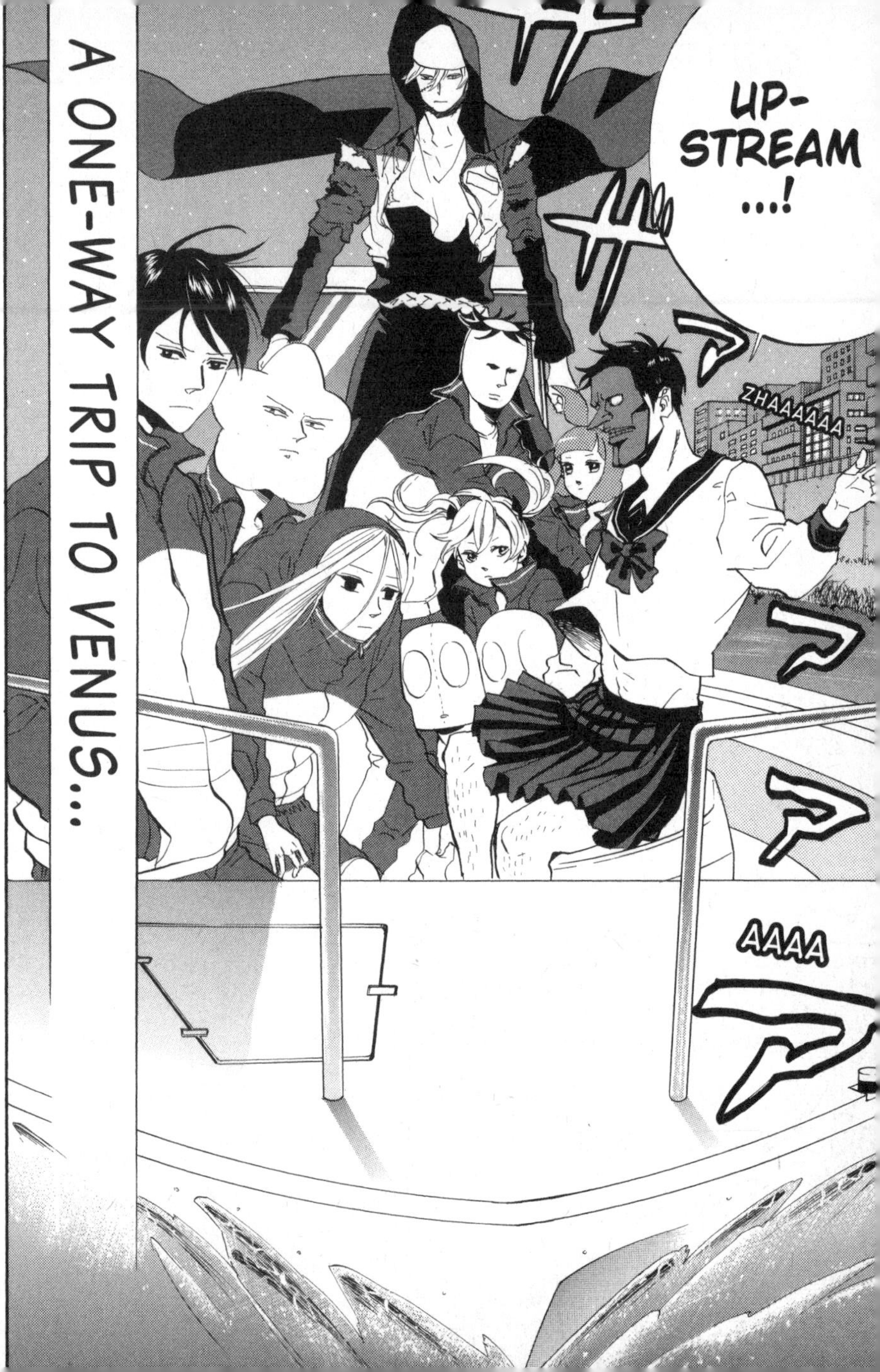
UP-STREAM ...!
ZHAAAAAAA
AAAA
A ONE-WAY TRIP TO VENUS...

Chapter 277: Genre

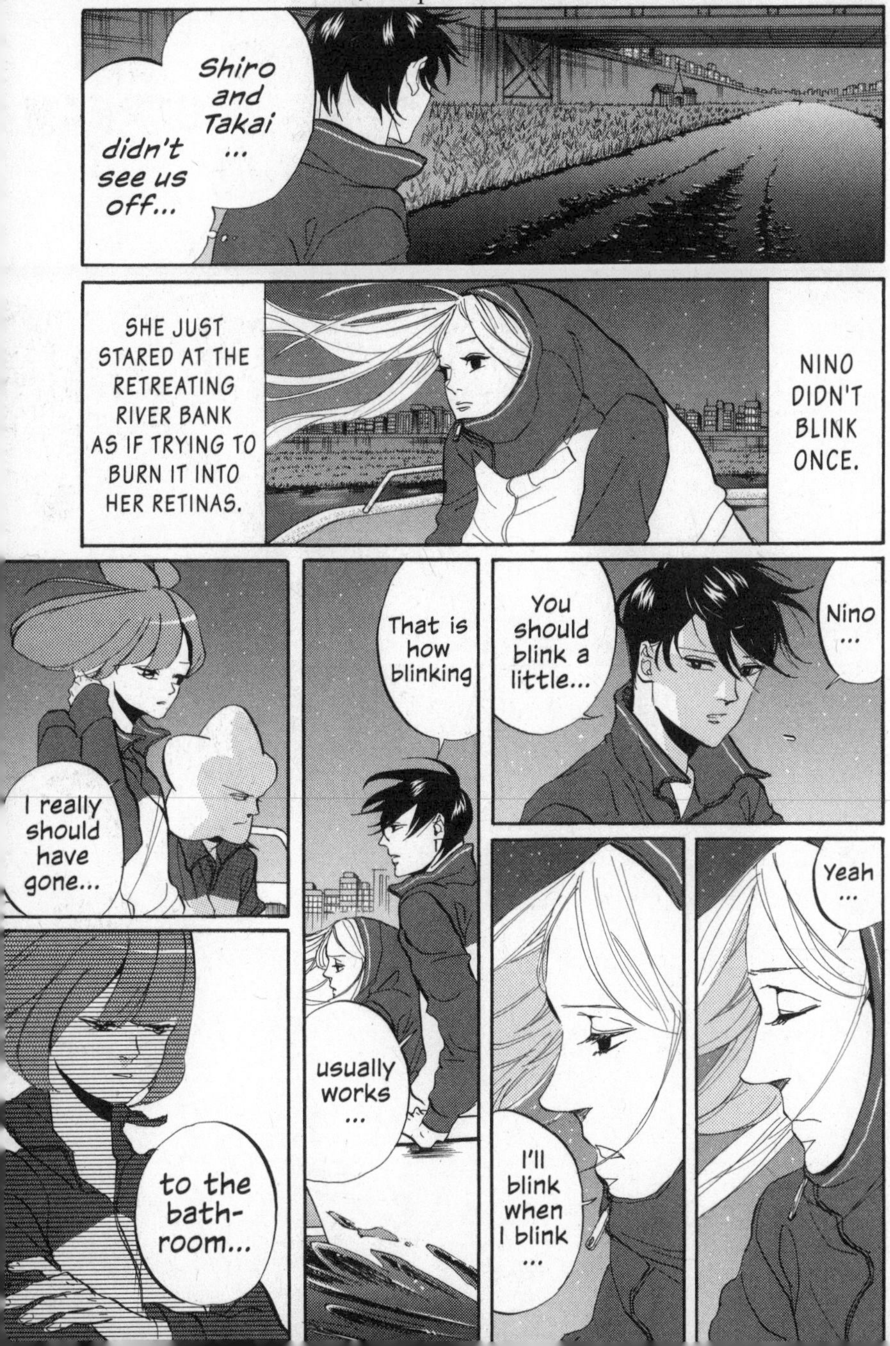
Shiro and Takai ... didn't see us off...
NINO DIDN'T BLINK ONCE.
SHE JUST STARED AT THE RETREATING RIVER BANK AS IF TRYING TO BURN IT INTO HER RETINAS.
Nino ...
You should blink a little...
Yeah ...
I'll blink when I blink ...
That is how blinking
usually works ...
I really should have gone...
to the bath-room...

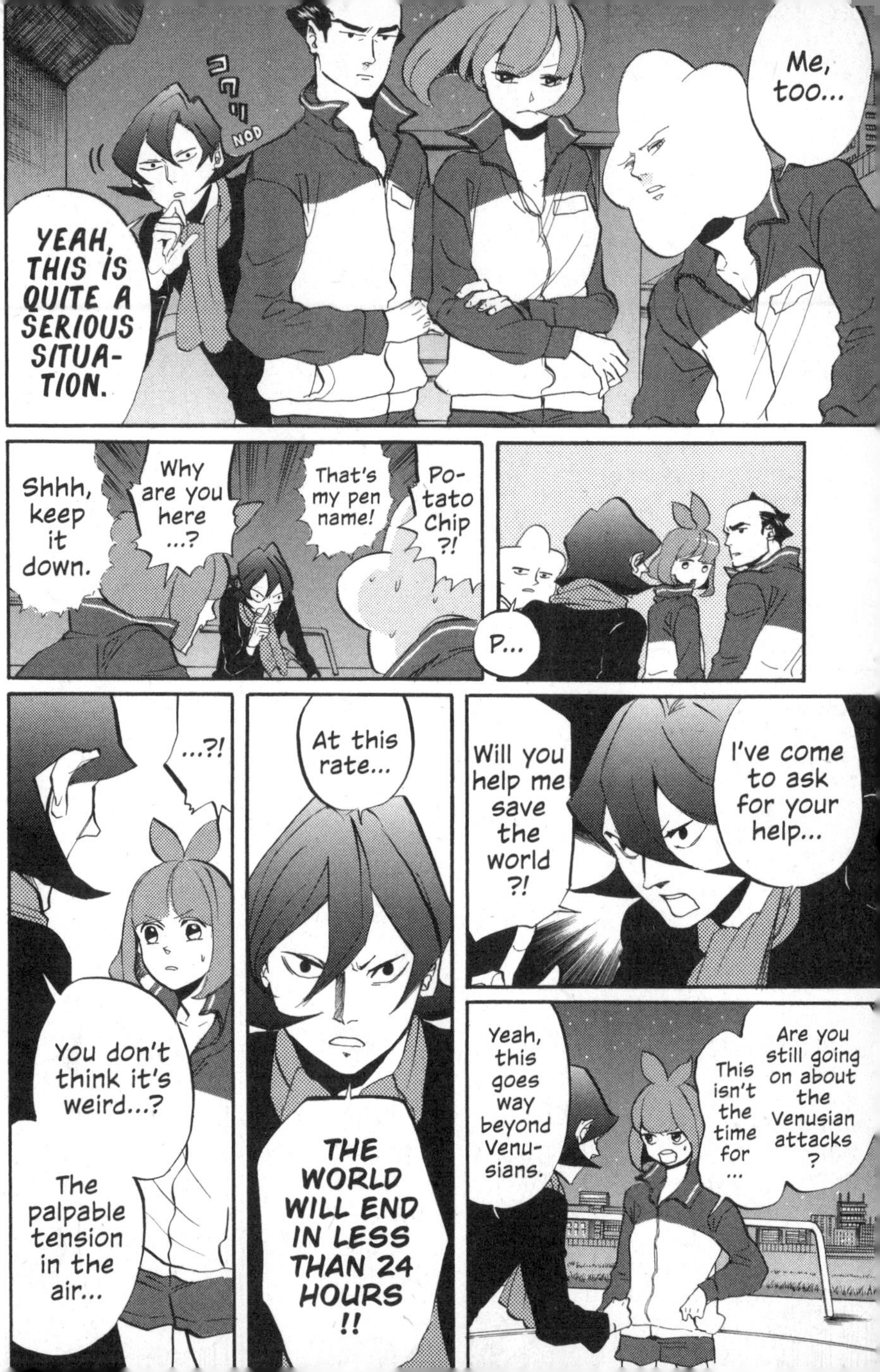
Me, too...
NOD
YEAH, THIS IS QUITE A SERIOUS SITUATION.
P...
Po-tato Chip?!
That's my pen name!
Why are you here...?
Shhh, keep it down.
I've come to ask for your help...
Will you help me save the world?!
Are you still going on about the Venusian attacks?
This isn't the time for...
Yeah, this goes way beyond Venusians.
At this rate...
THE WORLD WILL END IN LESS THAN 24 HOURS!!
...?!
You don't think it's weird...?
The palpable tension in the air...

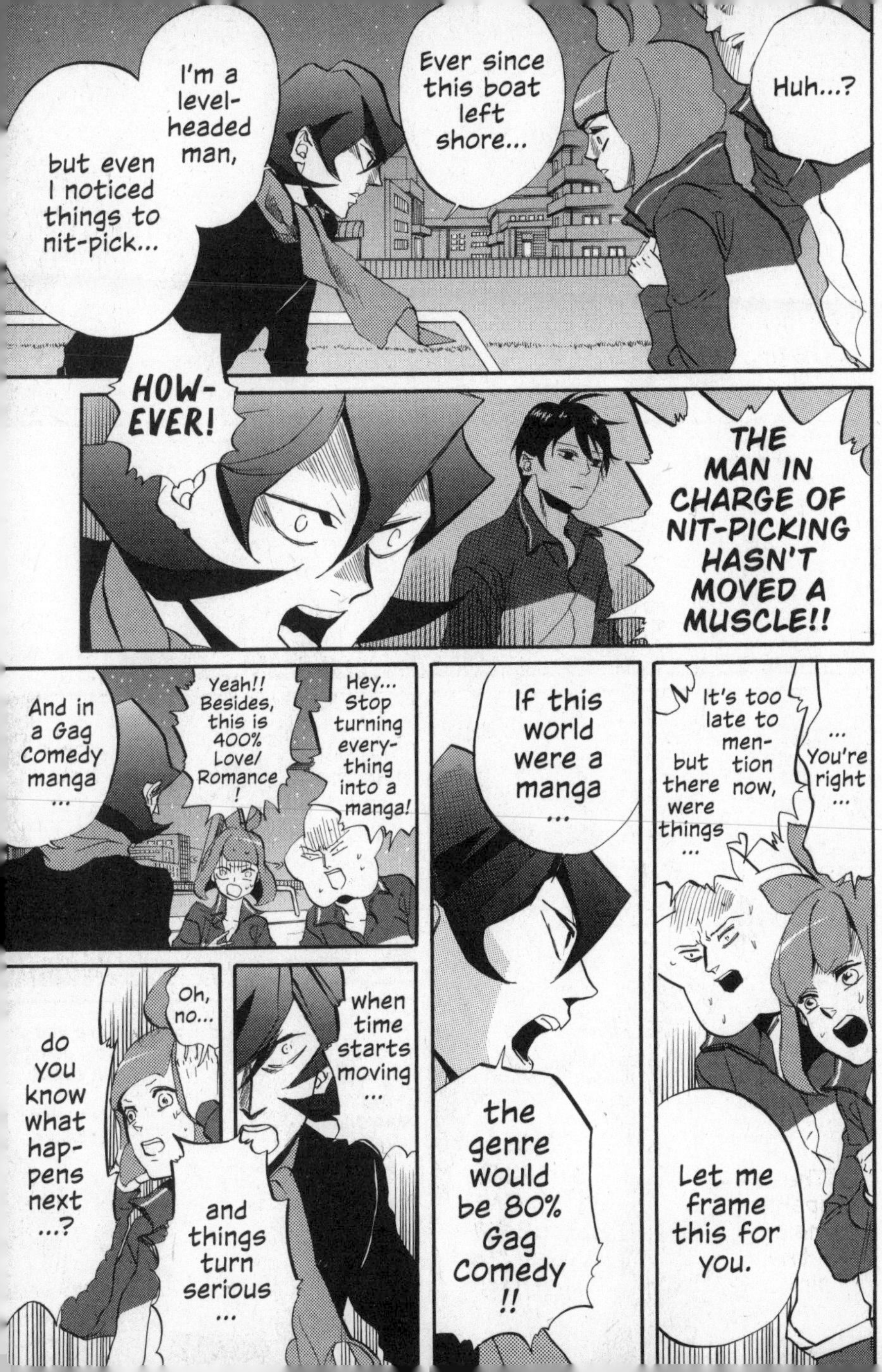
Huh...?
Ever since this boat left shore...
I'm a level-headed man,
but even I noticed things to nit-pick...
HOW-EVER!
THE MAN IN CHARGE OF NIT-PICKING HASN'T MOVED A MUSCLE!!
... You're right ...
It's too late to mention now, but there were things ...
Let me frame this for you.
If this world were a manga ...
the genre would be 80% Gag Comedy !!
Hey... Stop turning every-thing into a manga!
Yeah!! Besides, this is 400% Love/ Romance !
And in a Gag Comedy manga ...
when time starts moving ...
and things turn serious ...
Oh, no...
do you know what hap-pens next ...?

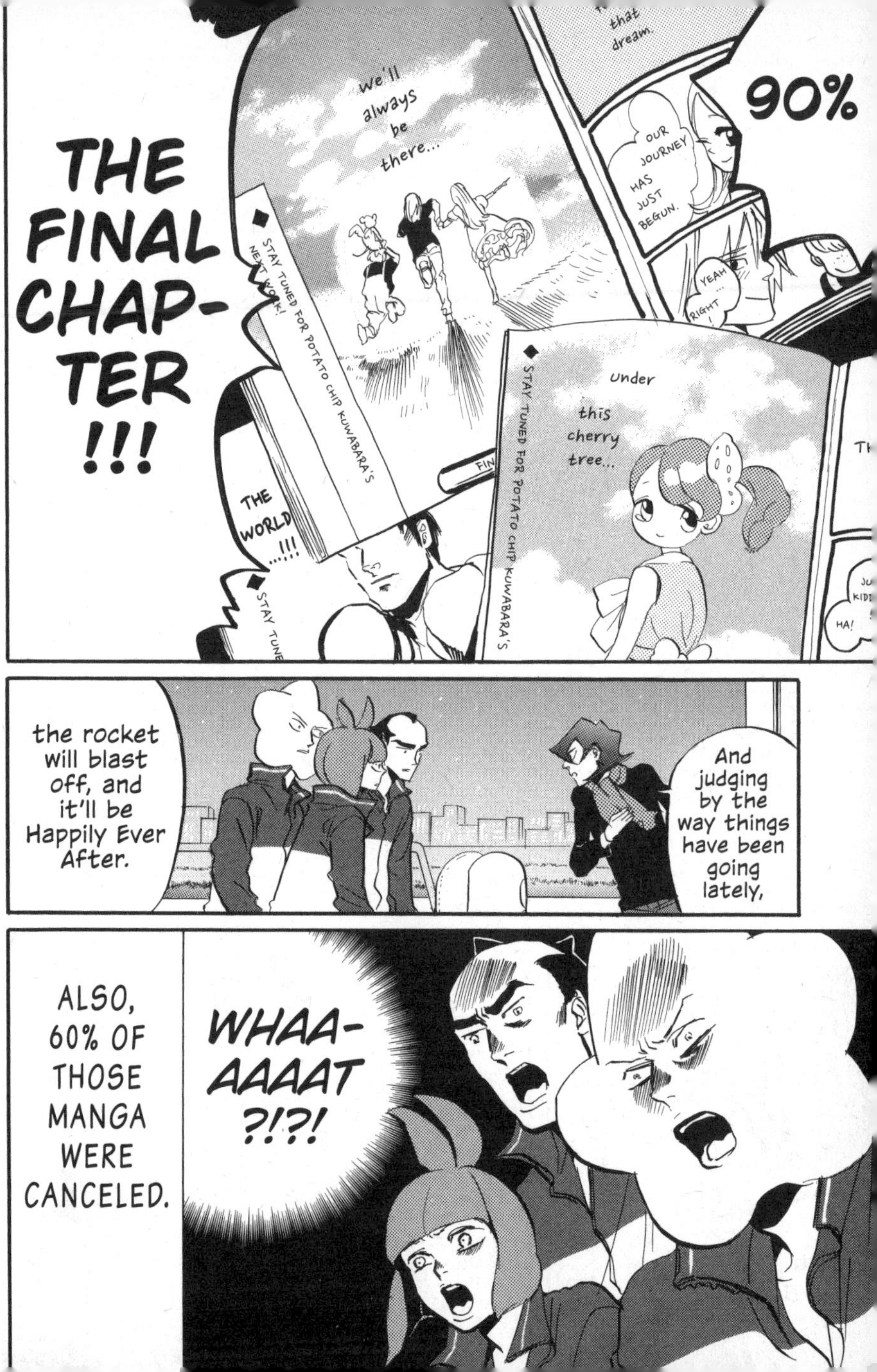

90%
that dream.
OUR JOURNEY HAS JUST BEGUN.
YEAH RIGHT...
we'll always be there...
STAY TUNED FOR POTATO CHIP KUWABARA'S NEXT WORK!
under this cherry tree...
STAY TUNED FOR POTATO CHIP KUWABARA'S
HA!
THE WORLD ...!!!
STAY TUNE
THE FINAL CHAPTER!!!
And judging by the way things have been going lately,
the rocket will blast off, and it'll be Happily Ever After.
WHAA-AAAAT?!?!
ALSO, 60% OF THOSE MANGA WERE CANCELED.

Chapter 278: Main Character

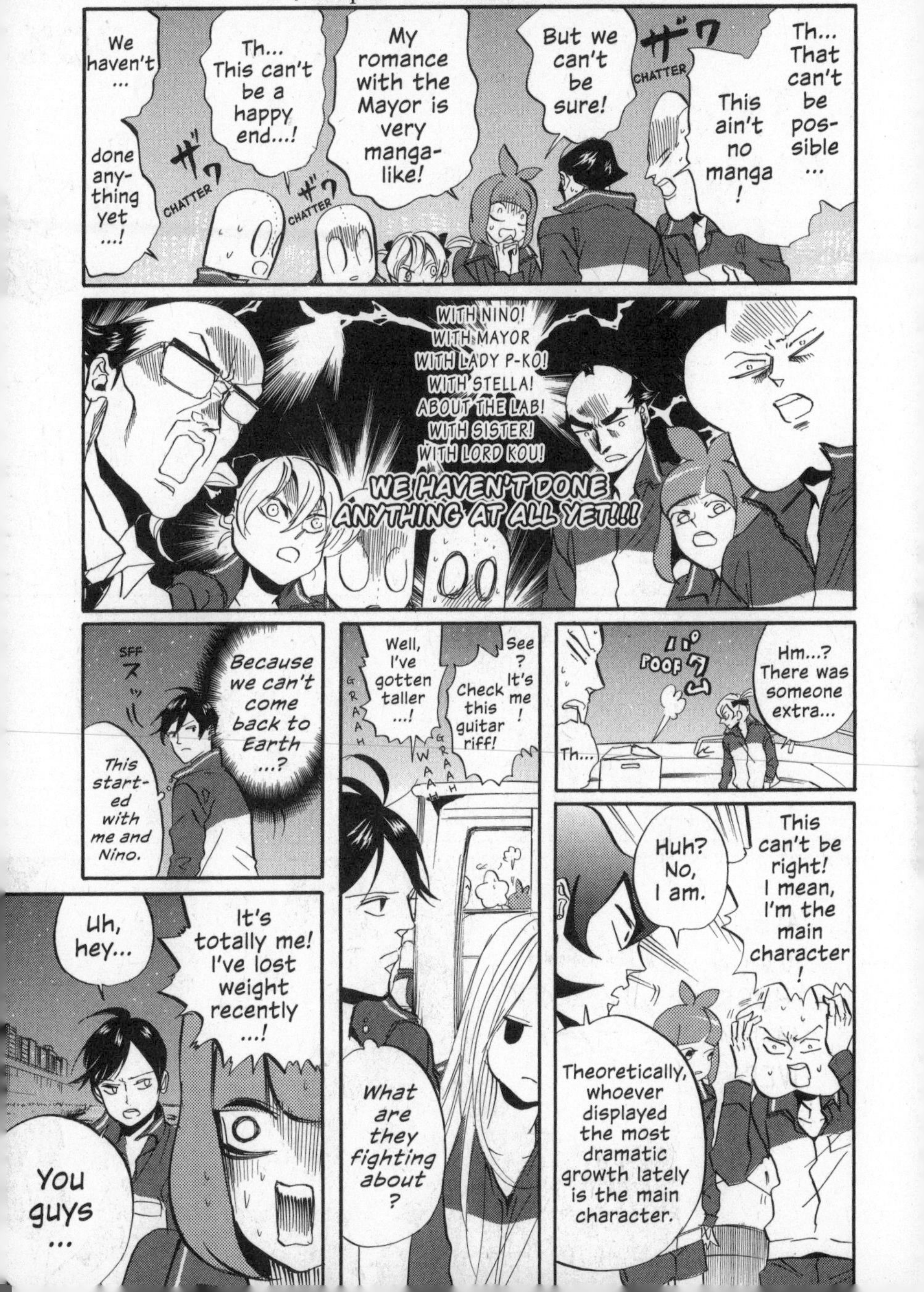

Th... That can't be possible...
This ain't no manga!
CHATTER
But we can't be sure!
My romance with the Mayor is very manga-like!
Th... This can't be a happy end...!
We haven't... done anything yet...!
CHATTER
CHATTER
WITH NINO!
WITH MAYOR
WITH LADY P-KO!
WITH STELLA!
ABOUT THE LAB!
WITH SISTER!
WITH LORD KOU!
WE HAVEN'T DONE ANYTHING AT ALL YET!!!
Hm...? There was someone extra...
POOF
Th...
This can't be right! I mean, I'm the main character!
Huh? No, I am.
Theoretically, whoever displayed the most dramatic growth lately is the main character.
See? It's me!
Check this guitar riff!
Well, I've gotten taller...!
GRAAAH
WAAAH
GRAAAH
What are they fighting about?
SFF
Because we can't come back to Earth...?
This started with me and Nino.
It's totally me! I've lost weight recently...!
Uh, hey...
You guys...

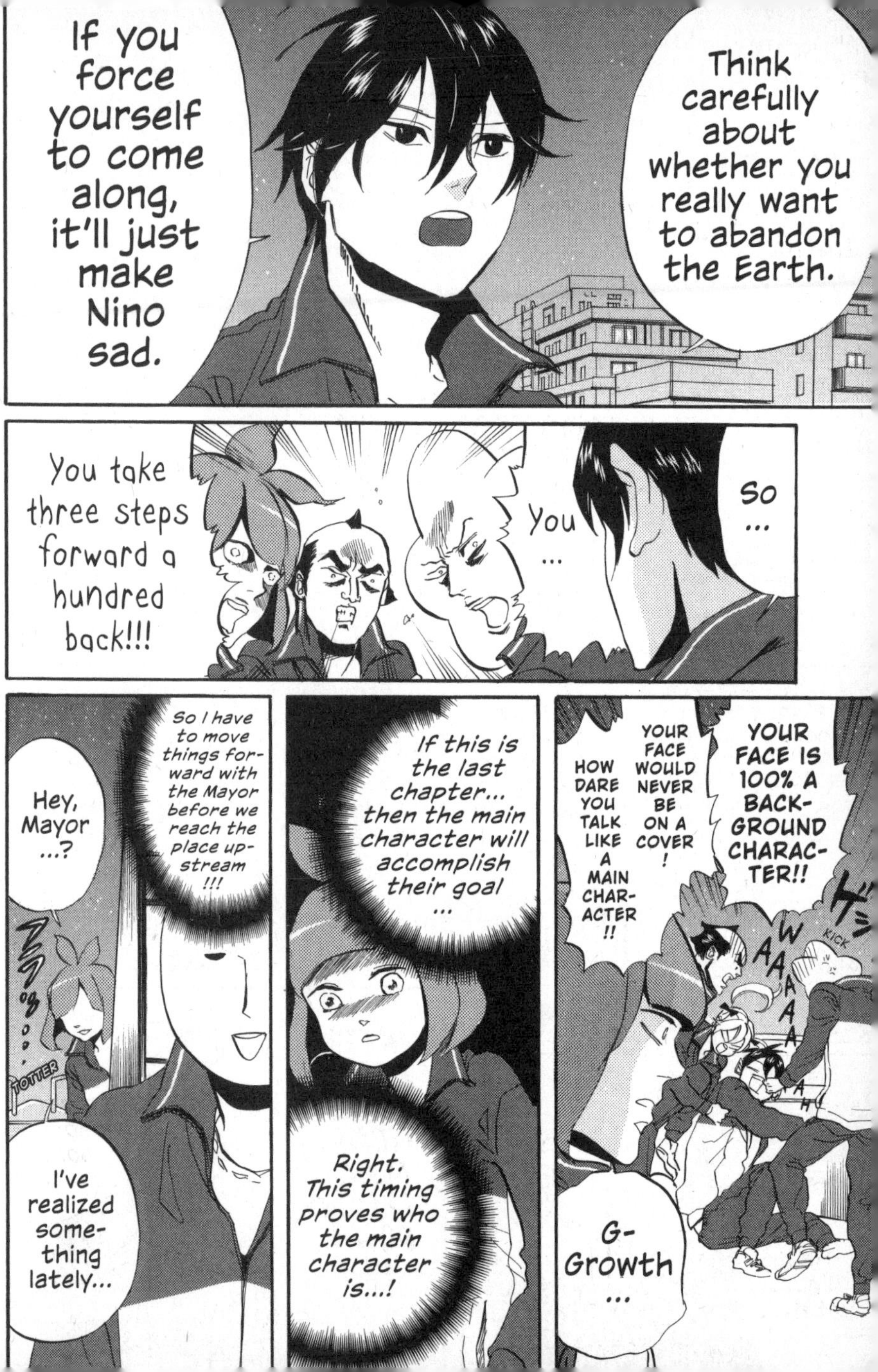
Think carefully about whether you really want to abandon the Earth.
If you force yourself to come along, it'll just make Nino sad.
So ...
You ...
You take three steps forward a hundred back!!!
YOUR FACE IS 100% A BACK-GROUND CHARAC-TER!!
YOUR FACE WOULD NEVER BE ON A COVER!
HOW DARE YOU TALK LIKE A MAIN CHAR-ACTER!!
KICK
WAAAAAAH
G-Growth ...
If this is the last chapter... then the main character will accomplish their goal ...
Right. This timing proves who the main character is...!
So I have to move things for-ward with the Mayor before we reach the place up-stream !!!
Hey, Mayor ...?
TOTTER
I've realized some-thing lately...

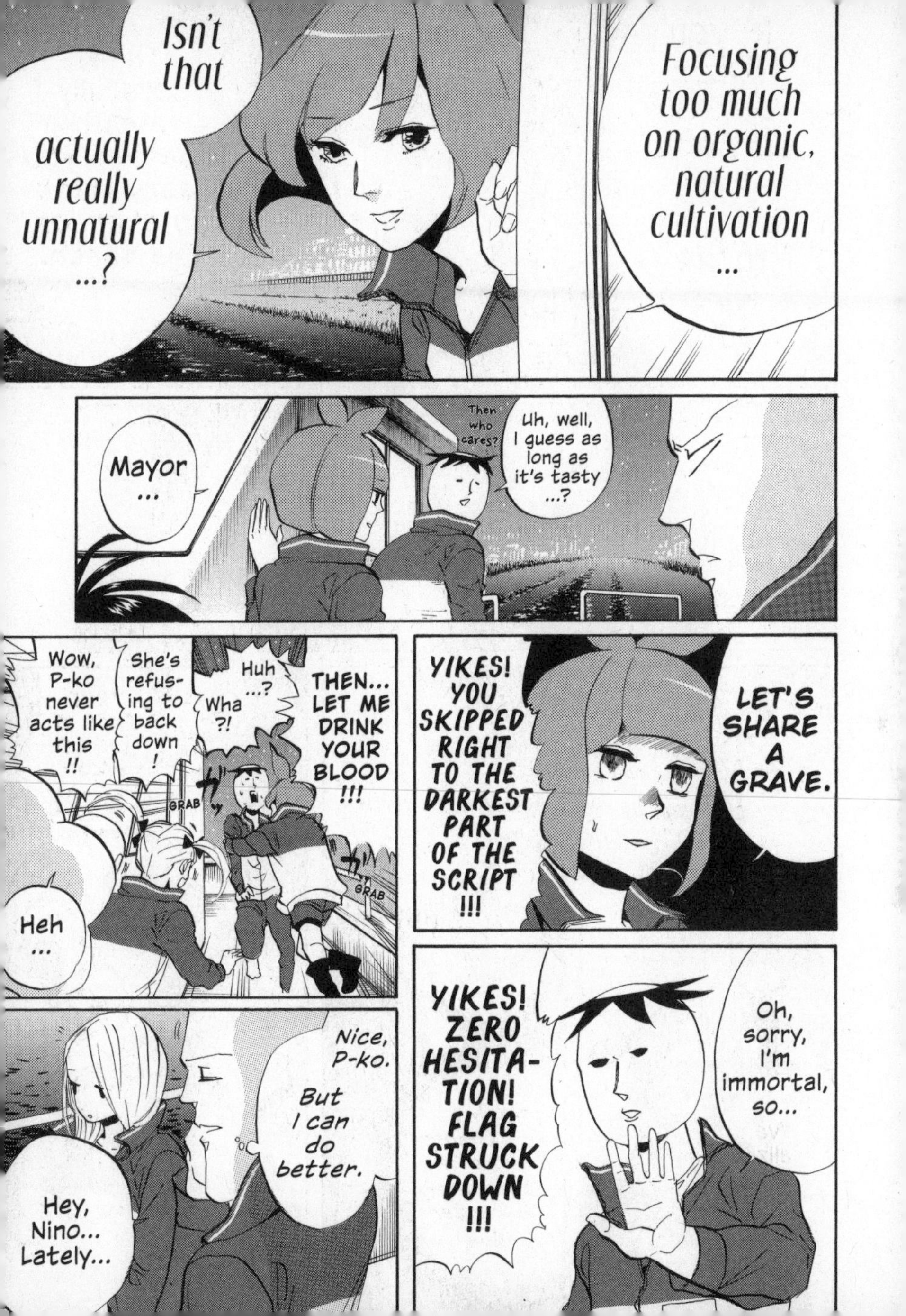

Focusing too much on organic, natural cultivation...
Isn't that actually really unnatural...?
Uh, well, I guess as long as it's tasty...?
Then who cares?
Mayor...
LET'S SHARE A GRAVE.
YIKES! YOU SKIPPED RIGHT TO THE DARKEST PART OF THE SCRIPT!!!
THEN... LET ME DRINK YOUR BLOOD!!!
Huh...?
Wha?!
She's refusing to back down!
Wow, P-ko never acts like this!!
GRAB
GRAB
Heh...
Oh, sorry, I'm immortal, so...
YIKES! ZERO HESITATION! FLAG STRUCK DOWN!!!
Nice, P-ko.
But I can do better.
Hey, Nino... Lately...

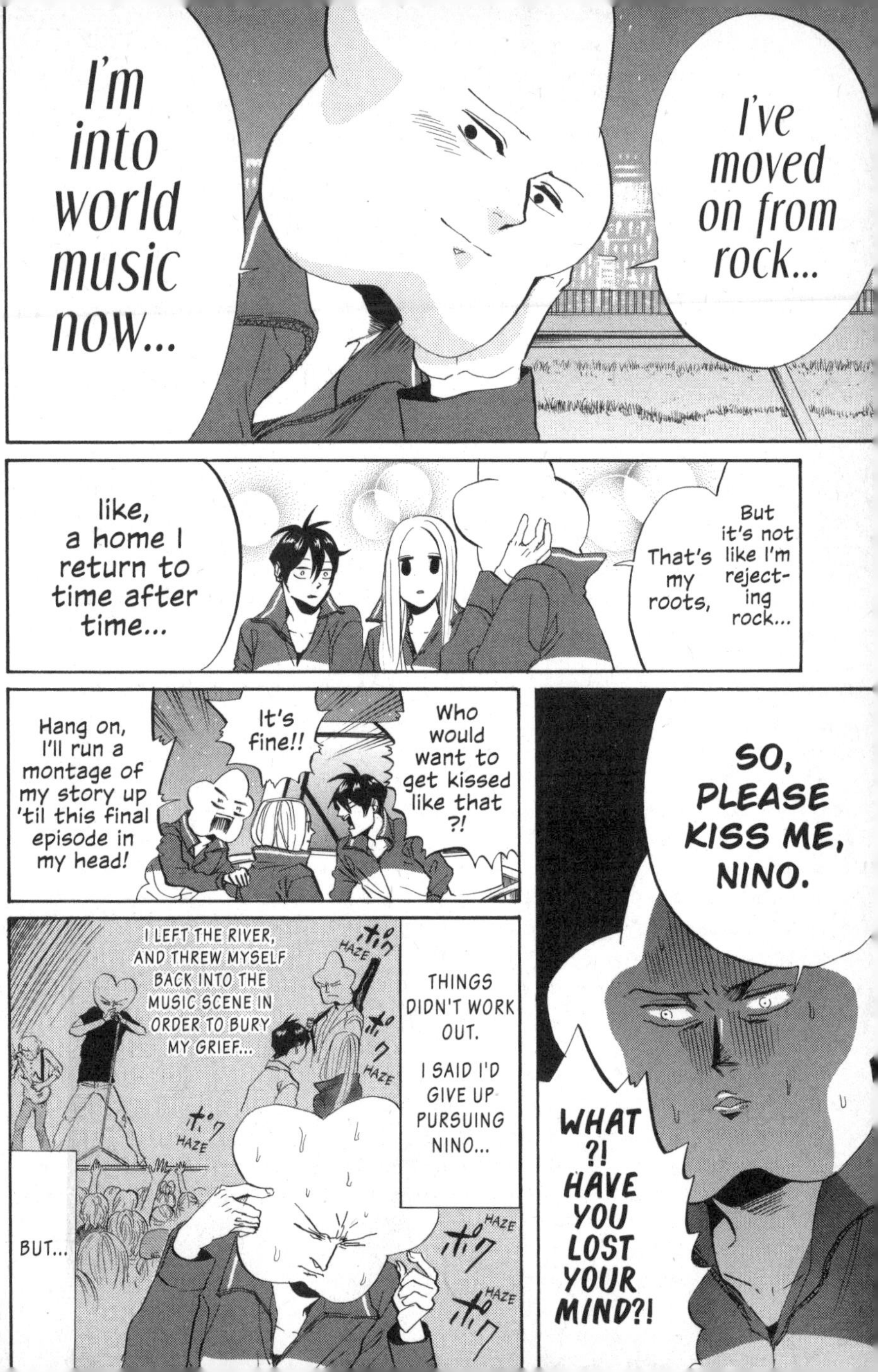
I've moved on from rock...
I'm into world music now...
But it's not like I'm rejecting rock...
That's my roots,
like, a home I return to time after time...
SO, PLEASE KISS ME, NINO.
WHAT?! HAVE YOU LOST YOUR MIND?!
Who would want to get kissed like that?!
It's fine!!
Hang on, I'll run a montage of my story up 'til this final episode in my head!
I LEFT THE RIVER, AND THREW MYSELF BACK INTO THE MUSIC SCENE IN ORDER TO BURY MY GRIEF...
THINGS DIDN'T WORK OUT.
I SAID I'D GIVE UP PURSUING NINO...
BUT...
HAZE
HAZE
HAZE
HAZE
HAZE

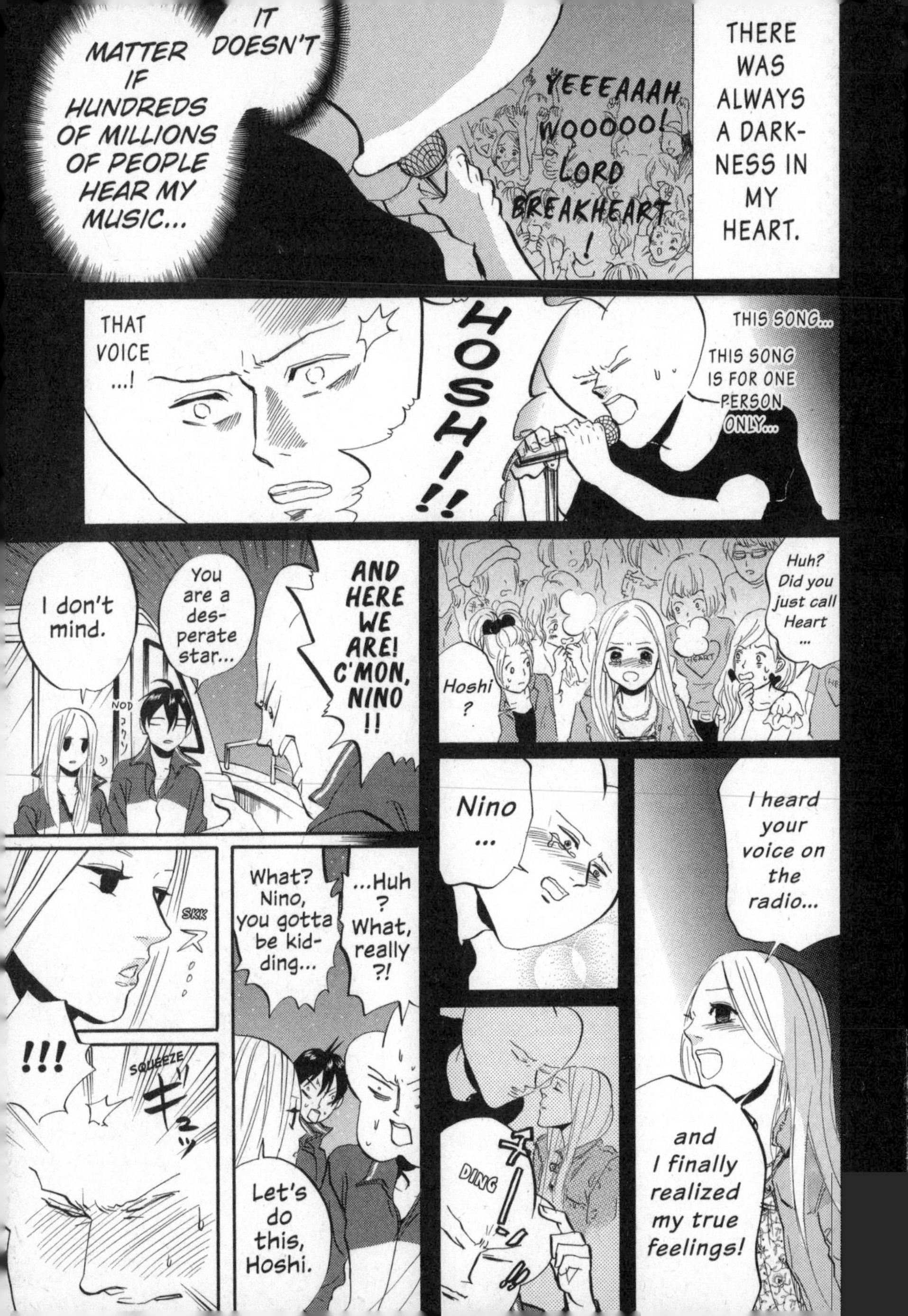
THERE WAS ALWAYS A DARKNESS IN MY HEART.
YEEEAAAH WOOOOO! LORD BREAKHEART!
IT DOESN'T MATTER IF HUNDREDS OF MILLIONS OF PEOPLE HEAR MY MUSIC...
THIS SONG...
THIS SONG IS FOR ONE PERSON ONLY...
HOSHI!!
THAT VOICE ...!
Huh? Did you just call Heart ...
Hoshi ?
AND HERE WE ARE! C'MON, NINO!!
You are a desperate star...
NOD
I don't mind.
I heard your voice on the radio...
and I finally realized my true feelings!
Nino ...
DING
...Huh? What, really?!
What? Nino, you gotta be kidding...
Let's do this, Hoshi.
SKK
!!!
SQUEEZE

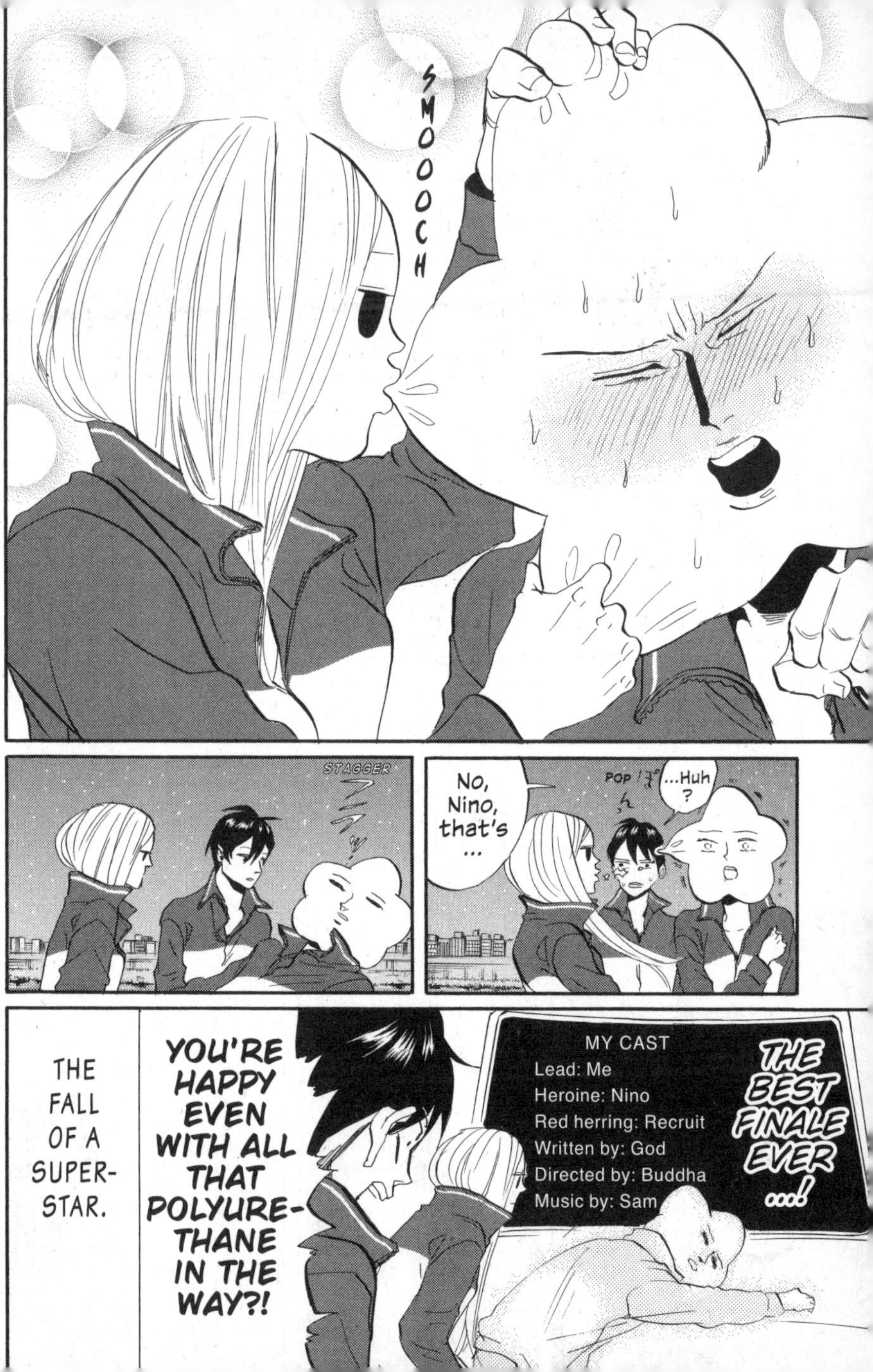
SMOOOOCH
...Huh?
POP
No, Nino, that's...
STAGGER
THE BEST FINALE EVER...!
MY CAST
Lead: Me
Heroine: Nino
Red herring: Recruit
Written by: God
Directed by: Buddha
Music by: Sam
YOU'RE HAPPY EVEN WITH ALL THAT POLYURETHANE IN THE WAY?!
THE FALL OF A SUPERSTAR.

Chapter 279: Story Help

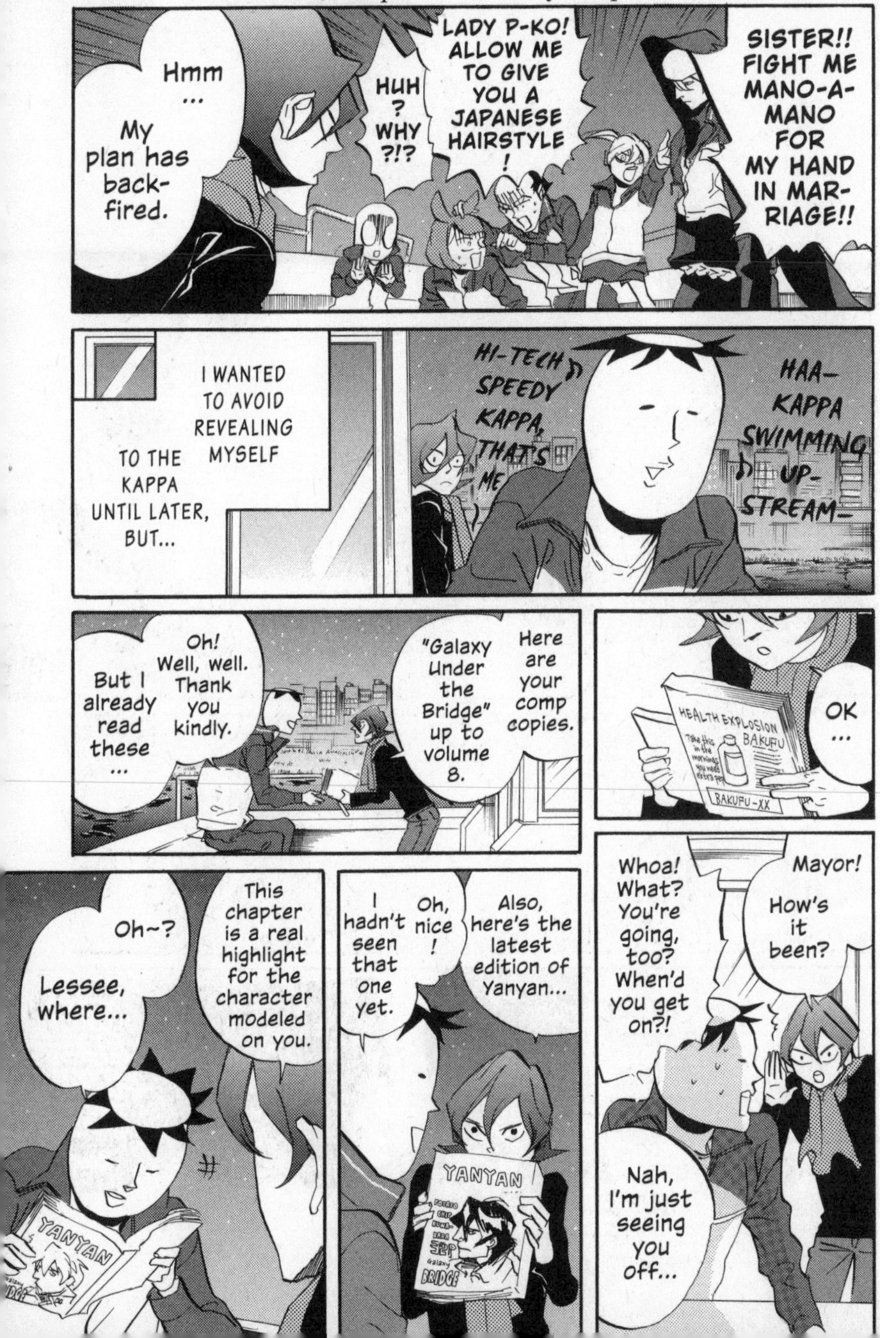
SISTER!! FIGHT ME MANO-A-MANO FOR MY HAND IN MARRIAGE!!
LADY P-KO! ALLOW ME TO GIVE YOU A JAPANESE HAIRSTYLE!
HUH? WHY?!?
Hmm... My plan has backfired.
HAA-KAPPA SWIMMING UP-STREAM-
HI-TECH SPEEDY KAPPA, THAT'S ME
I WANTED TO AVOID REVEALING MYSELF
TO THE KAPPA UNTIL LATER, BUT...
HEALTH EXPLOSION BAKUFU
BAKUFU-XX
OK...
Here are your comp copies.
"Galaxy Under the Bridge" up to volume 8.
Oh! Well, well. Thank you kindly.
But I already read these...
Mayor! How's it been?
Whoa! What? You're going, too? When'd you get on?!
Nah, I'm just seeing you off...
Also, here's the latest edition of Yanyan...
Oh, nice!
I hadn't seen that one yet.
YANYAN
This chapter is a real highlight for the character modeled on you.
Oh~?
Lessee, where...
YANYAN

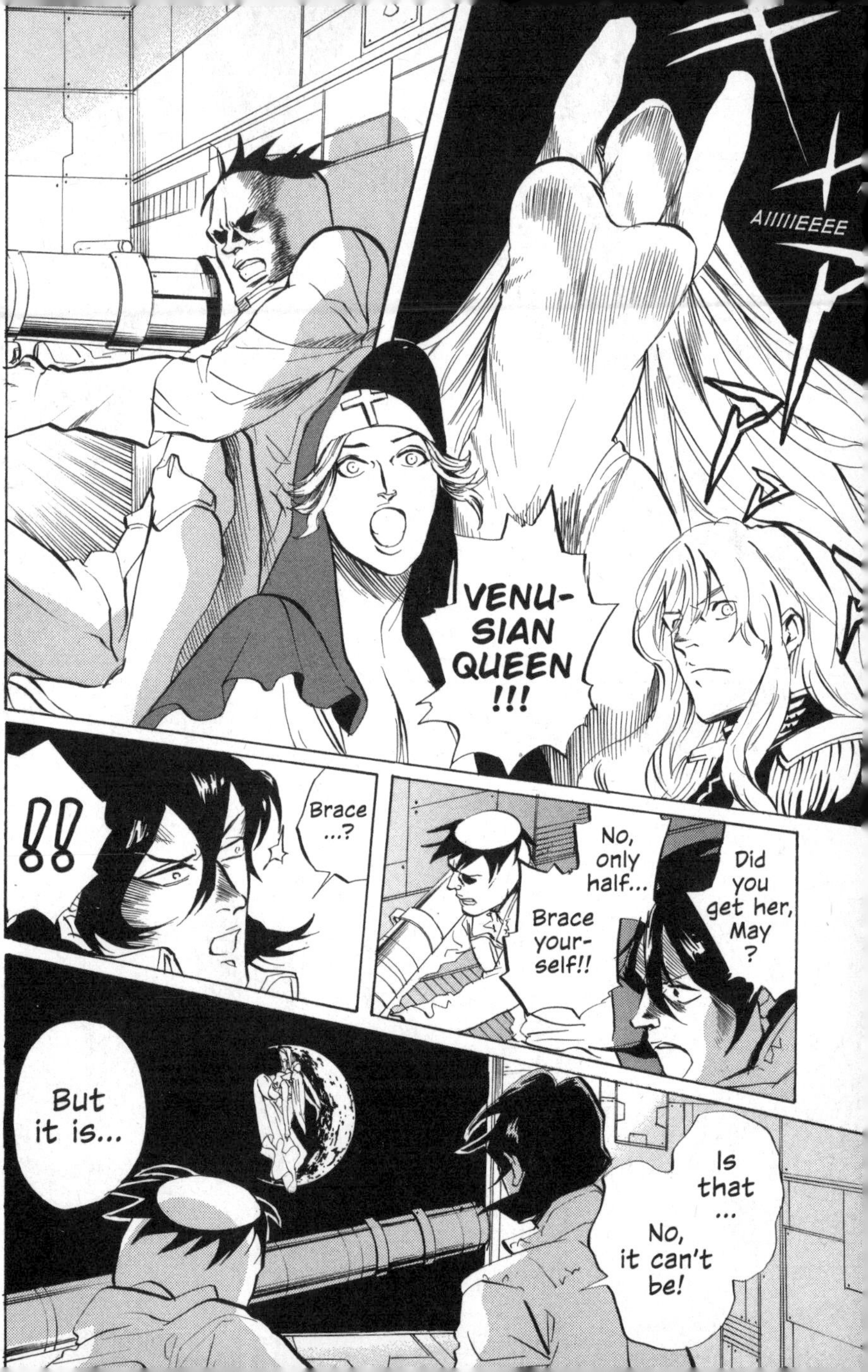
AIIIIEEEE
VENU-SIAN QUEEN!!!
Did you get her, May?
No, only half...
Brace yourself!!
Brace ...?
!!
Is that ...
No, it can't be!
But it is...

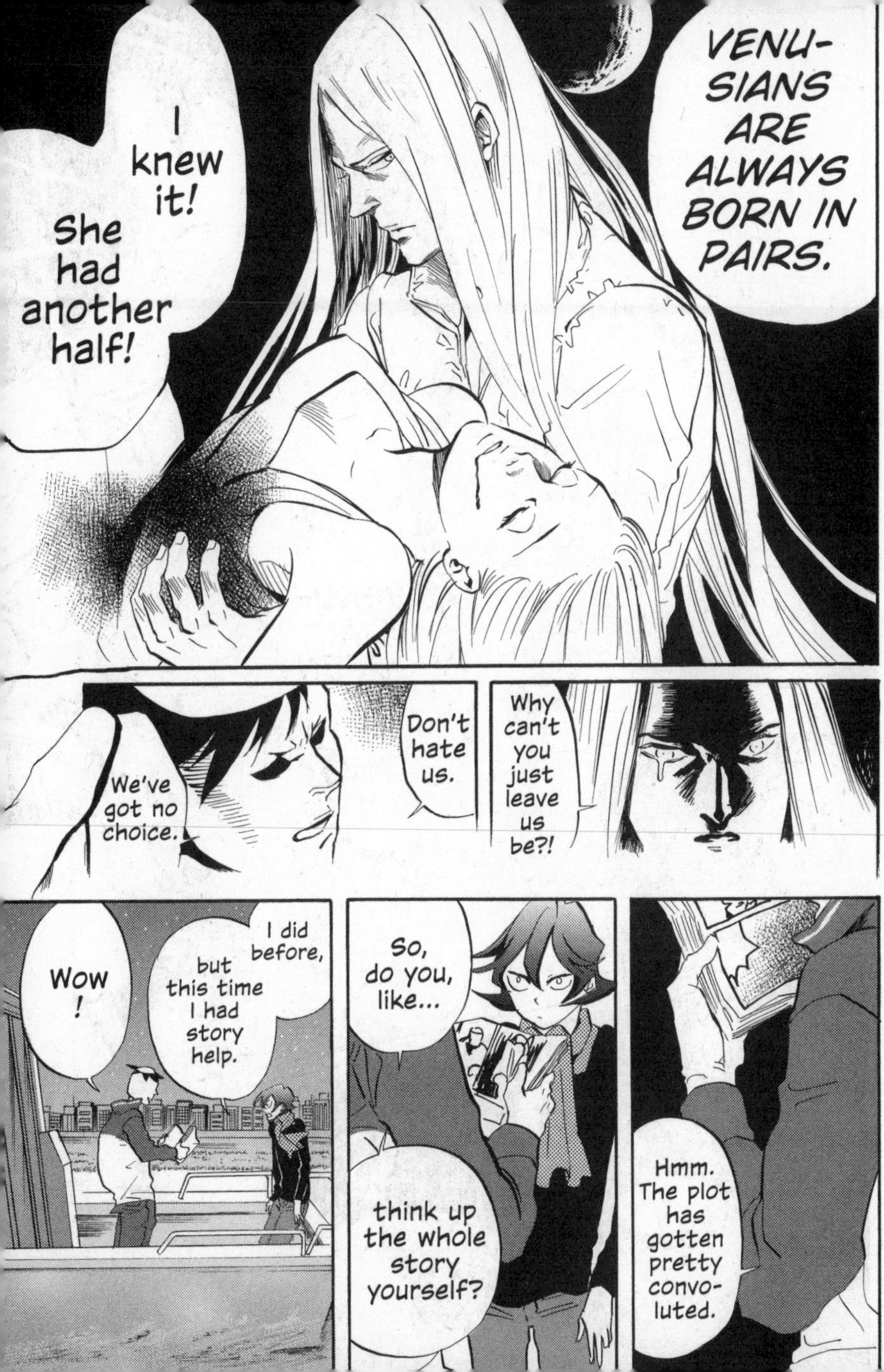
VENU-SIANS ARE ALWAYS BORN IN PAIRS.
I knew it!
She had another half!
Why can't you just leave us be?!
Don't hate us.
We've got no choice.
Hmm. The plot has gotten pretty convo-luted.
So, do you, like...
think up the whole story yourself?
I did before, but this time I had story help.
Wow!

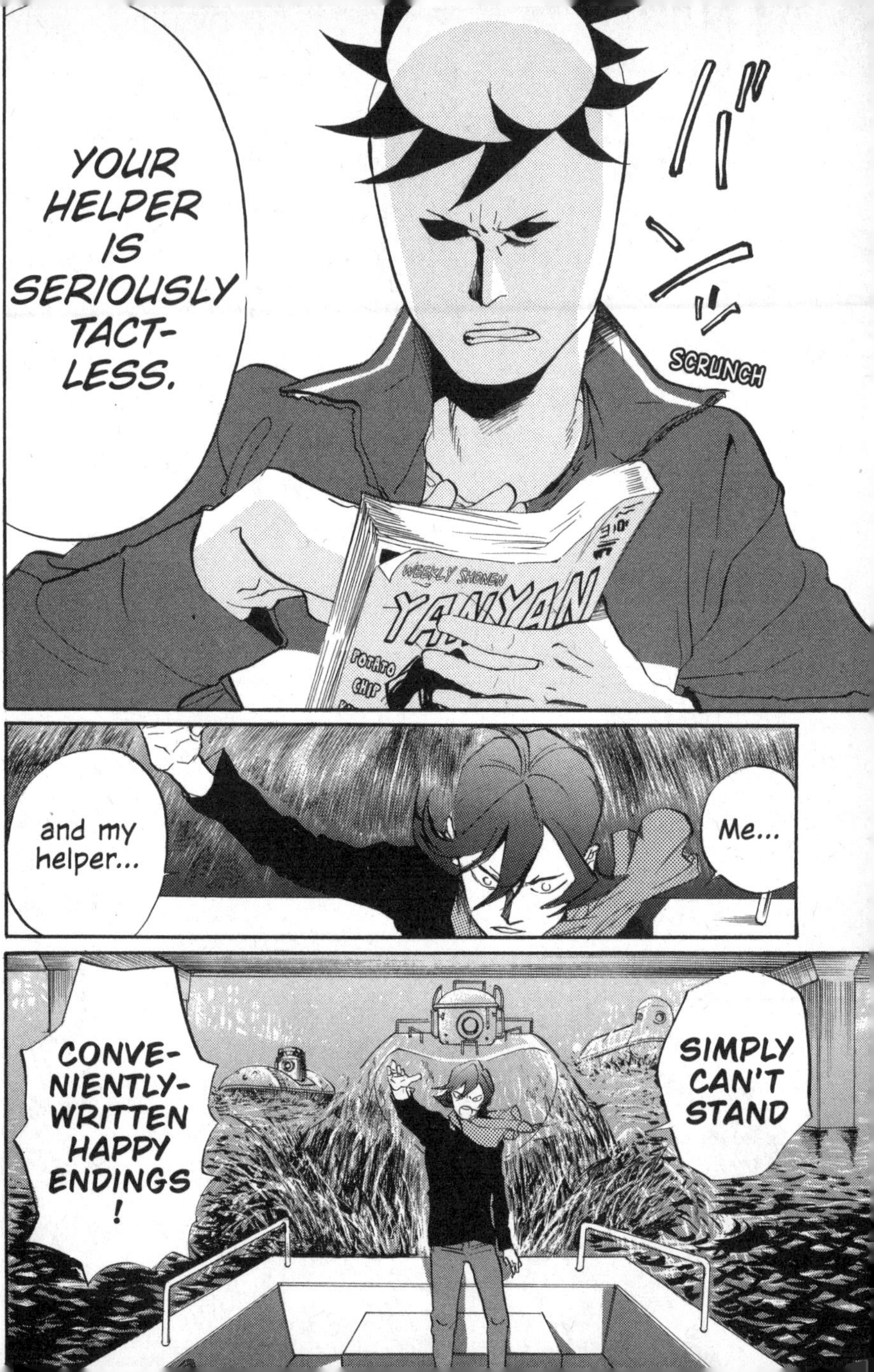
YOUR HELPER IS SERIOUSLY TACT-LESS.
SCRUNCH
WEEKLY SHONEN
YANYAN
POTATO CHIP
Me...
and my helper...
SIMPLY CAN'T STAND
CONVE-NIENTLY-WRITTEN HAPPY ENDINGS!

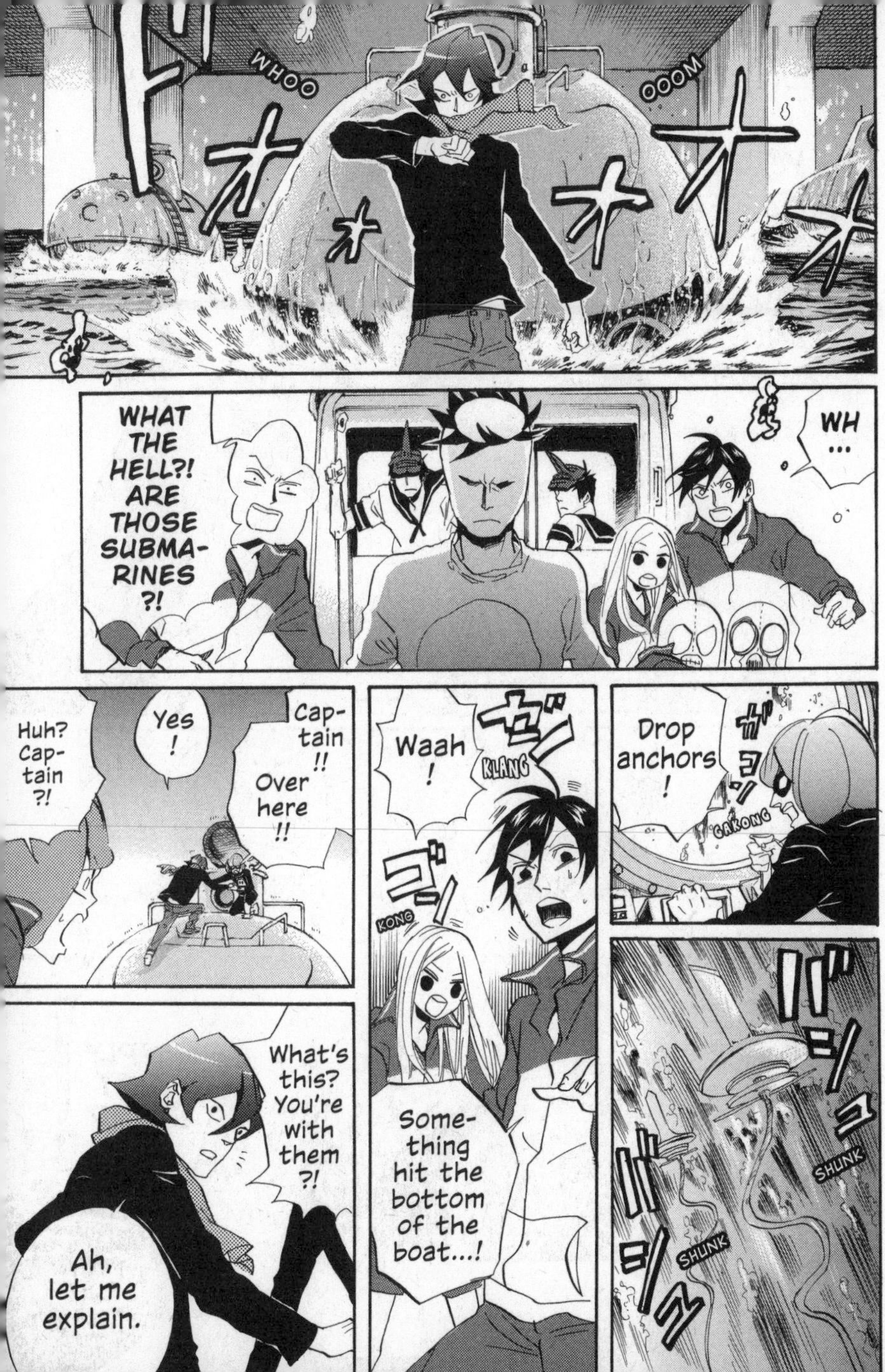
WHOO
OOOM
WH...
WHAT THE HELL?! ARE THOSE SUBMARINES?!
Drop anchors!
GAKONG
SHUNK
SHUNK
Waah!
KLANG
KONG
Something hit the bottom of the boat...!
Captain!! Over here!!
Yes!
Huh? Captain?!
What's this? You're with them?!
Ah, let me explain.

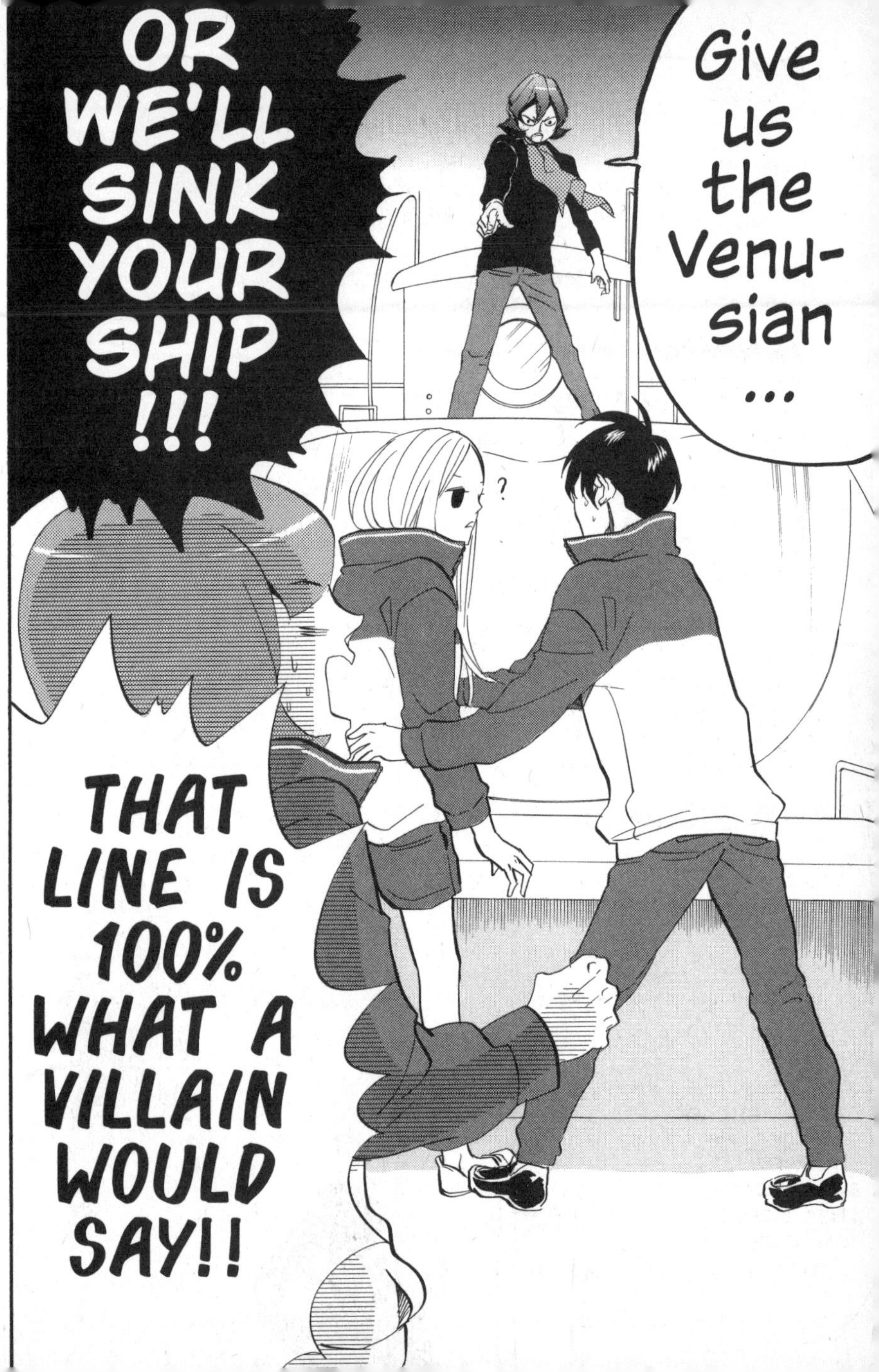
Give us the Venu-sian ...
OR WE'LL SINK YOUR SHIP !!!
THAT LINE IS 100% WHAT A VILLAIN WOULD SAY!!

Chapter 280: Countdown

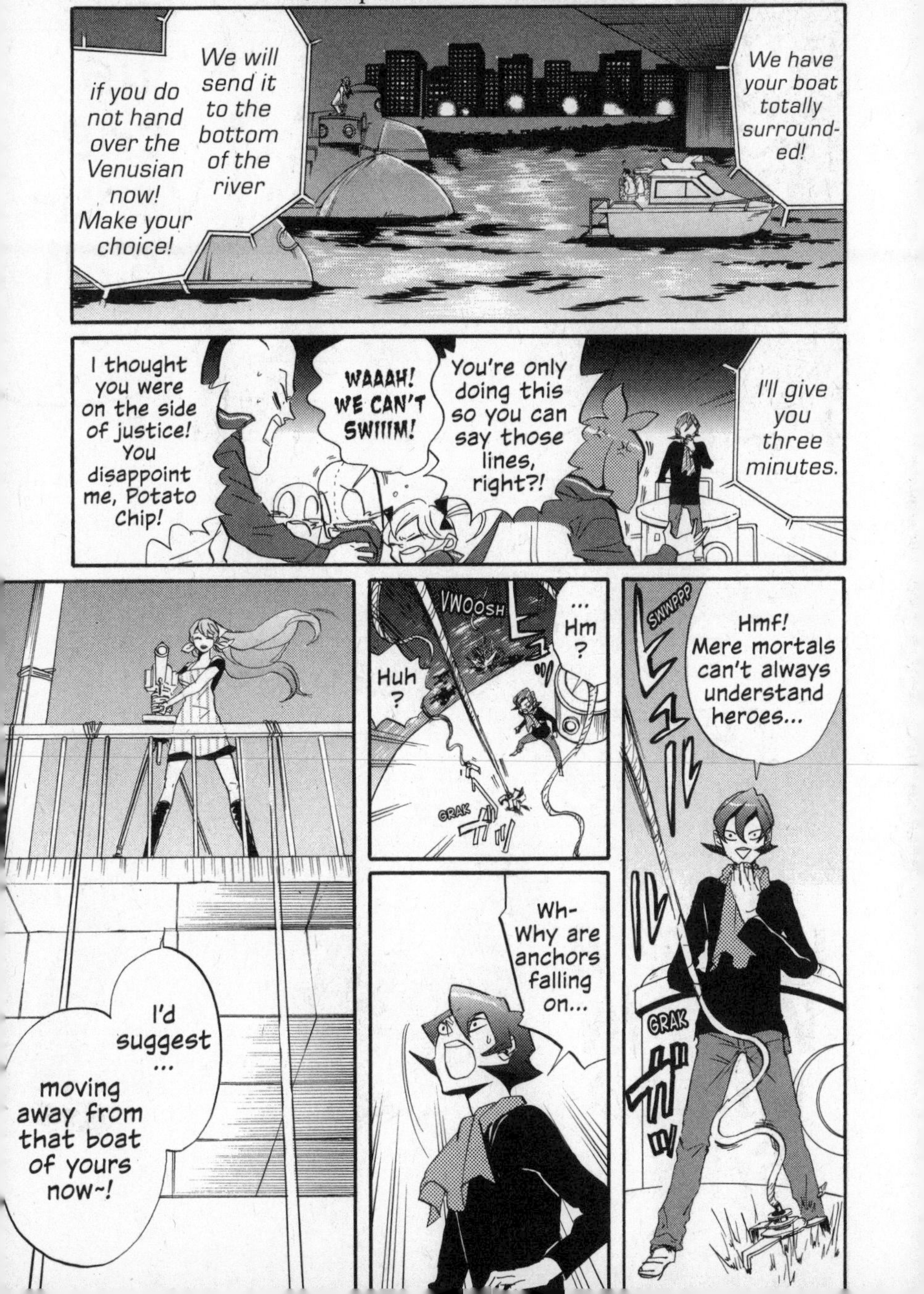

We have your boat totally surround-ed!
We will send it to the bottom of the river
if you do not hand over the Venusian now! Make your choice!
I'll give you three minutes.
You're only doing this so you can say those lines, right?!
WAAAH! WE CAN'T SWIIIM!
I thought you were on the side of justice! You disappoint me, Potato Chip!
SWNPPP
Hmf! Mere mortals can't always understand heroes...
GRAK
... Hm?
VWOOSH
Huh?
GRAK
Wh- Why are anchors falling on...
I'd suggest ... moving away from that boat of yours now~!

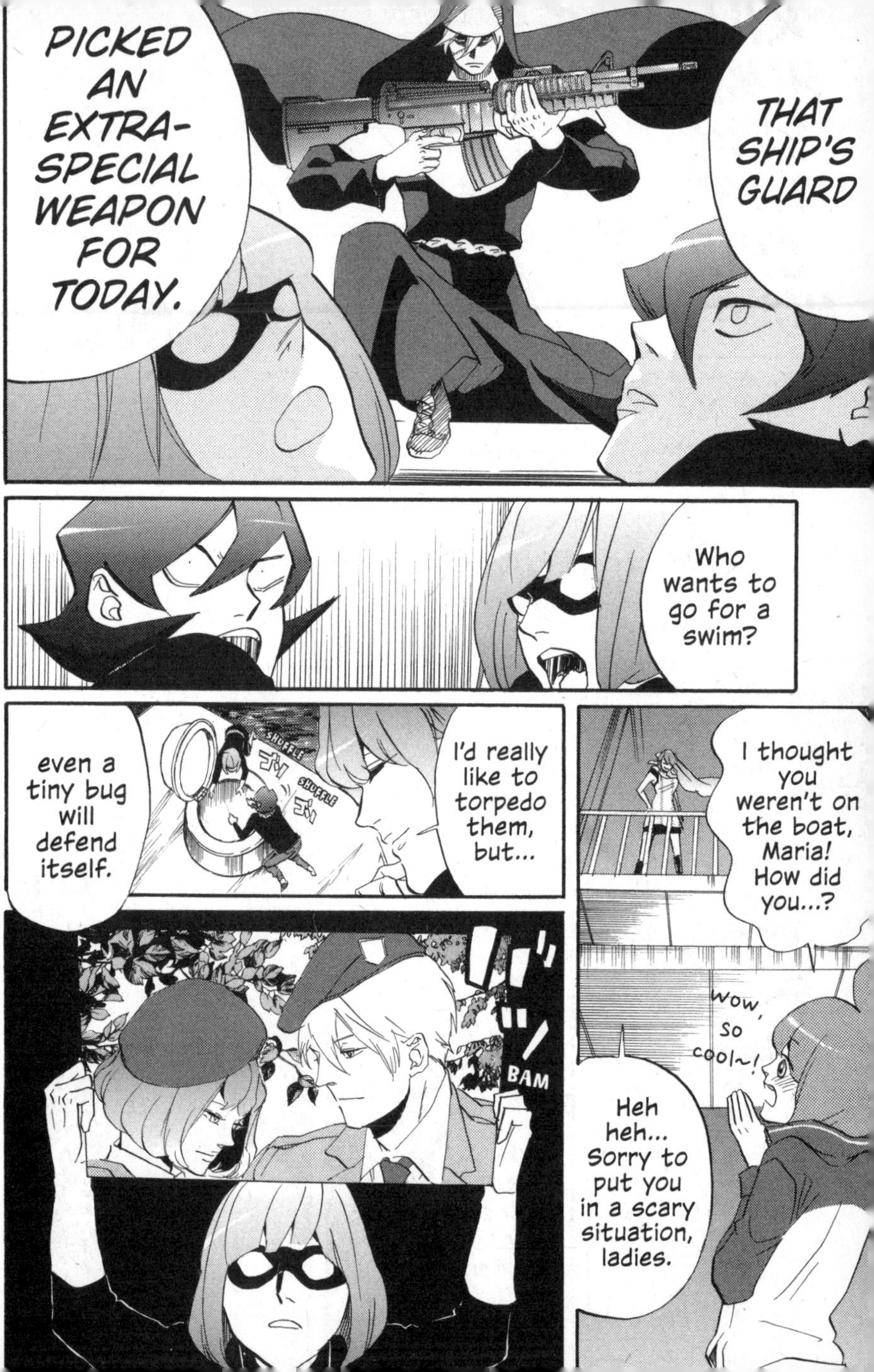
THAT SHIP'S GUARD
PICKED AN EXTRA-SPECIAL WEAPON FOR TODAY.
Who wants to go for a swim?
I thought you weren't on the boat, Maria! How did you...?
I'd really like to torpedo them, but...
SHUFFLE
SHUFFLE
even a tiny bug will defend itself.
Wow, so cool~!
Heh heh... Sorry to put you in a scary situation, ladies.
BAM

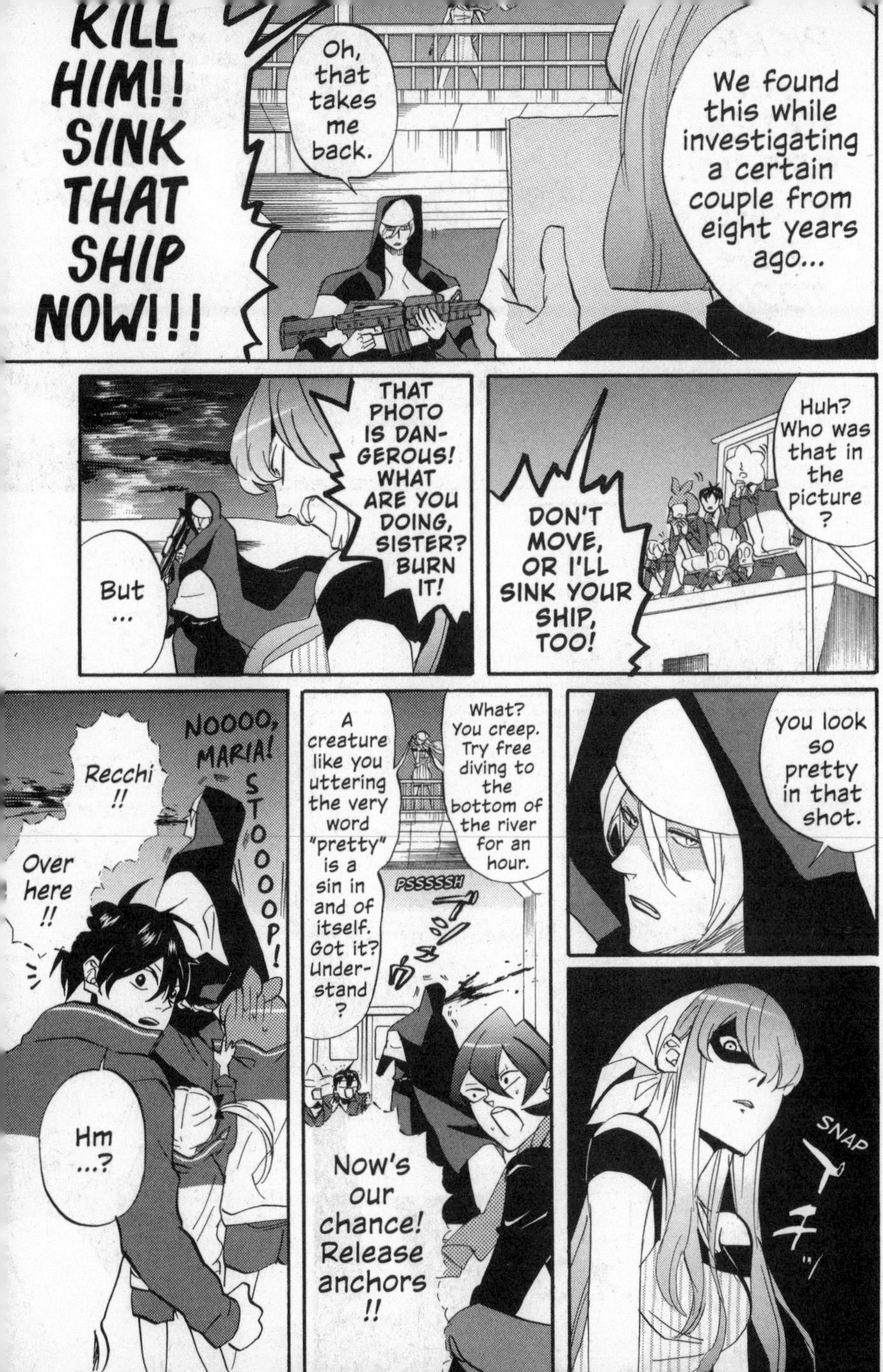
We found this while investigating a certain couple from eight years ago...
Oh, that takes me back.
KILL HIM!! SINK THAT SHIP NOW!!!
Huh? Who was that in the picture?
DON'T MOVE, OR I'LL SINK YOUR SHIP, TOO!
THAT PHOTO IS DANGEROUS! WHAT ARE YOU DOING, SISTER? BURN IT!
But ...
you look so pretty in that shot.
SNAP
What? You creep. Try free diving to the bottom of the river for an hour.
A creature like you uttering the very word "pretty" is a sin in and of itself. Got it? Understand?
PSSSSSH
Now's our chance! Release anchors!!
NOOOO, MARIA!
STOOOOOP!
Recchi!!
Over here!!
Hm ...?

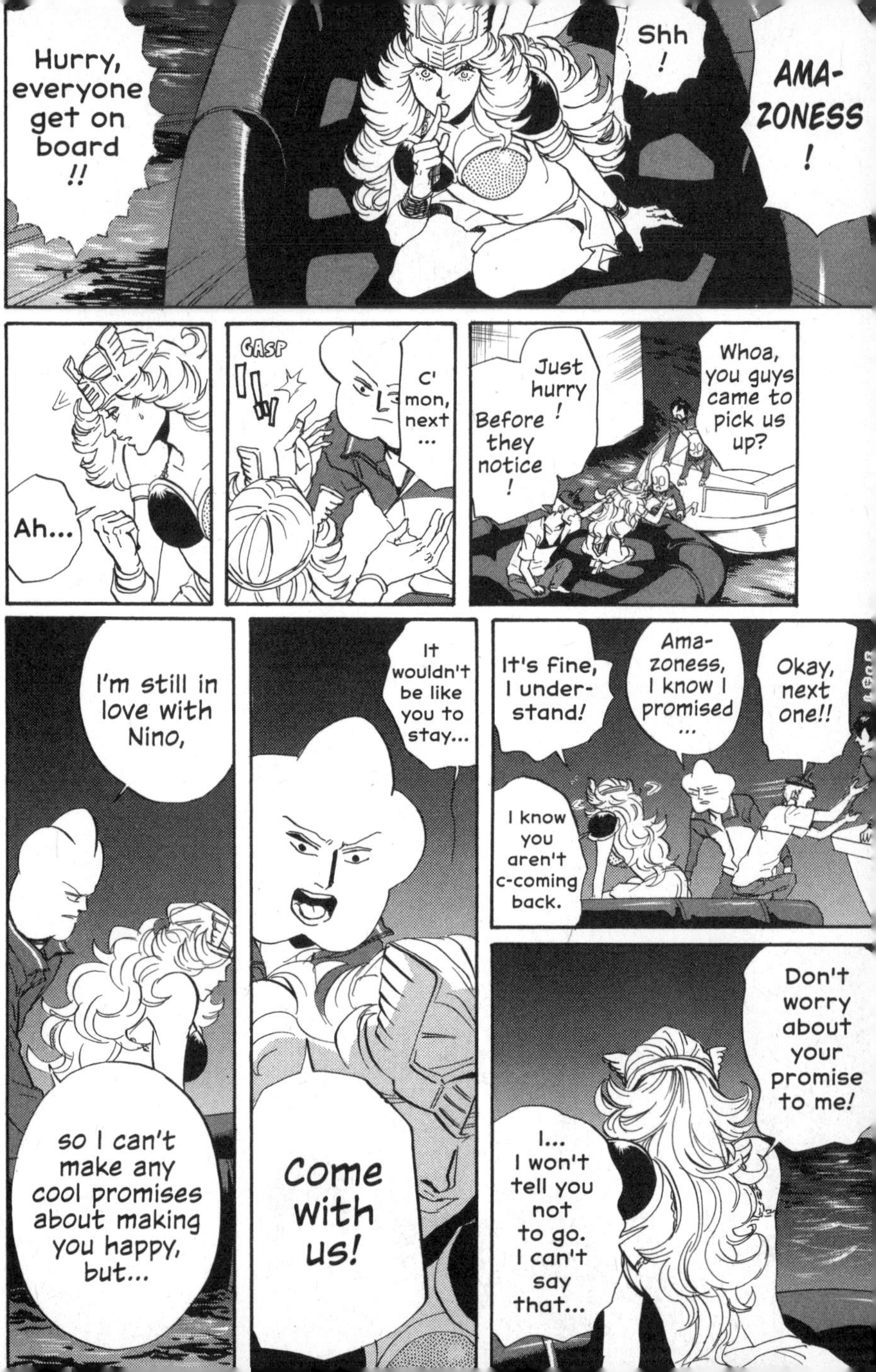
AMA-ZONESS!
Shh!
Hurry, everyone get on board!!
Whoa, you guys came to pick us up?
Just hurry! Before they notice!
GASP
C' mon, next...
Ah...
Okay, next one!!
Ama-zoness, I know I promised...
It's fine, I understand!
I know you aren't c-coming back.
Don't worry about your promise to me!
I... I won't tell you not to go. I can't say that...
It wouldn't be like you to stay...
Come with us!
I'm still in love with Nino,
so I can't make any cool promises about making you happy, but...

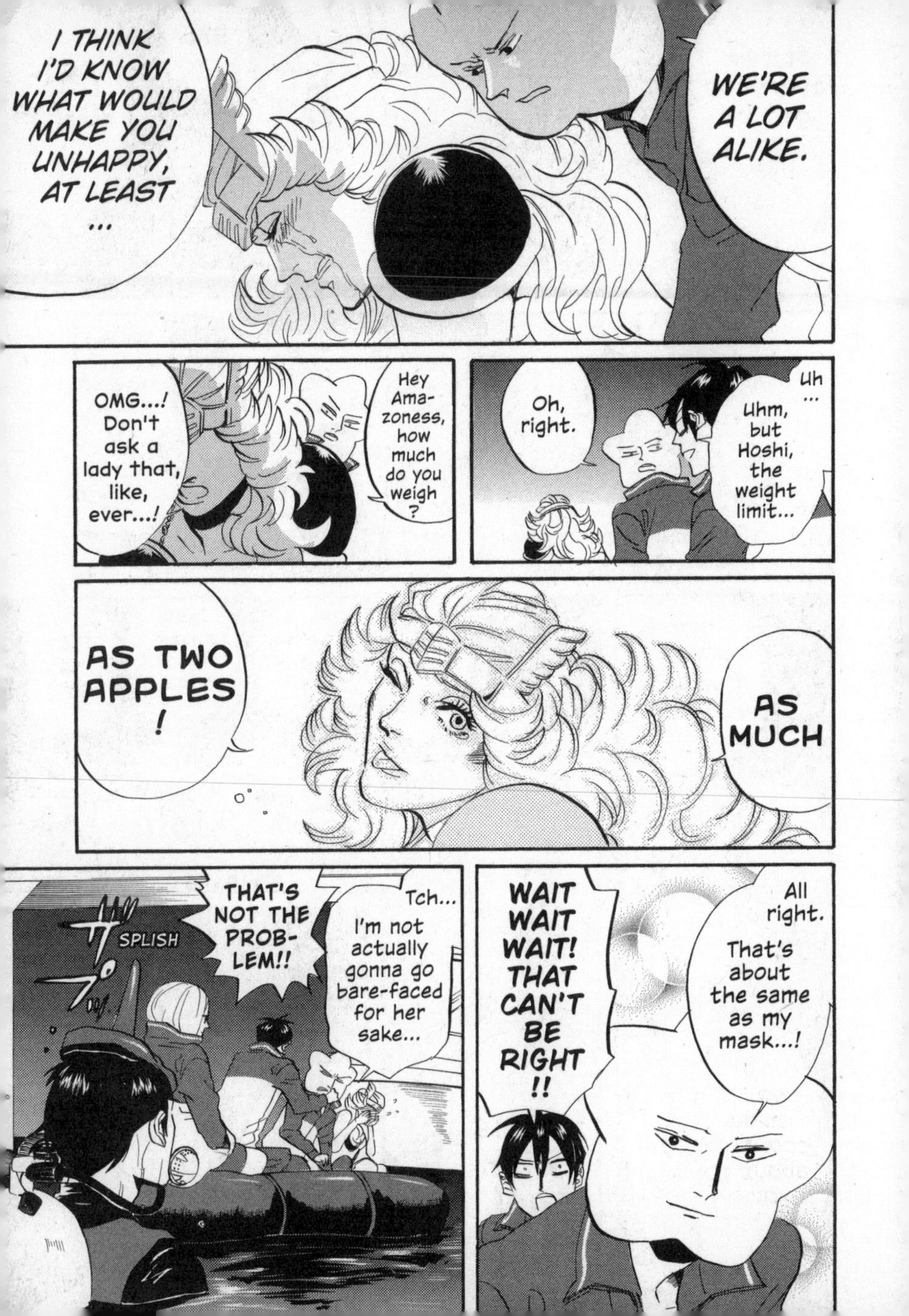
WE'RE A LOT ALIKE.
I THINK I'D KNOW WHAT WOULD MAKE YOU UNHAPPY, AT LEAST ...
Uh ...
Uhm, but Hoshi, the weight limit...
Oh, right.
Hey Amazoness, how much do you weigh?
OMG...! Don't ask a lady that, like, ever...!
AS MUCH
AS TWO APPLES!
All right.
That's about the same as my mask...!
WAIT WAIT WAIT! THAT CAN'T BE RIGHT!!
Tch...
I'm not actually gonna go bare-faced for her sake...
THAT'S NOT THE PROB-LEM!!
SPLISH

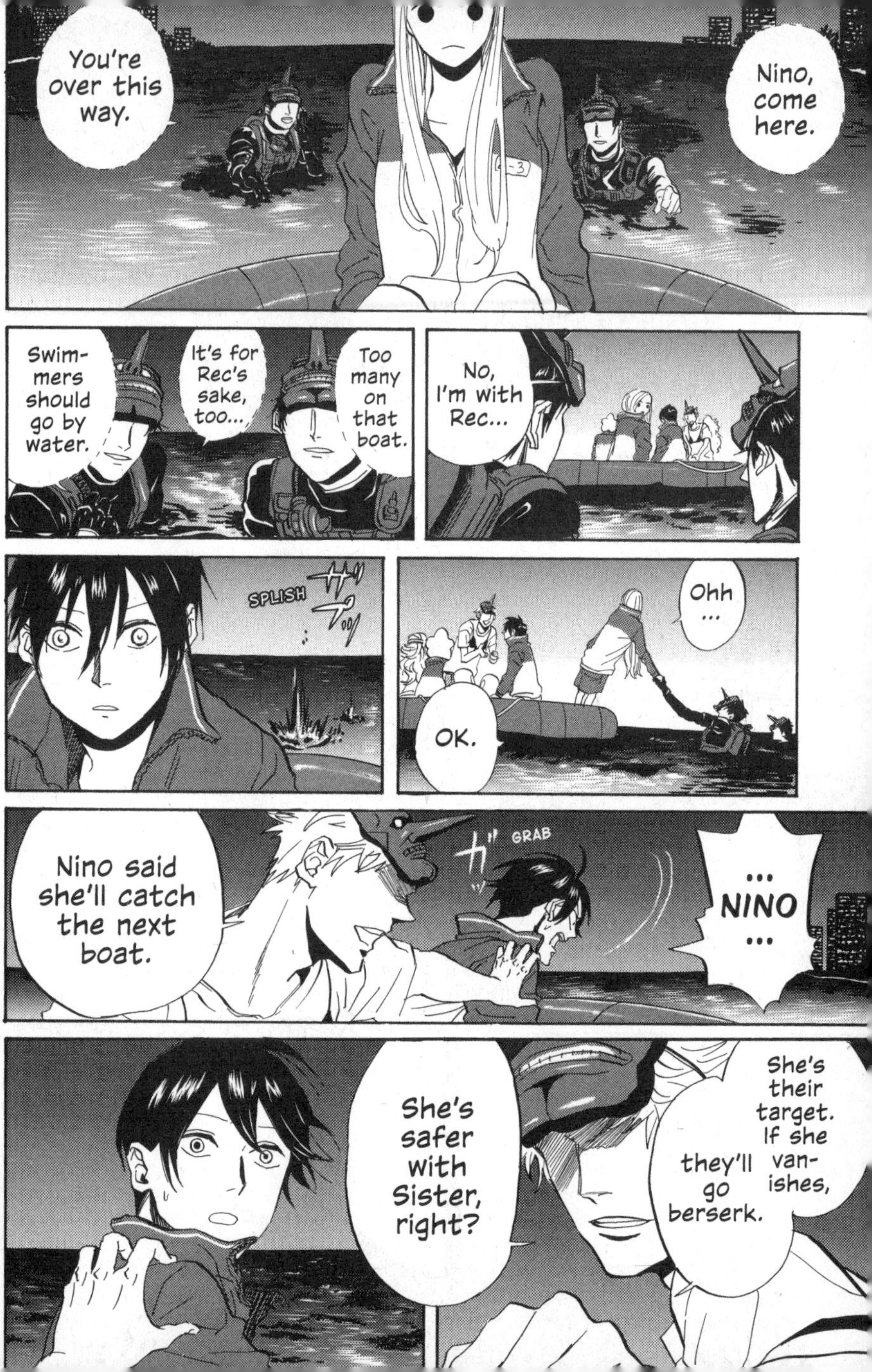
Nino, come here.
You're over this way.
No, I'm with Rec...
Too many on that boat.
It's for Rec's sake, too...
Swimmers should go by water.
Ohh ...
OK.
SPLISH
... NINO ...
GRAB
Nino said she'll catch the next boat.
She's their target. If she vanishes, they'll go berserk.
She's safer with Sister, right?

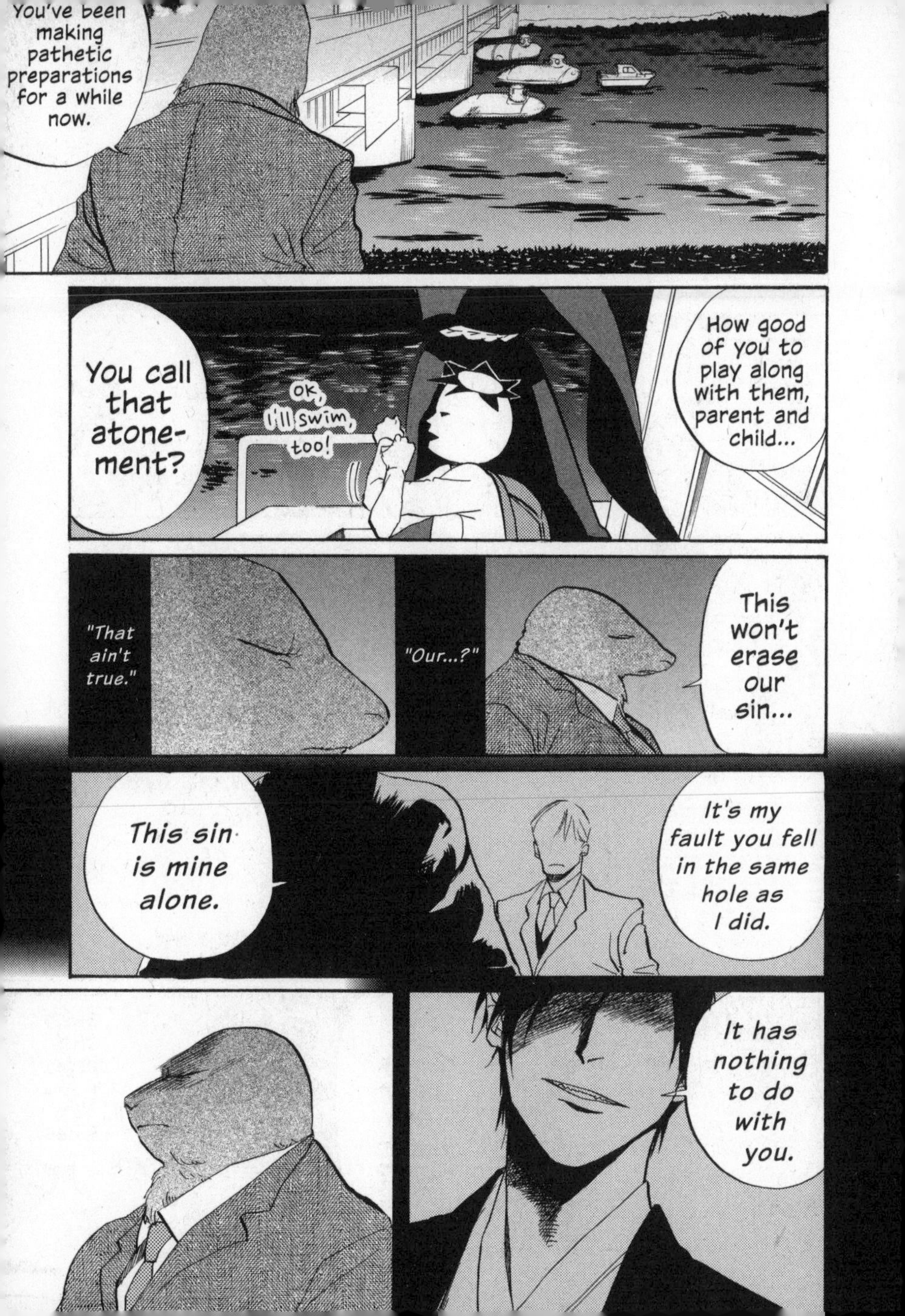
You've been making pathetic preparations for a while now.
How good of you to play along with them, parent and child...
OK, I'll swim, too!
You call that atonement?
This won't erase our sin...
"Our...?"
"That ain't true."
It's my fault you fell in the same hole as I did.
This sin is mine alone.
It has nothing to do with you.

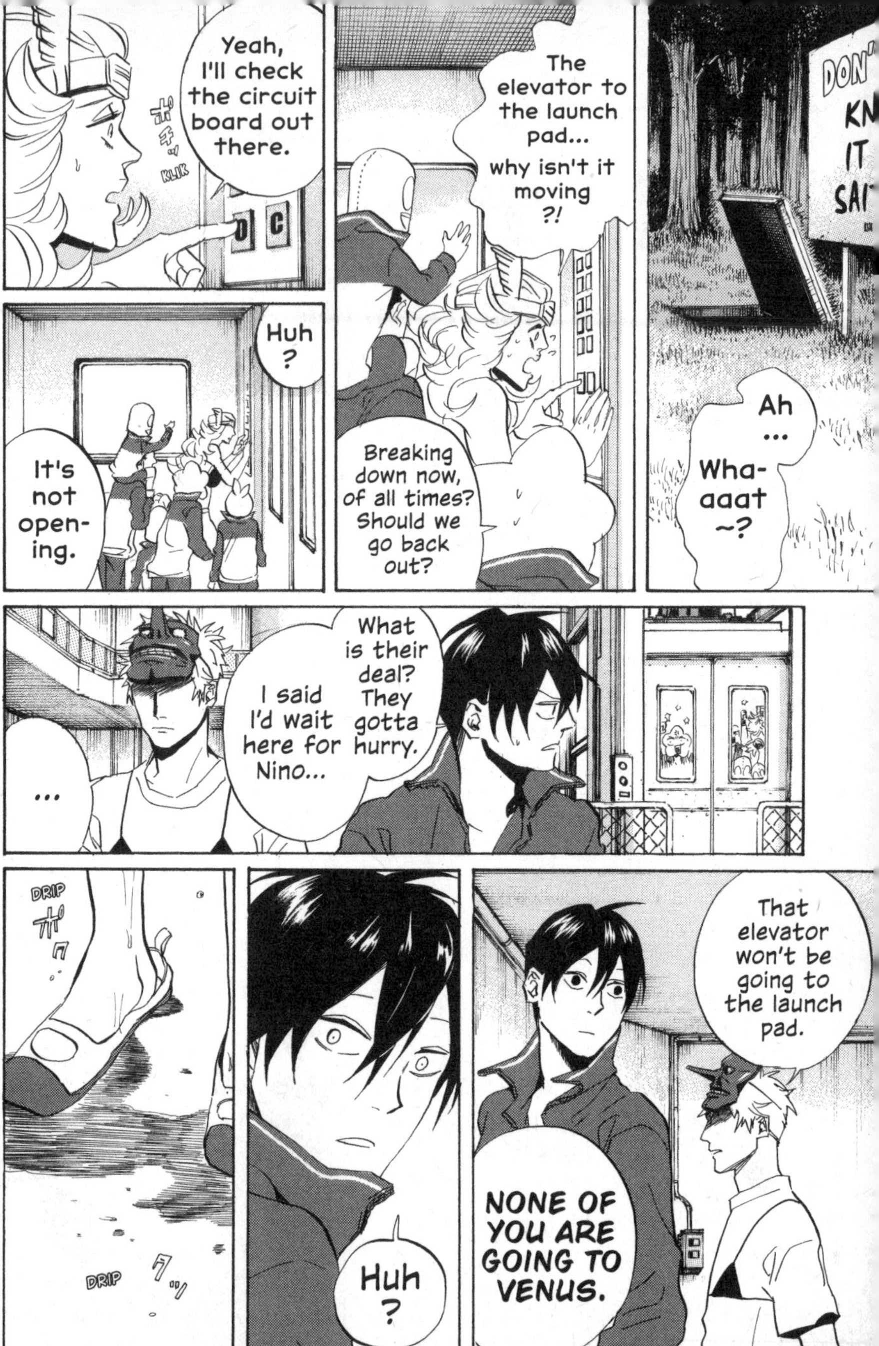
Ah ... Wha-aaat ~?
The elevator to the launch pad... why isn't it moving ?!
Breaking down now, of all times? Should we go back out?
Yeah, I'll check the circuit board out there.
KLIK
Huh ?
It's not open-ing.
What is their deal? They gotta hurry.
I said I'd wait here for Nino...
...
That elevator won't be going to the launch pad.
NONE OF YOU ARE GOING TO VENUS.
Huh ?
DRIP
DRIP

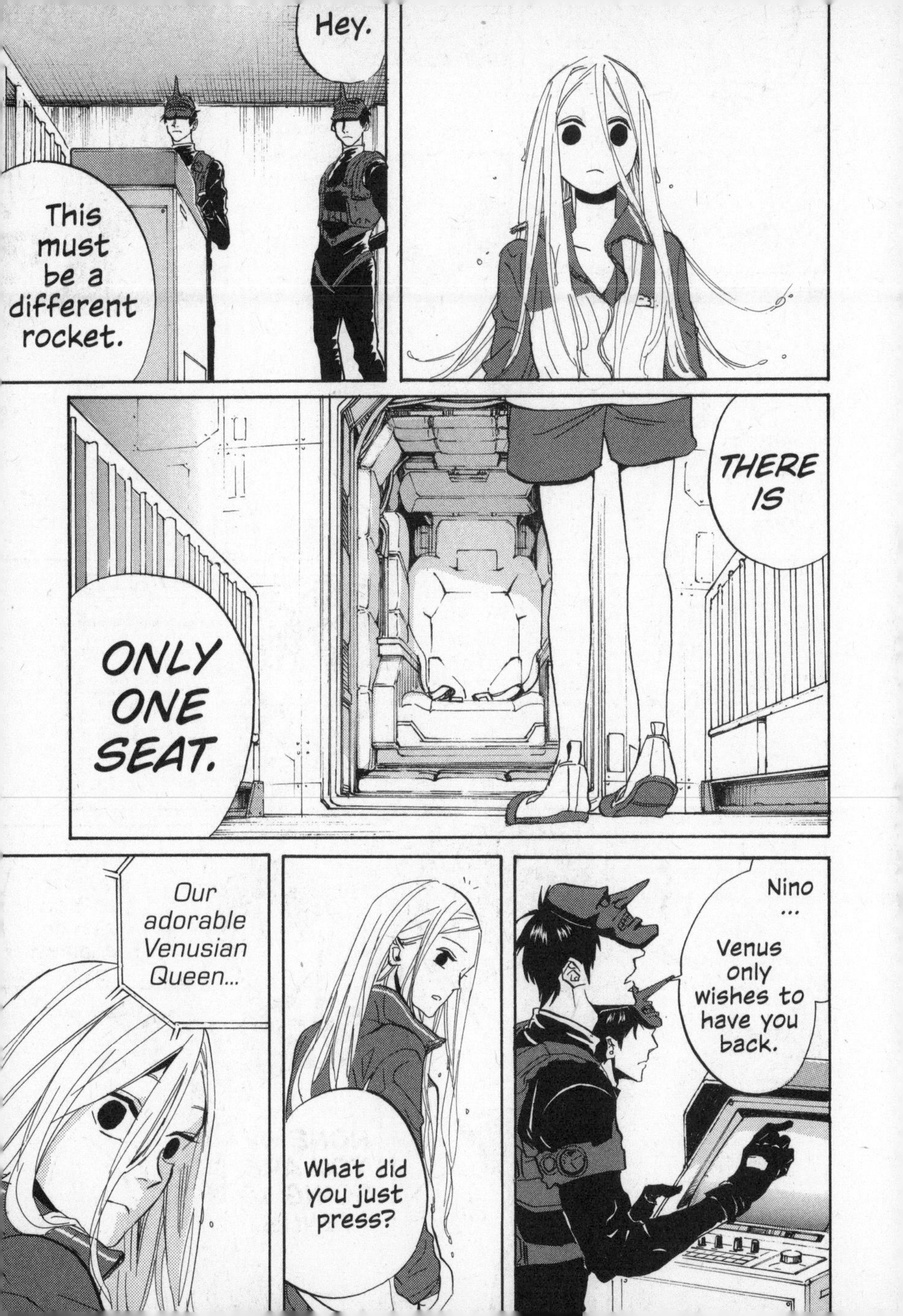
Hey.
This must be a different rocket.
THERE IS
ONLY ONE SEAT.
Nino ...
Venus only wishes to have you back.
What did you just press?
Our adorable Venusian Queen...

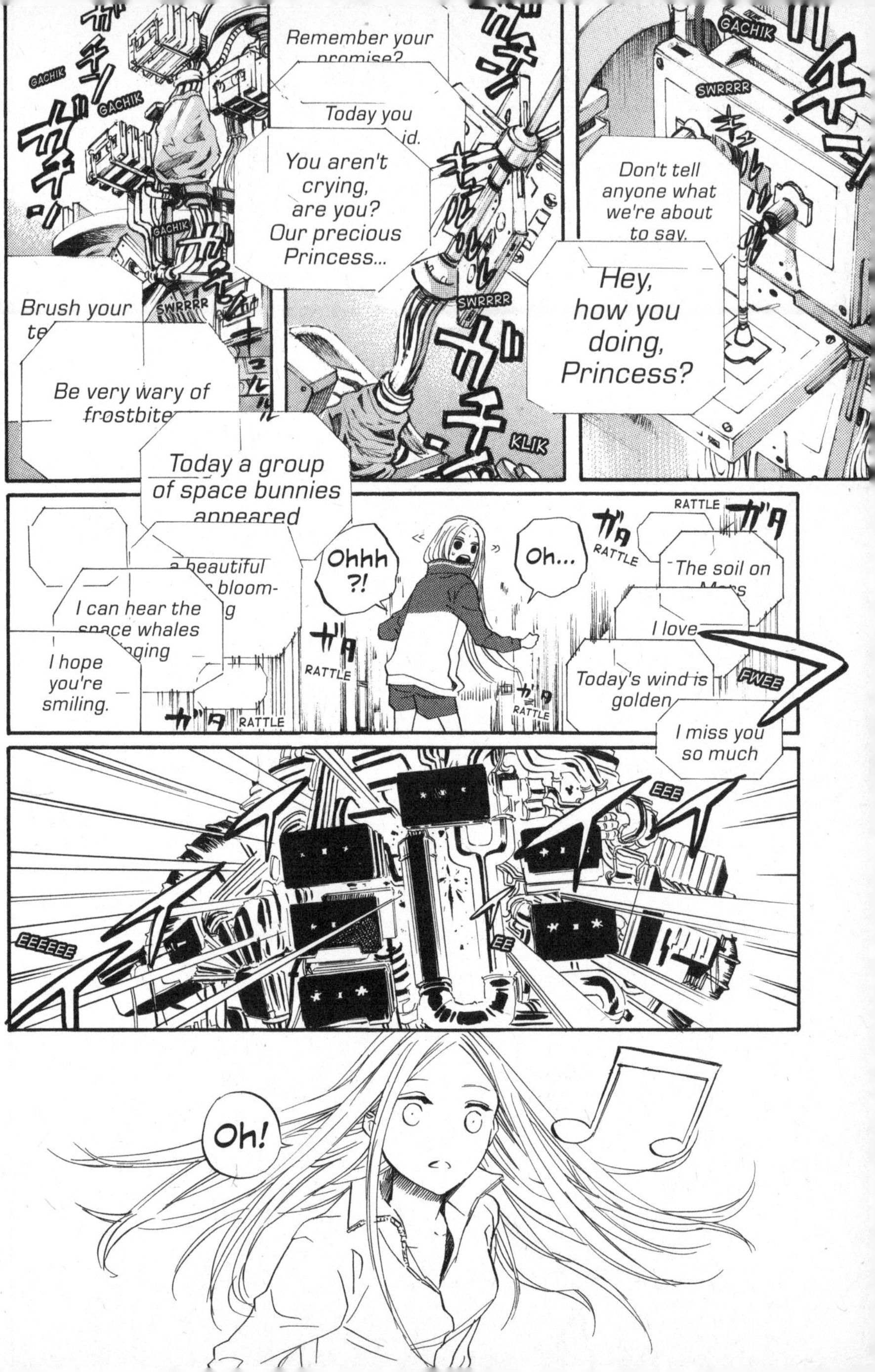
GACHIK
SWRRRR
Don't tell anyone what we're about to say.
Hey, how you doing, Princess?
Remember your promise?
Today you
id.
You aren't crying, are you? Our precious Princess...
SWRRRR
KLIK
GACHIK
GACHIK
GACHIK
SWRRRR
Brush your te
Be very wary of frostbite
Today a group of space bunnies appeared
RATTLE
RATTLE
The soil on
I love
Today's wind is golden
FWEE
I miss you so much
Oh...
RATTLE
Ohhh?!
a beautiful
bloom-
I can hear the space whales singing
I hope you're smiling.
RATTLE
RATTLE
EEE
EE
EEEEEE
Oh!

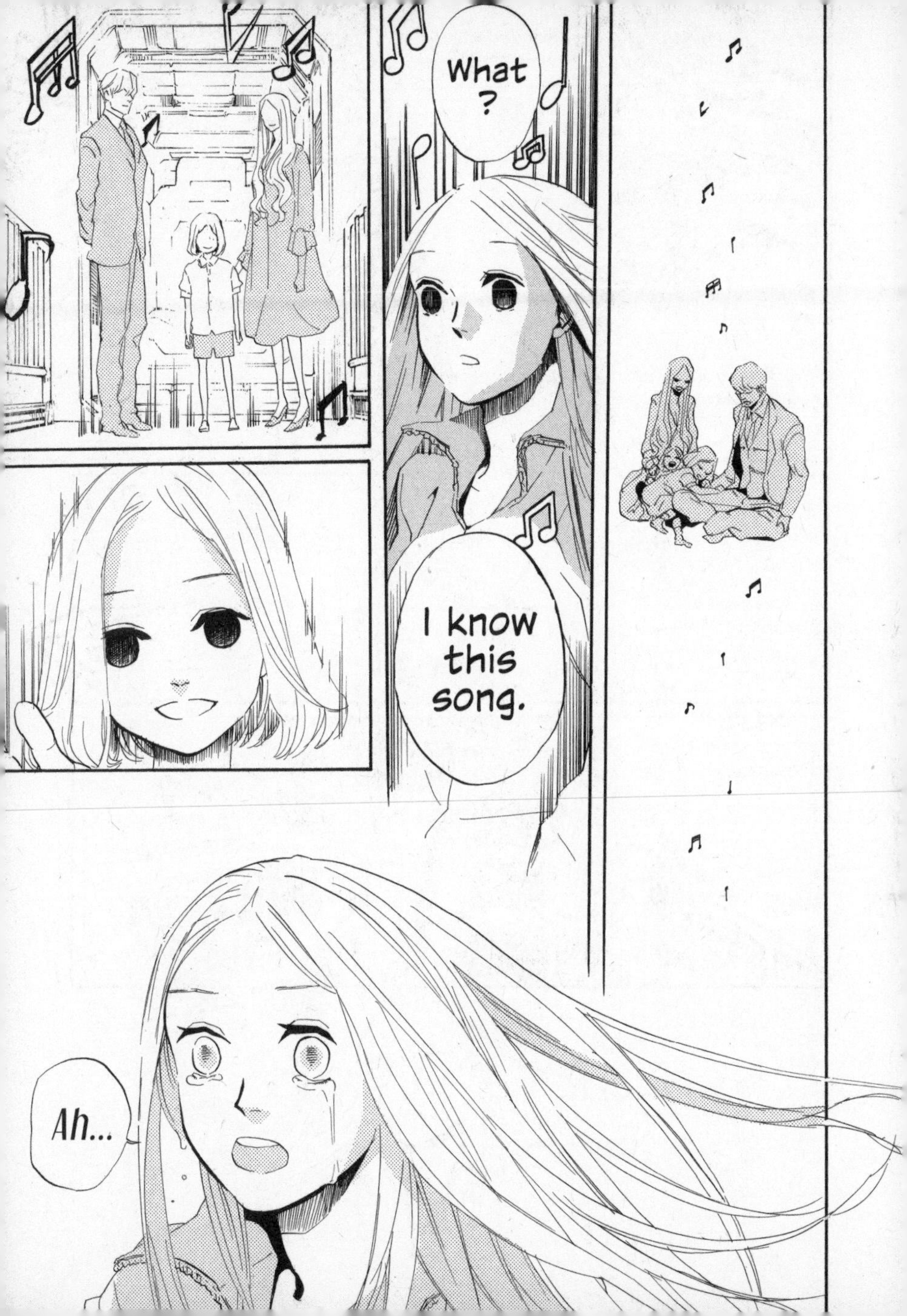
What?
I know this song.
Ah...

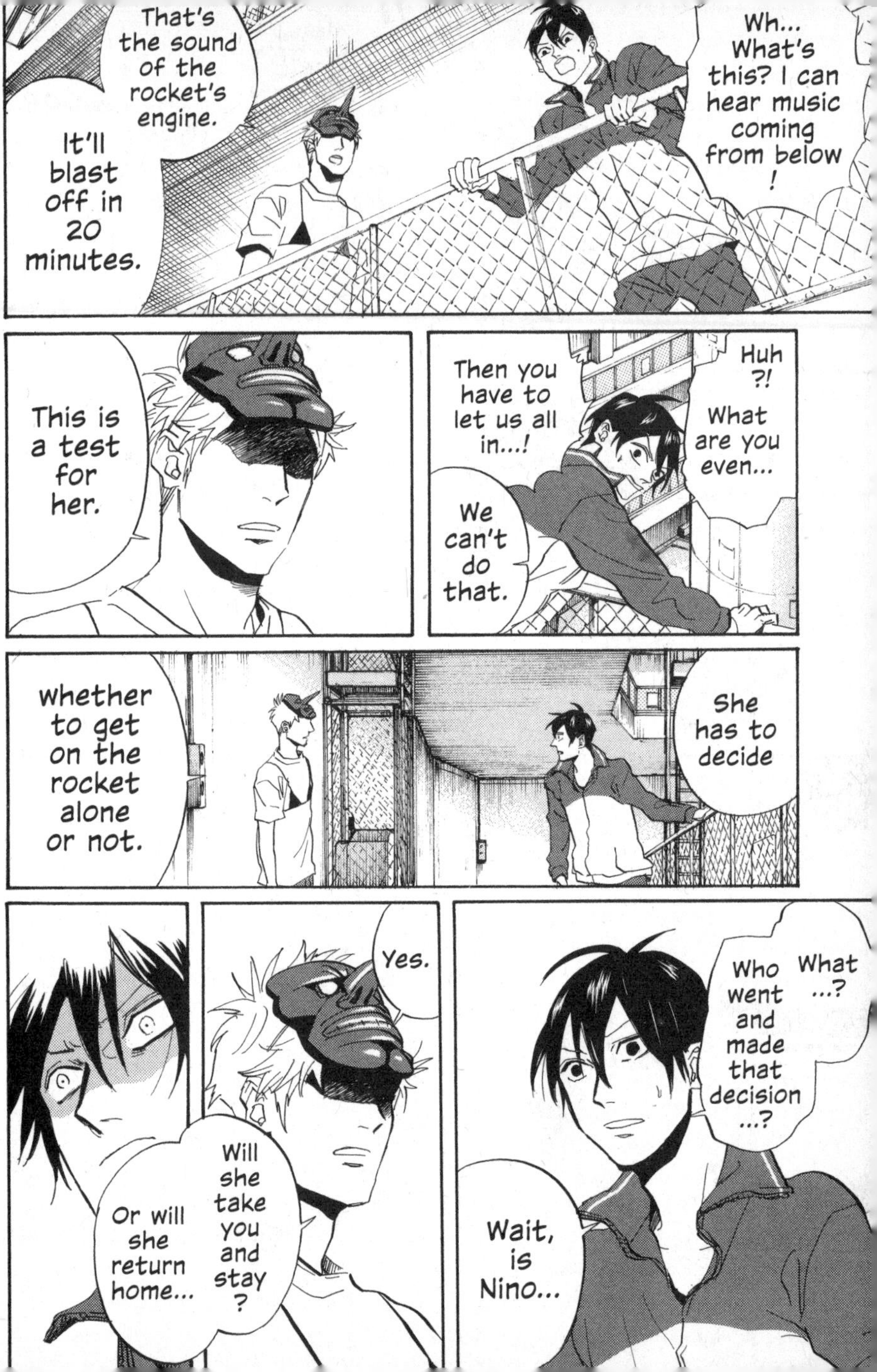
Wh... What's this? I can hear music coming from below!
That's the sound of the rocket's engine.
It'll blast off in 20 minutes.
Huh?! What are you even...
Then you have to let us all in...!
We can't do that.
This is a test for her.
She has to decide
whether to get on the rocket alone or not.
What...?
Who went and made that decision...?
Wait, is Nino...
Yes.
Will she take you and stay?
Or will she return home...

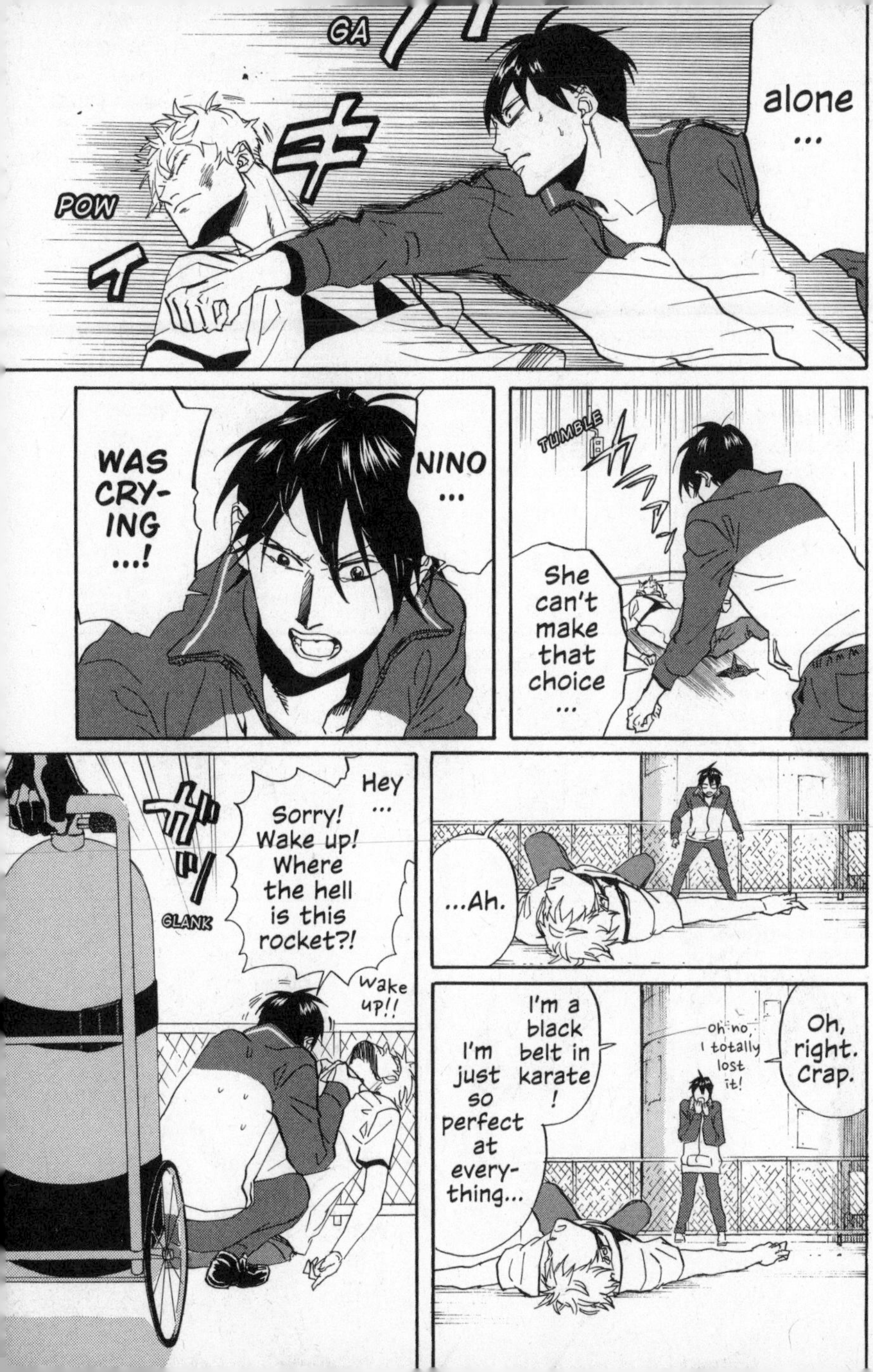
alone ...
GA
POW
TUMBLE
She can't make that choice ...
NINO ...
WAS CRY-ING ...!
...Ah.
Oh, right. Crap.
Oh no, I totally lost it!
I'm a black belt in karate!
I'm just so perfect at every-thing...
Hey ...
Sorry! Wake up! Where the hell is this rocket?!
GLANK
Wake up!!

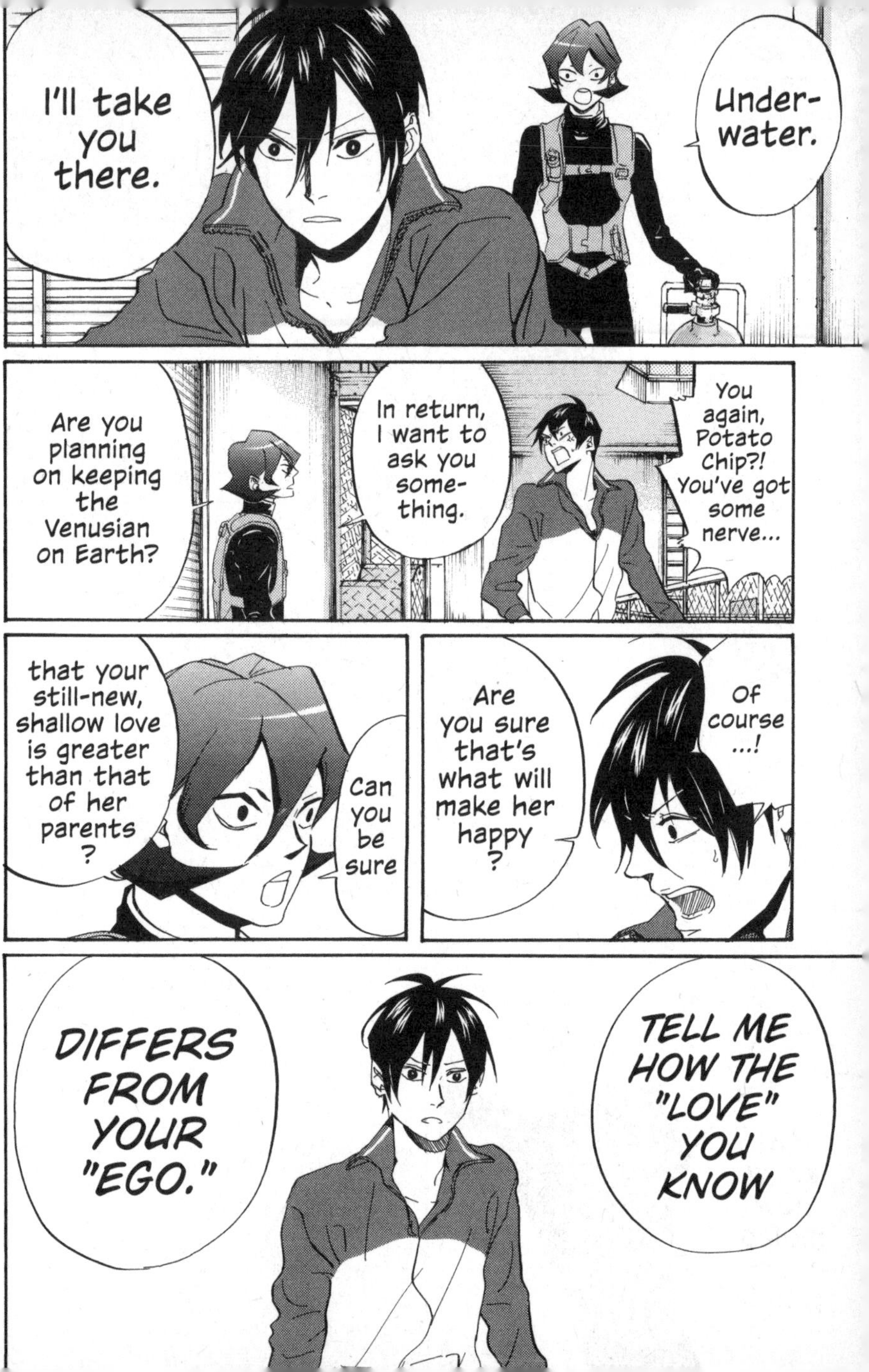
Under-water.
I'll take you there.
You again, Potato Chip?! You've got some nerve...
In return, I want to ask you some-thing.
Are you planning on keeping the Venusian on Earth?
Of course ...!
Are you sure that's what will make her happy ?
Can you be sure
that your still-new, shallow love is greater than that of her parents ?
TELL ME HOW THE "LOVE" YOU KNOW
DIFFERS FROM YOUR "EGO."

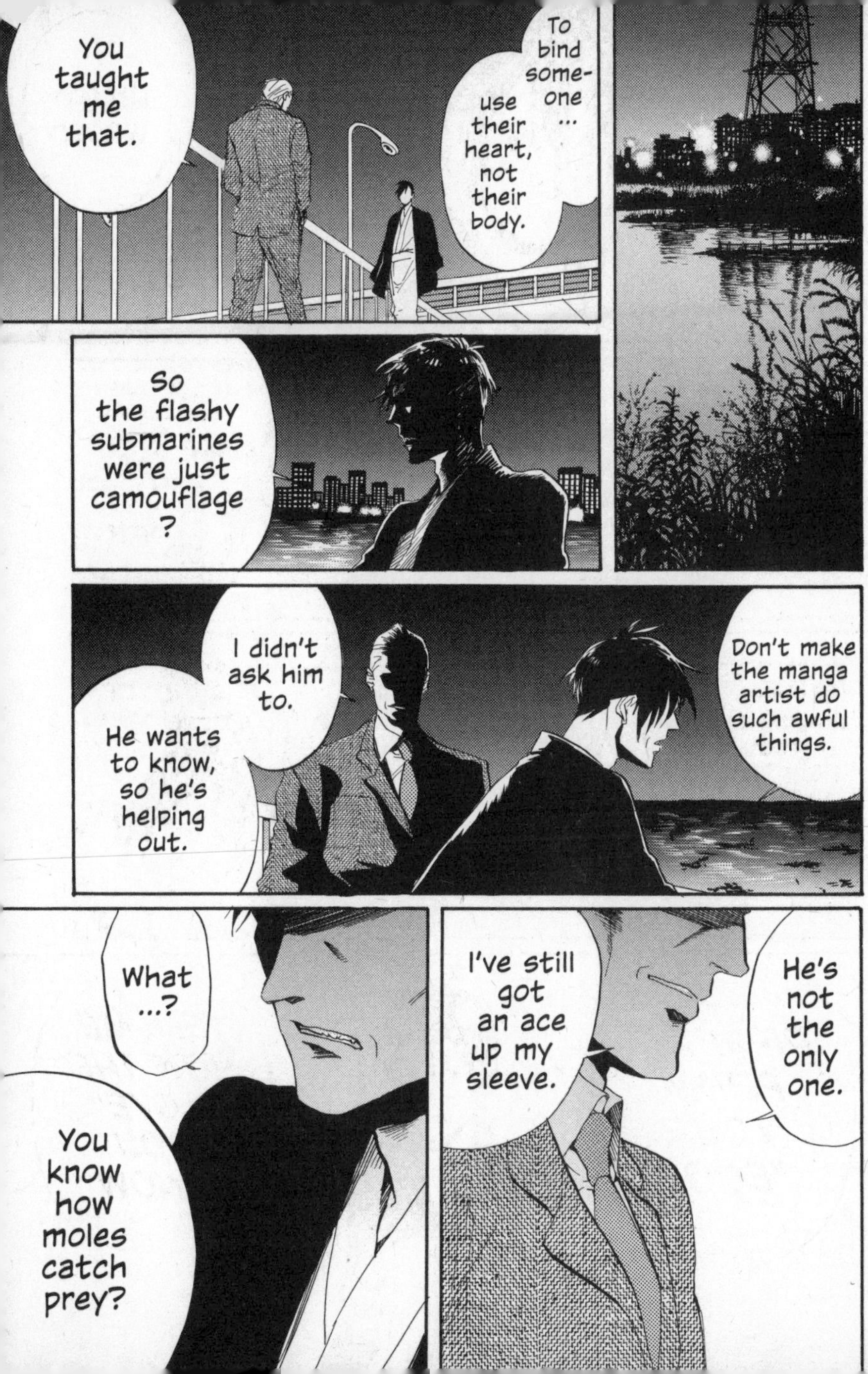
To bind someone...
use their heart, not their body.
You taught me that.
So the flashy submarines were just camouflage?
Don't make the manga artist do such awful things.
I didn't ask him to.
He wants to know, so he's helping out.
He's not the only one.
I've still got an ace up my sleeve.
What...?
You know how moles catch prey?

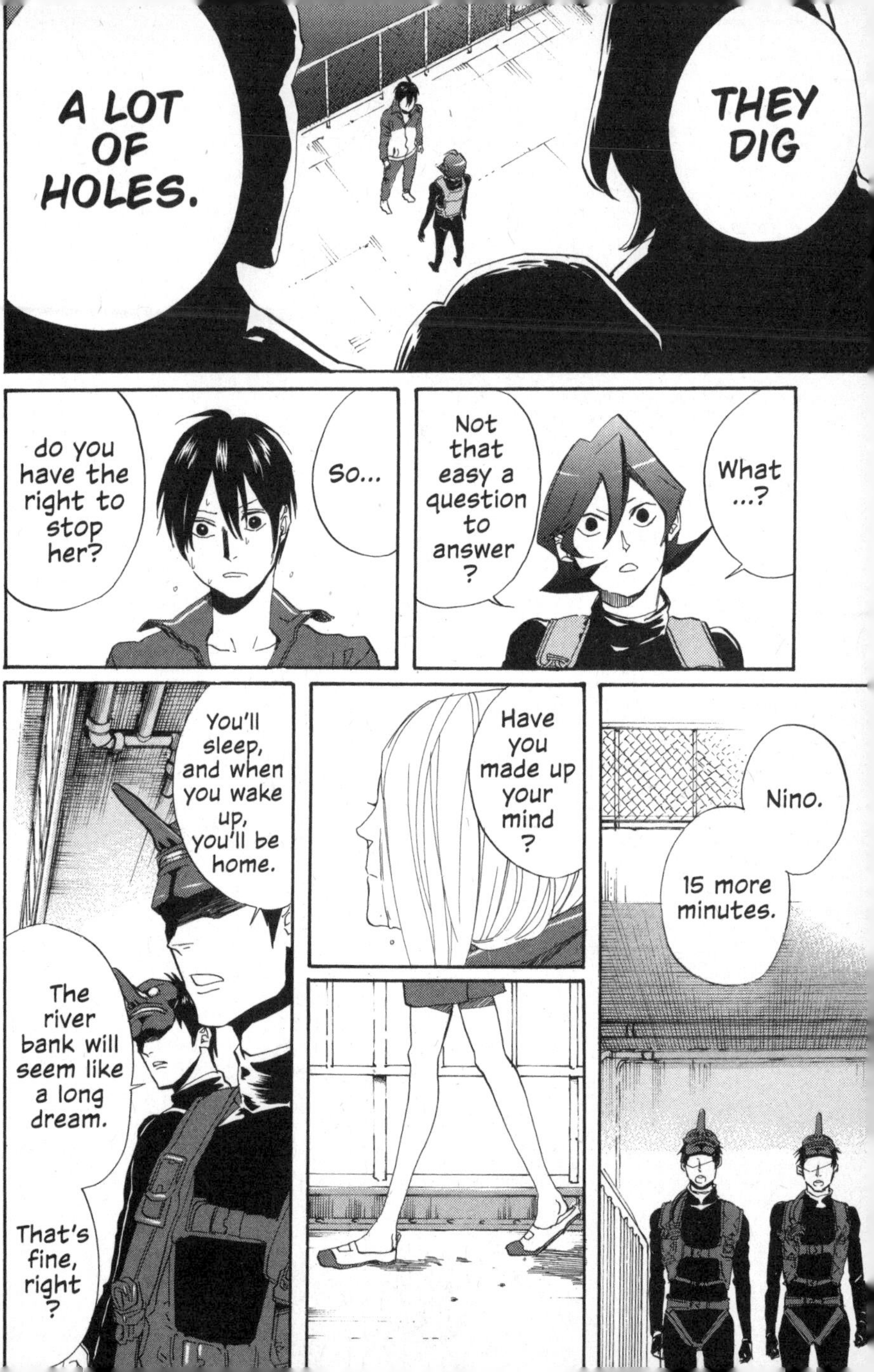
THEY DIG
A LOT OF HOLES.
What ...?
Not that easy a question to answer?
So...
do you have the right to stop her?
Nino.
15 more minutes.
Have you made up your mind?
You'll sleep, and when you wake up, you'll be home.
The river bank will seem like a long dream.
That's fine, right?

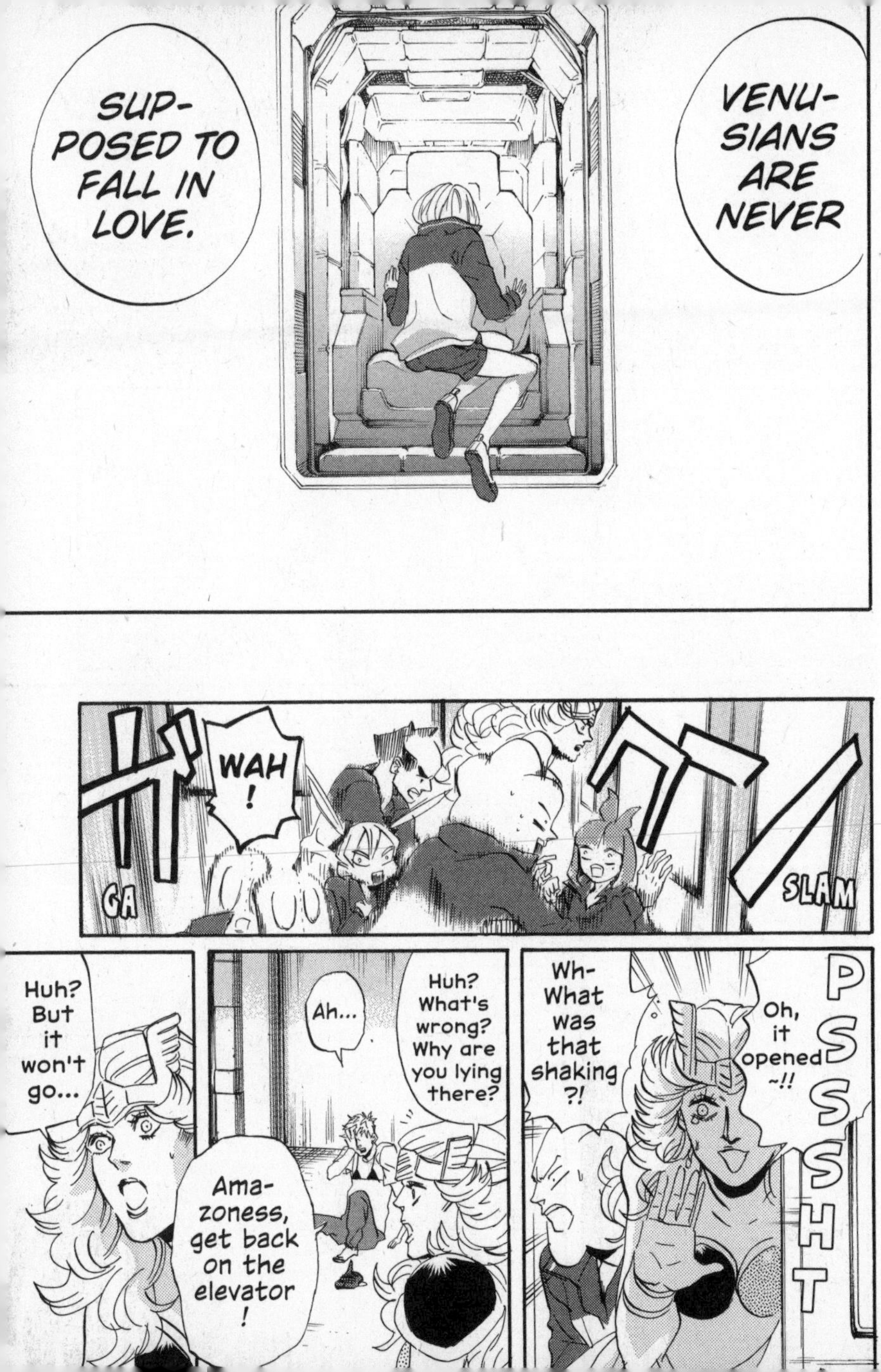
VENU-SIANS ARE NEVER
SUP-POSED TO FALL IN LOVE.
SLAM
WAH!
GA
PSSSHT
Oh, it opened~!!
Wh-What was that shaking?!
Huh? What's wrong? Why are you lying there?
Ah...
Amazoness, get back on the elevator!
Huh? But it won't go...

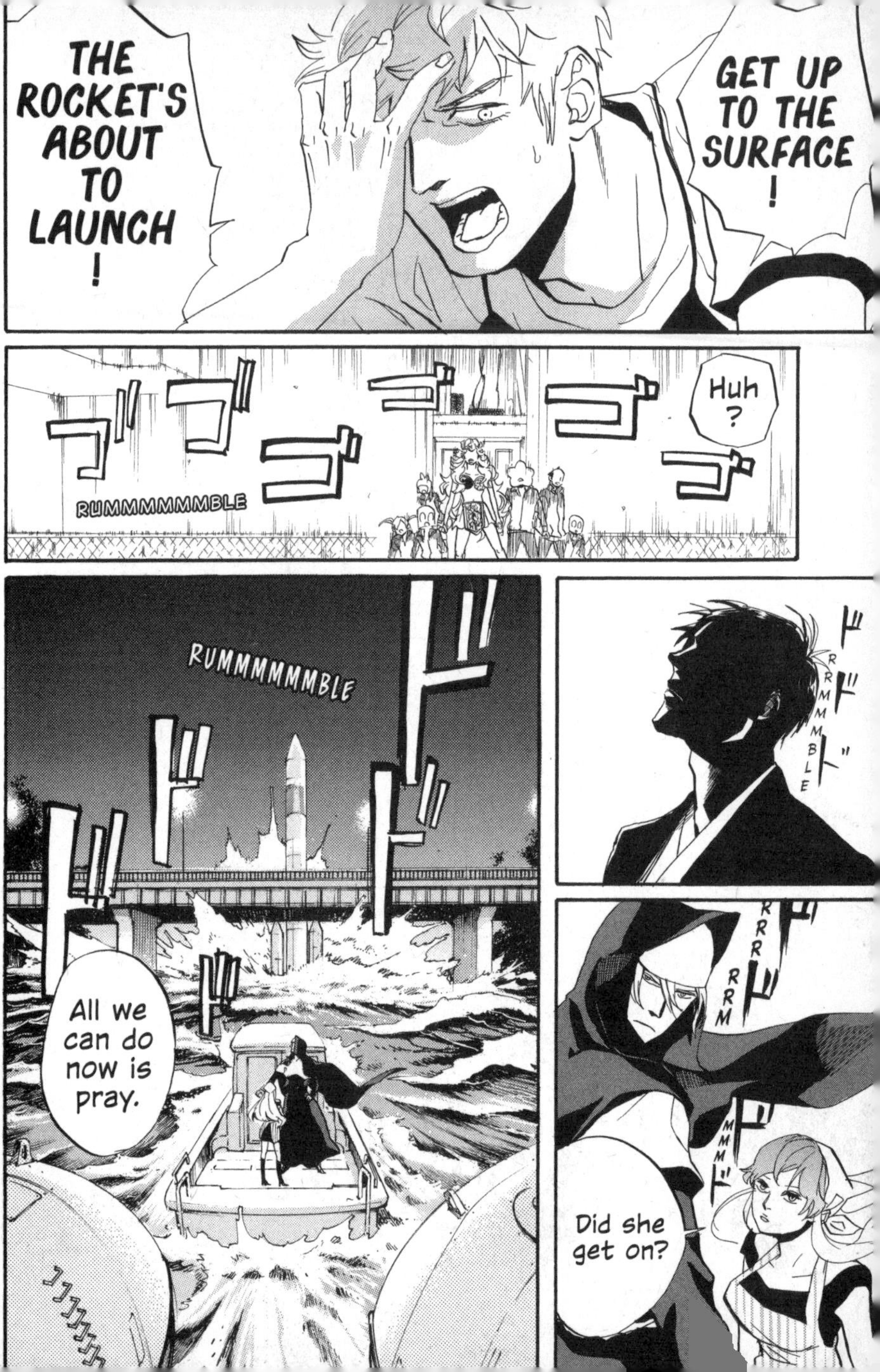
GET UP TO THE SURFACE!
THE ROCKET'S ABOUT TO LAUNCH!
Huh?
RUMMMMMMMBLE
RRMMMBLE
RRRRRM
MMM
Did she get on?
RUMMMMMMMBLE
All we can do now is pray.

Arakawa Under the Bridge 5 The End

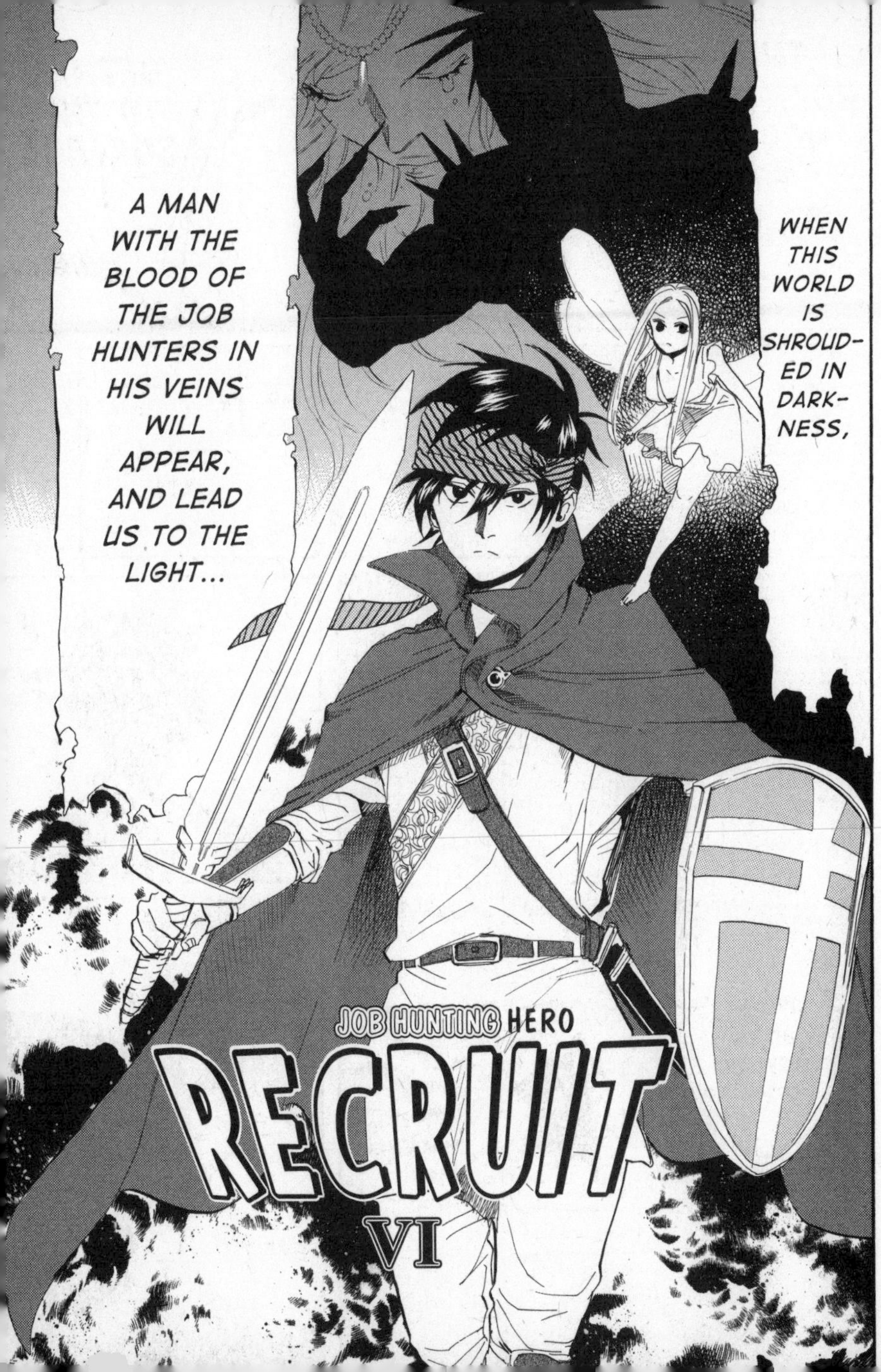
WHEN THIS WORLD IS SHROUDED IN DARKNESS,
A MAN WITH THE BLOOD OF THE JOB HUNTERS IN HIS VEINS WILL APPEAR, AND LEAD US TO THE LIGHT...
JOB HUNTING HERO
RECRUIT
VI

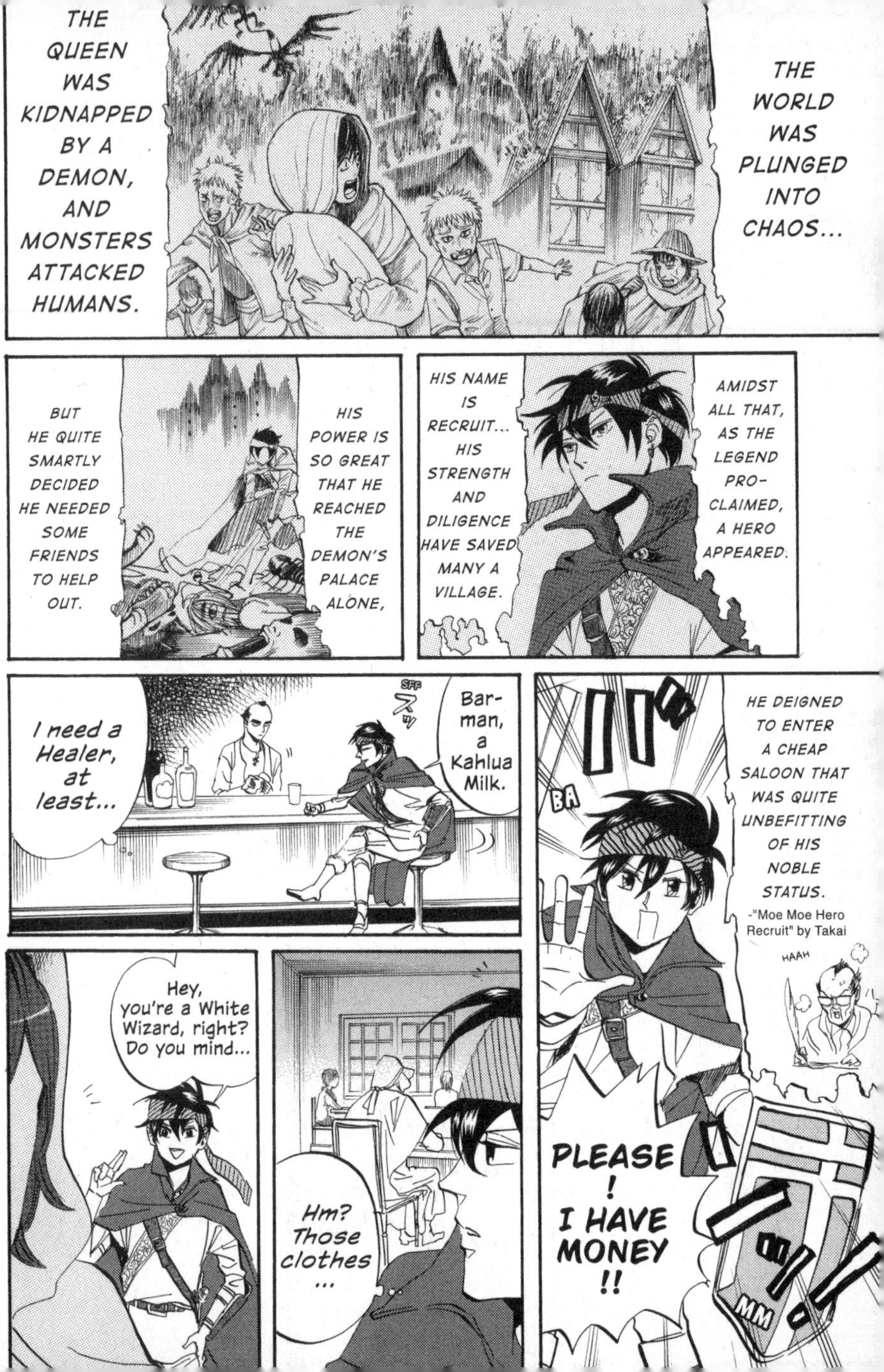
THE WORLD WAS PLUNGED INTO CHAOS...
THE QUEEN WAS KIDNAPPED BY A DEMON, AND MONSTERS ATTACKED HUMANS.
AMIDST ALL THAT, AS THE LEGEND PRO-CLAIMED, A HERO APPEARED.
HIS NAME IS RECRUIT... HIS STRENGTH AND DILIGENCE HAVE SAVED MANY A VILLAGE.
HIS POWER IS SO GREAT THAT HE REACHED THE DEMON'S PALACE ALONE,
BUT HE QUITE SMARTLY DECIDED HE NEEDED SOME FRIENDS TO HELP OUT.
HE DEIGNED TO ENTER A CHEAP SALOON THAT WAS QUITE UNBEFITTING OF HIS NOBLE STATUS.
-"Moe Moe Hero Recruit" by Takai
BA
HAAH
PLEASE! I HAVE MONEY!!
MM
SFF
Bar-man, a Kahlua Milk.
I need a Healer, at least...
Hm? Those clothes...
Hey, you're a White Wizard, right? Do you mind...

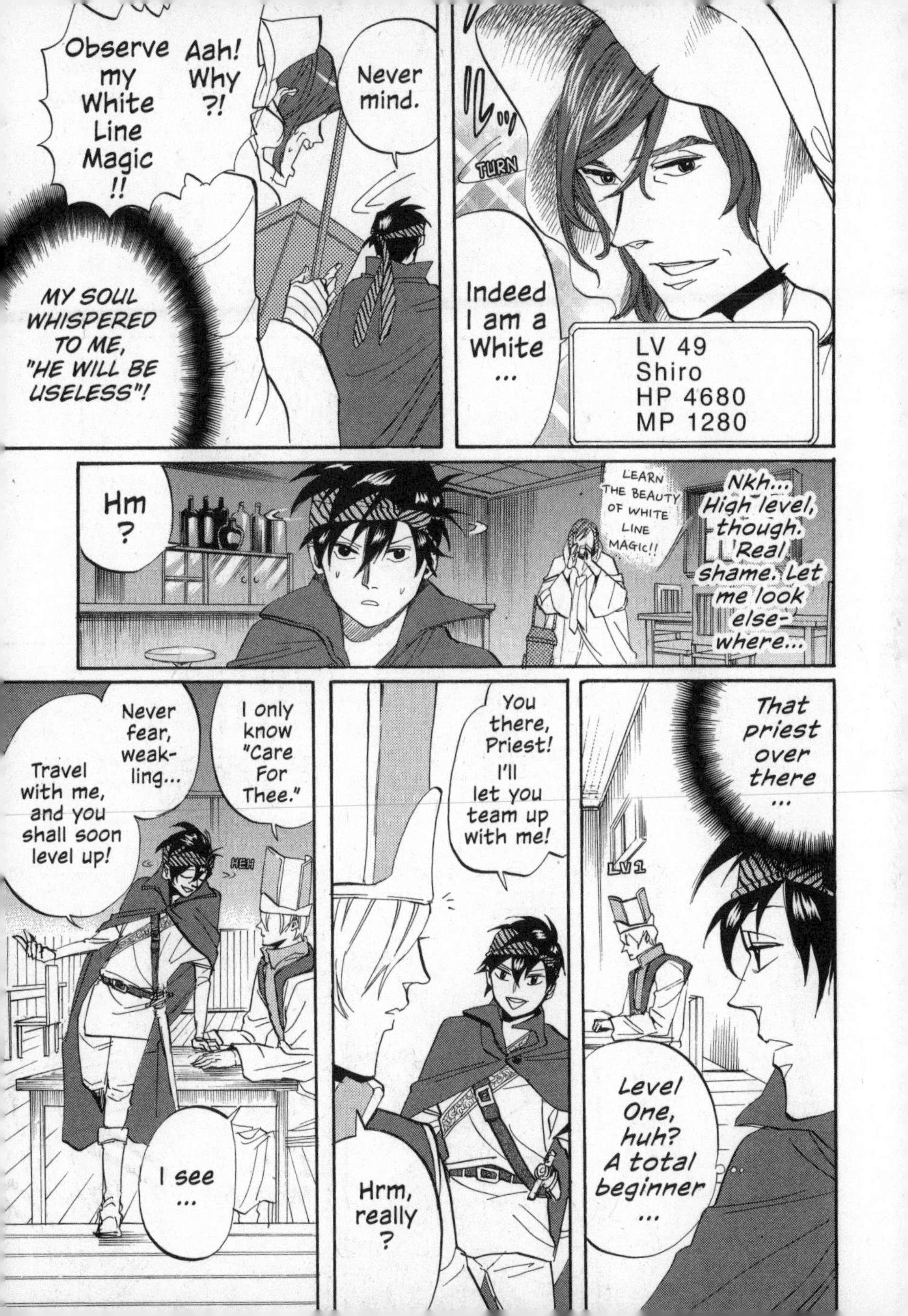
TURN
Indeed I am a White ...
LV 49 Shiro HP 4680 MP 1280
Never mind.
Aah! Why ?!
Observe my White Line Magic !!
MY SOUL WHISPERED TO ME, "HE WILL BE USELESS"!
Nkh... High level, though. Real shame. Let me look else-where...
LEARN THE BEAUTY OF WHITE LINE MAGIC!!
Hm ?
That priest over there ...
LV 1
Level One, huh? A total beginner ...
You there, Priest! I'll let you team up with me!
Hrm, really ?
I only know "Care For Thee."
Never fear, weak-ling...
Travel with me, and you shall soon level up!
HEH
I see ...

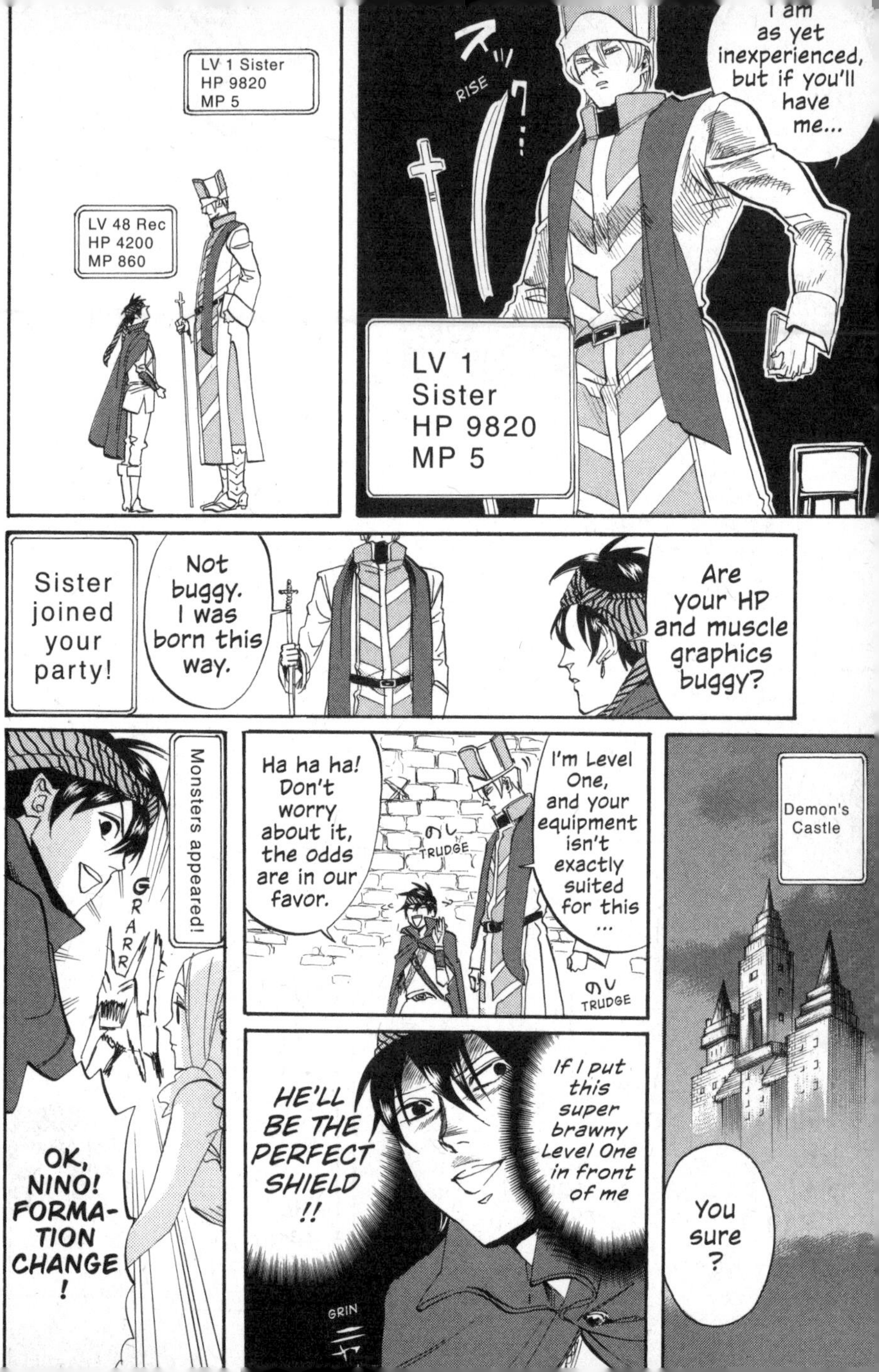
RISE
I am as yet inexperienced, but if you'll have me...
LV 1 Sister HP 9820 MP 5
LV 1 Sister HP 9820 MP 5
LV 48 Rec HP 4200 MP 860
Are your HP and muscle graphics buggy?
Not buggy. I was born this way.
Sister joined your party!
Demon's Castle
You sure?
I'm Level One, and your equipment isn't exactly suited for this ...
TRUDGE
Ha ha ha! Don't worry about it, the odds are in our favor.
TRUDGE
If I put this super brawny Level One in front of me
HE'LL BE THE PERFECT SHIELD !!
GRIN
Monsters appeared!
GRARR
OK, NINO! FORMA-TION CHANGE!

ADVICE TIME!

FAIRY NINO'S

Sister to the vanguard...

Weird... Why can't I move...

Vanguard Rec	Rear
	▶ ~~Sister~~

CHANGE THAT NAME TO "FAIRY NINO'S USELESS MEDDLING TIME"!!

GRRA AARR

ビッ ZWU

リ MM

You should put Level One allies in the rear and protect them...

I was in such great spirits that I headed right to the Final Boss's castle, and yet...

HAAA HAH HAH HAH! WELCOME, HUMAN SCUM!!!

Care For Thee.

Hey, look....! I'm in major trouble, here!!

+100

CHOMP

Too tiny!! That's not enough! My gauge is solid red!!

ガブ

CHOMP

CHOMP

Nkh... But offense is the best defense...!

Change of strategy!

NO!!

Sister, "Follow Orders"...

He refused?!?

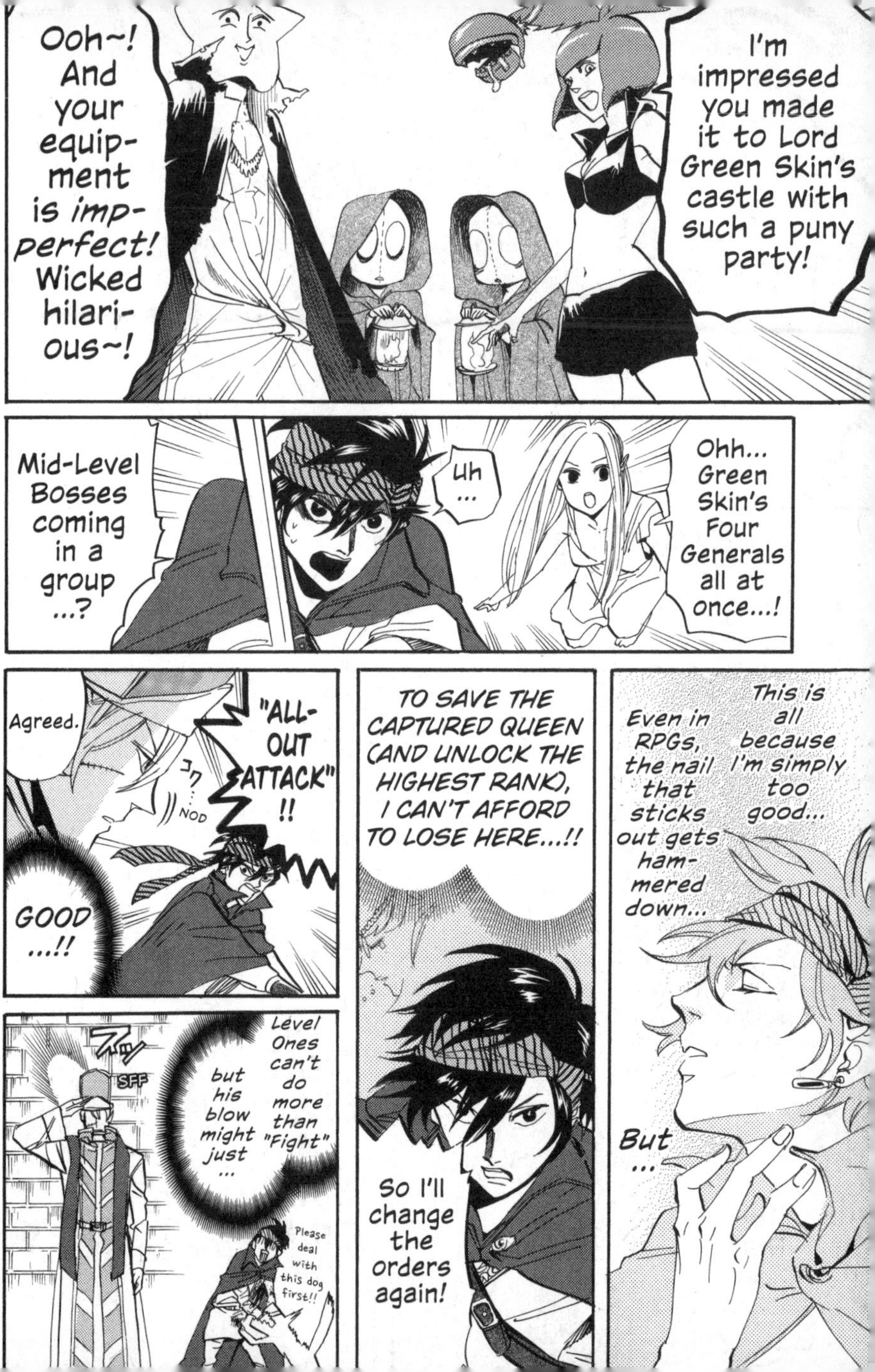
I'm impressed you made it to Lord Green Skin's castle with such a puny party!
Ooh~! And your equipment is *imperfect!* Wicked hilarious~!
Ohh... Green Skin's Four Generals all at once...!
Uh ...
Mid-Level Bosses coming in a group ...?
This is all because I'm simply too good...
Even in RPGs, the nail that sticks out gets hammered down...
But ...
TO SAVE THE CAPTURED QUEEN (AND UNLOCK THE HIGHEST RANK), I CAN'T AFFORD TO LOSE HERE...!!
So I'll change the orders again!
"ALL-OUT ATTACK" !!
Agreed.
NOD
GOOD ...!!
Level Ones can't do more than "Fight"
but his blow might just ...
SFF
Please deal with this dog first!!

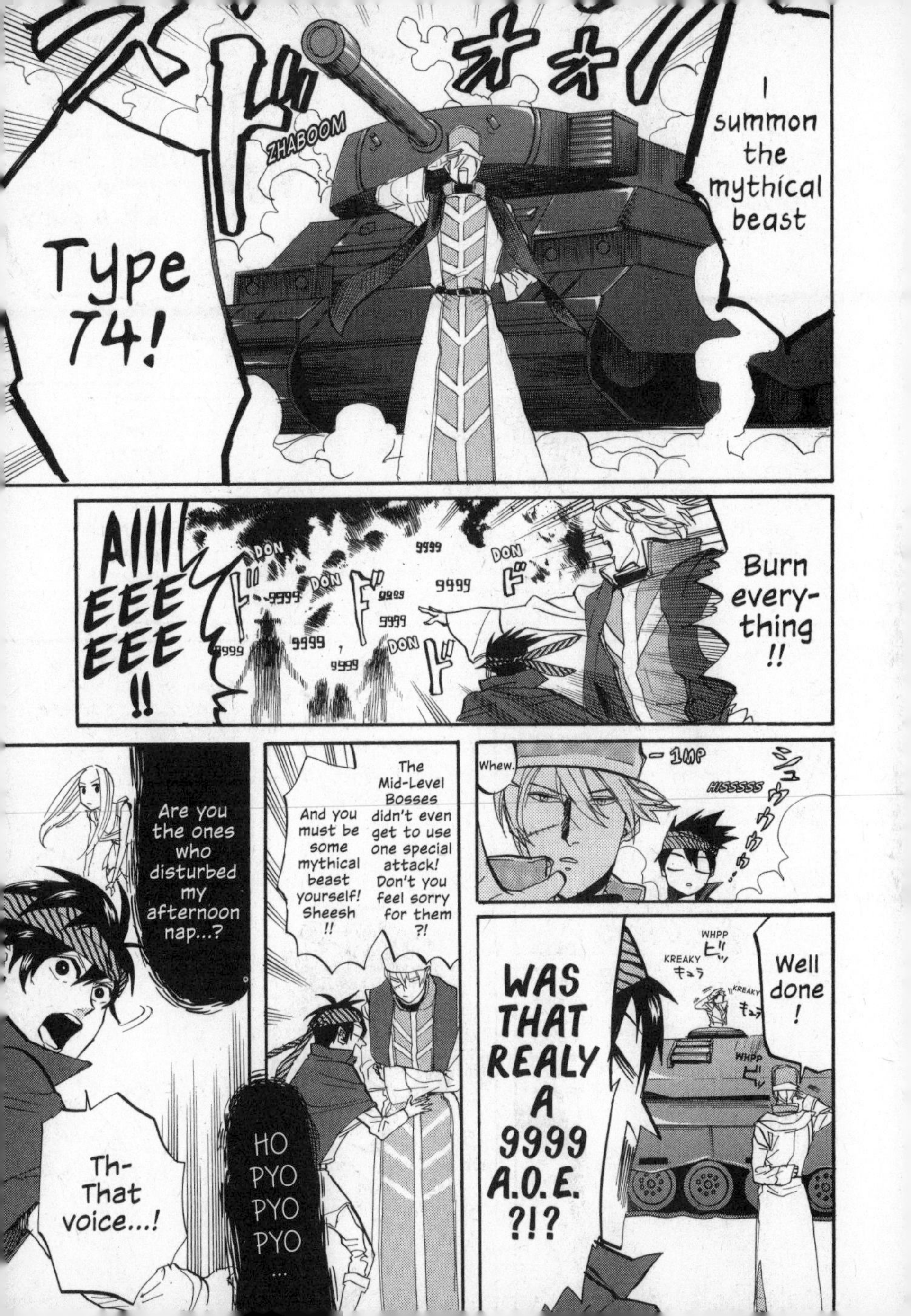
ZHABOOM
I summon the mythical beast
Type 74!
Burn every-thing !!
DON
DON
DON
9999
AIIII EEE EEE !!
Whew.
−1MP
HISSSSS
Well done!
WHPP
KREAKY
KREAKY
WHPP
WAS THAT REALY A 9999 A.O.E. ?!?
The Mid-Level Bosses didn't even get to use one special attack! Don't you feel sorry for them ?!
And you must be some mythical beast yourself! Sheesh !!
Are you the ones who disturbed my afternoon nap...?
HO PYO PYO PYO ...
Th- That voice...!

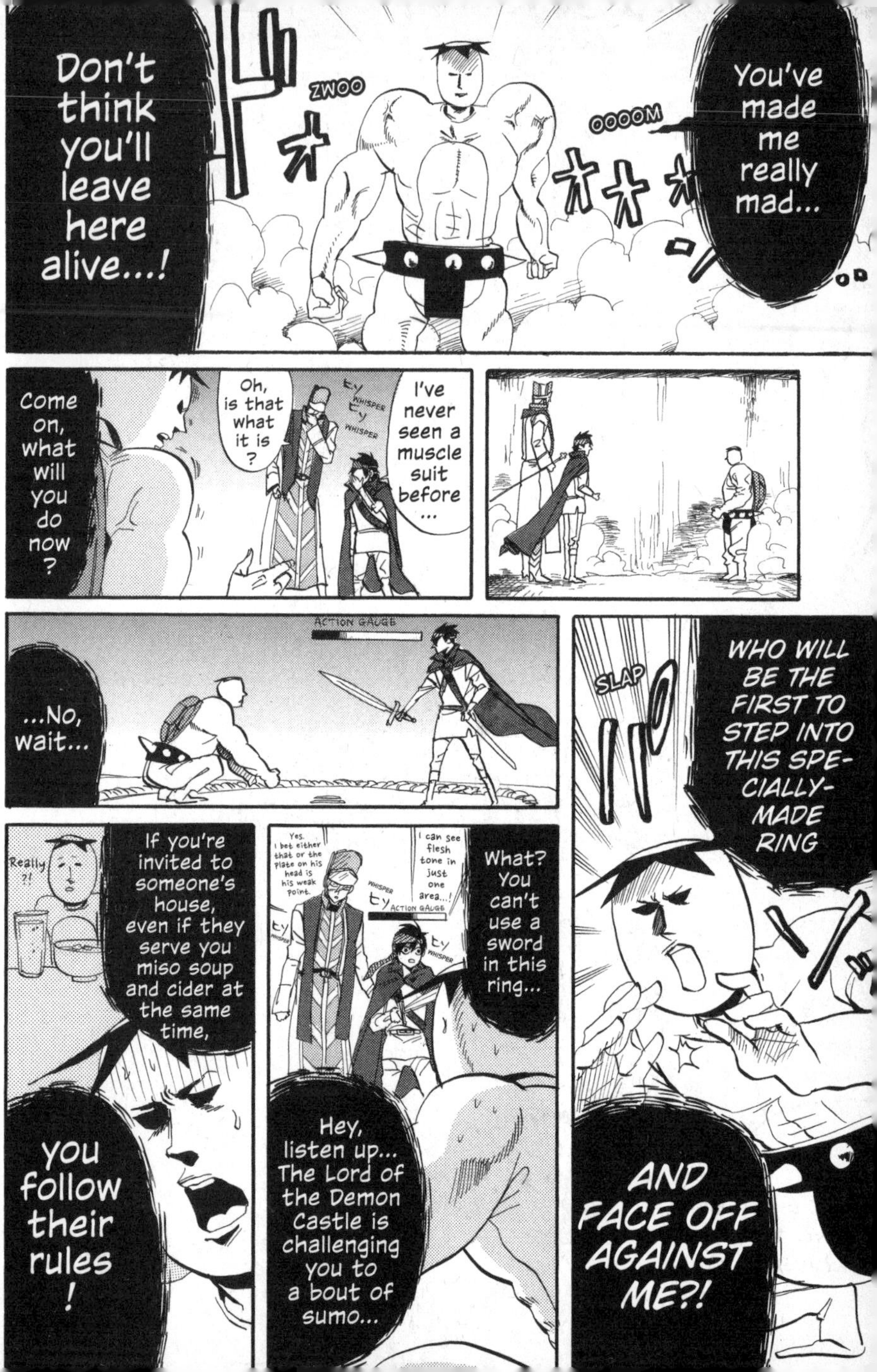
You've made me really mad...
OOOOM
ZWOO
Don't think you'll leave here alive...!
I've never seen a muscle suit before...
WHISPER
WHISPER
Oh, is that what it is?
Come on, what will you do now?
WHO WILL BE THE FIRST TO STEP INTO THIS SPECIALLY-MADE RING
SLAP
AND FACE OFF AGAINST ME?!
ACTION GAUGE
...No, wait...
What? You can't use a sword in this ring...
I can see flesh tone in just one area...!
Yes. I bet either that or the plate on his head is his weak point.
WHISPER
WHISPER
ACTION GAUGE
Hey, listen up... The Lord of the Demon Castle is challenging you to a bout of sumo...
If you're invited to someone's house, even if they serve you miso soup and cider at the same time,
Really?!
YOU follow their rules!

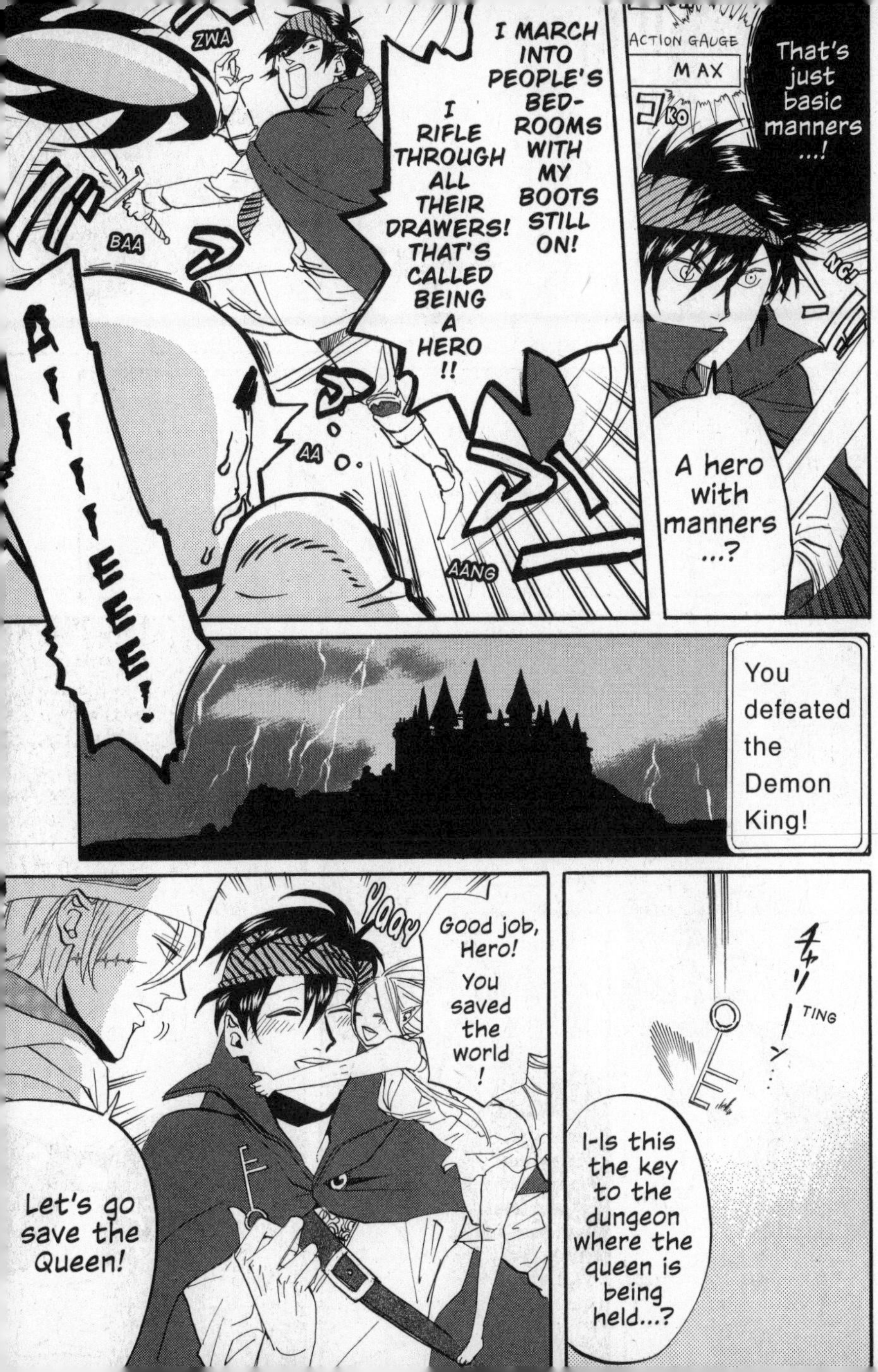
ACTION GAUGE
MAX
That's just basic manners ...!
KO
NG!
A hero with manners ...?
I MARCH INTO PEOPLE'S BEDROOMS WITH MY BOOTS STILL ON!
I RIFLE THROUGH ALL THEIR DRAWERS! THAT'S CALLED BEING A HERO!!
ZWA
BAA
AA
AANG
AIIIIEEEE!
You defeated the Demon King!
TING
I-Is this the key to the dungeon where the queen is being held...?
YAAY
Good job, Hero!
You saved the world!
Let's go save the Queen!

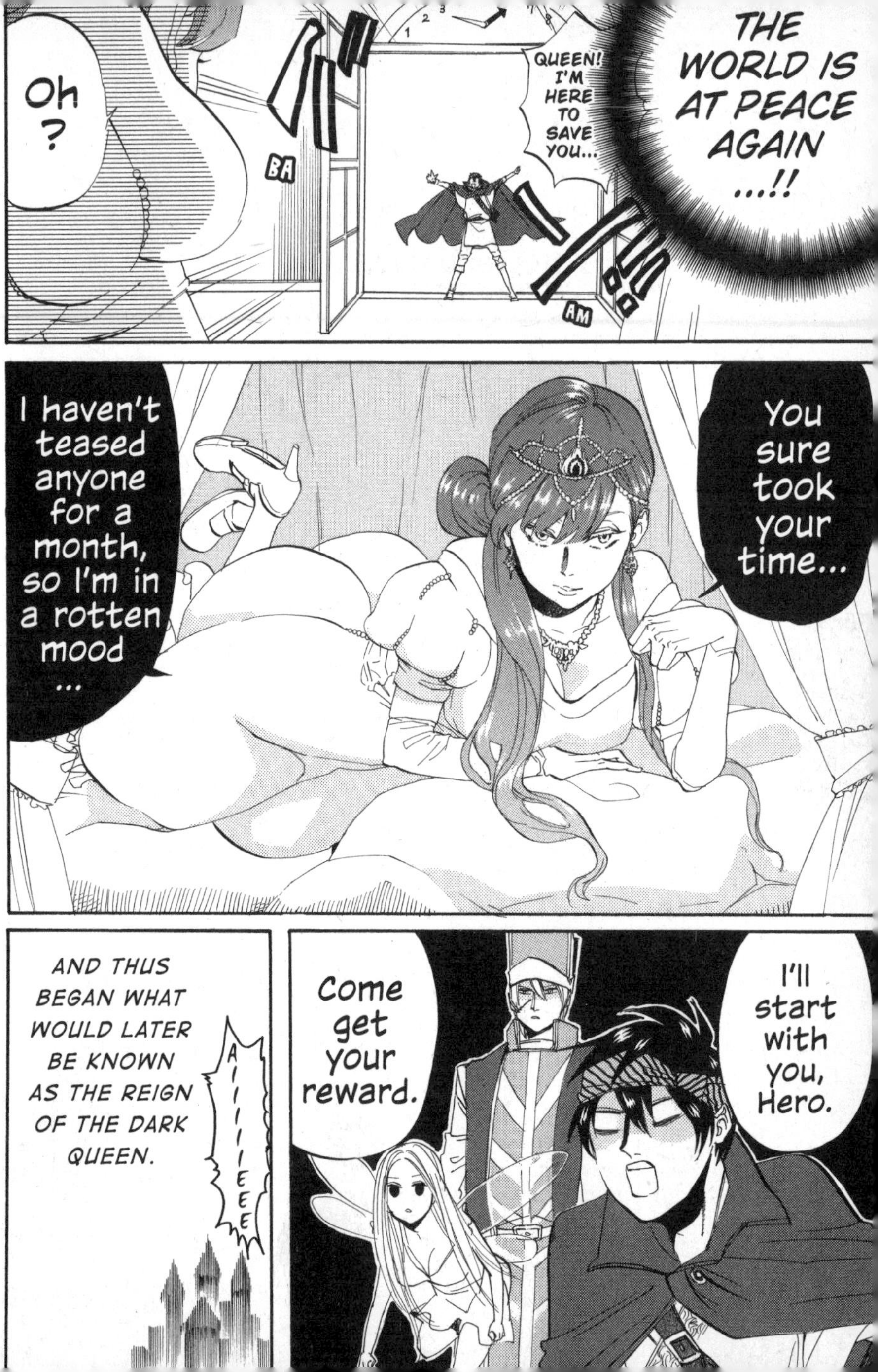
THE WORLD IS AT PEACE AGAIN ...!!
QUEEN! I'M HERE TO SAVE YOU...
BA
AM
Oh ?
You sure took your time...
I haven't teased anyone for a month, so I'm in a rotten mood ...
I'll start with you, Hero.
Come get your reward.
AIIIIIEEE
AND THUS BEGAN WHAT WOULD LATER BE KNOWN AS THE REIGN OF THE DARK QUEEN.

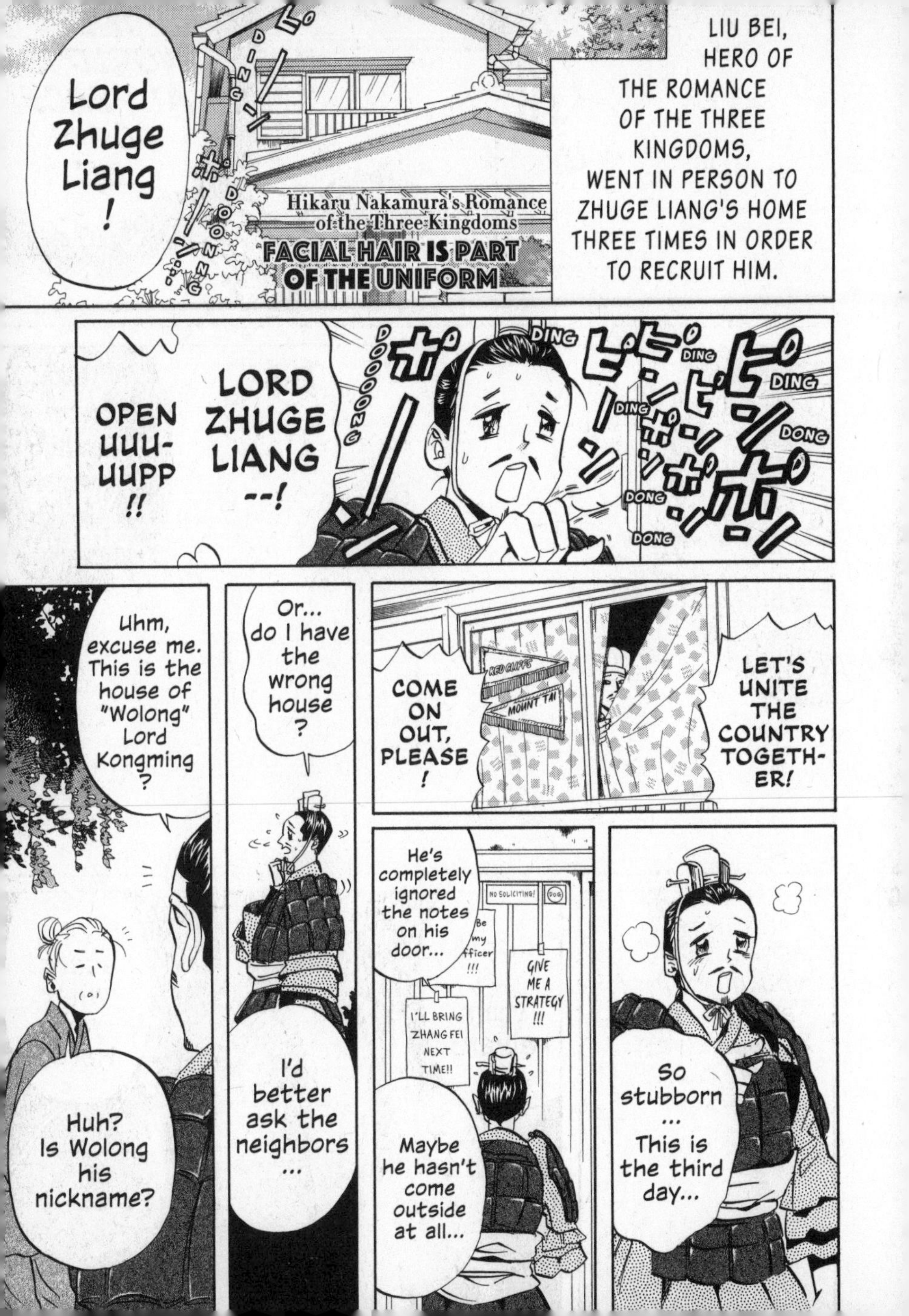
LIU BEI, HERO OF THE ROMANCE OF THE THREE KINGDOMS, WENT IN PERSON TO ZHUGE LIANG'S HOME THREE TIMES IN ORDER TO RECRUIT HIM.
Hikaru Nakamura's Romance of the Three Kingdoms
FACIAL HAIR IS PART OF THE UNIFORM
DING
DOONG
Lord Zhuge Liang!
DING
DING
DING
DING
DONG
DONG
DONG
DOOOOONG
LORD ZHUGE LIANG--!
OPEN UUUUUPP!!
LET'S UNITE THE COUNTRY TOGETHER!
RED CLIFFS
MOUNT TAI
COME ON OUT, PLEASE!
So stubborn... This is the third day...
He's completely ignored the notes on his door...
NO SOLICITING!
DOG
Be my officer!!!
GIVE ME A STRATEGY!!!
I'LL BRING ZHANG FEI NEXT TIME!!
Maybe he hasn't come outside at all...
Or... do I have the wrong house?
I'd better ask the neighbors...
Uhm, excuse me. This is the house of "Wolong" Lord Kongming?
Huh? Is Wolong his nickname?

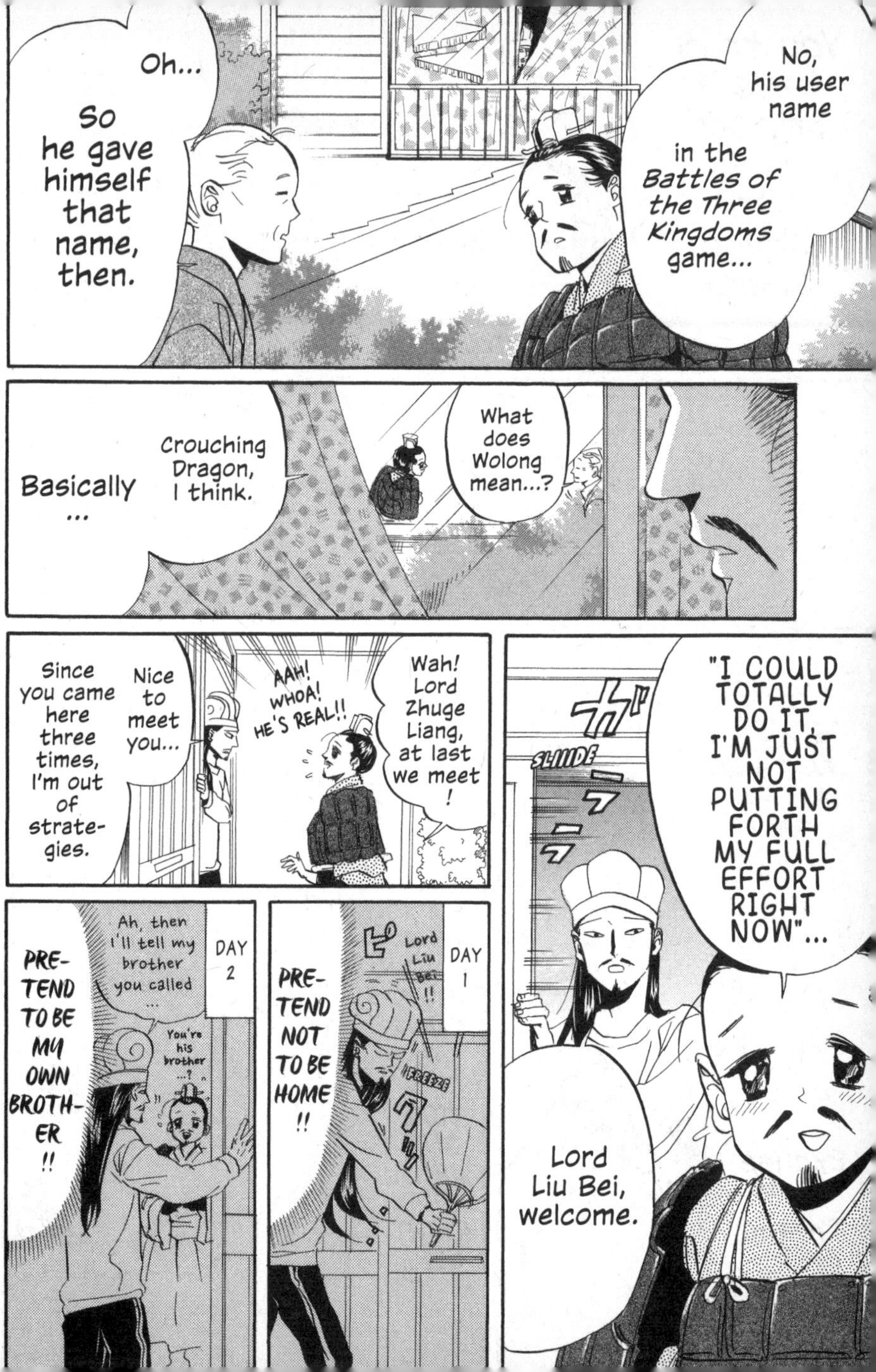
No, his user name in the *Battles of the Three Kingdoms* game...
Oh...
So he gave himself that name, then.
What does Wolong mean...?
Crouching Dragon, I think.
Basically ...
"I COULD TOTALLY DO IT, I'M JUST NOT PUTTING FORTH MY FULL EFFORT RIGHT NOW"...
SLIIIDE
Lord Liu Bei, welcome.
Wah! Lord Zhuge Liang, at last we meet!
AAH! WHOA! HE'S REAL!!
Nice to meet you...
Since you came here three times, I'm out of strategies.
DAY 1
Lord Liu Bei!!
PRETEND NOT TO BE HOME!!
FREEZE
DAY 2
Ah, then I'll tell my brother you called ...
You're his brother ...?
PRETEND TO BE MY OWN BROTHER!!

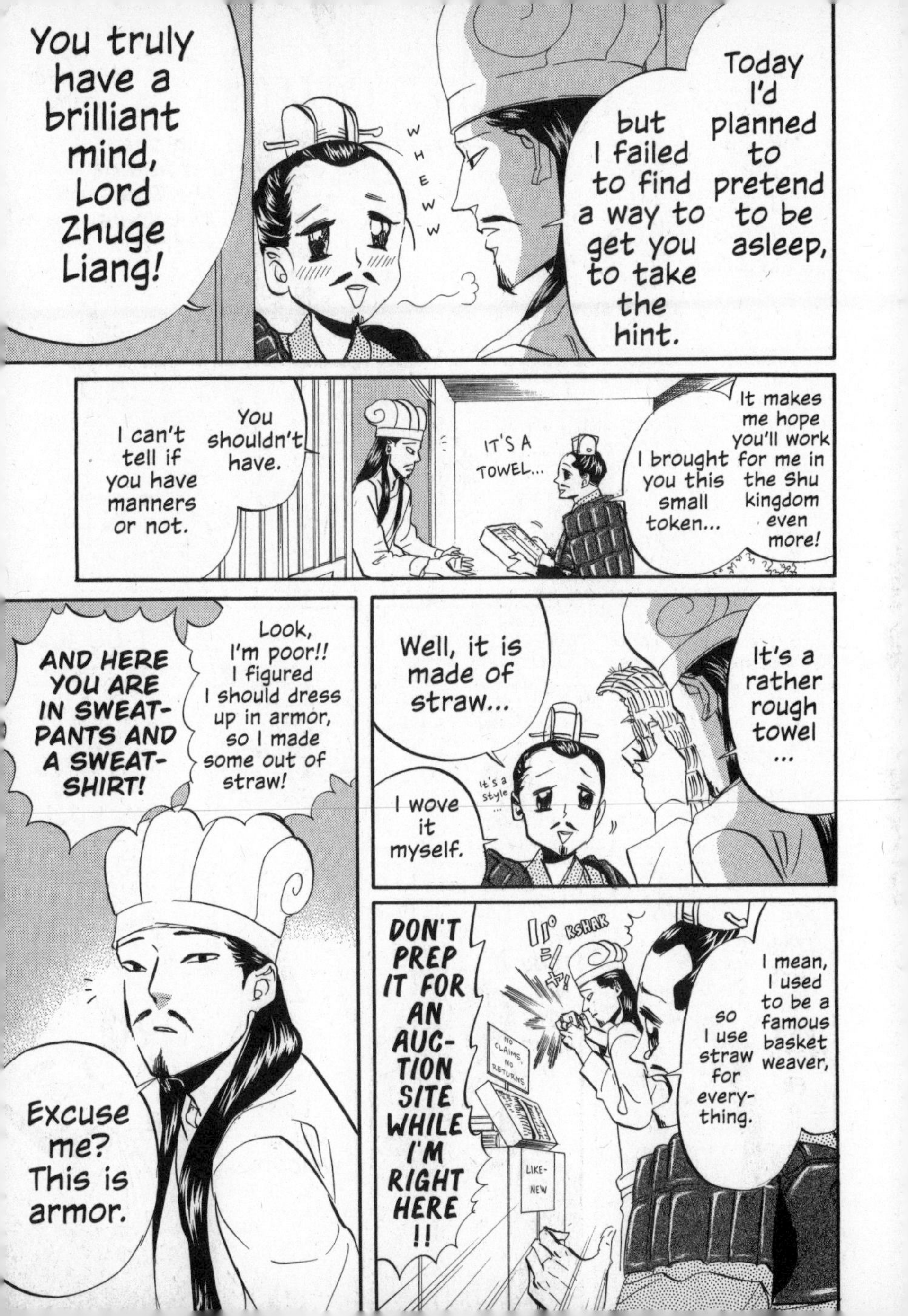

Today I'd planned to pretend to be asleep, but I failed to find a way to get you to take the hint.
WHEWW
You truly have a brilliant mind, Lord Zhuge Liang!
It makes me hope you'll work for me in the Shu kingdom even more!
I brought you this small token...
IT'S A TOWEL...
You shouldn't have.
I can't tell if you have manners or not.
It's a rather rough towel ...
Well, it is made of straw...
It's a style ...
I wove it myself.
I mean, I used to be a famous basket weaver,
so I use straw for everything.
KSHAK
NO CLAIMS, NO RETURNS
LIKE-NEW
DON'T PREP IT FOR AN AUCTION SITE WHILE I'M RIGHT HERE !!
Look, I'm poor!! I figured I should dress up in armor, so I made some out of straw!
AND HERE YOU ARE IN SWEAT-PANTS AND A SWEAT-SHIRT!
Excuse me? This is armor.

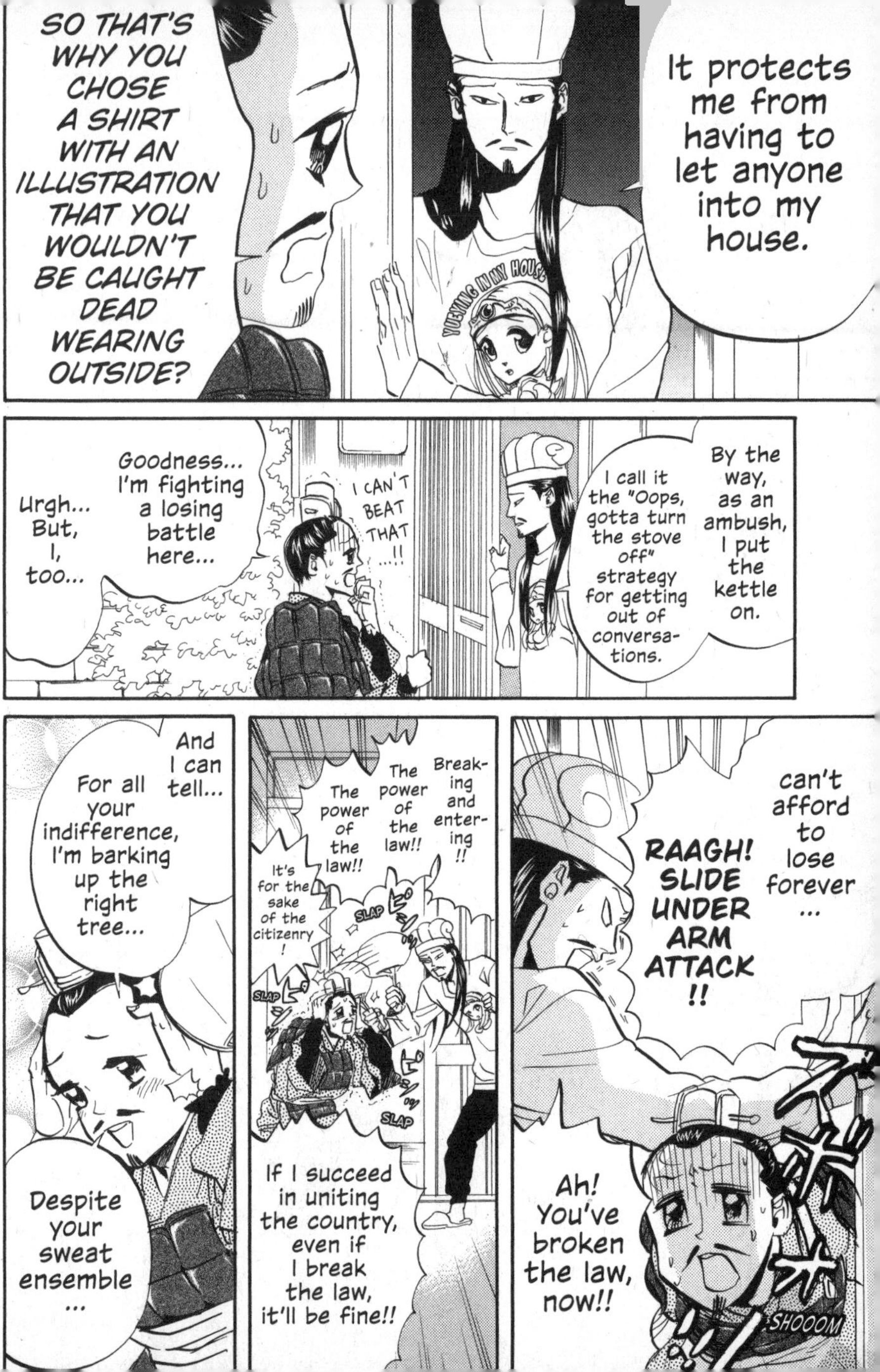
It protects me from having to let anyone into my house.
SO THAT'S WHY YOU CHOSE A SHIRT WITH AN ILLUSTRATION THAT YOU WOULDN'T BE CAUGHT DEAD WEARING OUTSIDE?
YUEYING IN MY HOUSE
By the way, as an ambush, I put the kettle on.
I call it the "Oops, gotta turn the stove off" strategy for getting out of conversations.
I CAN'T BEAT THAT ...!!
Goodness... I'm fighting a losing battle here...
Urgh... But, I, too...
can't afford to lose forever ...
RAAGH! SLIDE UNDER ARM ATTACK !!
Ah! You've broken the law, now!!
SHOOOM
Breaking and entering !!
The power of the law!!
The power of the law!!
It's for the sake of the citizenry !
SLAP
SLAP
SLAP
If I succeed in uniting the country, even if I break the law, it'll be fine!!
And I can tell...
For all your indifference, I'm barking up the right tree...
Despite your sweat ensemble ...

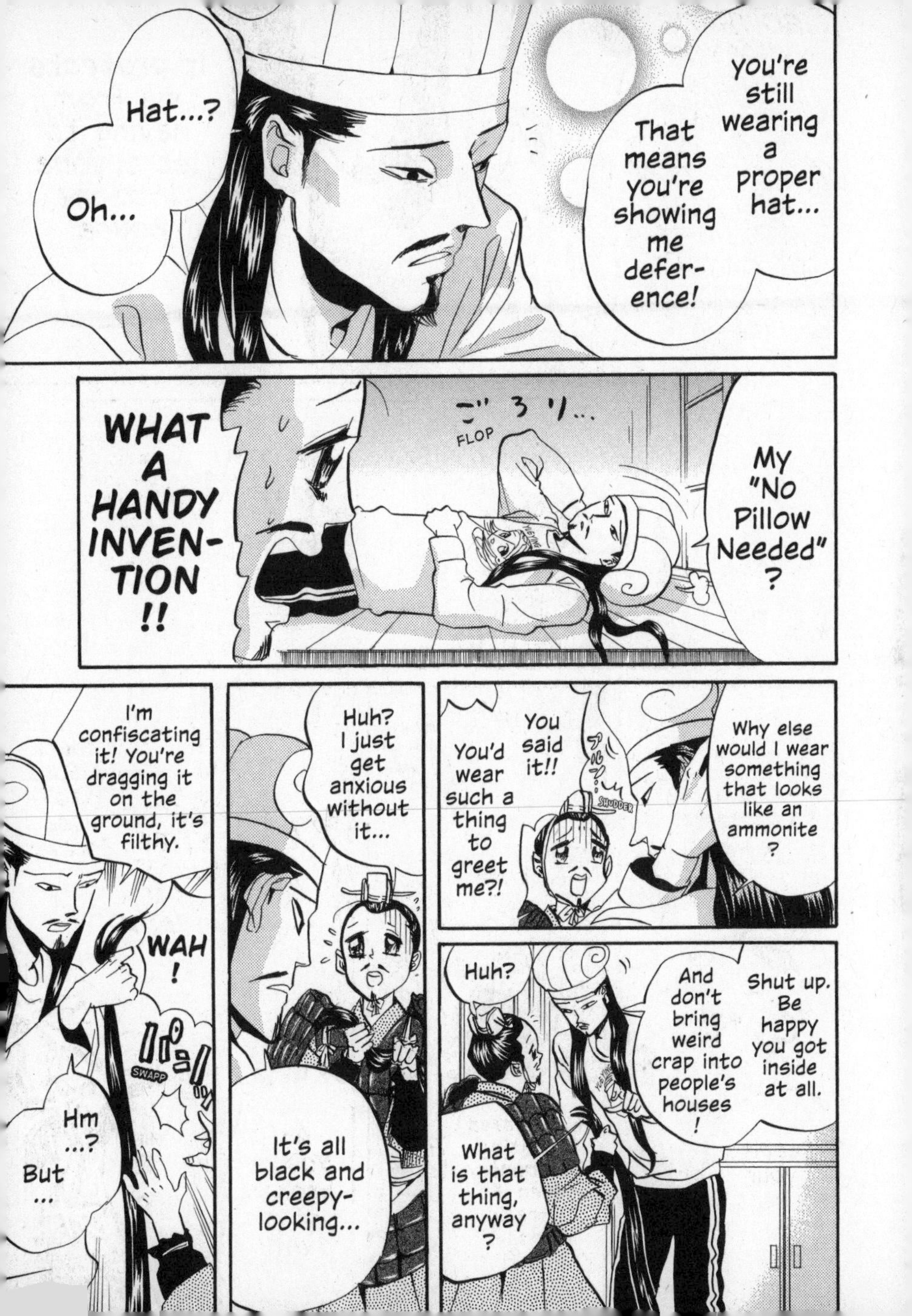
You're still wearing a proper hat...
That means you're showing me deference!
Hat...?
Oh...
My "No Pillow Needed"?
ごろり...
FLOP
WHAT A HANDY INVENTION!!
Why else would I wear something that looks like an ammonite?
You said it!!
SHUDDER
You'd wear such a thing to greet me?!
Shut up. Be happy you got inside at all.
And don't bring weird crap into people's houses!
Huh?
What is that thing, anyway?
Huh? I just get anxious without it...
It's all black and creepy-looking...
I'm confiscating it! You're dragging it on the ground, it's filthy.
WAH!
SWAPP
Hm...?
But...

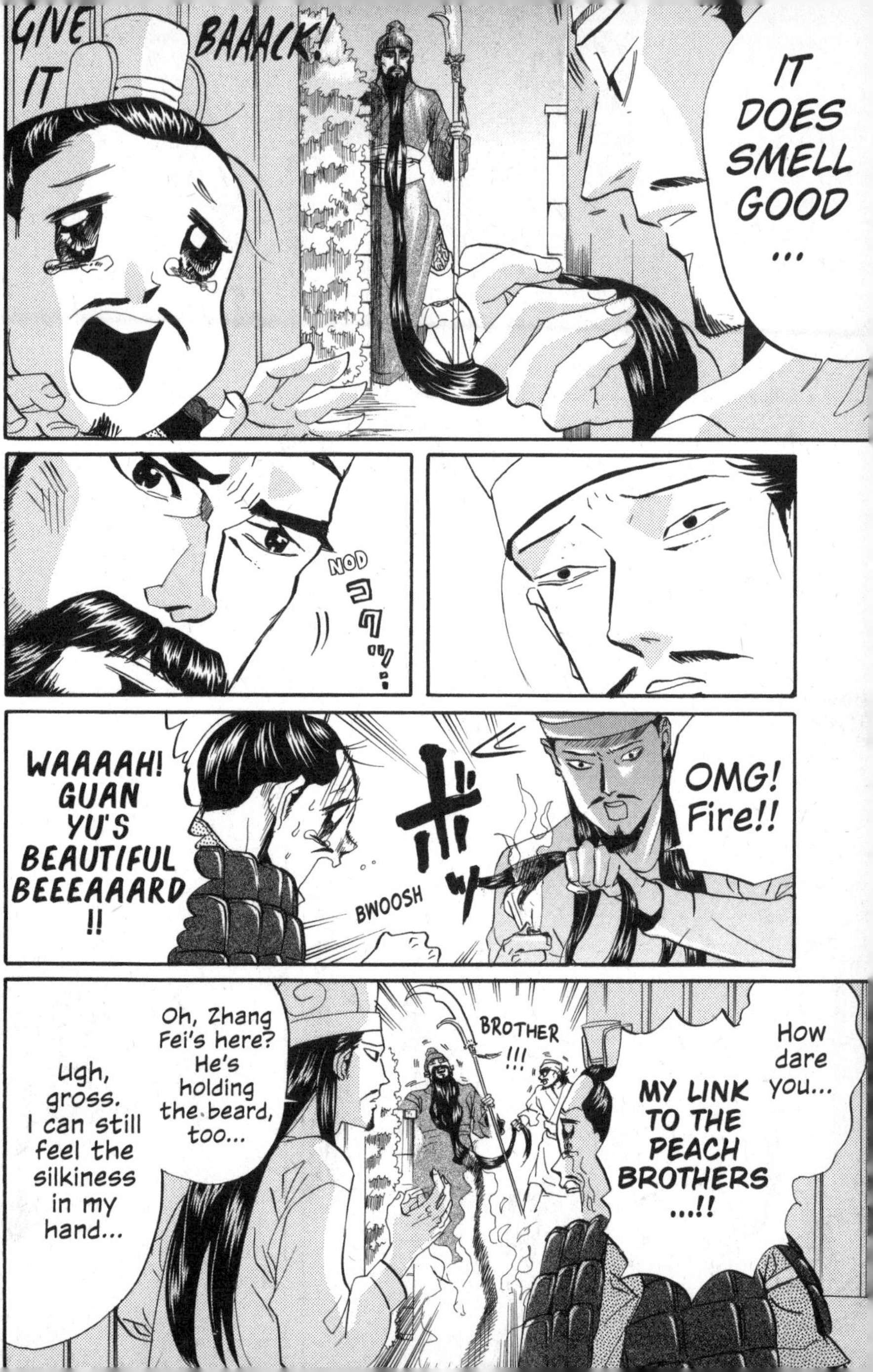
IT DOES SMELL GOOD ...
GIVE IT BAAACK!
NOD
OMG! Fire!!
ボッ
BWOOSH
WAAAAH! GUAN YU'S BEAUTIFUL BEEEAAARD !!
How dare you...
MY LINK TO THE PEACH BROTHERS ...!!
BROTHER !!!
Oh, Zhang Fei's here? He's holding the beard, too...
Ugh, gross. I can still feel the silkiness in my hand...

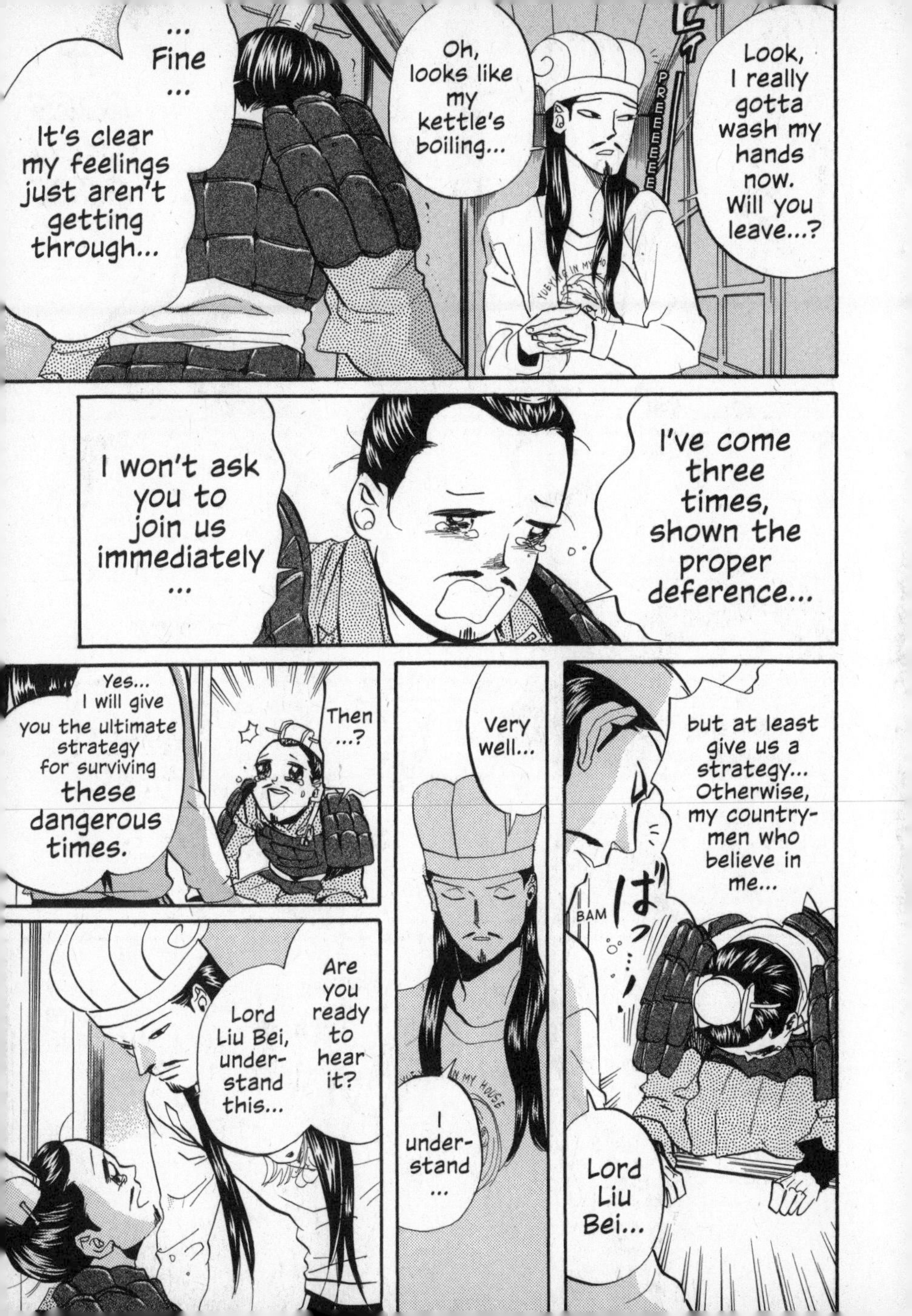

Look, I really gotta wash my hands now. Will you leave...?
PREEEEEEE
Oh, looks like my kettle's boiling...
... Fine ...
It's clear my feelings just aren't getting through...
I've come three times, shown the proper deference...
I won't ask you to join us immediately ...
but at least give us a strategy... Otherwise, my countrymen who believe in me...
BAM
ばっ
Lord Liu Bei...
Very well...
I understand ...
Then ...?
Yes... I will give you the ultimate strategy for surviving these dangerous times.
Are you ready to hear it?
Lord Liu Bei, understand this...

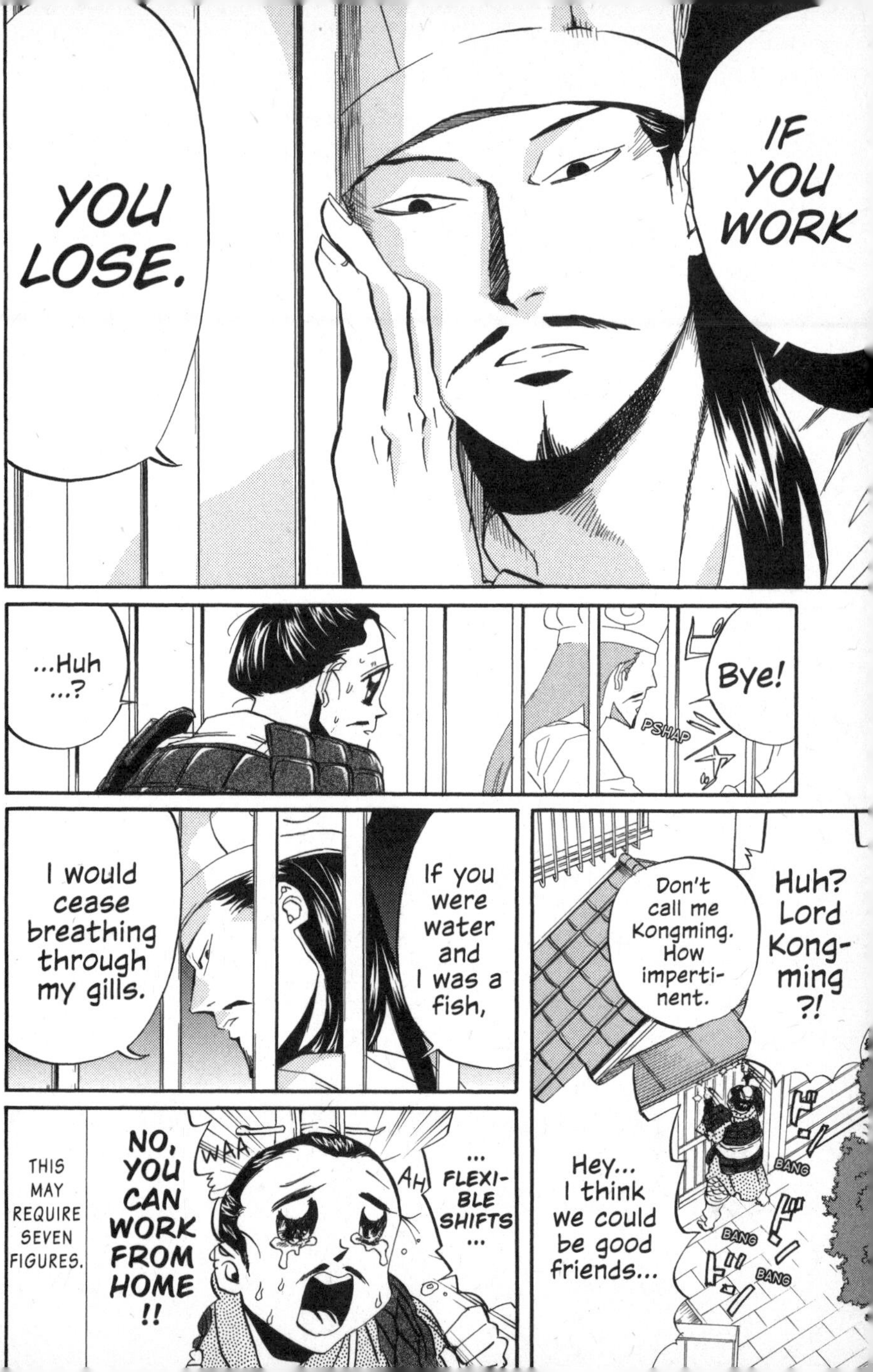
IF YOU WORK
YOU LOSE.
Bye!
PSHAP
...Huh ...?
Huh? Lord Kong-ming?!
Don't call me Kongming. How imperti-nent.
BANG
BANG
BANG
Hey... I think we could be good friends...
If you were water and I was a fish,
I would cease breathing through my gills.
... FLEXI-BLE SHIFTS ...
AH
WAA
NO, YOU CAN WORK FROM HOME !!
THIS MAY REQUIRE SEVEN FIGURES.

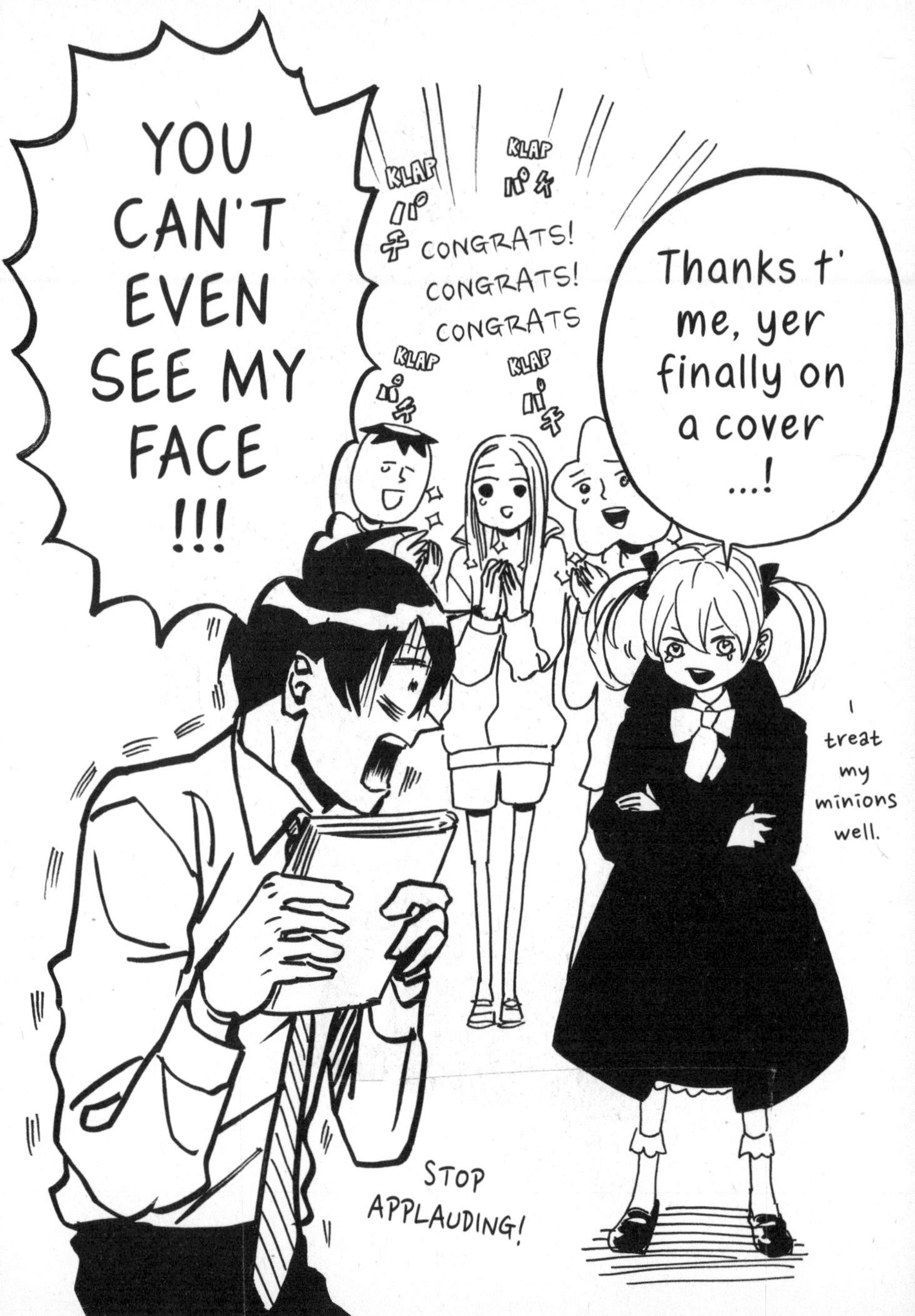
Thanks t' me, yer finally on a cover ...!
I treat my minions well.
KLAP パチ
KLAP パチ
CONGRATS! CONGRATS! CONGRATS
KLAP パチ
KLAP パチ
YOU CAN'T EVEN SEE MY FACE!!!
STOP APPLAUDING!

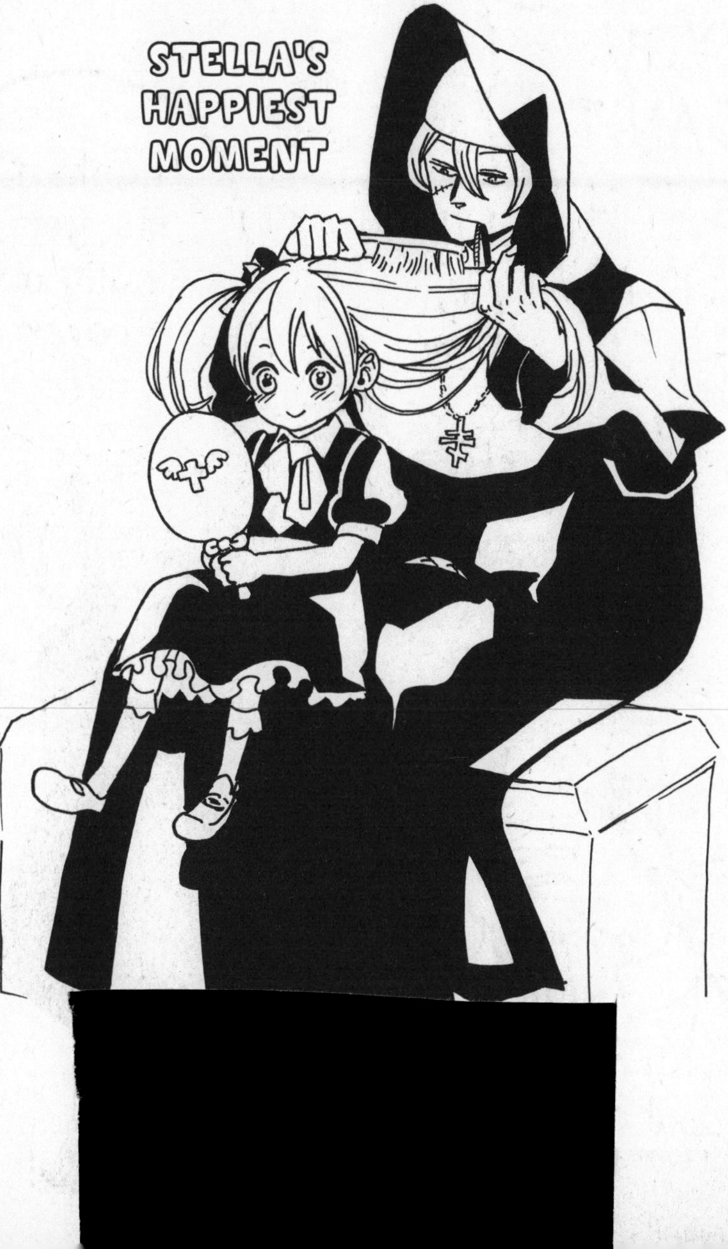
STELLA'S HAPPIEST MOMENT

AUG 19

ARAKAWA UNDER THE BRIDGE 5
Hikaru Nakamura

Translation: Andrew Cunningham
Production: Risa Cho
          Tomoe Tsutsumi

ARAKAWA UNDER THE BRIDGE Vol. 9 & 10
© 2009, 2010 Hikaru Nakamura / SQUARE ENIX CO., LTD.
First Published in Japan in 2009, 2010 by SQUARE ENIX CO., LTD.
Translation rights arranged with SQUARE ENIX CO., LTD. and Vertical, Inc.
through Tuttle-Mori Agency, Inc. Translation © 2019 by SQUARE ENIX CO., LTD.

Translation provided by Vertical Comics, 2019
Published by Vertical, Inc., New York

Originally published in Japanese as *Arakawa Andaa Za Burijji 9 & 10*
by SQUARE ENIX Co., Ltd., 2009-2010
Arakawa Andaa Za Burijji first serialized in *Young Gangan*, SQUARE ENIX Co.,
Ltd., 2004-2015

This is a work of fiction.

ISBN: 978-1-947194-24-3

Manufactured in Canada

First Edition

Vertical, Inc.
451 Park Avenue S█
7th Floor
New York, NY 1001█
www.vertical-comi█

Vertical books are █   █rvices.

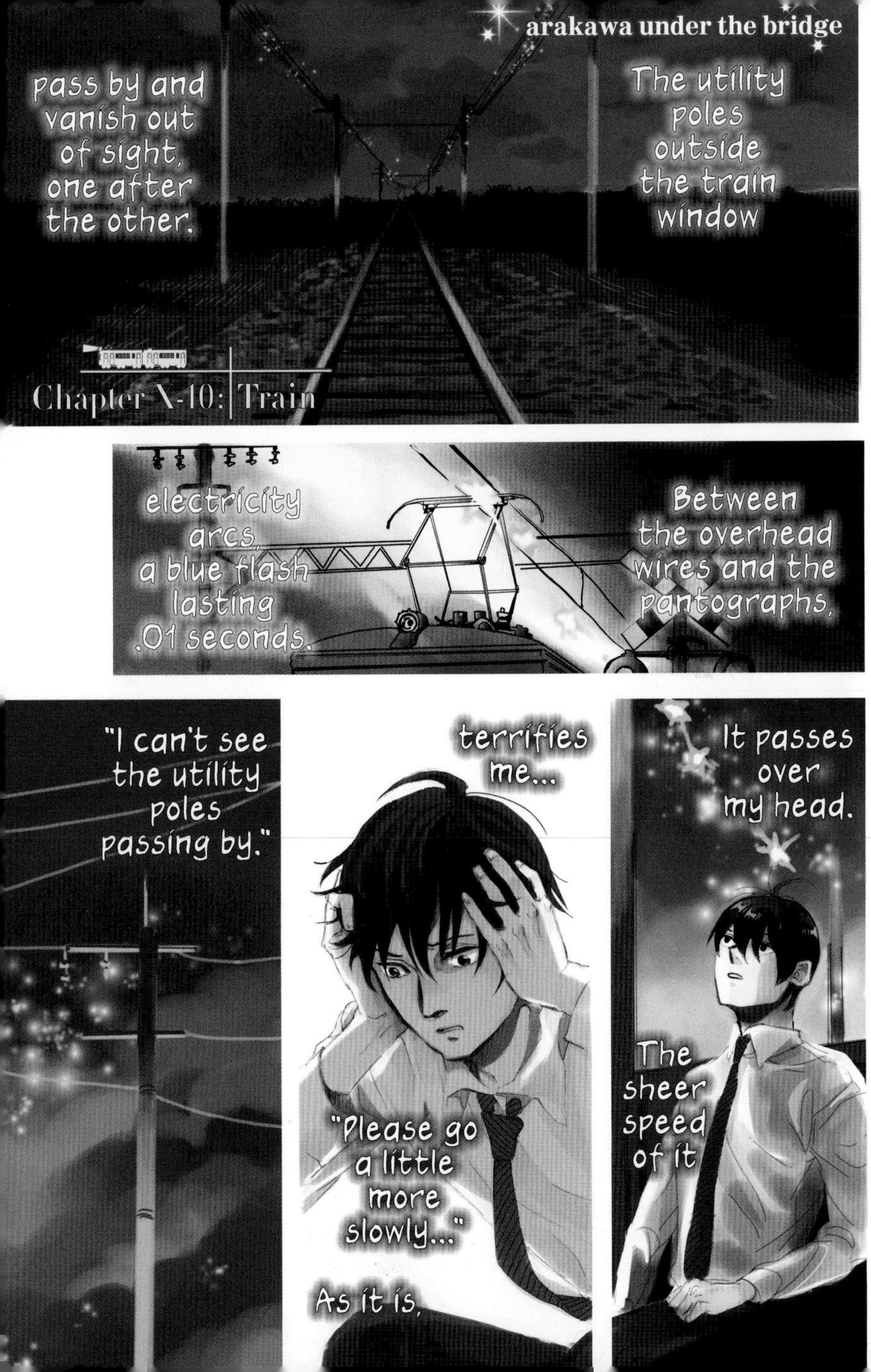
arakawa under the bridge
The utility poles outside the train window
pass by and vanish out of sight, one after the other.
Chapter X-10: Train
Between the overhead wires and the pantographs,
electricity arcs, a blue flash lasting .01 seconds.
It passes over my head.
The sheer speed of it
terrifies me...
"Please go a little more slowly..."
As it is,
"I can't see the utility poles passing by."

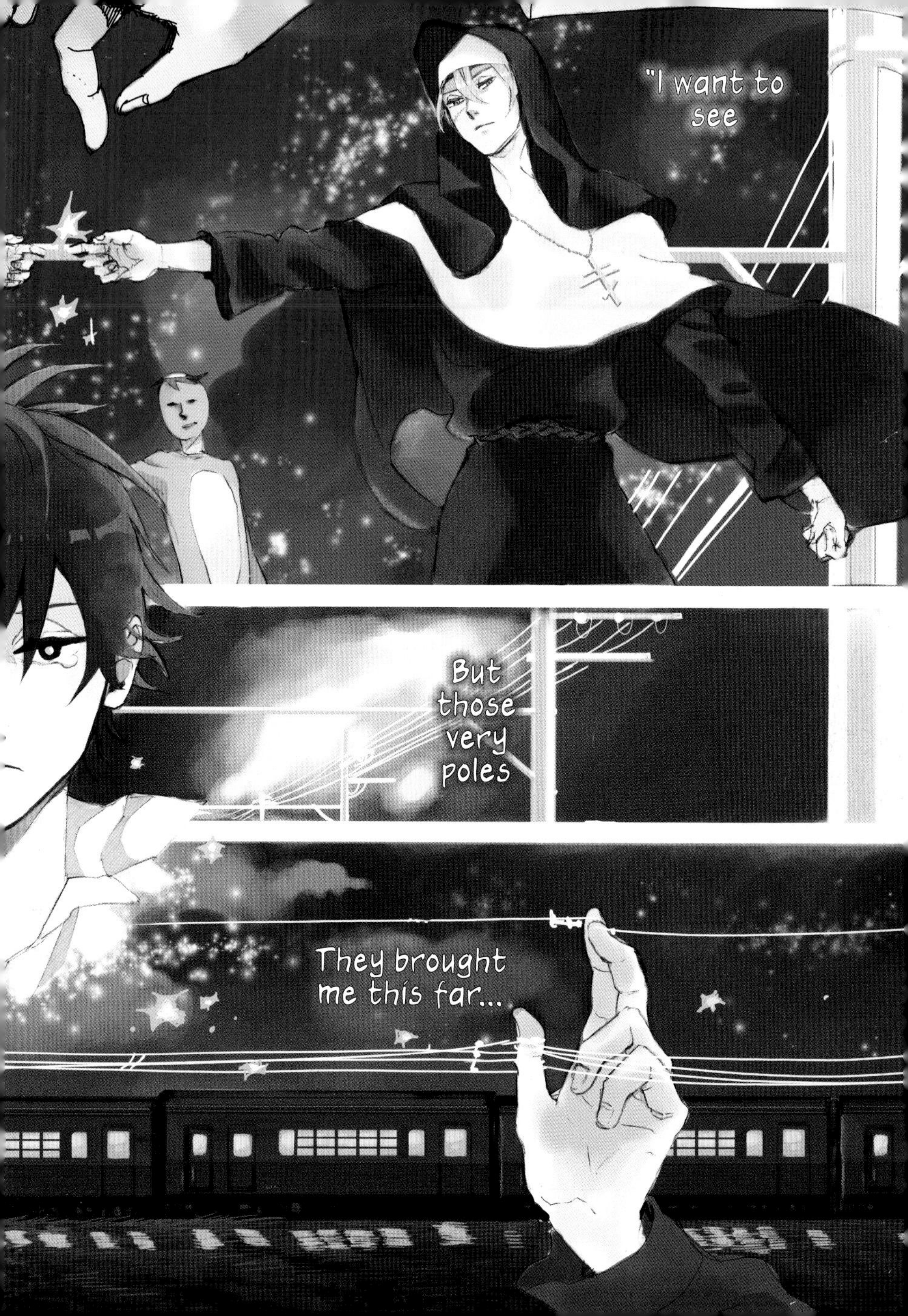
"I want to see
But those very poles
They brought me this far...

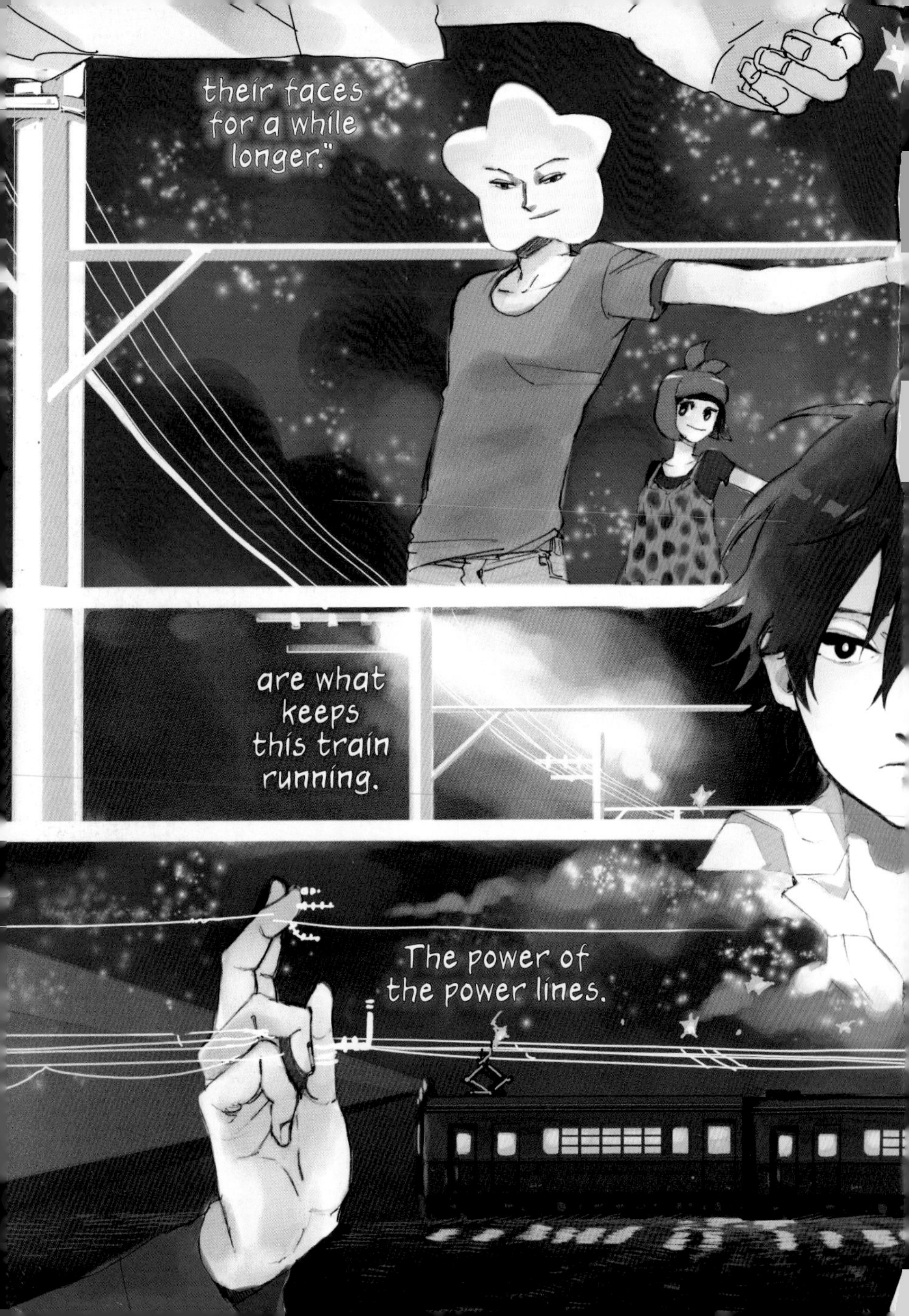
their faces for a while longer."
are what keeps this train running.
The power of the power lines.

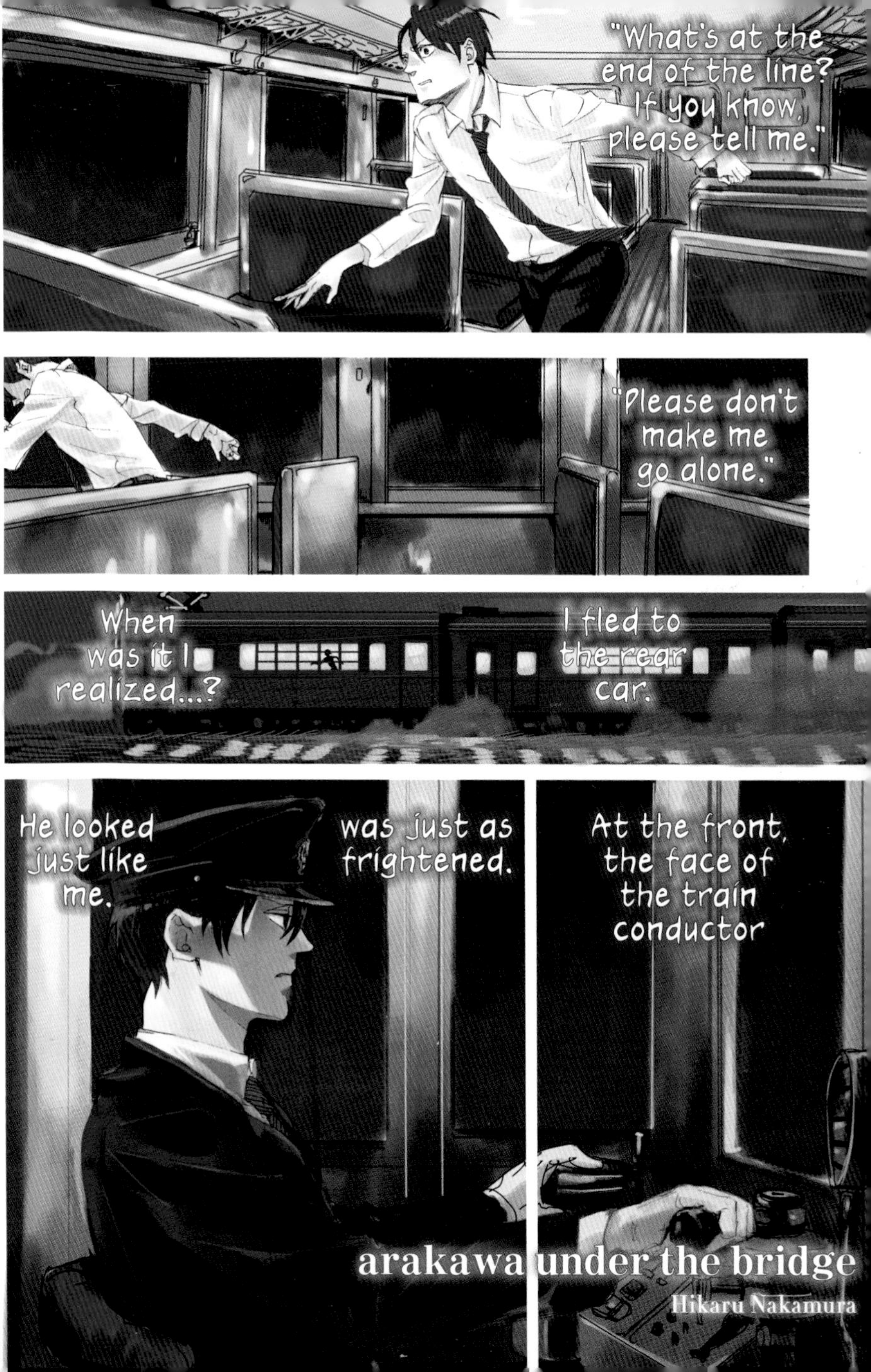
"What's at the end of the line? If you know, please tell me."
"Please don't make me go alone."
I fled to the rear car.
When was it I realized...?
At the front, the face of the train conductor
was just as frightened.
He looked just like me.
arakawa under the bridge
Hikaru Nakamura